RICHARD FRANCIS BURTON

EXPLORATIONS

OF THE

HIGHLANDS OF THE BRAZIL;

WITH

A FULL ACCOUNT OF THE GOLD
AND DIAMOND MINES

VOLUME I

D1354674

Elibron Classics
www.elibron.com

THE

HIGHLANDS OF THE BRAZIL.

THE FORTNIGHTLY SLAVE-MUSTER AT THE CASA GRANDE, MORRO VELHO.

THE

HIGHLANDS OF THE BRAZIL.

By CAPTAIN RICHARD F. BURTON,

F.R.G.S., ETC.

The aboriginal Indian (Tupy) of Brazil.

VOL. I.

LONDON:
TINSLEY BROTHERS, 18, CATHERINE STREET, STRAND.
1869.

EXPLORATIONS

OF THE

HIGHLANDS OF THE BRAZIL;

WITH

A FULL ACCOUNT OF THE GOLD AND DIAMOND MINES.

ALSO,

CANOEING DOWN 1500 MILES OF THE GREAT RIVER SÃO FRANCISCO, FROM SABARÁ TO THE SEA.

BY

CAPTAIN RICHARD F. BURTON,

F.R.G.S., ETC.

VOL. I.

LONDON:

TINSLEY BROTHERS, 18, CATHERINE ST., STRAND.

1869.

LONDON
BRADBURY, EVANS, AND CO., PRINTERS, WHITEFRIARS.

RIGHT HON. THE LORD STANLEY, P.C., M.P.

&c. &c. &c.

My Lord,

I HAVE not solicited the honour of prefixing your name to these pages. A "Dedication by Permission" might be looked upon as an attempt to take sanctuary after committing the crime of publishing harsh truths, and of advocating opinions which are not those of an influential majority. But I am irresistibly tempted to address a fellow-anthropologist, whose enlarged and enlightened world-knowledge, collected, not only in the Closet, but by the close inspection of travel, and by the study of mankind, promises to our native land the broad measures and the solidly based policy which during the last third of a century have shared the fate of other good intentions. The glorious year 1867, the commencement of a new era in the British Empire, may take as its device—

"Anglia surge,
Immo resurge, tuam refero tibi mortuæ vitam."

Your Lordship's name is well known in the Brazil; its fair report is that of a Statesman pledged to progress, who acts upon the belief that the welfare of his own country is advanced by the advancement of all other nations. If this my latest journey have the happy effect of drawing your attention to the Brazil, a region so rich in Nature's gifts, so abounding in still latent capabilities, and so ardent for development; to an Empire bound to us by the ties of commerce, and by its high and honourable bearing in matters of public credit; to a people which excites our admiration by its young and glorious history as a Colony, and by a perseverance, a patriotism, and a self-reliance in the last three years' war, of which the proudest of European races might be proud ; and to a community endeared to us by its monarchical and constitutional government, and by the friendly relations which date from its Independence Day, I shall not deem (to use the stereotyped phrase) that my time and labour have been expended in vain.

I have the honour to be,

My Lord,

Your most obedient humble servant,

RICHARD F. BURTON,
Ex-President Anthrop. Soc. London.

SANTOS, SÃO PAULO,
July 23, 1868.

PREFACE.

BEFORE the reader dives into the interior of Brazil with my husband as a medium, let me address two words to him.

I have returned home, on six months' leave of absence, after three years in Brazil. One of the many commissions I am to execute for Captain Burton, is to see the following pages through the press.

It has been my privilege, during those three years, to have been his almost constant companion; and I consider that to travel, write, read, and study under such a master, is no small boon to any one desirous of seeing and learning.

Although he frequently informs me, in a certain Oriental way, that "the Moslem can permit no equality with women," yet he has chosen me, his pupil, for this distinction, in preference to a more competent stranger.

As long as there is anything difficult to do, a risk to be incurred, or any chance of improving the mind, and of educating oneself, I am a very faithful disciple; but I now begin to feel, that while he and his readers are old friends, I am humbly standing unknown in the shadow of his glory. It is therefore time for me respectfully but firmly to assert, that, although I proudly accept of the trust confided to me, and pledge myself not to avail myself of my discretionary powers to alter one word of the original text, I protest vehemently against his religious and moral sentiments, which belie a good and chivalrous life. I point the finger of indignation particularly at what misrepresents our Holy Roman Catholic Church, and at what upholds that unnatural and repulsive law, Polygamy, which the Author is careful not to practise himself, but from a high moral pedestal he preaches to the ignorant as a means of population in young countries.

I am compelled to differ with him on many other subjects; but, be it understood, not in the common spirit of domestic jar, but with a mutual agreement to differ and enjoy our differences, whence points of interest never flag.

Having now justified myself, and given a friendly warning to a *fair* or *gentle* reader,—the rest must take care of themselves,—I leave him or her to steer through these anthropological sand-banks and hidden rocks as best he or she may.

ISABEL BURTON.

14, Montagu Place,
Montagu Square, W., London,
November, 1868.

THE LUSIADS OF CAMOENS.

CANTO VI.

STANZA XCV.

Amid such scenes with danger fraught and pain,
Serving the fiery spirit more to 'flame,
Who wooes bright Honour, he shall ever win
A true nobility, a deathless fame:
Not they who love to lean, unjustly vain,
Upon th' ancestral trunk's departed claim ;
Nor they reclining on the gilded beds
Where Moscow's Zebeline downy softness spreads.

XCVI.

Not with the viands new and exquisite,
Not with the wanton languid promenade,
Not with the varied infinite delight
Which can so much the generous bosom jade ;
Not with the never conquered appetite,
Which Fortune, ever delicate, hath made,
Which suffers none to change and seek the meed
Of Valour daring high heroic deed:

XCVII.

But by a doughty arm and weapon's grace
Gaining the glory which is all his own ;
With weary vigil, in the steel-forgèd case,
'Mid wrathsome winds and bitter billows thrown ;
Conquering the torpid rigours in th' embrace
Of South, and regions destitute and lone,
Swallowing the tainted rations' scanty dole
Temper'd with toil of body, moil of soul:

XCVIII.

Forcing the face, with fullest mastery,
  Confident to appear, and glad, and sound,
When met the burning balls, which, whistling by,
  Bespread with feet and arms the battle ground.
'Tis thus the bosom, nobly hard and high,
  Spurns gold and honours with contempt profound;
Gold, honours, oft by thrust of chance obtain'd,
And not by dint of virtuous daring gain'd.

XCIX.

Thus grows the human spirit heavenly bright,
  Led by Experience, truest, excellent guide;
Holding in view, as from some towering height,
  The maze of mortal littleness and pride:
He who his path thus lights with Reason's light,
  Which weak affections ne'er have might to hide,
Shall rise (as rise he ought) to honour true,
Against his will that would not stoop to sue.

CONTENTS.

xii

CONTENTS.

THE

HIGHLANDS OF THE BRAZIL.

PRELIMINARY ESSAY.

THE Brazil is, especially to the foreign traveller, a land of specialties. As he disembarks at Pernambuco the questions proposed to him, even from the guard-boat, are : Is he a Merchant? an Engineer? a Naturalist? a Doctor?—No! then—he must be a Dentist! And—I presume that he is not a Royal Duke or a "Bristol Diamond," with loan legibly written on his brow—he will do well, especially if bound for the Far West in the Land of the Southern Cross, to be or to become one of the five recognised castes.

Like the stranger herd, Brazilian authors have also been mostly specialists, each bound to his specific end. When the Annalists of the Jesuits and the Franciscans had had their day, the old travellers preceding the savans who were charged with the demarcation of the frontiers were explorers pure and simple ; who, if they wrote at all, wrote only Rotêiros or Itineraries. Among the Portuguese may be mentioned the celebrated naturalist, Alexandre Rodrigues Ferreira, sent in 1785-6 on a scientific expedition to the River of the Amazons. The active and intrepid Paulista, Dr. de Lacerda (1790), who, by-the-bye, was forbidden to use instruments by a certain D. Bernardo José de Lorena, Captain-General of the Province of São Paulo—a veritable Sultan of Waday—and who died at the Capital of the African Cazembe, was a mathematician and astronomer. Dr. José Vieira Couto (1800-1), of Tejuco, now Diamantina, was a mineralogist; so was the Pater Patriæ the Venerable José Bonifacio de Andrada e Silva, of Santos (1820). Major Coutinho, the experienced Amazonian traveller, is an officer of engineers.

The Netherlanders, in the olden days, sent the littérateur and historiographer, Gaspar Baerle, *alias* Barlæus ("Rerum per Octennium in Brasilia' gestarum Historia," Amsterdam, 1647), whose ponderous Latin folio has now an anthropological interest; Piso of Leyden, and the German Marcgraf (1648), who laid the foundations of systematic botanical study; Arnoldus Montanus (1671), plagiarised by the often quoted Dapper; and G. Nieuhof (1862). Amongst the Germans are Hans Stade (1547); the Prince Maximilian of Wied Neuwied (1815-1817), naturalist and ornithologist; and H.R.H. Prince Adalbert of Prussia, who travelled in Brazil; * the savans Spix and Martius (1817-1820),† the Humboldt‡ and Bonpland of Southern America; the Baron von Eschwege, a mineralogist; besides the elder Varnhagen and Schuch (senior), Langsdorff and Natterer, Pohl, Burmeister, and other names well known to science.

The French, not to mention the ancients, as De Sery (1563), the "Montaigne of the old travellers"; the Capuchin Claude d'Abbeville (1612), Yves d'Evreux (1613-14), and Roulox Baro (1651), have contributed the mathematician La Condamine; the botanist Auguste de St. Hilaire (1816-1822); the naturalist Count Francis de Castelnau (1843-1847); and the astronomer M. Liais (1858-1862). Besides these are the less reputable names of M. Expilly (1862), who, as his "Brésil tel qu'il est "§ tells us, came out as a maker of phosphorus matches; and M. Biard (1862), who came out as a portrait painter, and who produced a notable caricature.

The Anglo-Americans sent Messrs. Hernden and Gibbon, officers of their navy (1851), to reconnoitre the Valley of the Amazons. Mr. Thos. Ewbank (1856) was an engineer. The two valuable and now neglected volumes of Mr. Kidder (1845)

---

* Travels of H. R. H. Prince Adalbert of Prussia in the South of Europe and in Brazil, with a voyage up the Amazon and the Xingú. Translated by Sir Robert H. Schomburgk and John Edward Taylor. 2 vols. Bogue : London, 1849. The Counts Bismarck and Oriolla accompanied this traveller, who ascended the Xingú as far as Piranhaguára.

† Travels in Brazil, by Dr. Joh. Bapt. von Spix and Dr. C. F. Phil. von Martius. London : Longmans, 1824. 2 vols. octavo. I saw this translation at the little English Library, Pernambuco, but have never been able to procure the original.

‡ According to M. de Castelnau the Library of Rio de Janeiro preserves a curious document, highly characteristic of colonial days : this is an order to arrest and to deport Humboldt, if ever found upon Brazilian soil.

§ I cite with pleasure the judgment passed by M. Liais upon this disreputable production (L'Espace Céleste, 210): "C'est faire injure au bon sens de ses lecteurs que d'écrire de pareilles absurdités. Au reste le livre en question est rempli d'inexactitudes. Si l'auteur l'avait intitulé *le Brésil tel qu'il n'est pas*, il serait d'une vérité parfaite."

were written by a missionary, and the joint production of Messrs.
Kidder and Fletcher was the work of missionaries.* Of late
sundry "*opuscules*" have been published by "General" Wood,
Dr. Gaston, and the Rev. Mr. Dunn, colonists, and by Capt.
John Codman, who commanded a steamer upon the coast.

We English have given the "British merchant" Luccock
(1808-1818); the mineralogist John Mawe (1809-1810); the
accurate Koster (1809-1815), settled in trade at Pernambuco;
the Reverend Mr. Walsh, High Church and Protestant (1820);
Dr. Gardner, the botanist (1836-1841); Mr. Henry Walter
Bates, the accomplished naturalist and entomologist (1847-1859),
who, in his earlier labours on the Amazons River was accompanied by Mr. A. P. Wallace; Mr. Hadfield (1854), who visited
the coast and prospected for it steam navigation; the naturalist,
Mr. R. Spruce; and the engineer, Mr. William Chandless, who
are still pushing their adventurous way to the skirts of the Andes.
Nor must I conclude this skeleton list without mentioning Dr.
Lund, the learned Dane, who lived amongst the extinct Saurians
in the caverns of Minas Geraes, and the ichthyologist and
"man of pure science," Professor Louis Agassiz of Boston (1865-
1866), a traveller received with the greatest enthusiasm of which
the Brazil is capable.

In this brilliant assembly a mere tourist would or should feel
somewhat out of place. I, however, had also an especial object,
—e son pittor anch' io. H. I. Majesty had remarked with much
truth that Central Africa is fast becoming better known to
Europe than the Central Brazil.† Even at Rio de Janeiro few
would believe that the valley of the Rio de São Francisco,
popularly but ungeographically called the Southern Mississippi,
is in any but a state of nature. My plan then was to visit the
future seat of Empire along the grand artery; how I would

* Brazil and the Brazilians, portrayed
in historical and descriptive sketches by
Rev. D. P. Kidder and Rev. J. C. Fletcher.
Philadelphia: Childs & Peterson. London:
Trübner & Co. 1857. A new edition, with
corrections, has lately been issued by Messrs.
Sampson Low & Co., London.

This production has been somewhat
harshly described in semi-official documents
as an "elaborate fulsome puff which has
done much mischief." Its principal injury
to the public has been to engender an im-

pudent plagiarism, printed in 1860 by the
Religious Tract Society, 56 Paternoster
Row, London, and entitled "Brazil: its
History, People, Natural Productions, &c."

† I do not call the country "Brazil,"
when she does not; nor indeed does any
other nation but our own. Worse still is
the popular anachronism "Brazils," which
was correct only between A.D. 1572 and
1576, when the State was split into two
governments; and yet the error still lives
in the best informed of our periodicals.

make known the vastness of its wealth and the immense variety of its productions, which embrace all things, between salt and diamonds, that man can desire. In Minas Geraes alone the traveller finds a " country as large and a soil and climate as fertile and salubrious as those of England," * an atmosphere of " æstas et non æstus," where the "tyranny of nipping winds and early frosts " is unknown; and, finally, a *fit habitat*—or rather the old home †—for the nobler tropical man about to be, when the so-called temperate regions shall have done their work. "I hold to the opinion," says Mr. Bates, " that though humanity can reach an advanced stage of culture only by battling with the inclemencies of nature in high latitudes, it is under the Equator alone that the perfect race of the future will attain to complete fruition of man's beautiful heritage, the earth."

The date of my journey fell happily enough. The Seventh of September, that glorious Independence Day of the Brazil, worthily commemorated itself by throwing open to the merchant ships of all nations the Rio de São Francisco and the Sweet-water Mediterranean further north. The Minister of Agriculture and Public Works had despatched a steamer to be put together on the upper course of the stream. The President of Minas had lately granted to a Brazilian civil engineer a concession to exploit by steamer the tributary valley of the Rio das Velhas. An English surveyor was laying out a line of rails to connect the Capital of the Empire with the City of Sabará, the future St. Louis; thus it was proposed to link to the Southern Atlantic the water-way which receives a thousand streams, that drains 8800 square leagues of one province only, and which is ready to support twenty instead of the present poor two millions of souls.

Nor is this all. The youngest of empires and the only monarchy in the New World, so richly dowered with physical beauty and material wealth still buried in her bosom, so magnificent in geographical position, with a coast line like that of Europe between the North Cape and Gibraltar‡ appears to be

---

* The area of England is 57,812 square miles; of Minas Geraes 20,000 square leagues.

† "It is rather in the great alluvial valleys of tropical or sub-tropical rivers, like the Ganges, the Irrawaddy, and the Nile," (let me add, the Euphrates, the Niger, and the Indus), " where we may ex-pect to detect the vestiges of man's earliest abode." Falconer, Quart. Journ. of Geol. 1865. And the great Law of Progression is apparently evolving the future continents and islands of earth more rapidly within the tropical than in the temperate latitudes.

‡ M. Van Straten de Ponthez (Le Brésil, ii. 27). Sir John Herschel (Physical Geo-

Fortune's favourite child. In 1852,* when the importation of slaves became a nullity, the country was dismayed, and not without reason, by the prospect of a deficient labour-market.† Compulsory service was then the sole source of prosperity to the agriculturist; it was purely and simply his *gagne-pain*.

But her star, her " good luck," as say those hostile to the Brazil, prevailed. In 1860 South Carolina " retracted the connection of State and Union," and resumed her independence. Five years afterwards Southerners began to exchange for happier regions their desolate homes. The movement was fondly fostered by the Brazilian Government; and in January, 1868, the number of the immigrants was stated as follows :—‡

Province of Paraná§ (near Curitiba, Morretes, and Paranaguá)	. 200	persons.
São Paulo (Ribeira district, Campinas, Capivarhy, &c.)‖ .	. 800	„
Rio de Janeiro (in and about the capital) . . .	. 200	„
Minas Geraes (Rio das Velhas, &c.)	. 100	„
Espirito Santo ¶ (on the rivers Doce, Linhares, and Guandú)	. 400	„
Bahia	. 100	„
Pernambuco	. 70	„
Pará	. 200	„
Total . .	2700	

graphy, p. 87), informs us that South America has an area of 6,800,000 square miles, and a coast line of 16,500 (" 1 to 420 "—1 : 412 ?), and that it has " little to boast of good harbours." This cannot be said of the Brazil, which has some of the finest ports in the world.

* In 1850 the import slave-trade was prohibited by law; in 1852 the most active measures were taken, and since that time it has virtually been extinct. A committee of the House of Commons (July 19, 1853) gave the following figures :—

In 1847 imported 56,172
,, 1848 ,, 60,000
,, 1849 ,, 54,000
,, 1851 ,, 3,287

In 1853, imported 700 (of whom the greater part were seized by Government). In 1854 the only slave-ship was seized by the authorities in the Bay of Serinhaem (Pernambuco), and the cargo was set free. This was the effect of an enlightened majority, who, as M. Reybaud says, raised the cry, " No more traffic in slaves ! European colonisation ! " It was far from being the work of cruisers. On May 3, 1862, Mr. Christie reported officially to H. M.'s Secretary of State for Foreign Affairs that the importation had wholly ceased, and that its revival appeared an impossibility; and yet we have retained the Aberdeen Bill, one of the greatest insults which a strong ever offered to a weak people.

† A work lately published and attributed to H. I. M. the late Maximilian, who visited Bahia between June 11 and June 19, 1860, gives a melo-dramatic episode of a fight inside the Bay between a slaver and a cruiser. Unfortunately, it adds that the slaves who saved themselves by swimming were employed by the Bahian Railway, whose concession severely prohibits servile labour.

‡ My authority is Mr. Charles Nathan of Rio de Janeiro, who in 1867 contracted with the Imperial Government to bring out in 18 months 1000 families, or 5000 agriculturists. In the list given above he does not include " the New York thieves, &c., who generally work themselves to the Plate River in a few months." The change of steamer-embarkation from New York to Mobile and New Orleans has partly remedied the "scum " evil.

§ Principally settled by Missourians, who come with considerable capital, and who in a few years will make this centre very important.

‖ Mr. C. A. Glennie, long acting Consul at São Paulo, estimates the emigration to the Ribeira at 400—500 souls, and the rest who have passed through Santos, at 375 souls, or 75 families × 5.

¶ The Rio Doce is preferred on account of its magnificent scenery, facilities for transport, and superior soil upon which the plough can be used.

The official list of immigrants into Rio de Janeiro during 1867
gives :—

Portuguese	4822, or nearly half the total.
North Americans	1575
English	647
Germans	357
Irish	220
Other nations	2411
Total	10,032

The current year expects 10,000 : first-class planters appear
inclined to come out to a country where an equal area of ground
produces three times as much cane as Louisiana does. Sugar is
rapidly supplanting cotton, which has not been found to pay,*
and the "Southrons" in the Doce district are studying coffee,
which will probably become a favourite culture.

Thus has begun a steady inflow of hard-working, long-headed
practical men, accustomed to the use of machinery, and forming
in each settlement a nucleus around which European labourers
can cluster. As slavery diminishes so immigration will increase,
and it is good to bear in mind that the two cannot co-exist.
Presently the stream will set in of itself without extraneous aid :
the Germans will appear, the Anglo-Scandinavians, and in fact
whatever pullulates in the fecund North.† And thus the Empire,
despite the want of black hands, will gain labour and follow in
the path of the great Northern Republic.‡

In the Valley of the São Francisco River, the emigration
process has begun, and the pioneer of civilization is now on its
banks. M. Dulot has proved how well calculated is the sub-

---

* Thus one acre in cotton produces 12
arrobas (each 12 lbs.), when clean at
10$000=120$000 (say £12). The same
land gives in sugar, 35 arrobas at 5$000=
175$000, besides the coarse rum obtained
from skimmings and so forth.

† In February, 1868, a detachment of
53 persons was sent from London to Rio de
Janeiro, and a second party of Irish families,
making a total of 338 souls, was being
formed. Their passage money was found
for them, and the agreement was that they
should receive ten days' maintenance free on
landing in the Brazil, and have the option
of purchasing 100 acres a head at 2 shillings per acre, for the usual term of 5
years. In March, 1868, I heard that the
Government agent was about to send out

500 farmers with small capitals of from
£100 to £1000. The 391 souls above
alluded to were settled in the colonies
Principe D. Pedro (Sta. Catherina) and
Cananéa in São Paulo.

‡ The torrent of Irish emigration set in
towards the United States in 1847, when
the famine raged. On March 1, 1845, the
population of the island was nearly 8¼
millions ; on April 1, 1868, it was a little
above 5½ millions ; and it is calculated that
on April 1, 1871, it will hardly exceed that
of Belgium. During the 20 years succeeding that time (1866) the great Republic
had received an increase of 3,500,000
souls, or one-third the population of the
Brazil. The latter, it is computed, doubles
her population in 30 years.

tropical plateau of the Brazil to be a home for Frenchmen. How much more, then, for the swarming hive of Northern Europe and for the Anglo-Scandinavians, vulgarly called Anglo-Saxons, who, at an earlier and more energetic period of their history, would have asserted and proved themselves to be the natural colonizers of the South Temperate zones of the world?

It is evident in our present state that every pound sterling charitably wasted upon catechizing races about to perish, and upon the barren hopeless savagery of Africa and Australia, is a pound diverted from its proper purpose. We still devote fifteen vessels of war, 1500 men, and nearly a million of money per annum, to support a Coffin or Sentimental Squadron, which has ever proved itself powerless to prevent negro-export, whenever and wherever black hands were in due demand, and whose main effect upon West Africa has been to pamper "Sā Leone," that Hamitic Sodom and Gomorrah, to fill a few pockets, to act as a political machine for throwing dust into the public eyes, and greatly to increase the miseries of the slave and the misfortunes of his continent.

At the same time we boast of more than 900,000 paupers or persons in receipt of relief. Our poor-rates cost us per annum a total, actually expended, of 6,959,000l.: the increase of 1867 over 1866 varies from 4·8 to 19·6 per cent. Population advances in the old home in a geometrical, subsistence in an arithmetical, ratio. The plague-spot of England has been declared to be "over-suckling and under-feeding." Overcrowding produces the horrors of the Black Country, and of Terling and Witham in the "Calf County." Hence the state of "City Arabs," of bondagers and hop-pickers, of "Sheffield saw-grinders and Manchester brickmakers."

The million and a half per annum thus thrown away upon "propagating the faith" and maintaining a Squadron effete in its political use, would long ere this have grown to be a "removal fund." It would have made loyal emigrants of the unfortunate Connaught Irish, and would have supplied strong arms and willing hearts to our colonies, that still want, as does the Brazil, farm-labourers and house-servants. During the last score of years we have allowed millions to exile themselves from our shores and to become Fenians in the New World, a thorn in the side of the present generation, preaching to the world in words of fire the inefficiency, to use no harsher term, of our rule, and a scandal to future ages. But the fatal system based upon the tripod " *Quieta non movere,*" " *Après nous le Deluge,*" and the command of Glencrow so grateful to the feeble and the superannuated in body and mind, has allowed us to drift into this our latest and least excusable difficulty.

Half a generation ago, the Irish landlord, the propagator of constitutions and the supporter of " oppressed nationalities," must have known that at least about Sligo discontent was rife, that armed men were drilling at night, that Catholics had thrown off the trammels of the priest and the confessional, and that Irishmen were ready at any moment to strike a blow for what they held to be their rights.

It was not, however, judged proper to startle the many respectables into whose hands the fortunes of Great Britain had fallen since the year of grace 1832, and from whom only 1867 and its consequences can liberate us. The volcano might throb and boil under the feet of the initiated few, but they were bound to feel it and to make no sign. Every parliamentary question upon the subject was answered in a style the most jaunty, off-hand, and self-sufficient; no motion could be made without incurring personal ridicule or obloquy, and the result has been 1867.

Thus far the damage done is irreparable, but we may still prevent the evil from spreading.

The Anglo-Scandinavian and the Anglo-Celt have been described as the great "navvies" of the globe. Before them mountains are levelled; they dig rivers, they build cities, they convert the desert place into a garden—Utah becomes Deseret, the Land of the Honey-bee. The world still wants them; they, in turn, can find many a happier home than Great Britain, where, indeed, it is hard to understand how a poor man can consent to live. The workman coming to the Brazil a miner, a carpenter, or a blacksmith, becomes a mining-captain—perhaps a mine-owner—an agent or land-proprietor, an engineer. The petty shopkeeper in Europe here calls himself at least a merchant, possibly a capitalist. The hedge-schoolmaster is a professor; the clerk rises from 100*l.* to 300*l.* a-year. The governess, so far from being an upper servant, with a heart-wearying lot before her, too often becomes the head of the establishment, and rules it with a rod of iron.

To these and many others, especially to the unmarried of

Europe, the Brazil may say, in the words of Holy Writ—
"*Venite ad me omnes qui laboratis et onerati estis, et ego reficiam vos.*"

It has been said that the lower orders of Englishmen, which word includes Irishmen, do not, as a rule, flourish in the Tropics; that they are mostly, when "left to themselves," a race

> Of men degenerate surely, who have strayed
> Far from the lustrous glories of their sires,
> Deep-mired in vanities and low desires.

But these pages will prove that, with discipline and under strict surveillance, they can do wonders, and when Southerners from the United States shall have settled in the Empire, these men, so well accustomed at home to "drive" whites and to deal with the *prolétaires* and the *colluvies gentium* of Europe, will soon supply the necessary curb.

Hitherto the Brazil has suffered from being virtually a terra incognita to Europe. She is deficient in that powerful interest which arises from "nearness," and she subtends too vast an angle of vision. The books published upon the subject are mostly, I have said, those of specialists: they are, therefore, of the category "*biblia a biblia;*" and none can be catalogued as belonging to the class "which no gentleman's library should be without."

But as far back as 1862, the London Exhibition proved that this region excels all others in supplying the peculiar species of cotton which our manufacturers most demand. Since that time the fleeting thought of war perhaps did good to both countries by introducing them to each other. And now our ever-increasing relations, social and commercial, with this vast and admirable section of the South American Continent, must lead in time to a closer and better acquaintance than anything that we can now imagine. A great national disgrace was required to atone for the national sin of neglecting our East Indian possessions. The Brazil, I believe, now incurs no risk of being forgotten.

In 1864-5, whilst all other nations exported to the Empire 6,850,300*l.*, Great Britain supplied 6,809,700*l.* out of a total of 13,160,000*l.* During 1865-6, the figures became respectively 6,434,400*l.*, 7,375,100*l.*, and the united sum 13,809,500*l.* The year 1866-7 presents, notwithstanding large purchases of raw materials, a large decline.* This, however, is transient, the effect of depreciated currency and of deficient industry, resulting from a three years' campaign that drained gold and blood to a distant region—in fact, a Crimean affair in South America. Finally, Anglo-Brazilian debts amount to a little above 14,000,000*l.*

My motto in these volumes, as in others, has been—

> Dizei em tudo a verdade
> A quem em tudo a deveis.

And certainly the Public has a right to the writer's fullest confidence. It is, however, no pleasant office, when treating of the Gold Mines worked by English companies, to describe correctly the system which has " got them up." But it is not just that the Brazil should bear blame for the unconscience of those who "rig her markets;" and when " Brazilian specs are not favourites: all the Stock and Joint-Stock Companies connected with the country are at a discount;" whilst the money market Review threatens the Empire with the thunders of that monetary Vatican, the Stock Exchange; and when it is reported, even at this moment, that the Brazil, before effecting a loan, will be compelled to pay debts which she does not owe, it is only fair to show the cause, and to call wrong acts by their right names. Of course, unless the whole trick be told, it is better not to tell the tale at all. The reader, however, will perceive, it is hoped, that I have pointed to the system, not to individuals, and that in describing two successes amongst a dozen failures, I have done my best homage to honesty and energy.

While sketching the Highlands of Brazil as far as they were visited by me, my handiwork is totally deficient in the " beautification" of which " serious travellers" complain. It is mostly a succession of hard, dry photographs with rough lines and dark, raw colours, where there is not a sign of glazing. The sketch, in fact, pretends only to the usefulness of accuracy. The day must

---

* The Brazil imported from England—
During the half-year ending
    June 30, 1866 . . £3,789,882
During the half-year ending
    June 30, 1867 . . 2,738,460
But even with this falling off she stands eighth in the list of our customers, ranking below the United States, Germany, France, Holland, Egypt, and Turkey; above Italy, China, and Belgium, and far above Russia and Spain.

The progress of the Brazilian revenue may thus be laid down:—

In 1864-5	...	56,995 : 928$000
,, 1865-6	...	58,146 : 813$000
,, 1866-7	...	61,469 : 437$000
,, 1867-8 not less than		61,535 : 000$000

The estimates for the fiscal year 1869 are calculated to be—

Receipts .	73,000 : 000$000
Expenditure	70,786 : 932$000
Surplus .	2,203 : 067 $000

come when the outlines drawn by other pens will be compared with mine, which will thus afford a standard whereby the progress of the country may be measured. It was judged better to place before the reader certain portions in diary form, not to spare myself the toil and trouble of "digesting," but to present the simplest and the most natural picture of travel. The Brazilians, who, like most young peoples, have a ravenous and almost feminine appetite for admiration and tender protestation, will find my narrative rude and uncompromising. Foreigners here resident, who are gene-rally badly affected to the country,* and who hold it the part of patriotism and a point of honour to support a compatriot against a native, however the former may blunder or plunder, will charge me with "Brazilianism;" but the impartial will give me credit for a sincerity that refuses to flatter or even to exaggerate the gifts of a region which I prefer to all where my travels have hitherto extended. Thus I may escape the charge freely made against almost all who have written in favour of the Brazil, namely, that of having been "induced," or, to speak plain English, of having been bought.†

I have purposely used the word "sketching." My journey covered more than 2000 miles, of which 1150 miles in round numbers were by the slow progress of a raft. The time occupied was only five months, between June 12 and November 12 of 1867: as many years might most profitably be devoted to the Rio São Francisco alone, and even then it would be difficult to produce of it an exhaustive description. I have, however, been careful to collect for future travellers, who shall be masters of more time than my profession allowed me, hearsay accounts of the interesting natural features, the geological remains, and the rock-inscriptions hitherto unworked. Koster, in the beginning of the present century, drew

* Like every country struggling for recog-nition among the self-reliant nations of the world, Brazil has to contend with the pre-judiced reports of a floating foreign popu-lation, indifferent to the welfare of the land they temporarily inhabit, and whose appre-ciations are mainly influenced by private interest. It is much to be regretted that the Government has not thought it worth while to take decided measures to correct the erroneous impressions current abroad concerning its administration; and that its diplomatic agents do so little to circulate truthful and authoritative statements of their domestic concerns." (Agassiz, Journey in Brazil, pp. 515-6). "À Rio de Janeiro on ne connaît guère que Rio de Janeiro, et l'on méprise un peu trop tout ce qui n'est pas Rio de Janeiro," says Auguste de Saint Hilaire with great truth.

† This is at present the popular way to dispose of their opinions who think well of the Brazil. We find extensive reference to "paid puffers of Brazil, and lackeys of its Legation," even in the "Brazil Correspond-ence, with an Introduction." London: Ridgway, 1863.

attention to these "written rocks" in the bed of the northern Parahyba River. I believe that such antiquities are to be found in many parts of the north-eastern shoulder of the South American continent, which approaches nearest to the Old World. And I hope in a future volume to show distinct "vestiges of some forgotten people who possessed the country before the present race of savages (the Tupy family), and of whom not even the most vague tradition has been preserved."*

My second volume ends suddenly at the Great Rapids of the Rio de São Francisco instead of placing the traveller at its mouth. This is perhaps a caprice. But my pen refused to work upon the petty details of a few leagues of land travel and a mere steamer trip down stream, whilst my brain was filled with images of beauty and grandeur. Nor would further narrative have been of any especial service. A thousand vacation tourists will learn at length that yellow fever in the Empire is not an abiding guest, that her shores can be reached in ten days from Europe, that no long sea-voyage is more comfortable or so pleasant, that the Highlands of the Brazil, which popular ignorance figures to be a swampy flat, are exceptionally healthy, and have been used as Sanitaria by invalids who had no prospect of life in Europe, and, lastly, that a short fortnight spent in the country upon a visit to Barbacena in the province of Minas Geraes, viâ the D. Pedro Segundo R. R., will offer the finest specimens of the three great geographical features of the land, the Beiramar or seaboard, the Serra do Mar, maritime range or Eastern Ghauts, and the Campos, commonly translated prairies. They will not neglect to visit the Niagara of the Brazil, and they will find Paulo Affonso, King of Rapids, more accessible than northern Scotland. From the agents of the Bahia Steam Navigation Company at S. Salvador and on the lower São Francisco River they will meet with every attention, and at the office they will obtain more general knowledge of the country than can be packed into a handbook.

The Appendix contains a translation of a monogram by M. Gerber, C.E., describing Minas Geraes, one of the typical provinces of the Empire of the Southern Cross. It is simply a compila-

---

* Southey (History of Brazil, ii. pp. 30, 653). The laborious author adds, "Rocks sculptured with the representations of animals, of the sun, moon, and stars, with hieroglyphical signs, and if an incurious Franciscan may be trusted, with characters also, have been recently found in Guyana, the most savage part of South America, and hitherto the least explored."

tion. But it forms an excellent base for future labours, and it is a good specimen of the stores of local information now locked up from the world in the pigeon-holes of Brazilian literature. I failed to meet the distinguished author at Ouro Preto, and I am bound to make an apology for having translated him without his express permission.

Were I here to quote all the names, Brazilian and English, to which the pleasure and the profit of my journey are due, the list would occupy many a page. They have not been ignored in these volumes, and now they shall not be troubled with anything but the heartfelt expression of my liveliest gratitude.

To conclude. The kindly reader will not criticize the smaller errors of sheets which were not corrected in proof.* During my absence from England, my wife, who travelled with me through Minas Geraes, will take upon herself the work of revision, but the last " coup de peigne " must necessarily be wanting.

NOTE.†

THIS Essay has extended to an undue length, but it would not be complete without a list of the authors whose names I have used, and a few observations upon the subject of their labours.

John Mawe : the only edition known to me is " Voyages dans l'Intérieur du Brésil en 1809 et 1810, traduits de l'Anglais par J. B. B. Cyriès." ‡ Paris, Gide fils, libraire, 1816. I have not seen his " Treatise on Diamonds and Precious Stones, including their History, Natural and Commercial, to which is added some account of the best method of cutting and polishing them." 8vo. London, 1813. The Englishman in the Brazil must often meet his countrymen, if he would meet them at all, in the garb of the Gaul. Thus only have I seen the excellent volumes of Mr. Koster, so often quoted by Southey, and known in the Brazil as Henrique da Costa. The edition is

---

* Former travellers have noticed a "fatality" attaching to works upon the subject of the Brazil, the unconscionable number of errata required by Manoel Ayres de Cazal, MM. Spix and Martius, Jozé Feliciano Fernandes Pinheiro, Eschwege, Pizarro e Araujo, and the first publication by Saint Hilaire.

† In the following pages the names of certain authors will recur with unusual frequency. The object of these repeated quotations from what are now "standard works," is complimentary, not critical: no one knows more than myself how little my own errors and shortcomings justify me in criticising. There is a Hakluyt Society for republishing with annotations those who date from a certain number of centuries. The moderns, however, must be read as they wrote; and since the days when they wrote, many things have been changed. In due course of time they will all be deemed worthy of the Hakluyts, and, meanwhile, notices of their labours will be as valuable to future students as they are unpleasant to the reader in the present day.

‡ This venerable author has merited, by attracting to her the attention of Europe, the gratitude of the Brazil.

"Voyages dans la Partie Septentrionale du Brésil, &c., par Henri Koster, depuis 1809 jusqu'en 1815." Traduits de l'Anglais par M. A. Jay. Paris, 1818.*

"Voyage au Brésil dans les années 1815, 1816 et 1817, par S. A. S. Maximilien, Prince de Wied-Neuwied ; traduit de l'Allemand par J. B. B. Cyriès." Paris, Arthur Bertrand, 1821. "Prince Max." the Lord of Braunberg, has made *époque*, and his collections were valuable in illustrating the natural history of the Brazil.

M. Auguste de Saint Hilaire visited the Brazil in the suite of the Duc de Luxembourg, and during the whole six years between April 1, 1816, and 1822, he travelled over 2500 leagues. This author is respected by the Brazilians more than any other ; he is almost German in point of exactness and painstaking, and the only fault to be found with his narrative is its succinctness, an unusual offence. Of his works eight volumes are familiar to me, and I have quoted them under their respective numbers :

I. Voyage dans les Provinces de Rio de Janeiro et de Minas Geraes. Paris, Grimbert et Dorez, 1830.

II. Voyage dans le District des Diamans et sur le Littoral du Brésil. Paris, Librairie Gide, 1833.

III. Voyage aux Sources du Rio de S. Francisco et dans la Province de Goyaz. Paris, Arthur Bertrand, 1847.

IV. Voyage dans les Provinces de Saint Paul et de Sainte Catherine. Paris, Arthur Bertrand, 1851.

I could not meet with his "Flora Brasiliæ Meridionalis," which was edited with the collaboration of MM. Jussieu and Cambassèdes, nor with the "Plantes Usuelles des Brésiliens," nor with the "Histoire des Plantes les plus remarquables du Brésil et du Paraguay."

The last French author whose travels in the Brazil were of importance is the Count Francis de Castelnau, who directed the "Expédition dans les Parties centrales de l'Amérique du Sud." Paris, Bertrand, 1850. 6 vols. in 8vo.

I have often referred to Robert Southey, whose "History of the Brazil" has been admirably translated into Portuguese by a Brazilian.

The three folios, at present scarce and unpleasantly expensive, amply deserve another edition, with notes and emendations. This "great undertaking" of the Laureate's "mature manhood" is characterised in his two valuable volumes by Sr. A. de Varnhagen (Historia Geral do Brazil, ii. 344), "not so much a history as chronological memoirs, collected from many authors and various manuscripts, to serve for the history of the Brazil, Buenos Ayres, Montevideo, Paraguay, &c." †

---

* It abounds in the worst misprints, for instance in the first volume : Cava for Cará (Pref. xxxvii.), Assogados for Affogados (12), Poco for Poço (13), Alsandega for Alfandega (52), Alqueise or Alqueère for Alqueire (55 and 219), Jaguadas for Jangadas (93), Cacinebas for Cacimbas (131), Homems for Homens (214), Andhorina for Andorinha (232), Guardamare for Guardamór (295), Serra Pequeno for Pequena (333), and so forth.

† Sr. Varnhagen is open to somewhat the same objection. The historical part of his work is far less valuable than the portions devoted to general information, and the concluding chapters are exceedingly unsatisfactory.

Southey's History was continued in two volumes by "John Armitage, Esquire," Smith & Elder, London, 1836. The author was engaged in commerce at Rio de Janeiro, but he wrote under high official information, and his book will ever be most interesting. The English edition and the

"Notes on Rio de Janeiro and the Southern Parts of Brazil, taken during a residence of ten years in that country, from 1808 to 1818." By John Luccock. London, Strand, 1820. These "Notes" belong to the folio days of travel : we wonder what a "work" would have been. The laborious historian, Sr. Varnhagen (ii., 481), alludes to his not having been able to procure the volume, hence we may judge how little it is known.

"A History of the Brazil," &c., &c. By James Henderson. London, Longmans, 1821. This is also a folio ; it is 'rather a compilation than an original, and thus it wants the freshness and utility of its rival.

"Notices of Brazil in 1828 and 1829." By the Rev. R. Walsh, LL.D., M.R.I.A. London, Westley & Davis, 1830. The two stout octavos require correction with a liberal hand ; the author seems to have believed every tale invented for him, and he viewed the Empire through the dark glances of our rabid anti-slavery age, happily now past. He is one of the authors who, according to Saint Hilaire, have materially injured British prestige in the Brazil.

"Travels in the Interior of Brazil." By George Gardner, F.L.S., Superintendent of the Royal Botanical Gardens of Ceylon. London, Reeve, 1846. This estimable author spent in the Empire the years between 1836 and 1841. His forte is botany, but he was also a man of general knowledge, who wrote in a pleasant unassuming style, whose geniality is still appreciated.*

An immense mass of information touching the Brazil is to be found in the official and other documents published at Lisbon, especially in the "Collecção de Noticias para a Historia e Geographia das Nações ultra-marinas que vivem nos dominios Portuguezes, ou lhes são visinhas. Publicada pela Academia Real das Sciencias." Lisboa, na Typographia da Mesma Academia, 1812. The seven octavos are read by few 'but students, and at present the English public has everything to learn of the truly noble Portuguese literature. As a rule we dislike the language because it is nasal, and we have a deep-rooted and most ignorant idea that Portuguese, the most Latin of all the neo-Latin tongues, is a "bastard dialect of Spanish."

"Annaes Maritimos e Coloniaes, Publicação Mensal redigida sob a direcção da Associacão Maritima e Colonial." Lisboa, Imprensa Nacional. Of this valuable collection many series have been published. I was unable to purchase a copy at the Imprensa Nacional. The Royal Geographical Society of London objected to send their volumes beyond the Atlantic, and my debt of gratitude is to my friend the geographer, Mr. Alexander Findlay, F.R.G.S.†

Portuguese translation are both out of print, and well merit re-issue, if possible with notes and amplifications.

* The object of this note is not to notice contemporary English authors—Hadfield (1854), Hinchliff (1863), and others. I cannot refrain, however, from expressing my admiration of the "Naturalist on the River Amazons," by Henry Walter Bates. London, Murray, 1863. "Publishers say that our public does not care for Brazil," the author once told me : his volumes have certainly given the correction to this idea.

† It may be deemed curious that no mention is here made of the "Revista Trimensal," issued by the Instituto Historico Geographico of Rio de Janeiro. The publication is so carelessly supplied that it is well nigh useless. The library attached to the Faculty of São Paulo, one of the nearest approaches to a Brazilian university, has no complete copy, four years' numbers are wanting, and since 1866 no copies have been forwarded. As regards the Institute itself I can personally afford no information ; during my frequent visits to Rio de Janeiro the honour of an invitation to attend its meetings was never extended to me.

A ponderous but valuable work (which an index would make ten times more useful), in 9 volumes, is the " Memorias Historicas do Rio de Janeiro e das Provincias Annexas à Jurisdicçao do Vice-rei do Estado do Brazil," por (Monsenhor) Jozé de Souza Azevedo Pizarro e Araujo. Rio de Janeiro, Impressão Nacional, 1822. Another is the Corographia Brazilica of (the Abbé) Manoel Ayres de Casal, the "dozen" of Brazilian geographers. The book (printed in 1817) is well known, not so the author : his birth-place has never been discovered, and the only detail of his career which came to light is that he returned with the Court to Portugal and there died. He is now, despite of a few inaccuracies, one of the classics. Of purely geographical compilations we have the "Diccionario Geographico Historico e Descriptivo do Imperio do Brazil." Por J. C. R. Millet de Saint Adolphe. Paris, Ailland, 1845. This work, in two volumes, is a mere compilation and is exceedingly incorrect.

Works of local use are—

"Memorias sobre as Minas de Minas Geraes, escripta em 1801, pelo Dr. José Vieira Couto." This excellent little book, which is philosophical, unprejudiced, and not without eloquent and picturesque descriptions, was republished by MM. Laemmert & Co., Rio de Janeiro, 1842. It will frequently be referred to in the following pages.

"Viagem Mineralogica na Provincia de S. Paulo," por José Bonifacio de Andrada e Silva, e Martim Francisco Ribeiro de Andrada. I am unable to give the date, as my copy wants the title page, and none of the Andrada family could supply the information. It has been translated into French by the Councillor Antonio de Menezes Drummond, and it was published in the "Journal des Voyages."

"Historia do Movimento Politico que no Anno de 1842, teve lugar na Provincia de Minas Geraes." Pelo Conego José Antonio Marinho. The first volume was published by J. E. S. Cabral, Rio de Janeiro, Rua do Hospicei, No. 66, in 1844 ; the second in the same year by J. Villeneuve e Comp^ie, Rua do Ouvidor, No. 65. "Padre Marinho" was a red-hot Lusia or Liberal ; he was however much esteemed, and after the Revolutionary movement was crushed, he lived out the rest of his days, taking an active part in public affairs, at Rio de Janeiro. There is also a Chronological History of the affair taken from the opposite stand-point, and published under the auspices, it is said, of the President of Minas Geraes, Bernardo Jacintho da Veiga.

"Informação ou Descripção topographica e politica do Rio de S. Francisco," pelo Coronel Ignacio Accioli de Cerqueira e Silva. Rio de Janeiro. Typographia Franceza de Frederico Arverson, Largo da Carioca, 1860. Colonel Accioli has laboured hard and well in the field of local Brazilian literature.

"Almanak Administrativo, Civil e Industrial da Provincia de Minas Geraes, para o anno de 1864," organisado e redigido por A. de Assis Martins e T. Marquez de Oliveira. 1° anno. Rio de Janeiro, Typographia da Actualidade. A 2nd volume appeared at Ouro Preto, Typographia do Minas Geraes, 1864 (for the year 1865). I had hoped to see a 3rd in 1868, but it has not yet been issued.

"Rapport partiel sur le Haut San Francisco, ou Description topographique et statistique des parties de la Province de Minas Geraes comprises dans le bassin du Haut San Francisco, précédée de quelques aperçus généraux sur la même Province," par Eduardo José de Moraes, Lieutenant du Génie de l'Armée Brésilienne. Paris, Parent, 1866. Its object is a canal.

As regards the Tupy or Lingua Geral,* a subject now so deeply interesting in the Brazil, from whose settled portions the "Indian" element is so rapidly disappearing, I have used the—

"Grammatica da Lingua Geral dos Indios do Brasil, reimpressa pela primeira vez neste continente depois de tão longo tempo de sua publicaçao em Lisboa," por João Joaquim da Silva Guimarães. Bahia, Typographia de Manoel Feliciano Sepulveda, 1851.

"Diccionario da Lingua Tupy chamada Lingua Geral dos Indigenas do Brazil," por A. Gonçalves Dias. Lipsia, F. A. Brockhaus, 1858. The author was a linguist, a traveller, and a poet, and his early death cast a gloom over his native land.

"Chrestomathia da Lingua Brazilica," pelo Dr. Ernesto Fineira França. Leipzig, Brockhaus, 1859.

A useful handbook to those studying the Flora of the Empire is the "Systema de Materia Medica Vegetal Brasileira, etc., etc., extrahida a traduzida das Obras de Car. Fred. Phil. de Martins," pelo Desembargador Henrique Velloso d'Oliveira. Rio de Janeiro, Laemmert, 1854. It is something more than a translation of the Latin volume,† published by the learned Bavarian.

Upon the Rio de São Francisco I was accompanied by the—

"Relatorio concernente á Exploração do Rio de São Francisco desde a Cachoeira da Pirapora até o Oceano Atlantico, durante os Annos de 1852, 1853, e 1854," pelo Engenheiro Henrique Guilherme Fernando Halfeld. Impresso por ordem do Governo Imperial. Rio de Janeiro : Typographia Moderna de Georges Bertrand, Rua da Ajuda, 73. This small thin folio is of convenient travelling dimensions. Not so the enormous and costly—

"Atlas e Relatorio concernente a Exploração do Rio de S. Francisco desde a Cachoeira da Pirapora até o Oceano Atlantico, levantado por ordem do Governo de S. M. I. O Senhor Dom Pedro II.," pelo Engenheiro Civil Henrique Guilherme Fernando Halfeld em 1852, 1853, e 1854, e mandado lithographar na lithographia Imperial de Eduardo Rensburg. Rio de Janeiro, 1860. The plans do honour to lithography in the Brazil. His Imperial Majesty, an Honorary Member of the Royal Geographical Society of London, was pleased to forward, in 1865, a copy of this huge folio to our library.

For the Rio das Velhas I had provided myself with a copy of the—

"Hydrographie du Haut San Francisco, et du Rio das Velhas, résultats au point de vue hydrographique d'un Voyage effectué dans la Province de Minas Geraes, par Emm. Liais. Ouvrage publié par ordre du Gouvernement Impérial du Brésil, et accompagné de Cartes levées par l'auteur, avec la collaboration de MM. Eduardo José de Moraes et Ladislao de Souza Mello Netto." Paris et Rio Janeiro, 1865. This is a work having authority, and the style of the folio is worthy of its matter.

M. Liais tells us in his Preface (p. 2) that he has "collected numerous documents upon a crowd of other than hydrographical questions, and has

---

* The first publication upon the subject was the "Arte da Grammatica da lingua mais usada na Costa do Brazil," by the venerable Anchieta, published at Coimbra, 1595, and now of extreme rarity.

The Jesuit Padre Luis Figueira also printed an "Arte da Grammatica da

Lingua Brasilica," Lisbon, 1687. I have a copy of the 4th edition, Lisbon, 1795.

† "Systema Materiæ Medicæ Vegetalis Brasiliensis Composuit," Car. Frid. Phil. de Martins. Lipsiæ, apud Frid. Fleischer, 1843.

conscientiously studied the soil, the mines, the climate, the natural productions, the agriculture, and the statistics of the country." These he promises to issue with his Atlas, but in a more portable form. But besides five other Memoires upon various scientific subjects,* he has yet published, I believe, only " L'Espace Céleste,"† which contains notices of his travels and labours in the Empire.

     *   *   *   *   *   *

    This list of studies is not imposing. It would, however, have been even less so, but for the unwearied kindness of my excellent friend Dr. José Innocencio de Moraes Vieira, Librarian to the Faculty of Law (Faculdade de Direito) in the City of São Paulo.

    * These are, 1, "De l'Emploi des Observations Azimutales pour la Determination des Ascensions droites," &c. ; 2, "Théorie des Oscillations du Baromètre "; 3, "De l'Emploi de l'Air chauffé comme force motrice" ; 4, "De l'Influence de la Mer sur les Climats "; and (promised in 1865) 5, "La Continuation des Explorations scientifiques au Brésil."

    † Emm. Liais, Astronome de l'Observatoire Impérial de Paris. "L'Espace Céleste et la Nature tropicale, Description physique de l'Univers, d'après des observations personnelles faites dans les deux hémisphères." Preface de M. Bubinet, desseins de Yan' Dargent. Paris, Garnier Brothers (no date).

CHAPTER I.

WE LEAVE RIO DE JANEIRO.

"Rien au monde n'est aussi beau, peut-être, que les environs de Rio de Janeiro."
St. Hilaire.

I AM about to describe in this volume a holiday excursion which we made to the Gold Mines of Central Minas Geraes *viá* Petropolis, Barbaçena, and the Prairies and Highlands of the Brazil. Our journey has a something of general interest; in a few years it will have its Handbook and form a section of the Nineteenth Century "Grand Tour." And I venture to predict that many of those now living will be whirled over the land at hurricane speed, covering sixty miles per hour, where our painful "pede-locomotion" wasted nearly a week. Perhaps they may fly—*Quem sabe ?*

My project was, then, to visit the head-waters of the Rio de São Francisco, the mighty river here trivially called the Brazilian Mississippi, and to float down its whole length, ending by way of *bonne bouche* with the King of Rapids, Paulo Affonso. In this second act of travel, which is *not* a holiday excursion, the diamond diggings were to be inspected.

After eighteen dull months spent at Santos, São Paulo, I was graciously allowed leave of absence by the Right Honourable the Lord Stanley, Her Majesty's Principal Secretary of State for Foreign Affairs. By command of His Majesty the Emperor of the Brazil, I was supplied with a " Portaria "*—Podoroshna, or especial licence to travel; it bore the signature of His Excellency the late Councillor Antonio Coelho de Sá e Albuquerque, Minister for Foreign Affairs, a name immortalised by the decrees of December 7, 1866, and July 31, 1867, which admitted the

---

* In former times the Portaria dispensed the traveller with paying ferries, tolls, and other small charges. I did not attempt such trifling economy, and can hardly say whether it is still useful for "dead heading."

world to, and which regulated the inland navigation of the Brazil. The Minister of Agriculture and Public Works, His Excellency the Councillor Manoel Pinto de Souza Dantas, who took the liveliest interest in the journey, honoured me with a circular letter addressed to the authorities of his own Province, Bahia, where he had lately been President, and where his wishes were law. Finally, the eminent Deputy of Alagôas, Dr. Aureliano Candido Tavares Bastos, Jun., whose patriotic enthusiasm for progress has so urgently advocated the freeing of the coasting trade and the opening of great fluvial lines,* kindly gave me a variety of introductory letters.

Under such auspices we—that is to say, my wife and the inevitable Ego—with a negret answering to the name of Chico or Frank, after exhausting the excitements of the " Rio Season," left that charming but somewhat drowsy, dreamy, and do-little Capital on the fortunate Ember-day, Wednesday, June 12, 1867. Affectionate acquaintances bade us sad adieux, prognosticating every misery from tick-bites to kniving. What Dr. Couto calls the " old system of terrors " is not yet obsolete, and I was looked upon as a murderer *in posse*, because Mrs. Burton chose to accompany me. A " synthesis of cognate habits " induced Mr. George Lennon Hunt to see us embark, and he was not alone, for there are " good children " even amongst the John Bull-lings of the Brazil.

" Rio Bay," like all the beautiful sisterhood, from Cornish "Mullions " westward to the Bay of Naples, must be seen in " war-paint." Most charming is she when sitting under her rich ethereal canopy, whilst a varnish of diaphanous atmosphere tempers the distance to soft and exquisite loveliness ; when the robing blue is perfect brilliant blue, when the browns are dashed with pink and purple, and when the national colours suggest themselves : green, vivid as the emerald, and yellow, bright as burnished gold. Then the streams are silver, then the scaurs are marked orange and vermilion as they stand straightly out from the snowy sand or the embedding forest, then the passing clouds form floating islets as their shadows walk over the waters of the inner sea, so purely green. Then the peasant's whitewashed hut of tile and " wattle and dab," rising from the strand of snowy

---

* His book, " O Valle do Amazonas " (Rio de Janeiro, B. L. Garnier, 1866), is a valuable statistical study of the River, and amply deserves translation.

sand, becomes opal and garnet in the floods of light which suggest nothing but a perpetual springtide. And every hour has its own spell. There is sublimity in the morning mists rolling far away over headland brow and heaving ocean; there is grandeur, loveliness, and splendour in the sparkling of the waves under the noon-day sun, when the breeze is laden with the perfume of a thousand flowers; and there is inexpressible repose and grace in the shades of vinous purple which evening sheds over the same.

Combine with this soft and fairy-like, this singular feminine beauty of complexion, a power and a majesty born of the size and the abrupt grandeur of mountain and peak, of precipice and rock, which would strike the mind of Staffa, and which forbid any suspicion of effeminacy. Such effects of Nature, at once masculine and womanly, alternately soft and stern, necessarily affect the national character. The old sneer that the family of Uncle Sam must not hold itself to be a great people because Niagara is a great cataract, contains even less truth than such sneers usually contain. The "Aspects of Nature" are now recognized influences upon the ideality and the intellect of man. "Onde ha o grande e o bello," says Sr. Castilho, with eminent poetic instinct, "apparece logo a poesia;*" and now even we of the little island readily own that "size becomes in the long run a measure of political power." And is not the Beautiful the visible form of the Good? As these pages will prove, travel in the "Land of Dye-wood" resembles travel in no other land. It has a gentleness, an amenity of aspect which the sons of the rugged North see for the first occasion, and which they must never expect to see again. At the same time we shall find amongst the people pronounced traits of character, and an almost savage energy, which show bone as well as smoothness of skin.

There are, however, times and seasons when Rio Bay, the Charmer, bears a stormy dangerous brow, upon which it is not good to look. Again there are days, especially in early winter from May to June,† when her frowns melt into smiles, and when

* "Where the Grand and the Beautiful exist, there the Poet soon appears." This part of the Brazil is a just middle between those physical extremes which over-stimulate or which depress the imagination.

† The Europeanized seasons in this part of the Brazil, as "adapted to the Southern Hemisphere, are the normal four (the Aryan division being originally three, Winter, Spring, and Summer); viz.:—1. Spring, beginning September 22; 2. Summer, December 21; 3. Autumn, March 20; and 4. Winter, June 21. The Guarany "Indians," or indigenes, more sensibly divided the year into two halves, "Coaracy-ara," sun-season, and "Almana-ara," rain-season. "They are the divisions which we recognize now," says Sr. José de Alencar in

2 views - grim & lovel

tears follow her laughter. Of such sort was that Wednesday, the Ember-day, in the year of grace 1867; it came hard upon a terrible shipwrecking gale.

Rio de Janeiro, the "very loyal and heroic city," viewed from the quarter and station of the "Prainha," *alias* "Mauá's Wharf," *does* remind eye, nose, and ear of certain sites on the Thames which shall be nameless. You hustle through a crowd of blacks. You make the little jetty under a barrel roof of corrugated and galvanized iron, between piles of coffee sacks, whose beans, scattered over the floor, show that the ruthless "piercer"* has plunged in his scoop, withdrawn his sample, and stocked his home with plundered caffeine. Near the coarse pier of creaking planks lie swamped canoes and floating boats, a red dredging craft, sundry little black steamers, a crowd of loading ships, and a scatter of crippled hulks; a dead dog floats lazily past us, the smoke of Dover stifles us, the clang of hammers has power to *agaçer* our nerves, and we acknowledge the savour of that old Father who once harboured Le Brut of Troy. But here the picturesque "Morro da Saude"—the Hill of Health— sits by the shore clad in Tanga kirtle of grass and tree, whilst close behind, towering high in air, the gigantic detached block culminating in "Tijuca Peak," overlooks the scene like the monarch of mountains he is.

To the south-east are the yellow-ochre buildings of the Marine Arsenal, long and low, and Lisbon-like, with windows jealously barred. The surroundings are a tall red slip-shed, a taller black-shed, fronted by a big, antiquated, and green-painted crane; piles of coke and coal, rusty guns, and old tanks and boilers cumber the ground; in front floats a ship newly born to ocean life, and a mob of smaller craft are made to hug their great mother, the shore. But, again, the upper part of this picture is São Bento's stern old pile, with its massive square front of monastery pitted and dented by the cannon-balls of the stout French corsair,† with its pyramid-capped belfries, whose weathercocks have been weathered down to spikes, and with its gardens of rich sward and luxuriant banana stretching far away in our rear.

his admirable romance, O Guarany, vol. i. 361, "and the only seasons which really exist in the Brazil." Moreover it may be said that Rio de Janeiro, the city, placed in the interval between the Trades and the Variable winds, has no regular "dries"

or "rains," a result also brought about of late years by extensive cultivation and dis-foresting.

* O furador, the "sampler:" the word wants, methinks, a letter.

† Duguay-Trouin, who bombarded it in 1711.

And now the little steamer "Petropolis" is under way, making nine knots per hour, very unlike the "open boat"* affected by the travellers of 1808—1825. We rush past the Ilha das Cobras, "Snake Island," a little heap of green slope and granite scarp, with bran-new docks and ancient lines of fortalice and building, all ochre-tinted, to show public property; past the shipping channel, all hull and mast; past the big red Custom-house, said to have cost £300,000, and already showing a graceful sag of some four inches in the centre; past the low, solid buildings, not without the usual steeple, on the Ilha das Enxadas, or "Isle of Hoes," known to the Briton as the "Coal Island," which was sold for a song, and which is now worth a mint of pounds sterling; past the distance-dwarfed eastern wall of the Bay, in the upper part broken hills, by contrast hillocks, and below a town and outlying villages, with houses and villas, forts and churches; past the "Island of the Governor" (Salvador Corrêa de Sá), very properly called in the English "Long Island," from its length of twenty-eight miles, where the ant-eater† having been eaten out, the ant eats out the farmer; past Paquetá, of old "Pacatá," shaped like a figure of 8 —that "lovely insular gem," shady with mangos and cashews, and myrtles, and the olive-like Camará,‡ the coquette called the Capri of Rio—classical, charming, and happily without a Tiberius; past the bight of Magé, which deluded the first discoverers into misnaming this little Mediterranean "River of January," and which caused their descendants to miscall themselves Fluminenses, or People of the River; § past slabs of rock, each growing its one or two bunches of vigorous verdure, fruit of that mighty coition of equinoctial sun and tropical rain; past eyots of dull white granite boulders, the blocs perchés and roches moutonnées of De Saussure ("Verily," exclaims a friend, "its name is

---

* "Falúa."

† Especially the species called Tamanduá (*i.e.*, Taixi-mondé, ant-trap) Mirim, or little ant-eater (Myrmecophaga tetradactyla), as opposed to the greater ant-eater, Tamanduá Cavallo or bandeira (Myrmecophaga jubata, Linn.). The often recurring word miry, merem or mirim (Portuguese —inho—inha—sinho, etc.), a terminal borrowed from the Tupy-Guarany tongue, means small, lesser, least, opposed to osú, asú, wasú, guasú, ussu (it varies according to the syllable preceding it), magnus, major, maximus. The latter corresponds with the termination ão in Portuguese.

Anthropologists are advised to visit Long Island. It contains kitchen-middens of oyster and other shells locally called "Sambaqúis," and is rich in aboriginal skulls and stone celts.

‡ A Lantana, one of the Verbenaceæ, a common wild tree in the prairies of the Brazil.

§ Hence we still read in French and English "Gazetteers," and "Compendiums of Geography," "Rio de Janeiro, or Rio de Janario, on the Rio River;" "Rio de Janeiro, située à l'embouchure du fleuve du même nom." (Dictionnaire de la Conversation, F. Didot, Paris, 1857.)

boulder!")—some the size of a house, rounded and water-rolled, others acutangular, and brought on thin ice-rafts and floes by the Glacial Theory from yon towering range of Swiss physiognomy. We look behind us, and the glance plunges into the open sea through the portals of the Colossal Gate, sentinelled by an army of peaks. We look in front at a northern wall, the Serra do Mar, or Sea Range; to the north-east rise the Organ Mountains proper, with their four sharp needles of darker blue, silhouetted against the undefined vapoury background, and resembling anything but organ-pipes;* due north is the Star Range,† where a break and a knob of rock, the usual Cabeça de Frade, or "Friar's Head," mark the natural zigzag taken by the road; while to the north-west the pyramidal and sharply outlined peaks of the Serra de Tinguá prolong the mighty curtain in the direction of São Paulo. And now, eleven miles duly left behind, we dash towards a sprinkling of huts and a low line of mangrove, backed by the sub-range, heaps of dark green hill shaggy with second growth, and not unfrequently topped by a white church. This is the "Mauá Landing Place," and here ends Act No. 1 of to-day's travel drama.

Before we tread the shaky, creaky, little plank-jetty leading to the railway carriages, we may incidentally remark that Mauá Bay and Paquetá Island supply Rio with the best oysters. Bad, however, are now the best. The Riverines should, like their northern

---

* I may suggest that the discoverers called them Serra dos Orgãos from the huge tree cactus (Cactus arboreus, in Spanish Organo) which abounds in these mountains. As regards the altitude a popular error makes the Organ Mountains never to exceed 1300 metres. Professor Agassiz (A Journey in Brazil, chap. 2) tells us that the highest summits of the Organ Mountains range only from 2000 to 3000 feet, and in chap. 15, quoting M. Liais, who makes the maximum altitude observed by him 7000 feet, he ignores Gardner, who found a still greater height. According to Captain Bulhões the Alto da Serra is 883·21 metres, the road in front of the palace at Petropolis 842, and the Peak of Tinguá upwards of 2000. The Tijúca is 1050, and the Corcovado 664 metres.

† The Serra da Estrella is probably so called from the beautiful highlands of Central Portugal. It is part of the Serra do Mar or Maritime Range, which here corresponds with the Alleghanies, or Appalachian range of the northern continent. The chain begins in the north of Espirito Santo (S. lat. 16°—17°), where it continues the Serra dos Aymorés, and thence it runs some 150 miles from E.N.E. to W.S.W. It is a barrier cutting off the hot, damp, and fever-haunted maritime lowlands of the coast or Beiramar, from the dry and healthy highlands of the interior, and though only a score of miles from the capital it is still in a state of nature.

Estrella, the port at the foot of the range, and north of "Mauá," was a place of great consequence and bustle during the first quarter of the present century: all the imports and exports of the Far West passed through it, and large covered boats with flat bottoms connected it with the capital. It was then

"Differtum nautis, cauponibus atque malignis."

Now it has passed through the court, has obtained its discharge, and is hopelessly ruined.

brethren of Californian San Francisco, send for spat or oyster-seed to New York, or, better still, to Baltimore. The aboriginal mollusk might meanwhile be greatly improved by scientific ostrei-culture. Bed the bivalves for six months where there is no seaward current, but where the rising tide mixes salt water with fresh. There must be artificial collectors to prevent the spat being carried away and lost, and which will save the trouble and expense of removing it to another place. Feed them for the last fortnight with "farinha"* or other flour. So shall you see the long, thick, black beard give way to delicate meat, and the thin angular flatness become plump and rounded.

Here begins Act No. 2. The Mauá Railway, upon which the engine first whistled in the Brazil,† is a very small chapter in that latest and best Euangelion which began, one year before the Brazil was born, with the first "Stockton and Darlington Rail-way Act," April 19, 1821. Like other little things, "Mauá" had a mighty soul. At the Fête of Industry, when its godfather opened it, he is said to have exclaimed, "A Barra do Rio das Velhas." (En route to the valley of the São Francisco River.) But unhappily double the sum authorised—£60,000, instead of £30,000—was expended upon a road, not a railroad, and the prophecy has still to fulfil itself.

The engine pulls us slowly, feebly up a valley, or rather a gully, winding through the lowest sub-range. Then we come to a flat, a strip of the Pontine Marshes—a true crocodile country, all mud and mangrove, miasma and mosquitos, watery even during the driest weather, and in places sandy and sterile. Around the single station, "Inhomirim," the land bristles with the Piri-piri, or Brazilian papyrus,‡ tall and tufty as that of Sicilian Anapas, or

---

* When farinha, "*the* flour par excel-lence," is mentioned, the reader will under-stand that it is the "wood-meal" (farinha de pão), of the Euphorbiaceous "Manihot utilissima" (not "Jatropha Manihot"), the black or poisonous manioc. The French colonies call it Cassave, hence our Cassava, or Cassada. I will not describe the prepa-ration, this has been done by a century of travellers.

† In the Esboço Historico das Estradas de Ferro do Brazil (por C. B. Ottoni. Rio: Villeneuve, 1866) we are told that the contract was made on April 27, 1852; the trains began to run over the whole line in December, 1854: the rules and regulations

arranged for the Company on December 23, 1855, and the total cost was 1,743:764$121 (£174,300), or 105:683 $ 000 per kilo-metre (£10,568).

‡ "Piri-piri" resembles "papyrus" in sound, but the likeness is superficial. Piri is the common rush, and piri-piri (rush-rush) is the largest species. The Tupy language delights in the onomatopoetic or the "ding-dong," "bow-wow," or "cag-mag," and like many other barbarous tongues it expresses augmentation and magnitude by reduplication. Thus muré is a flute; muré-muré a large flute. Ará is a parroquet; ará ará, contracted to arara, (big parroquet), a macaw. As remarked

as the produce of the Whydah lagoon. It shows the saltness of the soil, and it has never yet made paper. The girding hills are dull green with poor second growth, fit only for hedges. On our left runs the "Estrella Road," and here and there a few palms and plantains, or a tall myrtle, brown with breathing bad air, and clad in rags of grey Tillandsia moss, show that the squatter or settler is not far off. As we approach the maritime mountains there are rich fields and clearings for cattle, all the work of the last two years, and made despite the deadly swamp-fevers. After eleven miles or more, exactly 16·5 kilometres, we reach the Root of the Range. Here we strangers stare wonder-stricken at the colossal amphitheatre of "Eastern Ghauts" that fronts us, with shaggy wall forested to its coping, with tremendous flying buttresses shot forth from the main mass, and with slides of bare granite, famous Montagnes Russes for Titans at play. How we are to get up is a mystery, till our courier, the indefatigable George F. Land, a Britisher withal, points from the flat to a kind of gap on the right, the path of a superficial torrential drain which feeds the rivulet Inhomirim.* It is the key-stone of the gigantic inverted arch, up which the admirable road constructed by Government painfully winds.

Now opens Act No. 3—the gem of the piece. Our well-packed carriage is drawn by four mules; thorough-bred horses could not stand such work. Up we go, blessing the projectors of this smooth, gutter-lined, and parapetted Macadam:† it is a Simplon with prodigious windings; the gradient is 1: 16. In places a man may address his friend in the third zigzag above or below him; and a pedestrian who takes the old mule-track will reach the mountain crest before the coach, which gallops over nearly the whole new way. Up we go under giants of the virgin forest, tall and slender as the race of man in these regions, all struggling with fierce energy, like the victims of the Black

---

by M. Gœtling the trick is found in most of the ancient languages. He cites πυρφύρεος (pro πορπήρεος) and πορφυρα, which are doublings of πύρ, and our modern pa-pa and bon-bon.

* Pizarro makes Inhomirim to be a corruption of Anhum-mirim, "the little field," and Mawe, a poor linguist, degrades it to "Moremim." The stream is also called from the port near its mouth, "Rio da Estrella," and the boats of bygone days plied up it towards the mountains: the

torrent of the zigzag valley may be considered its head waters. Some call it the "Fragoso River;" but Fragoso (the rugged) is the name of an estate upon its banks, still preserved by the single small station two kilometres from the Serra foot.

† The travellers of 1808—1816, mention the broad "calçada," or paved way of Estrella, but it was doubtless a very rude original of the modern edition.

Hole, for life, which is sun and air, each bearing the "strange device Excelsior" (not Excelsius), and each forming when old a conservatory, a hortus, but not siccus, a botanical garden of air-plants and parasites—along perpendicular cuttings of hard red clay based on blue gneiss, and mossed over with delicate vegetation (the Germans here grumble that weeds grow everywhere when grass will not)—below dank overhanging boulders, and past Troglodytic abodes, whose dripping approaches are curtained and fringed with a lovely pendent vegetation of ribbon-like fern, the maiden-hair or "feather-leaf" contrasting with the gaunt brake, five feet tall.* Everywhere the soft rush and plash, and the silvery tinkle and murmur of falling water, make music in our ears. This beautiful abundance is ever present in the Sea-range of the Brazil, ever ready to quench the traveller's thirst. Up we go, gradually relieved from undue atmospheric pressure, the air waxing thinner and more ethereal, and a corresponding lightness of spirits developing itself. The white road glistens in the sun as if powdered with silver, and fragments of crystallized quartz suggest diamonds to the Northern eye. At every turn there is a noble view of the lowlands, and happily, in this rainiest of spots,† we have a fine evening. Usually in the mornings, thick white vapours lie like the waters of a lake, or rise in smoky wreaths from spots where the foliage offers no mechanical obstruction. In the afternoon,

---

* A pest of the Brazil, locally called Samambaia (Mertensia dichotoma or Pteris caudata). I do not know why St. Hilaire III. i. 13, writes Camambaia : this is certainly not the modern orthography. Mr. Caldcleugh (Travels in South America, 1819—21. London, Murray, 1825) confounds this fern with the Umbahuba or Umbauba (Cecropia peltata, see chap. xxix.), "the tree which the sloths love to frequent." Gardner (p. 478) makes no such mistake.

† On a similar formation in the province of São Paulo we have the following results for January—December, 1867 :—

Months.	Santos, on sea level.	Alto da Serra, Maritime Crest.	São Paulo, 35 direct miles from the sea.
January . .	11·18 inches.	11·6 inches.	2·21 inches.
February . .	8·22 ,,	12·6 ,,	2·96 ,,
March . .	10·39 ,,	15·8 ,,	3·46 ,,
April . . .	3·04 ,,	9·5 ,,	1·77 ,,
May . .	8·86 ,,	13·3 ,,	3·43 ,,
June . .	4·85 ,,	10·2 ,,	1·10 ,,
July . .	13·98 ,,	17·9 ,,	5·04 ,,
August . .	4·57 ,,	11·2 ,,	3·00 ,,
September . .	12·20 ,,	15·2 ,,	3·19 ,,
October . .	6·88 ,,	11·8 ,,	2·67 ,,
November . .	10·00 ,,	13·8 ,,	2·76 ,,
December . .	6·24 ,,	4·9 ,,	3·90 ,,
Totals .	100·41	147·4	35·49

cold mountain mists, dense as chauldron-fumes, cling to the cliffs, course down the mighty sides, seethe up from the deep shaggy clefts and valleys, and, swift as racers urged by the hollow-sounding wind, scud and whirl over the dark and lowering hill-tops: you would think it a foamy ocean rushing to flood the world. Again about sunset, when the southern bay lies in all its glory, the Serra is often drenched by a sharp pitiless rainfall.

The noblest panorama is at the Alto da Serra, the summit of the Pass, some two thousand nine hundred feet above sea-level,* especially when a late shower has washed the air of mote, spore, and corpuscule. Here you stand, enchanted by the glories of the view. The picture is set in a monstrous "invert," whose abutments are on the right or west a gigantic cone of naked granite: to the left is a mountain shoulder clothed with dense forest, and capped with one of those curious knobs of bare rock,† gneiss, porphyry, or greenstone, so common in this Sea-Range. Between them, seen almost in bird's-eye view, is Rio Bay, reduced to tiny proportions: it is best described by its distances, which form a study for the perspectivist. The first is the jagged and gashed slope of mountain upon whose crest we are, with valleys and ravines hundreds of feet deep, and densely wooded, as if fresh from the Flood. It falls sharp and sudden upon the second, the Beiramar,‡ or maritime plain, chequered with bright green patches of field and marsh, and studded with hills like mole-earth, tumulous in shape: the Railway, springing from the red and black station, extends its straight and angular lines over the surface, and abuts on the edge of the Bay. Possibly we see the train, with its long white plume of steam streaming and tossing in its wake—no unpicturesque object at this distance is the final destroyer of moribund feudalism. The third is the silvery surface of placid inland sea, broken by the dark length of

---

* I did not measure it. St. Hil. II. i. 11, assigns to the Pass in the Serra up which he travelled an altitude of 1099·55 metres = 3607 feet. He makes Petropolis 732·80 metres = 2405 feet above sea level. As has been before shown, Captain Bulhoës gives a lesser height to the Pass, and a greater altitude to Petropolis.

† This is the "Cabeça de Frade" before alluded to. Throughout the Brazil it is the popular name for these naked knobs,

and it doubtless dates from the days when the bare-footed shavelings were giants in the land. There are also several "Rios do Frade," in which Franciscan and other missionaries have been drowned.

‡ Also called Serra Baixa, opposed to Serra Acima, the Highlands of the Brazil. The word corresponds with the Italian Maremma, the flats along the Mediterranean from Leghorn to Amalfi.

Governor's Island, still fronting bright Paquetá, both the centres of smaller satellite formations.   Backs this basin the white mass of City, sitting near the waves, with shipping that dots the shore-line: above it, beginning with the "little turn to the left" into the misty Atlantic, are all the well-known features of the majestic block, the Sugarloaf bending backwards from the Morro da Cruz; the fantastic Corcovado, here like a parrot's beak; the Gaviá Cube, even at this distance quaint and strange, and the lumpy dome of Babilonia's rock; whilst the Tijuca Peak, apparently double and bifid, towers with cloudless outline, deep blue upon a sky-blue ground.   And to the right there is still a fifth distance, beautiful and mysterious, where filmy highland blends with the lower heavens.

This is beautiful—a delight, an enchantment!   But there is no anorexia here, and certain materialisms, appetite for instance, are becoming impudent.   A cold wind rushes through the Pass, and the thermometer has fallen from 72° (F.) to 62°—shivering point in the Tropics.   We shoot the Barreira da Serra, the much misplaced toll-gate, loudly calling for a writ "de essendo quietum de Theolonio," and the station of Villa Theresa.   Then through the southern quarter of Petropolis, the "Ueberpfalz" of the German colonists, the northern town being their "Lower Pala-tinate."   We leave Maurin Valley to the right, and descending rapidly, we find ourselves, after a last stage of ten miles,* comfortably housed in the "Hotel Inglez," kept by Mr. and Mrs. Morritt.

Here the curtain falls upon a pleasant scene, composed mainly of a dining-room and a bed-room.

* Namely, eight miles to the summit of the range—the old road being three—and two to the hotel.

CHAPTER II.

AT PETROPOLIS.

Aqui pelo contrario poz Natura
Por Brasoĕs da primeira architectura,
Volumes colossaes, corpos enormes,
Cylindros de granite desconformes,
Massas, que não erguerem nunca humanos
Mil braços à gastar, gastar mil annos.

Assumpção Fr. Francisco de São Carlos.

I HAVE given a few pages to this Cockney trip, this Brazilian run down from London to Richmond. My object is partly that the thousands who well know the way may thus be able to test the accuracy of my descriptions. Books of travel, it may be remarked, depend for permanent character upon the opinion of "experts,"—that is to say, of those who live, or who have lived, amongst the scenes depicted. There is a well-known work, much read in England, but called in Egypt the "Romance of the Nile;" despite many editions, it is dying the death.

Moreover, as hinted in the last Chapter, vacation and other tourists will not long neglect the "Empire of the Southern Cross." The beauties of yesterday and to-morrow may be reached within three weeks of tranquil and varied voyage from Lisbon; and he who has coached from Rio de Janeiro to Juiz de Fóra will have seen Nature in equatorial Africa and in the lowlands of Hindostan. Some day the public will unlearn the "fact" that yellow fever is endemic in the Brazil,* and will

---

* It is partly the fault of Brazilian authors that this evil report has become chronic in Europe. Thus in the "Compendio Elementar" of Sr. Thomaz Pompeo de Souza Brazil (4th edit. Rio : Laemmert, 1864, p. 472), we read of the climate of Rio Janeiro, "É pouco salubre, principalmente depois da invasão da febre amarella, que alli ficou endemica." The little volume published by the Religious Tract Society in 1860 was as premature in declaring that yellow fever in the Brazil is an abiding guest. The disease between 1850 and 1861 appeared upon the coast without extending to the highlands, and then vanished suddenly as it came. It is regrettable to see such statements in popular books intended to "diffuse knowledge," and to think of the fate of the hapless scholar who, before he can *know* anything, is compelled to go through a triple process —to learn, to unlearn, to relearn.

master the truth that her climate, duly considering that it is distinctly tropical, is one of the healthiest in the world.

The reason which led me carefully to sketch the excursion from the metropolis to Petropolis, dispenses me with describing the latter. Yet, in this its hour of extremest need, when the D. Pedro II. Railway is threatening to annihilate the coaches by abstracting the passengers, and to shut up the Mauá line by withdrawing its salt and coffee; and when even Mr. Morritt, who, in 1841, horsed the last mail to Manchester, threatens to close his hotel and to give up his labours, commenced in 1853, Petropolis must have a few lines of praise from me.*

It is no small matter to find within five hours of Rio de Janeiro a spot where appetite is European, where exercise may be taken freely, and where you enjoy the luxury of sitting in a dry skin. No place can be better fitted for the Pedro Segundo College, which is now in the heart of the city, and the country to the west is invaluable as a sanitarium. Petropolis was left unscathed by the yellow fever of 1849—61,† and by the cholera of 1856. It abounds in mineral springs, especially the ferruginous; and in the "Municipality of the Court," the Columbia of the Brazil, many of both sexes suffer from gastric derangement, and want a "Bismarck"—blood and iron. Surely His Imperial Majesty will not abandon this St. Cloud, this city of his own creation, the "small, miserable village of Corrego Secco"—"Dry Stream Bed"—converted by him into a court and cascine.

Petropolis—or rather, the "City of S. Pedro de Alcantara"—may be said to date from 1844. She is a child, but old enough for a municipal chamber and aldermen, police authorities, and all the other material of self-rule or misrule. This lust for city-ship, a part of "fonctionmanie," is prevalent in the Brazil as in the United States. Mr. Bayard Taylor terms it a "vulgar, snobbish custom." I presume that boys everywhere long to shed their jackets, and that few men despise a "fat appointment." See her on a bright, clear day, and you will find her a "coolness to the eye." Down the main thoroughfares, "Emperor Street"

---

* Thus it is that in 1867, though the road has been paying steady dividends of about 13½ per cent., the value of the stock has not improved above quotation of 46⅔ per cent. discount. (Annual Report of Mr. Henry Nathan.)

† My authority is a short report upon yellow fever by Dr. Croker Pennell, Rio, 1850. Yellow fever in the Brazil apparently does not rise high: the city of São Paulo, also 2000—2400 feet above the sea-level, escaped the plague. In Venezuela, I am told, the fever line extends to nearly double that altitude.

and "Empress Street," pour bubbling, clear brown, gravel-floored streams, the Piabanha* and its feeding runnels, purer than those of Salt Lake City. Encased in lively green grass, they are crossed by black and scarlet bridges, and they will be shaded with velvety stapelias, feathery Brazilian cedars,† and quaint Barrigudos, the pot-bellied, spindle-like bombax. We are now in the land which produces the pine tree and palm, a more poetical and picturesque combination than the orange and myrtle, which here also are at home. Detached houses, villas and kiosks, chalets and cottages, extend themselves, form lines and fine off, giving to the place on paper the look of a gigantic crab, whose centre is where the Piabanha proper begins. Poly-chrome is the taste, and it is good—always excepting white pilasters upon dark chocolate ground. Many roofs are painted red—the Briton mutters "pigs' blood;" but the tint lights up, like the eye of a snake, the cool dark verdure of the hanging forest. In the flowery season the gardens are gorgeous; there are country walks in all rhumbs, and you can find a solitude within five minutes of your door. The naval officer who com-plained of Petropolis because he had always to look upwards, could easily have discovered points from which to look down upon wonderful glimpses and prospects of blue-green back-ground. Nor is it a hardship to gaze upon mountain sides and peaks so ununiform in shape; here with the virgin forest seen in profile from a partial clearing, there deep with gathered shade, twined and corded, throttled and festooned with all its llianas, tufted with wonderful epidendra and air-plants, bearded with gigantic mosses of grotesquest shape,‡ and rich in every vegetable form from the orchid to the cardamom, from the simple bamboo and palm to the complicated mimosa, from the delicate little leaves of the myrtle to the monstrous aroids and the quaint stiff cecropias or candelabra trees.

* It derives its name from a small fresh-water fish. Mr. Walsh has named it "Piabunda." I have been careful in ascertaining the meanings of indigenous words which ere long will be forgotten throughout the Brazil.

† Cedrella odorata, a fine scented tim-ber. The superstitious in the Brazil will cut it but will not burn this wood, which supplied the "True Cross." The trembling maple once enjoyed the same reputation in England.

‡ Called in the Brazil Barba de Páu. The people here ignore the use of this epiphyte, which makes excellent girths, surcingles, and bands that require elasticity and strength. On the other hand its astrin-gent properties are well known, after a bone-dislocating ride, or a heavy fall with a mule, the sufferer is put into a hot bath, in which the moss has been boiled, and he soon feels the benefit of the "tanning-process."

Nor is the population of Petropolis less pleasing than the scenery. We are not in the " Helvétie Meridionale," but in a tropical Ems, where the valleys are *thals*, the rills are *bachs*, and the hills are *gebirge;* where white-headed boys shout at us, and open-faced women smile at us, and where the broad accent of the Fatherland falls with agreeable reminiscences upon our ears. Compared with the formality, not to say the primness, and at times the moodiness, of the Luso-Latin race, these bees of the northern hive appear peculiarly genial, and my friend Mr. Theodore de Bunsen justifies me in asserting that as a rule the Creole Germans are here an improvement upon the Teuton at home.

CHAPTER III.

FROM PETROPOLIS TO JUIZ DE FÓRA.

" Au milieu d'une des vallées les plus accidentées du globe, véritable vallée Alpine, une route magnifique, aux pentes douces et régulières, comme il en existe à peine encore dans l'Europe même, œuvre gigantesque par les immenses travaux d'art qu'elle a occasionés, et qui fait honneur au Brésil, unit Pétropolis, ou mieux Rio de Janeiro, à Juiz de Fóra."—M. Liais.

THE dark of other days, when the difficulties of Brazilian travel were to be dreaded, used to spend half a week on mule-back between Petropolis and Juiz de Fóra. The distance is 91¼ miles, or, more correctly speaking, 146·8 kilometres. We shall see the end of it in nine hours, halts not included. It may be divided into three sections—forty miles of descent, twenty-one of flat, riverine valley, and thirty of ascent.

We were six in the jaunting car, Major Newdigate and his brother, " on the rampage," from Canada; a personage whom I shall call Mr. L'pool; and our host, Mr. Morritt. I never saw so good-tempered a man as the latter; it was admirable to mark the unflinching patience with which he stood the galling fire of inter- rogation from four persons armed with four several note-books, and each asking simultaneously his or her own question. We called him the " Angel Morritt."

At 6 A.M. on Saturday, June 15, 1867, the top-heavy mail, carrying seventeen passengers, and twenty-eight mail bags, a weight of three tons, left the Hotel Inglez, and revived many coaching recollections. It was purely English, rigged out *à la Brésilienne*. The panel was inscribed " Celeridade," instead of bearing Her Majesty's arms. The country bumpkins were slaves of both sexes, whose Garibaldian shirts showed that they were in process of sale. The guard mounted a glazed and japanned hat; coachey was a stout young German, and the team was composed of four fiery little mules. It is a spectacle to see their rearing and dancing, and when the ostler casts off, their frantic rush and plunge at the collar, especially in the cool of a Petropolis morning. "All right" is then a temporary "all wrong." On the other hand, no passenger can quote the old growl—

> "Heavy roads, and horses weak,
> Coachman drunk, and guard asleep."

We bowled in our char-à-banc through the city of D. Pedro, down the valley of the Piabanha, over the noble road known as the Uniaõ e Industria. The old highway to Minas Geraes, described by travellers, and still traced upon our maps, lies far below, to the right. It is marked by large deserted houses, and by huge hedges of the artichoke-shaped Pita,* curious in its flower, the last production of a long, hardy life. As early as 1840 Gardner passed over ten leagues of rolling road, intended to connect the Capital of Minas with that of the Empire; and the Provincial Assembly at Ouro Preto raised by law upwards of £40,000, to be recovered by tolls. The new line, whose thoroughness of execution is admirable, was laid out by the superintendent, Capt. José Maria de Oliveira Bulhões, of the Imperial Engineers, and his aides, Messrs. Flageollot and Vigouroux, assisted by the two Kellers, father and son.† I saw, without surprise, in the virgin forest, French road-rollers, civilized appliances which had not reached London by May, 1865, when the hoofs of blood-horses, and the costliest wheels from Long Acre, still did the dirty work.‡

The team was changed at the "Farm of Padre Correa," situated in a hollow surrounded by low hills. It is mentioned with gratitude by many a traveller.§ The good farmer-priest, so celebrated for

---

* Agave americana, or fœtida, also called yucca and bayonet plant, from its straight, stiff-armed leaves. Its fibre is well known, and the 'robust flower-stalk, thirty feet high, supplies the best of razor strops, and of corks for the insect-pinking naturalist. This is the part properly called Pita, a word popularly transferred to the whole.

† The germ of the idea was a railway survey made for the Barão de Mauá by an English engineer, Mr. Edward Brainerd Webb. The road was projected in 1857, under Sr. Mariano Procopio Ferreira Lage. When we travelled there, M. Audemar was resident engineer. Prof. Agassiz (A Jour-

ney in Brazil, p. 63) speaks of "French engineers," but omits the name of Captain Bulhões, which appears in every inscription. Thus foreigners in the Brazil often claim and manage to carry off the honours due to the natives.

‡ In April, 1868, road locomotives were tried upon this road with entire success: steam omnibuses for passenger traffic, and traction engines for heavy goods, are to be introduced in lieu of mules.

§ John Mawe (1809) speaks of Padre Correo, his negroes, his forges, and his hospitality. Luccock (1817) describes Padre Correio, his mansion-house and his ambition. St. Hilaire (1819), Caldcleugh (1821), and

his peaches, has long been dead, and the house, which formerly received royalty, now lodges the company's live stock. Now the aspect of the road waxes motley. There are mule troops (tropas), divided, as usual, into lots of seven or more, each "lote" being attended by its own "tocador," or driver. These ships of the luxuriant S. American desert are freighted with salt and sundries, forming the provincial imports, and they bring from the interior coffee and cotton, raw and worked. The brutes are our "black beasts;" they *will* stop and turn to us their sterns, and lash out fiercely, and huddle together, and dash down the middle of the road, as if determined to upset us. The "cachorro brabo,"* or fierce dog, here an "institootion," flies at us from every turn. The four-wheeled carts are palpably German, very unlike the Brazilian "plaustra," which have descended unaltered through modern Portugal from ancient Rome. Pigs meet us in droves: as usual in the Empire, they are fat and well-bred, especially the short-legged and big-barrel'd "box-pig."† Some of the goats, with dun golden coats and long black beards and points, remind me of Africa. The sheep are far from being Merinos; lean, ragged, and ram-horned, they justify the popular prejudice against mutton.‡ Black cattle are painful spectacles, scarred and eaten by the white grub of the local Tzetze.§ The day is coming when the

---

Gardner (1841), have not forgotten him, and the Rev. Mr. Walsh (1829) saw part of the Imperial family at the establishment.

* "Bravo"—wild, and sometimes "poisonous"—applied to fruits and plants, is generally pronounced "brabo." Hence our mutilated word "Brab," or wild date tree. This is a legacy from the "Gallego," who calls Vinho Verde "Binho Berde," as with us high hills become "'igh 'ills." The peculiarity is of old date, as Scaliger shows,

"Haud temere antiquas mutat Vasconia voces,
Cui nihil est aliud 'vivere' quam 'bibere.'"

† Porco Canastra, a term derived from "Tatu Canastra," the armadillo of that shape. It differs from the true Tatu (the black tatou of Azara, Essais, tome 3, 175), and from the tatu-peba, or flat tatu.

‡ "Mutton was, and still is," says Luccock (p. 44), "in small request among the people of Brazil, some of whom allege, perhaps jestingly, that it is not proper food for Christians, because it was the Lamb of

God which took away the sins of the world." St. Hil. (III. i. 44, 225) casts doubt upon the assertion, and declares that mutton is poor food in the hot parts of the Brazil. Mr. Walsh (ii. 54) confirms the assertion that there is a popular prejudice against mutton, and so we may remember there is in Naples. The objection is also mentioned by John Mawe (i. chap. 5, and especially in chap. 7.)

My second volume will prove that in one part of the Brazil, at least, mutton is preferred to beef, and is held to be the natural food of man; also, that the meat is excellent, not only in the highland prairies so well-fitted for wool growing, but upon the hot banks of the Rio de São Francisco.

As a rule, throughout the Empire, however, food prejudices are uncommonly strong, and the art of Soyer is uncommonly weak.

§ It is called "Berne." The word is generally explained as a corruption of Verme (worm), but I believe it to be of Guarany origin. The worm is mentioned by Azara, who believes that it penetrates the skin. Prince Max (i. 29) reasonably

fine beef of São Paulo and Paraná will supplant, at Rio de Janeiro, the over-driven, under-fed, and worm-blown meat which now scantily supplies her monopolised butcheries.

At the stations we find the usual varieties of the Gallinaceæ. There are a few Guinea fowls, sometimes pure white albinos. They are rarely eaten, not because they are bad, but because they prefer an ant diet. Pigeons multiply: here, as in Russia, they are a "holy emblem." The goose is a bird to be looked at, and is generally as safe from the Brazilian, who believes that the main of its diet is snakes, as from the ancient Briton. Unless fattened it is dry and tasteless as the turkey, perhaps the worst of all *volaille* in the Empire. The best are the ducks, especially the young "Muscovies" or "Manillas" (Anas Moschata, Canard de Barbarie, indigenous in the Brazil). There is another variety of almost anserine proportions, and these are often half wild, flying away from and returning to their homes. Of poultry proper there are the common breed, the knicker-bocker'd Cochin China, here not "A 1 for the table;" the "Pampa" or piebald, prettily marked with black on a white ground; the "Nanico," a pert, pretty bantam; the Gallinha napeva, a short-legged or "dumpie";* the "Sura," a tail-less variety—nothing to do with M. de Sora; the "Tupetuda" or "Cacarutada"; the "Polish" or "pollish," so called from its top-knot; and the Arripiado or frizzly chicken of the United States, used in African superstitions. The latter, when gaitered down the legs (emboabas or sapateiras), is an excellent layer of eggs. The tall thin bird, with a peculiar screaming and prolonged crow, which travellers have converted into a singing cock (musico), and which the superstitious believe to be a descendant from the bird which warned St. Peter, startles the stranger's ear.† There are also fowls with dark bones, which the people sell cheap, holding them as the Somal do all volatiles, to be semi-vulturine. We especially remark the gallinaceous hermaphrodites, hens with spurs, and the haughty

---

doubts this. Many tales are told of negroes losing their lives in consequence of the grub being deposited in the nose and other places : if squeezed to death and not extracted, it may, of course, produce serious results. The usual treatment is by mercurial ointment.

* This bird can hardly run, and fattens quickly. I found the breed in Unyamwezi, and I tried to bring home caged specimens, but they all died en route.

† The people say that this arises from "Gôgo," not the pip, but a thickening of the membranes of the throat. John Mawe tells us that in his day the bird was greatly valued when its voice was fine. The sound always appeared to me "croupy."

look of the cock.   One of the most interesting, and by far the ugliest, is the Gallinha mesticia, or da India, a lank, ragged bird, with yellow shanks and a dark bottle-green plume turned up with red; the crimson neck and breast are nude of feathers naturally, but appearing as if plucked.   A specimen of this bird is kept in the poultry-yard, as the hog in the Persian stable, to maintain its health by attracting all the sickness.   Hen-wives, and husbands afflicted with the hen fever, may learn that in the Brazil those neutrals, the capons, are remarkable as dry-nurses, tending chickens with a parent's care.   And the much-talked-of crane, the agami or ogami of the Amazonian basin, described as bearing the relation to poultry which a shepherd's dog bears to sheep, and locally called " Juiz de Paz."   Juge de Paix is, so far from being a feathered Quaker, and despite his "pretty looks and ways," the most turbulent and pugnacious of his family.

I reserve for a future book my observations upon the acclimatization of the magnificent Gallinaceæ of the Brazil.   Europe has borrowed but one bird from the New World.   Remain the curassoa (Hocco or Mútum, Crax Alector);   the many species of Jacú (Penelope), more gamey in flavour than our pheasant;   the Nambú or Inamba (Tinamus);   the Capoeira (Perdix guianensis or dentata) and many others.

Many roadside tenements appear to be, but are not deserted; the inmates are "cutting tie-tie,"* as the local slang is;   they have fled during the day from conscription into the bush.†   The third stage from Pedro do Rio to Posse (Possession),‡ becomes interesting.   The broadening River Valley affords a vista of the now respectable Piabanha, no longer a rowdy mountain torrent. Gigantic slides of forest-crowned granitic rock, bare-sided and smooth-sloped, except where pitted with weather-holes and tufted with Tillandsias and Bromelias, which seem capable of growing upon a tea-table, rise sheer in the brilliant blue-pink air of morning.   The climate is a notable improvement upon that of Petro-

---

* Tirando Cipó. This word, sometimes written Sipó, and erroneously Cipó (the til or cedille not being required), means in Tupy a root: Cipó im, for instance, is the climbing salsaparilla. In the Brazil it is equivalent to the Portuguese "trepador" (climber), to our "liana," and to the Anglo-negro "tie-tie." The best for making rope is said to be the Cipó cururu; but these climbers and vines are of course little studied.

† I would remind my readers, that during the Crimean war, when a conscription was talked of, it was declared that the population of certain works in Derbyshire would "flee to the mines, and lead a sort of Robin Hood life under ground."

‡ Guarda da Posse—the Guard of taking Possession—was an old name for military posts.

polis; there the warm damp sea breeze condensed by the cold mountain tops, drenches the Serra, and "tips over" into the settlement; here it is glorious summer, with the winter of discontent a few miles to the south. Coffee begins to appear, but in lowly guise, stunted and sickly; the soil is mean, and the shrub is too closely planted. "Clear sowing" would make the half better than the whole; moreover, field hands are wanting, the soil is rarely "beneficed,"* and the surface shows a carpet of weeds.

Posse is a place of some importance, which collects the rich produce of the districts about the Porto Novo da Cunha to the east. After Luiz Gomez, the sixth station, the land wants nothing but rotation of crops; and the cotton cure would heal all its present ills. From the roadside under the grassy humus of the River Valley, Professor Agassiz found "drift" in immediate contact with the floor of crystalline rock, and he observed that where it lies thickest, there the coffee flourishes most. It determines, he says, the fertility of the soil on account of the great variety of chemical elements contained in it, and the kneading process which it has undergone under the gigantic ice plough. The glacial theory has inserted its thin edge into the Brazil; the student, however, is puzzled to account for the absence of those grooves and striæ which in other lands show the gravitating action of the ice fields. Nor has any satisfactory explanation been given; the sun and rains of the tropics can hardly effect what the frosts and the sudden climatic changes of the temperates have failed to effect.†

The Piabanha now flows between heights of the blackest virgin forest; and the dark lush verdure, contrasting with the grey-yellow or pale-green of the poorer lands, shows its wealth. In the cuttings we find a paste of red clay‡ deeply tinged with oxide of iron, proceeding from the mica and based upon whitish grey gneiss. The banks are a double line of noble growth, the

---

* Bemficiado. Improvements made by a tenant are called "bemfeitorias."

† My excellent friend, Du Chaillu (2nd Exp., chap. 15), found these marks distinctly shown upon rocks close to the Equator: "Whilst I am on the subject of boulders and signs of glaciers, I may as well mention that, when crossing the hilly country from Obindji to Ashira-land, my attention was drawn to distinct traces of grooves on the surface of several of the blocks of granite which there lie strewed about on the tops and declivities of the hills. I am aware how preposterous it seems to suppose that the same movements of ice which have modified the surface of land in northern countries, can have taken place here under the Equator; but I think it only proper to relate what I saw with my own eyes." This testimony is the more valuable as the author seems not to see its import or its importance.

‡ Barro vermelho, of deep colour, like brick dust.

" vestimenta " or clothing by which the Brazilian farmer judges the soil. In places the precipices are so thickly covered with timber and undergrowth, that the river dashes unseen down its bed. Worth a million of money if within excursion trains of London or Paris is the bamboo-copse.* The cane appears in cones and live columns that invest the trees, in piled up feathery heaps, in serpentines and arches, in the most fantastic figures, and in those graceful waving curves upon which the eye delights to dwell. There is an immense variety, from the thorny large-leaved pinnated and thick-stemmed " Taquarussú," fifty to sixty feet long, to the tufty and lanceolate Criciúma, which cuts like the sugar-cane, whilst other species bend over the road, tapering in the semblance of a fishing-rod. Thyrsi of climbing plants, clinging to the dead trunks, suggest cypresses. The Cipó matador, or murderer lliana, is our old friend the " Scotchman strangling the Creole " on the Isthmus of Panama, and the " Parricide tree " of Cuba. Often thick as its victim, this vege-table vampire sometimes rises from the neck-compressing coil and stands up like a lightning conductor.† " Birds of the gaudiest plume vie with the splendid efflorescence of the forests which they inhabit;" especially the large-beaked black and orange-throated Rhamphastus (discolorus), of the exclusively American family. From the densest brake we hear his Tucano ! Tucano! but we cannot, like the travellers of 1821, convert him into a stew. Being eagerly hunted, these beauties are very timid, and perch on the tallest rocks and trees; for two years I have vainly attempted to rob their nests in order to observe whether the colossal bill is or is not found within the egg. They are easily tamed, they make excellent pets, and with their " Lord Hood's noses," they are comical as court fools.

Presently our old friend the Piabanha sweeps away to the right and we part for ever. It falls into the Parahyba do Sul‡ river at

---

* Locally called Taquára, or Tacoára, and in the dictionary, Tacúara (Bambusa To-goara, Mart.). Another Indian name is Tabóca. The Taquárussú is sometimes forty feet high, and thick as a man's arm ; the branches are armed with short, thick thorns, and the Botocudos, like the Hindus of Mala-bar, made vessels of it ,the joint-sept form-ing the bottom. I have seen Brazilians carrying long segments by way of canteen. When young, this large reed contains a

supply of sweet water, often useful to travellers. The siliceous exterior recom-mended the bamboo for arrow tips, and the savages, we are told, made of it their razors.

† St. Hil. III. i. 30. Bates, i. 50, well describes this parasitic fig, which he calls the " Sipó matador, or the murderer liana."

‡ Parahyba, called do Sul, to distinguish it from the stream that waters the northern province of that ilk, is usually explained to

Tres Barras, the three sister waters reminding us of "Nore, and Suir, and Barrow;" the Parahybúna, with which we are to make acquaintance, is the northernmost of the trio. Running along the flat valley we sight the Parahyba without fearing its register or custom-house;* this place was terrible to strangers, smuggling diamonds and gold dust, and it has consigned many an un-fortunate to life-long imprisonment or to Angolan exile. The river which I have seen so small near São Paulo, is here broad as the Thames at Battersea, and so stately a king of the valley that I can hardly claim acquaintance with him. "Engineer's art" is rarely artistic, but the Birmingham-built bridge, with 320 tons of iron and latticed girders painted red, put together by Mr. O'Kell, is an effective adjunct to the scenery; its vermilion sets off the deep luxuriant verdure, as the fisherman's cap becomes the glaucous waves. This fine bridge, and another at Parahyba do Sul, the city, which cost 800 contos, will be thrown out of employment, and three others have been built for the use of the D. Pedro II. Railway. Thus it is the money goes; and thus one river has three bridges, whilst half-a-dozen others have not one.

At 11·30 A.M., after four hours of actual travelling, we reached Entre Rios, "Betwixt the Rivers,"† the half-way house. Here a breakfast—and a bad breakfast too—awaited the pas-sengers. Whilst the "feijão" was being served up, I inspected the foundations of a railway station which will put to shame the hovels answering to that name on the majority of the Anglo-Brazilian railways: these remind me of the venerable remnants of Stephenson's line, the "Liverpool and Manchester," which still linger for instance at Newton Bridge. A few months after our visit, the railway was opened to Entre Rios, thus cutting across the fine macadamized road. And worse still, the D.

mean opposed to—"Catu," good; hence Southey's "Yguatu, or the good water," should be Ycatu, the bad river (Para, river, and Ayba, bad). Others make it a cor-ruption of Pirahyba, which would be "Bad fish river." Others deduce it from Pira and ayba, the fishy or scaly disease—leprosy. The "bad river" would be an excellent descriptive name. It is one of the most dangerous streams in the Brazil. Many of those working on the railway lost their lives in it. A description of its course and of its colonization by the English in days now forgotten, belong to the province of São Paulo.

Generally it is supposed in the Tupy or Lingoa Geral that Pará means a river—Paraná, the sea. If there be any distinc-tion between the words, the reverse is the case.

* Properly a post where, in former times, passports were visited and duties were taken.

† The name is equivalent to our Delta, to the Doab of India, and to the Rineon of Spanish America.

Pedro II. proposes to run down the Parahyba River some thirty-eight miles to Porto Novo da Cunha. A glance at the map will prove to the veriest tyro that the railway should be driven directly northwards to the head waters of the great Rio de São Francisco. But as usual the line is a party and a political question. Why not then trim—make the main trunk go north, and the branch eastward?

Entre Rios* declines to 610 feet above the sea-level; the air is bad, hot and damp, breeding fevers like grubs; the water is worse. A hotel, therefore, will kill as well as keep the keeper. Hereabouts the once luxuriant valley is " cleaned out " for coffee, and must be treated with cotton and the plough. The sluice-like rains following the annual fires have swept away the carboniferous humus from the cleared round hill-tops into the narrow swampy bottoms, which are too cold for cultivation ; every stream is a sewer of liquid manure, coursing to the Atlantic, and the superficial soil is that of a brickfield. Here too the land suffers from two especial curses,—the large proprietor, and from the agricultural system bequeathed by the aborigines, or from Inner Africa, and perpetuated by the slovenly methods of culture everywhere necessary when slave labour is employed. In the Brazil as in Russia and in the Southern States of the Union, where vast plantations must be merely skimmed, virgin soil forms a considerable item in the real value of landed property; the want of manure and the necessity of fallows admit only half of the whole estate—sometimes hardly even a tenth—to annual cultivation. This evil must be mitigated before the country can be colonized or greatly improved, but it is not easy to suggest a measure without the evils of " disappropriation."†

" Serraria," our next station, begins the ascent, and the road wisely as usual hugs the margin of the Parahybuna River.‡ This

---

* Below Entre Rios, and sixteen miles above the Porto Novo da Cunha, are rapids which fall about 120 feet in two miles. Where they end the Sapucaia streamlet enters the left bank, and opposite it is an islet rising some five feet above low water. Here agates and bloodstones have been found exactly resembling the formations which will be described in the São Francisco River.

† A Brazilian friend writes to me—"The iniquitous law of 1823, which put a stop to land concessions, caused substituous occu-pation to take the place of lawful titles. Thus the best lands were worked out and ruined."

‡ Luccock (p. 407) says, "it may probably be from the dark colour of the stones that the river derives its name, if it be written Parabúna ; or if Parahybúna be the proper mode, from the deep tinge of the water." Caldcleugh (ii. 200) translates it Para, river, and ibuna, black. Scholars make it a corruption of Parayuna, a river rolling black waves—at once a picturesque and remarkably correct description.

eastern drain of the Mantiqueira, or Trans-maritime Range, is a broad shallow stream of flavous hue, much resembling the Piabanha when we last saw it. The "Sawery" is important to the Company, as it taps the coffee districts of Ubá and Mar de Hespanha.

The "Union and Industry," white and glaring, sweeps along the tumbling river, which has cut deep irregular channels in the dark sunburnt rock. On both sides are layers of deep red clay, with imbedded boulders and masses of undecomposed feld-spar, covered with a dense wood of evergreens, that winter when, and only when, they please. We now pass through the Serra das Abóboras, or "Pumkin Range," and our attention is drawn to a local lion, the Pedra da Fortaleza.* This "Montagne Pelée," a giant amongst its colossal race, is a block, apparently single, of chocolate-coloured gneiss, springing 500 feet from the river gulley, where the stream makes an elbow; we run under a vertical wall, 100 yards high, which gathers up the sunbeams, and which radiates them like a furnace. Its grim brown but-tress, thinly bristling, where touched by weathering, with large Bromelias, which looked like bits of grass, suggested to my wife the idea of a church, and mere specks upon the airy summit denoted its capping of tall forest. As we wind panting round the base, with the canoe-less river on our right, we detect a russet-coated capyvara or water-hog, basking in the sun, and calmly prospecting the unclean stream.† Hawks and vultures

---

* Castelnau gives the total height 150 metres, with a vertical wall of 100 metres. He adds, "aucune plante ne poussait sur cette vaste surface," whereas the steepest walls are tufted over with air-plants.

It would be interesting to examine these rocks, which may belong to the ancient sedi-mentary strata, metamorphosed by heat to highly crystalline substances, known as the Laurentian, and the most ancient known on the North American continent. The "dawn-animal of Canada" has not yet been dis-covered in the Brazil; on the other hand, it has not yet been sought for.

† The Hydrochærus Capybára, or Cavia Capyvara (Linn.). The "Indian" name is as usual pretty and picturesque. "Capi-uara," or "Capivara," means the "grass eater," not as the T. D. says, "qui vive entre o capim." The origin is "Caapiïm," or "Capyi," corrupted to "Capim," the common Brazilian word for "green meat,"

whence "Capinar," to "cut grass," and "G-u-âra," "an eater," composed of "g," relative "u," "uu," or "vu," "to eat," and "âra," the verbal desinence which curiously resembles the Hindostani "wala." Hence the Argentine name "Capiguára" (Southey, i. 187) is more correct than the Brazilian : the Spanish-Americans gene-rally name it Capincho or Carpincho, and travellers corrupt it to Cabiais and Chi-guiré. I do not know why St. Hil. III. i. 181, writes "Capimvara," it is certainly not so pronounced. M. H. A. Weddell (Cas-telnau, vol. vi. 348) informs us, "Le vrai nom de cet animal en Guarani est Capu-qüã, mot qui signifie 'habitant des prés.'" In the interior, as will appear, the people confound it with the Caïtetú, or Tagassú, the peccari (Dicotylos labiatus, not the tor-quatus). The wild men used to wear its teeth as ornaments.

This rodent equals in size a half-grown

sought coolth in the upper æther, the kingfisher flitted over
the water, ducks and dabchicks sported in the smooth reaches,
wild pigeons whirred past us, small ground-doves ran along the
road, and thrushes, black and brown, balanced themselves upon
the spray, silent all, doubtless thinking "*il fait trop chaud.*"
The "bush" looked a likely place for game; we were told,
however, that the ounce remains, whilst the deer has been
killed off.

The Parahybuna now ignores gold working; its once eminently
auriferous sands were dredged for the precious metal and for the
white, pink, and wine-yellow topazes, once a branch of provincial
industry and now completely abandoned. The red ferruginous
soil and the rusty quartz probably still contain gold; but the
surface deposits have been exhausted. In Colonial days the
Government, *mirabile dictu!* interdicted mining upon this
streamlet lest the market value of the ore might be greatly
reduced through the habitable world. I heard the same expressions used in London when California proved to be the El
Dorado. Yet, as the old searcher said, "the night has no eyes,"
and the gold disappeared despite orders, and without affecting the
globe's exchange.

The large Parahybuna Station shows us the Register Bridge,
where duties are still taken upon imports into the Province of
Minas Geraes. In 1825 the tax was 3$640, or a little more than
17s. per cart; in 1867 it had risen to 20$000, then about 2l.
Thus the Province pays a compound impost, on the seaboard and

---

porker: it is an ugly half-finished brute,
somewhat like an overgrown Guinea-pig
(called "Guinea," because it is Brazilian).
The muzzle is bluff, and the jaw very deep,
like that of a fatted hog; it swims with
the square head carried high, like the
hippopotamus, and it is said to bear its
young on its back, as that animal does.
The grunt, not "bray," is a kind of ugh!
ugh! It is gregarious, living in packs of
10 to 60, and in old legends the chief
was mounted by a pigmy demon, called Caã-
póra, or "forest dweller." When rendered
shy by hunting, the Capyvara never quits
the water except to bask in the sun; in
captivity it thrives, but its habits are filthy
and ultra-porcine. In Spanish America it
is eaten, and M. Isabelle declares, with
many others, that the flesh is not bad, after
being placed for eighteen hours in running

water. The Brazilians use its leather,
rarely its meat. Humboldt (Voyage aux
Régions équatoriales du Nouveau Continent,
vol. ii. 217), found troops of 60 to 100,
and believes that these graminivors eat fish.
The Capivara appears in Brazilian poetry:
thus writes in his "Parabolas," Sr. José
Joaquim Corrêa de Almeida (Parabolas,
114)—

> Assim procede o politico
>   Que os principios não extrema;
> Calculadamente segue
>   Da Capivara o systema.

> Thus proceeds the politician,
>   Where principles go not too far;
> He right studiously pursues the
>   System of the Capivár.

at its frontier ; and the evil is little lessened by double loading each wheeled vehicle at the Rio de Janeiro side, and by a re-distribution of weight after settling the dues upon Minas ground. Every political economist must condemn this outlandish system of inland douanes. It keeps up the old Colonial habit of placing barriers between provinces, and it interferes with commerce by holding out premiums to bribery and contraband traffic. Many years ago it has been proposed to abate this nuisance.* But it is easier to advocate the suppression of the tolls than to show whence the equivalent in coin is to come.

This bridge has ever been an eye-sore. In 1842, when Minas and her parent, São Paulo, were "up," or "out," the officer in charge burned it down to prevent the advance of loyalist troops, and in 1843 Castelnau found it unrepaired. It is now composed of new timbers supported by old stone piers and abutments, and no longer roofed over. A little beyond it, a tattered hut marks the scene of another revolutionary affair : this Rocinha† da Negra, or "Little Clearing of the Negress," belongs, at present, to the Conselheiro Pedro de Alcantara de Cirqueira Leite. On the left is the Barra, or mouth of the Rio Preto,‡ the southern frontier-limit of Minas. Across this western in-

---

* St. Hil. III. i. 47.

† Rossinho da Negra (Mr. Walsh). Here I must trouble the reader with a few necessary explanations.

The Róça, or Roçádo, in the Brazil, is a *défriché*, a clearing for agricultural purposes ; generally, as in Africa, at a little distance from the farm house, or village : sometimes it has, often it has not, a thatched shed to shelter the day-labourers. In places "Rocinha" may be translated "country house in the suburbs." The Sitio is a bonâ fide farm with messuages. The chácara, or chácra, is a word borrowed from the Tupy : the indigenes applied it to their wretched huts, and in Peru "chacrayoc" means "Lord of the Field :" the South Americans transferred it to their pretty villas and country houses. Mr. William Bollaert (Ant. of Peru, &c., p. 67), defines it to mean in the Quichua tongue "estates, farms, plantations." Mr. Clements Markham (Quichua Gram. & Dict. sub voce), translates it by "Quinta" (a house and grounds), so called because the tenant paid one-fifth to the proprietor. The Fazénda is the Spanish Hacienda, the plantation of our tropical colonies, including the ground and the buildings. The proprietor is entitled "Fazendeiro," and the class here represents one of the landed county families of England, or the planters of the West Indies. In the Northern Provinces of the Empire, the Fazenda is called Engenho (Southey's Ingenio is Spanish), especially when it is a sugar plantation, and the owner is Senhor de Engenho, one of the local aristocracy, and not to be confounded, unless you want shooting, with the lavrador or farmer. The Engenhoca is a small Engenho.

‡ Caldcleugh (ii. 200) confounds the Parahybuna with the Rio Preto, which he says is a "mere translation of the Indian word Paraibuna." It is the Portuguese equivalent of Una (anciently Huna), "Blackwater River," properly Yg-una, softened to Y'-una. The Y, or Yg, meaning water, is omitted and supplied by Rio Una. These black, or rather deep brown, coffee-coloured streams, are always universal on the seaboard, but comparatively rare in the interior : the tinge is evidently due to decomposed vegetation, and often under the black sediment we find the snowy sand of the bed.

fluent lay the old road from Rio de Janeiro *viâ* Rodeio, Vassouras and Valença, into Southern Minas.

Further on, to the right, is "Rancheria," a village hardly ten years old. The normal church is at the head of the square, the normal big house is at the bottom, and the normal fountain is in the centre : whence the saying—

> "The chafariz
> John Anthony and the matriz." *

which described the constituents of these settlements. Around the *grande place* are Chácaras and dwelling houses, used by the rich planters on Sundays and fêtes : during the rest of the year they are shut up. There are half-a-dozen Vendas—onde não vendem nada. † As usual in the Brazil, the Cemetery occupies a conspicuous upland, and the dwellings of the dead are far better situated than those of the living. Also certain offices which with us mostly conceal themselves in a shame-faced way, here stand out solitary and eye-catching.

About "Rancharia" ‡ the land is modified by its distance from the Serra. The opulent water supply of the maritime heights disappears, the streams shrink, the ascents are longer and less abrupt, the rich red clayey soil of the Rio de Janeiro Province further south, now alternates with light-coloured loams, far drier dustier, and, as in Minas generally, much more porous and friable. The "Matas Negras," those luxuriant dark jungles, have made way for a yellow-green grass, and near the stream for bamboo-tufts, less magnificent than before. Travellers have found garnets imbedded in the underlying gneiss ; the stone is common as worthless.

---

* Chafariz is corrupted Mauro-Arabic (شكارِج Shakáríj) and the word is ridiculed by the Spaniards, who prefer the Latin "fuente." The Matriz is the parish church, with filial chapels under it.

† "A vending-place without vent." The word Venda will be explained in a future page.

‡ The old Brazilians used to apply the word Rancharia, "Ranchery," or collection of sheds, to the huts and wigwams of the aboriginal heathen villages. Prince Max (iii. 151), has by misprint Ranchario (rancharios ou villages de Camacans, iii. 34), and makes it synonymous—which it is not —with Aldôa, or Aldcia. The latter is derived from the Arabic الراوة (El-dáwat) ; in Portugal and in Portuguese Hindostan it means any village. St. Hil. III. i. 5, tells us that in the Brazil it is applied exclusively to a settlement of catechized natives, who are said to be "Mansos," tame ; or Aldeados, "villaged." This might have been the case in his days, the word is not so exclusively used now. Thus it was similar to the "Reduction" of Spanish South America,. especially when it could boast of a missionary.

The Capella de Matthias Barbosa, a hill chapel on the right, announces Mathias Station, umquwhile Registro Velho. It was in Colonial days the principal " contagem " where toll was taken, and even in 1801 the dues were called Quintos, (Royal) Fifths (of gold). Smuggling was then to the " miner " what robbery was to the ingenuous youth of Sparta. The Superintendent and his guard, with spies all over the country, kept a sharp look out for those who had not before their eyes the fear of jail or maritime Africa. The contrabandist stored his valuables in horsewhips and gun-stocks, in his provision of beans, and in the stuffing of his pack-saddles. Foreigners dreaded the ordeal. Luccock called the Superintendent " his Lordship," and Caldcleugh (ii. 202) tells the sad tale of what happened to a feminine votary of impromptu free trade. Here, for some time, lived my friend Dr. G——, whose successful practice in treating psora deserves notice. The patient, when a slave, was rolled in mud, and solemnly sundried into the necessity of bathing: to the " lady of fashion " the same receipt was applied with Quixotic gravity in the shape of viscid oil, which had the same effect.

Then came heavy inclines and a steep hill, sparkling with wild fuchsia and bright with lilies, parasitic plants, and a profusion of unplanted Maracujas, or Passion-flowers,* one of the gifts of the New to the Old World. Far below us the Parahybuna brawled down its apology for a bed. Houses and fields became more frequent, and the curse of great proprietors is no longer upon the land.† We changed mules for the last time at the Ponte do Americano, a bridge with solid timber girders, and we ran at a hand gallop up the river valley, which now bulges out into sites for settlements. A mortuary chapel in a new wall-less cemetery on the left, was for once a grateful spectacle, and ere the sun set, we rounded a corner, and sighted Juiz de Fóra.

The station is at the northern or further end, distant some two kilometres of wild bush, which clusters thickly round the city. We all stared, even when *blazés* by twelve hours of kaleidoscopic travel, to see a well-gravelled footway, with posts and wheeltires for rails, in front of a carefully trimmed quickset hedge

---

* Passiflora (incarnata ?) without perfume. The System enumerates ten wild species.

† Their effect is that which has been in France, which was in the Southern States of the Union, and which is in Great Britain. When will the political economist duly appreciate the benefit derived from the subdivision of land ?

that protected, not a neat park, but an undrained swamp. Behind it. on a dwarf rise, with pretty ground below, was a villa with a squat square tower, which looked as if brought bodily from Hammersmith. At last, dismounting with stiffened knees, we were led by Mr. Morritt to the "châlet," a cottage built in curious proportions of brick and wood, uncompromising materials. In due time every comfort appeared, and with tobacco and chat, assisted by Messrs. Swan and Audemar, C.C. E.E., we much enjoyed our first evening in Minas Geraes. And the sound sleep in the light, cool, pure air was the properest end of a coaching day.

CHAPTER IV.

AT JUIZ DE FÓRA.

And down thy slopes, romantic Ashburn, glides
The Derby dilly carrying six insides.
Byron?

THE proper style and title of Juiz de Fóra is " Cidade de Santo
Antonio de Parahybuna," but a colonial justice of the peace in
foreign parts, an official now obsolete,* having been sent there in
forgotten years, it will ever be known to the people by its trivial
name.   Mawe (1809) speaks of it as a Fazenda, calling it "Juiz
de Fuera." Luccock (1817) makes it contain a "small chapel
and a few poor houses."   In 1825 it was still a "Povoaçao," a
mere institution.   In 1850 it was promoted to the rank of "Freguezia" and "Villa," parish and township.   In 1856 it advanced
to cityship, and in 1864 its municipality numbered 23,916 souls,
including 1998 voters and 33 electors.   Such is progress in the
Brazil, where the situation is favourable and—nota benè—where
communications are opened.

The settlement consists of three distinct parts, "Santo
Antonio," the city proper; the station of the Company "Union and
Industry;" and the German colony, "D. Pedro Segundo."   The
situation is good, 2000 feet above sea-level.   On the east is the
winding river-plain.   Westward towers a forested height, commanding a view of the "Fortaleza" Rock, and the mountains of
Petropolis.   It is called Alto do Imperador, after the Imperial
visit, and a fair path winds up it.   From the lower levels of this
block a white thread of cascade, like the crystal waterfall in an old
Geneva clock of ormulu, hideous mixture ! trends towards the
main drain.   The German colony contained about 1000 souls in

---

* The Juiz de Fóra, according to Koster
(i. chap. 4), was named by the Supreme
Government for three years, and appeal
from his decisions was made to the
Ouvidor or Auditor Judge, another dignitary now obsolete.

whitewashed huts, and the inmates appeared poor and discontented.
In June, 1867, the Practical Agricultural School * seemed in no
hurry to be finished. I have since that time been informed that
the establishment has been completed, that stock has been imported, and that all is in the finest working order.

The station where we lodged prides itself on having nothing to
do with the "old town." It contains, besides the château on the
hill and the châlet, a chapel, two or three tolerable houses, a
small inn and stables, negro quarters, and huge stores where the
salt and coffee are lodged.

The city is the usual mixture of misery and splendour. Minas,
it must be remembered, is one of the three provinces not directly
colonized from Portugal : São Paulo is her progenitor, and the
son cannot yet boast of being better than the sire. Juiz de Fóra
is a single dusty or muddy street, or rather road, across which
palms are planted in pairs. Its sole merit is its breadth, and
when tramways shall be introduced by some Brazilian "Train,"
this good disposition will be recognised. The trottoir is a jumpery,
and the stranger hopping over the pavement seems to be practising "bog-trotting." The dwellings are low and poor, mostly
"door and window" † as the phrase is. Amongst them, however,
are large and roomy town houses, with gilt pineapples on the roof,
glass balls on the French balconies, fantastic water-spouts, pig-
tailed corners, birds of tile and mortar disposed along the ridges,
and all the architectural freaks of Rio de Janeiro. Here the wealthy
planters gather together; during the Saturday evening we saw
large parties of friends and families, men, women, and children ;
negroes, negresses, and negrets, coming into church. Not a little
play is done on these occasions : there are men who gamble like
Poles and Russians—Rooshuns, as they were called at the Old
Cocoa Tree—and the year's profits from coffee and cotton are not
unfrequently dropped at Monte or Voltarete. In Paris Baccarat
does it.

Very mean are the public buildings. The prison would not

---

* Paragraph 4, condition 2 of the contract dated Oct. 29, 1864, insisted upon
the establishment of this "Escola pratica
de Agricultura," by the "Union and Industry Company." These sensible institutions are gradually extending along Eastern
Brazil, and one of them will do more good
than all the colleges which annually turn
out upon the world a hungry swarm of
young "Doctors," LL.Ds. They will be followed, and it is to be hoped soon, by Schools
of Mines ; at present the sons of the Gold
and Diamond Empire must go to Europe
for study.

† "Porta e janella," meaning a ground
floor with a single door and window.

hold a London housebreaker for a quarter of an hour.   The Collectoria, into which the provincial revenue is paid, looks small.   The Matriz of Santo Antonio, at the bottom of a dwarf square, is in tolerable order, but the chapel on the hill is towerless and in tumble-down condition.   Here we see for the first time the tall black cross of Minas, introduced probably by the Italian missionaries, and recalling to mind Norman France; it is garnished with all the instruments of the Passion—ladder, spear, sponge, crown of thorns, hammer, nails, pincers, and a peculiarly wooden cock.

The day after our arrival, Sunday, was one of absolute rest. The station boasts of a neat chapel, unusually clean and free from tawdry ornament.   The inside has a plain altar and benches of polished wood, a picture of the Assumption, and three candles on each side of a silver crucifix.   There is no squatting on the floor, which is, moreover, closed to dogs, and does not require spittoons.   Expectoration, I may observe, is a popular habit in the Brazil as in the United States.   Most men do it instinctively: some, as they whistle, for want of thought; others, because they consider it sanitary, think thereby to preserve a spare habit of body, or hold it to promote appetite or drinketite.   My conclusion is that spitting is natural, so to speak, and refraining from it is artificial, a habit bred by waxed parquets and pretty carpets.

The most agreeable part of the day was spent in the château garden and grounds.   I had before met the owner, Commendador Mariano Procopio Ferreira Lage; during my second visit he was once more in Europe.   In 1853 he organised the União and Industria Company, of which he is still the hard-working chairman; he made Juiz de Fóra a city, the chapel was arranged by him, the châlet was his property, and he had laid out an arboretum and orchard upon what was twelve years ago a bog on the right bank of the Parahybuna.

Our fastidious English taste could find no fault in house or grounds, except that they were a little fantastic, the contrast with Nature was somewhat too violent—an Italian villa-garden in a virgin forest is startling.   The château, which cost 30,000l. or 40,000l., has too much colour and too many medallions; behind it, too, there is an ugly bridge leading to a prim summer-house, both of cast iron, and the former painfully like a viaduct.   The little lake, with bamboo-tufted islets, dwarf Chinese bridges, and paddled boat, worked by negroes instead of steam; the " Grotto

of the Princesses," the grotesque seats and arbours, and the rustic
figures of wood, are a trifle too artificial, and the Ema* and stags,
not pacing over the park, but caged along with monkeys and silver
pheasants, suggesting a menagerie. The European and tropical
plants, however, were magnificent, and we measured an arum-leaf
5 feet 4 inches long. What a contrast to its English representative, the little Arum maculatum, or cuckoo plant, whose berries
poison small children!

We wandered about the orangery, which was innocent of glass,
and found out the favourite trees;† we lay for hours upon the grass
eating the Tangerines, enjoying the perfumed shade of the myrtles,
and admiring the young Wellingtonias and screwpines. Mr. Swan
related to us the grand reception given by the Commendador to
Professor Agassiz, the man of whom prophetic Spenser surely
wrote:—

> O what an endless task has he in hand,
> Who'd count the sea's abundant progeny,
> Whose fruitful seed far passeth that on land.

When surfeited with the view of the waterfall and the "Emperor's Height," we drove to the city, passing en route the Hotel
Gratidão, by which probably no guest was ever rendered "truly
thankful." Juiz de Fóra was in gorgeous array, this being the
festival of its Padroeiro or patron saint, Santo Antonio, known
to Europe chiefly in connection with pigs. Here it is his duty to
find husbands for young women, and if he does not he is slapped

* The South American or three-toed
Ostrich (Rhea americana). It weighs from
fifty to sixty pounds, and is thus about one-
third smaller than the two-toed African,
that largest of known birds, and it wears
a dull grey, half-mourning dress, which
has been till lately neglected by the trade.
In the province of Rio Grande the word
"Avestrus," properly the African ostrich,
is used. "Ema" is a corruption of the
Arabic Neámah (نعامة), yet even the
accurate Southey (vol. i., chap. 5, p. 129)
and Gardner, to say nothing of the vulgar
herd, have corrupted it to "Emu." The
aborigines of the Brazil called it "Nhandú"
or "Nhundú." According to Prince Max.
(iii. 12), the Brazilians also know it as
"Touyou," and Southey adds, "Churi"
(i., 8, 253). I have not heard either
of these words, which are pure Guaraní.
† I know no oranges better than the

Brazilian. The tree, however, is very
uncertain, and the same shoots planted in
the same soil produce a very different fruit.
Each Province has its own, as, to quote no
others, the Selectas of Rio de Janeiro and
the Bahian Embigudas, which ladies call the
"Naval" orange. The most common is the
Laranja da China, which extends nearly
along the coast and far into the interior.
We shall pass through places on the Rio de
São Francisco where it will not thrive.
Pizarro mentions two sub-varieties of this
Chinese orange, of redder tinge, outside
and inside, than the other. São Paulo is
remarkable for its "Tangerinas," a name
popularly derived from Tangiers; they
resemble the small mandarins of China,
but they are not so delicate. There are
two varieties, the pequenas and the grandes,
and Pizarro distinguishes three sub-
varieties, which he calls, "da China, da
India, and da Terra, or Boceta."

and ducked in the well, and made to sleep in the chill night air. The peal of bells was well-nigh worn out by hard hammering. The Matriz was a Black Hole of worshippers, the flower of the flock being in the tribunes and prodigal of smiles to the couthless strangers. "The son of the quarter," says the Arabic proverb, "filleth not the eye."

At Juiz de Fóra I met the Commendador Henrique Guilherme Fernando Halfeld, of whom more in the next volume. He gave me some information about the Rio de São Francisco, and told me when taking leave of us that he, aged seventy-two, was about to marry a young person of sixteen. May the result be satisfactory!

CHAPTER V.

" À partir de Juiz de Fóra on ne trouve plus qu'un chemin inégal, aux pentes inadmissibles, dans lequel, pendant la saison des pluies, on peut à peine circuler à cheval, et avec la condition de mettre bientôt son animal hors de service."
M. Liais.

THE next day (Monday, June 17, 1867) witnessed the break-up of a pleasant party, and our farewell to " comforts " for a season. Mr. L'pool determined to accompany us northwards, Major and Mr. Newdigate with Mr. Morritt tend to the south. At noon we shall be separated by a century of miles, something of a consideration in the Brazil, where men move slowly. We are also to lose Sr. Francisco Alves Malvero, the cashier of the " Union and Industry Company," who, on his sole responsibility and with true New-World go-a-head liberality, had franked us to Barbacena.

At 6 A.M. on a raw, dark morning, the two coaches, duly packed, stood side by side fronting opposite ways, and ready to start at the same moment. Presently Godfrey, a stout young German, ex-sailor, from the then jeopardied Duchy of Luxemburg, handled the ribbons, and with a blast of the horn and waved hats we dashed at the way. Our light, strong mail, " O Barbacenense," was full. The insides were a Brazilian lady with two black girls, the normal two black babies, plus an Austrian ex-lieutenant, married and settled in the interior; the

* The stages are approximately :—	miles.	h.	m.
1. Juiz de Fóra to Saudade	6	0	35
2. Saudade to Estiva	10	0	55
3. Estiva to Chapéo d'Uvas	4	0	45
4. Chapéo d'Uvas to Pedro Alves	10	1	25
5. Pedro Alves to João Gomes	4	0	30
6. João Gomes to José Roberto	9	1	15
7. José Roberto to Nascimento Novo	8	2	15
8. Nascimento Novo to Registro	8	0	50
9. Registro to Barbacena	4	0	35

Total, 63 miles in 9 hours and 5 minutes ; the regulation speed is twelve miles per hour upon the good parts of the road, which are few and far between.

outsides behind were our two negro servants and a large collection of small baggage. We sat in the rear of the driver and the guard, with my wife packed between us in case of a "spill."

The first lot was poor land, and the line lay up the riverine plain, at times cutting across a high hill-spur that projected into the valley. The early world looked pale white with hoar frost; the effect arose from the velvety down of the well-known gramen, Capim Gordura,* the "grass of fatness," so called because the blades feel greasy and viscous. It was purple with flower and seed, and at once suggested stock breeding, but it will dry up in a few weeks and become poor forage; then the troop mules will suffer, and devour all manner of trash. Botanists rank it amongst the plants which follow the footsteps of man; it covers deserted roads, it occupies the ground when freshly cleared of virgin forest, and it takes possession of fields allowed to lie fallow for the five years that usually follow two successive harvests. According to St. Hilaire the "ambitieuse graminée" is not indigenous, and the people told him that it was a present from the Spanish colonies. They have now forgotten its foreign origin.

The land is rising rapidly, the receding woods become less dense, and the delicate "cabbage palms" †, with other growths of the Maritime Range, disappear. Air and soil are too cold for coffee and sugar, except a trifle raised for home consumption in the Quintal or sheltered and often manured courtyard. Rice and maize, however, are good; vegetables and tobacco flourish; every hut has its floor for drying beans; buckwheat, rye, and hops would doubtless everywhere be at home except upon the bald polls of the disforested hills; and, in the bottom lands, cotton might be grown to advantage. So rich is the Brazilian soil, even in its poorer phases.

* Tristegis glutinosa, or Melinis minutifolia (Palis.). It is also called Capim Catinga or of fetor, its peculiar odour being supposed to resemble that of the negro. I did not find it unpleasant. St. Hilaire, who has given an ample account of the grass (I. i. 195; III. i. 223—5, and in III. ii. 29, 31, 54, and 175), makes Capim Catinguero the same as Capim Gordura and the Capim Melado ("honied grass") of Rio de Janeiro and S. Paulo. He found it called Capim de Frei Luiz, the religious who introduced it with a view of benefiting the country; his name is now forgotten. According to Martius,

Capi-Catinga is one of the Cyperaceæ, the sedges. Some Brazilians hold Capim Catinga to be the young Capim Gordura. Gardner (475·7) observed that north of south latitude 17° it grows near houses only. I see no reason why this grass should not make excellent hay.

† Euterpe edulis, in Tupy Assahi or Assaï. The cylindrical spike or footstalk, long, green, and succulent, which contains the rudiments of future leaves, is the cabbage. Many palms yield this edible embryo; in the Brazil the Euterpe is the best.

We miss the neat Swiss Gothic stations with their fancy gables
and iron roofs painted red. At Saudade (why call it "Deside-
rium?") we find an old tiled ranch, or shed, with nothing to
recommend it but a semicircle of fine coqueiros.* Presently we
crossed for the last time the Parahybuna River, whose valley ran
up to the left. Though the soil did not improve, the views did:
there were pretty bits of "home scenery," grassy hills with
graceful rounded curves, and their groves of palm and other trees.

Animal life now became more conspicuous. The Urubú vulture
spreads its wings to the rising sun; the Caracará buzzard (Falco
crotophagus or F. degener or F. brasiliensis, the Chima-chima of
Azara) perched like the Indian Maina upon the backs of grazing
kine, or trotted after them, pecking at the ticks; this singular
bird of prey, revered by the Guaycurú Indians, was evidently
rendering an interested service. "Maria preta"—black Maria—a
kind of widow finch, in sable and snow, flashed across the path
from holt to holt. The Japé, or hang-nest, and the brilliant violet
oriole (Oriolus violaceus) trotted about, whilst the merlo or black-
bird (Turdus brasiliensis) and the Sabiá thrush (Turdus rufiventris),
that Brazilian nightingale of the flutey song, chanted their matins
with a will. Troops of the glancing purple-green, black, and grey-
white "anum," † chattering like starlings, shunned the trees as is
their wont, balancing themselves on the elastic shrub tops.

The Cupim-nests,‡ or termitaria, are lumpy pillars and pyramids
of clay, yellow or drab coloured, as may be the subsoil, and sometimes 5 or 6 feet high. They are scattered like tombstones,
occasionally in pairs or trios, as if a succursale had been added,
often shaped suggestively to a pious Hindu: nowhere in the
Brazil, however, do they constitute so conspicuous a feature, or
cumber the land as in the Somali country. The mounds near the
road appear to be deserted; and some suppose that the "white
ants" abandon their homes when made, which is absurd. Opened

---

* Not "Cocoeiro," as Professor Agassiz
has it. The Cocos butyracea, one of the
finest palms in the Brazil, was seen throughout the interior when I visited it, till the
Carnauba palm (Copernicia cerifera) took its
place.

† In the plural anuns. The word has
been much abused, turned into anuh, annù,
and so forth. The black anum is the Crotophaga ani (Prince Max). The white is the
Cuculus Guira (Linn.), or spotted cuckoo;

it is the Pirigua of Azara, and is said to
have reached the coast from the Highlands.
The large variety is the Crotophaga major
(Linn.).

‡ Properly Co-pim, from co, a nest, cave,
hole, and pim, to sting, a sting, dart, iron
point. Hence the error of M. de Suzannet,
whose bird "Coupy" is the termite: in
places it builds round the tree trunks and
branches clay nests which look like gigantic
wens. Azara also writes Cupiy.

they suggest a mammoth hotel as Asmodeus would see it, and a few stiff blows with a pick upon the hard crust of those which seem to be in ruins, brings from their burrows a frantic swarm as the said hotel would show at the cry of fire. The Cupim does little injury to the farmer, and has foes innumerable, especially the Myothera, the prairie wood-pecker (Picus campestris), the toad, the lizard family, the Myrmecophaga, and the armadillo. Some travellers make the ant-house a *ménage à trois*, and the same tale is told of the prairie dog villages. It is not, however, a happy family if it be true that the toad, after eating up the ants, is eaten by a serpent, and the serpent is devoured by a Siriéma,* a bird whose tastes correspond with the African "Secretary" (Gypogeranus africanus), but it wants the pens behind the ears, which made the Dutch give the latter so literary a name. Others believe that the young of the Cupim are carried off and enslaved, like West Africans, by the fierce plantation ant,† which thus represents the wicked and merciless white man. But the same tale is told of the "Quem-Quem" ant, and possibly the superstition may have arisen from the different sizes of the workers major and the workers minor.

The road, tolerably good for the Brazil, is execrable compared with the first day's line. In many places it is double or treble. These "deviations"‡ denote muds worse than those of a Cheshire lane. The surface is now hard and caky; about December it will be cut up by the regular tramping of the "boiadas" or droves of market cattle, into a "corduroy," a gridiron of ruts and ridges, locally called caldeiras or "caldeirões." § These "chauldrons," horrible to Brazilian travellers, consist of raised lines, narrow, hard and slippery, divided by parallel hollows of soppy, treacly clay; in the latter mules sink to the knee or to the shoulder, their tall-heeled shoes are often lost, and at times a hoof remains behind. Old and wary beasts tread in the mud, not on the ridges, which cause dangerous falls. The cure would be deep-trenching to drain the "chauldrons," bush clearing to

---

* The Siriema (Dicolophus cristatus, Illiger; Palamedea cristata, Gmelin) will be repeatedly mentioned in the second volume. It is about the size of a small turkey, for which it is often mistaken; it runs like a young ostrich; it goes generally in pairs, and it builds in low trees. Its "bell-note" is not unpleasant, and it is easily tamed. Others suppose the Termitarium bird to be a kind of owl (Strix cunicularia, or Campos owl), which is known to lay eggs in deserted armadillo holes.

† Alta cephalotis. The Brazilians call it Saúba, a corruption of the Tupy "Yçauba."

‡ Desvios.

§ The holes made by the waves in the coast rocks also have this name.

admit the great engineers Sun and Wind, and in extreme cases laying down logs across the mud. At present the forest presses upon the roads because travellers prefer riding in the shade. It is easy for them to choose the cool of the day; moreover, I never felt the least inconvenience, even from a "chimney-pot," in the heat of noon; and, finally, the Brazil, like Western Africa—probably for the same reason—is remarkably free from sunstroke. But in this stage of society, to "work for others"* stultifies a man exceedingly, and the real Portuguese of the old school would rather want than do anything incidentally likely to supply the wants of his neighbours.

We are upon the highway between the metropolis of the Empire and the Capital of the Gold and Diamond Province. In the rainy season, from November to April, the sloughs take off the coach. The annual cost of repair is 300$000 per league. The zelador or cantonnier, however, expects everywhere in the Brazil to draw pay and to do nothing, save perchance to vote. He is equal to any amount of "drawing," but *do* he will not. Upon this whole line, where there is not a single rood that does not urgently require a large gang, we found a single negro lad scratching his head, and sometimes tickling the ground with a hoe.

Throughout the Empire these lines of communications are divided into Imperial, Provincial, Municipal, and between three such stools accidents are ever happening. When a route is to be made the concession is granted sometimes in payment for political services to the applicant, who lays it out well or ill, as the case may be. It is then thrown open to the public, and is left to be spoiled. When worn down to the bone, and converted into rock-ladders, rut-systems, and quagmire-holes, where beasts are bogged and die—then, possibly, may be built alongside of the old road a new line, whose fate, in course of time, shall inevitably be the same. Often my Brazilian friends have remarked that men who travel by such weary ways need no future process of punishment.

Of course, after living three years in the Brazil, I know the difficulties of road-making. The pasty red clay which here as in Africa clothes Earth's skeleton demands metalling if the line is to

* Trabalhar para os outros. Every school in the Empire should put up the motto of the Free Cantons—
"Each for all, and all for each;"
and borrow a few Gaelic maxims, "One and all," "Union is strength," "I care for everybody, and I hope everybody cares for me."

last, and macadamizing is an expensive process, requiring constant repairs. The rivers and brooks are not those of a "well-regulated country" like England: they shrink to nothing, they swell into immense torrents, and the cost of bridging and controlling them is no trifle. Popular opinion, by no means thoroughly awake to the importance of highways and byways, is another obstacle; many think that a good road is that which enables you to ride your mule comfortably. Their fathers have done without mending their ways, and straightening their paths—ergo, so can they, et cetera.

These pages, however, will show that in this Empire, about to be so mighty and magnificent, communication signifies civilization, prosperity, progress—everything. It is more important to national welfare even than the school or the newspaper, for these will follow where that precedes. And travellers who wish well to the land must ever harp, even to surfeit, upon this one string.

After Saudade the country waxes lone. Besides a few roadside shop-sheds, which sell wet and dry goods, beans, flour, and the baldest necessaries of life, we find only two manor-houses belonging to a landowner known as " O Mirandão " and his son-in-law. The monotonous thud and creak of the "Monjolo,"* the only labour-saving machine bequeathed by Portugal to her big daughter, proclaims the rudeness of agriculture.† A heavy hill of the slippery clay, with its cuttings of purple, marbled or mauve-coloured ochreish earth, called in São Paulo " Taguá," delays the pace; and Godfrey must often " skid " and employ the patent break as we descend.

The next station, " Chapéo d'Uvas," is so called from some generous old vineyarder who allowed the thirsty to fill their hats with his grapes. A certain modern traveller related that somewhere between this place and Curral Novo, as well as in other wooded parts of the Brazil, there is a pigmy race about three feet high, white as Europeans, and with hairless bodies. This suggests the Wabilikimo or " Two-cubit Men," gravely

---

* Or Monjóllo. Mawe terms it Pre-guiça (the sloth), and gives a drawing of this rough water-mill, which is described by every traveller. Caldcleugh calls it Jogo, a game. St. Hil. (III. i. 121, &c.) erroneously writes the word "Manjola." It appears in Brazilian poetry, e.g. the Parabolas (No. 113, Wolf) of José Joaquim Corrêa de Almeida—

" Deputado vil comparsa
Representou de Monjolo."
" The Deputy, a vile compare,
Like the Monjolo beat the air."
† So in 1633, the first saw-mill built on the Thames, opposite Durham Yard, was taken down, "lest our labouring people should want employment."

located by the " Mombas Mission Map," within the seaboard of
Zanzibar; and the reader will at once recall to mind the detailed
notices of the " Obengo " dwarfs, lately brought home from
Ashango-land by my indefatigable and adventurous friend, Paul
du Chaillu.

Here the Caminho do Mato, the " Forest-road" from the
north-east, falls into the Caminho do Campo, the " Prairie highway," which trends to the north-west. The settlement is the
normal post-town," a single straggling street with a pauper
chapel : it can no longer claim to be " one of the prettiest and
most civilized spots seen since leaving Rio de Janeiro." It
could hardly supply grain to our five beasts; the people raise
enough for domestic consumption only, and travellers carry their
own slender stores. The waggons were standing in the thoroughfare, and the first glance showed wayfarers from the United
States. They had done what they would have done in Illinois—
they had brought traps and teams, and they were lumbering on
towards the setting sun.

The next stage showed us " Retiro,"* a bunch of huts tenanted
by negroes, who had hoisted a black saint upon the " Tree of St.
John." Here we first sighted the Mantiqueira Range, with
which I had made acquaintance in São Paulo. I have something
to say about this most interesting formation. It is not one line,
but a collection of systems, crystalline, volcanic and sedimentary.
Its southernmost wall is within sight of São Paulo, the city,
forming the Serra da Cantareira, a septentrional buttress to the
valley of the Tiété River. Thence it runs to the east with
northing, increases greatly in importance, and presently forms
the culminating point of the Brazilian Highlands. A little beyond
this point—in W. long. (Rio) 1° 20'—it obeys the great law of
South America, and indeed of the New World generally; and,
curving at an angle of 115°-120°, it becomes a meridional range,
not an east to west chain, as are mostly those of the so-called Old
Hemisphere. It bisects the Province of Minas upon the line of
Barbacena, Ouro Preto, and Diamantina, and it divides the
Atlantic watershed, the riverine basins of the Rio Doce, the
Mucury, the Jequitinhonha, and the minor systems from the

---

* St. Hil. (III. i. 233) translates " Retiro " by Châlet. In this part of the country
it confounds with our " shooting box :" on
the Rio de São Francisco it will bear another meaning.

Western versant, draining the Paraná, Paraguay, Plata, and the Rio de São Francisco. It affects the surface almost as much as do the Andes further to the occident; it arrests the rains which flood the lands on its seaward flank; it breaks up the ground, and covers earth with the densest forests. The inland slopes are more regular, prairies abound, and the vegetation is chiefly gramineous, and the low woods known in the Brazil as Caatingas and Carrascos.* North of Diamantina it becomes the Serra do Grão Mogor; it then forms in Bahia the Serra das Almas and the Chapada Diamantina, or Diamantine Plateau, after which it sinks into the broken plain on the southern bank of the Rio de São Francisco. Then it extends some 860 geographical miles between S. lat. 10° and 24° 20′. The southern portion runs almost parallel with and distant 30 to 50 miles from the Serra do Mar or Maritime Range. About Barbacena it has already greatly diverged, and its maximum distance from the shores of the Atlantic may amount to 200 direct miles.

The culminating point of Mantiqueira and of the Brazil generally is the Itatiaiossú, a highly picturesque word, interpreted to mean the "great flamboyant rock," from the flame-like outlines of its three loftiest crests. The chief peak is placed in S. lat. 22°·38′ 45″, and W. long. (Rio) 1° 30′. The "Revista Trimensal" (1861), of the Instituto Historico e Geographico Brasileiro, adopts the mean altitude of 3140 metres, or 10,300 feet. Dr. Franklin da Silva Massena has reduced the estimate to 2994 metres; and Père Germain, of the Episcopal Seminary of São Paulo, who visited it in May, 1868, increases it to 2995.† The formation is essentially volcanic, two craters and more than 200 caves have been found in it, and the explorers met with sulphur springs and large deposits of sulphur and iron pyrites.

* "Caatinga" must not be confounded with "Catinga" before mentioned. The former is derived from the Tupy "Cáa," forest, bush, leaf, grass; and "tinga," white. It admirably describes the scattered growth of dry clay or sandy plains, gnarled trees averaging 10—20 feet in height, or one-tenth of the forest-growth, and looking pale and sickly by the side of the dark virgin leafage. "Carrasco" in Portugal is a low stiff growth, and the word is supposed to be derived from Quercus and rusceus, "Carvalho picante," prickly oak. The Mineiros mostly apply it to a vegetation more scattered, stunted, and ragged than the Caatinga, ranging between 3 to 6 feet, and often rich in the Mimosa dumetorum, a true "Carrasquente" shrub. Both allow the sun to penetrate through their thin coats, and with the assistance of dew a little grass good for pasture grows about their roots.

† The number 2994 has been adopted by that excellent Brazilian geographer, Sr. Candido Mendes de Almeida. Père Germain found the altitude of the highest habitation to be 1560 metres.

The summits are annually covered with snow, which sometimes lies for a fortnight, and the plains are fields of wild strawberries. I shall have more to say upon this subject when describing the Province of São Paulo. Suffice it now to remark that this part of the Mantiqueira is a Sanitarium, lying at the easy distance of three days' trip from Rio de Janeiro, viâ the D. Pedro Segundo Railway and the Valley of the Southern Parahyba.

The Abbé Cazal calls the central and symmetrical range "Serra do Mantiqueiro." Dr. Couto very properly terms it "Serra Grande;" its peaks, the Itabira, the Itambé, and the Itacolumi, not to mention the Itatiaiossú, exceed in height all others in the Empire, except those visited by Gardner in the Serra do Mar near Rio de Janeiro. The popular name which appears upon our maps, and which is being adopted by the Brazilians, is Serra do Espinhaço* or Range of the Spine-bone. This generalization is, I believe, the work of the Baron von Eschwege, who in the last generation commanded the Corps of Imperial Engineers at Ouro Preto, and who has written extensively upon the geography and mineralogy of the country. But the so-called Espinhaço is not the spine of the Brazil generally, although it may be that of Minas Geraes. A nearer approach to a true Charpente dorsale would be the Ranges da Mantiqueira, dos Vertentes, and da Canastra; the Mata da Corda and the great ridge to the west of the Rio de São Francisco, known to maps as the Serra da Tiririca and da Tauatinga.† North of S. lat. 11° it forks into the so-called Serra da Borborema, trending to the north-east and the Serra dos Cerôados, diverging to the north-west.

The word "Mantiqueira," also written and pronounced "Mantiguira," is still unjudged. Usually it is translated "ladroeira," robbery, and is supposed to be local patois. Some derive it from "Manta," a (woollen) "cloak," and figuratively a "trick" or "treachery." In the early half of the present

---

* Not "Sierra Espenhaço" (Herschel, Physical Geography, 292).

† Often and erroneously written "Tabatinga," which would signify literally the white wigwam, and which the Dictionaries render by "smoke." The Tupy "tauá" seems to be the same word as "taguá" or "tagoá," which Figueira translates "barro vermelho"—red argil; whilst "tinga" is white. It is a pure white, or slightly yellow kaolin, sometimes mixed with sand; but more often pure, the degradation of felspar, and it has been mistaken by foreigners for chalk: when limestone is deficient, it is still used as whitewash. The older writers define it to be the "wunder erde" of Saxony, a hardened, argillaceous lithomarge. In 1800, a certain João Manso Pereira made, we are told, works of art from the material found at the Lagôa-de Sentinella, near Rio de Janeiro.

century it was a name of fear, as Apennines and Abruzzi are even yet. Old travellers are full of legends about its banditti, and mule-troopers still shudder at the tales told around their camp-fires. The Thugs used to lasso their victims and cast the corpses, duly plundered of diamonds and gold dust, into the deepest "cañons" and ravines: there is a tradition that one of these Golgothas was discovered by a fast-growing tree which bore a saddle by way of fruit. The guard assured me that when the last road was made, treasure was found in several places. The most noted bands in late years were headed by a certain Schinderhans; "O Chefe Guimarães," a "highly respectable" Portuguese of Barbacena: about 1825 he and his familiar friend, the gipsy Pedro Hespanhol, died in jail. Another actor in the tragedy was the Padre Joaquim Arruda, a rich man and well connected in this part of the Province. The fidus Achates, who everywhere stood by his Fra Diavolo, was one Joaquim Alves Saião Beijú, properly called Cigano Beijú, or Gipsy Manioc Cake.* The Reverend "Rue" (Ruta graveolens?) came in 1831 to a bad end after some seven years of successful villany; aided by his gipsy, he escaped from prison, hid himself in a cave near S. José de Parahyba, and was shot down by the detachment that pursued him.

But "Mantiqueira" is now shorn of its terrors, and very beautiful are the slate-blue summits which meet our sight. At its base we find the Half-way House, "Pedro Alves," where the normal breakfast, not, alas! "blessed pullets and fat hams" awaited us. I will at once observe that neither gourmand nor gourmet should visit the South American interior, especially the Highlands of the Brazil.

Refreshed with the "quantum interpellat," such as it was, we dashed down a steep, winding hill, where Godfrey remembered a broken arm and the guard two fractured ribs. Every hollow in the road made our vehicle buck-jump like taking a brook, and the swing and sway and the heaving to and fro as we rounded the corners equalled any Brighton coach in the early days of railways. The high wind prostrates bamboos near the road, and the wicked

---

* The gipsies of the Brazil, who are still numerous in Minas, take their names from food, birds and beasts, trees and flowers. Koster explains "Cigano" as a corruption of Egypciano; in fact, synonymous with "Gitano." Many English residents of long standing ignore the existence of gipsies in the Brazil.

little mules gave us the worst taste of their quality. We crossed the Rio do Pinho, one of the headwaters of the Rio das Mercês da Pomba, which feeds the Lower Parahyba, and drains the Eastern Mantiqueira. At the foot of the latter is the little countrified town "João Gomes," with palm-grown square, cross-fronted church, and Hotel da Ponte.

As we near the ascent water becomes again plentiful; here it is said to rain or to drizzle every second day. This Brazilian Westmoreland sucks dry the sea-born clouds, and does its best to make the Far West an arid waste. After sundry preliminaries of subrange and outlying buttress, we breast the slope that measures about four miles and occupies an hour. M. Liais prematurely wrote, "les ingénieurs de la Compagnie Union et Industrie ont trouvé un bon passage dans la Serra da Manti-queira," but he confesses to not having seen it. The facing is easterly, fronting the weather, and exposed to the full force of the north-eastern and south-eastern Trades, water-logged from the Atlantic. However, the Commission lately sent under command of the late Mr. John Whittaker, C.E., has found a pass of easy gradients and without the main fault of the present seaward-fronting line.

Gneiss and granite, thickly banded with veins of clear and smoky quartz, composed the under strata. The surface was the usual rich red clay, ferruginous with degraded mica and felspar; the cuttings showed boulders and "hard heads," peeling like the coats of an onion. Greenstone blocks appeared, especially upon rising ground, but not *in situ*. When the sun shone, minute fragments of silvery mica sparkled with a wonderful glitter. Caldcleugh found near the summit the old red sandstone, between which and the new red, the carboniferous formations of the Brazil are, I believe, mostly found. This would argue that we are now west of the great coal formation, which has been traced with intervals between Bagé of Rio Grande do Sul (S. lat. 31° 30′) and the Province of Pernambuco (S. lat. 8° 10).* If this be the case, the country between the Mantiqueira Range and the coast line must be explored for carbonic deposits.

The deep mud, sticky as coal tar, and engulfing our wheels to

---

* I do not pretend to fix the limits, the 23° in the text have already supplied specimens. M. Charles Van Lede (De la Colonization au Brésil. Bruxelles, 1843, chap. 10) has well described the coal mines of Santa Catharina.

the hub, dismounted all the men, who tried some short cuts and suffered accordingly. As we ascended, two crystal streams gushed out of the clay scarps on our right, and had been converted into fountains by some charitable soul who probably knew what thirst is, and who pitied thirsty man and beast. At the summit we waded through a pool of slush, and the team—all the kick was now taken out of it—halted with quivering flanks, streaming skins and prone muzzles. An opportune rock slab invited us to rest and be thankful for the panorama.

We are now at the eastern culminating plateau-point of the Brazilian Highlands, and from this radiate the headwater valleys of the Parahyba do Sul, the Rio Doce, and the Paraná, which becomes the mighty Plata. Below us lay the land mapped out into an infinity of feature that ranged through the quadrant from south-east to south-west. There was the usual beautiful Brazilian perspective, tier after tier of mountain, hill, hillock, rise, and wavy horizon, whose arc was dotted with the forms familiar to Rio de Janeiro—sugar loaves, hunchbacks, topsails, and parrots'-beaks. The clothing of the earth was "Capoeira," or second-growth forest*, so old that in parts it appeared almost virginal; the colours were black-green, light-green, brown-green, blue-green, blue and azure in regular succession, whilst the cloud-patches gathering before the sun mottled the landscape with a marbling of shade—travellers from the temperates prefer this mixture of grey to the perfect glory of the day-god. On the

---

* As in Intertropical Africa so in the Brazil, when the virgin forest is filled, a different growth, more shrubby and of lighter colour, rather herbaceous than ligneous, takes its place. The eye soon learns to distinguish between the two, and no Brazilian farmer ever confounds them. The virgin is darker, and more gloomy; there is less undergrowth, the ground is cleaner, and the llianas are larger, more numerous and more useful. The wood that has lost its virginity is far richer in flowers and fruits, in Orchids and Bromelias. Some botanists believed that the germs were hidden for countless centuries in the soil; others that the seeds are transported by wind and the animal creation, which appears more probable. This second growth is called "Capoeira," and when old "Capoeirão," an incrementative form; Capoeirinho means that it is young. It is said that after many years the characteristic vegetation of the virgin forest re-appears;

I have no opinion to offer upon the subject. The word "Capoeira" is derived from "Capão" (plural, "Capões"), a corrupted Tupy word. In Portugal it means a capon; in the Brazil it is derived from Caá-poam, a bush island, either on hill or plain; "Caá," a bush, and "poám" or "puam," from "apoam," subs. and adj. a globe, a ball, an island, also round, swelling. It is admirably descriptive of the feature which in classical Lusitanian is termed ilha de mato, mouta or moita; in French, bouquet de bois; and in Canadian English "motte." Thus "Capoeira" is opposed to mata, matagal, mata virgem, mato virgem, and in Tupy to Caa-etê. This would be literally the "very" or "the virgin forest," "etê" being a particle which augments and prolongs the signification of its substantive, as Aba, a man, Aba-etê a true or great man. Caa-etê undergoing slight alterations, as Caethé, Caithé, and so forth, is the name of many Brazilian settlements.

south-west a long high wall of light plum-colour, streaked with
purple and capped with a blue-yellow sheet, which might be grass
or stone, fixed the glance. This is the Serra da Ibitipóca*, a
counterfort of great "Mantiqueira," trending from north-north-
east to south-south-west. On its summit there is, they say,
a lakelet, and in the lakelet fish. The mountain tarns are very
common in the Highlands of the Brazil; they may be met with
even on the blocks that rise from the Maritime lowlands.†

I pushed on, determined to spare the mules, and reached a
dwarf basin, where dark mica slate and tufaceous formations
announced a change of country. *Obiter*, it may be remarked
that the Brazil is rich in turbaries, which have never yet been
used for fuel. As the turf is mostly modern, it must go through
a certain process, especially of compression ; and the late Mr.
Ginty, C.E., of Rio de Janeiro, took out a patent for working
the beds. At this place, 4000 feet above sea level, a ragged
hut protected a few roadside squatters‡ from the burning sun and
the biting wind. A short slope led to the great descent. The
soil was still deep black earth, decayed vegetable matter, the dust of
extinct forests forming peat. In the rains it becomes a tenacious
mire, in the dries a stiff cakey clay, which severely tries our
trusty English coach-springs. Half-way down hill I found what
suggested the wooden cart of Northumberland in the middle of
the last century. It had ten yoke of oxen, and the men, armed
with the usual goads, huge spur-rowels at the end of perches ten
feet long, had spent the day in pricking, cursing, and lashing the
laggers over the one league up the Serra.

At "José Roberto" the road became dry; we are now in
a lea-land. The new mules kept up a hand gallop to "Nascimento," a pretty "venda" in a dwarf plain or hollow, bright
with the greenest grass, tall waving Coqueiro palms, and the
glorious mauve-pink bracts of the Bougainvillea§ (B. brasiliensis)
which in Minas becomes a tree.

---

* My informant explains this to mean
"here" (iby) ; "it ends" (tipoca). The
derivation appears fanciful. "Iby" as a
rule means "earth," Iby-tira a serra or
mountain range, and Iby-tira cua, a valley.
Poc means to burst.

† For instance, Itabaiana in Sirgipe,
the Monserrate hills behind Santos, São
Paulo, and in various mountains of Minas

which will be mentioned. We remember
the Witch's Well that never dries on the
granitic Brocken or Blocksberg, the highest
point of the North German Hartz.

‡ "Moradores," literally dwellers.

§ The Prince Max. writes Bugainvillea
and Buginvillæa (i. 58). The accurate
Gardner Bugenvillea, which mutilates not
a little the name of the great circum-

After running eight miles from the Mantiqueira crest, and at the twelfth from our destination, we make the Borda do Campo or "Edge of the Prairie (ground)." A similar name and nature is found near São Paulo, the city; there, however, the Campo begins close to the Maritime Range, while here the Mantiqueira intervenes. I curiously compared first impressions: in Minas the land is more broken into deep hollows, glens, and ravines; and the "capões" or patches of forest are of superior importance. The minor characteristics I must reserve for another Chapter.

The dry season was now at its height, and the country looked faint and torpid with drowth. We caught a far sight of Barbacena, with its church-towers fretting the summit of a high dark ridge to the north, already purpling in the slanted rays of the sun. The situation at once suggested São Paulo, and we again breathed the cool, clear, light air of the Plateau, a tonic after the humid heat of the Mantiqueiran ascent. Large Fazendas lay scattered about: we were struck by the appearance of those called Campo Verde and Nascimento Novo.

Our eighth team, fine white mules for the run in, awaited us at Registro Velho. It is the first of the trio which, in colonial times, awaited the hapless wayfarer from Minas Geraes to the seaboard. The building is a large white affair of a rude wooden style; its ancient occupation is now gone, and it has found new industries. The "Gold troops" from the Anglo-Minas mines always night here, avoiding the city streets, where they lose their shoes and spend their money; the pasture, however, is execrable. The proprietor, "Capitão"* José Rodriguez da Costa, lodges travellers in his own independent way, turning them out if they grumble at high charges. Before visiting the several Companies, one marvels that they cannot combine to set up an establishment of their own. The captain, however, is trustworthy, or rather, being a wealthy man, he is much trusted.

---

navigator. French colonists unaccountably call the beauty Œil de Judas, and the Brazilians Porca Rota.

* Military rank is as common in the Brazil as in the Far West of the Union before the War, or in Great Britain since the last days of the Volunteers. Rarely it refers to the Line; almost always to the National Guard. The latter, organised in Dec. 31, 1863, consisted in 1864 of 212 superior commands, and a vast cadre of officers, with 595,454 rank and file, distributed into artillery, cavalry, infantry, and infantry of reserve. It formed, as in North America, a curious contrast with the regular army, which, till Paraguay rendered an increase necessary, numbered 1550 officers and 16,000 men, whilst the police in 18 provinces did not exceed 4467. These figures speak volumes in favour of the orderly and law-fearing character of the Brazilian people.

Here is a manufactory of cigarros,* celebrated from Minas to Rio de Janeiro. Two rooms contain the workpeople, men and women, and there is one cutter to each half-a-dozen rollers. The maize leaf is used instead of paper, a custom directly derived from the aborigines. "Après qu'ils ont cueilli le petem" (tobacco-leaf),† says De Léry of the Tupinambas (p. 200), " et, par petite poignée, pendu et fait sécher en leurs maisons, ils en prennent quatre ou cinq feuilles qu'ils enveloppent dans une autre grande feuille d'arbre en façon de cornet d'épices ; mettant alors le feu par le petit bout et le mettant ainsi allumé dans leur bouche, ils en tirent de cette façon la fumée." The tobacco is strong, and the "pinch of snuff rolled up in a leaf" soon cakes and must be unrolled and rerolled before it will draw. A large bundle may be bought for a shilling, and yet the profits of the establishment are about 160*l.* per mensem. Roll-tobacco, as a rule, in the Brazil is good, and this is remarkably good.

The next stage crosses the Rio do Registro Velho, a feeder of the Rio das Mortes—the River of the Murder-Deaths.‡ We are now, therefore, in the South Brazilian basin of the Paraná, Paraguay, and Plata rivers. Turning from the main road to the right we pass the wretched little colony "José Ribeiro." A landowner of that name sold the ground to the "Union and Industry," and the latter established a settlement of Germans. The only decent house was that of the Director. And now appeared the beginning of the end in a bittock of fine smooth macadam laid down by the Company. It was like rolling over a billiard table, and we galloped up it with a will, the breath of the mid-winter evening biting our faces and feet.

It was almost dark when we entered the city of Barbacena, which looked as lively as a mighty catacomb, and we deposited

* The Portuguese cigarro is a cigarette, the cigar (a Singhalese word) being called "Charúto," whence our cheroot.

† The tobacco plant and leaf, in the Tupy tongue, is called petúm, petume, or pety. Hence the corrupted popular Brazilian word "Pitar," to smoke. It is curious that the Portuguese should apply the word which Europe has derived from the Tobago-pipe to snuff only, and reduce tobacco to the vague generic word "fumo."

It is usually asserted that Brazilian tobacco contains, like that of the Havannah, only 2 per cent. of nicotine, a little more than Turkish and Syrian ; whilst that of Kentucky and Virginia averages from 5 to 6 per cent., and the produce of Lot-et-Garonne, &c., 7 per cent. As yet experiments have been made, I believe, only with that grown about Bahia. Both in São Paulo and Minas there are local varieties of the "holy herb," whose headiness suggests a far larger proportion.

‡ The origin of the ill-omened name will presently be explained. Mr. Walsh (ii. 235) calls the Rio do Registro Velho, "Rio das Mortes," which it is not, the lower course only being thus known. Here it was that the well-hoaxed traveller suffered his terrible comical fright about nothing.

the old lady and her innumerable parcels, with the slave girls and their *moutards*, before we could stretch our cramped legs at the Barbacenense Inn. Sr. Herculano Ferreira Paes, the owner, had unfortunately seen better days; he evinced it by giving us in perfect courtesy, sadly misplaced, not dinner but a damnable iteration of excuses. "The house was not worthy of us—we were such great personages—the town was so wretchedly poor—the people were such perfect barbarians." His sons were palpably above their work, they received every order under tacit protest, and they prospected us as their grandsires might have prospected John Mawe, who, in 1809, visited "Barbasinas." * But food came at last, and we found even the odious Spanish wine good. The sleeping rooms were small, the beds were *grabats*, the air was nipping, and the street dogs barked perniciously. Yet we slept the sleep of the just. It was a weight off one's shoulders that day of stage coaching, which had been uncommonly heavy upon the nervous collar.

* This error is unfortunately followed by that excellent geographer, M. Balbi.

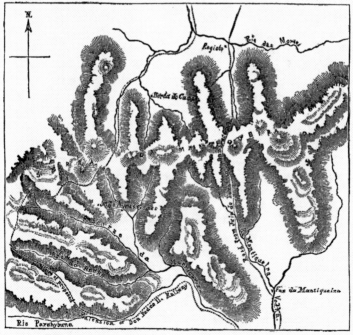

HOW THE FUTURE RAILROAD WILL CROSS THE MANTIQUEIRA.

CHAPTER VI.

THE CAMPOS OR BRAZILIAN PRAIRIES.

> The clouds,
> The mists, the shadows, light of golden suns,
> Motions of moonlight, all come hither, touch
> And have an answer—hither come and shape
> In language not unwelcome to sick hearts
> And idle spirits.   *Wordsworth.*

THE word Campo*—campus—is fitly translated Prairie. The formation, however, is not an elevated plain, like the "grass seas" of the Orinoco, the irksome steppes of Tartary, or the great flats of Russia and Poland, dead levels of lakes and morasses; nor in this parallel does it resemble the rolling uplands of Kansas and the trans-Mississippian territories. In the Oriental Brazil it is a surface of rounded summits between 300 and 600 feet high, generally of ungentle grade, and disposed without regularity, not in gigantic sweeps and billows like the broad swells of Cape seas. Each eminence is separated from its neighbour by a rift or valley, deep or shallow hollows which may often have been lakes, generally forested, and during the rains bottomed with swamp or stream. In the Province of São Paulo the surface of monticles has a lower profile and sometimes falls into the semblance of a plain, whereas Minas has rarely, except in her riverine lines, sufficient level ground for the site of a city. This sinking of the heights and shallowing of the depths continue progressively and uninterruptedly through the Province of Paraná, and

---

* In the Far West these features are called Campos Geraes or General Plains, often abbreviated to "Geraes." The word is supposed to express their fitness for agriculture and stock-breeding in general. Another modification of the Campo is the Taboleiro (table-ground), which when very large becomes a "Chapada" or plateau.

In Vol. II. Chap. 8, I have distinguished between the Taboleiro coberto and the Taboleiro descoberto. The "Campina" is a little formation in the Taboleiro, generally a slope towards water, where the soil is better and the grass affords superior forage.

reaches its maximum in the Pampas and Llanos, the naked or thistle-clad *landes* of the south.

The Campos form the third region of this portion of the Brazil, lying westward of the Maritime Serra and the Beira-mar or coast country. It is a sedimentary and stratified plateau 2000 to 2500 feet high, subtended to the east or seaward by the great unstratified and plutonic ranges, which average in height from 3000 to 4000 feet. In one place Gardner found the Organ Mountains 7800 feet above summit level, and thus in this section of the Brazil, as in Zanzibarian Africa, the summit line is not in the interior but near the coast.* Moreover, the mountains do not attain the altitude of those in Greece (8250 feet). Here we enter upon the vast Itacolumite and Itaberite formations which characterize the mountain chains of the interior, and which stretch, with intervals, to the Andes. The floor is of hypogeneous crystalline rocks, granite, and syenites, which in rare places protrude, and which are mostly seen where the beds of great rivers have cut away the upper deposits. Thus, to quote no other instance, in the Nile Valley, 400 miles long by 12 of breadth, granite forces its way at the Cataracts through the limestones and sandstones; in Unyamwezi I found enormous outcrops of Plutonic breaking through the Neptunian rocks. M. du Chaillu (2nd Exp. chap. xv. p. 292,) describes the same at "Mokenga" in Ishogo-land, about 150 direct miles from the West African Coast.

Resting, here conformably there unconformably upon this undulating basis, crystalline and stratified, both in the interior and on the coast, are, as natural gashes and artificial cuttings prove, layers of pebbles, chiefly quartz, now water-rounded, then sharp and angular, lying in level or wavy bands and seams, as if deposited by still waters and by ice action.† Superjacent, again, is the deep, rich clay which makes the Brazil, like Africa, an Ophir,

---

* The Itatiaiossú is, as I have shown, considerably higher; but at that point the Mantiqueira is also near the coast.

† The glacialists will recognise in this one of the many forms of drift phenomena. Probably the same will be found in the great basin of Central Intertropical Africa, with a tendency of glacial action towards the Equator, and the usual remarkable continuity. In the Brazil the clays and marls are sometimes based upon sand, which seems to be fresh from the sea-shore.

May not the glacial theory explain the "freddo e caldo polo" of Monti? We are, I believe, free to think that our solar system, a subordinate portion of the great stellar universe, may have traversed in its vast orbit spaces where the temperature was higher and lower than it is at present. The variations of the ecliptic, assumed to be one cause of the change of climate, require 25,000 years for their completion.

a red land, ochraceous, highly ferruginous, homogeneous, and almost unstratified, once a paste of sand and argile with pebbles and boulders scattered indiscriminately through the deposit. The surface is siliceous and argillaceous, poor and yellow, scanty in humus, and thinly spread with quartz and sandstones mostly containing iron. This formation happily secures them from the terrible dust-storms of Asia and Africa.

The first sight of these Campos reminded me strongly of Ugogo in Eastern Africa, the arid lea region robbed of its rain by the mountains of dripping Usagara. Then the analogy of the elevated trough formation of Inner Africa * with the Brazilian plateau suggested itself. The main point of difference is—a glance at any map will show it—that the vast lacustrine region of the parallel continent is here imperfectly represented, the drainage slope of South America is more regular, its "continental basins" have no great rock fissures like the Tanganyika bed, no vast hollows like those of the Victoria Nyanza. Thus the main arteries find in this æra of the world uninterrupted way to the ocean, and thus in South America, whose mountains and rivers equal or rather excel those of all other continents, there are no lakes, while North America and Africa, with their sweet-water inland seas and Nyanzas, have comparatively stunted Cordilleras. The lake in this country becomes the Pantanal or flooded Savannah, grounds watered by inundations, and often, like Xaráyis and Uberába, mere enlargements of great rivers, tranquil and shallow sheets where submerged bush and drowned forests form bouquets of verdure, where the dry tracts, like the little prairies in the dark seas of the African jungle, show charming fields sprinkled with flowers, bearing the palm and the magnolia; and where floating islands are bound together in impassable tangle with aquatic and semi-aquatic plants, Pontiderias and Polygonias, Malvaceæ, Convolvulaceæ, Portularias, tall Sacchara, and the rice known as Arroz de Pantanal (Oryza paraguayensis).† These swamps support a considerable population of canoe-men, and have been sung by the

---

* M. du Chaillu found in Ashango-land, on the West African coast, a range running from the north-west-by-west to south-east-by-east, upwards of 3000 feet in height, and dividing the waters that flow to the ocean from those trending to the interior, and thus exactly corresponding with Usa-gara. I also observed their continuation on the course of the Congo River.

† Those writers are in error who derive rice from Asia. A species grows wild in Central Africa as in Central South America.

poets of the Brazil. They form a characteristic feature of the central regions in Southern America.

A typical feature in these Prairie lands is that which Minas calls " esbarrancado," and São Paulo " vossoroca." * At first sight it appears as if a gigantic mine had been sprung. It is either natural or artificial, and an unpractised eye can hardly distinguish between Nature and Art. The former is generally, if not always, the effect of rain-water percolating through the surface into a stratum of subjacent sand or other material that forms a reservoir above the ground rock *in situ.* Presently the drought creates a vacuum; heavy rains then choke the enlarged cavity, and at last the hill side, undermined to the foundation, is suddenly shot forward by the water pressure with the irresistible force of an eruption, leaving a huge irregular hollow cone, sometimes shallow, sometimes deep, like the crater of an extinct volcano. Fatal accidents have happened from these earthen avalanches, which are not unknown to the British islands; † and in 1866 several houses near Petropolis were buried by huge fragments measuring several thousand cubic feet. After the fall a perennial stream generally issues from the water breach, causing a long fracture of the lower level, and creating a valley where before there was nothing but a mountain. The weather transforms the irregular gash into a quarry with a circular head, and thus in time a considerable portion of the high ground is swept down into the hollows, which centuries will convert to levels. Some of these landslips are " alive," that is to say in process of enlargement; they are known by their watery bottoms : their "death " is caused by grass, shrubs, and trees, whose roots and rain-dispersing heads arrest the growth.

These vast fissures, opening into highly irregular glens and ravines, have in some places made the Province of Minas a succession of impasses which time only can bridge. Nothing can be more interesting to the traveller than the puckerings and the

---

* Esbarrancádo, "broken into a precipice," from Barranco, a precipice, a river bank. " Vossoróca " is a local term for these hollows : hence the name of the city "Sorocaba," once celebrated for its mule fair. Cába or -aba terminal denotes place, time, mode or instrument. The common Tupy word for hole is coara (quára), as araraquara, the " Macaw's hole."

† I have heard of them in Ireland, where the vacuum or cavity is formed between the peat surface and the gravelly substratum. The late accident at Santa Lucia (Naples) was also partly due to the pressure of the sandy soil swollen by frequent rains and rocked by continual earthquakes.

spine-like processes, the vast arêtes, the fantastic spires, and the
florid ornamentation of a Gothic cathedral springing from the
vertical or sloping sides of these water-breaches, whose angles are
determined by the nature of the subsoil.   They are best seen
from below, and they reminded me of a section of a Deseret
" Kanyon."   The hues too are vivid as the forms are varied ; all
the colours of the rainbow are there, flashing with quartz and
mica, the detritus of ancient rocks.   The walls are banded with
colours resulting from decomposed metals : dark purple, from
chromes and ochres ; a rich red with pulverized sesquioxide of
iron, green with copper and pyrites, yellow with hydrate of iron,
snowy white with decomposed felspar, silver-coloured with talcose
schist, blue and violet with oxides of manganese, dark brown
with carbonized turfy deposits, charged with ulmic and humic
acids, and variegated with kaolins hard and soft.*   We soon learn
to distinguish the artificial feature.†   The soil of the latter is the
auriferous dark red limonite ; rubbish heaps and spoil banks of
pebbles and conglomerate show that the miner has been at work,
and frequently there are ruins of houses within easy distance.

The vegetation of these high grassy lands offers a wonderful
contrast to the dense forests of the seaboard and the Serra, where
the visible horizon may often be touched by the hand.   This
singular fecundity of vegetable matter, this " plica of growth," is
apt to deceive the stranger by suggesting an excessive fertility
and depth of soil.‡   If he will penetrate into the " lush," he will
find the true roots running along the surface so as to feed upon
every possible inch of shallow humus, and the shallow radical disks
of the prostrated giants show that no tap-root has been able to
strike down into the ferruginous argile of the huge red clay heaps
and mounds, whose core of blue gneiss often lies within a few
feet of the ground.   And when these trees, perhaps the produce
of a century, and forced by a hot-house atmosphere, with rain and
sun *ad libitum*, are once felled, they are followed, as has been said,

---

* " The red clay " (barro vermelho) in
the presence of organic matters, principally
decomposed plants, becomes black or blue,
by the partial de-oxydation of the red
peroxide of iron that passes into dark
peroxide.   If the red clay be in contact
with water, the peroxide changes to the
yellow hydrate, and thus under the influence of carbonic, pronounces the white

Tauatinga.   The granite-clays, moreover,
may be lively red, yellow, white, blue, or
black, and by their mixture russet or
brown."   "Decomposição dos Penedos no
Brasil."   Por G. S. de Capanema. Rio, 1866.
† Esbarrancado de lavras.
‡ This refers especially to the provinces
of Rio de Janeiro and São Paulo.

by a second growth of paler, yellower verdure, which at once betrays the poverty of the soil.

On the other hand, the Campo, apparently a heap of stone and stunted grass, inhabited principally by armadillos and termites, is apt to suggest the idea of stubborn sterility, which is far from being the case. I have not yet seen in the Brazil what Mr. Bayard Taylor calls the " spontaneous production of forests from prairie land." Botanists and travellers, moreover, do not agree about the original clothing of the country: some believe that it was always barren of timber; others that it was in old days a primæval forest. The truth lies probably between the two extremes. Doubtless, as about the Upper Congo and the Prairies on the Missouri, much of this Campo-land has been forested; but the trees, especially near the towns, have been fired or felled. Thus the rainfall, partly arrested by the weatherward Serras, has still further diminished; the streams, so abundant to the eastward, have shrunk and dried up; whilst the gales, finding no blocks or screens to oppose them, have increased in violence. The annual burnings, here about August, intended to act as manure to produce a succedaneum for salt, and to promote the growth of young pasture, destroy the soil, and leave nothing alive but the Cerrados,* stunted and gnarled trees, with coriaceous foliage and suberous bark, which after a course of ages have learned to resist the flames, the sun, the rain, the cold, the dew, the frost, the hail, the drought. In Piauhy and the northern provinces the Campo is either " Mimoso " or " Agreste "—comely or couthless; the former has annual grasses, tender, juicy, and pliant; the latter, which is probably a natural feature, is known by its coarse, wiry produce. The soil greatly affects the vegetation. Often, travelling over the Brazilian Campo, we cross a short divide, and find on the farther side that the growth assumes almost a new facies, without difference of frontage or other apparent cause. But everywhere in the Campos, however barren, there are rich bottoms admirably fitted for the cultivation of corn and cotton,

---

* The Portuguese Cerrado is a garden or an enclosure; the Brazilian Cerrado (when important called Cerradão) is defined to be " campos cobertos d'arvoredo curto e denso ;" the Spanish Chapparal, which Humboldt derives from a tree called Chaparro ; and both are applied to the formation of the ground as well as to the growth. Sr. Luiz D'Alincourt (in p. 129, " Sobre a Viagem do Porto de Santos à Cidade de Cuyabá," Rio de Janeiro, 1830) writes the word Serradão. The two forms of the same sibilant sound (c and s) are often used indifferently by Portuguese.

and in most of them Capoës* or tree clumps flourish upon the slopes, where they are sheltered from the wind and extend along the margins of the streams. Wood, after water the settler's prime want, will still last here for many generations.

Let us now cast a glance at the vegetation as it appears upon the Borda do Campo. The first remark is that the Campo is not so poorly clad as the Llano, the Pampa, and especially the Steppe : it will be sufficient here to mention the most prominent types.

The Cerrados or scrub, 10 or 20 feet high, and not unlike our hazels and crab-apple trees and the olives of southern Europe, are often Acacias and Leguminosæ. Such for instance is the Jacarandá do Campo, a Mimosa, whose wood is little valued ; such is the "Sicupira"† (Bowdichea major), a straight hard wood used for axles; the Angico (Acacia Angico), which produces catechu; and the small-foliaged Barbatimão or Barba de Timão (Acacia adstringens, Vellozo), whose bark is styptic and rich in tannic acid, and whose leaves are valuable for feeding the cantharides fly. That " antediluvian " growth, the noble and valuable Araucaria (A. imbricata or brasiliensis) ‡, the S. American pine, is seen only near settlements, and is probably an immigrant from Paraná, where it forms primæval forests. The distorted Piqui § (Caryocar brasiliensis) gives an oily mucilaginous fruit, containing a chestnut eaten in times of famine. The Tingui ‖ (Magonia glabrata, St. Hil.) is a useless growth, with a shapeless pendent fruit like a huge fungus. The Paú Terra and the large-seeded Patári supply good charcoal : the bark, leaf, and flower of the latter are used for dyeing black. The Cedro do Campo (?) and various species of

---

* The evil done by these bocages or bouquets de bois is the generation of ticks and flies that injure cattle : but this bears no proportion to the advantages which they offer.

† The name is variously pronounced : according to the Syst. it is rich in stryphnum (astringent principle), and much used in household medicine (Medicina Caseira).

‡ This Araucaria must not be confounded with the Araucaria excelsa of Norfolk Island and the Chile pine. Every part of it is useful, the fruit, the timber, the turpentine which has been used as incense, and the fibre which will be used as grass cloth. I reserve a detailed notice of it for my description of the São Paulo Province.

John Mawe and Prince Max. do not seem to have heard that this pine belongs to more southerly latitudes than Minas Geraes. Southey says (i. 119), that the native name is Curiyeh, with the last syllable aspirated. It is properly "cury" or "cory," and enters into the word Coritiba in Paraná. Also the "pine nuts" are not as large as acorns, but about three times larger.

§ St. Hil. (III. ii. 27) writes Pequi, but prefers Piqui, as it is so pronounced. In Tupy, Pequi means a small duck, a canneton. Gardner has Piki, an inadmissible form.

‖ Gardner writes Tingi, which in Portuguese would be pronounced Tinji.

wild Psidium are also common. There are several Solanaceæ: the Juá or Joá, vulgarly called Mata-cavallo and Rebenta-cavallo (burst-horse), whose yellow apple resembles the "wild bengan" of Africa; the Matafome,* an edible variety with red fruit; and the pleasant-scented Fruta do Lobo (Solanum undatum, S. lycocarpum, St.Hil.), said to be eaten by wolves and to poison cattle. The light green fruit, large as a foot-ball, is used as a detergent, and as one of the ingredients of soap. The most valuable tree and the king of the Cerrados is the Aroeira (Schinus terebinthifolius, or Schinus molle): the timber is of excessive hardness, resists weather admirably, and takes a fine polish. The leaves are used as epispastics, the decoction serves to alleviate rheumatic and other pains, and the gum rubbed on ropes preserves them from decay. The appearance of the tree when hung with its bunches of red currants is pleasing, but the people of the country avoid it. Tumours in the joints are, they say, produced by sleeping under it, and the highly sensitive who pass beneath it suffer from swellings in the face—this happened to the wife of one of my friends at São Paulo.† Unlike the true forest lands, the Serra and the Mato Dentro, the trees are mostly deciduous, and when they are bare the aspect is that of unpleasant nudity.

The clothing of earth near the road is the clumpy tussicky grass, known as Barba de bode (buckgoat's beard, Chætaria pallens). When young and green, this Stipea is eaten by cattle; it is, however, a sign of poor soil that has been much trampled upon. Capim redondo and superior grasses grow in the offing, and at Bertioga, to the south-west of Barbacena, there are, I was told, wild oats as in California, which ripen during the rains, and which suggest cattle breeding on a large scale.‡ The hardy lucerne of the United States, the Alfafa of the Argentine Republic and of Paraná, will some day be tried, and may succeed in making first-rate hay. In the hollows we find the tall grass of

---

* Juá or Matafome—"kill hunger"— is what Caldcleugh (ii. 208) calls Juan Matafome, and compares with a yellow gooseberry. In p. 210 he speaks of Mata Cavallos (kill-horse) as "a small bush covered with berries . . . like a Solanum," which it is. I am not sure that this plant is poisonous; a cultivated variety of it is a favourite in the Province of São Paulo, and I am told that children—who here eat what men will not—have eaten the Juá.

† The Indians used the green juice of the young branches for diseases of the eyes.

‡ Mr. Walsh (ii. 76) found that what he supposed to be an immense flock of sheep, "was nothing more than the wiry tufts of a species of wild oats, whose bending heads at a distance much more resembled a feeding sheep than the barometz of Tartary resembled a lamb." He also found an Avena sterilis near S. José.

several species, called by the people Sapé (Saccharum Sapé,
St. Hil.). It appears in richer soils when overworked, or where
the ground has been often fired. The Samambaia fern also,
which covers a large proportion of the prairies, grows under the
same conditions. Most of the shrubs and smaller plants are
medicinal, and the people* are well acquainted with their use.
Besides the true and false Chinchonaceæ, there is the Carapiá,†
valuable in chest complaints; it perfumes the air, as does the heath-
like Alecrim do Campo (Lantana microphylla Mart.), a Labiad,
which entered into "Hungary-water."‡ The Vassoura or broom
plant (Sida lanceolata), which supplies alkali and resembles rag-
wort, is used as an emollient in infusion and decoction. The
Assa-peixe branco,§ one of the Composites, acts like chamomile.
The aromatic Velame do Campo, "veiling of the prairie," (Croton
fulvus or campestris) is a powerful diaphoretic and resolvent
known to all. In the bushes there are many species of wild
Ipecacuanha called Poaya (Cephaelis ipecacuanha). The Labiad
known from its shape as Cordão de Frade, "Friar's Waist-cord"
(Leonotis nepetifolia, Mart.), is a powerful narcotic. The Composite
Carqueja (Baccharis, Nardum rusticum, Mart.), with triangular
elongated leaves and whitish buds at the angles, is a bitter tonic,
aromatic and antifebrile, much used in German-Brazilian beer.

I need hardly say that nothing can be purer than the perfumed air of these Campos; its exhilaration combats even the
monotony of a mule journey, and the European traveller in the
Tropics recovers in it all his energies, mental and physical. The
mornings and evenings are the perfection of climate; the nights
are cool, clear, and serene, as in the Arabian Desert without its
sand. Nor are the prairies deficient in the highest beauties of
form and tint. There is grandeur in the vast continuous ex-

---

* It is the fashion to deride the "Curan-
deiro" or simple doctor of the Brazil; yet
from the days of Pison's Marcgraf he has
taught the scientific botanist what knowledge he learned from the forest people.
As Prince Max. shows, the latter could
cure hernia, knew how to cup and bleed,
dressed the most dangerous wounds, and
practised the vapour bath, which like the
Wood and Stone Ages is almost universal;
the latter was effected in the usual savage
way by heating a large stone and by pour-
ing water upon it. "La malade se plaça

aussi près qu'elle put au-dessus de
l'endroit échauffé, ne tarda pas à transpirer
fortement par l'effet de la vapeur qu'elle
recevait, et recouvra la santé."

† Corrupted from Caa-pia, or pyá (heart,
liver), a Dorstenia, one of the Urticaceæ.

‡ Alecrim is derived from the Arabic
الاكليل الجبل El-iklil el-jabal, the
"Crown of the Mountain."

§ White "roast-fish;" the Eupatorium is
so called, I presume, because skewers were
made from it.

panse fading into the far distance. The eye can rest upon the scene for hours, especially when viewing from an eminence, whilst it is chequered by the afternoon cloud, whose eclipse seems to come and go, and this gives mobility to the aspect, as it walks over the ridged surface of the light green or pale golden earth-waves, upheaved in the intensely blue atmosphere of morning, or in the lovely pink tints of the " afterglow," from the shadowy hollows and the tree-clumps glooming below.   If we analyse the charm, its essence seems to be the instability of the ocean when we know that there is the solidity of earth.

CHAPTER VII.

AT BARBACENA.

Respirando os Ares limpidos,
A viração mais amena
Da liberal Barbacena   * * *
Padre Corrêa, Poesias, vol. iii. 11.

A HAPPY inspiration induced me to call upon Dr. Pierre Victor Renault of Sierck, Vice-Consul of France, Homœopathic Physician, Professor of Mathematics, Geography and History at Barbacena. He has spent thirty-four years in the Brazil, he knows by heart the byeways of Minas Geraes, especially about the Rivers Paracatú and Doce, and he has lived amongst and learned the languages of the wildest savagery. He once acted cashier to the Morro Velho Mine, and between 1842—6 he assisted M. Halfeld in opening the coach-road. He has married a Brazilian wife, and all the notables in the place are his " gossips."* What more could be desired in a guide? Although somewhat invalided by the bivouac and the field, he kindly and cordially placed himself at our disposal, took his stick, and led us out to look at the city.

Barbacena da Rainha lies in S. lat. 21° 13′ 9″·1, and W. long. 0° 49′ 44″·3 (Rio) in the culminating point of the Plateau, 3800 feet in "round numbers" above sea level.† The climate is essentially temperate; the annual maximum being 80° (F.) in the

---

* "Compadre" and "comadre," so called in relation to the afilhado or afilhada, the god-child, still form in the Brazil a religious relationship as in the days when our gossip was a God-sibb, or "akin in God." I have heard brothers address each other as Compadre, and the same term applied by wives to their husbands. These brother and sister sponsors may legally marry, but public opinion is as strongly pronounced against the union as the wise of England regard "confarreation" with the deceased wife's sister. If you intrigue with your comadre, you be-come after death a peculiar demon whose sole object in life seems to consist in frightening muleteers. Foreigners resident in the Brazil are compelled to fall into the custom, which has its bad as well as its good side. In small country places, for instance, all the inhabitants are connected by baptism if not by blood, and thus the ends of justice are admirably carried out the clean contrary way.

† M. Liais, the latest and the best authority, makes the height of Barbacena 1137 metres = 3730 feet above sea level.

shade. The Highland city began life as the Arraial da Igreja
Nova do Bordo do Campo, a halting-place for mule troops
between Ouro Preto (22 leagues) and Petropolis (40 leagues);
its chief trade was in cakes and refreshments sold by old.women.*
The site is unusually good for a settlement of such origin. In
the Brazil, cities founded by ecclesiastics occupy the best situa-
tions, hills and rises commanding fine views; the laity preferred
the bottom lands, near gold and water. It was made a municipal
town in 1791 by the famous or infamous Visconde de Barbacena,
Captain General of Minas, who baptised it after himself. Mawe
(1809) describes it as a village of 200 houses, governed by an
ouvidor or auditor judge. It was made a city by provincial law
of March 9, 1849.† Its municipal population in 1864 was
23,448 souls, with 1954 votes, and 39 electors, covering 1400
alqueiras of ground, each alqueira being 10,000 Brazilian
fathoms. The city numbered 5000 souls in 1849; it was then
a kind of central oasis in the desert, formed by the southern
Mato or forest region which we have traversed, and by the
northern prairies over which we are to pass. Travellers to and
from Minas loved to linger here; now they put themselves into
the Union and Industry coach. In 1867 the rude census gave
about 3600 souls within "Toque de Sino"—sound of the church
bell. This retrogrades half a century; in 1825 the population
was estimated at 3600, of whom 300 were whites, the rest being
blacks, mulattos, and quarteroons. Such, however, was the first
effect of the rail in Europe, and such will be the temporary consequences of improved communication in the Brazil. The white
element now greatly preponderates, and the slaves, it is said,
do not number 200 head.

In the last generation the Barão de Pitanguy made by commerce 400,000*l.* : no such fortunes are now open to industry. A
house which cost 2000*l.* in days when labour was cheap willingly
sells for 500*l.*, and this is a general rule in Minas. In 1864
more than 60,000 bags‡ of salt passed through the city; in 1867
this fell to 50,000.

The "Nobre e Muito Leal Cidade" began in 1842 a kind of
"Secesh" movement, which took the name of "The Revolu-

---

* Sr. A. D. de Pascual calls it the "Freguezia dos Carrijós" in 1792. This is, I
believe, an error.

† Castelnau (i. 198) says in 1841.

‡ The bag of salt weighs from 2 arrobas
(64 lbs.) to 2 arrobas 6lbs. I found the
average of 6 to weigh 2 arrobas 2 lbs.

tion of Barbacena." Minas, and her stalwart parent São
Paulo, were especially aggrieved by the law of judiciary and
electoral reform (Dec. 8, 1841), which, establishing chiefs of
police, delegates, sub-delegates, and inspectors of quarters, overspread the country with a cloud of preventive agents. They
cried out that these measures were in the interest of an oligarchy,
and that thus, the citizens were placed at the mercy of the
Government. Yet they repudiated republicanism, and professed
the greatest loyalty to the head of the State. Minas was also
furious with the Conservative Ministry of 1841, and even more
so with her provincial President, Bernardo Jacinto da Veiega.
The movement was precipitated at Sorocaba in São Paulo. Upon
this, the Municipal Chamber of Barbacena met (June 10, 1842)
and proclaimed Lieut.-Col. José Filicianno Pinto Coelho de Cunha
acting President of Minas, with Sr. José Pedro Dias de
Carvalho as Secretary. Pomba and Queluz at once rose, but the
acting or "intrusive President" instead of marching at once
upon Ouro Preto, the capital, wasted time upon a military promenade to São João d'El-Rei and elsewhere. The next two months
saw various *peripéties*; the "Massena" of the contest being the
present senator Theophilo B. Ottoni, who was proposed as Vice-
President. In early August the then Barão de Caxias, after
reducing São Paulo to order, appeared before Barbacena, and
the city bowed before its "manifest destiny."

Barbacena, the white town on the hill-top, has straggled into
the shape of a cross or T, with a random sprinkle around it;
the main street, Rua do Rosario, is the perpendicular, running
nearly north and south, whilst the eastern arm is truncated. The
two main thoroughfares are unpaved in the middle; lines of
stones rib their breadth, and at the sides are trottoirs of terrible
roughness. The chief squares, mere widenings of the streets, are
the Largo da Camara, where the palace of the municipality is;
the Praça da Allegria, behind the Matriz; and the Praça da
Concordia to the east. In one of them a piece of machinery,
intended for the Morro Velho mine, cumbers the ground; the
article is in a "fix;" the clay roads cannot convey it, and the
town-hall threatens to fine it for remaining there. The houses
are mostly "porta e janella;" the best belongs to the General-
Deputy the Barão de Prados, who, at the time of our visit, was
on duty at Rio de Janeiro.

We walked painfully up the main street, named after the mean chapel, Nossa Senhora do Rosario, an invocation much affected throughout the Brazil by slaves and negroes. It is generally known by a plaster crown on the façade, and beneath the crown, either detached or adjoined, is a rosary * ending in a simple cross. Beyond it was an Ermida or private place of worship, with a gilt bell; these little sacraria characterize all the older towns of Minas. Embryo inns still swarm; we counted half-a-dozen. The destructive and lucrative " Art of Healing " numbers many votaries : six allopaths, five apothecaries (and general practitioners), four midwives, known by the wooden cross nailed to the wall, and one homœopath. A square of white paper stuck inside the window shows " house to let," here apparently the normal condition of such property. The favourite building material is the well-known " adobe "—the sun-dried brick of Mexico and Salt Lake City : in Minas it is a mass of clay, often weighing 30— 32 lbs. A few of the tenements have stone foundations to prevent the damp and rains crumbling and washing away these unbaked masses of mud ; the houses' eaves are made to project abnormally.

We inspected the Matriz Nª Sª da Piedade, which fronts to the north-north east, and commands a good view down the main street, and into the open beyond. The sloping ground required for it a raised and stone-revetted " Adro "—platform or terrace. Here, as with us, was the earliest burial-ground, the churchyard under whose flags repose, *in pace Domini*, the ancient vicars and rude grandees. Thus Padre Corrêa (" Cavaco," p. 157, Woolf), sings :—

> " Dos cemiterios e do adro,
> Resuscita vaôs espectros." †

The Adro is adorned at the entrance and the corners with well-cut little pyramids, and " promiscuously " with seedy willows, all athirst, and the " scrimpy," stiff, and worse than useless " Casuarina." The stranger wonders to see this Australasian savage —ugly as a Scotch fir—naturalised amongst the glorious vegetable beauties of the Brazil and Hindostan ; its roots overspread and impoverish the soil ; where the neighbours gracefully droop their branches, it turns them up with impudent preten-

---

* The beads seem to awaken the negro's sense of home ; in Africa they compose his finest finery and his richest riches. Of course here I speak of the " Popó Bead."

† "From the graveyard and the platform, Praises he the empty ghosts."

blue steatite—check

sion, and its main purpose in Creation seems to be that of hous-
ing destitute crickets—

" A importuna monotona sigarra,"

jolly beggars, whose ceaseless chirping and hoarse whirring
drown the sound of the voice. The façade of whitewashed
adobe and stone has four windows; in the older Province of
São Paulo the number is a *sine quâ non*, five, the Trinity
occupying the front, as they did the three Gothic steeples,
Joseph and Mary the wings. A suspicious crack and a dangerous bulge appear about the entrance; they are attributed to the
sinking of the font-water. There are two square campaniles,
short and squat, after the fashion of the older Brazil, a cross,
and a broken statue. The profile shows the usual big nave and
broken chancel, a small barn backing a large barn, as in the
countrified parts of England. The material of the decorations is
the blue steatite * here abundant; it is often painted blue to
make it bluer, " and thus," exclaims a talented Brazilian author,
" thus they assassinate Nature ! " Like the lapis ollaris it may
be cut with a knife, and exposure to the air soon hardens it by
absorbing the " quarry water." Thus it is well fitted for carvings and coarse statuary. Some of the monolithic jambs are 14
feet long.

The entrance is guarded by the usual screen † of plain wood
and glass peepholes. The choir-balcony is over the door; under
it are two frescoes by a native hand, representing the Saviour's
Passion, two holy-water stoups, and in its own chapel, to
the left, a baptismal font of green-daubed granite.‡ Seven small
windows placed high up admit a dim light, and there are two
tribunes to accommodate the local magnificos. The wooden
flooring, a parquet of moveable parallelograms, six feet by three,
shows that it has been a cemetery, a custom which still lingers
in Southern Europe; here it lasted till a sensible law, one of
the benefits of yellow fever, put an end to the pious malpractice.
The walls are pasted with election papers and other public
documents, and on each side is a white and gilt pulpit in the
normal style, which may be called the " swallow-nest." The six
minor chapels § have altars of white, green, and gold; the

---

* Pedra azulada.
† Tapa-vento.
‡ Mawe, c. 10, says that there is in the
neighbourhood of Barbacena, " une carrière

de granit tendre, blanchâtre, dont on fait
des meules."
§ My wife took down the patrons, as
follows: Right side—

pillars of stone and wood rest upon consoles, but these have basal pedestals, and are not founded upon nothing, as in most Brazilian churches.

The chancel arch leading to the high altar shows a massive silver candelabrum, worth 120*l*., and presented by the pious Barão de Pitanguy. The curtain guarding the throne has a black cross on a white mortuary cloth of silk and wool, costing 100*l*., and given by the Barão's son. The altar cloths are worked by the Barão's sisters. And there is a good statue of Italian marble representing a guardian angel at his devotions, and placed at an expense of 360*l*. by the Barão in honour of his father.

Pietà

The high altar is of white and gold, with a " Dead Christ and Our Lady " on painted wood, and somewhat above life-size. The effect is not bad. There is a large tabernacle; four massive candlesticks of ormolu assist the tapers, and four tolerable modern oil-paintings represent the " Flagellation," " Our Lady at the Cross," the " Agony in the Garden," and the " Resurrection from the Tomb." I have lingered over this description; it will serve for all the churches in the " well-to-do " country towns of the Brazil, within the civilizing influence of the capital.

We next visited the church of (Nª Sª da) Boa Morte—of happy dispatch; it is a conspicuous pile on the western ridge, best seen from afar. The exterior of granite and steatite is grotesque, the towers have two clocks, apparently dummies, leaving work to the neighbouring sun-dial, and an ugly new sacristy of strange style has been stuck on to the original building, which bears date 1815. Thus Castelnau erred in supposing that the unfinished pile had been abandoned, like the Hyde Park Achilles. These places in the Brazil belong to Sodalities or brotherhoods, who proceed with them as fast or as slowly as funds permit; foreigners readily prophesy that progress has ceased, and moralize, when such process is uncalled for by the occasion, upon the decay of zeal in this our modern day. And yet they *do* move.

The interior is the normal barn—white and blue. Nª Sª da

No. 1. Saints Michael, Cecilia, and Luzia.

No. 2. Nª Sª do Carmo and Nª Sª do Rosario.

No. 3. Nº Sʳ dos Passos.

Left side—

No. 1. Saints Antonio and Rita.

No. 2. Nª Sª das Dôres and Sᵗª Barbara.

No. 3. Saints Sebastian and Joseph, with the "Menino Deus"—infant Christ.

Also there is a little separate chapel for the Blessed Sacrament, with a crucifix, &c., S. Vincent de Paul.

Assumpção occupies the caput, and below her is a recumbent
Virgin.   There are two stone pulpits painted azure, an organless
organ-loft, and three votive tablets on the wall.   To the west is
the cemetery, with its mortuary chapel, which owe their existence to our excellent guide.   This "colony of the dead," though
only three years old, is filling fast; catarrh and pneumonia, with
their numberless varieties, being the principal *causæ causantes*.
At the entrance we met a dead negro carried upon a stretcher
by four black brethren, who, laughing and chatting, tossed and
jolted the clay into a semblance of life.

Struck by the savageness of a white man beating a dog—a rare
sight in Brazil, where humanity to animals is the rule—I asked
who he was, and was told "an Italian."   There are many
of these emigrants in São Paulo—more in Minas—in fact, they
extend from Pará to Buenos Ayres.   They do not bear a good
report, and my friends often warned me against being suspected of
coming from the land which produced Cæsar and Napoleon, Dante
and Macchiavelli.   The *perfervidum ingenium,* the clairvoyant sub-
tlety of the Ausonian, is a plague to him in these countries: he is too
clever by half, or rather by three quarters.   He returns to the Italian
of the sixteenth century; he is dark, wily, and unscrupulous as
Rizzio.   Some answer to the old saying, "fur atque sacerdos."
A certain Fr. Bernardo is reported to have sold for the Virgin's
milk, "mosquito's eggs," as homœopathic globules are here
called.   The reader may think this a draft upon his credulity;
but official documents prove * that these ecclesiastics have sold
"veritable tears of Our Lady in rosaries," have passed off
rubbish as saints' relics, and have sold "passports for heaven"
at the rate of a sovereign a head.   The Mineiro † may sing with
Beranger:—

> What imperceptibles we have !
> Small Jesuits of the bilious hue.
> Hundreds of other clergy grave,
> Who little relics hold to view.

---

* Appendix to Presidential Relatorio of
Minas for 1865, p. 39.   Moreover most
large churches in these lands have a bit of
the True Cross duly supplied to them by
Italian speculators.

† Mineiro (from Mineira) is an inhabitant of Minas Geraes, the Province, and
must not be confounded by the stranger
with the African "Minas" of "St. George

del Mina" on the Guinea Coast.   Varnhagen (History, ii. 281) warns us that
at first the Mineiro was a term applied
solely to the gold miner.   A native of
Rio Grande is Rio Grandense; of São Paulo,
Paulista (substantive), or Paulistano (adjective), (not Paulense, as in the excellent
handbook, "Brazil: its Provinces and
Chief Cities," by William Scully.   London :

From the Boâ Morte we descended the vile Ladeira da Cadêa, Prison Ramp, and looked at the jail: the barred windows showed three women. In almost all cases of premeditated murder throughout the Brazil, two of the active actors are a woman and a negro. The last of the public buildings to be visited is the Misericordia Hospital, in a cold hollow to the north of the city. The entrance bears inscribed—

> Pauperis infirmi sit in ore Antonius Armond,
> Et pius, et magnus vir, pater egregius.

Queer Latin, but well intentioned! All honour to Sr. Antonio José Ferreira Armond (nat. March 11, 1798, ob. 1852), who in five years built the little chapel of Santo Antonio, and the charitable establishment to which he left 12,000*l*., an estate and fourteen slaves. In the absence of the priestly Curator the civil apothecary showed us about the building and allowed us to gather violets in the neat "Patio" or central garden-court.* The rooms were clean, and had six inmates: freemen pay about four florins per diem, and serviles half. The place has not a good name; patients are said to die for want of care, and Brazilians deride a "Misericordia" which charges for board and lodging. It is also far from good water, always a scarce commodity at Barbacena. The best is supplied by a fountain to the east of the city; the façade wall is inscribed with the name of the Camara Municipal for 1864.

We then inspected Dr. Renault's little garden behind the house, which vegetation spoke of a temperate climate; it is full of pinks, roses, violets, and verbena,† gladeoli, and heliotropes. The oranges were excellent, and from them our host made his "Tokay;" it cost about fourpence a bottle, and drunk with the Pinhão or Araucaria nut it suggested the best liqueur. At Morro Velho I obtained an excellent recipe; it is worth knowing in a country where millions of oranges and pine-apples, justifying Elia's rave,

---

Murray & Co., Paternoster Row, 1866.) There is a peculiarity in the use of the word Paulista; for instance, O fazendeiro Paulista is correct, Paulistano would not be idiomatic.

* Patio is Portuguese, derived from the Arabic بطحاء (bathah), even as Saguão, a vestibule, comes from صحن (Sahn). In the Brazil the Patio is usually called Quintal; the latter, however, also means a small garden attached to a messuage.

† An indigenous growth, the Verbena virgata of M. Sellow. It is a powerful sudorific, and in the treatment of "chills" it equals lemon-grass.

are left to decay upon the ground.* We were also shown good specimens of the heavy hand-made pots of steatite or pierre ollaire, for which Barbacena is celebrated. The best ollary talc comes from the Mello village six leagues distant, and from the Mercês do Pomba,† a town ten leagues to the east upon the seaward slope of the Mantiqueira Range. The formation is found in the talcose and micaceous schists : the first quality is tolerably free from the crystallized bits of hydrate of iron, which induce decomposition. It is easily quarried, it hardens rapidly, and lasting long it is in general use throughout the country. The price ranges according to size from fourpence to twelve shillings, some being large enough to accommodate a round of beef. The smaller pots (panellas) rival the West Indian pepper pot for stewing. Some day this soapstone will be worked with great profit, and pipe bowls, for which I inquired in vain, ought especially to " take."

---

* The Count Hogendorf, ex-aide-de-camp to the First Napoleon, who took refuge in Brazil, made this wine, which M. de Freycinet (Voyage de l'Uranie, i. 231) compares with Malaga. St. Hilaire also described the process of making, but very imperfectly (III. ii. 347). The following is the Morro Velho recipe for making nine gallons of orange wine :—Take two hundred sweet oranges, pare off the thin outer rind of fifty, and put them to soak in four quarts of water. Squeeze out all the juice, strain it well, and put it into the barrel with thirty-two pounds of white sugar. Fill the barrel with water, and stir and shake it well, add a quart basin of ferment, and as it works off replenish it with the water of the soaked peels, so that it may be always

full. As soon as the hissing ceases, put in a quart of old sugar brandy, restilo, bung up the cask, and let it stand for seven months before bottling it. It sometimes takes as much as three days to begin to work, and has continued working from thirty to forty days. To give the wine a colour, you may burn a teacup of sugar in restilo, before the barrel is bunged up.

† Some write Mercês da Pomba. The expression, however, contains one of those ellipses so common in Portuguese and so difficult to the stranger ; the full phrase would be (Nᵃ Sᵃ das) Mercês do (Rio da) Pomba. The Pomba River is an important northern feeder of the Parahyba do Sul, and the lands about it are known as the "Mata,"—the bush.

CHAPTER VIII.

GUP.—THE HOTEL.—THE MULES.

Jardins, vergeis, umbrosas alamedas,
Frescas grutas então, piscosos lagos,
E pingues campos, sempre verdes prados,
Um novo Eden fariam.
José Bonifacio de Andrada e Silva.

AMONGST the curios, the "bric-à-brac," shown to us by Dr. Renault, none was more interesting than the gold bar, the lingot d'or, formerly current in the Brazil. In the year of royalty 1808, according to Mr. Henderson, the circulation of gold dust,* then the medium of commerce, was prohibited—of course the use lingered long in the interior—and coins of the three usual metals were introduced. The bar kept up its circulation till 1832. The weight varied according to the quantity of gold brought by the miner to the Intendencia of Ouro Preto or elsewhere. The specimen which we saw was about three inches long, and valued at 15*l.* : sometimes it weighed several marcos, each marco=eight ounces. The ore was duly assayed, the Quinto or royal fifth was taken, and it was stamped with the number, date, royal arms, and standard (toque), 24 quilate or carat-gold being the purest. Finally it bore its value in ounces, octaves, and grains. It was accompanied by the usual paper, the "guia" or "guide," a kind of manifest given to direct the carrier; without this it could not leave the Province.

After the bars came the age of gold oitavas (eighth of the Portuguese ounce) and their subdivisions. In 1816—1822 the oitava was worth 1$500, but taxes reduced it to a current value

---

* "Canjica," the diminutive form of canja, a word in which the Anglo-Indian would hardly recognise the old familiar "congee" or rice-water. In the Brazil it is applied to a "rice-squash" soup, to husked and boiled Indian corn, to the granular gold and nuggets (pepitas) which St. Hil. says (III. i. 70) are called Maçamorras in the Uraguay or Banda Oriental; and, thirdly, to the diamantiferous gravel, as will afterwards appear.

of 1$200 (=7 francs 50 centimes), for which men now pay 3$500. The other coins were vintens d'ouro 0$037·5 = $23\frac{7}{10}$ centimes, half-patacas and patacas (=0$800), crusadas d'ouro (=0$750*), half-oitavas and oitavas. Some of these coins were mere spangles, like the Egyptian piastres, and the people complained that they were easily lost.

The golden age expired in 1864. During the last quarter of that year the many ruinous bankruptcies at Rio de Janeiro called for an exceptional measure. The Government permitted, and not for the first time, the Imperial Bank, a private establishment like that of England, to issue instead of specie payments a forced circulation of paper money in a treble proportion to the bullion at its command. The privilege has been renewed, and, as figures show, it has not yet been excessively abused.[†] But times were bad, the Paraguayan war was absorbing bullion and returning nothing, all the gold currency was withdrawn and substituted by Treasury notes. Brazilians soon remembered that there had been such things as assignats. In the short space of three years gold has completely disappeared from the Gold and Diamond Empire, and except in the Museums I have not seen a gold coin. Silver is rare, but not so rare, and of late there has been a new issue of somewhat debased small change. The principal bullion is copper, a metal introduced by the celebrated Vasconcellos, "great architect of ruins and scourge of Ministries:" the "dump," thus elegantly termed by the English, is a piece of 40 reis, the local penny. It is uglier and more barbarous than its British representative, but it is on the point of making way for a neat bronze piece, with 95 parts of copper, 4 of tin, and 1 of zinc.

The place of gold and silver is thus taken by "flimsies," which begin at the minimum of 1$000, and the maximum of 500$000, the latter but lately issued. Every bullionist, in the United States sense of the word, will understand the result of this

---

* St. Hil. III. i. 366.
† In April 1, 1867, the whole issue of paper money in the Brazil was as follows :

National notes .	.	42,560 : 444 $ 000
Bank of Brazil	. .	73,476 : 710 $ 000
Other banks .	.	2,461 : 700 $ 000

Total . . . 118,498 : 854 $ 000
This sum had increased on March 31st, 1868, to 124,686 : 209 $ 000.
In this session, however, a bill was

passed empowering the issue of forty-five millions (mil-reis) in notes.

The paper money does not present to the traveller as many difficulties in the Brazil as in the United States. His only chance of loss—if at least he wisely prefer imperial paper—will be that incurred when old notes are called in. Private bank-paper will cost him 2 to 5 per cent. everywhere, except at the place where it is issued.

unsound paper currency. It is fatal to economy, it doubles small
expenses, and its effect is that whilst the Brazil exports to Europe
gold and diamonds, coffee and cocoa, cotton, tobacco, and sugar,
she receives in return nothing but "trash," the refuse of the
markets delivered at the highest possible prices.*

More disastrous still, on account of the national fears and sus-
picions, has been the effect of this paper upon the mil-reis. Travellers assure us that in 1801 this, the practical unit of value, was
worth 5 shillings 7½ pence. In 1815 it represented 6 francs 25
centimes. In 1835—36 it was 30—32 pence. When I landed at
Pernambuco, June 1865, it was at par=27 pence. It has in 1867
fallen to 13¾ pence, and under actual circumstances there is apparently nothing to prevent it sinking, like the dollar of the South
American Republics, to twopence.

But the Brazil is a young country, eminently rich in resources
still unexploited. A debt of 60 millions of pounds sterling, the
"ballast of the ship," is to her literally a flea-bite, considering
her enormous excess of exports over imports, that is to say,
of income over expenditure. If she ever become bankrupt, it
will be because, with enough to pay off a score of such debts, she
has not kept ready money enough in hand for household expenses.
She has clerical property to be secularized, public lands to be
sold, a system of direct taxation to be introduced, import dues to
be taken in gold when such process will not discredit her own
credit, and mines of precious metals waiting to be worked. All
bullionists will agree with me that the sooner her paper is replaced by gold the better. As early as 1801 Dr. Couto proposed
to raise the value of the metal by making the oitava represent
1$500 instead of 1$200, a far-sighted policy. We have all witnessed what a small premium upon gold has done in France,
where it was treated as an article of commerce, not as an in-
flexible standard—the old English view. This measure would
save the discount upon paper, and the heavy expenses incurred
by the Caixa de Amortizacão, that peculiar South American form
of sinking fund.

---

* The least being double the market
value in Europe. Again the mil-reis
(Anglicè milrea) is a financial error like
the rouble of Russia and the rupee of Hindostan; everything costs a mil-reis. Thus
in Europe we find that the carlino and the
paolo do the duty of franc and shilling.

I am perfectly aware that the "absurdity
of discouraging the exportation of precious
metals" was disclosed some two centuries
and a half ago. But it is contended that
new countries mostly present exceptions to
the economic law, or rather to its operations,
and that of these lands the Brazil is one.

The monetary system of the Brazil, arithmetically considered, is good, because it has rendered decimals familiar to the people. Strangers forget this when they complain of the long array of confusing figures.   The true unit of value is the *real* (plural reis) written 0$001 ;* a "conto," or million of reis, is written 1:000$000, or without the three dextral ciphers, 1:000$, and as in Brazilian arithmetic generally, a colon is placed to the right of the thousands.

The old Portuguese subdivisions of the mil-reis are mostly conventional, like our guinea.   They are, 1, the testão (testoon) = 100 reis, or the tenth of the mil-rei ; 2, the patáca = 8 "dumps" = 320 reis (what a tax upon memory!) ; 3, the crusádo, once half-a-crown, now = 10 dumps = 400 reis ; 4, the sello (rare) = 1½ pataca = 480 reis ; 5, the half mil-reis = 500 reis ; 6, the patacão = 3 patácas = 960 reis.   The hideous copper coinage is 1 vintem (a score of reis, plur. vintens) = 0$020, and the dois vintens, or "dump," = 0$040.   The older travellers were obliged to have a mule for the carriage of this Spartan coinage.

We dined together at the *table d'hôte*, a motley group, the Austrian ex-lieutenant, the driver, and sundry citizens of Barbacena.   All harmonized well, and in the evening our good guide gave me the following items of information.   I must premise, however, that the Doctor is an enthusiast for his adopted country.

The Campos of Barbacena, the broken plains beyond the Mantiqueira Range, raised 3000 to 3500 feet above sea-level, are evidently well fitted for stock breeding.   The principal use of black cattle is at present to produce the cheese, which is exported to the capital of the Empire.   About six square acres are allowed for each cow ; thirty-two bottles of milk yield 2 lbs. ; the women and children of a family easily make half a dozen loaves per diem, and colporteurs sometimes collect 200 from a single establish-

---

* The monogram of dollar ($) precedes in the United States, and in the Brazil follows the figure.   In the older Brazil it is sometimes written U.   This favours the idea that the mark is a contraction of U. S.   Others believe it to stand for a "piece of eight" (reals), the Spanish dollar which gave birth to the American dollar, and that the parallels were drawn across the 8 to distinguish it.   Others again derive it from the columns and scroll of the Spanish pillar dollar, which the Arabs liken to a window or to cannon.   Another minutia is prefixing Rs. (reis not rupees) to large sums, *e. g.* Rs. 100:000$000.

N.B. Since the above was written, on Sept. 5, 1868 a decree authorized the Minister of Fazenda to issue 40,000,000$000 of further paper money.   An act of Sept. 28,'67, authorized an issue of 50,000,000$000.   Of this, all has been emitted but 3,614,000$000.

ment. St. Hilaire's account of the rude process is not obsolete;
the cheese material is hard and white, equal perhaps to the
Dutch "cannon-ball," but not to be mentioned with Stilton or
Roquefort; like Parmesan, it is good for grating. It awaits improvement in the dairy and even in the churn, which John Mawe
tells us was not known before 1809.

The cereals flourish in the richer soils: wheat,* the maize or
"corn," which in the Brazil takes the place of oats; rye and
buckwheat, also called black-wheat: the two latter are hardy, and
require little care. Tubers abound. The American potato, here
known as "English" or "Irish," gives two crops per annum;
and the batata or sweet potato (Tuber Parmantier), four. There
is also the Inhanu (Caladium esculentum); the Mangarito† or Mangareto (Caladium sagittifolium) and the well-known and excellent
Cará (Dioscorea alata, St. Hil.). I saw, for the first time, the Jacutupé ‡ and the "Topinambour," "Tupinambur," or "Taratouf."§
Of the fruits, pears, apples; plums, white and black; cherries,
chesnuts, damsons, and peaches, grow well, and are worth improving. The grape, especially that called the Manga,¶ or American, bears twice; the vintage is poor in July, but in December
the bunches are marvellously large and numerous. The unripe
crop makes good vinegar; the ripe yields a thin, rough Bur-

---

* Wheat will grow at these altitudes in the sub-tropical regions, but it is always liable to rust (ferrugem).

† Prince Max. (ii. 76) calls the plant "le mangaranito (Arum esculentum)." St. Hil. (I. i. 402), speaks of the "Manga-reto branco," and a variety of a violet colour known as "Mangareto Roxo."

‡ According to Dr. Renault, Martius has not yet named the Jacutupé. It is evidently a legumen with papilionaceous flowers, creeping on the ground with a root 4—5 decimetres long, by 1—2 in diameter. The flower of blue-violet is followed by siliquæ, each containing 4—5 beans, re-sembling the "fève de marais" (Windsor beans ?). These are very poisonous, killing animals in a short time. The toxic sub-stance may be a new and especial alkaloid, or as it seems by analogy, perhaps Brucine. Its tonic properties are supposed to be the result of a great disengagement of carbonic acid. The beans are planted in September, and the roots are edible after six months; when taken up they cannot be kept long. The well-rasped fecula makes excellent starch, and is used by the Brazilian house-

wife for thickening soups and for making sweetmeats, which much resemble con-serves of the cocoa-nut. The Jacutupé flourishes most in light lands where there is shade.

§ Dr. Renault tells me that this Helian-thus tuberosus is also called "Artichaut de Canada" and Poire de terre; it belongs to the great family of Synanthereæ, order Radi-aceæ, genus Helianthus. It has been often confounded with the sweet potato (Con-volvulus Batatas), as in both plants the tuberosities of the roots are mere swellings. Some derive it from Chili, others make it a native of the Brazil, where however it is little cultivated, and only in gardens. It is a hardy plant, which would thrive in Europe. Dr. Renault says that the root would be a blessing to the poor, and opines with the philosopher that a new dish is of more general importance to humanity than the discovery of a new star or planet.

‖ I have not yet seen a cherry in the Brazil.

¶ The well-known fruit which we call Mango.

gundy; and the raisins give excellent brandy, like the Raki of Syria.

Mulberry trees thrive; they do not lose the leaf in the cold season, but continually renew it; after the second year they can be utilized. I am told that M. Abricht, now at the colony of Joinville, has found five indigenous species of silk-worm. Castelnau (146) declares that the true Bombyx mori is nowhere to be met with in the Brazil; he observed, however, many large species of the "Saturnia," known to the Chinese and to the Hindus. The Urumbeba (Cactus spinosus), also called Figueira do Inferno, grows wild; and the cochineal insect* appears spontaneously, showing that the fine Mexican or Tenerife Nopal might be naturalized. Both soil and climate are propitious for the hop, which is now imported at a heavy price from Europe. The hardy and almost indestructible tea-plant gave crops of fair market value; this industry was destroyed by the fall of price at Rio de Janeiro. Cotton, both the herbaceous and the so-called arboreous, has been grown on the "Capão"-lands, and, intelligently cultivated, it will be wealth to the Province. The tobacco of the Rio do Pomba, 15 leagues from Barbacena and the Rio Novo, won the medal at the Industrial Exhibition of Rio de Janeiro; that of Baependy, especially the "Fumo crespo," is a dark strong leaf, well fitted for making "Cavendish" or "honey-dew;" and the "weed" flourishes throughout Minas Geraes. The soil will be much improved by compost: and the produce by being treated in Virginian style, delicately dried in closed barns with fires. Indigo grows everywhere wild, and gives that fine purple gloss which rivals the produce of Hindostan.† Dr. Renault declares that every hive of the European bee "gives from twelve to fifteen

---

* In many parts of Minas Geraes the "prickly pear" Cactus grows without prickles; it is eaten by children, not as at Malta by all classes and ages, who hold it during the hot season to be a wholesome cooling fruit eminently fitted for breakfast. As regards cochineal, the dye which has made obsolete the Tyrian purple, Dr. Couto, writing in old times, says, "A Cochinilla, planta em que se cria esta tinta igual ao ouro no valor, e da qual temos tanta abundancia, cresce inutilmente entre nos." "Cochineal, a plant upon which is raised the dye that equals gold in value, and of which we have such an abundance, grows useless on our lands." A small exportation of cochineal was tried between 1800—1815,

but adulteration with flour soon crushed the attempt. Prince Max. ("Voyage au Brésil," vol. i. chap. 3) found that at "Sagoarema" it had been cultivated and fetched 6 $ 400 then = 31 francs. I shall have more to say about cochineal when descending the Rio de São Francisco.

† In 1764 a law was passed exempting from duty the indigo of Pará and Maranham. Under the Marquez de Lavradio, third Viceroy of Rio de Janeiro (1769—1778) the exportation was attempted from the Captaincy of Rio de Janeiro; the article was excellent, but as was the case with cochineal, the excessive adulteration disgusted the trade. The plant was mostly the Solanum indigiferum (St. Hil.).

swarms (enxames) per six months; 1½ lb. of wax with 20 litres of honey; whilst each litre of the latter produces four litres of excellent aqua vitæ." Nothing, I may remark, is more wanted in the Brazil than *la petite culture*, bees, silk-worms, cochineal, seed-picking, which will work the hands of women and children.

The Barbacenense Hotel, pronounce 'Otel, even as Uncle R—— will say " an *h*otel," is the usual guest house of the countrified Brazil. As it is frequented by strangers there is salt upon the table, here not the general usage, and a huge joint of beef appears, if possible, by the side of the grilled and boiled-with-rice fowls, the hunches of pork, the sausages, the chopped cabbage-cum-lard (Couve picado), and the inevitable haricots of the national cuisine. The worst part of it is the " addition," which has all the " beauties of dearness;" unless there be a special agreement the multiplication of items would read a lesson to a " Family Hotel " in Dover Street, Piccadilly, or any other place where that obsolete institution, an ancient English inn, lingers out its dishonest old age. Brazilians, like Russians, take pride in a generosity verging upon recklessness and profusion; moreover, the exceeding courteousness of manner that characterizes the people prevents the Cavalheiro observing openly that he has been plundered. He therefore pays with apparent cheerfulness, departs, and grumbles.

The " Maje," as our host would be called in the Far West, further north, sent us in an unconscionable bill; possibly he was excited by the abnormal appearance of Mr. L'pool. The costume of our fellow-traveller consisted of (firstly), a tall broad-brimmed cone of felt, brigand-like, adorned with a cockade of rare feathers; of (secundo), the threadbare shooting jacket and frayed waistcoat and terminations, worn only by the wealthy Britisher; of (thirdly), a broad silk sash, splendid as a marigold, over which was buckled (fourthly) the " Guayáca," a belt of untanned leather, in which the wild Guacho of the Pampas carries his coin when he has any. In this case it was furnished with (fifthly) a loaded Colt's six-shooter: and (sixthly), with a bowie knife of Brummagem silver, very " low" in Brazilian eyes; (seventhly), there was a pair of " tamáncas," wooden pattens, used only in the house, and these had been provided with leather thongs like the sandal ribbons worn by our venerable feminine parents in the days when Charles Dix was yet Roi. Add to

this a " capánga,"* or pouchlet of coarse canvas, in which the
muleteer stows away tobacco, flint and steel, pack-thread, and as
much miscellaneous cargo as is contained by the schoolboy's
pocket. Thus equipped, the wearer was the model of an English
travelling gentleman.

The Brazil may be improvident, profuse, reckless, but not so
North Britain. Mr. L'pool scrutinized, with underwriter eyes,
the " little bill," and at once detected charged to us 32 bottles
of beer, which the " Maje " had drunk to drown his sorrows.
Poor little old man, his family allows him no "trink-gelt!"
When remonstrated with, he offered seriously, but in bitter irony,
to reduce his account to nothing—to one quarter—to half. But
the fine satire being utterly thrown away upon the son of that
city where men seem to be born with brown paper parcels under
their arms, he took off 14 shillings from as many pounds sterling,
and thus ended the Battle of the Bottles.

Good news awaited us at Barbacena. Mr. J. N. Gordon,
Superintendent-in-chief of the great English mine at Morro Velho,
had kindly offered to send mules for us to Juiz de Fóra; our
delay had caused the troop to march northwards, and we were in
no small fear of missing it. Hired animals are here paid 5$000
per diem each, including a mounted guide. But they are seldom
good, never safe, especially where a riding-habit is in the case;
and the first comfort of travel in the Brazil depends upon your
beast and your saddle. It was therefore with no small satisfaction
that we found ten good beasts under the charge of Mr. Fitzpatrick,
whose sole duty it was to look after them and their furniture. In
Persia we should call this Master of the Morro Velho Horse a
Mirakhor, Chief of stables, here he is an Escoteiro or Ecuyer—
all I shall say of him is that he kept his men sober, and that he
made us thoroughly comfortable.

Every traveller complains of the testy and petulant mule;
every traveller rides mules, a necessary evil, as horses cannot
stand long marches in this part of the Brazil. The beast may be
learned by studying the mulatto and the eunuch: like those
amiable monsters, it appears to eye all creation with a general
and undistinguishable hate. It will not become attached to the

---

* This bag is taken from the Indians,
who when hunting slung it over the
shoulder like a kind of carnassière ; it was
of cotton cords knotted and plaited and
dyed alternately yellow or red brown, with
the " catona " bark.

master, treat he it never so kindly; the rider can never be sure of it, and of all animals it is the most violently agitated by fear. Its tricks are legion, and it seems to feel a consciousness that its treachery can always get the better of a struggle : elderly men, therefore, prefer horses to mules. It is a mistake to believe in the brute's hardiness : here at least I find that the sun soon tires it, and that it requires much grain, plentiful drink, and frequent rest.   During my travels in the Brazil one fell with me through a bridge, despite the vaunted muline sagacity; another dropped on its side ;* a third, a vicious little mule (macho), gave me as I was sitting loosely in the saddle a hoist which made me ask the day o' week for an hour afterwards; and briefly, I never rode a hundred miles without my monture kissing the ground once, twice, or thrice.   In one point, however, the quadruped mule surpasses the biped. The former looks up to the nobler side of the house, and will follow the lead of a horse rather than the wake of a brother bastard. The latter learns—curiously enough the father's family teaches him the lesson—not to do so.

Our little caravan consisted of two " tropeiros " or muleteers, the almocreves of Portugal, and arreiros of Spain. Miguel was the driver (tocador), whilst Antonio acted guide. There were three baggage mules, including " Falloux," the scapegoat, and Estrella, the " star-faced," an incarnation of vice, ready to kick the hand that fed her. They had the old Brazilian packsaddle, described in detail by Mr. Luccock and Prince Max., girt on by skilful hands over masses of heterogeneous packages, stuck as if plastered. They will value the comfort of good loading who, by engaging some dunderhead European, have lost all patience and alternate half-hours. The riding beasts were " Roão " the chesnut, " Machinho," a small grey mule, " Estrella No. 2," a good sun beast, and Camandongo the "male mouse," stout and willing, old, and therefore tolerably safe. Thus each had a single remount : nothing like the change after a few hours in a hottish sun. There were three horses, " Castanha " the bay, " Alazão " the roan, and an old white guide (madrinha) named " Prodigio," the sole prodigy being its age. All were in good condition, with sound eyes and teeth, frothing their bits to show their spirit; there are no "parrot mouths," and there are few shiny places upon their backs. "Lombo limpo," says the proverb, "bom arreiro." †

---

* Pranchear-se is the Brazilian term.   † " Clean back (shows) good muleteer."

A word before leaving Barbacena. The observations of
M. Liais found no difficulty in running a line of railway viâ this
city to Santo Antonio de Rio Acima and Sabará on the Rio das
Velhas ; indeed he declares this to be the shortest and readiest
road. If so, the dull old town has a future. Juiz de Fóra may
be called gay, because it has a daily arrival and departure of the
mail. Barbacena is galvanized by a bi-weekly coach, which keeps
up a theatre for amateurs and a billiard-room. We are now
about to see the outer darkness of places to which mules are the
only transport.

THE LINGOT D'OR.

Royal Arms.	N 1470	(1815)	B
	Toque 22 * * * 4 — 1 — 18		

Length	.	.	.	.	88 millimetres.
Breadth	.	.	.	6	,,
Thickness	.	.	.	4½	,,

CHAPTER IX.

FROM BARBACENA TO NOSSO SENHOR DO BOM JESUS DE MATOSINHOS DO BARROSO.*

"S'il existe un pays qui jamais puisse se passer du reste du monde, ce sera certainement la Province des Mines."—*St. Hilaire*, i. 4.

WE now digress from the most populous part of Minas, which lies almost due north between Barbacena and Diamantina. The direct, or north-west road, about 150 miles, between us and the Morro Velho Mine has been trodden to uninterestingness.† I therefore took a liberty with the mules, and resolved upon making a right angle to the west, with a base of thirty and a leg of ninety miles as the crow flies.

The good Dr. Renault supplied us with letters, not forgetting one for Sr. Francisco José de Meirelles, innkeeper of Barroso, the "muddy" where we intended to night. In this country "recommendations," as introductions are called, may often prove more valuable than bank-notes. He accompanied us on horseback for a few miles,‡ and I felt sad when taking leave of him. A man living upon conversation and exchange of opinion, and to whom talk is bliss, he must find Barbacena as it now is, a penance, a purgatory.

* Time and approximate length of stages from Barbacena viâ S. João and São José to Morro Velho :—

1. Barbacena to Barroso	.	.	. hours	5° 30'	statute miles	24.
2. Barroso to S. João	.	.	. ,,	7° 10'	,,	24.
3. S. João to S. José	.	.	. ,,	1° 30'	,,	6.
4. S. José to Alagôa Dourada	.	.	,,	6° 10'	,,	24.
5. Alagôa Dourada to Camapuan	.	,,	5° 15'	,,	15.
6. Camapuan to Congonhas do Campo	,,	8° 0'	,,	24.
7. Congonhas to Teixeira	.	.	,,	5° 0'	,,	14.
8. Teixeira to Coche de Agoa	.	.	,,	8° 25'	,,	24.
9. Coche de Agoa to Morro Velho	.	,,	3° 0'	,,	12.

Thus the total time was fifty hours expended in covering 163 statute miles : the rate was, therefore, 3⅓ miles per hour. When I travel alone my men are always mounted, and thus we easily get over six to seven miles an hour.

† In 1825 Caldcleugh (ii. chaps. 17—18). Mr. Walsh (1829) travelled viâ S. José. Castelnau was the last in 1843.

‡ This complimentary escort is known as the "despedida," and as in the nearer east is general throughout the interior of the Brazil.

To-day's march will be about five leagues,* and occupy the usual time, as many hours. Had the road run along the Valley of the Rio das Mortes, the distance between Barbacena and São João would have been shortened, it is said, from forty-eight to thirty-six miles. But the ancients adopted the custom of the savages—a custom with which the African traveller is painfully familiar. They made the ascents and descents as short as possible by taking a bee line, and by disdaining a zigzag. The object, of course, was to strike the plateau as soon as they could, and to keep it as long as possible. The Paulista saying is, "Ride slowly up the hill for the sake of your beast, prick fast over the level for the journey's sake, and ride gently down hill for your own sake." Accordingly, our bridle-path cut over hills and dales covered with thin grass, glowing with light, but lacking the glare of Arabia and Sindh. The horizon was evidently of the same contour, but flattened by distance into knobs and knuckles. The surface glittered painfully at times with débris of mica and crystallised quartz ; there were ugly descents of white earth, with rolling pebbles, and the water breaches (esbarrancados) were of monstrous size.

Antonio, the guide, having declared that he knew the way, lost no time in losing it. At one of many critical turns he broke to the south, and led us to the "Fazenda de Canyagora."† Through a woody bottom, over a bed of carbonate of lime, flowed the little Rio Caieiro, "Limestone Creek," an affluent of the Rio das Mortes. This dolomite, covering sixteen square leagues, sells for 0$280 to 0$320 per bushel at Barroso. It is good for building purposes, and the burnt lime fetches 2$000 to 3$000 at Juiz de Fóra.

We found two "Campeiro"‡ lads, herders of black cattle, and offered them coppers in vain. They were going in their rags to the Campo—a juvenile taradiddle—they had not time to guide us, but they condescended to show us how to guide ourselves. We

* When speaking of inland leagues, I refer, unless it is otherwise specified, to the old Brazilian, a little more than four English statute miles. Popularly it means an hour's ride. Assuming the animals stride at one yard, and two strides per second—less uphill and more down, or *vice versâ* according to the beast—we have 3600 seconds = 7200 strides or yards, 160

yards over the four miles (7040 yards). Concerning the leagues and other measures of length, I have given all necessary information in the Appendix of Vol. II.
† My friend Mr. Copsey informs me that the Fazenda in question is generally known as "do Mello," or "dos Caieiros."
‡ Prince Max. (iii. 89 and elsewhere) calls them Campistos—an error.

passed a large lime-kiln, and shortly before sunset we made a long
descent from the barren highland into a pretty picturesque basin.
A bird's-eye view showed an oasis (of Fiction) in the desert. All
was bright with Capim Angola (Panicum altissimum), and with
roses and the Poinsettia, whose brilliant red bracts, always the
highest light in the picture, give it a centre, as it were, and illuminate up like lamps the tints of tamer flowers. The vegetation
of the basin ranges between England and India, from the weeping
willow, the Sicilian cactus, the orange, and the palm, to the plan-
tain, the coffee-shrub, and the sugar-cane. Nor was the "utile"
forgotten; the gardens smiled with yams and various greens. The
little village boasts of a church, Nosso Senhor do Bom Jesus de
Matosinhos (of thickets) do Barroso ; of a chapel that accommo-
dates Nᵃ Sᵃ do Rosario, and of a half-finished square, with the
normal two shops of seccos and molhados—dry and wet goods.
The brightly whitewashed tenements are disposed as usual in
single lines and scatters. Each has its quintal, or "compound"
of flowers, fruit-trees, and vegetables, with a few coffee-plants and
a patch of sugar. Such was Barroso when we visited it. Once
the Fazenda do Barroso, whose last possessor was the Capitão
José Francisco Pires, it has now become a district in the Municipality of Barbacena.*

A curious contrast there was in the beauty and elegance—
excuse the word—of this Brazilian village, and the homely,
unlovely auburns of modern England and France and of "New
America."

We presented our letter to Sr. Meirelles, who condescend-
ingly bade us alight,† otherwise we had remained in the saddle.
A "dirty-picturesque" mob of muleteers pressed to the door and
eyed us as if we had come from one of the "foreign parts" which
Virgil described. The establishment was the common compound
of the third and fourth phases assumed by venal hospitality in a
land where every second gentleman keeps open house.

No. 1 is the Pouso, a mere camping-ground, whose proprietor

---

* In 1829, when Mr. Walsh passed
through "Barroza," as he calls it, the place
was still a Fazenda. Curious to say, in the
map of M. Gerber (1862), it is placed upon
the north or right bank of the Rio das
Mortes, in this case the wrong bank. In
the chart of M. Burmeister (1850) it does
not appear.

† "Apear :" it would be "indecent
haste" to dismount without such invitation, especially at a private house. And
here all the honours and ceremonies of the
private, are expected by the public, house,
whilst the host is at least as exigeant as
his dwelling.

does not object to let troopers water their mules and tether them to stakes. In the first quarter of the present century travellers were often condemned to nights *à la belle étoile* in these germs of accommodation, which have now become populous villages and towns.

No. 2, the Rancho, represents the "Traveller's Bungalow," lacking, however, cot, chair, and table, Thugs and Dacoits. Essentially it is a long, tiled shed, sometimes fronted by a verandah on wooden posts or brick pillars; at other times with outer walls, and even with inner compartments, formed by taipa* adobes, or clay and wattle. Here the muleteers unload; the beasts wander undriven to the pasture, whilst the masters build a fire, hang their kettle, gipsy fashion, from a tripod of sticks, strew on the ground by way of bedding the hide covers of the cargoes, and make a snuggery with parallel partitions of neatly-piled panniers† and pack-saddles. The Brazilian poet describes the Rancho—

> E por grupos apinhoados,
> Em seu centro estão arreios,
> Sacos, couros e broacas.‡

It requires the skin of a "tropeiro" to sleep in such places: all swarm with strange, outlandish vermin, which burrow into your flesh, and which make their homes under your nails.

No. 3 is the Venda, or shop, a decided advance, but not "thoroughly respectable." I was once reproved for owning to having enjoyed the opposite extremes of Fazenda and Venda. It is the "pulperia" of the Hispano-American colonies, the village emporium of England, combined with the grocery and the public-house; it sells "a' things," from garlic and prayer-books to gin and rum, cake and candles; sometimes it is double, with

---

* The pisé of Brittany and puddle of England, found from Devonshire *viâ* Dahome and Sindh, &c., to Australia. The way of making it is almost everywhere the same; I will not, therefore, describe the process. When the clay is stiff and contains small quartz pebbles, it forms a good wall. It always requires, however, to be, as the phrase is, well hatted and booted—supplied with wide eaves to save it from the rain, and a stone or brick foundation to prevent the moisture of the ground eating away the base.

† The Jacá is made of the bamboo bark

split and plaited: it is a flat parallelogram containing the sack of salt or coffee, and fitting close to the cangalha or pack-saddle. The "broaca" is a bullock's hide softened in water, shaped and sewn into a rude box with cover, and allowed to dry, when it becomes hard as wood. The word is written by old writers Boroacas, by the moderns Bruacas and Broacas. Prince Max. (ii. 365) prefers "boroacas, sacs de peau de bœuf durcie."

‡ "And in the middle, heaped and grouped, are mule trappings, bags, hides, and skin-boxes." (Bacharel, Teixeira).

one side for wet, and the other for dry goods. A counter,* over which swings the rude balance, bisects the length. Between it and the door are stools, boxes, or inverted tubs. The customer touches hat to the proprietor, and is hereupon told to sit down. Behind the "balcão" is sacred ground, admitting to the gynecœum. The shelves of untrimmed wood are laden with mugs, cans, and other pottery, and on both sides with full and empty bottles, upright and couchant. On the floor are salt-bins and open kegs of coarse sugar and beans, a box or two of maize, piles of lard and salted meat—the popular "carne seca," a rope of black tobacco curled round a stick, and tins and demijohns of the local rum. The items are umbrellas, horseshoes, hats, mirrors, belts, knives, long pistols (garruchas), cheap guns, ammunition, and sewing gear—in fact, everything that can be wanted by rustic man or woman. The Venda has usually a room where strangers are accommodated with a large platter† for ablutions, a wooden bunk, a long-legged table, and a low bench.

No. 4 is the Estalagem, or Hospedaria, the inn where we shall lodge at Marianna; and No. 5, and last, is the more pretentious hotel, or 'ôtel, with which the reader has made acquaintance at Barbacena.

We had omitted the advisable precaution of sending forwards to order dinner, and two hours' delay converted it to a supper. The menu was the usual thing. The flesh is represented by a hunch of roast pork, which no stranger in the Brazil will touch after he has seen the behaviour of St. George's pet animal. The bazar pig of India is a better specimen of education. There is usually a tough stewed fowl, au riz,‡ with head and neck, giblets and four shanks, but wanting probably a wing and a thigh. Œufs au plat§ are common as pigeons and omelettes in Italy. The Brazil, like England, is a land of one sauce, red and yellow peppers‖ gathered from the garden, and bruised in broth and

---

* Balcão.

† Gamella, a hollowed bowl of some soft tree, generally the Gamelleira (Ficus doliaria), at times six or seven feet in circumference. See Chap. 21. sect. 2, for a further notice of this popular article. In the house it is of various shapes, round, square, and oblong, deep and shallow, and it much reminded me of the platters which I saw at Harrar in East Africa.

‡ Gallinha ensopada, usually tolerably done, but always a "sudden death."

§ Ovos estrellados; thrown upon a hot plate, copiously larded, and often swimming in brown liquid.

‖ Molho de pimenta (capsicum). Of these there are many varieties known to, and cultivated by, the aborigines; the "System" mentions ten species. The best is probably the yellow-skinned rounded Pimenta de Cheiro (of perfume, C. ovatum or odoriferum, also Juá), superior, in my opinion, to that of Nepaul. There is also the Cheiro' Comprido, or long smeller,

limejuice. The feijoada, locally called "tutú de feijão,"* is the staff of life in the many places where wheaten bread is unprocurable, and corn bread is unknown. I have heard an Irishman call it a "bean poultice," and, 'faith, the unsavoury simile fitted exactly. It is a mixture of farinha with haricots, flavoured with toucinho (cutis and suinus), the oil and cooking-butter of the country. This adipose tissue of boned, disembowelled, and unfleshed pig, slightly salted, is hygienically well adapted to beans, combining carbon with nitrogen ; unfortunately it enters into almost every dish, and it does no good to the digestion of " Young Brazil." The same may be said of many places in the Western United States and in China, where people are almost made of pork. Apparently it is a favourite food in young lands. In Europe we are told during many centuries the only animal food generally used was pork; beef, veal, and mutton being comparatively unknown. The rice is sensibly cooked. Brazilians know the knack, whereas the English and the Anglo-Americans still persist in eating the husk.†

For dessert‡ appears a tureen-full of canjica—boiled maize, and sweetmeats, of which all orders and ages are exceedingly fond. Canjica is "kitchen'd" with brown sugar, with quince conserve,§ or with guava cheese.|| The two latter are served up in wooden boxes, or in flat tins. They are universal favourites, supposed to facilitate digestion, and they accompany salt cheese,

and the Cheiro doce. Strangers often bring with them from Europe a nursery prejudice against this excellent stomachic, superior for opening the appetite to all absinthe. Prince Max. was wiser : " Dans ces forêts humides . . . . cette épice est excellente pour la digestion, et peut aussi passer pour un fébrifuge très salutaire" (iii. 6). So is Paul du Chaillu (Ashangoland, chap. 3.) "The pepper itself I believe to be a very useful medicine in this climate, for I have often found benefit from it when unwell and feverish, by taking a moderate quantity in my food." Brazilians are exceedingly fond of pepper, as were their Indian predecessors, who used "muita somma de pimenta." Amongst the ten well-known kinds we find the Pimentão, or large pepper (Capsicum cordiforme, or in Tupy, Quiyá-açú, also Pimentão comprido), much cultivated by the savages. Yet the Brazilians do not seem to enjoy the large boiled pods of which the Spaniards are so fond. In old

books we find many native names for the different species : Pimenta-poca, Poca doce, Quiyaqui, Quiyá-apuá (corrupted to Cujepia), Quiya-Cumari, or Cumbari, Quiya-açú (corrupted to Cuihemoçu), Inquitai, Pesijurimu, Sabaa, and others. The generic name in Tupy was Quiya or Quiyuha ; in Carib " Axi ;" in Peruvian "Api."

* The Feijão (Phaseolus vulgaris) here takes the place of the Egyptian Fúl (Mudammas, etc.) It is of many kinds, mulato, fidalgo, preto, rôxo, incarnado, cavallo, and so forth.

† I have explained all this in the "Lake Regions of Central Africa," i. 393, yet the British rice-eater still feeds like the Prodigal Son in distress.

‡ Sobre-mêsa, literally on the table.

§ Marméláda, not to be confounded with our marmalade.

|| Goiabáda, from goiába, whence our guava (Psidium pyriferum).

even as cheese and pudding go together in ancient Yorkshire.
The wine, where there is any, calls itself Lisbon, and is dyewood,
molasses rum, and half a tumbler of the worst juice of the Bar-
celona grape ; the popular name for it is "caustic." Sometimes
there is Bordeaux, and then we may inquire, as did the Teuton
of his ecclesiastical host, "Senhor Batre, esde e binho ou binakre ?"
Every feed invariably ends with a cup of coffee, not "water
bewitched," as in England, but, though rich, badly made. The
bean is burned to blackness, as in Egypt; it is pounded, not
ground, as in England ; but it is always strained, boiling water
being poured through the charged bag. Moreover, the popular
sweet tooth makes it into a syrup with treacly Rapadura, and
"Rapadura—coisa dura,"* justly observes the Brazilian Mr.
Merryman. Of course there is as little sitting after dinner as in
Utah or a little Russian town.

Such is the Jantar (dinner), the prototype of Almoço, or breakfast. The latter, however, in the better inns ends with a
sobre-mêsa of tea and café au lait, the milk always scalded, with
bread, or that failing, with biscuit† and Irish butter. The people
are like King George I., who preferred his oysters stale, and the
good citizens, who love to "taste" their fish and eggs, complain
that the fine fresh butter made by the Germans lacks flavour, and
I have seen many a man temper it, as Suez people do the Nile
water, with a pinch of salt. This adjunct to the minor meal
reminds me of our "fasts" at Oxford, where the day was known
by meat plus fish.

My wife was allowed to swing her hammock in an inner room ;
we passed the night on and under rugs in the verandah. The air
was cold, colder than at Barbacena. We had been gradually
descending, and a stranger would have expected warmth from
this snug hollow. In the Brazil it is the reverse. The first-
comers, I have said, when not priests, built dwelling-houses
which afterwards became villages, towns, cities, in bottom-

---

* "Rapadura, thing t' endure." The
word means "scrapings;" the thing is
a preparation peculiar to South America, a
brick of uncrystallized sugar from which
the molasses has not been drained. The
word in Peru is Chancaca or Raspadura
(St. Hil. III. ii. 266), where it also means
sugar with the syrup expressed from the
clayed or cured stuff, and allowed to drain
or drop into a vessel, being thus cast like

bullets. The traveller must use it in the
far west of the Brazil. Its sole merit is
that of being very portable. I never saw
it in the United States, or in other sugar-
growing lands.

† Generally Rosca, our "rusk," too
often resembling the "rock of ages," as
the war biscuit was called in the United
States.

lands, where water for mills ("monjolos") and home uses was near and plentiful. Evaporation being excessive made the hollows rawer than the heights by night, and as the sun is not yet coloured German-silver in the Brazil, the cold was followed by the other extreme. A small difference of altitude here determines the worth or worthlessness of landed property. When men say that the soil is "cold" they mean that it is low-lying and subject to frosts, which destroy coffee and sugar : it may be geologically the same as its neighbour on the other side of the hill, yet it is unfit for any but such pauper culture as cotton and cereals. Long ago Theophrastus* observed that it freezes less on hills than on hills, and it is an old remark that the ascent of warm air preserves vines and other plants on heights when they would perish in the valleys.

* Theophrastus, v. 20. I quote from p. 74 of a valuable book which was obligingly sent to me by the Editor, "Essay on Dew," by William Charles Wells. Edited by L. P. Casella, F.R.A.S. London : Longmans, 1866.

CHAPTER X.

FROM BARROSO TO SÃO JOÃO D'EL-REI.

"Of all inventions, the alphabet and the printing press alone excepted, those inventions which abridge distance have done most for the civilization of our species."—Macaulay.

RISING before dawn on the next day, we found from the blood-clotted hides of our animals that they had suffered severely from the vampire (Vespertilio Naso, or Phyllostomus Spectrum), a Phyllostom, locally called by the generic name of "Morcego" Andira or Guandira. These big ruddy-brown bats, of ghostly flight and cannibal tastes, are confined to the American continent, and they unaccountably prefer particular spots. I found many of them in the island of São Sebastião (São Paulo), where there is no cattle-breeding. They seem to select the neck, shoulders, withers, and hind-quarters of animals,—in fact, to attack where they can least be disturbed.* When a "raw" exists it is chosen before other places. The muleteers declare that the phlebotomy does no harm. I remarked that it always enfeebled the patient. In São Paulo and Minas no case of a man having been bitten by the "ugly spectre-bats" came under my notice. They did, however, much damage to the earlier European settlements in the New World. Cabiza de Vaca (1543) was wounded by the leaf-nosed maroon-coloured monster near the Lake Xarayes. Messrs. Bates and A. R. Wallace, and my excellent friend Mr. Charles H. Williams, of Bahia,† suffered in person on the Amazons, where the rhinophyll appears to be decidedly anthropophagous. Koster mentions the use of an owl-skin to preserve animals from the leaf-nose.

The mode of the vampire's attack has of late years become

---

* Southey, i. 144, relates that they bit the ears of horses and greatly terrified the animals. Prince Max. (ii. 61), never saw men bled by them.

† All his party of three were phleboto-mized in the big toe during a single night. Mr. Williams felt the bite of the brute, and found a punctured wound about one-eighth of an inch in diameter.

the subject of debate. The wound is softly and skilfully inflicted—I never saw my horses or mules terrified by it. Prince Max. asserts before the doubting days, " Ce vampire (Phyllostomus) fait avec ses dents un grand trou dans la peau des animaux." Gardner believes the puncture is made by the sharp hooked nail of the thumb. Lieutenant Herndon thinks that the tusks bite, whilst the nostrils are fitted for a suction apparatus. Others trace the wound to the papillæ of the tongue, an organ of action. The armature of the jaw, however, speaks for itself. It must be like a Vision of Judgment to awake suddenly and to find upon the tip of one's nose, in the act of drawing one's lifeblood, that demonical face with deformed nose, satyr-like ears, and staring fixed saucer eyes, backed by a body measuring two feet from wing-end to wing-end. No wonder that it suggested to the simple savage the subordinate fiend " Chimay," who thinned him by draining the sap of life.

We set out at 4·30 A.M.—the latest time that should be allowed even at this season—when nothing injures mules so much as travelling in the post-meridian sun. The bridle-path led over the same style of Campos, gleaming yellow with coarse low grass, and perfumed with the hardy wild rosemary.* Even the gramens had lost the culms of fructification seen below the Mantiqueira. Everything except the sun told us that mid-winter was at hand. We forded sundry veins, all running northwards to the main artery : near one of them we enjoyed a roadside breakfast, and we persuaded the tropeiros of a neighbouring gipsy camp to refresh us with coffee. We might easily have fed at the halfway ranch at the Rio Elvas (P.N.)† Here is a bridge in the style of ancient Minas, with central ridge, huge balustrade, and roof of ponderous tiles.

As we trudged along slowly in the fiery sunshine, Ollaria and other out-stations, nestling white in the cool verdure of the hollows, made us sigh for their shade. At noon we saw with a thrill of pleasure far below the Valley of the Great River of the Murder-deaths,‡ whose sources we passed in the Mantiqueira Range, to the south-east of Barbacena. Here its valley, even at this dry season, was much cut up with water : during the rains it

---

* Rosmarinho do Campo, a Lantana (?)
† Or Rio do Elvas, popularly pronounced Ervas ; hence some travellers write it "Hervas." Can it be the " Widasmaoth,"
which Mr. Walsh (ii. 227) places near Barroso ?
‡ Rio das Mortes Grande and Pequeno.

must be a lake. A little further on it will receive a southerly influent, the Lesser Rio das Mortes, and the two anastomosing west of S. João, will form the true Rio das Mortes. This, again, falls into the Rio Grande, also called the Paraná, being the head-stream of that mighty artery, and dividing the Provinces of São Paulo and Minas Geraes.

About six miles to our right rose the craggy lines of the S. José mountains. Far to the left was "St. John of the King," bristling with a dozen churches, spread like a white sheet upon a hill-side, grim and jagged as the Togi's bed. Under our feet, upon its little river-plain lay the Arraial* de Matosinhos, a charming suburb, distant a mile and three-quarters—more exactly, eight hundred Brazilian fathoms—from the city. We passed up the neat principal street, and entered a main square formed by the best houses, each with its flower garden, set off by a few coffee shrubs of prodigious size, and the richest verdure.† There is no priest, but the church of the Espiritu Santo appeared, externally at least, in good order. Here during its fête pilgrims flock from the country for the spiritual refreshment of praying through the day and night.

Matosinhos stands where once stood the far-famed "Capão de Traição"—Tree-clump of Treachery—a term dating from the days which named its stream "River of the Deaths," or rather murders. At the end of the seventeenth century, the Paulistas, especially the Taubatienses, or people of Taubaté, a Paulistan city in the Valley of the Parahyba do Sul, found gold diggings in most parts of their captaincy, now the Province of Minas Geraes; and they incontinently claimed all the rights of discovery. One of their Poderosos, named Manoel de Borba Gato, arrogated to himself the title of Governor of the Mines, and he was supported by his countrymen. They determined to expel, some say to massacre, the Forasteiros or Foreigners, meaning the emigrants

---

* Arraial (Arrayal), or Reál, means properly the royal head-quarters in a camp. Thus Camoens (iii. 42)—

"Já no campo de Ourique se assentava
O arraial soberbo e bellicoso."

"Now on Ourique's field was pitched and manned
The Lusan 'campment proud and belli-cose."

Thence it came to signify a field of battle. In Minas Geraes the word was applied to the povoaçaõ, or village of olden days, because it was mostly fortified, and it was generally in the presence of the Indian enemy.

† In these places, which are usually well watered, if not manured, fruit-trees and shrubs thrive exceptionally. Café de Quintal, for instance, means something much more luxuriant than what is grown in the open.

from Portugal and Europe.   The latter, nicknamed the " Phari-
sees of Minas," chose as their Governor the Portuguese Manuel
Nunes Vianna (Viana), " White Man and European," and thus
began, in 1708, the celebrated wars of the Caboclos* and Em-
boabas†—" Red-skins and Feather-legged fowls."

Vianna, then the " Grey-eyed Man of Destiny," sent from
Ouro Preto a thousand miners under a blood-thirsty villain,
Bento do Amaral Coutinho, to assist his party the Forasteiros.
The Paulistas, who were hutted in the Tree-clump of Treachery,
were persuaded to lay down their arms, and were foully massacred
to a man by the mob of slaves and cut-throats who followed
Amaral.   The Governor and Captain-General of Rio de Janeiro,
D. Fernando Martins Mascarenhas de Lancastro, who succeeded
Artur de Sá, went to the Arraial with four companies of troops : he
was met as an equal by Vianna of the will of bronze, and he was
presently induced to retire.‡   In 1708 the Governor was succeeded
by Antonio de Albuquerque Coelho de Carvalho—a man of
different stamp.   He mastered Vianna, and permitted him to
retire from the Mines, and to live upon his property near the Rio
de São Francisco.   " Whether his merits were rewarded by the
Court," says Southey,§ " is nowhere stated; they are, however,
acknowledged in (his ?) history."   Albuquerque, it is generally
believed, pardoned Vianna by order dated August 22, 1709.
The King (D. João V.) subsequently revoked this, and directed
that both the ringleader, with Amaral and · his secretary, Fr.
Miguel Ribeiro, should be arrested.   Some say that Vianna died
at large, others in the prison of Bahia. These civil discords breed

* According to the exact Varnhagen "Caboclo " or " Cabocolo " means " peeled,"
or " plucked," because the aborigines removed the body hair as the Christian
Brazilians used to do, and as Oriental
peoples still do.   Marcgraff (Hist. Nat.
Braz. 268) applies " Caribocas " and " Ca-
bocles " to the mixture of white, negro,
and Indian : in this he is supported by
Gardner (p. 22).   Prince Max. calls civilized Indians " Caboclos " (i. 30), and
elsewhere (i. 110) makes the word equivalent to Tapouyas, pure " Indians. St.
Hil. (III. ii. 253) asserts that Caboclo or
Caboco is contemptuously applied to the
pure Indian.   On the Amazons, as the "Naturalist " informs us (i. 35), the civilized
Indian is called Tapuyo or Caboclo.   According to my experience the word now
means a man with a mixture of red blood,

and it is applied insultingly, somewhat
like our " nigger."   Yet I have known a
man nick-name himself " Caboclo." Prince
Max. (i. 30—1) says that the mixture of
white and Indian produces the Mamalucco,
the negro and Indian Ceribocos (popularly
Cafuz, corrupted to Cafuso), the pure Indians Indios, the civilized red-skins Caboclos, the wild Indians Gentios, Tapuyès or
Bugrès.

† Some write Embuaba.   It is rightly
explained by Cazal (i. 235).   See Southey
(iii. 885).   In many parts of the Brazil a
" knickerbocker " fowl is still termed
"Emboaba."

‡ Local tradition says that Vianna with
4000 men met D. Fernando at Congonhas
do Campo, and compelled him, with
threats, to march back upon Rio de Janeiro.

§ History (iii. 83).

long-lived results. The Paulistas and Mineiros are cousins; but the two branches are still alienated by the battles for gold on the Rio das Mortes and elsewhere.

Beyond the pretty suburb lay the "Agua Limpa," pure as the Neva : well it deserves its name. The pebbly bed is now forded, and during the rains a "pingela," or "pingella," a beam, often an unsquared tree-trunk, oftener without than with handrail, suffices for communication.* Higher up is a broken bridge dating from the days when Matosinhos had a flourishing gold mine : it ended with the bursting of a dyke like the "Sadd El Arem." Reaching the Municipal Palace and Prison, we were arrested by the normal procession on the fête of Corpus Christi; we pulled off our hats and we sat in the sun till it passed.

There was nothing remarkable in the "function." All the Irmandades† Sodalities, or Tertiary Orders, were there,—white men in red cloaks, brown men in green, and black men— naturally—in white. Not wanting were the Anjinhos, or little angels, chits in short crinolines, frilled pantalettes, satin shoes, and fancy wings, all under ten, apparently the *ne plus ultra* of the angelic age, and all learning vanity with a will. There was a profuse waste of wax taper, and very little of art in the images. The principal ecclesiastic bore the Host under an embroidered canopy, and military with music brought up the rear.

These processions were much patronised by Nobrega and the great Jesuit lights of 1850. Doubtless the show, the melody, and the mystery, won many a stray Tupi sheep for the Fathers' fold.‡ These ardent votaries were followed by men who thought with Hosius, "Strip the Church of its pomps and pageantry, and its doctrines will become as the fables of Æsop." The rite presently declined, became a system of farces and masquerades, "irreverent ceremonies, and ridiculous mummeries.§ In these

---

* The Indians of the Brazil, like those of the Orinoco, made suspension bridges of llianas, woven together in the simplest fashion, and allowed to oscillate above the water. A "hand-rail" of vine or creeper enabled the passenger to steady himself.

† Mistaking this institution, Mr. Walsh (ii. 134) locates at São João two convents at a time when religious orders were not permitted to establish themselves in Minas Geraes.

‡ "Les naturels ne connaissent de la re-ligion que les formes extérieures du culte. Amateurs de tout ce qui tient à un ordre de cérémonies présentes, ils trouvent dans le culte chrétien des jouissances particulièrès." Prince Max, ii. 395.

§ St. Hil. (III. i. 100). I use his words, for he was a very Catholic and a "Professor," as far as a scientific man can be. So in the Province of Pasto, amongst the Andes, Humboldt saw the Indians dancing, masked, and hung with bells, round the altar where a Franciscan was elevating the Host.

days it is perfectly and dully decorous, and it subserves the useful purpose of "bringing people together." It combines the promenade, the visit, the pic-nic—in fact, it is the one outlet, the grand parade, for poor human vanity, here so little, when in Europe so copiously, aired. And wherever in the Brazil the citizens have, primo, little to do with the outer world, secundo, little to do at home, there this style of devotion flourishes. At São João we heard the bell-ringing of Oxford: all the day and half the night was made vocal by the "dobrar," slow-tolling, the lever being used, and "repicar," ringing in triple bob-major, when the tongue is hammered with the hand. It was a "furnace of music," a "tempest symphony."

We followed the Praia, or Eastern Quay, stone revetted, whilst the opposite side is not. This *en revanche* has a picturesque bit of aqueduct lately repaired. The Rio de São João, descriptively but erroneously termed by some travellers Rio Tejuco,[*] flows through the city to the common reservoir on the north-east. At this season it is a film of water trickling down a foul bed, doggy and catty. Like many a once rural stream in England, it wants only breadth, volume, and washing. Two old-fashioned bridges of solid stone, each with three arches of about twenty feet span, cross it : to the east, and near the Camara, is Ponte Novo, looking very elderly, and capped with a cross. Westward lies the Ponte do Rosario.

Seen from its streamlet, São João is strikingly picturesque. The snowy buildings of the northern section spread out, trigon-shaped, upon the Quay; thence, rich in tall houses, massive fanes, and clumps of wondrous verdure and startling flowers, they swarm up their wild and remarkable background of Serra, once the El Dorado, the focus of auriferous deposit. To the left, also lending its foot for the city to rest upon, is the Serra do Lenheiro, said to be 3000 feet above sea-level.[†] It is ridged and ribbed with that hard talcose slate soon to become so familiar

---

[*] Rio Tejúco would mean "mud river." The Tupi (or Lingoa Geral) "Tyjuca," also written Tijuca, is applied to many places in the Brazil where the first explorers found a bad Tyjucopába or Tyjucopão, in Portuguese atoleiro or lamaçal, a slough or quagmire. The Dict. translates Tyjú "escuma," froth or foam ; and Tyjuca "lama," barro podre or apodrecer—mud, rotten clay, to rot. At São João the Rio Tejúco is a small influent from the north, which, joined by the "Barreiro" from the east, joins the "Rio Acima," the western section of the São João stream.

[†] Some say 5700—6000. But the city is only 1290 feet (Aroeira) above sea-level, and about 2300 feet below Barbacena. I regret not having made observations for altitude, as the temperature seems to suggest nearly 2000 feet.

to us, the thinnest brownish brushwood, finds place there, and the system looks like a magnified thistle, a vast teazle. To the right is the "Bocáina," or Gap, the water-gate of the River of the Murder-Deaths; and further still, the Serra de São José, a brother of the Lenheiro, walls in the view.

We deposited our very hot and dusty selves in the Hotel Almeida, kept by Sr. Joaquim José de Almeida, and sent our "tickets" to the Capitão Custodio de Almeida Magalhaẽs, who obligingly insisted upon our "cutting our mutton" with him. Presently, lounging at the doorway, we espied, in the act of riding by, an indubitable British hat—white, massive, and broad-brimmed. Unlike Eothen, but very like other Englishmen in similar circumstances, we took the liberty of asking the wearer's nationality, and when surprise at the sudden process had worn off, we found ourselves sitting and chatting with Dr. Lee, a Kentish man, or a man of Kent. He had married, settled, and spent thirty-three years, "on and off," at São João. Presently he introduced us to Mr. Charles C. Copsy, of Cambridge, who there had known some of my undergraduate kinsmen. He also had passed through the Church; he was a lieut.-colonel of real Brazilian volunteers, seventy-four stalwart youths, well armed and uniformed; moreover, he was Professor of English, geography, and mathematics at the Lyceum.

It was pleasant to fall so unexpectedly upon these two culti-vated English gentlemen, to brush up reminiscences, to exchange adventures, and to hear the chaff of our own land. More pleasant still to find that their home habits had not permitted themselves to become Brazilianised. Brazilian is good, and British is good; the mixture, as is said of other matters which shall be nameless, spoils two good things. It much suggests the old saw,—

Un Ingleze Italianato
E il Diavolo incarnato.

Also, "on n'a que trop souvent à rougir des compatriotes que l'on rencontre dans les régions éloignées." And, for the personal kindness of my fellow-countrymen of São João, I can only beg them to receive our heartfelt thanks.

Before ending in sleep the uncommonly satisfactory evening, we may prepare for an inspection of the city to-morrow.*

* I have borrowed freely from the Apon-tamentos da População, Topographia, e Noticias Chronologicas do Municipio da Cidade de S. João Del-Rei (sic), Provincia de Minas Geraes. Por José Antonio Rodrigues. S. João D'El Rei (sic). Typ.

When Sebastião Fernandes Tourinho discovered in 1572 the emerald mines which proved to be ridiculous grass-green tourmalines, the Brazilian interior was at once traversed by intrepid bands of explorers and pioneers, mostly Paulistas. The names generally quoted are those of Bartholomeu Bueno da Silva,— by cognomen O Anhanguera, popularly translated Old Devil, and suggesting the Shaitan Ka Ohai of Sindh; his brother-in-law, Antonio Rodrigues; Arzão, of Taubate; Fernão Dias Paes Leme, his son-in-law; Manoel de Borba Gato, before alluded to; and Thomé Pontes. The first lodes and veins[*] were found in and about the stream now called Rio das Mortes, and the abundance of ores caused the land to be named Minas Geraes— General Mines. Chroniclers delight to repeat that in those golden days a peck and a-half of corn cost sixty-eight oitavas of gold, now = £23; farinha-meal was worth forty oitavas; whilst a horse or a bullock fetched thirteen to fourteen ounces. These prices, they state, effectually killed out all agricultural industry. I should think that the reverse would be the fact.

The Arraial do Rio das Mortes began life as a village in 1684. In 1712 (*alii* Jan. 29, 1714) D. João the Magnificent named it Villa de São João d'El Rei.[†] On December 8, 1713 (*alii* 1715) its proprietor, the Governor and Captain-General of São Paulo, sent to it the first Ouvidor-Judge, Dr. Gonçalo de Freitas Baracho. By Provincial Law No. 93, of March, 1838, it became a city, the chief place of a Comarca,[‡] and the headquarters of the electoral district. In 1828 Mr. Walsh gave the municipality 9000 to 10,000 souls. This figure had risen in 1859 to 21,500, of whom 15,200 were free, 100 were strangers, and

de J. A. Rodrigues, 1859. The author still practises as an advocate. His monography is one of the many valuable pamphlets which appear in the Brazil: they are little known to the Geographical Societies of London and Paris, and the traveller should be careful to collect them.

[*] The veeio (hardly a pure Portuguese word) is a vein of metal. Veeiro means the corpo do metal, the lode; and veta is also a vein. The usual word is veã (vena), *e.g.* "veas de quartzos que são os veeiros."

[†] This is the only correct way of writing the name; all the others, as Del Rei, Del Rey, D' El Rei, and numerous modifications, are obsolete or erroneous. The Arabo-Spanish article El is reserved in Portuguese for *the* king, and it commands

a hyphen: the particle "d'" cannot claim a capital letter, and the modern Portuguese write Rei, not Rey, which is now Spanish.

[‡] In colonial days the Comarca was a district within the jurisdiction of a Corregidor. The latter name is now obsolete, and the chief legal authority is the Juiz de Direito, or Juge de Droit. Thus also the Juiz Municipal has taken the place of the Juiz Ordinario, from whom an appeal lay to the Ouvidor. The Comarca or arrondissement of the Rio das Mortes is composed of the municipalities of S. João, S. José, and Oliveira. The municipios of a Comarca again are divided into freguezias or parishes, and these also into districts (districtos).

6200 slaves, an element rapidly decreasing.* There were thirty-nine electors, of whom sixteen were chosen by the city, 800 jurymen (jurados), and 1600 voters. The city is about two miles long from north to south, and contains ten squares, twenty-four streets, and 1600 houses, of which eighty are two-storied (sobrados). The census of 1859 gave it—

Men, free	3,150
Women, ditto	4,650
Foreigners	50
Men, servile	260
Women, ditto	390
Total . . .	8,500

I am unwilling at this late hour to make reflections savouring of Mormonism. But what think you, reader, or what would Milton and Priestly think, of such relative numbers as these in a poorly-peopled country? Is it not a waste of productive power? In fertile Pará feminine births average, I am informed by my friend Mr. Williams, four or five to one masculine. Is it not lamentable to see men blinded by the prejudices of education, thus neglecting the goods the gods provide? Surely it is time for some Illmo Senhor Dr. Brigham Joven to arise in the land.†

* In 1867 I was told the number of slaves in the municipality is about 1350, in the city 500. This is not unlikely in a pastoral land, where free labour is preferred to the brutal negligence of the African, and whose hands have mostly been sold off to the agricultural districts of Rio de Janeiro, which still calls for more.

† The text may appear paradoxical to those, to the many, who still believe cannibalism and human sacrifice, slavery, and polygamy, abominations per se, the sum of all villanies, and so forth. I look upon them as so many steps, or rather necessary conditions, by which civilized society rose to its present advanced state. Without cannibalism how could the Zealander have preserved his fine physical development? Certainly not by eating his bat and his rat. Without slavery how could the Antilles and the Southern States of the American Union have been cleared of jungle? White men could not, and free black men would not have done it. Without polygamy, how could the seed of Abraham have multiplied exceedingly? At the utmost they would have doubled their numbers in half a century. In the Old World a return to the state of its youth would be a retrograde movement, a relapse into barbarism. But it is not the same with new lands, which represent numerically the conditions which we have forgotten centuries ago.

CHAPTER XI.

Hásta los palos del Monte
Tienen su destinacion ;
Unos nacem para santos
Otros para hacer carbon.*

THIS quotation, borrowed from Dr. Rodrigues, refers somewhat vaguely to the past and future of São João. Hereabouts, shortly after the great earthquake at Lisbon (1755), it was proposed to transfer the seat of government. In 1789, as will appear, the patriotic movement in Minas fixed upon São João for the site of their Washington, and Ouro Preto for the University.† Unfortunately, there is hardly a place of importance, or even without importance, in the Mining Province which does not assert its claim to the Imperial Metropolis. I may briefly quote Campanha, Baependy, Minas Novas, Paracatú, Guaicuhy, and even the savage site of the Pirapora Rapid, on the Rio de São Francisco.

In history these things repeat themselves. The Brazil will not always rest satisfied with her present capital, exposed as it is to the attacks of all first-rate maritime Powers, and far more vulnerable than was St. Petersburgh before the Crimean war. Presently the oldest claimant, São João d'El-Rei, will see her name once more thrust forward. But I doubt whether the project will be seriously entertained ; the many advantages of

---

* It may be thus translated :—

Even the tree in forest glade
  Each has its several lot ;
While this to make a saint is made,
  That fain must warm the pot.

The sentiment is Horatian. Quum faber incertus scamnum faceret ne Priapum maluit esse deum.

† Varnhagan justly calls this a great thought, and proposes both a Capital and a University in the Province of Minas. The Brazil can afford to "wait awhile" for her metropolis, but she should not be patient about her Alma Mater.

the situation are counterbalanced by its uncentral position.* The Valley of the São Francisco will, one is inclined to prophesy, be in the course of time the chosen seat for the metropolis of the Diamond Empire.

On the shortest day of the year we set out to visit the little city, marshalled by Mr. Copsy; his local knowledge made all things easy. In the Rua Municipal we found the town-house, a large pile, whose ground floor boasted of barred windows, and whose upper front showed imperial arms and Justice in relief; moreover, it was unaccompanied by a shop. In Brazilian towns, as in Spanish colonies, a practical homage is rendered to commerce in almost all the best houses, by converting the lower half into a store. This, the Municipal Palace, was also the common jail— another "institution." It is somewhat barbarous, a flavouring of jealous Begum Sombre, to hold sessions over the heads of the buried alive; and the demoralizing prominence and publicity of mendicant incarceration should be abolished, and will be abolished, as soon as the municipal funds, at present much depressed, permit.†

The building, stone below and adobe above, is polychrome, and not without beauty. The frontage numbers 110 palms by a depth of 120—not the normal square or the popular claret case. It has five entrances, all iron-railed; the central adit cúrves outwards, and shows traces of the sentinel. We visited the state-room, 100 palms × 50, where an iron railing divides, as usual, the jurymen from the aldermen in session. The western ceiling was shored up, confessedly wanting repairs. To the north is the Public Library, open every day, and grimly decorated with the portrait of a local benefactor. Baptista Caetano, Mr. Walsh's "hog in armour," is dead; the present librarian is stone deaf, and ignores the number of volumes under his charge. We guessed 3200, and were corrected by the

* São João lies twenty-four leagues south-west of Ouro Preto, capital of Minas, and sixty leagues north-north-west of Rio de Janeiro. It is popularly said that a line through Bom Jardim, eighteen leagues to the south, would reduce the sixty to fifty leagues. They reckon from São João twenty-eight leagues to Rio Preto, the frontier of Rio de Janeiro, and thirty-four leagues to the mine of Morro Velho.

† In 1859 the annual revenue of the Camara ranged from 6 : 000 $ 000 to 7 : 000 $ 000. The taxes (impostos) were—

Per Provincial Collectorship 21 : 000 $ 000
,, General (Imperial) do. 22 : 000 $ 000

Total taxes . . 43 : 000 $ 000

Not including imports and exports dues, and toll bars (Barreiras), which may amount to as much more. Thus, says Sr. Rodrigues, the municipality contributes to the public coffers more than one hundred contos of reis (£10,000) per annum.

" Almanak," which says upwards of 4000. The mental pabulum consists mostly of old and now hardly legible folios and squat quartos, which have fed the minds of churchmen and the bodies of brocas—bookworms. Here, as in old Rome, the library may sing aloud,—

> Constrictos nisi das mihi libellos,
> Admittam tineas trucesque blattas.

São João has reason to remember her literary men. One of her sons, Manoel Ignacio d'Alvarenga, wrote the " Gruta Americana," and, under the name of Alcindo Palmireno, he was a member of the " Arcadia Mineira."* The second notability was João Antonio Ferreira da Costa, and the third was the satirical Padre Manoel Joaquim de Castro Viana. Add to the three poets a number of " sacred orators," the " terrors of sin," and eloquent " echoes of the Gospel." Besides these, an architect, a painter, and a sculptor are quoted by the curious. There are two choirs, and four " professors of the piano." Every person of education is, more or less, a musician.

We then proceeded up hill to the Externato de São João. This establishment dates from 1848; it was originally called the " Duval College," after the founder, Mr. Richard J. Duval,† once an *employé* in the mines of São José, under his cousin, Mr. G. V. Duval, once Director of Gongo Soco. He was followed by a Frenchman, M. A. M. Delverd, and the school was entitled Lyceum by the Councillor Carlos Carneiro de Campos. The site, on the extreme south of the city, is admirable, and commands a noble view. The old building once contained the inspection of gold (Casa da Intendencia), the smelting-rooms (Fundição)‡, the Residency of the ouvidors, and barracks for the regulars. Wholesome and orderly, it has one serious disadvantage. In these lands, where Art has not yet acquired sufficient power to control Nature, the violent hurricanes that open the Rains, ordeals of fire and water, are dangerously electrical. About four

---

* He was imprisoned by the Count Resende in the subterraneous dungeons of the Ilha das Cobras, but he must not be confounded with another famous plotter, the lyrical poet, Ignacio José de Alvarenga Peixoto (Plutarco Brasileiro, por J. M. Pereira da Silva, pp. 323—330. Rio de Janeiro, Laemmert, 1847). See chaps. 35 and 36.

† Mr. R. J. Duval made money here,

became Inspector of Traffic on the Dom Pedro Segundo Railway, and died in 1861. His son is, I believe, established in commerce at Rio de Janeiro.

‡ Mr. Walsh (ii. 138) gives a good and detailed account of the gold melting. He says, however, erroneously, that in old Minas each Comarca had its Intendencia, and its Casa de Fundição. The error has been noticed by St. Hilaire.

years ago the fluid struck the Lyceum; a bolis, like that which entered the church of Stralaund,* split one of the gable ends, and only by a miracle all the eighty pupils escaped. I should suggest £5 worth of lightning rod.

We assisted at the geographical lecture delivered by Professor Copsy, and I supplemented a few remarks upon the subject of Eastern and Central Africa. The ingenuous youths were of the upper ten thousand,—the porcelain not pottery of Society, well-born, well-dressed, well-behaved, and apparently well disposed to learn. Besides this aristocratic establishment, São João has humbler schools. There are two "Minerva Lodges." One, the Nª Sª das Mercês, in the north of the city, presided over by D. Policena Tertoliano d'Oliveira Machado. The second is in a central situation; its inspector-general is São Francisco, and the directress is D. Antonia Carolina Campos d'Andrade.

Our next step was northwards to the Santa Casa de Misericordia, one of the oldest in Minas. It was built in 1817, upon the site of a Poor-house, by Manuel de Jesus, a Spanish monk, whose funds did not exceed £2. Presently it obtained all the privileges enjoyed by the sister hospital, Lisbon; large sums were left to it, and it added to itself a pretty whitewashed chapel, under Nª Sª das Dôres. It has also annexes for the insane, for lepers, and for contagious cases. For a free man the charges are 2$000 per diem, and 1$500 for slaves. The sick annually treated are between sixty and seventy.†

We then turned westwards, passing by the Church of São Gonçalo Garcia, belonging to the Confraria Episcopal de São Francisco e São Gonçalo, aggregated to the convent of Santo Antonio do Rio de Janeiro. To this Order men of all colours and classes, except the servile, belong. The building is a mere shell, an unfinished ruin of much exposure, and doubtless it will take time to become

---

* These fire-balls are a frequent form of lightning assumed in the Brazil as in Eastern Africa, and deserving careful observation. At São Paulo I have often seen the electric fluid ascending in the south-eastern sky, and at the height of about 60° projecting a number of globes, like a monstrous Roman candle. Houses are often struck by them, as I have personally witnessed, and nothing but the bolis can explain the mode in which one of my maps was burned.

† In 1864—5 the hospital funds were 95:941 $ 019. The receipts were 10:357 $ 654, the expenditure was 7:800 $ 983, and the balance in favour was 2:556 $ 871. The Recolhimento de Expostos (Enfans trouvés) made 13:241 $ 000 expended 500 $ 000, and had a surplus of 12:741 $ 000. The hospital entrances were 224; the deaths, 51; the cured, 124; and the number under treatment, 49. Of the "exposed" during the same period five out of the ten died.

a decent House of God. Near it is a magnificent Cambucaia tree, resembling a Eugenia myrtle four times magnified. Hereabouts also are two noble lofty Sapucaias (Quatele or Lecythis Ollaria), vestiges of the forest primæval, which once adorned the land. The aborigines used to extract from it a " cauim "* or wine; the leaf reminded me of the two huge Mangos in H.M.'s Consulate Fernando Po. The heavy pot-like fruit, evidently the model of the Indian or indigenous pottery, and so celebrated as a monkey trap, and so loved by the Macaw, renders it as dangerous to sleep under as an African Calabash, a Hindostani " Jack," or a Borneo Doriyan. The mighty arms bear the neat little mud-huts of the Furnarius, here known as João de Barros (John Clay, Merops rufus or Turdus Figulus). The tenements are shaped in miniature like the items of a Kafi Kraal, and the single small entrance is not faced in any particular direction; neighbours often turn their backs to each other, civilized as Londoners or Parisians. This reddish yellow merle often amuses travellers. I have felt in society when seeing them hopping on the road before me, evidently to attract attention, and chattering amazingly, with the apparent hope of a reply. In this case we certainly need not ask J. J. Rousseau† if birds confabulate or no.

As we are about to inspect the show-Church of São João, if not of Minas Geraes, a short sketch of ecclesiastical architecture in this part of the Brazil may be advisable. In former times the first thought of the successful gold miner or speculator was to build and to endow a temple; hence the inordinate number of fanes in the older cities, and the exceeding rareness of a modern building. But though masons were easily procurable, architects were not; consequently the churches speak well for the piety and intelligence of the ancient Mineiro, but badly of his " instruc-

---

* The T. D. explains Cauím by Vinho, and Cauim tatá, literally " fire-water," by agua ardente. The word is generally derived from Caju (the Cashew tree, Anacardium occidentale) and yg water : that fruit supplied the favourite fermentation. " Cauim," like " Koumis," is so differently written by travellers that it can hardly be recognized; for instance, Caoni, Caouy, Caowy, Kaawy, etc. It is a generic term, and applied to some thirty-two different preparations of manioc, plan-

tains, maize, pine-apple, sweet-potato, and sugar-cane, cultivated or wild. Prince Max. (i. 115) compares the chewed form with the Ava or Kava described by Cook in Oceanica.

† The last view of this celebrated character, the " eleuthero-maniac," is taken by Sr. Castilho (Excav. Poet.)—
" João Jacques (certo animal
Que trata de educação)."
" John James, a certain animal who of man's education treats."

tion." The style mostly introduced by the Jesuits is heavy and couthless; it tries to combine the vertical lines of the Gothic with the horizontal length of classical architecture, and it notably fails. The traveller must not expect to find the pillared aisles, the clerestories, the Lady Chapels, the Strypes, or the Chapter Houses of the Eastern Hemisphere. When the building is sub-cruciform, the arms of the transept are concealed by sacristies, corridors, and other conveniences which occupy the space between the double walls. Few also are carved and coffered ceilings; a plain curtain covering the throne takes the place of altar veils, frontals and super-frontals; there are no desk or pulpit hangings, no book covers or elaborate markers—in fact, ecclesiastical frippery shines by its absence.

Nothing like the Pantheon or the Cathedral of Rouen has yet been attempted here. The Church Brazilic is the humblest form of that Palatial Hall of Justice and Sacred Temple which Brazilian enthusiasts derive from the Tabernacle in the wilderness. The integrity of the Palace, however, has been split up into nave and chancel. This plan may be grandiose enough when its dimensions are those of the old cathedral at Bahia. But generally the first effect upon the stranger is that he stands in a large barn, and the effect is very humble when it lacks the physical element of grandeur—greatness.

On the other hand, the Church in the Brazil has the advantage of not requiring any frontage-rhumb; from this region Jerusalem lies north, south-east, or west. It is almost always built on the highest and prettiest site, and there is a fine open space in front for which St. Paul's and Westminster must sigh in vain. The dangerous encroaching system of older cities is unknown, the acid-laden staining atmosphere of our towns is absent, and where not a chimney can be found, the "gathered gloom" of "smuts" is not to be dreaded. The sombre sadness of an iron-railed London square, with its "prison-look," is of course wanting. Finally, the rapid growth of trees, and the admirable supply of water, form natural and artistic ornaments always at hand.

The Church of the Third Order of São Francisco, our old Grey Friars, opposed to the Black Friars or Dominicans, belongs to a brotherhood numbering upwards of 5000 members, mostly males. Like their brethren of the Carmo, they are independent of parochial jurisdiction; and their accounts are forwarded for inspection to their head-quarters at Rio de Janeiro. The temple is built on the highest part of its square, the approach has a fair flight of stone steps leading to the paved "Adro" or platform. There is a two-beaked fountain fed by the southern hills, and symmetry demands a corresponding feature on the other side. The Cemetery of the Brotherhood lurks behind the church, and the modest Hospicio dos Irmãos da Terra Santa—Hospice of the Brothers of the Holy Land—acts as a foil to the pile.

It has been said that the architect of the São Francisco used no rule but a compass; there is not a straight line save the vertical; the chosen form is oval, the division is into bays, and even the tiled roofs are curved. The dimensions are 240 by 64 palms, and masonry is so solid that the walls contain the flights of pulpit steps, which are some three palms broad. An inscription over the main entrance gives the date of birth 1774. Local tradition declares that it was built over a humble chapel which was allowed to remain, like the old woman's hut under the Palace roof of Anushirwan the Just. What an easy way to win fame! The façade is two-windowed, the pediment is crowned with the two-armed Grecian or Sepulchran Cross, and the tympanum bears Jesus Crucified, St. Francis receiving the Stigmata, and sundry accompaniments. Over the main entrance are the instruments of the Passion, and the "arms," literally and metaphorically, of the "Orago," or Patron Saint; the pyramid is capped by a Nª Sª da Conceiçao in stone clouds amongst fat-faced cherubs, who display upon a substantial roll,—

> Tota pulchra es Maria, et
> Macula originalis non est in Te.

This shows how early the Iberian dogma, erst so popular in Catholic England, had been recognised by the Brazil, and how readily the "progressive doctrine" of the co-redemptoress will be accepted.

The material is excellent, a fine steatite, blueish, and at times of an apple green, which, when the usual bits of octohedral iron are rare, takes a high polish. The sculpture suggests woodwork, with very laborious alt-reliefs; it is the handicraft—Hibernicè—of a handless man, whose labours we shall find scattered throughout this part of the Province. He is generally known as the

Aleijado or Aleijadinho *—the Cripple or the Little Cripple ; some call him O Ignacinho, little Ignatius, others Antonio Francisco. His work was done with tools adjusted by an assistant to the stumps which represented arms, and his is not the only case on record of surprising activity in the trunk of a man, or of a woman. Witness the late Miss Biffin.

The " clocheria," is 150 palms high, and of a shape peculiar to and very common in Minas Geraes—parallelograms made quasi cylindrical by pilasters fitting close to the angles ; the capitals are quaint, partly Corinthian, partly composite. exceedingly. This may be called the "round-square" tower style, and it has nothing but the originality of eccentricity to recommend it. Young peoples, like young people, should learn that genius begins by imitating, and ends by creating ; when the latter process precociously precedes the former, the results are apt to be taste-less, ungraceful, grotesque. The capital defects of the belfries are their domes, mere ovens, apparently copied from the white ant's nest or the hut of " John Clay." Both should be pulled down and replaced by something harmonising with the body of the church. They are easily ascended, an iron railing makes them safe, and the peal of four bells is better than usual.

Passing round the polished " Tapa-vento " of neat workman-ship, the gift of the good Mrs. Lee, we sight a hall of which Sr. Rodrigues says, "nada deixa á desejar." † Let me softly whisper, coloured glass and finished panels to begin with. The blues and whites look cold and raw, even in this glorious sunshine, and the beautiful cabinet woods of the Brazil are washed and painted to resemble marble run mad. The balustrade of the upper gallery, whence candelabra are hung, is tinted red. And from the centre hangs a huge lustre with some thirty-six lights, much more fitted for theatre than for fane.

The choir, as usual in the Brazil, overhangs the entrance. It is supported by a low, dark splayed arch of such a span, and so shallow a sag, that it merits the title of Manoelesque, as seen in glorious Lisbonian Belem. Syenite enables it to stand despite all the thrust, and the designer's initials deserve a place upon it.

---

* O Aleijadinho was, I believe, the nickname of a painter, José Gonçalves, who lived at Rio de Janeiro (Pequeno Pano-rama da Cidade do Rio de Janeiro, por Moreira de Azevedo. Rio : Paula Brito,

1861. Vol. i. p. 77). There is a life of this worthy, but I have never been able to procure it.

† It leaves nothing to be desired.

There are the normal six-side altars.* Of the Sanctuary (Capella Môr) we may remark that chancel and nave have different ceilings. The curved steps and the pavement are of polished stone. The throne and its lateral niches display twisted and festooned columns of white and gold, much cut and carved with painted cherubs of unpleasantly "jolly" expression.† The Retable is the Santissima Trindade in life-sized figures. The Creator is distinguished from the Preserver by a red cloak and a gold triangle for a crown, a Dove in red and white hovering between them. Underneath is a large figure of Nª Sª da Conceição supported by Santa Rosa de Viterbo, and Santa Isabel Rainha de Portugal. " Tudo," says the guide-book, "infunde respeito." ‡ What would my old tutor Mirza Mohammed Ali, the Shirazi, have said to all this ?

The Brazilians have to a considerable extent inherited the art of wooden statuary, in which Ebro-land has excelled the world. Here the chef-d'œuvre is São Pedro de Alcantara, torn dress and all, cut out of a single block. The most worshipful is the Senhor Bom Jesus do Monte Alverne, of which the following tale is told. The Order being simultaneously in want of a statue and of funds, issued tenders; an unknown Person offered himself, and required for earnest-money only the material and the implements of his craft, rating his labours at a fair round sum. In due time he presented his work to the Sodality and disappeared. Sensible men suppose that it was some sinner who took this curious path of penance for the health of his soul. We waited to see the image, but of the Sacristan the only obtainable tidings were " 'Sta na rúa," §—a general

---

* The altars on the right are,—
No. 1. S. Luiz de França, S. Boaventura (St. Good Luck), Santo
Antonio and the Menino Deus.
,, 2. S. Pedro de Alcantara, Santa
Quiteria and S. Bento (not to
be confounded with S. Bene-
dito).
,, 3. Jesus crucified kissing S. Francisco de Assis (the patron of
the missioners who built Californian San Francisco), supported by S. Francisco de
Paulo and a Pope. In the
base of the altar S. Francisco
de Assis, dead.
On the left the altars are,—

No. 1. S. Francisco do Assis, S. João
Nepomuceno and the Holy
Family.
,, 2. S. Lucio, Santa Bona (who was
married), S. Domingo, and S.
João Evangelista.
,, 3. Santa Margarita do Cortona, S.
Roque, S. João and Nepomuceno.
The system of six side altars appears to
be general throughout Minas, where some
churches aro crowded to accommodate
them.
† " Serafins de semblantes risonhos."
‡ " All inspires respect."
§ "He is at present in the street," i.c.,
not at home—unconventionally.

reply to enquiries touching whereabouts in a Brazilian country town.

Further south, and commanding a noble view, is the poor chapel of Sr. Bom Jesus do Bomfim. It is fronted by four palms, and the knobby hill is thinly grown with wild grass * and the smaller Grama,† both yellow with hunger and thirst. By this way, on June 17, 1842, the revolutionists marched in from Elvas and had the city at their mercy. A month afterwards the Provincial deputies met here and solemnly approved of the movement. The acting President made the common fatal error of leaving 500 men under Alvarenga, one of his best officers, to do garrison duty instead of taking the field. Finally, here, on September 7, the Sociedade Ypirunga meets to celebrate Independence Day.

Descending the hill we enter the Post Office, a gauge of civilization in the Brazil. We find one room, and three clerks who never heard of "postal delivery." ‡ This is a poor allowance in a city which has, like old Ilchester, a dozen churches, which burns 4800lbs. of wax per annum, and where there is a specialist tailor who makes Padres' clothes.

---

* Capim do Campo.
† Graminha.
‡ Until very few years past, travellers in the United States made the same com- plaint. The Twopenny Post in England dates only from 1683, when David Murray of Paternoster Row projected it.

CHAPTER XII.

THE NORTH OF SÃO JOÃO D'EL-REI.

"Não ha uma pedra posta pela mão do homem no centro de suas Cidades, que não exprima uma idéa, que não represente uma letra do alphabeto da civilisação."
Sr. Manoel de Araujo Porto Alegre.

WE completed the circle of the northern town by visiting our compatriots in the Rua da Prata, the local Belgravia, and the best street in the city. They loaded us with small presents, the Balanus tintinnabulum, and specimens of gold from the old pit, magnetic iron, and water-rolled jasper, the true diamond formation of Bagagem.[*] We carried off a valuable prescription, which I have called Dr. Lee's pills,—a single seed of the Ricinus communis taken every third hour, the third being generally the colophon. He deserves a medal from the Humane Society for making so easy what is to some almost impossible. We were shown the "Azeitona da Africa—African olive tree—a shrub fifteen feet high, with a tea-like flower and dome-shaped foliage. It produces at all seasons round capsules containing some five three-sided almonds, about the size of a quarter hazel nut : proportionally they are more oleaceous than the Palma Christi.[†] A quarter of a bushel gives five bottles of clear odourless oil, fit for culinary purposes.

We also saw the Brazilian copal, of which there are large deposits in Minas and São Paulo ; these came from near Oliveira, sixteen leagues to the north-west. This "Brêo," or pitch as it is vulgarly called, is the produce of extinct forests, composed of various Hymeneæ, and semi-mineralized by heat and pressure. Like that of East Africa, it shows the "goose-skin," or imprint of sand ; it often contains flies, and bits of bark ; it is

---

[*] Dr. Couto named the place Nova Lorena in honour of his patron, but this was not endorsed by the people.

[†] I saw only one shrub in the garden of D. Maria Benedicta, and did not recognize it as an African growth.

affected by spirits of wine, and it almost dissolves in æther and chloroform. This most durable of varnishes was exported to Europe early in the present century, before the African coasts, east and west, supplied an article preferred by the trade. It will again appear in our markets when the labour-market in the Brazil shall become moderate. The aborigines used to make from the live-green, or raw copal—the " chakazi " of Zanzibar—" labrets," or lip ornaments of the brightest amber colour; they were subconical cylinders, a foot long and of finger thickness, a hollow tube of bamboo thrust into the tree serving for a mould. They were fixed by a diminutive crutch to the lower lip, and they hung down like pump handles to the wearer's breast.

We were also shown specimens of indigenous Vanilla, prepared by our hosts. The pods are strung upon a line, hung to dry in the sun and air every day, but not till too dry; twice, with an interval, the oil of the " Azeitona da Africa " is applied by means of a feather. Some split them and insert sugar or salt. This valuable growth has long been known in the Brazil; a colonial law of 1740 forbids it to be cut. The author of the poem " Caramurú," first printed in 1781, sings of it (Canto 7. st. 47)—

A baunilha nos sipós desponta,
Que tem no chocolate a parte sua :
Nasce em bainhas, como páos de lacre,
De um suco oleoso, grato o cheiro e acre.*

But whilst the Spaniards exploited Vaynilla (Epidendron Vanilla), even in their age of gold and silver, the Portuguese, especially the Paulistas and Mineiros, systematically neglected it, and our popular books ignore it. Yet the plant grows wild in the greater part of the intertropical Brazil, and in places perfumes the air. It seems, therefore, to be reproduced without art.† The pods given to us at São João were large, fleshy, and very dark; they preserved their characteristic fragrance for months.

We resumed our way over the Ponte do Rosario to visit the Southern city. To our left are the ruins of " São Caetano," a church which fell in or about 1864, and which has not been

---

* "In lliana-shape hangs the vanilla, which takes her place in chocolate. She is borne in sheaths, like sticks of sealing wax, with an oily juice and a grateful pungent smell."

† Prof. Morren of Liège proved that the reproductive organs of the Vanilla planifolia have peculiarities which require artificial fecundation; in Mexico this process is effected by an insect.

restored. A hopeful sign! That old saw, the nearer the kirk the
farther from grace, is of general significance, and throughout
the Brazil, the Age of Faith must be followed by the Age of
Work; moreover, roads will build churches, but churches will not
make roads. The peculiarity of that temple was a chancel—
o altar mór—much larger than the nave. A certain Guardamór, or local Commandant, commanded the architect to make it
so, and silenced the objectors of "irregularity" with " Tudo
quanto é mór, e maïor."* The same church bore the insolent
inscription, " O Rey depende de nós, e não nós delle,"—" The king
depends upon us, not we upon him." My authority remarks
hereupon, so prodigal of fidalguia or gentility were these men
who, mostly arrant roturiers in the Old World, purchased titles
and "founded families " in the New.

We proceeded up the Rua da Prata—with difficulty. There
is sometimes a raised sideway in the flagged streets, but both
street and way are equally atrocious. The black kidney-shaped
cobble-stones† are as slippery as they are hard, and the new
comer's gait suggests that of one practising hop-scotch. The
effects upon the hallux and the digit minim of the São Joã-
nensis must be sensible—and might not all or much of the evil be
remedied by a few cart-loads of gravel, or well bruised macadam?
Of course not a wheeled vehicle is to be seen; " carriage people "
must content themselves with an old-fashioned sedan chair, or
a " bangué,"‡ an overgrown palanquin carried by two mules. En
revanche the city is well supplied with water, and if money were
expended every square and street could have its fountain. At
present there are three large Chafarizes, and springs whose waters
men prefer, are still scattered about the neighbourhood. Some,
we were told, have disappeared, and the rains, which as usual in
these Highlands of the Brazil, formerly began in August, now
defer their break till the end of November—the cause is probably
disforesting.

We find ourselves thoroughly well morgués by the juvenile
population ; stared at with ten-Cornish power; we have our por-

---

* " Whatever is greater must be bigger."
It contains an untranslatable jeu de mots.
The same idea, expressed by *grand* and *gros*,
passed between Napoleon the Great and his
librarian, when the latter objected the
bigness of a volume.

† Pedras de ferro.

‡ The word is the Hindostani "Banghi."
The article is the Takht-rawan of the
Meccan pilgrimage, of humbler form and
without camels. I have published a sketch
of the camel litter in my "Pilgrimage to El
Medinah and Mecca" (vol. i. 305).

traits taken mentally, as if each pair of eyes belonged to a turn-key. At Barbacena the youth prospected us open-mouthed; here they furthermore protrude the tongue, not wantonly, how-ever, but in mere wonder. The citizens are described as high-spirited, intelligent, fond of study, and anxious for information; the curiosity of the juniors promises well,—without curiosity there is no enquiry. We remarked sundry scattered Ermidas, or small oratories. On the other hand there is no fixed market, and the Quitanda,* or res mercatoria, is exposed in the usual "Quatro Cantos," or place where four streets meet. The tailors' favourite place is on the sweet shady side of the way. This we understand when told that for the last four years the minimum of temper-ature has been 42° (F.) and the maximum 88° (F.) Many houses were to let, and there were signs of depreciated property at São João, since the end of its second and last aurea ætas. A "palacete" built for 5000l., at a time too when labour averaged less than half its present price, now sells for 750l. But here as elsewhere, there are three distinct estimates; viz., that of the buyer (−), that of the seller (+), and that of the appraiser (± or =).

Sighting the Nª Sª do Rosario, we did not require to be told that it is the especial worship-place of the "Homo niger." It shows tawdry coarseness in colour and form; there are no cam-paniles, the last belfry having been pulled down to prevent its coming down; a silver lamp, weighing 900 ounces, lately stolen, and probably by one of the brotherhood, has left the order poor. The Hamites have a better cemetery than church; over the door-way of the well chosen situation is a skull, not dolichocephalic as it should be, based upon the distich,

> Eu fui o que tu es,
> Tu serás o que eu sou. †

to which we anthropologically demur.

At the wall base of the Rosario we were shown a "Deusa Astréa," or figure of Justice, in stone, half decapitated, and

---

* In the Bunda tongue Kwitanda, by the Portuguese written Quitánda, is the market-place; and Standa is explained as venda, venditio, also Feira, or emporium; thus, "to the sale" would be somewhat like the "Eis tén polin," which became Stamboul. in the Brazil, Quitanda, is not the site of sale, but invariably the thing sold (mon marché, as the French cook says) and "Quitandeira" is the woman who sells it.

† "I was what thou art: thou shalt be what I am." São João has not yet estab-lished a branch of the Anthropological Society of London.

lying upon the ground; this elicited some small wit. Presently we reached the Igreja Matriz, whose patroness is N^a S^a do Pilar, and which unites the brotherhoods " dos Passos (the Passion), do Sacramento, da Boã Morte, de São Miguel, das Almas (the Souls, *i. e.* in Purgatory), and de Santa Cecilia." I will spare description of it after São Francisco. The building dates from 1711, except the modern façade, the work of Sr. Candido José da Silva.   There are six side chapels and one upstairs for the sacrament.   The high altar is, like the two pulpits, of old wood thickly gilt, and its ceiling is gilt, painted and panelled, whilst that of the nave is the simplest tunnel or half barrel; and, curious to say, the temple is finished. As the Provincial Government votes small annual sums to the " Matrizes," the latter generally want a last touch.

We rested in the house of the Latin Professor at the Lyceum, Dr. Aureliano Pereira Corrêa Pimental.   That high literary tastes are not extinct in São João, may be proved by the fact, that this gentleman is teaching himself Hebrew and Sanskrit. He kindly gave me the satires, epigrams, and other poems of Padre José Joaquim Corrêa de Almeida,* and he recommended to me for translation the Assumpção of Frei Francisco de São Carlos.†   Some noble traits are recorded of the Professor.   I will spare his modesty the pain of seeing them in print; but there are few men with more family than substance, who will unasked reduce the interest upon an inheritance from fifty per cent. to five.

The end of our long peregrination was to the church of N^a S^a de Carmo, administered by the Third Order of that invocation; its principal benefactors were the Barão de Itambé and the late João da Silva Pereira Gomes.   The façade ornaments of cut steatite, with fanciful initials and cherubs worked by *the* Cripple, the round-square towers with composite pilasters, and the internal consoles and columns were those of São Francisco. Its interior was being refitted with cedar wood, cut by a self-taught man, Sr. Joaquim Francisco de Assis Pereira; it will

---

* Rio de Janeiro, Laemmert, 1863.

† A Assumpção da Santissima Virgem, now a Brazilian classic, published Rio de Janeiro, 1819. The author was born in the Franciscan Convent of the Immaculate Conception, August 13, 1763, and there died, or rather exhausted himself by mortifications, on May 6, 1829.   It was his object to mix, with praises of the virgin, descriptions of his "beautiful country" (*nosso bello paiz*), and he has certainly succeeded.

assuredly, despite all our deprecations, be whitewashed and gilt. Pity that routine forbids it to be left au naturel; the theatre should be as brilliant as possible, but the dim religious light far better becomes the delubra deorum.

The Terceiros (Third Order) of the Carmo, have housed their dead better than their living, in above-ground catacombs some eighty feet west of the church. The square cemetery measuring 400 palms in circumference, with walls 28 palms high, has good grated doors,* with the initials of the Portuguese artist, J. J. F. (Jesuino José Ferreira). A small mortuary chapel fronts the entrance, the interior has cloisters like the Campo Santo of Pisa in miniature, and in the thickness of the walls are tiers of catacombs, family vaults apparently often wanted.

We had worked like horses through the livelong day, and we were only too glad to house ourselves. Professor Pimental dined with us, our fellow-countrymen were also there, and the result was a highly satisfactory symposium with a musical clooping of corks. Rare indeed are they—these noctes cœnæque deûm. We separated as the small hours chimed, promising to breakfast at Matosinhos on the morrow.†

Before leaving São João I ascended its Serra of notable memory, under the guidance of a Rio-Grandense, the Capitão Christão José Ferreira. There is a fine bird's-eye view of the city at the top of the step-flight, some 150 feet long, leading to the Capella dos Mercenarios, whose confraternity, black and indigenous, is entitled Nª Sª das Merces. From this place on the rough slope we could see the General Cemetery crowning the hill on our right, the old Matriz below, with the northern city clustering around it, and bottoming all the rivulet that

picciol fiumicello
Lo cui rossore ancor? mi raccapriccia,

---

* "Ramagem," our "ramage"—branchery.

† Future travellers, who have more leisure than we had are advised to visit the fall or rapids of the Carandahy river, and the "São Thomé das Litras," eighteen leagues to the south-west, and nine leagues from Campanha. It is described as a little town, built upon the serra of the same name. The literary name comes from a rock within sight of the square, and inscribed with the letters S T (São Thomé). The educated at the spot declare that this and other curious shapes, especially an ounce perfectly outlined, are produced by decaying roots and vegetation. The material, however, is laminated sandstone, elastic or non-elastic (Itacolumite), and the infiltration of oxide of iron produces between the slabs these dendrites. I have seen them in railway cuttings near São Paulo.

whilst on the mound opposite, the show-church, São Francisco, pride of the southern quarter, completed the prospect.

Thence, ascending a jagged hill, where building stone was being blasted, we sighted the ancient gold "diggins." This was the true El Dorado of El Dorado, the focus of the auriferous foci, all gashed and pierced for gold, with pits, fodinas, and quarries, now filled with sand, and broken down by weather into ravines which drain the Serra at right angles. The birth-place of the ore was the upper rock-ridge; thence it was weathered into the lower levels. There was also a formation called Jacutinga, of which more hereafter; suffice here to say, that it is 75—84 per cent. of micaceous iron, based probably upon specular or oligiste, with free gold in lines and potholes. To our left lay the Nª Sª do Monte, a hideous chapel, like the colonial fanes of modern Spanish colonies, double windowed (two red shutters being the windows), single doored, and suggesting a noseless face. Near the Igreja do Carmo we found no traces of the large muddy pool, or waterpit. At the quarry bottom there, says Mr. Walsh, the citizens used wistfully to peer for drowned and buried treasures, and we asked in vain for Dr. Such his tank. After inspecting the waterworks we returned "home," viâ the Rua da Allegria, "of gladness," which till lately bore, said our guide, the "less honest" name of Rua da Cachaça, or Rum Street. Thus, chez nous, Grass Church Street became Grace Church Street.

We are about to visit the "St. John Del Rey Mining Company (Limited)," which here began its operations; and these we may prospect in situ. Its birth date was April 5, 1830, and on May 4 it sent from Liverpool to Rio de Janeiro nineteen men, under their commissioner, the late Mr. Chas. Herring, Jun. The contract* gave permission to work the mineral grounds immediately north of the city. The deposits were found in a great lode parallel to a valley 1320 yards long by 150 broad, and in small veins perpendicularly offsetting from it. The native workings had consisted of an open trenching,† and their miners had opened at Dr. Such's tank an irregular quarry 110 feet deep. Their pumping gear of bucketed wheels, each worked by eight

* As security for the gold duty being paid, the licence required a deposit fund of 50 contos of reis in Brazilian apolices or Government bonds, to be used by the Imperial treasury without paying interest. These were sold in 1834 for £3,713 13s. 11d.

† Talho abero.

or ten men, had failed, and the pit was soon filled up with mud and water to within thirty feet of the edge.

In August, 1830, an open-cut, adit-level, faced on both flanks with stone work, was begun from the rivulet side to the east. It proved the main lode, whilst its course cut the cross-veins below the depth reached by former miners. Moreover, it drained the surface water deposited during the rains. In those days the dry season above ground began in April, underground in July, and this gave but four clear months. The "shaft of St. John" was sunk about the same time in favourable ore ground, west of the tank. On the east was commenced a second shaft for sump or drainage. Both served for ventilation, and were provided with "whims" or "gins,"* for pumping and drawing stuff. Dams were erected to secure washing during the dries, and dwellings, store-houses, offices, and other "surface-works," were put up. The superintendent and mine agent obtained rights to water courses, and then commenced the normal operations of blasting, pulverizing, and fanning in the Batêa,† followed by the more scientific process of smelting and amalgamating the pyritiferous matter, which was sent to London for assay.

The total salaries for the first year amounted to £2,310. The works, however, did not pay; and in 1835, after incurring a loss of £26,287 18s. 4d., Mr. Herring transferred himself to Morro Velho. Thus ended, at São João, the aurea ætas No. 2, and since that time the "mother of gold"‡ has reigned with little molestation. Up to late years a small quantity of the precious metal, about £2,000 per annum, has been exported by the municipality.

The industry of the city is at a low ebb. São João has a banker, the Capitão Custodio de Almeida. Cotton and woollen

---

* The drums round which are wound the ropes which draw up the ore. The "gin race" is the level "horse round" where the animals work.

† This Batêa corresponds in gold working with the Calabash of Guinea and the pan of California and Australia. In the Brazil it is of various shapes, sizes, and kinds of wood; usually it is a circular platter of cedar, 1½ feet in diameter, concave, with a dip of 3-5 inches, and forming in the centre of the flattish cone a little hollow (pião da batêa "the angle of the pan"), into which the diamonds or the gold dust settle. It is worked with the usual rotatory motion that requires some practice, and the water and lighter dirt are removed by tilting over and with the fingers. The washer sometimes adds raw rum or aloe juice, or an infusion of the plants called Capoeîra and Itámbâmba, which, sprinkled over the contents of the pan, is supposed to clear them mechanically, as cold water or the contents of an egg clarifies coffee.

‡ Mãi de Ouro, a Brazilian pixy, who guards the virgin treasure. She is rather whimsical than malevolent; but at times she does a little murder. So the Indians of the Manitoulin Islands believe that the Manitou has forbidden his children to seek for gold.

cloths, plain and striped, are made by the hand. They are stained with indigo urucú (the well-known Bixa orellana), and other dyes in which the country abounds. These stuffs are strong, and out-last many lengths of machinery-woven stuffs; but they are expensive, and the supply hardly suffices for home use. Tea was grown, and the Padre Francisco de Paula Machado's preparation, from his chacara on the Barro road to Oliveira, is largely bought at São João, and is appreciated at Rio de Janeiro.

Cereals thrive, and tubers everywhere abound. Hard woods* are of various kinds, but they are now produced in small quantities. The high lying and healthy campos grounds make stock breeding the favourite industry; black cattle are tolerably good, the horses and mules want fresh blood, and the same may be said of the hogs that supply the prized "lombo" and "toucinho." Cheese is also exported. There are large tracts of bottom land admirably fitted for growing cotton, which might be made a source of wealth. A little "tree-wool," cleaned and uncleaned, together with hides and leather, is exported to pay for salt, the principal import.† Of this indispensable article, some 100,000 alqueires are annually introduced for sale and consumption, and it is brought up by mule troops belonging to the planters and traders.

Sugar-cane supplies spirits and vinegar, with a small surplus for trade. In 1859, the municipality contained 48 Engenhos, or boiling establishments, 30 worked by water and 18 by bullocks. In the same year the city numbered 64 stores for goods, native and foreign, 1 inn (hospedaria), several taverns (locandas), and 4 druggist's shops (boticas), "Carne seca" (charqui) and pork are as usual much consumed, and four bullocks are slaughtered daily.

Early in the last century, São João was haunted by a Familiar of the Holy Office, appointed by the Inquisitor General, Cardinal Nuno da Cunha. A certain Padre Pontes, it is related,

---

* Here called "wood of the law" (Madeira da Lei), because in colonial days it might not be felled without permission. The Portuguese Madeira is the Latin "Materia" used by Cæsar and others.

† The exports in 1859 were :—

Industry	.	.	.	1,292:000$000
Commerce	.	.	.	2,216:800$000
Total	.	.	3,508:800$000

The imports in 1859 were :—
Salt, iron, pottery, wet and dry goods,

| Total | . | . | 2,305:900$000 |

Thus showing in favour of produce a total of 1,202:900$000 (=£120,000 per annum, assuming the milreis = 1 florin).

found himself in the Holy Tribunal's grip. Wishing to change his condition, he had forwarded the following questions to the Vigario da Vara, the Vicar with juridical powers.

"Pedro the Priest wishes to intermarry with Maria, having a dispensation from his Holiness to that effect. Query, can Pedro the Priest so do?"

The Vicar, an intelligent man, replied:—

"To me it is a virgin case, but if Pedro have the dispensation, Pedro can so do."

And Pedro, presenting a forged dispensation, went and did it: he was married with all the honours by the Padre Sebastião José da Freiria, the Padre Francisco Justiniano assisting as witness. The affair was presently bruited abroad, the deceit was discovered, the Inquisition was an edged tool in those days, and the hot amourist was consigned to confinement with ugly prospects. Escaping, he became "Doctor Vieira," and travelled to Rome, where, the matter being taken in jest, he was pardoned. The actors suffered more than the author of the farce, both were placed in the hands of the Holy Office; or, in plain English, thrown into the dungeons, now happily turned into stage and green-room. Padre Sebastião returned home, after justifying his innocence. Padre Justiniano remained with the Holy Office: and it is still doubtful whether he was "relaxed" (relaxado), that is to say, strangled and roasted, or he died in the course of nature, a captive and an exile.

CHAPTER XIII.

TO AND AT SÃO JOSÉ D'EL-REI.

"Capitania tão largamente prendada da natureza, em mil recursos uteis ao
Estado e aos particulares, e tão cahida até ao presente em desemparo e descuido."
Dr. Couto.

IT was Saturday—begging day by ancient usage in the Brazil.
We were strangers, and therefore fair game. The Praia was
beset by cripples of every kind, and some wore the weekly " property dress "—I had never yet seen so much mendicancy in so
small a place. Was with me a person who still believes in the
Knightly and middle-aged legends about alms, and even a share
of bed unwittingly given to individuals of exalted rank in the
Spiritual Kingdom : one of these wretches might be St. Joseph,
or something higher. All, therefore, received coppers, and the
results were a glorious gathering of Clan Ragged, the expenditure of small change, the *not* seeing St. Joseph, and the
frequent seeing " Saint Impudence."

Mr. Copsy took advantage of his midsummer vacation, and
joined our party. It is no light matter to take leave of a
Brazilian wife, especially when young and pretty : these ladies
determinedly ignore innocent gipsying, and carefully scrutinize
the gait of the returning mate as he " turns in." He was not,
therefore, sans soucis, till he had " crossed the first Córrego," *

---

* "Córrego" (with the acute accent,
which raises the voice-tone) is pronounced
by the people " Córgo," and sometimes so
written in poetry and by the unlearned.
The English turn it to " Corg," upon the
same principle that mato becomes " mat,"
restilo, "restil," dono, "don," pardo,
"pard," and doce, "dose." Their ears do
not distinguish the semi-elision of the
final vowel. And here we may see the
wonderful richness and the exceptional
variety of the Luso-Latin tongue, which
almost ignores general words and whose
specific terminology tax so heavily the
stranger's memory. The Córrego is a rill,
not to be confounded with the Sangradouro
(and the smaller feature Bebedor or Bebe-
douro), the natural drain of a lake or high
ground, nor with the arroio or arroyo (Arab.
الرويه) a fiumara, nullah, or intermittent
mountain stream. It is somewhat larger
than the Regato or rivulet, which again
must not be confused with Rego, a leat or
water-course. Next is the Ribeiro, a brook,
whose feminine form, Ribeira, classically

where, as demons and witches dislike running water, Atra Cura stayed behind.

Reaching Matosinhos, the Memorious suburb, we breakfasted with Dr. Lee and his very agreeable São-Joãnense wife, whose kind manner and hospitality, in the shortest possible time, won all our hearts. We wandered about the fine large garden, where the orange is the most banal of fruits, and we found the " Sneezer " * growing with Egyptian luxuriance, and a leaf-green rose with undeveloped petals, very fragrant was the Verbena (Verbena Virgata, Sellow), a powerful sudorific, used externally and internally as a cure for snake bites. As a parting present, Dr. Lee gave me a mastiff-pup, answering to the name of " Negra," lank in body, with brindled coat, square head, broad shoulders, and huge hands and feet. This is the breed called in Minas Cão de fila, and I have seen specimens which much reminded me of the thorough-bred English bull dog, not the toy animal which now goes by that name. " Negra " nearly reached the Rapids of the São Francisco River before I was compelled to part with her.

Bidding a regretful adieu to our excellent hosts, we struck up the Valley of the Rio das Mortes Grande. The stream was stained possibly by gold washing, and the Ponte de Sant Iago remained as described thirty years ago, a crazy frame-work of patched wood, with tiled roof and gravelled footway sixty yards long. The local authorities have lately bought it for 600l., and thus it runs every risk of ruin : these instruments of civilization should in the present age of the Brazil be farmed to contractors upon conditions of moderate tolls and regular repairs. The road was especially vile, and after rain it must be almost intransitable. I have already spoken of Brazilian lines of communication generally. In this Province the Imperial are rare : †

---

means a river bank, like Riba (or Ribanceira, a tall bank). In parts of the Brazil it is improperly applied to a large navigable river, e. g. the "Ribeira de Iguape." Follow the Riacho, a stream ; the Ribeirão, a large stream ; and the Rio or river, which latter is arbitrarily applied to minor features. Many Rio Grandes are mere "creeks." Each term has its incrementative and diminutive forms, the latter much affected in these lands. Sometimes both are united whimsically, but with a specific signification.

"Ribeirãosinho," for instance, means a big small stream. It is applied to a water of the class Ribeirão, but small for its Ribeirão-ship.

* Espirradeira, Nerium odorum, or Oleander. The word is sometimes applied to the sternutative Ortelão do mato (Peltodon radicans, one of the Labiadæ?) The people do not much admire the Oleander, and happily ignore its poisonous properties.

† I know only one, that of Philadelphia.

funds were voted for a highway to Goyaz, but the municipal chambers could not combine, and thus it has not emerged from the paper stage.

We passed many Chácaras now in ruins, and recalling the opulent days of São João. A classical site lies some two miles below the bridge, hugging the right bank of the river, and on the western road to the Alagŏa Dourada. The lone spot is now known as the Vargem (Meadow reach) de Marçal Casado Rotier, a French-Portuguese. It has been often pointed out as the future metropolis of the Brazil.

On the left rose the Serra do Córrego, a south-eastern spur of the São José Range; the jagged mass of lime and sandstone grit still conserves, they say, gold and rock crystal. At its base crouched "Córrego," a rugged hamlet of poor huts and rich fruit trees, and a little farther on the chapel of Nª Sª do Bom Despacho (of happy conclusion); it was a neat little place when gold was abundantly washed from the "Córrego," and it had a pompous annual festival; during the last fifteen years it has been in ruins. Beyond the northern hills are the Caldas or Thermæ de São José, best known as the Agoa Santa. According to Mr. Copsy, the springs have a temperature of 72° (F.), and are rich in carbonate of soda; he compared them with those of Buxton, 82° (F.), good for the rheumatics, and rich in muriate of magnesia and soda. Mineral waters are found in many parts of Minas, but hitherto "balenary establishments" have been greatly neglected, and patients have had to "rough it" without even lodging. Of late, however, energetic steps have been taken in this matter so important to the common weal.*

Presently we crossed the Morro da Candonga,† a lump lying

---

* In the Relatorio, or Annual Report of the President of Minas (Rio Typographia Esperança, 1867), we find (p. 68), that measures have been adopted to secure accommodation at the mineral waters of Caxambú, in the Municipality of Baependy, and at the "Aguas Virtuosas" of Campanha. The waters of Baependy are distributed into nine fountains already known. "They contain," says Sr. Julio Augusto Horta Barbosa, "free carbonic acid, carbonates, sulphates of alkaline base, traces of sulphate of iron and sulphuric acid, probably due to organic decomposition, and much esteemed in cutaneous diseases. The following is the analysis of the waters in the Serra do Picú.

Acid, Sulphuric	0·072
,, Carbonic	0·126
Chlorine . .	0·032
Silica . .	0·043
Lime . .	0·145
Magnesia. .	0·035
Soda . .	0·142
Organic, iron, alum, &c. }	0·035

Total . 0·630 in 1000 grammes, or 1 litre."

† The word means in Portuguese slang, deceit or trickery, hence a trickster is called Candongueiro, an intriguer. It has probably come from the coast of Africa.

south of the São José Range, and deeply pitted with huge ravines like craters of extinct volcanoes. From the summit we saw to the right of the road the calcareous formation known as the Casa de Pedra,* or more fancifully as Gruta de Calypso. Presently the Trindade church, and São José, the city, lay below our feet, singular and romantic. The basin is traversed by the Córrego de Santo Antonio, a tributary of the Rio das Mortes; though higher than São João,† it must accumulate heat in hot weather, cold in cold weather, damp in damp weather. Stretching from north-east to south-west rises the Serra de São José, which divides the valleys of the Rio das Mortes and the Carandahy; it forms, they say, a double line, a gigantic rut bisecting the centre. The perpendicular wall, 200 feet high, ultra-Cyclopean in architecture, and towering 500 feet above the basin, is a Jebel Mukattam, and not unlike the Palisades on the Hudson. Its crest bristles with curious projections, stiff points, pikes, needles, and organ pipes, while the débris fill the low lands with felspar and clay slate. It is the first of many which we shall presently see, their right lines intersecting the country divide it into vast compartments, and supply to it gold. The precious metal is still washed about Nᵃ Sᵃ da Conceição de Prados,‡ under the Ponto do Morro, to the north-east.

The pavement of the steep " Calçada " was even worse than that of São João; and we reached the house of Mr. Robert H. Milward, to whom our introductory letters had been sent forward, thoroughly prepared to dismount. But no such luck was in store; Mr. Milward was out of town, and Mrs. Milward was

---

* The usual term for a cave. Mr. Walsh (ii. 223), visited and described the feature. Mr. Copsy places it at six miles equidistant from São João, and São José and near the Rio Elvas. The site is an isolated, calcareous upheaval, some 300 feet raised above a mere brejo, or swamp, and about 440 yards long. The natural tunnel is the model of a subterraneous river bed. The ceiling has stalactitic jags, and saw-teeth, the sides are worked and turned by the water bath, and the bottom is clay, still preserving the bones of extinct animals. The party walls of thin calcaire, form the usual curios. The "pulpit" of Gothic style, and the "Church," lead to a dark passage, opening upon the "Gruta do Lustre," Grot of the Chandelier. Behind this are a limestone column and another chambered bulge: the latter

communicating with the open. I am tired of glancing at caverns, after the Mammoth and Adelsberg, and there was no pic-nic to justify the loss of a day.

† This is proved by our ascending nearly the whole way. M. Gerber does not give the altitude, which is popularly supposed to be 5300—5400 feet. We may reduce it to 2500 feet, a little below that of Barbacena.

‡ Prados, nine miles from São José, is likely to become important, as one of the stations on the future railway, viâ Alagôa Dourada to the head waters of the Rio de São Francisco. At present the speciality of the little town is saddlery, supplied by 20 workshops, employing 150 hands: the articles are sold wholesale for 20$000 each.

not visible to us, although we were thoroughly visible to her. We retraced our steps upwards through a sprinkling of "Jacubeiros,"* some of them "Gente de Casaca."† Their only occupation, when not making shoes, seemed to be playing "petéca," ‡ a kind of hand shuttlecock, in favour with both sexes. We did not expect to find "chicken-fixins" at the inn kept by the Capitão Severino, better known as "Joaquimsinho," and we were not disappointed. Happily for us, however, Saturday is beef day at São José.

Whilst the beef was being manipulated, we walked to the southern slope of the basin and inspected the Matriz dedicated to Santo Antonio. According to the chroniclers,§ it is the most beautiful and majestic in the province; it is finely situated, facing the mountains, the town, and the Riverine valleys and lowlands to the east. According to local tradition, it was built about 1710, by the Marçal Casado Rotier, and the sacraments were first administered in 1715. In those days of pristine piety the wealthy founder sent every Saturday night a gang of 200 slaves, each carrying a pan of auriferous earth; hence the puddle walls are mixed with gold as the pisé of the Dahoman palace is kneaded with rum or human blood—honoris causâ.

The style is the barocco or old Jesuit, and resembles the São Bento of Rio de Janeiro; it is, however, more primitive, tawdry, and grotesque. The nave is rectangular, with frescoes of very poor art, life-sized saints, Gregory and Ambrose, Augustine and Jerome, with the Annunciation, the Magi, and the crèche or crib of Bethlehem. The ceiling is a half hexagon, with panels

---

* Jacubeiros de São José, a highly invidious term, equivalent to country-bumpkin, applied by the neighbouring São-Joãnenses. Disputes about "urban precedency" here ran high as they ever did between Perth and Dundee. Jacúba is servile food, and Padre Corrêa sings of a bad lot. (Epistola, p. 24.)

"Nem agradece a jacuba
Que não comeria em Cuba!"

"Nor likes he the Jacuba
Which he would not eat in Cuba!"

It is also affected by mule drivers, and especially by the boatmen on the Rio de São Francisco. The simple "mets" is maize flour mixed with rapadura sugar and cold water. St. Hil. (III. i, 270,) omits the sugar.

† "Coat people," opposed to those who wear jackets or shirt sleeves. The garment is generally understood to be of broadcloth, invariably black.

‡ In Tupy, the word primarily signifies a "beating." It is explained in the Dict. by "volante" or "supapo," made of maize leaves. The phrase "fazer peteca de alguem" means to use another as a cat's-paw. The Botocudos had the football made of a stuffed sloth's skin. (Prince Max. ii. 274.)

§ Casal (vol. ii.) and Pizarro (vol. viii.) especially. Of course the dead were buried around and within it. The custom was not abolished in Rome and Naples till 1809.

and paintings not badly executed. There are six side chapels, the third left containing a large cross. Two pulpits attached to the side walls are poor and naked, with highly ornamental canopies, suggesting those "African gentlemen" whose sole costume to speak of is a tall blue chimney-pot hat. On the left is a curiously-shaped choir or organ loft, supported by queer caryatides and cornucopiæ, and copiously festooned and painted. The organ is tolerable, and indeed it is said to be the best in Minas; the organist kindly gave us a specimen of his art. Under the choir are two fancy figures weeping bitterly without a cause. Above it is a projecting branch for lights, a heraldic full-sized wooden eagle—somewhat like those which support our lecterns— whose beak supports a lamp chain; of these Jovian birds there is one before each altar.

The sanctuary is a mass of gilding and carving, and the ribbed roof shows a quadripartite vaulting. On the right-hand wall is the Marriage of Cana, to the left the Last Supper, large paintings, but not equal to the popular treatment of the subjects. The retablo under its canopy of gilt wood is Saint Anthony, performing the miracle of the animals. He holds up the monstrance. The people, doubtless "sceptics" and "shallow infidels," refuse to adore, but the once Typhonian donkey, new type of the zeal without knowledge, falls on its humble knees. It calls to mind the old hymn—

> Cognovit bos et asinus
> Quod puer erat Dominus.

Three steps lead up to the throne of the Santissima, a fine piece of wood and gilding, always, however, excepting the fat boys dressed in gold-wash, who put out the eye of taste. Above it is a figure of our Lord ascending to Heaven.

The Miracle room showed a votive offering, dated 1747, the men in periwigs and full skirted red coats, were wild brethren to

> Sir Plume, of amber snuff-box justly vain.

The sacristy contained the usual old fountain, decorated with an impossible head, a few insignificant pictures, and old prie-Dieu chairs of fine black-wood, with seats and tall backs of highly embossed leather. These articles are common in the

churches of Minas, some of the country clergy affect them, and I
have found them at times in laical houses. They are picturesque,
but who, in the name of comfort, sits off the dorsal angle? a
nursery stool would be preferable! This property room is rich
in thurifers, chalices, and other items of the ecclesiastical plate
service; it is said to contain 1280 lbs. of silver and silver gilt.
The most grotesque part is the Capella de Sete Passos, the
seven principal stations of our Lord's passion, beginning with
the garden and ending at the crucifixion. The figures were life-
size, of painted wood, and nothing can be more like a Buddhist
temple in those lands where Buddhist art does *not* excel.

We then strolled about the place, and inspected the minor
lions. The Casa da Camara, opposite the Matriz, is certainly
the best of the 300 houses. We counted, besides the parish
church, 1, São João Evangelista, 2, Rosario, 3, Santo Antonio
dos Pobres, 4, the chapel of São Francisco da Paula, and 5,
the Mercês, still under repair; a total of seven, and a tolerable
allowance for a population of 2500 souls.* Descending the
calçada, we crossed over the neat little stone bridge, and worked
round to the principal Chafariz. The entrance to its flagged
platform certainly dates before the days of crinoline; the front
shows three masks and two spouts, still surmounted by the arms
of Portugal. All is like the garden of black Hassan, but the
place would make an admirable bath.

Beyond this the red land is cut and hacked by the gold-washer.
"St. Joseph of the King" (D. João V.) was the wildest solitude
during the seventeenth century, when the Paulistas and Tau-
batéenses began to push their bandeiras or commandos into the
vast mysterious interior. Guided by the brave and energetic
adventurer, João de Serqueira Affonso, a party of explorers
seeking red-skins and "yellow clay," reached the margins of the
Rio das Mortes, and founded the usual "Arraial." Its golden
treasures attracted emigrants, and on January 19, 1718, about
two years before Minas Geraes was raised to an independent
captaincy, it became a villa and a municipality under the Governor D. Pedro de Almeida, Count of Assumar. In June 1842,
it acknowledged the insurgents, and in 1848 it was degraded to
a mere "povoação," a "one-horse" affair. But Resurgam was

---

* In 1828 it contained, we are told, 2000
souls. In 1864, the population of the
Municipality numbered 24,508 souls with
1209 voters and 35 electors.

its motto, and on October 7, 1860, it took upon itself the noble obligations of cityhood.

In April 1828 S. José became the head-quarters of the General Mining Association, that had secured three leagues of auriferous soil, and whose interests were looked after by Mr. Charles Duval.* In 1830 a tract of ground was also secured by the "St. John Del Rey." But water was found to be very abundant in the mine and very scanty on the surface; consequently, stamping and washing went on slowly. Two years afterwards the directors gave up the diggings in disgust, the "plant" was bought by Mr. Milward, and grass now grows abundantly in the streets.

The trade of São José, except in Jacuba and Petécas, is at a stand-still. Once it had five fabrics of native flax, seventy looms, (theares,) where 30,000 metres of country-grown cotton were woven, five potteries of good clay, and eight kilns, which produced per annum 3000 bushels of lime. In 1855 the municipal judge calculated the exports at 450 : 000 $ 000, and the imports at 250 : 000 $ 000.

Nature, in one of her usual freaky moods, produced at "São José of the Jacubeiros," no less a personage than José Basilio da Gama, ex-Jesuit noviciate, favourite of Pombal, member of the Arcadia Mineira, author of the celebrated epic, or rather metrical romance, "O Uraguay," and glory of his native land. As might be expected, however, under the circumstances, the place of his birth never recorded his natal date, which is supposed to be about 1740; the names of his parents have only just been discovered, and where there are seven churches, there is not a slab to honour the greatest of the Brazilian poets.

His "Exegi Monumentum" shall conclude this chapter.

> Uraguay! men shall read thee: though some day
> Brood o'er this vision dark, eternal night.
> Live thou and 'joy the light serene and clear!
> Go to Arcadia's groves, nor fear to be
> A stranger stepping on an unknown shore.
> There 'mid the sombre myrtles freshly reared,

---

* Mr. Charles Duval, who was married to a Polish lady, still remembered in the country, afterwards became Chief Commissioner of Gongo Soco, and died about 1857. Mr. Walsh (ii. 117—8) fully describes his system of treating the quartz and pyrites: having failed to see Mr. Milward who, in those days had charge of the operations, I can neither add to nor correct his information.

Not all Mirêu * the sad urn shall hold.
Raise from the foreign sky and o'er it strew
With peregrine hand the wreath of barbarous flow'rs ;
And seek thy follower to guide thy steps
Unto that place which long thy coming 'waits.

* His poetical, or pastoral name.

CHAPTER XIV.

TO THE ALAGÔA DOURADA OR GOLDEN LAKE.

"Aeris tanta est clementia ut nec nebula inficiens, nec spiritus hic pestilens, nec aura corrumperes ; medicorum opera parum indiget."—Gerald. Cambr., Chap. 9.

THE beds of São José were not downy. We agreed to rise at 1 A.M., and most of us spent the night talking over old times. Mules, however, will stray, and with the thermometer showing 36° F. negroes will feel torpid. Yet we effected a start at 4·50 A.M. The road at first traversed wooded lands ; at least, so we thought in the darkness of mid-winter. It was almost like riding up an endless wall of stone, slightly slanting, and sliding down on the other side. Presently it began winding through a gap in the grim Serra de São José ; bad it was to ascend, worse to descend, and the raw damp of early dawn was not favourable for the exercise of any faculties, perceptive or reflective.

At 8 A.M., desperately sleepy, chilly and comfortless, we reached the Rio Carandahy, which, draining the westward face of the meridional range north of Barbacena, falls into the Rio das Mortes Grande, and thus into the Rio Grande and the Paraná. The name is trivially explained by the cry on sighting a drowned man, "A cara anda ahi !"—here goes the face ! The term is probably Tupy, and Cara-andahy would mean the "hawk's hook," or curve. In the Brazil, as in "the East," there is an abundance of folk-lore philosophy, superstitious, fanciful, descriptive, and facetious. Thus, "araxá," town, so called because it is a "sun facer," "ara" being day, and "echa" that looks at, is popularly derived from "ha de se achar," he (or it) must be found, alluding either to a Quilombeiro* (maroon negro), or to the gold reported to be abundant.

* The Quilombo may be a corruption of the Bunda word which Fr. Bernardo Maria de Cannecatim (Lisbon, 1804) writes in his well-known dictionary, Curiémbu (Ku Riémbu), *i.e.*, povoar, to populate. In the Brazil it is applied to the bush settlements of fugitive slaves and other malefactors : some of these Maroon villages, as the Quilombo dos Palmares, will live in history. "Calhambola," "Carambola," or "Qui-

Having breakfasted at the Carandahy Bridge, we ascended to a kind of plateau, or table-land. This taboleiro was grassy, and thinly wooded above with stunted trees like the ilex and arbutus of the Tyrolese glade; whilst the slopes and hollows showed the huge red water-breaches and the bouquets de bois of the Minas Campo. There were only two fazendas upon the thousands of square acres, well supplied with small streams in little glens. The path was all up and down, nor did it want the usual quagmires.

Three mortal long leagues delayed us till nearly sunset. After many an "anathema esto," we reached an outlying settlement on a hill-top, primitive as a Tupy taba.* Thence descending a steep winding path, we found ourselves in something more civilised, the Freguezia de Santo Antonio de Alagôa (vulgarly Lagôa) Dourada.† It appears in the shape of a single street, a favourite form in old-fashioned parts of the Brazil, this long town reminding one of a settlement on the Gaboon or the Congo River, and survives in the suburbs of such civilized places as (São Salvador da) Bahia. Some fifty one-storeyed houses, with far-projecting eaves, which suggest, when viewed from below, a colossal flight of steps, stretch straggling from north to south, and spread along the meridional bank of a brook traversing a dwarf bottom. This is one of the head waters of the Brumado, the brumous, or foggy, called by the elders Córrego, or Ribeirão de Inferno, or "Hell Creek." After six or seven leagues it falls into the Paraopéba. According to some, it is the main stream, and we are now in the basin of the Rio de São Francisco. Crowning the square-like street are the remains of a new church, intended for St. John; it is highly effective as it now stands—a ruin before it became an edifice. Further down is the Matriz de Santo Antonio, old and with the antiquated belfry, a detached wooden framework. Also,

---

lombola," and in Prince Max. (i. 281), "Gayambolos," which I can only consider to be further debasements; one of them, however, occurs in the Cartas Chilenas, a celebrated Brazilian satire, the "Draper's Letters" done in verse,—

E manda a hum bom cabo, que lhe traga
A quantos *quilombolas* se apanharem
Em duras gargalheiras.

A sturdy corporal he sends to bring
All the Maroons on whom he can lay hands
In hard neck-irons.

* The Taba is the Kraal or Indian village, a collection of "Ocas," in Portuguese Cabanas—wigwams. The Ocara is the open space, generally circular, surrounded by the lodges.

† According to the Diccionario Geographico, sub voce, it was originally the Alagôa Escura—the Dark Lake. Dourada is sometimes erroneously written Doirada: the Portuguese diphthong "ou" is mostly sounded "oi," to the great confusion of foreigners.

for the population of 600 souls and Sunday visitors, there are two chapels of ease, the Mercês and the towerless Rosario.

We passed on to the further end of the straggling village, and "ranched" at a kind of cottage that bore the "strange device"—

CASA HOSPERIA ASAO, (sic, the word reversed.)
Dom Miguel da Assumpção (sic, cão a Dog) Chaves.

The kennels serving for bed-rooms were foully dirty, the floor was foot-tamped earth, and the ceilings were in Mineiro style, strips of bamboo bark about an inch in diameter crossing at right angles. This rough matting has its advantages; it is cheap, clean, and not close enough to prevent ventilation; in the better establishments it is fancifully patterned, stained, and chequered. The beds had, for all coverture, bits of thin, coloured chintz, not pleasant with the mercury at 35° F.; the occupants usually shiver in thin "ponches,"* or cloaks; of course we had not forgotten to bring railway rugs.

It was Sunday, June 23, the "vespera" (eve or vigil) of St. John, perhaps the oldest "holy day" in the civilised world. It is, I need hardly say, the commemoration of the Northern Solstice of the Mundi Oculus, when his "Dakhshanáyan" begins. It is the feast of the mighty Baal (or Bool בעל: 1 Kings xviii. 22—24), the great "master," the "husband" of the moon, the mighty "Lord" of light and heat, the sun of this great world, both eye and soul. We find him called Bel and Belus in Assyria and Chaldea, Beel in Phœnicia, Bal amongst the Carthaginians, Moloch (*i.e.*, Malik, or king) amongst the Ammonites, Hobal in Arabia (Drs. Dozy and Colenso), Balder (Apollo) in Scandinavia, Belenus in Avebury, and Beal in Ireland.† The flaming pyre is in honour of the Mundi Animus, the solar light. Thus we read in

* The Poncho of Spanish America. Here it is a heavy sleeveless cloak of blue broadcloth lined with red baize : when the stuff is fine, the garment of many uses is preferable to any macintosh or water-proof, and it protects from the sun as well as from rain. A "ponche" of white linen is used by the wealthier classes when riding during the heat of the day.

† I know it has been stated that nearly all the Bels, Bals, and Bils, which come so handy to the support of the Baal theory, are forms of Bil, good, Bally, a township, Bile, a tree, Bealach, a road, and Bil or Beul, the mouth of a river. But the pagan Irish certainly worshipped with hills, trees, wells, and stones, the heavenly bodies. The Bel-aine, "little circle of Belus," was their year. How then could they have omitted the sun, that object of universal adoration? The Baldersbad of Scandinavia are described by many a traveller, and Leopold von Buch found them in northern Norway, they are seen on both coasts of the Baltic, and they extend into Prussia and Lithuania. I cannot understand how a festival which is universal should be termed characteristic of the insular Celts. (Athenæum, No. 2073, July 20, 1867). The furthest point south at which I

the " Quatuor Sermones," " In worship of St. John, the people waked at home, and made three manners of fires: one was of clean bones, and no wood, and that is called a bonfire; another is clean wood, and no bones, and that is called a wood-fire, for people to sit and wake thereby; the third is made of wood and bones, and that is called St. John's fire." So the sun-worshippers of northern England, the central counties, and of Cornwall, kindled on their highest Lowes and Torrs, at the moment of the solstice, huge *feux de joie*, and called them " Bar-tine." And at this moment, whilst we in the heart of the Highlands of Brazil, are watching the piling up and the kindling of the pyre, semi-pagan Irishmen in Leinster and Connaught, even in Queen's County: they are dancing round, and their children are jumping through their memorious Beal-tienne* (Baal-fire). And still the Round Towers in which the signal fires were lit, are looking on.

Here also we see illustrated the effect of climate upon great national festivals. The northern yeule, or yule—merry Christmas —the Feast of the Southern Solstice, has scant importance in these latitudes, where the weather is hot and rainy, and the roads are bad. Midsummer is the cool of the year; the temperature is then delightful, and the ways are clean. People meet at the church towns from every direction; each place has its bonfire, bands promenade, and people sit up all night, and gleefully renew the " Tree of St. John." † They keep the feast in utter ignorance of its origin, and indeed I have often asked of European ecclesiastics the meaning of the bonfire, but in vain.‡ Educated Brazilians have inquired how is it that men

found the fires was at Guimar in beautiful Tenerife: there every person named John must on Midsummer Day "stand liquor" to all his friends. The Solstice day has probably made St. John's name so popular at the baptismal font throughout Christianity; hence too our Jones (*i.e.*, John's, the same form as Johnson) and Evans, the genitive of an old Welsh name equivalent to John. St. John seems especially to have favoured the Basque country. In his pyre is placed a stone which serves him as a " prie-Dieu;" on the next morning it is found to preserve some of his hairs, which naturally become relics. The fire is of herbs, and those who jump through it do not suffer from "itch."

* Till lately live coals from the fire were strewed over the fields to produce a good crop.

† The "mastro de S. João" is a tall, thin tree-trunk, sometimes left growing and merely trimmed; more often it is felled, stripped, and replanted. This is generally done a week or so before the festival. Attached to the top is a vane about two feet square, of light frame-work filled with calico, upon which is painted a figure of the Saint, and amongst negroes he is often black. This "mast" reminds the English traveller of our "shaft," or May-pole. The bonfire (fire of joy) was known to the indigenes of the Brazil, who called it "Toryba," from Tory, a faggot.

‡ The Equinoxes, as well as the Solstices, were honoured with memorial fire-festivals, *e.g.*, Easter-day or May-day, the Holi of India, and the Irish La Beal teinne; also All-hallow-een (Oct. 31). And if Christianity had an astronomical origin, so have

walk over the St. John's fire without burning the feet?* Of course, the answer is that those who pass through the flames always pass quickly, and often with wet soles. Girls throw the contents of eggs into water, and see in the forms which they assume the faces of their *"futurs."* † They all judge of their luck, of course matrimonial, by twisting paper-slips, which are opened or not by the cold. Uneducated men believe that St. John sleeps through his festival, and happily so, for were he to wake he would destroy the world. Poor saint! They sing lengthy songs beginning with—

> São João se soubéra que hoje e seu día,
> Do Ceo descería com alegria e prazer.‡

And the fiery fête is more pleasant in the country than in the towns, where bell-ringing, discharges of fireworks, begin before dawn. You are deafened with the ridiculous rockets, and the moliques or niggerlings make the streets unpleasant by throwing "feet seekers" (buscapés) or squibs, which do their best to injure your legs.

The village is a mean place, but its situation is remarkable, and the inhabitants say that it is the highest "arraial" in Minas; whilst the Serra das Taipas§ is the loftiest range, and Itacolumi is the monarch of mountains. It occupies one of the highest plateaus—perhaps *the* highest—not only in Minas,

---

all other advanced faiths. For religion, or the belief of things unseen, began on the earth with earthly matters and ended in the heavens with the Great Unknown.

* This is the legitimate Irish Bil-teinne, good or lucky fire through which cattle are driven and children are passed to guard them against the maladies of the year.

† In Ireland "Brideogh," a picture of St. Bridget, properly Brighid, a Vestal Virgin. It was made upon the eve of that apocryphal saint "by unmarried wenches with a view to discover their future husbands." So in Germany the maiden invites and sees her destiny on St. Andrew's Eve, St. Thomas' Eve, Christmas Eve, and New Year's Eve. Before midnight on St. Andrew's Eve, melted lead is poured through the open parts of a key whose wards form a cross into water drawn from the well during the same night, and the metal takes the form of the tools denoting the craft of the spouse to be.

‡ St. John could he but know that we honour him this day,
Down from heaven he would stray in his gladness and his joy.

The metre is a favourite with the country people, so is the rhyme; the consonance is of the first line end and of the syllable that ends the third hemistich, whilst the couplet terminates unrhymed. In this way are mostly composed the "Modinhas" which we may translate "ballads," and when recited, as the fashion is, not sung, the peculiarity favours a pathetic or sentimental dropping of the voice suitable to the theme. Curious to say, the same kind of couplet and triplet also may be found amongst the wild Sindhís. I have given instances in "Sindh and the Races that inhabit the Valley of the Indus," pp. 88 and 116.

§ Some call it Alto das Taipas. It is the north to south ridge connecting the heights of Ouro Preto with those of Barbacena, and Burmeister calls it Serra de Barbacena.

but in the Brazil, as is proved by the waters flowing from it to the northern and southern extremities of the Empire. And yet this "wasser-schied," which separates two of the mightiest river systems known to the world, is of moderate altitude, not exceeding 4000 feet. A similar anomaly of Nature is often to be seen in the divisions between highly important basins, witness the Rio Grande-Tocantins, the Madeira-Paraguay, the Nile-Zambezi, the Missouri-Colorado, and the Indus-Bramhaputra.

The name, the lay, and the trend of this great "Linha Divisoria" are still in confusion. The people, who are poor in general names, call it "Espigão Geral," the General Ridge.* Thus they distinguish it from the "Espigão Mestre," or Master Ridge, to the north-west, the divide of the Tocantins and the southern Paranahyba. Baron von Eschwege has connected the two by a vast curve, which heads the Valleys of the Amazon, the Paraná, and the São Francisco, and he has named the Espigão Mestre "Serra das Vertentes," or Range of Versants. In this he is followed by Burmeister, whilst St. Hilaire, after the fashion of French departments, preferred calling it "Serra do São Francisco e do Rio Grande.†

This mountain plateau forms in Eastern and Equinoctial South America the third and innermost transverse range, the others being the Serra do Mar and the Mantiqueira. Running in a direction roughly to be described as east to west, it connects the great north to south ridges. It begins at the Serra Grande, alias do Espinhaço, about W. long. 0° 30′ (Rio de Janeiro). It then runs on a parallel between S. lat. 20° and 21°, throwing off large streams to the north and south, and presently becoming the Serra do Piumhy.‡ It continues to trend west for a total of 180 miles, till it reaches the box-shaped mass called the Serra da Canastra, lying about W. long. 3°—3° 30′ (Rio) and 47° (Green.). Some maps, following Spix and Martius, extend the Serra da

---

* It is perhaps more generally known as the Serra da Alagôa Dourada.

† A name afflictingly common in the Brazil. This "big river" is the eastern head water of the Paraná-Paraguay-Plata. The Paraná is formed by the junction of this stream with the Paranahyba, which I call the Southern to distinguish it from the Great Northern Paranahyba of Maranhão and Piauhy.

‡ The word means Water of the Pium or

Sandfly. St. Hil. (III. i. 169) renders it "Water of the Swallow" (Mbiyui). Many however of his derivations are farfetched, and taken from vocabularies. Thus he derives (III. i. 166) Capitinga from the Guarany Capyi, grass, and pitíunga rank smelling (T. D. Piteú, bafio, fortum, rankness): it signifies simply white grass. So (III. i. 238) he makes Peripitinga to be "fetid rush:" it is "flat rush," pitínga, flat, not pitíunga.

Canastra to the Serra Negrá of Sabará, and thence north to the division of waters between the Rio de São Francisco and the Southern Paranahyba. M. Gerber and the majority prolong the Serra da Canastra to the " Mata da Corda," which extends to S. lat. 17°, and whose last buttress we shall see on the Rio de São Francisco.

CHAPTER XV.

AT THE ALAGÔA DOURADA.

> "Crám-bi-ba-bámbali-i-i."
>
> *Brazilian Drinking Song.*

WHEN our traps were settled in the dog-holes, I walked off to the Palacete da Commissão, which housed the surveyors of the great future line of rail, which will soon end the present "hideous waste of power" between the Valleys of the Parahyba and the São Francisco. Mr. John Whittaker, C.E., was then in charge, with two first assistants, Messrs. Thos. Hayden and Chas. A. Morsing, besides a number of underlings. Everything was in admirable and business-like confusion; mules tramped about the court, saddles hung from the walls, boxes strewed the floors, and instruments were stowed away in the corners. It was the signal of separation, half the party going north and the other south.

On the Fête of St. John we made a halt, and were invited to lay the first chain. At noon we proceeded to the brook, heading a little crowd of spectators, whose wives and children eyed the outlandish proceeding, as usual, from their windows. The peg was duly planted, my wife giving the first blow, and breaking the bottle. A chain was laid down, and sights were taken to "N. 74° W.," and "S. 73° E." The inauguration passed off well; flags flew, the band played its loudest, we drank with many vivas—pam! pam! pam! pams!—and hip! hip! hip! hurrahs! to the healths of the Brazil, of England, and especially to the prolongation of the Dom Pedro Segundo Railway; many complimentary speeches were exchanged, and the music escorted us back to our "ranch."

The scene of the ceremony was the site where the Dark became the Golden Lake. When first discovered it covered the lowlands upon which the houses now stand, and in order to drain it, the old miners practically solved the geographical problem of connecting two versants. By means of deep gap-like cuttings, which still remain in the lowest levels, they turned the feeders of the Carandahy, which flows south, into the Brumado, which runs north. Here the greater part of the precious metal was discovered, and there are many traditions of its former wealth. Mr. Walsh* gives an account of the old diggings now in abeyance; he mentions a forty-pound nugget, which proved to be the common nucleus of fibres ramifying in all directions.

As regards the line to be taken by the railway through the " Paiz Camponez," three termini have been warmly advocated by their several partisans, and the Commission was sent to see and survey for itself. The three valleys which claim the honour are those of the Pará, the Paraopéba, and the Rio das Velhas.

The Pará passes to the west of Pitanguy, and falls into the São Francisco about S. lat. 19° 30.′ Unfortunately, the Great Dividing Ridge, which must be crossed *viâ* Santa Rita, Lage, and Desterro, puts forth a succession of lateral buttresses, with numerous and important surface-drains, requiring long turns, tunnels, bridges, and similar expensive works. Moreover, when it reaches the São Francisco the latter river is completely unnavigable, and cannot in these days be made navigable.

The Paraopéba,† which runs to the east of, and almost parallel with, the Pará, has some advantages. From the Rio das Mortes to the Carandahy, the distance is only five leagues. At the Alagôa Dourada the ground is favourable; thence it would run down the Brumado valley, and enter that of the Paraopéba after eight leagues. This line would pass fourteen leagues west of the present capital of Minas, through campos where agriculture flourishes, and where there are backgrounds of unoccupied forests.‡ On the other hand, M. Liais has proved that the Paraopéba does not, like Sabará, lie nearly on the meridian of Rio de Janeiro, and that being far to the west it necessitates a useless detour. Moreover, the Paraopéba River is practicable only for thirty, some say twenty, leagues§ between the mouth

---

* (ii. 162).

† " Paraopéba," which Dr. Couto writes "Paropeba," and others "Paroupeba," is said, I do not know with what authority, to mean the "river of the leaf."

‡ Mato Geral, of which more presently.

§ The Riverines of the Paraopéba declare that it is navigable for canoes below the Salto (cataract) of Sᵗᵃ Cruz near Congonhas do Campo for almost double the distance mentioned in the text.

of the Betim (S. lat. 20° 10′) and the Cachoeira do Chero—the
Rapids of Lamentation*—in S. lat. 19° 30′. Finally, here again,
as Liais has shown, the Rio de São Francisco cannot be made
safe, even for tugs, from the debouchure of the Paraopéba to the
terrible Rapids of Pirapora.†

During the afternoon we walked up and down the banks of
the baby Brumado. Here the batêa produced a few spangles
of gold; the owner of the land is said to take at times three
to four florins' worth per diem, which barely pays. The day
ended as great days always do amongst true Britons—with a
grand dinner given by Mr. Whittaker, and he managed it wonderfully well. The good vicar, Rev. Francisco José Ferreira, who had
duly said mass at 11 A.M., took the head of the table; my wife
was at the foot, and the sides showed seventeen Brazilians and
eight strangers. The food was, as usual, represented by messes
of chickens and meat, feijão, rice, farinha, and pepper sauce,—
in fact, "Mexiriboca," ‡—with cheese, beer, and port from the
engineers' stores. The only peculiarity was the system of
toasts, after the fashion of old Minas. Immediately after the
soup, each one made a little speech, and sang in the most nasal
of tones a little scrap of a sentimental song, generally a qua-
train and a bittock. The following are specimens:—

> Aos amigos um brindo feito
> Reina a allegria em nosso peito
> Grato licor, allegre, jucundo,
> Que a tudo este mundo,
>
> desafria o Amor !§

All the audience takes up the last word, and joyously prolongs
with a melancholy murmur—"Amo-o-o-r." Follows, perhaps:—

> Como he grata a companhia,
> Lisonjeira a sociedade,
> Entre amigos verdadeiros,
> Viva a constante amizade—
>
> Amizade! (chorus.)‖

---

* Reminding us etymologically of the "Bab-El-Mandab"—Gate or Gut of the Weeping-place.

† This is not the place to treat of the Rio das Velhas, which will be described in the first chapters of the second volume.

‡ Mexiriboca is a ludicrous term like our "hodge-podge," meat, rice, beans, farinha, and other matters mixed and eaten with a spoon.

§ A toast to this good company,
Where every heart beats high with glee;
The generous wine flows fast and free,
For nought in all the world we see
  That is not won by love.

‖ How happily we here are met,
  How pleasantly the time hath passed
Amid the friends we ne'er forget—
  Ever may constant friendship last,
    And amity.

Sr. Cyprianno Rodriguez Chaves greatly distinguished himself both in the singing* and the speechifying. All kinds of healths were drunk and redrunk. At last the married men were proposed; the bachelors objected, and then began a general fight, friendly and furious; the Centaurs and Lapithæ bound over to keep the peace. At such time,—

> *   *   *   The whole table,
> With cheers and tigers, was a perfect Babel.'

After dinner we removed our chairs, and took coffee in the street. Soon the temperature became nipping in these hollows of the Brazilian Highlands; thin ice forms over shallows, and in places a soup-plate full of water will be frozen in the night. We removed to the ranch, where Mr. Copsy made for us a "Crámbámbali," † a native brûlé, highly advisable in these frozen altitudes, and we " sampled " sundry glasses of it. The " vigil " fires were not lit again, but the band of ten men promenaded the streets, and ended with giving us a serenade. We did not separate till late, and we sat till " *Sat prata biberunt.*"

I have spent many a less merry Christmas in Merry England, and we shall not readily forget Midsummer Day at Alagòa Dourada, in the year of grace 1867.

---

* This singing at meat has been universal in Europe. In old Germany, when sitting after dinner all the guests were obliged to recite some rhymes under pain of being obliged to drink off a bumper. I believe that the practice was introduced into the Brazil by the Hollander invaders during the 17th Century. It is not known on the seaboard, where Portuguese "speechifying" is the rule, but parts of the interior still preserve it. What would say to it the accomplished author of the "Art of Dining?"

† I will give the receipt in the words of the compounder:—" Pour into a large deep dish a bottle of the best white rum, add a quant. suff. of sugar, fire it and keep stirring. Gradually add a bottle of port, and when the flame weakens, put in a little cinnamon and a few slices of lime. Blow out and you will have the very perfection of Crámbámbali."

CHAPTER XVI.

TO CONGONHAS DO CAMPO.

Vem se dentro campinas dileitosas,
Gelidas fontes, arvores copadas,
Outeiros de crystal, campos de rosas,
Mil fructiferas plantas delicadas.
Caramurú.

THOUGH joy lasted to the small hours, sorrow came in the morning. Mr. Copsy was compelled by professional engagements to turn his back upon us. " Prodigio," the old white "madrinha," leaped a ditch during the night, and was not followed by the rest, a rare circumstance. The intelligent animal doubtless cherished tender memories of good feeding at late baiting-places, and feebly determined to renew the pleasure. We rose at 4 A.M., and we could not mount till hot 9 A.M. We were accompanied by the engineers, nor could, indeed, we have gone far alone. Nothing is easier in the Campos generally than the " errada "—for which the popular phrase is " comprar porcos "—to buy pigs. The land is often a net of paths—a kind of highway from nothing to nowhere. When you ask about the way, the inevitable answer is, " Não tem " (pronounce "teng ") " errada "—you can't go wrong, and behold ! you at once come to a point where four or more roads cross or meet. The people know every inch of ground ; they *cannot* " stravague," and they cannot conceive that you can.

Moreover, we are now on a mere bridle path, without commerce, communications, or comforts ; the few inhabitants are naturally intelligent, but they never rise above semi-barbarism. If you inquire the hour, the replier will look at the sun and say 9 A.M. when it is noon. If you desire to know the distance, the answer will probably be, " One league, if the gentleman's beast is a good one ; if not, one and a half." Koster sensibly divides his leagues into legoas grandes, legoas pequenas, and legoas de nada—of nothing, which may mean four miles.

Crossing the old Lake-site, we ascended the northern hill by a hollow lane of red clay, and soon debouched upon the Campo. From the higher ground appeared, far in the blue north-east, the lofty wall of Itacolumi. The surface is much broken with "cluses," wooded and boggy ravines, generally struck by the path at a right angle. Railroads here must find, perforce, and follow the bed of some stream ; otherwise it is a "bad look-out."

After marching five miles, we forded a small water, and ate together our last breakfast. The occasion was not solemn. In these lands, where all wander, men do not say, "adeus" (fare-well), but "até a primeira," "à tantôt," or "até a volta" (pronounced "vorta"), till the return ; and I have long learned to substitute for adieu, *au revoir*. In fact, we all expected to meet again, and some of us met before we expected to meet. Mr. Whittaker then mounted his mule, and, followed by the minor lights, went his way, whilst we went ours.[*]

Two hours took us to Olhos d'Agua,[†] so called from a lakelet on the left. We rested at a cottage, and found the women busy at the old spinning-wheel, working the cotton that grew before their doors; this is a passe-temps as general throughout Minas as in ancient France. When cooled with oranges and plantains, we resumed, and sighted, deep down in a romantic hollow, a Fazenda belonging to the Padre Francisco Ferreira da Fonseca. It was a charming hermitage, embosomed in its hills, and beautified by its luxuriant weeping willows, its feathery palms, and its stiff Araucaria pines. The Bombax (Paineira) rose sturdy with its slightly bulging stem,[‡] tapering at the top, and armed with short and stout, sharp and curved cock-

---

[*] I leave these words as they were written. We did meet again, more than once, and with pleasure, and little expecting what was about to happen. On June 21, 1868, Mr. John Whittaker died at Rio de Janeiro, mourned by all his friends, and by none more than ourselves.

[†] "Eyes" of water—a term probably translated from the Arabic : in the Brazil many places are so called.

[‡] Another species of Silk-cotton tree, "le fromager ventru," is called from its prodigious central pot belly, the "Barri-gudo" (Chorisia or Bombax ventricosa,

Arr.). There are in the Brazil, as in Africa, many kinds of this tree, some with wrinkled but unarmed bark, others with thorns : the flowers are white pink, or white and pink, they easily fall like the blossom of the Calabash ; the leaves are either entire or have one to two lobes. The bole gives a viscid gum, and in some species the soft spongy centre is filled with large larvæ, which the savages used to eat. The fruit, about the size of our largest pears, yields a cotton of which no serious use has yet been made.

spurs, over which no one but Dahoman Amazons can pass. The large palmated leaves set off a profusion of pink and white blossoms, resembling the richest tulips, and these are soon followed by pendants of useful, but not yet utilised, cotton-pods. On the road side was the Chapel of N^a S^a da Lapa; the gossip tree opposite it was a magnificent Gamelleira, a pyramid of cool green shade, almost equalling the sycamore of Halmalah, or the piles of wild fig which adorn the eastern borders of wild Ugogo.

About mid-afternoon we reached Camapoão* district and streamlet, the latter crossed by a dangerous bridge. The little chapel was under repairs, and a few fazendas, large and small, showed that the land could bear coffee and sugar. We now entered the cretaceous formation, which corresponds with that of São Paulo, and scattered upon the path lay dark flints embedded in white chert.

At the end of the march we inquired for a resting-place, and were shown a deserted Ranch-shed, green with decay, and crying fever and ague. One José Antonio de Azevedo presently took us in, and proved himself a bitter draught—a very "niggard and misknown knave," the model of grumbling incivility and extortionate rapaciousness. This old wretch startled us. The traveller in these lands becomes so accustomed to the affable, hospitable Brazilian ways that he feels acutely those displays of small churlishness which he would not remark in a French or English boor. And how rare are such bad manners here may be judged by the fact that this Azevedo was the sole base exception to the rule of kindness and obligingness.

This day we suffered much from the Carrapato,† and "realised" the popular jest levelled at the Mineiro, namely, that he is known by his patent boots and—"fiddle." The nuisance is of the genus Ixiodes of Latreille, and entomologists still dispute whether it be of one or of two species. The people declare that the Carrapato grande is different from the miudo, a small and hardly perceptible insect. Spix and Martius take this view,

---

* Or Camapúam, translated "seins arrondis," opposed to Camapiréra, "peitos cahidos." Cama signifies the breast, and "apoam," contracted to poam, round.

† Not Carapatoo, as written by Mr. Walsh, nor Garapato, as by the Religious Tract Society. The former remarks (ii. 8)

that the insect, on account of its resemblance to the ripe bean of the Palmi Christi, was called by the ancients κροτον and ricinus. It is the vincucha of Paraguay, the tique of French Guiana, and the ricinus of old authors.

and Pohl named the former Ixiodes americanus, and the latter Ixiodes Collar. St. Hilaire (III. ii. 32) and Gardner (293) believe that there is only one kind, which greatly varies at different ages.* It is the "tick" of the Mississippi valley, and when fully developed it is not unlike our sheep-tick. *Ticks!*

This acaride, seen under the glass, shows a head armed with a trident of teeth, serrated inwards; the two external blades of the terebro when entering the flesh bend away, forming a triangle with the base outwards and downwards, and rendering it difficult to remove the plague. The three pairs of short and one of long legs are all provided with sharp and strongly-hooked claws, the flat body is coriaceous and hard to smash; the colour is a dull brownish red, like the cimex. The young animal in early spring is a mere dot, with powers of annoyance in inverse ratio to its size. It grows fast, and when distended with blood it becomes somewhat bigger than a marrowfat pea.

In most parts of Minas and São Paulo the nuisance is general; it seems to be in the air; every blade of grass has its colony; clusters of hundreds adhere to the twigs; myriads are found in the bush clumps. Lean and flat when growing on the leaves, the tick catches man or beast brushing by, fattens rapidly and at the end of a week's good living drops off, *plena cruoris*. Horses and cattle suffer greatly from the Ixiodes, and even die of exhaustion. The traveller soon wears a belt of bites, like the "shingles" of Lancashire. The tick attacks the most inconvenient places, and the venomous, irritating wound will bring on a ricinian fever, like the pulicious fever of Russia. Thus in East Africa Dr. Krapf found a "P'házi bug," which he declared to be mortal; it was the papázi, or tick, which sometimes kills by incessant worry. In East Africa I used to scatter gunpowder over the hut-floors, and to blow up the beasts before taking possession. The excitement of day travelling makes the nuisance comparatively light; but when lying down to sleep the sufferer is persecuted by the creeping and crawling of the small villain, and the heat of the bed adds much to his tribulation.

The favourite habitat is the Capoeira, or second growth, where cattle graze. The low scrubs known as "Catinga" and "Carrasco" are also good breeding grounds. Annual prairie fires

* Its youth is said to commence with the dry season.

destroy millions; but the Capoës, or bouquets de bois, act as preserves, and the branches are incrusted with them. The tick does not exist at certain altitudes; yet, when ascending Jaraguá Peak, near São Paulo, I found my overalls coloured pepper and salt. Below certain latitudes, also, the Ixiodes disappears. It loves most of all cool, damp places, on the dry sunny uplands, where it acts like the mosquito of the hot and humid Beiramar, and is less common in dry and sunny spots. On the upper waters of the São Francisco River the ticks were a mortification; when I descended the stream about half way they suddenly ceased, and reappeared only at intervals. It is difficult to lay down precise rules as regards their presence. Water is fatal to them, and animals are freed from them by swimming broad streams. Travellers are also advised to take off the infested clothing, and to hang it up in the hottest sun.

The stranger, with his body painted like an ounce, or like a child's horse plastered with red wafers, applies for a remedy, and receives a dozen prescriptions. All have a common object, to cause the beast's claws to retract, and not to leave the head in the skin, otherwise the result may be a venomous sore, which may last for months and even years, at times inducing dangerous cutaneous diseases. Some apply mercurial ointment; others bisect the tick's body with scissors; some insert into it a red-hot pin. The people apply snuff at the end of a cigar, and when much bitten they wash with spirits and a strong infusion of tobacco, followed by a tepid bath to remove absorbable nicotine.* In many places, when attacked by a score at a time, I found these methods too slow; the easiest plan was to pluck off the animals before they had taken firm hold, and to wash away the irritation with country rum and water.

The general cure for the plague will be clearing the country of its ragged and tangled thicket and wood, here called Mato Sujo, or dirty forest, and by substituting a cleaner growth. There are many tick-eating birds; for instance, the Caracára buzzard, that performs kindly offices to cattle. Unfortunately, they are not protected by law in the Brazil.

The decrepit greybeard, our host, after venting upon us his independence, consented to cook some beans, rice, and onions,

---

* I met in the Brazil a French traveller who was painfully intoxicated after rubbing his skin with a mixture of tobacco and native rum.

which he added to the contents of our provision basket. His
hovel was filthy as his person, and his kitchen excelled the
average pigstye, yet he was miserly, not poor. Though seventy
years old, he was living with two negresses; there was only one
bed in the house, and no amount of coaxing, not even a glass of
Cognac, would persuade him to vacate it. He was in years,
and required his comforts. He had lately suffered from the
"amarellão,"* a kind of jaundice here common. He would
hardly permit a hammock to be swung, for fear of injuring the
walls of stick and mud. The conversation between him and his
charmers lasted nearly all night. I was roused from my wrappers
on the table by seeing a bowie-knife and a repeating pistol make
their appearance. My wife had been kept awake by a curious
kind of whispering, and by hard listening she had heard the dark
and ominous words, "Pode (pronounced paude) facilmente
matar a todas"—Easy to kill the whole lot. She had forthwith
armed herself, and the dog "Negra" began to growl in sympathy. Of course, nothing occurred ; the slaughter alluded to
was probably that of the host's chickens, whose murder he feared
at our hands. Whatever may be the désagrémens of Brazilian
travelling in these bye-paths, the traveller is, as a rule, perfectly
safe.

Next morning we left the old Pongo, whom the troopers called
"son of Ganha dinheiro," and "grandson of Paga me logo,"†
grumbling that we had stolen his posts and rails for firewood.
The dawn light showed us an ugly mud hole, which would make
the hair of an easy-going man stand upright; the animals
plunged through it panting, and "Chico," the negret, stuck
till he was rescued. Presently we were stopped by a wide ditch,
where a gate had been. This arbitrary proceeding is common in
the wilder parts, and at São Paulo it has lost me a whole day's
march. Fazendas and plantations were scattered about ; we
passed a neat white establishment belonging to Senhor João
Lopes Texeira Chaves. He had been described to us as
"homem muito brábo," who, if "in the humour," would have
refused the "pouso." I ought to have tried the experiment,
and doubtless we should have rested comfortably ; unfortunately

---

* In pure Portuguese "Amarellidão."
Koster (ii. 19) alludes to this complaint,
which he identifies with jaundice. According to him, Africans in the Brazil are very
subject to it.

† "Gain-Coin," and "Pay-me-quick."

we had no Brazilian in our party, or everything would have been made easy.

This part of the Highlands is a cold, red land : the Araucarias become numerous and luxuriant ; beans and hulls heaped upon the well-swept floors fronting the cottages, show that "mantimento" * is the principal industry. There are signs of stock-breeding, and pigs, gaunt and long-legged, uproot the soil. At 8 A.M. the view reminded me of a sunrise seen from the Peak of Teneriffe. Below us lay a silvery water, flowing and curling before a gentle three-knot breeze ; from the distinctly marked shores jutted green tongued capes, and stony headlands ; feathery islets protruded their dark heads from the white flood, and far, far off we could faintly discern the further blue coast of the Straits. The deception was complete as the Arabian Bahr-bila-Ma, or " sea without water," and the Mrig-trikhná, or " deer-thirst " of the Hindus. † Descending, we found the water to be a cold fog, or rather a thin cloud, with distinct and palpable vesicles condensed by the ground. At this season the phenomenon appears almost every morning.

We then breasted a hill-ridge, up which straggled red paths, over a quarter of a mile in breadth. A single house was on the summit, but, gaining it, we were surprised to find Suasuhy,‡ a street of some 300 houses, and banded with broad lines of rough pavement to prevent the red clay being washed down. The lay was east-west, and it was backed by gardens and orchards. In the middle of the lower thoroughfare was the Matriz of S. Braz upon a raised platform of stone, two belfries with a pair of bells, and a restored front copiously whitewashed. The women were in jackets of scarlet baize, the favourite winter wear, and the children hid themselves behind the doorways as we passed by.

---

* A term locally applied to all kinds of "Munition de bouche."

† The Mirage. The Arabs also know it as Bahr-el-Ghizal, the Deves' Sea, Bahr-el-Mejánin, the Sea of Madmen (who expect to drink of it), and the Bahr-el-Ifrit, or Fiend's Sea.

‡ St. Hil. (III. 2, 262) makes Çuaçu mean a deer in the Indian dialect of the Aldêa de Pedras : thus we should translate Suasuhy, " deer's water." The celebrated naturalist, Alexandre Rodrigues Ferreira, explains the Indian word for stag, Suha assú—may it not be Suia assú, large game ?—to signify " big head ; " but he derives it preferably from Cúu, to ruminate : Çúu assú then would be a ruminant,

and its young " Çuaçu Merin " (not minor in the sense of small). Casal writes " Sassuhy : " Pizarro " Sassuhy " and " Suassuhy," Spix and Martins " Sussuhy," and St. Hil. (I. i. 400) derives it from "Cuchu" petit parroquet, and " yg " water—Rivière des petits parroquets. Mr. Walsh writes " Sua-Suci, or Sussuy," and heard about it some tale which reminded him of the Aræ Philenorum—he was, it seems, a greedy recipient of "humbug," that reverend man. Burmeister prefers Suassui, the " Almanak " Suassuhy. Vulgarly it is written Sassuhy and Sassui, and is translated " Veada com filho," doe and fawn. In the Province of São Paulo there is a "Sua-Mirim," explained to mean the little doe.

Senhor Antonio José Cardoso, of the Hotel Nacional, gave us hot water, clean towels, and a good breakfast, all much required.

At 11 A.M. we remounted, and felt the sunheat after the cold damp dawn. The nearest ascent, where stands the Chapel of N^a S^a dos Passos and the village school, gave the first of many pretty back views. The road was a rough cross-country affair, over a succession of ground waves, divided by rivulets that feed their main drain, the Paraopéba. After a short hour we crossed the bridge of this stream, which was red with gold-washing; even after discharging into the São Francisco, it is said to preserve for some distance its ruddy tinge. Near the fazenda of Senhor Col. Luis Gonzaga we found a dozen gipsies, all men, resting tentless on the ground, whilst their beasts grazed on the road-side grass. These mysterious vagabonds are rare in São Paulo, and numerous in Minas, where they are horse-chaunters and hen-stealers, as everywhere between Kent and Catalonia. They are evidently a different breed from the races around them, and their long, wavy hair is the first thing remarked. I shall reserve for another volume a detached notice of the Brazilian " Cigano" —that object of popular fear, disgust, and superstition.[*]

Passing the Piquiry stream, we found the land greatly improved. It produces several kinds of manioc, and the red variety (Mandiora roxa) here ripens in five months. There were long slopes green with grama (Triticum repens), and the thickets were rich in climbing Cyperacea sedge, which, mixed with the young Capim Gordura, makes excellent forage. This plant is known in the Brazil as " Andrequiá," " André's knife," a mixed word, Luso-Indian,[†] which well expresses its powers of cutting. The road was hedged with a gorgeous growth of golden broom, profusely blossoming, and reminding the European not a little of his honeysuckle. The people call it the " flower of St. John,"[‡] because it is most beautiful in their mid-winter, when floral beauties are comparatively rare. It has justly claimed a place in poetry.

> Outra engraçada flor que em ramos pende
> (Chamão de S. João,)[§]

---

[*] So little is known about the subject that the usually well-informed Anglo-Brazilian Times ignores the presence of gipsies in the Empire.

[†] According to Captain Speke (Journal, &c., chap. xiii.), Mtesa, the despot of Uganda used to have his subject-criminals cut to pieces after death, not with knives, which are prohibited, but with slips of sharp-edged grass.

[‡] Flor de S. João.

[§] Another graceful flower with pendent twigs
(Named " of St. John ").
Caramurú, vii. 36.

says Fr. José de S. Rita Durão. Remarkable, too, were the snowy petals and the long green pods of the leguminous shrub with cloven-hoofed leaves (Bauhinia forficata, the mororó of the Indians) ; here it is called " unha de boi," or, as some prefer, " de vaca."* Another pretty growth is the Poaya, a kind of Ipecacuanha,† " the little plant near the path," which it beautifies with its small red and yellow trumpets. Here I noticed that our Brazil-born Africans had preserved their home custom of barring the wrong path with a twig laid transverse.

The little village of Redondo has a chapel dedicated to Nª Sª de Ajuda, and, better still, a charming prospect. Beyond the foreground of forest and green grass springing rankly from the ochreous purple soil, a colour here known as sangre de boi,‡ falls a basin of regular slope and sole, rising on the far side to the feet of a bluff stone wall towering in the air. This range, now to our east and north, is called in some maps " Serra de Deus te livre,"— of God help you !—doubtless from the perils of the path. It is more generally known as the " Serra de Ouro Branco," from a town on the direct highway—we see its white line threading the ravines—between Barbacena and Morro Velho. The grand pile will long remain in sight, but a bulge in the ground concealed from us the settlement.

Santo Antonio was first, and is still entitled White Gold, in opposition to Ouro Preto, or Black Gold. The latter§ is darkened by a little oxide of iron. The former is naturally alloyed with platinum ‖—a rare formation. The new metal discovered only two centuries and a quarter ago, and now used even for watchworks, is supplied in Minas by the gravels of streams flowing

---

* "Bullock's Hoof," "Cow's Hoof." The System prefers Unha de Boi, and ranks it amongst the astringent mucilaginous plants.

† Poaya is in the Brazil a generic term for this species of Rubiaceæ. The true emetic root is distinguished as Poaya Verdadeira, or de botica—of the apothecary's shop. The System derives "ipecacuanha" from ipé-caá-goéne, " the little plant near the roads : " it is rather "the little plant which excites emetism " (goéne), and doubtless the wild mediciners well know its use. Being much used in certain feminine complaints, it may mean "the little plant of the woman" (Cunha). The word has been corrupted to Epicaquenha and Picahonha. There are many kinds,

the Ipecacuanha-preta (I. officinalis arruda) ; the I. branca (Viola Ipecacuanha, or Pombalia Ipecacuanha Vandelli).

‡ " Bullock's Blood."

§ Mr. Walsh (ii. 125) says that black gold "contains an alloy of *silver*, which acquires a brown tarnish by oxidation when exposed to the air." This is anything but correct.

‖ D. Antonio de Ulhoa, a Spanish savant travelling in Peru (1748), speaks of it as the third perfect or noble metal. The name originally given was " Platina," little silver, the diminutive of "Plata," which, in Portuguese, would be " Prata " and "Pratinha." Europe has, I presume, preferred the barbarous " platinum " to assimilate it with ferrum and cuprum.

through table-lands and low hills. A piece weighing half an ounce was found in the Lavras, or diggings of the Barão de Itabira, near Marianna. Harder than iron, and much resembling gold, it gave great trouble to the old founders who wasted upon it their solimão (corrosive sublimate), and wondered to see the pale brassy bars which "touched," however, twenty-two carats. Dr. Couto says that about 1780 an unknown individual took a portion (parcella) of it to the Government melting-house at Sabará. As it was uncommonly refractory, as it split in two, and cracked round the impression, the officer declared it worthless. The disappointed miner disappeared, remarking that he never thought that it could be valuable, as he could find horse-loads of it. Although it was conjectured that he came from near the little village of Santa Anna dos Ferros, the valuable deposit has never been brought to light. The mineralogist examined the ingot which he found at the Intendency of Sabará; it weighed thirty to forty oitavas, or eighths of Portuguese ounces, and was platinum, with a fifth part of gold. Some local paper credited me with having rediscovered the mine—I wish that I had.

About 3 P.M., as the ride was becoming delightful, we came to a hill crest, and Congonhas showed itself suddenly, as Trieste is, or rather was, sighted from the old carriage-road. The situation is on the southern side of a charming valley, an oval whose long diameter, from north-east to south-west, is formed by the Rio Maranhão,* or "Skeiny Stream." The silvery water flows over land set in emerald verdure, a rich margin of meadow land, rare in Minas, where the bottoms are narrow. Jags and gashes of white, red, and yellow clay on the upper bed are the only vestiges of the once rich gold mines. To the north is a vast rugged ridge, straight and wall-like; it is called Serra (de Nª Sª) da Boa Morte, from a village and a chapel of that invocation. Its culminating point is the Peak of Itabira, which we shall presently see, and here it forms a semicircle extending to the Congonhas Mountains, a massive pile to the west. Eastward is the great chain of Ouro Branco, which alters strangely at the different angles of view.

At first glance Congonhas appeared to be all one church and

---

* Maranhão (anciently written Maran-ham) is a skein, a tangle: "arvoredo emmaranhado," for instance, would mean "matted bush." The little stream rises to the S.E. near Queluz, and winds round to the Paraopéba River.

convent. Presently a second temple appeared on the further side of the riverine valley; it was double towered, and the colours were white, bound in black, like the Nᵃ Sᵃ do Monte, Madeira, which strangers and seafaring men will call the "convent." Lime-washed houses dazzling in the slanting glance of the sun were scattered in a line on the transverse axis between the two fanes. We descended a rocky and paved ramp of most unpleasant pitch, and soon found ourselves under the roof of the Alferes (Ensign) Gourgel de Santa Anna. He made us grateful to him for ever by giving us warm baths and "planter's coffee,* and he kept us waiting for dinner only three hours.

* "Café de fazendeiro;" coffee which the wealthy planter drinks, not the "agua de Castanha," Chesnut water, of Portugal, not to speak of other lands. The former leaves a yellow tinge when poured out of a white cup, the latter does not.

CHAPTER XVII.

AT CONGONHAS DO CAMPO.[*]

Distante nove legoas desta terra,
Ha uma grande Ermida, que se chama,
Senhor de Matosinhos.

Cartas Chilenas, IV.

"Some nine leagues, stands a great oratory, which is called The Lord of Matosinhos."

Nᴬ Sᴬ ᴅᴀ Conçeicao, here a favourite invocation of the Bona Dea and the Magna Mater, is a Mineiran Loretto ; one cannot but wonder to see such labour in a hamlet of 600 souls, unassisted, moreover, by angelic hosts. The gold-washings explain the cause ; a deserted tenement still shows the well-carved scutcheon of some old Fidalgo ; moreover, at the beginning of the last century the Indians, now extinct, were still in the land, and worked willingly, or were made to work, at ecclesiastical architecture. The Brazilian traveller often finds in wild places solid and stately buildings which could not be attempted in the present day. The church of Congonhas has no grounds or estates settled upon it : moreover it has lately lost a dozen of its few slaves, and the general opinion of enlightened Brazilians is decidedly against the successors of the Apostles binding persons to service. But from the 11th till the 14th of last September is its Romaria, a mixture of " patron " and pilgrimage. Some 7000

---

[*] Congonhas is called "do Campo," to distinguish it from Congonhas de Sabará. The name is common in the Brazil, having been applied by troopers and travellers to the many spots where they found the several varieties of Ilicineœ, of which the most valuable is the Mate, or Herva do Paraguay (Ilex Paraguayensis, despite St. Hil. who, III. ii. 249, obstinately defends the incorrect old form Paraguariensis). I will not describe the shrub, this has been done by every writer from Southey downwards. The Brazilian term " Congonha " is generic, meaning all the shrubs that make "Paraguay tea." It is also specifically applied to the Ilex Congonha, common in Minas and in Paraná. The Congonha Cimarrão is only the infusion, drunk without sugar. Caraúna is Congonha of an inferior kind. In Mr. Luccock (p. 523), we read "Congonha is, in writing, commonly substituted for Caancunha. The name is derived from a plant, an infusion of which is held to be an excellent remedy in female complaints." Thus he confuses with Ipecacuanha the Congonha, which in the Tupy tongue was known as Caa-mirim, *the* little leaf.

souls then lodge in the houses which lie empty for the rest of the year, and the free gifts of many coppers and a few notes amount to some £2000 per annum, here worth £20,000. The brother-hood of Bom Jesus de Matosinhos distribute the alms amongst the people of the holy hamlet. There was no better way—be it said with due respect for popular belief—of founding a town in the old Brazil than by instituting a Growing Stone, a Healing Cross, or a Miracle-Working Image:* these things were found easily, as we now create a Spa by burying rusty nails with quassia and charging sixpence for admission.

The director of the college being absent, we called upon his vice, the Rev. Padre Antonio José da Costa, a son of São João; he had resided here only a month. He kindly reproved us for going to an inn, when there was so much vacant lodging for True Believers, and, calling for his key-bunch, he set out to show the lions.

We will begin with the beginning. The steep and badly-paved calçada which we descended yesterday has a branch to the right: this places the stranger at the base of a tall brow, upon which the Loretto is charmingly situated. In front is the church; to the right or westward is a long range of double-storied buildings, white above and yellow-ochre below: the third or eastern side of the hill-square is formed by poorer buildings, "porta e janella," also pilgrims' quarters.

Ascending the hill—typical, I presume, of "the hard and narrow way"—and bisecting the square," is a dwarf avenue of buildings called the Sete Passos, the Seven Chapels of the stations. The two lowest are old, the next pair is modern, and three are yet to be built when the contributions of the pious shall suffice: this last contains two of the normal fourteen, "stacions of Rome;" and, when finished, the place will be used as a burial ground for those who can or will afford it. In former days the fine pavement of cut stone round the temple cost a total of £40: now a single station represents £600. The expense is solely in the labour, the whole country is building material.

These oratories are low squares of solid masonry whitewashed,

---

* Such images are called apparecido, or apparecida, from their "appearing" on the sea-shore, in streams, in caverns, et le reste. It is the fashion now to deny that Catholics worship images; this is a truism as regards the educated; with the vulgar it is distinctly the reverse of fact. And by the operation popularly called counting noses, how many of these are found in proportion to those?

with terminals at the four angles, and "half-orange" domes and finials. Windowless and entered by a single door, they suggest the humbler sort of "Kubbah," which protects and honours the remains of Shaykh and Wali in Arabia and Sindh. The lowest, number 7, lacks inscription, and represents the Last Supper. Wooden figures, mostly mere masques or "dickies," without bowels or dorsal spine, dressed like the traditional Turk of the Christian Mediterranean type, are seated round a table richly spread with tea (or maté) pots, cups, liqueurs, and meats. Our Lord is saying, "One of you shall betray me." All look with quaint expressions of horror and surprise, except Judas, who sits next the door, hideous of aspect, and caring as little to disguise his villany as Iago upon an English stage. My wife complied with the custom of the place, took the knife from Judas his platter, and dug it into his eye, or rather into a deep cut which cleaves his left malar bone, and then smote with it his shoulder. This poor Judas! who, upon the D'Israelitic principle duly carried out, merits the affectionate gratitude of a Redeemed Race.

The next station, the Agony in the Garden, presents a peculiar inscription, which is supposed mysteriously to be Greek. I have copied it for the benefit of Grecians :—

ETIOα(*sic*) CTVS Iπα(*sic*)

Goπiα FIOLIXIVS

Oiαβαт

The first of the new stations shows the mercurial and somewhat Hibernian St. Peter striking off the ear while the Saviour is about to heal the wound. The inscription Tanquam ad latronem, &c., does not merit notice ; the Pagan soldiers do. Surely such Roman-nosed warriors never could have existed unless they used their proboscis as the elephant uses its trunk. But grotesque as they are, and utterly vile as works of art, these wooden caricatures serve, I have no doubt, to fix their subjects firmly in the public mind, and to keep alive a certain kind of devotion. The civilising, or rather the humanising, influences of the parish service and the "patron" have already been alluded to.

The church is reached by four semicircular steps, guarded by an iron railing : here an inscription commemorates the origin of the pilgrimage.

MDCCLV.

VAD₄
BUN₄ JESU MATUSINOR₄
P₄ R₄ BENED XIV
PRIMUS HIC CULTUS OBLATUS
A . MDCCLVIII.
R₄ N₄ F₄ JUSEPHO₄
TEMPLUM CONSTRUCTUM
MDCCLXI.
TANO₄ REÆDIF
CUI FAXIT
ÆTER-
NITAS.

The beginning was a rough way-side cross of dark wood bearing a rude figure of our Lord, and dedicated to Nᵒ Sʳ. do Matosinhos. About 1700 it began to work miracles ; the ground was consecrated, and a small chapel was built, the germ of the present church and seminary.

Before the entrance a double flight of broad steps diverges and meets upon the adro, the usual spacious paved area, fronted by a handsome stone balustrade, and commanding a lovely view. At the angles of the sets of steps, and at intervals in the front of the platform, are twelve gigantic* figures of the four major prophets ; sundry of the dozen invidiously distinguished as the minor being nowhere. Each figure is habited in conventional Oriental costume, bearing a roll engraved with some remarkable passage from his book, in Latin and large old letters. The material is steatite, found in the neighbourhood, and the workman was the ubiquitous Cripple, who again appears upon the façade. The group has a good effect at a distance, and in the Brazil the idea is original : it compares, however, poorly with the Bom Jesus de Braga, near Oporto, and the humblest of Italian holy places.

The façade is of course whitewashed, all except the cut brown stone at the corners : there are two windows assisted by a very simple rose-light : small apertures also are made in both the flanking towers. These belfries are domed and finished with extensive terminals, an armillary sphere supporting an angel

---

* The height is a little above 8 feet. On the right are Jeremiah, Ezekiel, Hosea, Joel, Nahum, and Habbakuk, fronted by Isaiah, Daniel, Amos, Obadiah, Jonah, and Baruch the Scribe. Thus the four "great prophets" are not in order of precedence.

All agree that the statues are twelve, yet in a memorandum given to me I find them thus described : to the right Ezekiel, Habbakuk, Hosea, Joel, and Nahum ; on the left Baruch, Daniel, Jonah, Amos, and Obadiah.

who bears a cross. The entrance is floridly carved in the greenish saponaceous stone, so common in these parts; the cherubs and the instruments of the Passion are better executed than usual. The most artistic features are the doors of massive hard wood, cut in highly relieved rays, and painted ecclesiastical green. I saw this style for the first time at old Olinda, and greatly admired it: some of the bosses were raised five inches.

Little need be said about the interior : the walls are panelled and frescoed with tawdry paintings, and hung with penny prints, whilst the images are below criticism. There are four side chapels, the first on the left shows St. Francis de Assis, the favourite St. Francis of the Brazil, and the second on the left has a S. Francisco de Paula, supposed to be a life-like copy of the Parisian statue. The organ-loft, over the principal entrance, has a small instrument, and the choir, on its left, projects into the body of the church. There are two pulpits of bare stone standing upon Gothic animals ; the lateral cherubs are well cut, but the canopies are inferior. There are two box and two open confessionals : the former generally contain a curiously pierced stool. The latter, sometimes made portable, are boards with a sieve-like grating, supposed to separate the seated saint from the kneeling sinner. Perhaps this religious exercise of olden date might in these ages be modified to a good purpose, by insisting that priest and penitent should be strangers to each other, and as both would doubtless strongly object to and abhor this measure, it would add to it another and a fresh charm of mortification.

The sanctuary has a tunnel roof frescoed with two curious productions—" the Trinity in Heaven, and the Burial of our Lord." Here also are the fourteen stations of the Passion. The high altar shows a large figure of Nᵒ Sʳ do Calvario : it is supported by Santa Anna tending the Virgin, S. Domingos, Sta. Luzia, Sta. Veronica with the veil, and the Roman soldier with the lance. In the base is an altar-tomb, and when a board is removed it exposes the Cadaver, the grand object of the pilgrimage, the full-length effigy of Nᵒ Sʳ De Matosinhos—a dead Christ, with angels kneeling and praying. The faithful prostrate to it, and kiss the hand with immense devotion, as is proved by the sinking of the floor close in front. On one side is a small " presepio " or crib of Bethlehem.   Four fine chandeliers of massive silver illuminate the high altar and the body of the church.

The sacristy has the usual small lavatory and manutergia, with pictures, like the rest of the building, and two bishops of Marianna upon the ceiling.   On the east is the Miracle-room,—a long, low hall containing *exvotos* in hundreds, memorial tablets recording cures and escapes, and waxen models of unsound limbs made whole.   Here is preserved the old original wooden cross upon which is cut—

INRI

(the crucifix)

NO. S. D.

MATVZINHOS.

Outside and east of the church are two stones embedded in the area close to the walls; they appeared to me quartzose granite.   One is the Growing Stone, which, despite the annual attraction of many kisses, steadily increases; the other is not crescive in its faculty.   Our priestly guide sensibly remarked, he would not answer for the fact, but that it might be, as all things are possible to the Creator.   This explanation, since the days of "numquid Deo quidquam est difficile ? " is still popular from London to Pekin; unfortunately it is wholly beside the question; no one denies that the Almighty has power to do what we often doubt that He does.   At Iguápe, on the sea-board of São Paulo, there is a brother-stone with like gifts.   In both cases the parts around the mineral are trodden upon, scraped, and carried away as relics and remedies.   Hence, possibly, the growth.   The harmless superstition reminds us, amongst other instances,* of the rent—one foot wide—in a granite rock near St. Levans, when big enough to allow an ass and panniers— homely fancy !—to pass through, we may expect the end of the world, viz., the conclusion of the present quiescent æra of earth, and a recommencement of its convulsions, if convulsionists say truth.

We then visited the college, which began about thirty-seven years ago.   Its founder was the late Reverend Padre Leandro de Castro, a Portuguese Lazarist, who also instituted the D. Pedro

---

* Exempli gratiâ, the venerable London Stone of many fables.   Doubtless these petral marvels originated in the Tu es Petrus, &c.

Segundo establishment at Rio de Janeiro. Over the doorway is the date 1844, showing the latest addition. The building is large, with ten front and some forty side windows; but we saw nothing of the curiosity described by Mr. Luccock: "Behind the church is another sacred singularity,—a garden in imitation of Paradise, where Adam and Eve, beneath the cross, are sitting beside a fountain, in all the nudity of innocence."

The present director is the Rev. Padre João Rodriguez da Cunha, a native of Sabará, and his salary, I was told, is 180*l.* per annum. The Provincial Government is supposed to contribute a yearly 400*l.*; but our guide complained that the assembly had not paid it for two years. There are seven professors and three priests for spiritual matters; the pupils average between sixty and seventy, and all wear the Soutane. There can be no better situation for a college. During the last three years, neither doctor nor apothecary has been known at Congonhas, and as often happens to passengers and crews of ships without surgeons, the want has not been felt. Of course we were told all about the normal old woman who had outlived the century.

It is said that the Capuchins proposed to take charge of this academy, but added an impossible condition—exemption from civil law, and subjection to their diocesan only. This was judged—procaciter atque injuriosè?—"a tendency to obsolete theocracy," a "revival of the days of Gregory VII. and Innocent IV." Sensible Brazilians have an aversion to the ecclesiastical Alma Mater, with her curriculum of Trivium and Quadrivium; where youth is taught by esercizi spirituali contempt for worldly matters; where politics are subject to religion; where state becomes handmaid to Church which inculcates unquestioning belief, blind obedience, austerity, asceticism, and self-abnegation,—virtues wholly unfitted for the citizens of a free commonwealth: they exclaim against philosophy being made the ancilla of theology, and to traditional fancies usurping the place of the teachings of nature; they do not wish to see human reason represented as a deceiver, and liberty of the press condemned with the "deluge of infernal ink," and seventy-eight other "modern errors." Moreover, there are not a few ugly reports of a peculiar hygiene being introduced into these seminaries, such as nitre being mixed with the dietary.*

* Appendix to the Presidential Relatorio of Minas for 1865, p. 38. A very able paper.

On the other hand there is no doubt of the superior teaching and discipline imported by the regular clergy of Europe into the Brazilian establishments. And here, not being entitled to offer an opinion upon such points in any country but my own, I leave this great dispute, which is not likely to be settled for a handful of years.

We then descended the rest of the steep calçada, passing on the right the ruined chapel of São José. At the bottom is the little river Maranhão, which formerly divided the Comarcas of Villa Rica and Rio das Mortes, it is crossed by the usual wooden bridge. On the northern bank is the hamlet of Matosinhos fronting Congonhas, " in the same manner that Gateshead does with respect to Newcastle-upon-Tyne." It has a Matriz dedicated to N^a S^a da Conceição, with a tolerable façade, and near the entrance an emblematic coat-of-arms cut in soapstone. The interior was still under repairs. About thirty years ago it was struck by lightning, and one man required the " triste bidental."

I visited the old gold-diggings, and found them of little importance. Caldcleugh has left an account of the industry[*] which was still thriving, in 1825. The precious metal, twenty-two carats fine, was found in the pores and cavities of friable or rotten quartz injected into green-stone. Mr. Luccock detected dust-gold " among schist-clays, and the other component parts of the ground," and the latter contained the ore " with equal certainty and in nearly equal quantity, whether of the prevailing red hue or any of the shades of brown or yellow." The matrix was crushed by stamping-mills, and the freed gold was made to run in the usual way down streakes or inclined plains, where hides placed in a contrary direction to the lay of the hair caught the heavy particles.[†]

We returned our best thanks to the amiable vice-director ; his attention and affability deserved all our gratitude. Before shaking hands he gave us, by way of memento, a parcel of toothpicks made of a highly-prized lliana, locally called " Cipo de salsa." How comes it that the " palito," cleanly and comfortable, is still obnoxious to popular prejudice in England?

---

[*] Travels, ii. 227. Mr. Walsh (ii. 173) passed through Congonhas, describes the Paraguay tea, but says nothing of the temple or the gold mines. Yet he had travelled amongst the Turks, and had written a book upon Turkey.

[†] This old system is still in use at Morro Velho. I reserve a longer notice of it for a future chapter.

CHAPTER XVIII.

TO TEIXEIRA.

São pois os quatro, A A por singulares
Arvoredos, Assucar, Agoas, Ares.
Manoel Botelho de Oliveira.

IT was early noon when we left Congonhas. Once more we descended the hill and crossed the Maranhão; we then struck up the little valley of the "Ribeirão de Santo Antonio," a surface drain of the "Serra da Bôa Morte." The soil was mostly chalk-white, like kaolin, and the banks of the hollow ways, once level with the ground, and now sunk many feet below it, worn down by torrential rains, and by the tramp of man and beast—still showed stiff deep red clay. The cross-country track abounded in artistic views of "salvage soyle." Congonhas, like a pearl set in emeralds, lingered long in sight, and the Ouro Branco Range yet gleamed high, towering in the limpid air.

At this season the weather is regular as a chronometer. The nights are raw and foggy in the low-lands; in the upper levels cold and clear, with high raised skies, planets that make the moon look very dowdy, and sparkling stars that have not forgotten to twinkle because we are so near the equator.[*]

Aurora comes in clouds, and yet the cloud
Dims not but decks her beauty :

Between 9 and 10 A.M. we have the full benefit of the day-orb, whose effulgence ignores a thread of cirrus, a vesicle of vapour. After three or four hours of the solar distillation, wool-pack and boulder clouds gather in the east; they float high in the blue immensity, then they coagulate as it were, forming mackerels' backs, and finally they weave purple hangings, innocent, however,

---

[*] In fact, I often thought on the Rio de São Francisco, even when the air was driest, that they danced more merrily than usual.

of thunder or rain.   At times we prepare for wind and wet, but all agree that the signs are the signs of increased cold.   It will not always be so.   At 3 P.M. we have no more reason to complain of the heat, and the sunsets are cool and clear, delightfully tranquil, the evenings of the lotos-eaters.

After a couple of hours, we entered a land of iron, all black and red spangled with mica.   The darkest soil was a degradation of the mysterious " Jacutinga," and the yellow-brown ruddy colour came from hæmatite, clay iron stone, often worked up in nodular or botryoidal pieces; there was also compact martite or magnetic iron, which often yields perfect specimens of the double pyramid, and in places a crust of the quartzose amygdaloid, called " canga." The chalybeate water ran splendid as gems over its bed of mineral.   Only two houses were in sight, the Fazenda do Pires, with its avenue of Araucarias, and deep embosomed in the hills, an iron foundry belonging to the Commendador Lucas Antonio Monteiro de Castro.

We then began to ascend the Serra de Santo Antonio, an east-west buttress of the Ouro Branco Range.   The little block lies on a parallel with and about thirty miles north of the Espigão Geral or Serra das Vertentes.*   It is a mass of huge clay mounds ribbed at the sides with outcrops of finely laminated clay-shale and building slate; the deep hollows separating the bulgings are densely timbered and luxuriantly green, the effect of the water-courses and the nightly mists.   The uplands sparkle with bud and blossom, mostly pink and yellow, and the grass carpet looks smooth enough to be stroked by the hand.   At this season it is a sheeny surface of greenish yellow, with dashes of broken colour, and the edges seen against the air look worn like frayed velvet. The path wound along the sides of these mound-hills, and a false step would have entailed a roll of 250 feet.   Not a sign of habitation was in sight, except some roofless ruins in a hollow to the right, which suggested the haunted house.   In fact the scene was unusually wild and romantic.

From the summit of the basin rim we saw far below us a forked stream threading the hills between avenues of thick tangled

---

* In Burmeister's map, the Serra de Santo Antonio is the apex of the angle formed by the Serra de Ouro Branco from the south-east, and the Serra da Cachoeira from the north-east.   Thus it appears as a great westerly bay in the Serra Grande or do Espinhaço.   In Geber's map neither the feature nor the name is found.

growth. The main branch flowing west to east was faintly blue; it receives a streamlet whose waters, slightly green, enter from the south-east. They drain the northern wall of the Santo Antonio Range, which here separates the Valleys of the River Paraopéba and the northern Rio das Velhas.* Both rivulets are described as " córregos desconfiados "—not to be trusted—and the angle of descent shows that their floods are dangerous. Anastomosing a little about the ruins of a bridge, which was carried away by a freshet in January 1867, they take the name of Rio da Prata.

Here then under our eyes is the task which is to occupy me some three months of river navigation. The people declare these baby waters to be the head waters of the Rio das Velhas. As will be seen, a larger volume comes from a section of or bulge in the Serra Grande (do Espinhaço), called " Serra de S. Bartholomeu," and lying about thirty miles to the north-east. The Silver River, however, can boast of superior length; it is in the south-easternmost division of the great basin whose main drain is the Rio de São Francisco.

Of undefinable interest is the first sight of a newly born stream in these new lands, suggestive as the sight of an infant, with the difference that the source must grow to riverhood, whereas the child may never become a man. A panorama passes before the eyes. The little stream so modestly purling down its channel shall presently become a mountain torrent with linns and kieves and cataracts and inundations that sweep all before them. Then will it widen to a majestic river, watering acres untold, its banks clothed with croft and glade, with field and forest, and supporting the lowly hamlet and the mighty city. Last in the far distance spreads the mouth and looms the port, busy with shipping, the link in the chain of communication which makes all nations brothers, and which must civilize if it has not civilized mankind. Standing at the small fount we see these vistas with a thrill of pleasant excitement, not unmixed with a faint sensation of anxiety. How many risks and hardships are to be undergone, how many difficulties are to be conquered before the task can be accomplished, before we can see the scenes of what is about to be.

---

* It must not be confounded with the Southern Rio das Velhas, another considerable stream visited by Castelnau. The latter river rises near Dezemboque, flows to the north-west, and discharges itself into the Southern Paranahyba, the great northern fork of the Paraná-Paraguay-Plata. For the future, whenever the Rio das Velhas is spoken of, Northern will be not expressed but understood.

The Rio das Velhas, River of the Old Women, derives its name, says local history, from the three old squaws found squatting upon its banks by the Paulista explorer "Old Devil," Bartholomeu Bueno, when in 1701 he first struck the stream at Sabará. The etymology is somewhat loose and lame. The red men, we are told by Sr. Rodriguez Valerio, a competent authority, called it "Guyaxim," and a corruption of this word becomes Guaiculiy,* still found on obsolete maps. This would mean the "old squaw's stream" (in the singular), and probably the early explorers mistranslated it into a plural, whilst their descendants invented the now classical three old women.

We forded the two forks that form the "Silver River," and, when in them, the waters appear crystal clear. The beds and the strips of riverine valley were strewed with alluvium galettes, water-rolled stones and pebbles. The harder talcose clays were cut into peculiar shapes : some resembled the balls and eggs used by the Indian slingsmen ; others were not to be distinguished, except by the practised eye, from our rude drift-hatchets. They probably suggested the weapon to the aborigines, and were formed by nature as artistically as the celts used by the seaboard tribes to open their oysters and shell-fish. On a future occasion I shall have something to say about the "Stone Age" in the Brazil, which like every other great division of the globe hitherto explored, distinctly shows the epoch :† it shows every variety, from the rudest palæolithic wedge (coin) of sandstone to the neatly chipped arrow-head of rock-crystal, and the neolithic or polished stone axe, rivalling any Celtic hatchet. Moreover, in the far interior it has not yet been thoroughly superseded by the Age of Iron.

We toiled up the very red further side of this interesting basin,

---

* The word is apparently an agglutination of Goiamim, old (woman), cunha (woman), and ig (water). Possibly it may be Cacuao-ig, which would bear the same signification. Yves D'Evreux gives the six ages of womankind :—1. Peïtan, babe ; 2. Konguantinmiry, child ; 3. Konguantin, adolescent ; 4. Konguanmoucou, woman ; Konguan, woman ; 5. Konguanmoucoupoïre, woman in force of age ; and 6. Ouaïnuy, old woman.

† The Brazil has a well-defined age of wood, and the indigenes still use wooden clubs and swords. I am happy to find the universality and ubiquity of the "Stone Age" asserted by that sound anthropologist Mr. E. B. Tylor, "Researches into the Early History of Mankind, and the Development of Civilization." These rude drift-hatchets are alluded to in "Notes on the Antiquity of Man" (pp. 85—87, Anthropological Review, No. 1, May, 1863, Trubner & Co.) ; and the literature upon the subject is becoming imposing.

To me the era is especially interesting, because it embraces the period when men had not, or what is much the same, knew not that they had souls. The soul, indeed, seems to have been the discovery of the Bronze Age.

guided by a mamelon cresting the spine. Another large hollow lay in front and beneath us; the surface where not cut up by the esbarrancados or water breaches, showed low timber above and large tree clumps in the depths, a test of superior soil and better shelter than its southern neighbour. On the right was the little mining village, "São Gonçalo do Bação," with white church and brown huts. The lowest level was a green patch known as Teixeira, rich with palms and bananas, maize and manioc, cotton and the fibre-bearing Yucca or bayonet plant: it looked the quietest of spots, where a man might most easily be consumed by age.

The northern background was a picture. We now stand full in the presence of the great Itacolumite and Itaberite formations. The sinking sun, canopied by snowy cloud lined with lively crimson, cast a glow of gold upon the castled crag, "Itabira do Campo,"* the Stone Girl of the prairie, which the Cornishmen called the Peak of Cata Branca. Early in the march we had seen it, and it then looked like a hill crowned with two blocks of masonry somewhat out of the perpendicular. From the basin rim of the Silver River, looking north-north-west, the rocks that jagged the summit appeared to form a single block. Here the head has a trident of three tall black prongs, and when winding eastward we shall often see it rising sudden and single like the Chimney Rock of the Plata River. Its form and plan recalled to mind many a half-forgotten legend of enchanted stronghold and magic mount, and curious tales are told about water springing from its base, and a shaft sunk by Nature in its depth.

---

* Dr. Couto, who found crystallized copper upon its flanks, translates the name "Moça ou rapariga de pedra." St. Hil. renders Yta bira "pierre qui brille." "Yta," more often written "Ita," occurs in many Brazilian compound words borrowed from the aborigines, and means rock, stone, or metal, especially iron; whilst "bera," or "berâb," is to flame. The usual explanation of "Itabira" is pointed stone. Castelnau calls it "Itabiri," but the loss of his MSS. compelled him to write much from memory. The distinctive "do Campo" prevents confusion with the Itabira do Mato dentro ("of the interior forest"), a magnificent pile to the north-east. We shall find also Catas Altas do Campo opposed to the Catas Altas do Mato Dentro.

This geographical feature will be noticed in Chap. 30.

From these Itabiras, the reader will remember, is derived the name of the mineral "Itaberite," a slaty rock of granular quartz and iron of several varieties, often pure oxide. Eschwege, who fathered the word, describes the mineral as ferruginous schist, and makes it the matrix of the diamond. At this Itabira do Campo begins the westernmost iron-Cordillera, described in this portion of Minas Geraes. It will run to Curral d'El-Rei, cross the Rio das Velhas at Sabará, and near it form the Serra da Piedade. In its lower slopes gold is abundant, mostly associated with iron.

We passed a ranch, whose tall and long-bearded owner, with felt broad-brim pulled low over his brows, regarded us surlily and vouchsafed no reply to questions concerning the night's rest. This individual, known as "João Militão," has the reputation of being a "valentaõ" or country bully, and, worse still, he is spoken of as a "capánga," a bravo or professional assassin. The latter gentry, relics of a barbarous age, are unhappily not yet extinct in the provincial parts of the Brazil. The Pundonor being still a mainspring of action, and the duello being unknown, men use the services of the hired ruffian with little squeamishness, and the enemy is potted from behind a tree like the Irish landlord of the last generation. As education advances and manners are softened by increased intercourse with the world, the disgrace will, like the old Poderoso, become obsolete. We behaved to the Sr. Militão at least as roughly as he did to us, and the next morning he civilly entered into conversation about the parroquets which we were shooting.

Happily we found next door lodgings in the house of José Teixeira, a saddler: he was evidently not rich, but he was kind and attentive, and his wife aided him to make us comfortable upon our little beds of sticks and straw. The third and last "morador" or squatter in this green patch presently came in, armed with a gun, and much excited. Upon the road we had met a small white cur, running purposeless and looking fagged: one of our party struck at it with a hunting whip: it did not cry or leave the path, but kept doggedly on without attempting to injure any one. Seeing its skin wet I did not suspect hydrophobia, but arrived at Teixeira, we were told that it had been rabid for some days, and had bitten sundry animals.

CHAPTER XIX.

TO COCHE D'AGUA.

O China allegre, fertil e jucundo,
E o chão de arvores muitas povoado :
E no verdor das folhas julguei que era
Ali sempre continua a primavera.
Eustachidos, by Manoel de Santa Maria Itaparica.

To the right or east of, and about a mile and a half from Itabira Peak, there is a gentle rise, the site of the mines and the village of Cata Branca.* A few details concerning its former fortunes may be interesting : it now belongs to the Morro Velho Company, and better days may again dawn upon it.

The ground, belonging originally to poor settlers, Brazilians and Portuguese, passed into the hands of the Count of Linhares, who sold the concession to the late Dr. Cliffe, an Anglo-American. The latter, a man of true trans-Atlantic energy and self reliance, parted with his right to the "Brazilian Company," raised Jan. 28, 1833, and during that year the superintendent, Mr. A. F. Mornay, completed the purchase.

The mining estate, including the fazendas of "Santo Antonio," which was bought, and "Arédes" (P. N.) which was rented, lay favourably, 4350 feet above sea-level,† within two miles of the

---

* "Cata" is sometimes erroneously written Calta; it is derived from "Catar," nearly synonymous with "Buscar," to seek, but with the sense of hunting. The miners applied it to a pit sunk in the upper strata till they reached the auriferous matter, whatever the formation might be.

Castelnau (1843) visited, and has left a good historical description of the mine from the observations of M. Weddell. My notes are taken from the Reports of the Brazilian Company 1833—37, modified by reliable information.

† Doubtless much exaggerated. Mr.

Gordon, of Morro Velho, took the observations with a Pelissher's aneroid upon the Serra, not the Peak of Cata Branca. They were on July 12, 1864—

1. Bar. 27·40   Therm. 59°   11 A.M.
2. ,, 27·37   ,,. 63°   1 P.M.

This would reduce the height in the text to about half. Mr. Gordon also makes the "Itacolumi Peak" of Ouro Preto to bear due east of Itabira. The maps of MM. Burmeister and Gerber place the former east-south-east (39°) from the latter.

Córrego Secco village, four miles or six miles by the long road from Itabira town, and 35 from the provincial capital. The soil was poor, but within a league were large roças or farms in Campo land, which supplied provisions to Ouro Preto.

The Serra of Cata Branca trends where mined from east of north, to west of south. The containing rock proved to be micaceous granular quartz with visible gold, as in California. The strike was N. 15° West, and the dip from 80° to 85°; in some places the stratification was nearly vertical, in others it was bent to the slope of the mountain, and generally it was irregular. The lode, narrow at the surface, widened below from 6 to 18 feet, and the greatest depth attained was 32 fathoms. The quartz formation was of many varieties, soft sugary, hard smoky, common white, and blue, which proved to be the richest; and the sides were hard quartzose matter equally bad for spalling and blasting. The south-eastern end was most productive. On the western side of the quartz were found the ferruginous formations "Cánga" and Jacutínga;" the latter was struck by drivings made below the Serra ridge, here a mass of iron peroxide : the works, however, wanted ventilation, and were abandoned.

The lode, which could not be called a " constant productive," abounds in "vughs" or vein-cavities, tubes, pipes, and branches, called by the Brazilian miner " olhos "—eyes, surrounded by a soft material, mainly running vertically, and richer in free gold than the average. Near these pockets, but not disseminated through the vein, was a small quantity of auriferous pyrites, iron and arsenical. A little fine yellow dust, oxide of bismuth, ran down the middle of the lode, and gave granular gold. The best specimens averaged from 21·75 to 22 carats, our standard gold.

The Santo Antonio lode lay parallel with and east of the Cata Branca. The Arédes mine, 8 miles to the south-west, was beyond the Peak : here the Serra is covered with boulders of hard quartz, very numerous at the base of the great vein. They rest on the common, soft, various-coloured clays of the country, and are intersected with lines of sugary quartz, which gave a little very fine gold. This formation extends far to south and west of Itabira : openings were made in it, and one, the " Sumidouro," was successful. Arédes showed also a small formation of Jacutinga containing red gold, sometimes alloyed with palladium, and accompanied with oxide of manganese. The soil was good, and it contained 1—2 square miles of arable land that produced all the cereals of Europe.

Mr. Mornay, afterwards Superintendent of Cocaes, and Vice-Director of Cuiabá, began with a salary, besides house and all civilized luxuries, of £3000 per annum, and this was paid out of a capital of 6000 £10 shares. In November, 1833, he was followed by Commander Cotesworth, R.N., who afterwards died at Liverpool. The latter was like all the " Service " superintendents, then such favourites at home, a strict disciplinarian, active and energetic, fond of riding horses till they broke down, tetchy on the subject of his rights, and " zealous in the discharge of his duty,"—which led to disputes. Finding the mine an immense hole, he had to fork* the water which filled the shafts, and to level, dial,† and measure afresh. The mine began with the antiquated practice of "stamping," or rather " crushing," by horizontal millstones of hard, tough, quartzose matter; presently the best machinery in the Empire was put up. In 1835, besides hired labourers, " Cata Branca " employed 38 Europeans, 76 negroes, and 34 negresses.

In 1844 the mine fell in. The sole had become sloppy, and the liquid Jacutinga could not be drained by any mechanical force; the ground was not properly timbered, and the side-thrust increased till it was enormous. The general account is that thirteen workmen, one of them an Englishman, were killed: some increase the number, which others declare to be exaggerated.

The " Cata Branca " failure, one unfortunately of very many, resulted from two causes. Firstly, there was an utter absence of economy, and as Mr. Moshesh justly observes, with peculiar applicability to Minas, even gold may be bought too dear. Secondly, the mine was badly worked. Jacutinga was then an unknown formation, but English miners, especially Cornish men, have learned everything, and consequently they will brook no teaching. Those who do not judge them by their own standard are willing to grant that they have acquired by rule of thumb

---

* To " fork," is to reduce the water to its proper level till the mouth of the pump hose can be seen.

† The sons of old Kernou used to call the theodolite a dial, hence " dialling " is applied to underground levels and surveys from a fixed station.

something of mineralogy, nothing of geology. But since the days of Howel or Houël, "king of small Brittany," they have been heaven-born miners with the airs of omniscience. Who can forget the naïve speech of the Cornish gang-captain, who told Robert Stephenson that a north country could not possibly know anything about mining? I have seen the offer of a "practical Cornishman" to do for £50,000 what a "theorist," that is to say a professional man, educated in the scientific schools, could not effect for £100,000. Mr. Practical was believed by a practical public— in England still linger old superstitions about rule of thumb, which makes men easily take the bait—and the consequence was that the practical shareholders soon found themselves safe in Chancery. The fact is that Tre, Pol, and Pen are good men and true, but they must take to heart what was asserted a little farther west, namely, that—

> John P. Robinson, he
> Said they didn't know ev'rything down in Judee.

We shall trace these same two evils, reckless expenditure and want of exact knowledge, in the history of many other mining adventures. Hence it is that in this land of boundless mineral wealth, so many companies have come to grief, and so many a mine has been, to use the technical word, "knocked."

After a delightfully bracing night, we rose with the dawn ; again however the old white garron had strayed, the mules had followed, and the glorious morn had waxed hot before it saw us in the saddle. The bridle-path fell at once into the valley of the Rio da Plata, a baby brook in a sandy and gravelly cradle, a world too wide for its shrunken stream. Six times we forded the limpid waters which ran northwards, we cut the throat of two big bends, each with its drain from the west, swelling the main line, and we halted for breakfast under a fig tree, upon the banks of the Córrego do Bação. The little Arraial of that name, rich in vegetables and fruit trees, was hard by, and the miners came out of their huts to stare and chat. The valley, when we struck it once more, was floored with loose sand, and heaped as usual with "spoil-banks," and mounds of washed red clay. Another hard pull up the left buttress was enlivened by the beauty of the vegetation, and our ears were refreshed by the under-murmur and the bubbling of abundant streams. The birds were more numerous

than usual; the parroquets chattered from tree to tree, a noisy
woodpecker* screamed in the bush, and hawks floated high in the
mistless air. We then walked carefully down a hideous causeway of rock, paving stones, white earth and sandy dust which
rose in suffocating clouds. A hollow lane of incipient sandstone
and, here and there, dry walls, told us that we were approaching
a settlement.

After about four hours of actual riding we sighted "Itabira do
Campo" in a punch-bowl below us. The stream which divides
it, running from east to west, is crossed by a tolerable stone
bridge, and the banks are used as bleaching-grounds, white with
raiment and black with washerwomen. On the south of the
"Freguezia" are the chapels of Nª Sª das Mercês and Bom
Jesus de Matosinhos; to the west is the Rosario, whilst the
body of the village contains the matriz of Nª Sª da Boâ
Viagem and Stª Theresa. In fact the church accommodation
would lodge the whole population, though hardly with comfort;
most of the buildings are in a ruinous condition.

We breasted another steep slippery causeway, the entrance
street; here there were good houses, but all bore inscribed over
their doors the Desolation of Dulness. The heat of the sun
induced us to dismount at a shop in the square of Santa Thereza,
whose steeple with its tiled roof and splayed eaves suggested a
chapel in Switzerland. The people were exceedingly obliging,
and gave us coffee with the least possible delay; they had long
tales to tell of palmy days, now set in night, when they established their sons, married their daughters to Englishmen, and
enjoyed the excitements of loss and gain. "Itabira" throve with
the "Cata Branca" mine, and it decayed when "she" was
"knocked." The Itabirenses linger on, barely supported by the
Morro Velho market, and the memories of better times hardly
suffice to keep alive hope for the future.

Though warned that we could hardly reach "Coche d'Agua"
before nightfall, and well acquainted with the horrors of a Brazilian cross-cut after dark, and on an unknown line, we set out at
1 P.M. Another causeway, a turn to the left, and we were again
in the Valley of the Silver Stream. It was now a "hobbledehoy" in the worst and most unmanageable phase, turbid, noisy,

* Known as the Pico chão-chão.

and shallow. Six miles of unusually good road placed us at
Mazagão,* the iron foundry of the Capitão Manoel França.
From this place to our destination is only six miles, but the
bridge was broken down, there is no road along the precipitous
left bank, and we were driven to a detour of a useless league and
a half westward, north-westward and northward.

Ladders of clay and rock led up the ascents of remarkably steep
pitch ; the ground on both sides was clad in " dirty forest." A single
house, with a little croft, belonging to one Pereira, was the only
proof that all was not a desert. We met but one party, probably returning from some family festival, wedding or baptism.
The girls rode on before their parents, as they are made to walk
in the old-fashioned towns of Italy and the Brazil, Pa and Ma
bringing up the rear, and marking down with four eyes every look
given and received. One maiden, a pretty specimen with nut-
brown skin, blue-black hair and roguish glance, was seated in the
manner masculine, a sensible practice now obsolete here, except
amongst the Caipiras†, and the slaves. Yet I would recommend it
to women who tempt the byeways of Brazil; here side-saddle and
skirts are really dangerous to limb and life.

Trotting over the table land, which we found much too short,
we dropped by another long and tedious descent into the river
valley. To the end of this march the hills are bluff southwards,
and fall in long gentle grassy slopes to the north. The path

---

* This word has spread over the Portuguese colonies between the Brazil and
Hindostan, where we write it " Maza-
gaum," as if it had any connection with
" Gaum," a village. The name is Moroc-
can, and commemorates the Christian vic-
tories at the Port of " Mazagan."

† In São Paulo " Caipíra " is preferred ;
in Minas, " Caipóra." The " Caypor " of
Mr. Bates, i. 89, is, I presume, a misprint.
Both are corruptions of " Caá," a bush,
and " -póra," who inhabits. Thus the
term literally means " bushman," or
savage. " Tapúya-Caápóra " would be a
wild (brabo) Tapuya, " abá-caapora,"
homme des bois. Amongst the Aborigines
" Caa-pora " (not Caypora) is a spirit or
demon that lives in the forest, a wood-imp
reputed to be malicious, and fond of robbing children, which he stores in a hollow
tree. In old authors we find Curupiora:
the old Jesuit Simão de Vasconcellos interprets the word " dæmon of thought,"
spirit of darkness ; others, " spirit of the

woods," opposed to Jurupari, or Jurupory,
the Devil. Evidently there is a confusion,
physical and metaphysical. Sr. J. d' Alencar
explains Curupira by Curumim, a pappoose
or Indian child, and pira, bad ; it was
usually represented as a dwarfish imp.
Jurupari is from Juru, a mouth, and apara,
crooked. In popular use Caipira is applied
contemptuously to both sexes, and corresponds with our Essex Calves, Kentish Long-
tails, Yorkshire Tikes, and Norfolk Bumpkins. A man will facetiously use it to
himself or to his family, but others must
not. The civil name for a backwoodsman,
a voyageur (Canada), a Coureur des Deserts,
or Coureur des bois, is " Sertanejo," which
classical authors write " Sertanista," from
Sertão, the backwoods, the Far West, a
term which will be explained in its proper
place. Southey (Explorations, &c., iii.
900) makes " Sertanejo " an inhabitant of
the " Sertam," and " Sertanista," a person engaged in exploring the " Sertam."

was a zigzag of the worst kind; again we hit the river, now a
flood in hot Achillean youth.

> Impiger iracundus inexorabilis acer.

A swirling torrent, not exactly yellow, but dark and flavous,
hardly to be swum or forded.   From the grassy slopes above, the
rush of water was imposing, banked with bluffs 800 feet high, and
shaded with gigantic trees, hanging woods and wonderful virgin
forests, a scene that would surprise the admirers of poor little
Dart, the wonder of Southern England.   The bridge was unsound, but it bore us across.   I felt no little anxiety.   The sun
was already streaming his last rays over the mountain tops, three
conspicuous knobs in the north, a kind of "Three Sisters," illu-
minated by the reflection.   Night follows sundown like a shot at
this height, and in these low latitudes; the slope was desperately
long, the mules were jaded, and in places holes twenty feet deep
yawned across the path.

At length, after much straining of the eyes, we descended the
last pitch of road, and ere day was burnt out we entered, with
no small satisfaction, Coche d'Agua.   Here we found Mr.
L'pool, who had hurried on, determined to be under cover before
dark.

And here I venture to offer advice with the view of forming a
"comfortable traveller."   Let every thought be duly subordinate to self.   Let no weak regard for sex or age deter you from
taking, or at least from trying to take, the strongest beast, the best
room, the superior cut, the last glass of sherry.   When riding
lead the way, monopolise the path, and bump up against all who
approach you—they will probably steer clear for the future.   If a
companion choose a horse, a saddle, or a bridle, endeavour to
abstract it—he had evidently some reason for the choice.   In the
morning take care of No. 1; muffle your head, wrap up your
throat, stuff your boots with cotton.   As the sun rises gradually
unshell yourself—"good people are scarce"—open your umbrella
and suck oranges, not omitting all the little contrivances of refec-
tion which your ingenuity will suggest.   Never go to a hotel if
there be a private house within a league, and above all things
keep the accounts.   Finally, if you invite a man to dine, score up
his liquor on the wall, staring him "in the face," so shall or may
it deter him from the other bottle.   And thus your trip will cost
you 123 milreis, when your friend is minus 750 milreis a head.

CHAPTER XX.

TO THE GOLD MINE OF MORRO VELHO.

"Cultiva se em Minas precisamente como se cultivam no tempo dos Paulistas e dos Emboabas."—*Pres. Report of Minas Geraes for* 1865, *Appendix*, p. 25.

"A VARGEM do Coche d'Agoa"* — the River-reach of the Water-trough—humble name for a humbler spot, is so called from a stone cistern, still visible in the now ruined house of the late Lieut. Domingos Souares, a small "Creoulo"† planter. Dr. Couto (1801), mentions it as a "sitio" and station on the old western road from Ouro Preto to the then Tejuco. Actually it is a scatter of some sixteen huts in a hollow which grows bad sugar-cane, good potatos, and plentiful fuel for the great English mine.

José Clemente Pereira, our host, had been presented by his wife with twelve sons, and their increase was fifty grand plus five grandchildren; the family populates the place. This "creating souls" and breeding citizens for the commonwealth, advances here as elsewhere in Minas, by geometrical rather than arithmetical progression. I shall revert to the subject. We all intended to sleep like humans who had earned their rest; but the night air was raw and nipping, the poor great-grandmother had a bad cough, and Negra, my mastiff-pup, snored grimly, till made thoroughly intoxicated by cachaça, poured upon it with that intention.

And here let me explain what cachaça is before we enter

---

* Caldcleugh (ii. 269), writes Coxo de Agua, and the Almanak Coxo d'Agua. The reader will have remarked before this that the etymology of the remarkably rich Portuguese language is still unsettled. This is naturally the case with a tongue spoken from the upper waters of the Amazons to Macao and Japan. The elision of the letter terminating the genitive sign is remarkably arbitrary.

† Creoulo, or Creolo in the Brazil, is applied to negroes and things grown in the country, and to persons either born in the Empire, but not of mixed blood.

civilized houses, where the word and the thing are equally abominable.

"Cacháça," or "Caxáça," the "cachass" of strangers, is the "tafia" of French writers, a pretty word wilfully thrown away, like the Spanish "tortilla," that means "scone." It is the korn-schnapps, the kwass of the Brazil. The commonest kind is distilled from the refuse molasses and drippings of clayed sugar, put into a retort-shaped still,* old as the hills, and rich in verdigris. The peculiar volatile oil or æther is not removed from the surface; the taste is of copper and smoke—not Glenlivet—in equal proportions, and when the "catinga" or fetor has tainted the spirits it cannot be removed.† Otherwise it would be as valuable to Europe as the corn brandy of Canada, and the potato brandy of Hamburg, from which is made the veritable Cognac. There are two kinds; the common, made from the Cayenne‡ cane, and the "Creoulinha" or "Branquinha," the old Madeiran growth; the latter is preferred, as the "cooler" and less injurious. Brandy, said Dr. Johnson, is the drink of heroes, and here men drink their Cachaça heroically; the effect is "liver," dropsy, and death. Strangers are not readily accustomed to the odour, but a man who once "takes to it," may reckon upon delirium tremens and an early grave. Its legitimate use is for bathing after insolation, or for washing away the discomfort of insect bites. Your Brazilian host generally sends a bottle with the tub of hot water.

The "Canninha," in Spanish "Cana," is a superior article, made from the cane juice fermented in souring tubs; it is our rum, and when kept for some years, especially underground, the flavour reminds one of Jamaica. Old travellers usually prefer this "Pinga" to the vitriolic gin and the alcoholic Cognacs which have found their way into the country; as the bottle is sold for a penny to twopence, there is no object in adulterating

---

* Archaically called Alambique.

† A more careful process would probably obviate much of this evil. At present imperfect heating and cooling of the rough machine, cause the irremediable empyreumatic taint. I never could light a spirit lamp with the second distillation, much less with the first.

‡ "On a d'abord cultivé dans le canton la canne de Cayenne, mais quand on a connu celle de Taïté, on lui a donné la préférence." (Prince Max. i. 83). Most writers declare the Cayenne (Cayena), to have been brought from "Otaheite;" about 1832 this "Otaheite Cane" was introduced into Louisiana and Florida, which formerly had the "Ribbon Cane," the Creoula of the Brazil. The author above mentioned tells us that in his day the commonest kind was called "Agoa ardente de Canna" (opposed to the agoa ardente do reino, i. e., rum, gin, Cognac, &c.); when better distilled, "Agoa ardente de mel," and the best "Cachaza" or "Cachassa," both wrongly spelled. These expressions are now quite obsolete.

the contents. Drunk in moderation, especially on raw mornings and wet evenings, it does more good than harm. The people have a prejudice against mixing it,* and prefer the style called "Kentucky drink," or "midshipman's grog;" they are loud in its praise, declaring that it cools the heat, heats the cold, dries the wet, and wets the dry. When did man ever want a pretext for a dram?

The "Restilo" is, as its name shows, a redistillation of either Cachaça or Canninha, and it removes the unpleasant odour of the molasses spirit. This form is little known in São Paulo; in Minas it is the popular drink, and the planter calls it jocosely "Brazilian wine;" he prefers it, and justly, to the vile beverages imported at enormous prices from the "Peninsula." There is yet a third distillation, "Lavado," or the washed. It is said to be so strong and anhydrous that if thrown up into the air it descends in a little spray, and almost evaporates. It is not, however, distilled over burnt lime, and thus it never becomes absolute alcohol. †

The effects of this rum upon the population, and the frequency of the Cachaçada or drunken quarrel, often ending in a shot or a stab, will be found noticed in the following pages.

It was 5·15 A.M. on Saturday, June 19, 1867, the ninth stage from Barbacena, and the sixteenth day after our departure from Rio de Janeiro, when we were summoned to mount and to measure our last march. A thick white mist blurred the moon's outline, here a sign of cold, not of rain. Our escoteiro, however, knew every inch of the road; we followed him with full confidence over a freshly repaired bridge, up and down hills like palm oil, and across sundry short levels, where the River Valley, which has now wound from east to north, widens out. Again I call by courtesy a valley this longitudinal furrow which splits the mountain range into two meridional chains; on its right crowd the westernmost buttresses of the "Serra Grande," or "do Espinhaço," whilst the eastern flank of the chain connecting Itabira Peak with its brother apex Curral d'El-Rei, hems in the left.

---

* Mr. Walsh (ii. 8), gravely chronicles concerning "Caxas:" "Our host informed me that it was a wholesome and excellent cordial when taken raw, but he warned me against mixing it with water." Despite which sound advice the traveller presently tried it "hot with" and pronounced it to be a by no means contemptible beverage.

† The Restilo is the best for preserving specimens, but it affects the delicate colours of the coral snakes for instance, and thus erroneous descriptions have become current. If cachaça be used, the spirit must be changed after a few days.

morning Star

Brazilian Tanager

As Lucifer sparkled aloft between the Crescent and the horizon, bright as should be the sun's herald in the Highlands of the Brazil, and the air became sensibly colder, and the pale brassy dawn-light waxed faintly green; when red reflections lined the fragments of cloud land, and the merry " Cardinal "* began to chirp his matins, we again saw on our left the baby brook, the hobbledehoy, the hot young torrent of yesterday, now become the Rio das Velhas, and stamped with the signet of middle age, a respectable fluviatile, progressing steadily three miles an hour, broad-waisted as the Richmond Thames, not ignorant of the canoe, and presently about to call for connection with and settlement by a steamer.   Dr. Couto calls it O Vermelho Rio, showing that the banks were then much worked and washed for gold; now it is of muddy yellow hue.

An hour's ride, ending with a steep incline, placed us at the arraial and freguezia of " S^to Antonio do Rio das Velhas."† Its birthday is unknown, the date was probably when the Batatal, ‡ the Socco, the Engenho de Agua, and the Papamilho Mines gave abundant golden yields.   In 1801 it had a hundred houses; in 1820 the population was numbered at 1200; in 1847, Sr. Silva Pinto § gave it 1086, and the Almanak (186–,) proposes 1300, an estimate based on 115 voters and three electors.   At present it has some forty-five tenements, scattered about the river's right bank.   We found it a village of the dead-asleep; vainly the mules halted unbidden at the familiar venda, and the Company's private ranch.   The little Matriz was silent, dumb, and so was its filial chapel—we had no desire to disturb their echos.   The village has shops and mechanics; it breeds and it cultivates " some," but the price of transport smothers exportation.   Sunday, when the parish meets to discuss its scandal and to do its worship, galvanizes it into a manner of life, and at times a drunken miner from Morro Velho performs a lively piece, ending with a " dance of all the characters."

The next hour lay over a mud which in the rains becomes the matrix of a small iron mine of mules' shoes.   It was lately re-

---

* A pretty red Tangara (Tanagra episco-pus ?), locally called Cardeal.

† Alias Santo Antonio do Rio Acima, " up-stream," thus distinguished from " S^to Antonio do Rio Abaixo," another village " down-stream."

‡ This name, common in the Provinces of Minas Geraes and São Paulo, means that the gold nuggets found there were common as sweet potatos (batatas).

§ This gentleman's work was promised to me at Ouro Preto.   Unfortunately the promiser forgot to keep his promise.

paired, and in parts newly laid by M. Gerber, C.E., of Ouro
Preto. The "troopers," as usual, prefer the old familiar way, consequently both lines are abominable. The end of the league
showed us, on the left bank, a little white-washed church, Sta
Rita, and in the stream were two piles, once a bridge built by
men who ignored the art and mystery of pile driving. Beyond
it lies the Morro da Gloria Mine, belonging to five proprietors;
the pyrites, finely crushed by six head of old Brazilian "chápas,"*
yields per ton ⅗ths of an ounce of 21-carat gold. Here, too, is
the "Morro de Santa Rita" Mine, once an "open cut," now
fallen in, fast closed, and no longer exploited.

Sta Rita is said to be one league from Morro Velho; if so it
is the longest league I ever did ride. Opposite it, the Estalagem, a big ranch, leads to the Santa Rita Mine, proprietrix
D. Florisbella da Horta, a widow who has worked her property
with the Brazilian energy of an earlier day. This "Lavra," or
washing, which is still at times washed, is partially pyritic, and
yields also brown auriferous oxide of iron with leaves of quartz;
it is quarried with an open face like a stone pit, then stamped
and finally straked.† The loss of negroes was great; Dr. Walker,
third superintendent of Morro Velho, informs us that in an
exceptionally short time, twenty-four out of forty seasoned men
died of dysentery and inflammation of the chest.

Here the river-bed is cumbered with grave-like mounds and
masses of gravel, coarse and fine; it is mostly grown with thin
vegetation, sown by the hand of Time since 1825, when all these
diggings were in decay. The hard ferruginous material locally
called Marumbé, ‡ darkened the soil. Presently we turned sharp
to the left from the Sabará road, and crossed the Rio das Velhas
by the Santa Rita bridge. The footway is 270 feet long, with
nine spans supported by trusses or trestles, the girders being
stiffened and prevented from warping by diagonal chains. Built
in 1853, it has frequently been repaired by the English Company;
in 1859 Mr. Gordon gave it the last touch, since then two supporting posts have given way, making an ugly sag. A bolster or
felling-piece of wood placed over the cap-piece would remedy the

---

* "Stamps," of which more hereafter.
† This use of the word may not be correct; but it is very convenient, and amply
deserves to be made a passed and accepted
verb.

‡ Dr. Couto declares these Marumbés,
or Marumbís, which he writes "Marom-
bés," to be copper ore of the ash-coloured
(cinzenta) species. But he certainly had
copper on the brain.

defect; but the municipality would take a year of Sundays to think and talk over the matter.

Beyond the bridge, northern energy and capital were seen to assert themselves. Here, three miles from Morro Velho, begins the estate of "Fernam Paes," bought in 1862 by the Great Company for 11,583*l*. The mines, mostly pyritic, are those of Gaia, Guabiroba (valuable ground), Samambaia, Serviço Novo, Mato Virgem, and minor deposits. The new proprietors have cleared a twenty-feet road, have laid a tramway for bringing the ore to the stamping mills, and have cut a leat* through very hard ground; the stamp site has been excavated, the framework is being put up, so as to begin work at once, and the old manor-house on the right of the thoroughfare had been repaired for the English miners; their sturdy northern voices greeted our guide from afar.

We ran for a short distance down the River Valley, which bagged to the left, and showed signs here of a "tip-over," there of regular flooding, as far as the hill foot. Part of this ground belongs to the Company, part does not,—which, to speak mildly, must be a nuisance. We then toiled up a red clay ridge, crept down an incline of similar formation, and up another bad chine, justly called "Monte Vidéo."† This Bella Vista shows the first glimpse of our destination, and joys our hearts. High in front towers the peak-capped wall of Curral d'El-Rei, bearing its timber cross. On a nearer and a lower horizon rises Morro Velho, "the old mount," also cross-crowned, and supporting on its brown shoulders "Timbuctoo" and "Boa Vista," the white-washed and red-tiled negro quarters.‡ At our feet is the pit filled by the little town Congonhas, whose site is an irregular mixture of bulge and hollow, sprinkled with church and villa, with garden and orchard, and beautified with its threading of silver stream. On the ridge to the right is the Bella Fama farm, where the Company keeps its "great troop" of mules, used to bring in stores and provisions. On the left are other ridges and other peaks, which we shall presently see to better advantage.

Nothing can be more suave than this view on a fine clear

---

* An artificial water-course, here called "Rego."

† Not Monte Vídéo, Anglicè : the vulgar derivation is Montem Video—"I see a mount."

‡ Here called by the African name, "Senzallas."

morning; but those who first descend it in a Monte Vídeo fog,
will shudder at the portal of a Brazilian Staffordshire,—a Black
Country. The angle of the road is that of a roof, and set in the
red clay is a dark slatey patch of finely pulverized or treacly-
muddy argile, which looks from afar like a vast pall. The
colouring matter is a trifling portion of cubical and unauriferous
iron pyrites, the clay is useful for plumbago-coloured pigments,
and in Europe the mineral is made to yield sulphuric acid, and
to serve many technological purposes.

Red ridge and black ridge might both be avoided by running
a road for 1·25 miles down the river-bed, below Santa Rita
bridge, and then by hugging the Ribeirão do Morro Velho.* The
latter is the main drain, the natural zigzag, and the best approach
to the great mine, which certainly deserves a carriage road instead of the present mule path.

A deep hollow lane, with the rocky remnants of an antiquated
ramp, a few huts, the little Bomfim chapel, and the large house
of a charcoal contractor, lead into the town. We rumbled over
the Ribeirão bridge, and thence we clattered over the slippery
kidney stones, with their black capping of iron, that pave the
sleepy little old settlement. It rarely opens its eyes before 8
A.M., when a few hundred yards beyond it, hundreds of men are
working night and day: those citizens who were awake were
probably but half awake, they looked very cross, and not a
slouched hat was fingered.

"Nª Sª do Pilar de Congonhas de Sabará"—here names are
long, apparently in direct inverse ratio of the importance of the
place or person named—though very drowsy, is tolerably neat,
and wears a kind of well-to-do-in-the-world look. The main
square has some two-storied and ornamented houses, and the
village dignitaries have taken the trouble to prop up that necessary of Brazilian town-life,† the theatre, decrepit though only
fifteen years old. The Matriz, repaired by the late Fr. Francisco de Coriolano, shows a three-windowed façade, and a cross-
crested pediment; the belfries have Swiss roofs, pig-tailed at the
corners, and turned up after the mode of Chinese Macao; pos-

---

* Formerly the Ribeirão de Congonhas,
which flowing from west to east has been
diverted to work and drain the English
mine.

† I believe that the Brazil, with about a

third of the population of England, has as
many theatres—166. It will be time to
abuse them when we have improved our
own.

sibly it is an unconscious derivation from the image dearly beloved by the heathenry of Pomeco and Tlascalla. At the railing door there is a quaint screen, quaintly painted with the Passion-events, whilst the ambulatory has fourteen station-crosses nailed to the walls.

Commerce flourishes in twenty shops, including a laboratorio and sundry pharmacies. The Inner Brazil, like the Western United States, and very unlike the Bananas* of the coast, still requires the dinner pill of our grandfathers and Dr. Kitchener's "peristaltic persuaders." May not this partly account for the spirit so *tenax propositi,* with which both nations have waged wars for years, when we wax weary of fighting and yearn for "home" after a few months' campaign? The apothecary in these parts is never a poor apothecary. 200*l.* worth of bad drugs brings him 2000*l.,* and keeps him for life; strange to say, men who can be dosed gratis by the Company, prefer the "botica" and—quingenties.

Congonhas has been cured of the "decádence et abandon" in which St. Hilaire found it forty-seven years ago. Built by mining, it fell with mining, and by mining it has been "resurrected." In 1830 it lodged 1390 souls; in 1840 about 2000, with three churches, one an unfinished ruin; in 1847 (Sr. Pinto) 913, of course Morro Velho not included; in 1864, 6 electors, 211 voters, and 4000, allowing 1000 miners. Since that time the number has certainly not fallen off.

From the square we turned to the left, compulsed by an ugly stony climb, impudently rising straight in front, and cutting over the ridge that separates the basin of Congonhas and Morro Velho. By the partially paved road there was a neat store and the Hotel Congonhense, where M. Gehrcke, an old English-speaking German employé of the Company, receives the destitute of introductory letters; here also an Italian portrait-painter lives upon his art. High above us to the right is the Rosario Church, filled though it is no fête. The dark towerless front of the mouldering fane frowns in stone like a bit of bastion; an unfinished crown of Portugal and a bald place for the "Quinas" beneath, tell their own tale. The nave and the high altar glare with whitewash, the ornamentation is pauper and gaudy—negro taste.

---

* The Cockneys of Rio de Janeiro are so called by the hardy Paulistas. The extensive use of aloes in the interior is noticed by the "System."

Lower to the right is the store of Messrs. Alexander and Sons, who brew their own "yel," called "Inkermann," which rapadura sugar makes a trifle more capitous than the pawkiest of Scotch barley braes, and which has rolled over many a stout fellow neatly as could a Russian gun. Beer, which ancient Egypt, although she had no pale ale, sensibly preferred to the vine, should be heavily backed in Minas against spirits, especially Cachaça. Mr. Henry D. Cocking, of the Smiths' Department, brews at home; he must, however, import his hops. To judge by the success of the Germans in western São Paulo, here also the fine tonic would flourish. Opposite Messrs. Alexander's is the large ranch of Mello and Co., where the black miners make their purchases; further on lies the old hospital, with its garden now occupied by the mining captain Andrew, and by Sr. Antonio Marcos da Rocha, once a servant of the Gongo Soco establishment, now "Ranger of Woods and Forests" at Morro Velho. The road is protected by tree-trunks laid obliquely across it, and faced up with clay to serve as watercourses; this is a common contrivance in the Highlands of the Brazil, and on some lines, especially in São Paulo, horses must step over a bole with every second pace.

Here the near view becomes passing pretty. The descent runs through an avenue of Coqueiro palms, whose drupes, large as a score of grape bunches, hang about their necks. On either side is a meadow of " Angola grass " (Capim d'Angola, Panicum guineense), each rich green leaf eight inches long, by one and a half broad; it is planted by joint-cuttings of the cane-like culm, and in the season it supplies per week three tons of sweet and succulent fodder. Unhappily this fair site is the very centre of diphtheria. Above the meadow, and crowning a red yellow hill, is the Rev. Mr. Armstrong's parsonage, white and neat as his neck-tie. The wonderfully thin lancet windows, and a cross ultra-Rumic, distinguish the chapel amongst the scattered villas and rows of houses.

To the right, on the near bank of the Ribeirão, heaps and banks of grey ore and crushed stone denote the "Praia Works."* A little tramway, 800 yards long, piercing the hillocks and crossing a pair of bridges, with one heavy filling and cuttings to

* I shall return to those " Praia Works " in Chapter 26.

the extent of 788 cubic fathoms, connects them with head-quarters, and conveys from the spaling floors "poor stuff"* to be worked should an accident close the upper mines.   Here also "launders"† or flumes with great fleet or inclination, bring down slimes and refuse-tailings.   The machinery which re-treats them consists of two wheels, and stamps housed under a long tiled shed.

Ascending a dwarf hill—our last, let us be thankful!—we pass a neat Anglo-Indian bungalow, occupied by Mr. James Smyth, superintendent of the Negro department.   On the other side of the Ribeirão gully are the brown tents denoting the "Mingú diggings," pyritiferous like the main lode.   Further on are the large new Hospital and the medical quarters, where lodge Doctors M'Intyre and Weir.

"Tranquillity House" has the prettiest of prospects; but lovelier, ah! far lovelier, are the charms of "Galashiels," says Dr. Weir, who with filial reverence hangs to his wall a print of the uncouth Scotch village.   Still further on is the Catholic Chapel, literally all crosses; outlying crosses, inlying crosses, crosses in the air,—even the windows are crosses.   To the primitive Christian what a scandal this would have been !   North of the valley is the "Morro Velho;" a dark red scaur in its southern slope shows where the Brazilian owners hit their first gold, and where sundry huts were buried by a land-slip.   The tall black cross was put up by Mr. Gordon, to ease the burden of his people; formerly, on days ordered by the priest, they pilgrimaged over three rough miles, to the apex of the Curral d'El-Rei.   The "Old Mount" gives a beautiful panorama, but in the "dirty bush" the King of the Carrapátos holds his court, and he will hold it till ejected by Bahama grass, or some similar immigrant vegetation.

Leaving to the left, on an eminence, the big white store of the Company, presided over by Messrs. George Morgan and Matthew, we find the "Casa Grande," which must not be con-founded with the "Casas Grandes" of the Gila Valley.   Here it is the Superintendent's quarters, red tiled, painted with official yellow, vine-grown, and fronted by a verandah built to receive

---

* "Mina Pobre."
† Native miners call the launders "bicáme," from "bíca," a spout.

His Imperial Majesty. To the west, and facing at right angles, is the Sobrado, which acts "Guesten House," and where, although intending that our visit should last a week, we shall presently pass, on and off, a pleasant month of busy idleness, the "best of all earthly blessings." This hospitable adjunct is found in all the old-fashioned establishments of the Brazil, and in the country towns, even now, a man will not take a tenement which wants the detached quarters where friends and strangers can be entertained.

The scene strikes my unfamiliar eye as a mixture of Brazilian Petropolis and Neilgherry Ootacamund; there is something English in the neat cottages, fronted by railed flower-beds, and the dark slatey stream; with a savour of Switzerland in the high clear air, and the meshes of yellow pathways on both sides of the Ribeirão Gorge. But can we be within earshot of the Great Mine? Where are the familiar features, the poisonous smoke, the vegetation "fuliginously green?" All around us are dottings of varied verdure, here a row of gigantic aloes, like the Socotrine, whose gold-green bands gain for them in the Brazil the title of "Independence Shrub." There we see a cedar, sole survivor of its ancient and noble race, proving that this valley was covered at one time, like the rest of the country, with virgin forest. The splendid snow-white trumpets of the Datura, popularly called Fig-tree of Hell,* depend from masses of verdure twelve feet high; the fatal use of the seed, so common in India, where a caste of professional poisoners is called "Dhaturíyah," here belongs to negroes. The Melastomaceæ, of various species, vary in size from a mere bush to a tall tree: the Flôr de Quaresma, or Lenten flower (Lasiandra mutabilis)† is beautiful in bloom of white, pink, and dark lilac, and the mauve-coloured bracts of the Brazilian Bougainvillea, here of unusual stature, are set off by the wild Fuchsia, brilliant with bloom of the richest scarlet, whilst the humbler growths of homely England act foil to the gorgeousness and the splendour of the Tropics.

---

* Figueira do Inferno.' This and "trombelleira" (trumpet-tree), are the general names for all varieties of the Datura Estramonio, or Stramonium. The common arbust is the Brugmansia candida.

It has probably been introduced from Hindostan into Minas.

† The bark of this tree is used as a black dye.

We have been riding four hours, we are hungry as hunters, and so, with another glance of admiration at externals, we bid *au revoir* to our good " master of the horse " and all his mules, we enter the hospitable house, and after the warmest of receptions, we suggest breakfast, which does not keep us waiting.

CHAPTER XXI.

NOTES ON GOLD-MINING IN MINAS GERAES.

"Quand la population sera plus considérable, et que les Brésiliens sauront exploiter leurs mines d'une manière regulière, on en tirera des avantages qu'on ne procurerait pas aujourd'hui sans faire d'immenses sacrifices."—*Eschwege, Pluto. Bras.* 78.

SECTION I.

GOLD.

BRAZILIAN travellers of the pre-Californian epoch, St. Hilaire[*] and Walsh for instance, firmly believing that Dives must ever go to the Devil, were fond of exalting, à la Fénelon, those silly pseudo-virtues, the golden mean, Frugality, Simplicity, Content, La Pauvreté, sa mission dans l'église, and so forth. They moralised, like St. Paul and Pliny, *ad libitum* upon the evils which gold does to mankind, and especially upon the evils which gold-digging has done to Minas and other places, by scratching up a vast extent of country, and by diverting industry from more profitable and enduring pursuits. They adopted the sentimental view of the metal. Mammon still looked upon the trodden gold of Heaven's pavement. They remembered their "gold alone does passion move;" their "auri sacra fames," the "aurum irrepertum," "et sic melius situm," the "auri sanies," and "bane for the human race;"

---

[*] "Gold mines discovered by audacious and enterprising men, swarms of adventurers settling upon riches announced with all the exaggeration of hope and desire ; a society formed in the midst of every crime, reduced into a semblance of order by military law, and softened by the burning sun and the effeminate indolence of the climate; some moments of splendour and prodigality ; a melancholy decadence and ruins —such is briefly the history of the Province of Goyaz ; such is the course of events in almost all gold-bearing countries." (St. Hil. III. i. 308—9).

Sentimentalism is *per se* irrefutable ; it is to common sense what metaphysics are to physics. But the amiable author forgot that Goyaz, a type of the inner Brazil, would have remained a luxuriant waste tenanted by cannibal "Indians" had not its mines attracted colonists. He ignored the fact that the labours of these men have laid the foundations for a vast superstructure of progress, by taming the ferocity of Nature, and by liberating posterity from the thraldom of mere animal wants. Thus in our day desert California has become under the gold-digger's hands the great wine-growing country of the West.

whilst they forgot that the precious ore is a mere matter of traffic like timber, corn, and wine. They probably expected men to cultivate the miserable potato when their grounds grew guineas in diamonds and gold : they perhaps wished the peasant to throw back, on philanthropic principles, his gold and diamonds into the stream that yielded them. They instanced the decay of mining cities and villages, as though ruin were the result of disturbing the bowels of the earth—"a dispensation of Providence," as they call it who assume the pleasures and duties of directing the course of "Providence." Even the civilized Castelnau laments the "hochets de la vanité humaine," which prizes the diamond, ignoring the fact that it is a mere coin of higher value, an unburnable bank-note.

Far wiser in their generation were the Brazilian writers, who considered the miner, like the tiller of the ground, one of the State's twin-pillars. They justly attributed the decay of the mushroom mineral settlements to ignorance of physical science, and to the workings of a destructive political system. They looked forward to the days when "deep mining" will leave more land for agriculture, but they also knew that land is here a drug, and that mining soils are, as a rule, not worth cultivating. And they dismissed objections against mines of diamonds and gold as readily as if they had been levelled against mines of coal, copper, or lead.

These chapters will show, I trust, that the exploitation of gold and diamonds has but just commenced in Minas Geraes, and indeed in all the Brazil. Martim Affonso de Souza, after touching at Pernambuco, Bahia, and Rio de Janeiro, cast anchor on August 12, 1531, off the island of Cananéa, now called Ilha do Abrigo—Isle of Shelter. There he found a certain Francisco de Chaves, known as the "Bacharel," who is said to have lived thirty years upon the seaboard, and who truly informed him that gold abounded in the near interior. The great voyager sent on September 1 of the same year a party of eighty men, commanded by Pedro Lobo. This, the first Bandeira,* was destroyed

---

* "Bandeira" is primarily a flag, secondarily a troop under a flag; the word gained a wide significance in São Paulo, which, between 1550 and 1750, sent forth those redoubtable Comandos which explored and conquered the interior. Southey (i. 43) has left a sadly garbled account of the first Bandeira. "Martim Affonso made an unsuccessful expedition southward into the interior, in search of mines, from which he returned with the loss of eighty Europeans." The great captain, who seems never to have failed, sailed from Cananéa on Sept. 26, 1531, explored the Rio da

by the barbarous Carijós and Tupys; a second set out to punish
the savages, and thus the extraction speedily followed the discovery
of the precious ore. Yet it may be truly said, that during these
three centuries and a quarter, nothing has been done compared
with what remains to be done. In California, we are told by
Mr. J. W. Taylor, that "notwithstanding the skilful application
of hydraulic power and other improved machinery, the production
of gold by placer-mining* has diminished from sixty millions of
dollars in 1853 to twenty millions in 1866." In most parts of
Australia also, the surface-washings are exhausted, and the pick
and pan men must make way for companies with machinery and
large means. The Brazil has still many an undiscovered
"placer," but her great wealth lies deeply buried under ground.

The gold-diggings of Minas Geraes, and especially those of
Morro Velho, correct a popular scientific error. I remember
how, a few years ago, a distinguished President of the Geological
Societies used to show the gold formation with the wrist upturned
and the fingers downwards, other metals being supposed to be
deposited in the inverse way, little above and much below.† Dr.
Couto's generalization is also, I believe, based on insufficient data,
when he supports his favourite Lehmann's belief,‡ that the sun is
the principal agent in the alchemy of gold, by asserting that mines
here lie on the eastern slopes of mountains, rarely on other
"rhumbs." On the other hand, here, as in Cornwall, the
tendency to an east to west direction of metalliferous veins has
been remarked. It is popularly explained by the "generally
westerly direction of voltaic currents, connected with the general
meridional direction of the magnetic needle." In the Brazil also
the auriferous mountain chains are mostly meridional. Pliny
(xxxvii. 15) is right in asserting that the diamond, if his hexahedral "adamas" be not corundum, but a true diamond, is
mostly found in close proximity with gold. And we may remark

Plata, and did not return northwards till
January, 1532. In the Discours prélimi-
naire prefixed by M. J. B. B. Eyriès
to "Jean Mawe," we read (p. xvi.) "Ce
fut en 1577 que l'on trouva les premières
mines de ce métal." The popular error is
that gold was first found in Jaraguá, a mountain within sight of S. Paulo the city.

* "Gold ledges are not more liable than
ordinary metalliferous veins to become impoverished in depth." (Mr. J. A. Phillips,

"The Mining and Metallurgy of Gold and
Silver,"—I quote from a review). The
same error, it appears, prevailed touching
the stanniferous deposits of Cornwall.

† Art des Mines (i. 11). The theory in
the Brazil was that the soft yellow clay was
gradually dried, ripened, and "aurified."

‡ The faults and dislocations which intersect and upheave metalliferous veins, and
which consequently are posterior in date,
often intersect them at right angles.

that, in this part of the Brazil at least, gold is invariably accompanied by some form of iron. The same may be said of diamonds.

The gold deposits of Minas Geraes may be divided into three formations, all the produce of primitive and metamorphic rocks.[*] These are :—

1. Quartz or Cascalho gold ;[†]
2. Jacutinga ; and
3. Pyritic formations.

All the specimens of quartz-gold shown to me at once suggested California and the Guinea Coast, and the works which I saw on the São Francisco River were of the rudest description. Brazilians divide it into three kinds. The first is Ouro do Rio or da Córrego, "stream ore" : it is either loose or embedded in pebbles, galettes, and kidneys of quartz, sandstone, granite, gneiss, "Itacolumite," talcose-schist, or the conglomerate called Cánga.[‡] This gold, being deposited at different epochs by "rain

[*] The auriferous quartz veins on the Pacific coast have proved that the deposits of ore are not confined to the Silurian epoch, as contended by Sir Roderick Murchison, but are also extended into the Jurassic period. I found no fossils which could mark the date of the Minas rocks.

[†] "Cascálho," or "Pedra de Cascalho," when large "Cascalhão," is a coarse gravel composed of many varieties of quartz, and supposed to be the matrix of gold and diamonds. I may suggest that it is the Spanish Segullo, the Segutilum of Pliny : the dictionaries, however, usually derive it from "quassus" and "calculus," making it synonymous with "pedregulho," or gravel. It is always rounded and water-rolled, opposed to the angular gurgulho— of which I shall presently speak. Some writers use the word, perhaps correctly, with great latitude. "Ó Cascalho he compacto de fragmentos angulosos de quartzo e mineral de ferro argiloso, a que os mineiros chamão pedra de Canga" (José Bonifacio, Viagem Mineralogica, p. 9). So Southey (iii. 53) explains "Cascalho" to be "hard gravelly soil in which the ore was embedded," and in another place (ii. 669) a "compost of earthy matter and gravel." Both definitions are equally incorrect. The "Cascalho" may rest either upon the stone core which underlies the Neptunian formation, or upon the common

clays of the country, or upon the loose sand called "Desmonte."[1] There are minor divisions of "Cascalho" as "Cascalho de Taboleiro," found on river banks and high lands : this is either rounded or angular. The "Cascalho do veio do rio" comes from the stream bed, and is always water-rolled. Again the "Cascalho corrido" is that which is much worked by water, opposed to the "Cascalho Virgem" when it is pudding-stone shape.

[‡] The word must not be confounded with the Portuguese "Canga," a yoke. It is evidently a mutilation of "Acánga," in Tupy a head ; thus we find the names of places "Cáia-Cánga," monkey's head, and "Tapanhu 'acanga," nigger's head, from "Tapanhúna" (vulgar corruption), a negro or negress. John Mawe (ii. 24) erroneously writes this "Tapinhoa-Canga," and says "Conga est le nom de quartz ferrugineux." We have seen José Bonifacio give it to angular quartz fragments in argillaceous iron. It is a general term for any stone with an iron capping, and therefore called "Pedra de Capote" (cloaked stone) in São Paulo. Dr. Couto declares that it has often been applied to what is really ochraceous copper.

We find in Pliny (xxxiii. 21) an allusion to these upper formations, the "gold that is thus found in the surface crust is known to the Romans as 'talutium.'"

[1] For the latter the reader may see Vol. 2, Chapter 8.

and rivers," extended from the surface to twelve and even twenty feet below it. As a rule, however, it was soon exhausted. The second formation was known as "Ouro de Gupiára," gold of the roof, a term very variously explained.* Here the ore was mixed with the superficial clay, generally red, rarely black; it was easily extracted and soon. The third kind of gold was termed "Ouro de Pedreiro," gold in stone, and was supposed to be supplied by little veins of quartz ramifying through rock. This, therefore, was the only true mine ; all the others were mere washings.

In the Jacutinga, as in the quartz, the gold is visible and often free. But the precious ore is so minutely and mechanically disseminated in the pyritic formations, that it seems to be another metal. This is the nature of the Morro Velho mine, and this for ages to come will be the auriferous stone quarried in the Brazil. My account of it will be somewhat tedious. Deep gold-digging in arsenical and other pyrites is, however, so interesting, and the difficulty of separating the precious ore is so great, that every mite of information has its value. The description of the minerals will be mainly taken from the "Annual Assay Report for 1861," an able article by M. Ferdinand Dietzsch, the principal Reduction Officer of the Morro Velho Company.

The auriferous ore delivered by this mine is composed of magnetic iron and arsenical pyrites, in a containing rock of quartz. The specific gravity of the lode ranges between 3·8 and 4·0. The composing minerals may be quoted in the following succession with respect to their metallic properties and relative value. It must be borne in mind that the formations pass into one another almost imperceptibly.

---

* I believe this word to be a corruption of the Tupy "Copiára, explained by the Dict. as "alpendre, varanda, a shed or awning (verandah):" the people on the São Francisco River still use it for a tiled roof supported by posts and without walls. José Bonifacio (Viagem 8) writes Guapiara (in which he is followed by Castelnau) and translates it "cascalho superficial," which follows conformably the irregularities of the ground. St. Hilaire (I. i. 247) has rightly asserted, "on designe ce cascalho par le mot de gupiara, à cause de la ressemblance qu'offrent la forme et la position de sa couche avec les véritables *gupiaras*, petits toits triangulaires qui s'avancent au-dessus du pignon des maisons,"—he had better have said attached to the wall of the dwelling-house. In Gardner we find "copiara" corrupted to "copial," a verandah ; but that good naturalist and observant traveller gave little attention to languages. Burmeister prefers "Grupi-ara," a common corruption in many parts of the country. Mr. Harry Emanuel (p. 56) explains "Grupiara" as "an alluvial deposit whose surface shows it to be the unused bed of a stream or river," whereas it alludes to the eaves-like side of a hill. I observe that that excellent scholar, Sr. J. de Alencar (in Iracema, p. 100, and other works) writes "Copiar," and Moraes (Diccionario da Lingua Portugueza), "Gopiara."

1. Arsenical pyrites or mispickel* does not form a large proportion of the mineral, but it is the principal gold-bearer. Some specimens have yielded when assayed from twenty to forty oitavas† per ton. More generally it is mixed with the magnetic pyritiferous matter, when it gives from sixteen to twenty oitavas of gold in assay, and from five to seventeen in reduction. It is the usual silvery-white or steel-coloured mineral, shining with metallic lustre, finely diffused in specks and dots, with a specific gravity when pure of 6·20. The Brazilian miner calls it "antimonio," a word explained by Dr. Couto to mean copper-pyrites, with iron and sulphur, cubical or hexahedral, well crystallized and coloured like pale gold. The country people declare "that there is much fire in it." It is evidently subject, when joined with other bodies, to combustion, as shown by the old experiment of making artificial volcanoes by burying in the earth a paste composed of iron-filings and sulphur, kneaded together with water.

2. Common iron (Martial) pyrites (Fe Su²), Marcasite or Mundic,‡ is more abundant than No. 1, but it is far inferior in auriferous yield. Almost pure specimens, with a slight admixture of quartz, give eleven oitavas per ton, the yellow stone of the "West Quebra Panella Mine" gives only six, and when the grains of the larger crystals are embedded in quartz, the per-centage is even less. A superabundance of iron pyrites is almost as antagonistic to gold as a preponderance of the quartz leaven.

---

* According to Berzelius (Fe S^2 + Fe As^2), or (Fe S^2 + Fe As). The proportions are variously stated, e.g.

Iron	36·04	86·00
Arsenic	42·88	42·90
Sulphur	21·08	21·10
	100·00	100·00

† The old Portuguese gold weights, still preserved, are,—

2½ grains	=	1 vintem.
5 vintens	=	1 tostão or tustão.
32 vintens	=	1 oitava (= $1\frac{7}{16}$ drachm avoirdupois).
8 oitavas	=	1 onça or ounce.
8 ounces	=	1 marco.
2 marcos	=	1 lb.

The popular gold weight is the oitava = the eighth part of 8·6742 of our ounce Troy, and 104 oitavas = 1 lb. Troy.

I cannot understand why the English Mining Companies in the Brazil persist in sending in large accounts calculated by oitavas instead of ounces and pounds. What can be more ridiculous than such figures as 8 oitavas (=1 oz.), 16 oitavas, and so forth?

The oitava of course varies with the quality of gold and the rate of exchange. That of Morro Velho, averaging 19 carats, is now (July, 1867) = 3 $ 454, and the ounce is 27 $ 632.

‡ Cornishmen have stated that "mundic rides a good horse in the Brazil as well as in Cornwall." This is true of many minerals, but not, I believe, of gold.

A working miner compared the latter to the soil, the former to
its manure. It is liable also to spontaneous combustion when
decomposed by contact with moisture. The mineral has the
normal metallic lustre and brassy yellow colour, it is found in
minute dots of well diffused metal, in cubes and in crystallized
masses, each face half an inch and more in breadth. Although
it readily tarnishes, the ignorant often mistake it for gold, and it
is scattered in large deposits about the valley of the São Francisco
River, and in the Provinces of Minas and São Paulo. My distinguished friends, the Commendador José Vergueiro of Ybicaba,
and the Deputy Antonio de Souza Prado D. C. L. of São Paulo,
showed me specimens of it. The former found them upon his
estate near Rio Claro, the proposed terminus of the Santos
and Jundiahy Railway, and the latter brought them from the
Cavern of Paranapanema, about eighty direct miles west-south-
west of São Paulo the city.

3. Magnetic iron pyrites * or proto-sulphuret of iron, forms
the largest yield of pyritic matter, but in assay it shows small
gold contents, rarely exceeding 1·50 to 2 oitavas per ton. It
occurs in the usual hexagonal crystals, foliated, sometimes
massive and of fine brassy lustre.

4. The quartz matrix is mostly white or greyish, sometimes
smoky, blue-black, and black. Pure and without pyrites, it was
formerly supposed never to contain gold; but of late six pieces,
some say two or three pieces divided into six, have been found
with the precious ore embedded in them. Quartz is generally
mixed with pyrites of the highest auriferous qualities, and when
it forms the staple, as in the West Bahia and the Champion
grounds, the whole body yields a fair average. It was soon
remarked that the ore often appears poor in pyrites, but that the
pyritiferous matter produces as much as 3·66 oitavas per ton.
In places the quartz is invaded by "capel," hard, white, and
poor quartzose matter, greatly distorting the contiguous containing rock, and presenting in cavities magnetic iron pyrites,
spathose iron, and crystallized copper pyrites.

---

* The formula is (Fe Su² + 6 Fe Su) or (Fe² Su³ + 5 Fe Su) : the proportions
vary, e.g.

Sulphur	.	.	.	36·5	40·4
Iron	.	.	.	63·5	59·6
				100·00	100,00

5. Clay slate, sometimes chloritic (micaceous), mostly talcose (magnesia and silicic acid), called by the English miner "killas." It is amorphous or laminated, generally of dull leaden colour, and exceedingly hard; it traverses the containing rock in places and protrudes into the lode, "teeth" or small branches, "horses" or large masses, and "bars" or dividing walls. Much of it has no auriferous pyrites, and even the highly charged parts rarely afford more than two to three oitavas of gold in assay, or one half to three-quarters of an oitava at the works. The yield is pronounced bad when the killas and quartz exceed the pyrites, middling when they are nearly equal, and good when the pyrites is in excess.* This clay slate is separated as much as is possible from the ore before the latter is forwarded to the stamps, and thus the whole body of mineral is brought up to a higher standard than the bulk received from the mine. As the subjoined figures will show,† the large quantities of valueless stuff cause great delay in the "spalling floors;" and "killas" stamped together with rich stone, occasions a heavy loss in fine free gold.

The gold daily treated in the Reduction works is derived from an intimate mixture of these minerals. The rarer formations are—

Calcareous spar, commonly called "pearl spar." This system of carbonate of lime is found in modified rhombohedra, hard but cleavable, usually white and crystalline, but sometimes of a delicate pink, with the appearance of marble. I saw a specimen of it adhering to the lode in its transition to killas.

---

* Sometimes, however, the richest ore does not contain more than fifty per cent. of pyrites.

† About 300 tons of stuff, more in the wet season, less in the dry weather, pay the daily expenses of the mine : 400 tons give a fair profit.

During the six months, March to August, 1866, we have the following computation :—

The mineral raised from the mine, a total of	53,698	tons.
During the previous six months	46,629	,,
During the six months ending August, 1865	40,014	,,
The killas rejected at head-quarters, but re-treated at the Praia Works amounted to . . . . . }	22,383 tons, or 40 per cent. on quantity raised.	
During the previous six months .	17,108 ,,	36·6 ,,
During the six months ending August, 1865 . . . . . }	12,117 ,,	30·2 ,,
The average yield of gold per ton raised was	5·974	oitavas.
During the previous six months	6·328	,,
During the six months ending August, 1865	4·885	,,
The average yield of gold per ton stamped was	11·048	,,
During the previous six months	9·988	,,
During the six months ending August, 1865	6·458	,,

Spathic ironstone, or carbonate of iron. It appears in obtuse rhombohedra, with faces often curvilinear. Some pieces, of a dirty yellow colour, stand erect, and resemble fish scales.

Chlorite is found in large lumps of a copperas-green colour; it sometimes stains with a pretty, light glaucous tinge the adjacent rock-crystal. In Morro Velho it contains iron pyrites, but no gold; this, however, is not the case throughout the Province of Minas.

Arragonite, in white vesicular crystals. Curious specimens are shown with magnetic iron pyrites adhering to the surface.

Traces of copper, crystallized and amorphous, have been found in the lode and the containing rock, but they have not been examined.

Silver in Minas, as elsewhere, is the general alloy of gold.[*] The mine which the Jesuits anciently worked near Sorocaba was, some say, this "electrum;" others believe it to have been galena highly argentiferous. The ore of Morro Velho contains silver in chemical combination with other substances, and it is not extracted on the spot. A report once prevailed that silver attained the proportion of 16·50 per cent. of the lode. The bar, or ingot, contains 19⅓ to 20 per cent. of silver.

interesting

SECTION II.

THE BRAZILIAN MINING SYSTEM.

Portugal, the western terminus of Rome's conquests, remains to the present day the most Roman of Latin countries. Her language approaches nearest to the speech of the ancient mistress of the world. Her people still preserve the sturdiness and perseverance, often degenerating into dogged obstinacy; the turbulent love of liberty; the materialism and unartistic spirit; the conservatism and love of routine; the superstition and the lust of "territorial aggrandisement," which distinguished the former conquerors of the world. Even in the present day, the traveller in Portugal sees with astonishment the domestic life of Rome, her poetry and literature, her arts and sciences; and the archaic form of civilization has extended even to the Brazil; here,

---

[*] "In all gold ore there is some silver, in varying proportions : a tenth part in some instances, an eighth in others." Pliny somewhat overstates the universality, but he errs only in degree.

although so far removed from its ethnic centre and mixed with a variety of jarring elements, it is easily recognized.

The admirable old naturalist, Pliny, telling us how "gold is found," describes three different ways. The first is by washing the sand of running waters for stream ore; the second is by sinking shafts or seeking it among the *débris* of mountains; and the third method of obtaining gold ("which surpasses the labours of the giants even") is by the aid of galleries driven to a long distance. The following sketch of gold-mining in the Brazil will show how little the Roman system has been changed since A.D. 50.

The first exploitation was by simply panning the auriferous sand taken from the stream-beds, and this we shall see practised to the present day. The next method was the "lavra," or superficial washing. The humus was stripped off with the hoe, and the red-gold clay, or the auriferous "cascalho" (gravel and sand) was cut into squares and lines by shallow trenches. The washers always chose an inclined plane, and a head stream was conducted to the cuttings by split bamboos or hollow trees. This simple "hydraulicking" carried down the free channel gold—the canalicium, or canaliense of Pliny—which was arrested by grass sods or blankets; these were afterwards washed in a "coche," or trough; the dust was then panned in a gamella, or carumbé,* and this ended the simple process. A slight improvement in these "stream works" was made by the "canôa," an oblong of bricks, tiles, or rough planking, which facilitated the washing of the "pay-dirt." In the Far West this industry still prevails; it disappears with the exhaustion of those superficial deposits of gold which more or less have existed in every known country of early formation. The effect of such washing was to leave the land a "caput mortuum of stubborn sterility" which can only be cured by manuring,† an operation beyond the means of the actual Brazil. Other wild "washing"

---

* The "Gamella" used in gold-washing is larger than the "batêa" (explained in Chap. 12), flat, round, and lacking the hollow point in the centre. The "Carumbé," or "Carumbeia," is a small gamella. According to St. Hil. it is the "Indian" term for the "écaille de tortue." In the country parts the dorsal armour of the armadillo is still used as a pouch or calabash.

† It is said that even in these brick-like soils coffee and sugar, at any rate manioc and maize, can be grown in holes filled with a mixture of earth and manure. The pits are dug at intervals of six feet, they are one foot in diameter and about the same depth. I have not had an opportunity of seeing a gold field thus treated.

contrivances will be noticed in the following pages, as they present themselves on the river and the road.

The "cata," or pit, has already been alluded to ; from these holes gold in grain and nuggets—the pelagæ and palacurnæ of Pliny—was extracted, after which the ground was supposed to be worked out. This system, like the "lavra," was peculiarly the work of the "Garimpeiro,"* the contrabandist and free lance. The first improvement which required more hands, and especially slave-labour, was the open cut called "talho aberto," or Socavão. Some of these works, the "Carapucuhu" at Jaraguá, for instance, near São Paulo, are extensive ; but sufficient slope was not given to the banks, shoring up was not judged necessary, and the sides being well undermined, fell in. Thus a few negroes were crushed ; their "almas," or ghosts— much dreaded in the Brazil—haunted the spot, and soon hunted away the stoutest hearts.

The most enterprising tried the "Serrilho," which we translate "shaft ;" † it was, however, generally an inclined plane, a mixture of shaft and gallery. The precious metal was attacked with charges half powder, half sawdust ; the slaves bore in buckets or wooden platters auriferous matter to a water-mill, working, perhaps, a pair of iron-shod stamps upon a hard, flat stone. The operations were carried on under a shed, always placed for better surveillance near the owner's house. When the "batêa" and "gamella" had done their work, a rude amalgam was sometimes tried, as in early California, and the loose mercury was recovered by squeezing through leather. They retorted it by placing the amalgam in a heated brass vessel, covered with green leaves. The latter, when parched, were removed with the sublimated globules on the inner surface. But the Brazilian

---

* Sometimes written as pronounced, "Grimpeiro :" it is the Spanish "Gambusino," made familiar by M. Gustave Aimard and Captain Mayne Reid. The "Garimpo " is the place where he works, the word is still applied depreciatingly to any digging on a small scale. Garimpeiro corresponds with our "night jossecker," men who employ the hours of darkness in robbing rich holes of superficial gold. According to the Dictionaries, which ignore "Garimpo," "Garimpeiro " is a Brazilian word : Moraes suggests that it is a corruption of Aripeiro, from Aripar, to collect pearls which have fallen from decayed piles of oysters into the sand.

† "Shaft " is here used of wells or pits open to the surface, whether perpendicular or not, the "whin-shaft " raises the ore to the surface : "sinkings " are downward excavations, "levels " when horizontal, or nearly so, and "risings," those that ascend. The "adit," or "adit-level," is the chief drainage tunnel cut to the surface at the lowest convenient spot : "levels " generally are horizontal galleries excavated in metalliferous veins, and "cross-cuts " those in non-metalliferous.

miner was ever careless about timbering and walling; he little regarded lighting or ventilation; the Davy and the Geordie were equally unknown to him; he ignored pumping on a large scale, and thus, when his mine became watered, he was compelled to quit it. Rude, however, as was his system, we shall see that it has been adopted by all the best English miners of the present day, and that the latter have been satisfied with a few and unimportant improvements.

SECTION III.

ENGLISH GOLD-MINING IN MINAS.

The first English Company dates from 1824, and was known as the Gongo Soco, or "Imperial Brazilian Mining Association." The diggings, which we shall presently pass, were in S. lat. 19° 58′ 30″, and W. long. 43° 30′,[*] about forty-eight miles north-west of Ouro Preto, and twenty-four miles south-east of Morro Velho. Barometric measurements by the Austrian mining engineer, M. Virgil von Helmreichen, place it 3360 feet "above the sea at Rio de Janeiro." Gongo Soco was in the then municipality of Caethé; now in that of Santa Barbara.

The first owner was a Coronel Manoel da Camara de Noronha, who dug about the middle of the last century.[†] His son Isidoro, who died in poverty, sold it about 1808 for 9000 crusados to the Commendador and Capitão Mór José Alves da Cunha, a Portuguese, and to his nephew by marriage, the Barão de Catas Altas. The former, about 1818, pushed levels into the true lode, on the flanks of the "Tejuco Mount;" and it is said that before 1824 he extracted in one month 480 lbs. of gold. The Baron inherited the property, bought out by private arrangement all others who had claims upon it, and offered it for sale.

Mr. Edward Oxenford, who had travelled in the Brazil as a Mascate, or itinerant merchant, returned to England, advocated the purchase, and was sent by the Association to examine the site, in company with Mr. Tregoning, as chief mining captain.

[*] The observations were taken by Mr. William Jory Henwood, F.R.S., F.G.S., Chief Commissioner of the Gold Mines of Gongo Soco, Cata Preta, etc., etc.: this scientific man is still, I believe, living. His papers were printed in the Phil. Mag. 1846, xxviii., pp. 364—6, and in the London, Edin., and Dub. Phil. Mag. and Journal of Science, June, 1848.

[†] Mr. Walsh is in error when he asserts that a Portuguese named Bittencourt, and father of Isidoro, first worked the banks of the Gongo River.

The reports were favourable. The Baron parted with his rights for £70,000 (others say £80,000), and the sanction of the Imperial Government was obtained on Sept. 16, 1824, on condition of receiving the annual "quinto,"—curiously high, twenty-five per cent. of gold extracted. This was close upon the "all-speculating year, 1825," when one of 999 speculations was the "Potosi, La Paz, and Peruvian Mining Association." How little creditably to national honour ended that "grande et belle entreprise," the reader may see in the lively pages of Mr. Edmond Temple.*

In 1825 Gongo Soco was visited by Caldcleugh, who could not enter the mine, the owner being absent. In March, 1827, the first superintendent, Captain Lyon, took command. This is Lieutenant Lyon, R.N.,† who travelled to the Fezzan, where Mr. Ritchie, chief of the mission, died of anxiety and bilious fever, on Nov. 20, 1819. He also bought the Morro Velho ground from its owner, Padre Freitas, and sold it to the "S. John Del Rey" Company. The speculation prospered. In December, 1827, the quint paid at Ouro Preto was £20,982. Gongo Soco had become an English village in the tropics, with its church and chaplain consecrated by the Bishop of London, and the forty original hands had increased to 180 Englishmen, assisted by 600 free labourers and blacks.‡ Mr. Walsh, who visited the place in 1828, draws a pleasant picture, and the ground is said to have already produced 736 lbs. of gold.

In 1830 Captain Lyon was succeeded by Colonel Skerrett, who, by judicious military discipline, kept the mine in "apple-pie order;" he introduced the excellent system of making the negroes their own "feitors," or overseers. Colonel Skerrett left because his salary was not increased from £2000 to £3000; the Company, as often happens, showed itself penny wise and pound foolish, and thus lost a valuable servant. The decline and fall of the establishment at once began.

---

* "Travels in Various Parts of Peru, including a Year's Residence in Potosi," by Edmond Temple, Knight of the Royal and Distinguished Order of Charles III. In 2 Vols. Colburn and Bentley, 1830. The narrative makes one blush for the Potosi &c. Mining Association.

† Dr. Gardner calls him the "Northern Voyager."

‡ During the first year, when the greatest depth was three fathoms, the employés, including forty Englishmen, numbered 450. The highest number was 217 Europeans, 200 Brazilians, and 500 slaves. When the mine was "broken" there were 14 Europeans and 447 slaves.

After Colonel Skerrett came Mr. George Vincent Duval, in 1840-2.   About this time it was visited by Dr. Gardner, who describes it as a thick stratum of ferruginous Itacolumite, with an inclination of 45°, and based upon clay slate, containing great masses of ironstone.   Upon the Itacolumite lies a bed of auri-ferous Jacutinga, fifty fathoms thick, and upon this again is Itacolumite.   About half a mile to the south of the mine he found a couch of crystallized and highly stratified limestone, cropping out at the same angle and in the same direction as the other rocks.   He visited seven of the nine levels, each separated by seven fathoms, and thus he saw 294 of 378 feet.   These galleries, pierced through the soft Jacutinga, were four to five feet wide and five to six feet high; they were strongly lined with eighteen-inch timbers of the hardest Brazilian wood, yet the logs were broken and crushed by the weight.   The chief vein ran east to west; there were, however, many shoots or ramifications which gave gold in bunches—as much as 100 lbs. had been taken out in one day.   The rich ore was washed and pounded in mortars.   It was concentrated at first by common panning, afterwards by amalgamation; the poorer stuff was sent to the stamping-mills, and then washed.   Dr. Gardner found the machinery here inferior to that of Cocaes.

But now appeared the truth of the Miner's axiom, "Better a low standard and high produce, than a high standard and low produce."   From 1837 to 1847 the Brazilian Government libe-rally reduced its quinto to twenty per cent.   Jacutinga is essentially a "weather-cock mine;" unlike those whose matrix is the rock, it may be rich to-day, and worthless to-morrow. The deep running lines could not be followed, and the expense of posts and stanchions, walling every foot, was enormous. Mr. Henwood then assumed command, and was followed by a committee consisting of Mr. John Morgan (senior), Dr. Hood, and others.   This republican rule ended the matter, and reads a valuable lesson.   In 1850 the Government compassionately diminished its claims to ten per cent.; in 1853 to five per cent.; and in 1854 foreigners were placed on the same footing as national industry, and laboured untaxed.   The large working capital—too large, indeed, at first—became insufficient, and between 1854-6 the Company expended the whole of a reserve fund which had accumulated for years.   The water entered; the

matrix was sopped to the foundations, and the workmen were
drowned out,—the fault of nobody but of the drainage. In
1857 the Commendador Francisco de Paula Santos, to whom
150 contos were owed by the property, embargoed the negroes,
as he had a right to do by Brazilian law, and presently
became owner of the mining property. Gongo Soco died deeply
regretted ; it had spread itself into the branch mines of Boa
Vista, Bananal or Agua Quente, Socorro, Campestre, Catas
Altas, Cata Preta, and Inficionado ; it had fed and fee'd the
country for thirty leagues around, and it had netted nearly
£1,500,000.*

Followed (April, 1830) the " St John Del Rey," of whose
origin I have given an account. In 1835 it was transferred to
Morro Velho, whilst still preserving the name which appeared
in the Company's original contract. The misnomer sounds like
the " Exeter Mine at Truro." I retain, however, the complicated barbarism, which distinguishes it from another São João
mine, merely remarking that such hybrid words should be
banished from all our maps. For ten years after its removal
the " St John " did little, and often that little was in the wrong
direction. In 1845 its royalty was lowered from ten to five per
cent. ; in 1855 a reduction of one per cent. per annum was made
till the extinction of the tax ; and after 1859 it was relieved of
the onus. During that year it began to yield five oitavas per
ton, where before it had given two ; the reader will presently see
the reason why.

In due succession came up the " Cata Branca " (1832-3), with
the Morro das Almas, in the municipality of Ouro Preto ; the
great Cocaes Company (1833-4),† in Santa Barbara, including
its branches Cuiabá, Caethé, and Macahúbas, with its neighbour,
Brucutú ; and the short-lived Serra da Candonga Company, in
the Sêrro do Frio, which ended after two to three years.

---

* The figures usually given show a national benefit of some £333,180, thus expressed :—

Paid royalty to the treasury £310,777 }   (Lt. Moraes, £338,180).
    ,, export duty . . 22,403 }

According to Lt. Moraes this Company extracted 34,528,098 lbs. of gold (20-carat),
thus laid out :—

Expenses £1,013,253
Income 1,388,416
                                              —————
Profit £375,163
† Gardner, Chap. 13. I have given some details in Chap. 41.

Except Cocaes, which still lingers on, these associations lasted till 1844-5 and 1850. The failures affected the London market, and gold-mining in the Brazil was not looked upon with favour. Here, as elsewhere in South America, the vast treasures promised by Montesquieu, Robertson, and Humboldt, were not realised, or rather were realised to a certain extent, and—diverted. Convey the wise it call.

After 1859, when Morro Velho had "rehabilitated" speculation in the Brazil,—which bore blame when she deserved every praise,—other Companies cropped up. Minas had five: the "Este Del Rey," including the Lavras do Capão and the Papafarinha, near Sabará,* and the Paciencia and S. Vicente, near Ouro Preto; the Norte Del Rey, in the Morro de Santa Anna, including the Maquiné Mine;† the London and Brazilian Gold-Mining Company (Limited), at Passagem, near Marianna;† the "Rossa Grande Company," in the municipality of Caëthé,‡ and the Santa Barbara-cum-Pari,‡ in the municipality of that name. There is a sixth—the "Montes Aureos Gold-Mining Company (Limited)," establishment in Maranhão; but I see that it is already in the market. The total capital of these establishments is usually set down at £600,000. Only two, the Morro Velho and the Maquiné mines, have as yet paid; the Passagem Mine has not paid, but probably will pay, and the rest have been failures—a dozen and a-half losses to two and a-half successes.

In the Brazil a gold mine may begin work economically enough. The owners of diggings which are supposed to be exhausted will generally sell cheap, and many would be contented with a fair per-centage on profits. The sum of £46,000 suffices for purchasing stock and rolling stock, for building, and for putting up one set of stamps,—say thirty-six head, which work, during the twelve hours, fifteen tons of ore, through grates of a sufficiently fine bore. Assuming the average yield of gold at five oitavas per ton, this would produce annually £10,000; the mine might be put in proper stope within the third year, when it should begin to pay. This easy effort of prudence would test its aptitude for good or evil, without seriously damaging the shareholders, so often victimised under the present reckless system, and without giving to the country an undeserved bad reputation in the markets of Europe.

* Chap. 41.   † Chap. 34.   ‡ Chap. 29.

I have been in this mine !

After reading a variety of reports,* I am able to describe the actual way of "getting up" an English Gold-mining Company, Limited (as to profits), in this section of the Brazilian California. A "chief commissioner," quasi self-created, one of the "Twenty-years-in-the-country-and-speak-the-language men," begins by laying before the British public a synopsis of advantages to be derived by the *actionnaires*. His experience must tell the following flattering tale in seven chapters. My readers need not suppose from this Democritic treatment of the subject that I am not in earnest. So was old Rabelais when he wrote, "En ycelle bien cultre gouste trouuerez et doctrine plus absconce;" and no one laments more than I do the dishonour which such charlatanism has brought upon the English name in the Brazil, to mention no other parts of South America.

1. The mine to be is situated in a good central district, close to the capital and to other great cities—the "astu" here is a mere village in Europe. If not so placed by Nature, it can easily be made so by the simple process of subtracting distance.

2. The pasture, the supply of timber and fuel, and especially the water, are abundant and of the best quality.

3. The ore, the lay of the lode, and the formation and the mineral characteristics generally, are similar to those of "St. John Del Rey." It may be well to invent some such high-sounding and well-known names as "West Del Rey" or "South Del Rey," upon the same principle which till late years called all coal "Wall's End." If invidious comparisons are required, an allusion may be made to the failures of Gongo Soco, Cocaes, and Cuiabá.

4. The original Brazilian owner made a large fortune before the works fell in, and the miners were drowned out. Anything, however, can be "done by an English Company and Cornish miners."

5. The lode is from ten to thirteen feet wide at grass; it is at as shallow an horizon as possible, situated above some valley, so that the facility of draining by adits and openings is "of no common order."

6. The dwelling-houses are in a very dilapidated state, neces-

---

* I can especially commend the Report of the St. John Del Rey Mining Company, (Tokenhouse Yard, now, presented half-yearly at the meeting of the Proprietors): the system is excellent, and it gives at a glance all the information required.

sitating *quam primum* a Casa Grande for Mr. Commissioner, and similar outlay.

7. This splendid field for mining operations must prove immediately remunerative to shareholders; it is an " affair of facts and figures "—an " investment rather than a speculation." Finally, if the pretensions are to be of the highest order, there must be diamonds and other deposits of which the reporter " abstains from speaking."

Thus the Company will be formed; money will be spent, nothing will be made, and, in due time, dissolution will be the *dénouement.* Emphatically true in modern Minas Geraes is the Spanish proverb :—

" A silver mine brings misery, a gold mine ruin."

Nothing is easier than to suggest a ready and efficient remedy for this undesirable state of affairs. The simplest exercise of induction and deduction of reason and experience shows the necessity of obtaining accurate knowledge before entering upon such speculations. There ought not to be any difficulty in finding a confidential man sufficiently versed in mining and mineralogy, and, to speak plain English, above taking the bribes which will assuredly be offered to him. His report should be final, without any regard to the small fry of local traders and shopkeepers,—all, of course, merchants and esquires—who, expecting to profit by the outlay, volunteer golden opinions touching the new mine.

It is said that the Englishman going to India, left his conscience at the Cape, and forgot to take it up on his return. I know not where Europeans deposit these troublesome articles when bound for the Brazil, or whether they care to recover them when *en route* homewards. It is, however, a melancholy truth that, in this country, honesty seems to be the smallest item of the adventurer's stock-in-trade. In the mines, as in the railways of the Brazil, the fault, the cause of failure, lies, I repeat, not with the Brazilians, but at our door. There has been the grossest mismanagement both at home and abroad. Private interests have been preferred to public; in certain notorious cases a system of plunder has been organized; impossible schemes have been floated through the market; the merest speculators have waxed rich; economy has been wholly neglected, and money has been buried as though it were expected to grow. The most lamentable result is the false conviction in Europe that the seed of capital cannot be sown profitably in the Brazil, when there is no country where, properly husbanded, it would bear a better crop.

The Morro Velho Mine has opened a new chapter in provincial history, proving that, even under adverse circumstances, much may be effected by men of honesty and energy, combined with scientific and practical knowledge of their profession; and I may end this sketch by expressing my conviction that we have well-nigh killed the goose that lay the golden eggs, and that until the present process shall be radically changed, it is better to leave the gold in the bowels of the earth.

On the other hand, I have something to say about the attitude of the Brazil in this matter.

"What does the mine pay to the State?" ask the well-educated. "These strangers carry all the gold out of our land," say the vulgar, who would see unmoved a shanty surmounting a gold mountain. Lt. Moraes* speaks of seven English companies, "exploitant au profit de l'Angleterre les richesses incalculables que la Nature a enfouies dans le sol brésilien." He calculates that between 1860-3 the Morro Velho Mine should have enriched the Treasury by "près un million de francs."

But in its highly liberal policy the Brazilian Government was emphatically right. The educated and the vulgar, who look only to monies actually paid, and who fancy that enormous indirect benefits mean nothing, are as emphatically wrong. Had the Imperial impost not been removed from the Morro Velho and other establishments these must have been ruined. Those in power happily had the courage to assist their "Do ut des," in opposition to the "dog-in-the-manger" policy, which is that of all half-civilised peoples. ·

"Brazileirismo" in the Brazil, and Americanismo in the Hispano-American republics, are never so rampant as when boasting of their country, a vanity even vainer than that of vaunting one's birth. The "torrão abençoado" (Heaven-blest soil) has past into the category of chaff. The sun, the moon,

---

* Rapport partiel sur le Haut San-Francisco (Paris, Parent, 1866). This officer calculates that between 1860—1863 (four years), the Morro Velho Mine should have paid into the Brazilian Treasury one million of francs (400 contos or £40,000). And he would have thrown it all away on a fanciful canal between the Rio Preto and the Parnaguá Lake, in order to imitate the Hudson-Champlain.

the stars, are subjects of popular braggadocio. "You have no such moon as that in France," I heard a Brazilian say to a Frenchman.

"No," was the reply: "we have a poor old night-light, well-nigh worn out; but it is still good enough for us."

Hence there is prodigiously "tall talk" concerning the magnificent Empire, the wondrous Land of the Southern Cross, with its mighty wealth and its splendid destiny. Whatever the latter may be, the riches are still in the ground, and the nation is undoubtedly poor. The capitalist will not, it is a truism to say, hazard money in a far country, when it would make as much at home; and the many risks to which he is exposed must raise his per-centage of profits.

I conclude, therefore, that if the Brazilian Government listen to that bad adviser, the General Voice, it will not deserve better fortune than what has befallen English mining and English railways in the Brazil.

As yet, however, let me repeat, the Government in question has displayed exceptional sagacity.

CHAPTER XXII.

LIFE AT MORRO VELHO.

"The best time I can get for maturing a commercial scheme or planning a sea-voyage, is at church, while the preacher is preaching. Away from the care and bustle of business, under the soothing sounds of the sermon, I have nothing to disturb my meditations."—*Frank Dodge, quoted in "The Model Preacher," by the Rev. H. Taylor.*

My notes taken at the Queen of the Minas Geraes Mines will not, I hope, prove uninteresting. They show what is English life in the heart of the Brazil, and they supply some details about a place worth studying.

The pretty site of the establishment is an irregularly shaped basin, about three-quarters of a mile long by half a mile in breadth. The narrow valley ends westward in an *impasse*—Voltaire forbids us to call it a *cul de sac*—formed by high ground, and the surrounding hills rise 700 to 900 feet above the Ribeirão. This stream, winding eastward, rolls a furious torrent during the rainy season, and in the dry half year the shallow water, thick with mundic and arsenical slime, must have a deleterious effect. The land around has been all disforested, and the vegetation is a mean second growth; much of the humus has been drained off by the Rio das Velhas, and the often fine soil has been much impoverished. The romantic beauty of shape is still there, and on bright days the sun and air make the colouring a pleasure to look upon.

To the north-west rises the Morro Velho, or Old Hill, that is to say, the place first worked, backed by the majestic Curral d'El-Rei, bearing 270° from the Casa Grande. To the north-west of the modern shafts are the first excavations made by the "antigos," and which duly fill in. About one mile east, and beyond the "Mingú Mount," is the "Morro Novo." The latter has a quartzose vein, bearing "south 60° east;" it was held to be poor, but it may still work well. Indeed, in most parts there is gold stone at a shallow horizon; but the question is, will it repay exploitation? Situated in a contracted, overcrowded space, the nucleus of the works is on the western slope of the valley; here are the huge water-wheels; the long, dark sheds covering spalling floors strewed with grey ore; engine-houses, and small whitewashed kiosk-shaped buildings, where the brakesmen sit and control the hauling speed with hand gear. But there is no iron furnace blowing off sooty smoke by day and belching lurid flames by night; the trees are not poisoned, and the lips do not taste of chemicals. The bustle and the rattle of the stamps is no unpleasant sound by day, and in the dark hours the song of the water-wheels reminded me of the autumnal waves sporting and tumbling upon the Scheveringen shore.

The buildings extend from the northern bank of the Ribeirão up the ridge-spur, to an altitude of about 450 feet: here are the highest negro quarters, "Timbuctoo"—gentle reminder of what may have been motherland, and here live the Cata Branca blacks. Midway up are the various grim entrances to the big mine, and below it spread the appurtenances, smithy, spalling floors, and mining office. This side of the stream is of somewhat easier slope than the other. A conspicuous whitewashed building is the blacks' kitchen; the eastern part is assigned to the Padre Petraglia. High up, and safely placed, is the gunpowder house, and near it the cemetery where three Europeans were buried during our stay of one month. A little bridge (Amalgamation House Bridge) crosses to the southern bank, where the Amalgamation House is; a rocky ramp rises to the stables higher up, and at 60 to 65 feet of greater elevation is the "Casa Grande." The hill that backs the latter is occupied by the Company's store,* and beyond it, scattered over a mile or so, are the quarters occupied by most of the officers. The medical men, the assistant storekeeper, the Catholic chaplain, and the captain in charge of the mine, lodge on the northern bank.

As a rule, the houses are comfortable, with broad verandahs, and similar tropical appurtenances. But the situation is unwholesome; in front, the tall Morro Velho, the "impasse" to the west, and the high ranges to the north and south, must impede circulation. The low-lying locality has a climate the

---

* Properly called the "Armazém"—popularly the "Venda."

reverse of what a climate here should be : the sun burns by day, the nights bring sudden chilliness, and, as the sojourners in the Highlands of the Brazil complain, the four seasons of Europe come and go in twenty-four hours. The head-quarters and the officers' bungalows might easily be removed to higher ground ; for instance, to the level a little above the Company's store. Many would doubtless declare that the place is too far from their work, but I hold this to be an advantage. All own that during the first months of residence they took regular exercise, and were in the best of health. Presently the Tropics asserted themselves ; the daily ride or walk became a bore, the northerners became " caseiros"—stay-at-homes—and the end of inertia in the Brazil is liver. Much moral courage is required for the daily solitary constitutional over a path whose every plant and pebble are familiar to the eye ; but the alternative may be thus laid down— inevitable " liver," loss of energy, loss of memory, loss of nerve, loss of health, and even loss of life. Equally difficult is the change of place which I vainly proposed at Sierra Leone and Bathurst. In those pest-houses man is content to be "left alone" to die. He loathes the idea of change, as the queer passenger does fat bacon, or the elderly Englishman a " new view of the subject ;" to propose any alteration is personally offensive to him, and he duly hates the meddler who does it.

Morro Velho is sub-tropically situated in S. lat. 19° 58' 6"·7, and the approximate longitude is W. 43° 51' (Gr.).* The altitude is that of São Paulo, the city, a little over 2000 feet. Its dry season begins, according to the rule of the Southern Hemisphere, in April, and ends with October. During this period the thermometer ranges between 61° and 72° F., and the air contains from 0·811 to 1·000 of moisture (Mason's hyg.). Water is seldom colder than 39° F. Hoar-frost, however, appears on boardings and on the grass. Droughts would burn up the fields but for the dense morning fog, often thickening into a drizzle, which chills the body. The mist disappears first from the lower levels, lighted by the sun of 9 to 10 A.M.† Then comes a great

* The latitude was taken with a reflecting circle by Sr. Henrique Dumont, C.E. Dr. Walker with an Adie's sympiesometer made the altitude 2300 feet : Mr. Gordon 2832, and another observation with the sympiesometer (air reading 68°, liquor in tube 59°, and attached thermometer 72°), gave 3411 feet. I made the first floor of the " Guesten House " 2233 feet (B. P. 208°, temp. 63°).

† In Dr. Walker's Sanitary Report of 1850 we read that these mists "cover even the summits of the heights." I believe this not to be the case.

and sudden change of temperature. Dr. Birt, whose acquaintance I made *en passant* at Bahia, found during the first two years of his service that the difference in the shade amounted to 20° to 23° F. Dr. Walker's observations give during four months and a-half a minimum of 46°, and a maximum of 80°.[*]

There are usually midsummer showers, called the Rains of St. John. The first fire-fly appears about the end of July, and the last in early May. August has a few heavy downfalls. In early September the peasant begins to burn his fields, the large South American swallow[†] appears, and the Sabiá (Turdus Orpheus, Lin.), the kokila of the Golden Land, *not*, however, an "American robin," ushers in the wet season with song. "About the same time," says Mr. Henwood, then of Gongo Soco, "the humming-bird ceases its low, monotonous chaunt, which during the cold season may be heard from every low, sheltered bush in the open ground (campos) between Gongo and Catas Altas."

Thunderstorms, here called "trovoadas,"[‡] sometimes accompanied by heavy falls of hail, usher in the tropical rains, which set in with a will about early November. As usual in the Brazil, the discharge greatly varies. For ten years the average was 68·28 inches; the smallest remembered was 51·57 in 1863; the average between 1864-6 was 63·00.[§]

About the end of January, or in early February, is a fair-weather interval, like our St. Martin's summer; it is called the "Veranhíco," little verão, or summer: during a fortnight or three weeks the rains cease, and there is cloudless sunshine. I travelled through the Province of São Paulo during the "Indian

---

[*] For March   Therm. Min. 65°   Max. 80°   Adie's Symp. 27·90 — 28·40 inches.

    ,, April   ,,   49°   ,,   68°   ,,   28·22 — 28·59 ,,

    ,, May   ,,   46°   ,,   68°   ,,   28·17 — 28·60 ,,

    ,, June   ,,   49°   ,,   72°   ,,   28·40 — 28·66 ,,

   For half July   ,,   47°   ,,   70°   ,,   28·56 — 28·75 ,,

The sun is in aphelion, July 2nd—the coldest season in these Highlands of the Brazil. This temperature reminds us of the results obtained by Dr. Blanc at Magdala in Abyssinia.

[†] The "Andorinha." It is also known by its Tupy name, Taperá or Majoi. The former must not be confounded with Tapera, which the T. D. translates Aldeia Velha, or Sitio Abandonado, and remarks that according to Pison it also means the "Andorinha," which it does not.

[‡] These trovoadas must not be confounded with the African "tornado," our corrupted word applied to a very different meteor.

[§] The following are the figures for three years :—

           In 1864 fall = 61·98 inches.

           ,, 1865 ,, = 61·98   ,,

           ,, 1866 ,, = 65·14   ,,

summer" of 1867 ; overhead all was delightful ; under foot everything was detestable.

The only pretty part of the Casa Grande is the outside. Its
terreiro, or compound, is a flat space laid out with good gravel
walks and with attempts at turf—an Anglo-tropical lawn. The
edge of this grassy bank fronting north, and looking down upon
the rivulet valley, is adorned with oranges, limes, and the ever-
brilliant Poinsettia. Eastward are earth-banks, once a heap of
rubbish, now bright with coffee and bananas. Behind in a deep
gorge, with its irrigating stream, is the garden. The upper part
shows foreign trees and flowers, which here suffer from two
plagues. The "plantation ant," which the old Portuguese called
the king of the Brazil, is a perfect "liberal," which here means a
"know-nothing." It injures the produce of the country, but it
"eats up" the stranger. The mistletoe-like "Herva de Passa-
rinho,"* with its yellow-red bunches, resembling currants, is
more fatal to trees. The main climber from the root embraces
the trunk, and puts forth tendrils which penetrate the bark and
suck the life-blood. It is hard to kill; if cut across it renews
itself, they say, and the seed is often deposited upon the upper
branches, especially by the "Bemtivi."†

The kitchen garden, under Mr. Fitzpatrick, who is handy at
all things, from killing a sheep to culling a bouquet, gives excellent salads and cabbages. The radishes are rather tough and
woody, the potato does not thrive. For nine years Morro Velho
has had a horticultural society, with the requisite president,
committee, and treasurer ; it meets in the first weeks of February
and August, and useful articles are then given as prizes. Mrs.
Gordon, who has lived in Jamaica, has introduced the "cassareep," and her "pepper-pot" equals any curry, and far excels
"palm-oil chop." Brazilians mostly throw away the juice of the
poisonous manioc, of which so many uses may be made. Every
old book has a chapter "wherein is declared how terrible is the
water of Mandioca," and never fails to tell you that it produces
large grubs with which the good wives of the Indians, and—this
is insinuated *sotto voce*—even white women, have eased off their
husbands. Yet, curious to say, the savages knew how to evapo-

* "The herb of the small bird."
† This amusing little wretch (Lanius
pitangua), whose noisy cry expresses, "I
saw you well," or "Welcome !" is mentioned by every Brazilian traveller. Prince
Max. (i. 63) also gives the name Tectivi.

rate the volatile acrid principle; they concentrated the juice with
the Crumari cumbari, or Cumari, the Capsicum frutescens, a wild
"bird pepper," and they made Cassareep,* which they called
"Ticupi," or "Tucupe." † This "tempero," a sauce to be compared with soy, is still known, I am told, to the backwoodsmen
of the Northern Brazil.

The Casa Grande is the old house of the Padre Antonio
Freitas, of course altered and added to. Caldcleugh (ii. 275)
describing the senior and his nephew, Padre Joaquim, remarks
that the padre's wife was very beautiful, with black eyes, and
"nice and fat." ‡ The padre, after having the grace to settle
D. Silveria in the neat little Fazenda de Santa Anna, on the
Sabará Road, died at Congonhas, but during Lent he revisits his
earthly home, and freely takes what he wants from the cupboard.
So Pedro, his grey-headed slave, with simple African fetish
faith, places meat upon the table, and often sees the "larva"
passing from room to room. Uncharitable persons have opined
that the good priest has been transferred to a locality where
walking exercise is not permissible, but tenets will differ upon
so weighty and obscure a subject.

The Superintendent's quarters, I repeat, should be changed.
The situation is close to the stream—one of the hottest, the
coldest, and the dampest of tenements. The Company's store
was once the Casa Grande; it might return to that honour.
Nothing is more injurious to the prosperity of the mine than a
frequent change of commanding officers; and the climate, combined with the peculiar influences of the place, requires that

---

* The following is the recipe for making "Cassareep," and it is a good action to
make it public :—

"To 1 gallon of brine from salted beef
add 2 galls. of (poisonous) manioc juice,
which must be as fresh as possible.
Simmer in earthen pot for six or seven
hours. After the third hour add 1 lb. of
unground black pepper corns, ½ lb. of
allspice, ¼ lb. of mace, 4 nutmegs pounded
in mortar, and 2 ounces of cloves. If not
hot enough add bird peppers whole. Pass
through a fine sieve, bottle and seal.
"Pepper-pot" is simply meat and vegetables
put into "Cassareep;" it must be sim-
mered every day, whether used or not, and
the wastage compensated for by adding as
much Cassareep (a wine-glass full or so)
and as many peppers as required. The

vessel should be a flattish pot of the most
porous clay, which will easily imbibe the
Capsicine.

† The Tucupi is still used in the Amazonian regions where the "Red" blood
remains. I have heard that beasts which
take a long time to chew can with impu-
nity eat manioc, whose poisonous juice
flows out of their mouths.

‡ "Bem gorda :" fatness, amongst all
the Southern Latin race, including the
Brazilian, being equivalent to fairness.
Possibly the mixture of Moorish blood
causes the taste—who can forget Clapper-
ton's widow Zuma, the "walking tun-butt?"
Ugly, old, thin, are the positive, comparative and superlative of contempt addressed
to the woman of the Mediterranean.

every attention be paid to health. Having once got a valuable man, keep him alive.

To the north-east of the Superintendency, and half hid by shrubbery, is the "Station Library," as we should say in India, externally a little octagon, tiled and whitewashed. There are 920 volumes, 800 for loan, and the rest for school purposes. The librarian is the chaplain, a clergyman licensed by the Bishop of London. The shelves show some good books of reference; unfortunately, nearly all those of local interest, as Spix and Martius, and Lyon's Journal, are missing. They should be found, and the delinquents fined. A few paces beyond the Library lead to the Company's offices. Here at 9 A.M. daily is held the officers' conference. I consider the system worse than a council of war. Here, too, on the first Saturday of every month, pay is issued to the Brazilian miners and labourers, free and unfree. The Europeans receive their money every two months, the day being appointed by notice.

The only level walk in or about Morro Velho is along the "Rego de Cristaes," or Crystal Leat. Risking many a tic—douloureux—you ascend the Store Hill, and enter the "Retiro" village, built upon a well-drained slope. Here whitewashed cottages of Brazilian aspect rise, row behind row, each fronted by its garden patch. These are the quarters of the English miners and their families. The rent varies from 0$500 to 1$500 per mensem. Others are placed at Mingú, behind the hospital; three families (August, 1867) are living near the Praia Gateway, and some are close to Congonhas. The Company has built beyond the Retiro village cottages for the Brazilian and German miners, but the house accommodation generally is poor, and might be improved with small outlay and great profit.

Entering the gate we strike the Rego, along whose right bank Mr. Gordon has laid out a neat road. Here in the hot evenings young Cornwall repairs to bathe. The water rises in the Cabeceiras Hills, nearly four miles distant along its course, from near the ridge leading to the Paraopéba* district. This part of the country is high. The south-western extremity of the "Morro das Quintas," *alias* "do Ramos," rises 1200 to 1800 feet above

---

* The Paraopéba River runs on the other side of the ridge, about eleven leagues westward of the Rio das Velhas, and here the lay of the two valleys is nearly parallel.

the stream, and on the south-east there is a still loftier block, the "Morro do Pires." Formerly the stream discharged through Congonhas; it was bought by Captain Lyon, and was taken up at a level to command the mine. It is one of the many courses which collect the waters of the adjacent streamlets. Undine is thus compelled to turn the huge wheels, to raise the ore, to wash it, and to deposit through flumes the tailings of the Praia. The process is costly, extending over twenty-nine miles, and the tents are continually suffering from floods, earth-slips, and that riva miner, "parvula . . . magni formica laboris." The Cristaes crosses in launders the Retiro Ravine, flows in a water-course round a hill to the receiving cistern, and then passes over by one of the finest works in the establishment, the deep gorge known as the "Criminoso." Inverted iron syphons plunge into the depths, and deliver 2000 cubic feet per minute about 182 feet above the Ribeirão, which finally drains off the water.*

Returning from the walk, we pass the little Protestant chapel. As a rule, it is tolerably attended in dry weather, when the congregation may number 100 souls, although Tregeagh some-times does complain that he has lost "all relish for his prayers." The mechanics sit on the right side, the miners on the left. I found the singing to be that of the country church in Great Britain generally, suggesting the question, why should men who cannot sing a song, sing psalms and hymns? After not hearing the English Litany for a length of days, we cannot but think of the dictum of Dr. Newman, the Oratorian, namely, that "Pro-testantism is the dreariest of possible religions, and that the thought of the Anglican service makes man shudder." Surely it might be altered for the better, but is there any middle term between the God-like gift of reason or the un-reason of Rome? †

On the next Sunday I tried the Padre Francisco Petraglia,

---

* Length of Cristaes inverted pipes from cistern to cistern   .   740 feet   5 inches.
  Height of framing from surface of water   .   .   .   .   81 ,,   6 ,,
  Difference of level on the opposite sides   .   .   .   .   23 ,,   11 ,,
  Height of pipes from the lowest part to the upper end of }   120 ,,   0 ,,
       the discharge, about   .   .   .   .}
  First set of pipes have internal diameter of   .   .   .   14 inches.
  Second ditto   ,,   ,, ...   12 ,,
  Thickness of iron in upper part   .   .   .   .   . $\frac{5}{16}$ths of inch.
  Ditto   ,,   lower ,, ... $\frac{3}{8}$ths ,,
  Pressure on lowest part about 45 lbs. per square inch.   This highly civilized aqueduct was put up by the head mechanic, Mr. Rouse.

  † "The rational form of thought must necessarily be the last of all." M. Cousin Cours de 1828, p. 28.

who affects the other side of the Ribeirão of Bŏa Vista. The chapel
was licensed by the Most Reverend the Bishop of Marianña. The
first incumbent was a Portuguese; in August, 1860, he was succeeded by the present, a retired Garibaldian. My wife was much
scandalised to hear that the altar lacked its stone; but the church
has not been consecrated, and there is such a thing as " commu-
nier en blanc." The ornaments are not rich, the monstrance is
merely a watch-case, with metal rays, and there is some want of
" a vessel with hyssop for the aspersion of the church and to
keep the holy water." The Padre does not disdain the early
weed, and is much liked by all, except those who resent the
immense superiority of his fireworks over the national article.

Mass was to be celebrated at 10·30 A.M., and we found a small
crowd, mostly black, gathered about the chapel. A few Brazilians rode up; they had probably sent or walked two or three
miles to catch the horses which they had used for 200 or 300
yards—thus far like the old Mameluke Beys, who would not
cross even a street on foot. Some delay was caused by collecting
grist for candles, and for the ecclesiastic mill generally. A table
loaded with heaped coppers stood inside the western entrance,
fronting the huge altar. It had been pay-day, and each one, as
he or she went in, knelt, kissed the offered stole, and delivered
his or her mite. A bald-headed black sacristan directed, from
his cunning eyes, a probing look at every coin, and with sneer
and leer, and indescribable gibe and jeer, corrected the few braves
who would not "lend to the Lord," or who lent too prudently.
The satirical Sr. Antonio Marcos declared that in every chapel
roof there is a hole, through which the drop * percolates into the
priestly pocket.

This hardly decorous scene ended, we all entered, the whites
taking station in front, the blacks behind; men standing and
women squatting on the floor. This old custom still prevails in
country places: only the most civilized cities in Brazil afford
benches. All were dressed in Sunday attire; the chapel was a
bed of tulips, with tall sable stamens and a few. whitey-brown
stigmas. The conduct of the flock was in every way creditable,

---

* The word used was "Pinga," whence
is derived the verb pingar, to take a drop,
often used with Pitar, to touch one's pipe.
The sentiment suggests the Basque proverb
"On-gosseac guiçon bat hilic ines seguin
eliça-barnera, eta esta gueros hautée atera,"
Avarice having slain a man, took sanctuary
in the Church, and since that time has
never left it.

their singing was better in time and tune, and there was more
fervour than in the rival establishment. Perhaps the cause may
be that the service is short and the sermon is shorter; yet in
matters of homiletics the good Mr. Armstrong does not require
a sermon-meter. Padre Petraglia inculcated very severely
Faith, Hope, and Charity, and demanded alms for a white
porcelain St. Sebastian, who, grilled with arrows, occupied a
table hard by: those who would not " down with the dust " were
all " burros and cachorros " *—donkeys and dogs. This was
suiting language to modified intelligence with a witness. Unhappily the Reverend has forgotten Italian and has not learned
Portuguese—here a common phenomenon, and not a little
puzzling to Hamitic comprehension.

---

* The strange primness and "respect-
ability" of the old Portuguese forbade
them to pronounce the indelicate word cão
(dog) on the same principle that a Maltese
peasant when speaking of his wife says
"saving your presence." He therefore
preferred Cachorro, a low corruption of
the Latin Catulus, and made "pup," like
"post-boy" or "drummer-boy," do duty
for its senior. Thus also all the Neo-
Latin tongues have taken the name of
a horse, not from "Equus," but from Ca-
ballus, " a nag."

A similar primness may be observed in
our "Philistine" English of the present
century. Sketch, for instance, the figure
feminine. She has a bosom but no breasts,
a stomach and a spleen, but no belly nor
kidneys. I believe that she has legs, but
no thighs; she has certainly ankles, but
she wants calves: and so forth.

CHAPTER XXIII.

THE PAST AND PRESENT OF THE ST. JOHN DEL REY MINE AT MORRO VELHO.

"Brazil does not contain any gold-mine."—Ure's Dictionary, sub voce.

THE Morro Velho Mine was first worked in 1725 by the father of Padre Freitas, who bought it with 150,000 cruzados, £600 of our money, but in those days a very different sum. The Padre sold it, as has been said, to Captain Lyon, and the total cost of the estate has been £56,434 12s. 7d.

Our earliest notice of it is in 1825, when Caldcleugh visited "the gold mine of Congonhas da Sabará." He describes it as an immense "quebrada" or ravine, worked almost through the heart of a mountain, whose upper stratum, disturbed by the earlier miners, was a *débris* of quartz, iron, and red earth. The lode was a highly-inclined mass of auriferous chlorite slate, intersected by quartz veins, where gold resided in ferruginous and arsenical pyrites. The walls of the mine were encrusted with white acicular crystals, an impure sulphate of alumine. The Padre blasted his ore, and when short of powder he used the Hannibalian method of rock-splitting—with water, however, not vinegar. The metal was stamped in five mills made progressively powerful, and they produced 25—30 oitavas per diem of poorish gold, seldom exceeding 19 carats. The chief work was the "Vinagrado" lode, so called from the reddish colour of the stone, and it is said that the owner extracted from it in two months 24:000$000. This was done with seventy slaves, each hand receiving 1½ oitava of gold per week.

Gardner, memorably ill-received by Mr. Goodair, Superintendent of Cocaes, was welcomed to Morro Velho by Mr. Crickitt, Acting Chief Commissioner for Mr. Herring. The traveller spent a month there in 1840, and has left an interesting account of the mine in its younger days. He found the auriferous vein

occurring in greyish-coloured clay slate, and consisting of quartzose rock, mixed with carbonate of lime, and strongly impregnated
with iron and pyrites of copper and arsenic. The lode, whose
general direction ranged east to west, was about seven fathoms
wide, a little to the east of the central workings. Here it divided
into two branches running to the westward, whilst two others
which had been more deeply mined, extended to the east. The
ramifications gradually diverged, took a north-easterly direction,
and then ran parallel to, and about 100 feet from, each other.
The quantity raised varied from 1500 to 1600 tons per month,
and each ton gave a mean of 3—4 oitavas, and a maximum of 7.
The Tyrolese Zillerthal, a running amalgamation process of
revolving-mills, had been tried at Gongo Soco, and had abolished
the batêa. Here they failed. The arsenic formed with the gold
an alloy which rendered the operation difficult, and the waste of
quicksilver was excessive. Roasting and calcining the ore had
also been abandoned, the arsenical fumes having proved dangerous, and it is said that a black was poisoned by them when treating
the refuse sand.

The early Reports of the present Company describe the main
body of the metalliferous mass as occupying the southern flank of
a high mountain, whose contour it follows in parallel lines : at
the eastern extremity it bends north, and becomes too small to be
worth pursuing. The mine consisted of three adjoining workings in the same lode. The easternmost was the "Arsenical,"
ten fathoms deep: in the centre was the principal open cut called
the Bahú, or "box-hole,"* whilst westward, also ten fathoms
deep, was the now deserted Quebra Panella, or break-pot, so
termed from its uneven surface.

Mr. Herring proceeded to push with all possible force an adit
for unwatering the mine at a deeper level; to apply draining
and stuff-hauling machinery, and to sink the lode and break it by
stope-work. As a guard against falling, "letting arches remain"
proved successful. He also set up "Arrastres" or triturators,†
each of which worked in the twenty-four hours four tons of refuse

---

* The "Bahú," the French "Bahut,"
a travelling trunk. In the Brazil it is
applied to many features, such as a square
rock rising from the water, or a cubical
block upon the summit of a mountain. In
mines it is the hollow where the drainage
gathers and forms a well : thus it is opposed to a "Cachoeira," ground where the
water falls over and does not sink. Hence
many great mines have a Bahú and a
Cachoeira.

† In Chap. 26 I have explained this
arrangement.

sand. From an average of twenty-seven head of stamps, the yield in December, 1835, was 27 lb. 11 oz. of gold. In 1838 communication was opened between the Bahú and Quebra Panella. Mr. Herring proposed to call them the " United Mines," but the old names were perforce retained. In July, 1838, the former workings of the Gambá,* a northerly off-set from the main lode, and lying to the eastward of the United Mines, were cleared out, and the " Vinagrado " was abandoned. At the same time, the " Cachoeira " or easternmost section of the great vein was opened. Presently was discovered the important fact that the whole mass of lode lies downward in nearly a true eastern direction, and the dip carries it forward some five feet ten inches for every six feet sunk when stoping.

In 1847, after his long service, Mr. Herring went home and died. Morro Velho has lost all her Commissioners in the prime of life. He was succeeded by Mr. George D. Keogh, formerly Secretary to the Company, an active energetic man, but without practical knowledge. In his day (1846) Mr. Thomas Treloar became the Head Mining-Captain, and the Company sent out a chaplain, the Reverend Charles Wright, who was sensibly directed not to trouble himself with conversion, but to open a school for the children of their European employés. In 1855 Mr. Thomas Walker, M.D., became Superintendent. An amiable and honourable man, he dreaded responsibility, and he trusted much in others: thus, as the gold returns prove, his rule was not very successful. He also died, and in 1858 Mr. Gordon took charge. No more gold-weighing in private was allowed, and the boast that three Superintendents had been got rid of, and that the back of the fourth would soon be seen, was notably stultified. The prospects of the Mine presently improved, and the consequence was a dividend.†

* Gambá, in French "Sarigue," is a Brazilian marsupial which does the duties of a fox (Dedelphis carnivorus or Azaree). It is applied opprobriously to a negro as well as to a mine.

† The following is an abstract of the gold produced by the Morro Velho Mine under its several Superintendents : my information comes from the best source—the Company's Annual Reports.

Mr. Herring (1837—1847).

In 1837 Morro Velho produced	.	.	41,861 oitavas of gold.
,, 1838	,,	,,	.	. .	60,472 ,,
,, 1839	,,	,,	.	. .	63,842 ,,
,, 1840	,,	,,	.	. .	76,908 ,,
,, 1841	,,	,,	.	. .	70,945 (= 68 lbs. 1 oz. Troy).
,, 1842	,,	,,	.	. .	92,744 oitavas of gold.
,, 1843	,,	,,	.	. .	127,834 ,,

It is easy to superintend in England establishments which have been drilled for years, perhaps for generations ; far otherwise in these regions, where the weight rests on one "pair of shoulders." Directors of future Companies, if they would benefit shareholders rather than promote friends and relations, should be as careful in choosing a Superintendent as they have been in the selection of a reporting engineer. At the mine he should possess the absolute power of a colonel commanding a French, not an English regiment, and receive daily reports from his officers, instead of meeting them in consultation : he should be entitled to make and unmake all his subalterns, and should be expected to take upon himself all responsibility. The subaltern might be allowed to send him complaints against his superiors, and if unable to substantiate them, he should at once be dismissed.

It is pleasing to see the excellent arrangements of Morro Velho amongst a people so defective in the organising and administrative capacity as are the English—at least in the Brazil. Let me cite, as an instance, a certain Anglo-Brazilian Railway,

March 1, 1844 to February 28, 1845 Morro Velho produced 124,432 oitavas of gold.
   ,,   1845 ,,   ,,   1846   ,,   ,,   128,515   ,,
   ,,   1846 ,,   ,,   1847   ,,   ,,   154,584   ,,

Mr. Keogh (1847—1855).

March 1, 1847 to February 28, 1848 Morro Velho produced 175,439   ,,
   ,,   1848 ,,   ,,   1849   ,,   ,,   230,136   ,,
   ,,   1849 ,,   ,,   1850   ,,   ,,   270,488   ,,
   ,,   1850 ,, March 10, 1851   ,,   ,,   278,654   ,,
   ,, 11, 1851 ,,   ,,   1852   ,,   ,,   324,279   ,,
   ,,   1852 ,,   ,,   1853   ,,   ,,   353,761   ,,
   ,,   1853 ,,   ,,   1854   ,,   ,,   372,679   ,,
   ,,   1854 ,,   ,, 11, 1855   ,,   ,,   364,428   ,,

Dr. Walker (1855—1858).

March 11, 1855 to March 21, 1856 Morro Velho produced 346,031*   ,,
   ,, 21, 1856 ,,   ,, 20, 1857   ,,   ,,   307,261   ,,
   ,,   1857 ,,   ,, 19, 1858   ,,   ,,   261,247   ,,

Mr. Gordon (1858—1866).

March 20, 1858 to March 18, 1859 Morro Velho produced 285,615   ,,
   ,, 19, 1859 ,,   ,,   1860   ,,   ,,   363,214   ,,
   ,,   1860 ,,   ,, 19, 1861   ,,   ,,   428,166   ,,
   ,, 20, 1861 ,,   ,, 20, 1862   ,,   ,,   543,637   ,,
   ,, 21, 1862 ,,   ,, 22, 1863   ,,   ,,   529,193   ,,
   ,, 23, 1863 ,,   ,,   1864   ,,   ,,   476,005   ,,
   ,,   1864 ,,   ,,   1865   ,,   ,,   247,663†   ,,
   ,,   1865 ,,   ,,   1866   ,,   ,,   522,119   ,,

* On March 7 about 170 tons fell in from the roof and south wall of the Bahú Mine. The borers and kibble-fillers all escaped.

† On February 13 a fall of killas took place in the West Cachoeira, and on April 19, eight miners were killed in the Cachoeira Works.

which consisted of four independent kingdomlets.   Mr. Superintendent was not allowed to give an order, and thus he superin-
tended nothing.   Mr. Chief Engineer commanded the road.
Mr. Mechanical Engineer was lord supreme over a few carriages
and inclined planes, whilst Mr. Transport-Manager, who was also,
curious to say, Mr. Storekeeper, ruled as absolutely as the chiefs,
his neighbours.   The Brazilian gazed with wonder.   But Mr.
Gordon is an Irishman, and the "individuality of the individual"
is less bristly, less tyrannous in this section of the Keltic race than
in the Anglo-Briton.

We have seen that the three great mines form a single continuation of the same line of mineral.   The Quebra Panella is
westernmost; next to it is a small affair, the Champion ground,
—so called from a person, and not used in the common mining
sense; in the centre is the Bahú, divided into east and west,
whilst over the Bahú and easternmost lies the Cachoeira,* also
having two sections.   The "Box-hole" and the "Rapids" are in fact
one mine.   The early workers left a large wedge or bar of killas
between them, but this, after due consideration, was removed in
1860.

The breadth of the lode varies from four to sixty feet.   The
general direction where worked is west to east, with northerly
shiftings.   The dip is 45°, rising to a maximum of 46° 30', or
47°.   The strike is from south 82° east to south 58° east.   The
cleavage planes of the killas are in some places transverse to, in
others parallel with the lode.   In certain sections of the mine-walls
they bear north 36° east, but the average is more easterly.   The
direction is south 46° east, and their dip is at angles varying from
43° to 70°.   Parts of the walls have been found to be baulk and
unsound, jointy and scaly, but in the early Reports the evils were
greatly exaggerated.   The underlay or underlie dip, or inclination
of the mineral vein, is 6° in the Bahú and 8° in the Middle
Cachoeira.   Its dip varies from south 82° east to south 58° east,

---

* In July, 1867,

The vertical depth of the Cachoeira Mine was   .   .   189 fathoms.

  ,,   depth on the dip of the lode   .   .   .   264   ,,

  ,,   length of excavation (E. and W. of the Sump)   .   66   ,,

The width of the excavation varied from 6 to 45 feet, average 29 feet.

  The vertical depth of the Bahú is   .   .   .   .   179 fathoms.

  ,,   depth on the dip of the lode   .   .   .   207   ,,

  ,,   length of the excavation (west of Sump, or lowest } 50   ,,

       part of the shaft)   .   .   .   .   .   .   }

The width of the excavation ranged from 11 to 90 feet, with an average of 44 feet.

and the inclination from 42° to 47°, but everywhere parallel with the striæ. The richest part of the lode is still in the eastern Bahú. There may be good lody matter nestling to the south-east, and in that direction "dead works" are being carried on with zeal. Much had been expected from the western extremity, but a shaft sunk there gave very poor results.

During the half-year between September and March, 1866—1867,* the net profit on the working of the mines had been £49,131. After making all reductions, there remained available for dividend £54,434, and the Directors "had the satisfaction" of recommending the payment of £4 5s. per share, free of income-tax, and independent of the 10 per cent. carried as usual to the reserve fund. In this prosperous state I left the mine. But shortly after, in the night of November 21, 1867, a fire broke out, and despite all efforts considerable damage was done.

* The following are the figures between March 23 and September 21 of 1866 : —

9 days in March yielded	19,627	oitavas.
April	50,046	,,
May	60,454	,,
June	52,076	,,
July	48,405	,,
August	52,016	,,
September (21 days)	32,028	,,
Total	314,652	

	£	s.	d.
The net profit on the working was	50,566	9	8
Interest on moneys unemployed	1,570	0	0
Balance of undivided profits	743	11	4
Total	£52,880	1	0
Deducting the London expenses	1,193	16	3
Remain for dividend	£51,686	4	9

During this half-year 7000 tons were raised in excess of the previous half-year, or 53,698 to 46,629, and this is the greatest amount yet quarried. On the other hand it had 41·6, and the latter only 36·6 of the valueless killas.

CHAPTER XXIV.

"Ipsaque barbaries aliquid præsentit honesti."

A PECULIAR sight, and very fit for a photograph, is the Revista or muster of the Blacks, which takes place every second Sunday. When we were there about 1100 out of 1452 attended in the "Compound" fronting the "Casa Grande." Both sexes were bare-footed—everywhere in the Brazil a token of slavery. The women, fronted by a picket of twelve young girls, were ranged in columns of six companies. They were dressed in the "Sabbath" uniform, white cotton petticoats, with narrow red band round the lower third; cotton shawls striped blue and white, and a bright kerchief, generally scarlet, bound round the wool. On the proper right, perpendicular to the column, are the "good-conduct women." The first year's badge is a broad red band round the white hem, and replaced by narrow red stripes, one for each year, till the mystic number seven * gives freedom. We saw ten women and as many men officially apply for the preliminaries to manumission.

Ranged behind the women, the men are clothed in white shirts, loose blue woollen pants, red caps—Turkish or Glengarry—and cotton trousers. The "jacket men," as the "good conducts" are called, stand on the proper left of, and at right angles with, the battalion of Amazons. They wear tailless coats of blue serge, bound with red cuffs and collars, white waistcoats, overalls with red stripes down the seams, and the usual bonnets; each has a medal with the Morro Velho stamp, the badge of approaching freedom. Children of an age to attend the Revista are clad in the same decent comfortable way; a great contrast they offer to the negrolings that sprawl about the land.

---

* The customary period is 10 years, but it has been humanely reduced.

The slaves answer to the roll-call made by the heads of the respective departments. This done, the Superintendent, followed by the Manager and Assistant Manager of the Blacks, and the two medical officers, walks down the companies and minutely inspects each individual. I observed that almost all the " chattels " were country born; there was only one Munjolo,* distinguished by the three scars of his race; the other "persons held to service " call him " Papagente " or man-eater.

After inspection, a pay-table was spread before the door, and the girls and small children received their allowance of pay and soap. The three coppers (0$120) of former days have been raised to 6—8 for those employed on the spalling floor, and the stone carriers get 12 "dumps" of "obligation." By extra earnings and overtime,† the pay will increase to 16—20 coppers. Each takes per week half a pound of soap; the cost of this article to the Company ranges between 300$000 and 400$000 a month, or annually 360l. to 480l. The men and married women are paid at the Public Office. The former anciently received 4 coppers, now they get double, and by industry they may gain from 8 to 10 patacas each of 8 coppers. The average of rewards and overtime paid to the blacks amounts to 1600$000 per fortnight, or about 3840l. per annum.

Muster over, both sexes and all ages are marched off to church. The day is then their own. The industrious will look after house and garden, pigs and poultry; they will wash and sew, or fetch water, wood, or grass for sale. The idle and dissolute will keep the day holy in African fashion, lie in the sun, smoke, and if they can, drink and smoke hemp, like the half-reclaimed savages of "Sā Leone." Dinah here and elsewhere is proverbially fond of trinkets and fine rags. Parade over, she will doff her regimental attire and don a showy printed gown and a blazing shawl, the envy of all beholders.

Once the negroes showed us what in Hindostan is called "tamasha," in Spain and Portugal a " folía," in Egypt and Morocco a " fantasíyah," and here a " Congáda " or Congo-ry. A score of men, after promenading through the settlement, came to the Casa Grande. They were dressed, as they fondly imagined, after

---

* A well-known race from the lands east of the Congo regions. St. Hil. writes the word Monjolo, thus confounding the animate with the inanimate machine.

† Technically called "fazer horas."

the style of the Agua-Rosada House,* descended from the great Manikongo and hereditary lords of Congo land. But the toilettes, though gorgeous with coloured silks and satins, were purely fanciful, and some wore the Kanitar or plumed head-gear, and the Arasvia or waist fringe, and carried the Tacape or tomahawk belonging to the red man. All were armed with sword and shield, except the king, who, in sign of dignity, carried his sceptre, a stout and useful stick. The masked old man, with white beard, trembling under-jaw, chevrotante voice, and testy manner, was cleverly represented by a young black from Sabará. On his right sat the captain of war, the Premier; on his left the young Prince, his son and heir, an uninteresting negrokin. Of course the buffoon of the Dahoman court was there, and the fun consisted in kicking and cuffing him as if he were one of our clowns or "pantaloons."

The "play" was a representation of the scenes which most delight that mild and amiable negro race, orders for a slave hunt; the march, accompanied with much running about and clashing of swords, which all handled like butchers' knives; the surprise, dragging in prisoners, directions to put to death recreant ministers and warriors, poisonings and administering antidotes—in fact, "savage Africa." His Majesty freely used his staff, threshing everybody right regally. The speeches were delivered in a singsong tone; the language was Hamitico-Lusan, and there was an attempt at cadence and rhyme. Slaughtering the foeman and drinking his blood were the favourite topics, varied by arch allusions to the Superintendent and his guests. After half an hour they received their bakshísh and went to show their finery elsewhere.

The ceremonies of the Sunday ended with five couple bringing up as many newly baptised bits of black, to receive the reward of fertility. Payment for progeny is a good idea; as a rule the Brazilian slave girl says, "What has a captive† to do with

---

* It sounds like "chaff," this rose-water title adopted by full-blooded negroes, but it is pure history. An interesting account of the dynasty, and a sketch of "Nicolas, Prince of Congo," has been lately given by M. Valdez. (Vol. II. Chap. 2, "Six Years of a Traveller's Life in Western Africa." London : Hurst & Blackett. 1861.)

† "Cattivo" (Cattiva, fem.), euphuistic for "escravo," or "escrava," which is opposed to "forro," a freeman, the Arabic ‫حر‬ A similar pretty term for buying slaves is "resgatar," to ransom, because officially they are supposed to be thus saved from being murdered by their hostile captors.

children?" At Morro Velho, on the contrary, negresses desire issue because they are temporarily taken off work. Unfortunately, when the second babe is to be born, the first is neglected, and the doctor is rarely sent for till death is at hand. It is an object to nurse only one child, and to be ready for bearing another when required. Thus the hospital books* for the first six months of 1867 show that the death-rate of negroes has doubled the birth-rate : with a total of 1452, 16 were born and 32 died.†

The sires of "occipital race" are in a state of wonderful grin— "patulis stant rietibus omnes." The mothers, in marvellous gold chains, are marshalled by a big black Meg Merrilies, who seems omnipotent over her sable flock. Each matron receives a mil-reis, a bottle of wine, and a bit of the best advice from the Superintendent. When the ceremony ends, the scamp of the party—he is ever foremost on such occasions—proposes three cheers, and a tiger for Mr. Gordon, and all depart in high feather.

A slave muster is also held daily in the great hall of the "Blacks' Ranch," which is lighted up during the dark season. The bell sounds at 5 A.M.; half an hour afterwards, the Brazilian assistants, in presence of Mr. Smyth, call out the names, first of the men, then of the women, and lastly of the new comers, who, being sometimes rebelliously inclined, are being broken to harness. Breakfast is cooked overnight, and each labourer carries off his meal.

I also visited the hospital, which is under the charge of Mrs. Holman, the matron, and inspected the reports, transmitted monthly and yearly to the directors. The building is as well situated as any other, and is clean and new, spacious and conve-nient; whilst the medical men live close by. Yet the blacks have, like Sepoys, an aversion to it,' and prefer to die in their own huts; consequently many of them are brought in only when moribund. There is a white ward, but Englishmen are usually treated at home, and they get sick leave, if absence from work be deemed necessary.

The medical reports take, I think, rather too favourable a

---

* Since December, 1866, Dr. Weir has kept a register of Births and Deaths of all whites and negroes, free Brazilians, who work in the establishment, not included. Before that time births were registered,

deaths were not.

† Castelnau (i. 184) is of opinion that the birth-rate does not balance the death-rate of slaves in the Brazil, and I quite agree with him.

view when they declare the black population of Morro Velho to
be "as a rule healthy." Dr. Robert Monach remarked in 1843,
"When we consider the constitution of the negroes, the modified (?) texture of their skin, performing a greater extent of function
than in the European, and recollect to what great and abrupt
changes of temperature they are continually exposed, from a very
variable climate,* their great carelessness, and the nature of their
occupations, it must be granted that the mortality is small, a
circumstance which affords the best proof that every care is taken
to preserve them in good health." In 1846 a "remarkable circumstance" was observed, namely, that of the 14 deaths 1 only
was from the English negroes of Cata Branca, 2 were of 244
"Company's Blacks," and 4 were of 141 hired from Brazilians.
It was suggested that the disproportion arose from good living
after poor diet suddenly changed; and yet many have testified
that the negroes improve in flesh, colour, and personal appearance after a few months at Morro Velho. In 1848 Dr. Birt
remarks that "in England the per-centage of deaths, including
the whole population, is not less than 3 per cent; ours is a little
more than 2½ per cent." † Dr. Thomas Walker, "Physician to
the Forces," who in 1850 reported upon the sanitary condition
of the Morro Velho blacks, found them decimated by pneumonia,
a very common and treacherous malady in the Highlands of the
Brazil. He regretted that he could not use more freely the
lancet, from which the blacks seem instinctively to shrink, and
thus sometimes they save their lives in the teeth of science.‡

From the Reports it appears that about every ten years there is
abnormal mortality produced by the "nature of the climate and
local situation, and by the social condition and peculiarities in
the constitution of the blacks." Diseases of the brain and bowels
are severe; dysentery and pleurisy carry off many victims, whilst
pneumonia is sometimes epidemic, and often latent, leading to a
rapid development. Of the 90 men and women in hospitals,
several suffered from malignant ulcers of the extremities, aggra-

---

* The drainage of the Central African
plateau, or raised basin, I have remarked
less regular than that of the Brazil. In
other points the climates remarkably resemble each other. I have often been
reminded of Usagara on the Serra do Mar,
and of Unyamwezi in Minas Geraes and

Saô Paulo.
  † For the official average rate of mortality, see Appendix 1, Section A.
  ‡ His paper has been printed in the
Twenty-first Annual Report of the Company. (London: R. Clay, Bread-street-
hill.)

vated perhaps by the mundic water, which is said to cause
gangrene in wounds. The loathsome "bôbas" or yaws, hardly
known to northern Europe, except in marine hospitals, are here as
common as on the Guinea Coast; the people dread the disease,
and declare of it "não se pode dizer 'tíve bôbas'"—"no man can
say 'I have had yaws.'" What Caldcleugh calls "atôa (or
chance) connections"[*] amongst the slaves, are energetically re-
pressed by the Superintendent, and the officers set an example of
scrupulous good conduct: yet as at "Sá Leone," so here, the
majority of cases are venereal, and even children are born with
corona veneris. But such is the negro everywhere out of his
own country, and in it also where Europeans have made
colonies.

> What wondrous scene the future then shall view.
> The links, half human, ruling sea and strand,
> Feigned human by the philanthropic few.
> A monstrous, foul, deformed and fetid band.
> Males, bestial all, and females all untrue,
> Lust, perjury, superstition, taint the land :
> Such fortune, " Sá Leone," becomes thee well,
> Thou negro paradise, thou white man's hell ! [†]

Women about to become mothers are taken off work and are sent
to hospital in the fourth month. After confinement they are
relieved from hard labour, and they work sometimes for half a
year in the sewing department. Those familiar with the condition of the Lancashire "bloomers," of the Cornish women who
assist in dressing the tin ores, and of the English agricultural
labourers' wives generally, will own that the slave-mother is far
better treated at the Morro Velho mines. The young children,
tended by an elderly woman, play under a large tiled shed in the
great square of the Bôa Vista Quarters. But the negro in the
Brazil is an exotic, he is out of his proper ethnic centre ; it is
difficult to keep him alive, as the next quarter century will prove,
and when young he requires every attention from the parent.[‡]

---

[*] A word often misleading strangers in
the Brazil, and appearing as the name of
plants and other things. It is properly
à tôa, the literal meaning "by tugging,"
or "towing;" the secondary signification
is "Sem governo," uselessly, inconside-
rately, and the popular meaning is bad,
worthless, unimportant, uma cousa à tôa,
thus converting it into an adjective.

[†] *Not* in Camoens, Canto V. 12. Like
my friend the author of " Wanderings in
West Africa," I have adopted the nigger
form "Sá Leone," which is merely a corruption of a word already corrupt.
[‡] Nothing can be more erroneous than the
assertion of St. Hil. (III. ii. 72, and other
places), that in the Brazil the negro race
"tend à se perfectionner." Equally abroad

The Brazilian planter who would not see the number of his slaves diminish, allows the children to be with their mothers, and the latter to be off work for two and even for three years.

One of the most interesting visits at Morro Velho is to the cotton-spinning department in the Company's store. The hands are negro girls, and mixed breeds, often free : they work by the task, and they feed and lodge themselves. They are paid at the end of each month, at the rate of 0$300 to 0$400 per lb. of spun yarn, and each averages 4—5 lbs. per week. The material is mostly brought from the dry regions lying west of the Diamantine district, and from the banks of the Rio das Velhas, especially Santa Quiteria, in the municipality of Cruvello. The plant, which the Indians called "Aminüü," is the black-seeded, preferred in the old Brazil to the herbaceous. The lint is more easily separated by the simple bow of Hindostan, still used, whilst the fibre is believed to be stronger and more easily spun. An arroba (32 lbs.) of seed-cotton, worth 0$100 per lb., yields after whipping 7—8 lb. of clean fibre, whose value rises to 0$400 and 0$500. During the last three years prices have been raised by increased demand at Rio de Janeiro ; and, as the following pages will prove, the Brazil, and especially the Province of Minas, with her parent São Paulo, has, in her cotton lands, a mine of wealth which wants only machinery and lines of communication.

The seed is removed from the lint by a charkha, a mere toy, two little cylinders of smooth hard wood, about 1 foot long, of broom-stick thickness, set close together in a diminutive frame, and worked contrary wise by winches.* These are turned by two children, whilst a third presents the cotton, which passes between the rollers and comes out free. I afterwards saw an improvement upon this rude and venerable hand-machine : a water-wheel worked by means of pulleys and bands, eight sets of cylinders, each served by a slave, who cleaned 96 lbs. per diem. By adding a hopper to supply the cotton, a whipper to remove, and a fan to

---

was the learned and eccentric Dr. Knox. "From Santo Domingo he (the negro) drove out the Celt ; from Jamaica he will expel the Saxon ; and the expulsion of the Lusitanian from Brazil is only an affair of time." As in the United States, emancipation will annihilate the African race, which, with very rare exceptions, is viable as a slave recruited from home, not as a freeman in lands occupied by higher blood. It is impossible not to notice the curious self-contradiction of Dr. Knox, who threatened with extinction the Anglo-American (not to mention others), because removed from his proper habitat, and yet who promised a mighty and productive future to the African under the same circumstances.

* There are many varieties of the wheel, many have only one winch.

transport the lint, one pair of hands might do the work of eight.

In nothing does nationality display her differences and peculiarities more notably than in cotton-cleaning machinery. The Brazilian and the Hindu chiefly rely upon Nature's instruments, and the best of all instruments—the fingers. The English invent good, dear, solid articles, safe enough, but tedious, tardy unto impossibility—

> And the trail of the slow worm is over them all.

The North-American contrivances, the popular saw-gins for instance, are cheap, poor, easy to manage, and work at railway speed, but they tear the fibre to pieces. I believe that the old cylinder of the Brazil would with certain improvements become superior to any yet invented.

Captain Joaquim Felizardo Ribeiro, whose mill is about three miles distant, contracts to supply at a fixed sum the Company with gunpowder, of which £200 worth per mensem is consumed in blasting. He finds the hard-wood charcoal; he receives from England, at cost prices, the best sulphur and saltpetre; and he prepares the article in the proportions required by the establishment. Mr. Gray, an Englishman, makes the safety-fuse, which is always charged with gunpowder from home. The other fuses are worked by the black spinsters. Blasting-oil or nitro-glycerine has not yet, I believe, been tried.

The Company's store also contains the theatre, which is always fully attended, and which deserves well of the moralist as a civilizing agent—in fact, what Salt Lake City holds it to be. Mr. Wood, assistant *pro tem.* in the Reduction Office, and Mr. White, jun., were the stars at the time of our visit. The "house" is a long room with two lines of benches; on the left are the officers; to the right sit the mechanics and miners, with their wives, and fronted by their children. The stage is a boarded platform, opposite a raised orchestra at the other end; we had all kinds of fun,—nigger minstrels, the Nerves, and every latest comic song. After hearing the shouts of laughter which greeted every screaming farce, the author would have modified his old saw—

> Anglica gens,
> Optima flens,
> Pessima ridens.

Such, reader, is life at Morro Velho, in the heart of the Brazil. We intended, I have said, to pass a week there; such however was the cordiality with which our countrymen received us, and such their kindness and hospitality, that we could not tear ourselves away till the month was ended.

CHAPTER XXV.

DOWN THE MINE.

At noon-day here
'Tis twilight, and at sunset blackest night.

MR. GORDON made every arrangement for our safe descent. Mrs. Gordon also, who had never before ventured under grass, kindly consented to accompany my wife. It was settled that Mr. L'pool and I should descend first, and receive the rest at the bottom of the pit. Mr. James Estlick, the captain in charge of the mine,* saw us properly clad in heavy boots for protecting the ankles, and in stiff leather hats to guard the head from falling stones, and to carry a "dip" stuck on by a lump of clay; the rest of the toilette was "old clothes," for the wearing out of which my Hibernian cousin defined Rome to be a capital place. A small crowd of surface workmen accompanied us to the mouth of Walker's inclined plane, a hot and unpleasant hole, leading to the Cachoeira Mine. The negret Chico gave one glance at the deep dark pit, wrung his hands, and fled the Tophet, crying that nothing in the wide, wide world would make him enter such an Inferno. He had lately been taught that he is a responsible being, with an "immortal soul," and he was beginning to believe it in a rough theoretical way : this certainly did not look like a place where the good niggers go.

Mr. John Whittaker, who reached Morro Velho just in time to be of the party, and the Superintendent, thought it *infra dig.* to descend otherwise than by the footway.† Yet even Geordy Stephenson did not always despise the "corve." The miners run up and down like cats, much preferring the ladder, because here they depend upon themselves, not on the chain; the stranger

---

* The Superintendent prefers not to have a head mining captain, and in this I think he is right. There are four captains, who change every week in taking the day and night work.

† Meaning the ladders for ingress and egress, including the space around them.

will take some four hours, and next day or two his knees will
remind him of the feat. I preferred, despite all the risks spoken
of, the big iron bucket which weighs nearly a ton, and carries
some nineteen cwts of ore; the Cornishmen call it a "kibble,"
the Brazilians, a "caçámba."* It hangs to a carriage, running
on a shaft of iron-shod wood, descending at an angle of about
46°, and it is lowered and raised by a haul-wheel worked by
water-power. There are two breaks, Cornice "drags," in the
traction machinery for arresting progress suddenly, and should
the chain snap, there is a catch, to which, however, one must not
trust. The big tub careers helplessly forwards and downwards,
"with a surge," till the strong rivets give way, and the affair
becomes a ruin; the fate of a man dashed into this apparently
fathomless abyss of darkness may be imagined. When the
kibble has reached the hauling station where the shaft ends,
self-acting springs detach it from its carriage; it then descends
vertically and is filled with stone.

Accidents have been exceptionally rare in the Great Mine; few
have required the epitaph—

> Here lies the body of Jan Trenow,
> Killed underground, we can't say how.

And there has been no loss of life between July 1, 1865, and
November, 1867. The contingencies have arisen chiefly from the
breaking of dishonestly made chains, which should last two years,
but which have often struck work after six months. The links
fail owing to defective welding of the scarf, the mere skin of
outer surface soon wears through, and imminent danger is the
result. At first wire-ropes were tried and failed; improved
manufacture and different conditions of application have now
rendered them safe. Under any average circumstances, however, a trip in the "kibble" is not more risky than to descend
any one of the four terrible inclined planes, those glissades of
death, which make the stranger "squirm" on the Santos and
São Paulo Railway.

Presently the bucket was suspended over the abyss, and we
found in it a rough wooden seat, comfortable enough. We were

---

* This must not be confounded with the Angolan word "Caçímba," meaning a pit for water, sunk generally in the bed of a nullah, very common on the lower São Francisco.

advised by the pitmen not to look downwards, as the glimmer
of sparks and light-points moving about in the mighty obscure
below, causes giddiness and sea-sickness. We did look down,
however, and none of us suffered from the trial. More useful
advice was to keep head and hands well within the bucket,
especially when passing the up-going tub. We tipped and
tilted half over only once against a kibble way drum, placed to
fend off the "Caçámba." Those who followed us had three
such collisions, which made them catch at the chains, and
describe them as "moments of fearful suspense;" they had
been lowered in a kibble with a superfluity of chain. A stout
young fellow, Zachariah Williams, one of the "lads below," kept
within hail of us, descending the footway as fast as we rattled
down in our novel vehicle.

I could not but marvel at the mighty timbering* which met
the eye as it dilated in the darkness visible—timber in brackets,
timber in hitches or holes; timber in the footways and sollars
or resting places; and timber in the stulls, platforms for depositing ore, for strengthening the wall, and for defending the
workmen. All was of the best and hardest wood, and it is
hardly conceivable how in such damp air it could have caught
fire. The immunity of Brazilian cities and towns results mostly
from the use of timber more like heart-of-oak than our deal-
tinder. The sight suggested a vast underground forest, but

---

* Woods of the first quality are—

Aroeira	Canella Vermelha	Landim
Angelim	Cangerana	Moreira
Brauna, Parda	Folha de Bolo	Massaranduba
Do. Preta	Gonçalo Alves	Paroba Vermelha
Balsamo	Ipé	Liquorana
Capebano	Jacarandá, Tãa	Tinta
Cycupira (Sicupira)	Do. Cabiuna	Tamboril
Cedro	Jatobá	

Amongst inferior growths are reckoned—

Angico	Canella Amarella	Goiabeira
Angá	Do. Preta	Mangue
Bagre	Do. Sassafras	Oleo Vermelho
Cabui	Do. Loura	Pinheiro Vermelho
Canafistula	Cycupiruna	Paroba Branca
Cochoá	Coita (Açoita) Cavallo	Vinhatico
Catoá	Camboatá	

The cost of 5 cubic feet of first quality is 2$000 ; of second quality, 2$000

,, 50	,,	,,	60$000	,,	45$000
,, 100	,,	,,	190$000		
,, 70	,,	,,	—	,,	70$000

a forest torn up by terrible floods, and dashed about by cataracts in all directions, with the wildest confusion. The mighty maze, it need hardly be said, was not without a plan, very palpable at the second look. Terrible was the thrust; in places the vastest trunks of the Brazilian forest giants have been cloven or crushed. These are at once removed and replaced by others. The work is never allowed to get into arrears; everything must be kept tidy as well as safe, and the masonry is as carefully watched as the timber. After a short delay one point becomes weak, another dangerous, the water comes in, the mine works flat, and presently something gives way.

The sight explains why those who are jealous of the mine threaten it with exhaustion of wood for fuel and propping. Of this, however, there is no present danger, the whole Paraopéba district is still untapped, and the Rio das Velhas will yield large supplies for many years. We shall pass charcoal on the way to Sabará, and quantities are to be found at Macácos to the south of the Morro Velho estate.

In this part of the Brazil, young wood, and especially that of small girth, does not last, if cut during the rainy season. The people here fell it from May to August, preferring June, and avoiding, as they say, "months which have no R's," as we shun oysters in months which have them. The rationale is easily understood; in the cold season, when the " dries " have well set in, the sap leaves the bole and returns to the ground. It is not so easy to account for the general belief that wood cut during the moon's wane is not liable to the worm;* even the Indians will not fell trees for their canoes when the satellite is full. In England, I believe, our ancestors who did not wish to be bald, objected to their hair being cut while the moon was waxing. Lunar action, despite northern scepticism, is everywhere in the Tropics a matter of faith. We may treat it like mesmerism, as the effect of latent electricity, or blind sympathy of some unknown force, or, best of all, with De Quincy's 'ἐποχή, or suspended judgment.

---

* "He que cumpre nos minguantes serem derrubadas." Silva, Lisboa Annaes, iii. 153. I am pleased to see that the question of lunar influence has of late years been considered unsettled. Dr. Winslow adduces evidence to prove that as regards its effect upon the insane, much may be said on both sides. With respect to its pernicious action upon sleepers, we are now told that the "moon's rays contain polarised light, which carbonises, and is therefore antagonistic to the sun's rays, which oxygenate."

The timbering does honour to Mr. John Jackson, the captain in charge. It is worked mostly by contract, at so much per log. The men who undertake the job receive no pay, but are supplied with candles, and each pair has a negro gang of 30—40 head. If they "tip" the slaves it is on the principle—or want of it—which makes us tip the railway guard. And here a white man striking a black is very properly fined.

We made an easy descent through this timber avenue of monstrous grandeur, and a bit of lighted tow tied to the bucket-chain showed us all its features. There was no "rattle his bones over the stones," and the trip lasted fifteen minutes. At the bottom the kibble stood still, began to roll like a boat, and descended perpendicularly till we were received by Mr. Andrew, the stopes captain, now on duty. To-night Mr. Williams will relieve him. Our eyes being here unaccustomed to the new gloom, we applied them to the unwatering system, as we stood in the "sump," which to collect the drainage was a little sunk below the deepest workings. There are two pumps, one in the Cachoeira, the other in Bahú, each with five sets of plungers, worked by water power. The rods of the Bahú are 649 feet 2 inches from the centre of the crank nipple pin to the middle of the pin at the surface bob. A hose from the stope-bottom is filled by a "lift" or suction-pump, which feeds a cistern above; higher up the process is carried on by plunger-bolts, until the water is conveyed through the sump-shaft to the surface. This is a decided improvement upon the Brazilian "bomba" and "macácu," which perpetuates the old "hund" or "hund-slauf" of the Freyberg miners.

Presently Mrs. Gordon and my wife, habited in brown-holland trowsers, belted blouses, and miner's caps, came down delighted with the "kibble" travelling. The hands did everything to banish alarm; showed lights at the stulls; spoke and cheered as they passed, and were attentive as if in a drawing-room. They were received with friendly welcomes to the mines, and loud "vivas." We were then joined by Messrs. Gordon and Whittaker, who will suffer from what the Peruvian miners call "Macolca."* When our eyesight had become somewhat feline, we threw a general glance around. Once more the enormous timbering under the

---

* A painful soreness of the muscles, particularly in the fore part of the thigh.

bar, or to the east of the shaft, called to it everyone's attention.

The mine was utterly new to me, and most unlike the dirty labyrinths of low drifts and stifling galleries, down which I have often crawled like one of the reptilia or the quadrumana. The vertical height, 1134 feet, and the 108 feet of breadth, unparalleled in the annals of mining, suggested a cavern, a huge stone quarry, a mammoth cave raised from the horizontal to the perpendicular. Looking eastward, where the lode is sloped and bends up a trifle northwards, before us arises a black ascent, besprinkled with lights, glittering like glow-worms upon a tall embankment; some scattered over the lower levels, some fixed higher up, with their lamps of Ricinus * oil dimmed by distance. Candle-burning, the usual test, detected nothing abnormal in the atmosphere; the air was free, the ventilation was excellent, and sulphuretted hydrogen can be found only after blasting. Right pleasant to the shareholder's ear would have been the merry song of the stope-cutter and the boisterous mirth of the borer. Presently they were silenced, the Superintendent made a short speech, and proposed the visitors; this was received with loud vivas and cheers that sounded strange in the abysm, in the bowels of the earth. Of course our feet were "wiped," and physically speaking they wanted wiping. The floor was wet, the mud was slippery, and locomotion seemed like an ascent of the Pyramids, although the ground was pretty level considering.

Then turning to the west we ascended a stope or two leading from the Cachoeira to the Bahú Mine; here was a trickling streamlet which in a few days would have drowned out the old men.† The water is slightly ferruginous, perhaps from contact with the iron tools; it does not, however, much oxydise or corrode metals. Testing its temperature at various successive horizons, Mr. Gordon found the water at the bottom of the mine colder than that on the surface. He carefully rejected the elements of error arising from animal temperature, lights, fires, and the higher temperature within the sumps. Many observations have induced him to question the existence of that inexplicable and indeed inconceivable caloric formerly located by M. Cordier and others

---

* In this mine all the works under the surface are lighted with Ricinus oil.

† "Os Antigos," as they call those who preceded the grandfathers or the great-grandfathers of the present race.

at the centre of the earth.* It is always a pleasure to see the old, the highly respectable, the "time-honoured truths" of our childhood shattered and cast to the winds. It is satisfactory to learn that we do not know everything about the solar parallax ; and that we have even something to explore about the moon. It is a treat to unlearn that, despite the teachings of Artesian wells and of volcanoes, of earthquakes and of thermal springs, we are inhabiting a kind of mundane egg-shell, a solid crust, an orange skin of badly conducting matter, a bomb stuffed with impossible contents. Mr. Glaisher's adventurous balloon ascents have severely damaged Humboldt's ratio of thermal decrement in elevation. Let us hope that Mr. Gordon may unmask that pretentious caloric, lend aid to the solid rocky skeleton theory, and thus light up another dark place for the rational eye.†

As we went forwards the roof of the Cachoeira, especially about the sump and at the middle section, seemed to impend considerably, with protuberances which excited astonishment. Of late, part of the northern hanging wall has been somewhat baulk and unsound, whilst much killas has appeared in the southern side ; thus the lode has somewhat contracted and diminished. Yet the inherent strength of the roof is judged to need little artificial support, and we were shown the remnant of the bar or tongue of killas slate which separated the two great mines, and which was long left as a prop. For the future the capel and other valueless matter will be left in the "Cachoeira," thus avoiding the trouble

---

* The gradual increment of heat is supposed greatly to vary according to the nature of the rock. The difference in fact has been stated to be as much as 12 to 35 metres per 1° (Cent.). We may assume the average of 1° Fahr. = $\frac{5}{9}$ Centigrade at 70 feet—54 feet (Ansted), to 90 feet (Herschel). A mile of depth usually represents 117° (F.) = 65° C. ; at two miles water boils, at 2700 metres it becomes steam, at 3000 metres sulphur would be fused, at 6500 metres lead would be melted, at 9 miles all substances are red-hot, and at 30—40 miles all matter is in fusion or incandescence. What then can there be 300—3000 miles below the surface ?
According to Lt. Moraes (p. 42), the surface temperature of Morro Velho is 75° (F.), and at the bottom 81° (F.), and he remarks that the general opinion represents it to be very hot. He makes the mean annual temperature of Morro Velho

20°·65 (Cent.), and this gives—
Temp. 7 metres below surface. 20°·65 (C.)
  „   at bottom of mine . . 27°·22 (C.)

Difference . . . 6°·57 (C.)
The depth being then 264^m·6 (i.e., 271^m —6 or 7) gives 1° (C.) to 40^m·27 of depth.

† Mr. Gordon is, I understand, about to publish the results of his labours. Meanwhile, he kindly gave me leave to use an extract, which will be found in Appendix 1 (Section B). The figures show great irregularity both in the water and in the air. Dr. Julius Schvarcz, the Hungarian anthropologist, has also, I believe, attacked "internal heat," and has supplanted the doctrine of a central fire by an entirely new argument. (Anthrop. Review, July—October, 1867, p. 372.) The skeleton theory, with pores and cavities containing fiery fluid, is, I believe, gaining ground.

and expense of raising it, and utilizing it in parts of the excavation, where hitherto for safety much timber has been expended.

And now looking west, the huge Palace of Darkness, dim in long perspective, wears a tremendous aspect; above us there seemed to be a sky without an atmosphere. The walls were either black as the grave or reflected slender rays of light glancing from the polished watery surface, or were broken into monstrous projections, half revealing and half concealing the cavernous gloomy recesses. Despite the lamps, the night pressed upon us, as it were, with a weight, and the only measure of distance was a spark here and there, glimmering like a single star. Distinctly Dantesque was the gulf between the huge mountain sides, apparently threatening every moment to fall. Everything, even the accents of a familiar voice, seemed changed, the ear was struck by the sharp click and dull thud of the hammer upon the boring iron, and this upon the stone; each blow invariably struck so as to keep time with the wild chaunt of the borer. The other definite sounds, curiously complicated by an echo, which seemed to be within reach, were the slush of water on the subterranean path, the rattling of the gold stone thrown into the kibbles, and the crash of chain and bucket. Through this Inferno gnomes and kobolds glided about in ghostly fashion, half-naked figures muffled by the mist. Here dark bodies, gleaming with beaded heat-drops, hung by chains in what seemed frightful positions; there they swung like Leotard from place to place; there they swarmed up loose ropes like the Troglodytes; there they moved over scaffolds, which, even to look up at, would make a nervous temperament dizzy. This one view amply repaid us. It was a place—

Where thoughts were many, and where words were few:

but the effect will remain upon the mental retina as long as our brains do their duty.

At the end of two hours we left this cathedral'd cavern of thick-ribbed gold, and we were safely got like ore to grass.

CHAPTER XXVI.

THE BIRTH OF THE BABE.

. . . . . longæ
Ambages, sed summa sequar fastigia rerum.

WE have just seen the stone sent up by the kibble fillers. The whole process between the lode and the ingot will now be under the charge of the Reduction Officer, Mr. Dietsch, whose department employs some 550 hands. We will accompany that " Good Lord deliver us," and witness the birth of the babe.

The embryo is placed in the tram-waggons connecting the mines with the spalling-floors. The latter are four in number, long airy sheds, completely guarded from rain and sea. Here begins the first process of mechanical pulverization. To each floor is allotted a feitor or overseer, and under him the sledgers break the larger pieces to the size of a man's fist. The women, who are four to one man, then reduce it to the size of moderate macadam, about 1½ inch square, small enough to pass through the hoppers feeding the stamp coffers. Their hammers are long-handled, with lozenge-shaped steel heads, weighing 1½ lb., and a first-class woman breaks a ton and a-half a day. They easily learn to "pick," to separate the rich from the poor ore : the latter has no metallic lustre, no iridescence. An over-abundance of slate and quartz at times causes delay, which is employed in rest. Each spaller must fill up one or two wooden funnels, containing 16 cubic feet, and during the six days a supply for the seventh is accumulated. The men labour only whilst it is light ; the industrious can finish their tasks on Friday evening, and thus they have the Saturday for themselves. Women and fresh hands are spared, and they can usually "knock off," if they please, at 2 P.M. They suffer from the stone dust, but this could be easily remedied with fans.

At first sight 350 hands engaged in spalling seems a sad waste of power. But it is not easy to improve upon the system, which has lasted since 1767. The roads, it has been shown, are unfit to bear heavy machinery. The use of steam has been rejected, water being by no means plentiful. "Bagg's steam spalling hammer" was tried, and failed. Now the Superintendent is about to set up another labour-saving contrivance, "Blake's stone crushing machine,"* of which we saw a portion in the square, Barbacena.

For further pulverization the spalled stone must be stamped.† The amount treated at head-quarters is 200—210 tons per diem, more in the rains, less in the dry season. Half an ounce of gold per ton pays, and the present rate, nearly one ounce per ton, is highly remunerative. Also, I have said, to clear off expenses (400l.) 300 tons of stuff must every day be raised from the mine, and to give dividends, 400. This gives a fair view of the work done.

The poor ore, as we have seen, goes by a tramway to the Praia. The rich spalled stuff is thrown into a row of wooden funnels, which, opening below, discharge into tram-waggons working in a tunnel. These carts are shunted up to the Stamp Passes, and are tipped over into enclosed slides of wood, each a general reservoir, which, assisted by a central "lifter," feeds all its stamps for a day and a fraction. The Passes are regulated by hoppers, with weighted arms acting as springs. The stamps, divided into sections of three heads each, are worked by the simple old water-wheel‡ and horizontal axle, whose cogs or cams raise, 60 to 78 times per minute, upright shafts ranged in row like capstan bars, or the pestles of an African housewife. Each

---

* The Brazilians call it "Comedor," or stone-eater, on account of its moveable limb or jaw.

† The ore stamped between March and August, 1866, amounted to 29,037 tons. During the 6 preceding months, 29,542 tons. During the 6 months ending August, 1865, 30,268 tons. In June, 1867, some 6020 tons were stamped.

‡ The wheels vary from 35 to 50 feet in diameter. There are 10 at head-quarters, viz., 6 for the stamps, 1 for the tritura-tors, and 1 for amalgamation. The stamps are in batteries of 3 each, and 4 at the Praia. At head-quarters there are 6 sets (or 135 heads), named the Addison, Herring, Powles, Lyon, Cotesworth, and Susannah. At the Praia are 2 batteries (56 heads). Thus the total is 191 heads, distributed into 61 batteries.

The Praia has 2 large "pressed wheels," upon whose centre the water impinges. The larger, 32 feet in diameter, and 9 feet 1 inch wide, drives the Hocking stamps, 32 heads and 2 triturators; the smaller, 26 feet × 7 feet 8 inches, works the Illingsworth, of 24 heads and 4 arrastres. The Praia stamps are not self-feeding, manual labour does the hopper's work.

"lifter" has a "head" of country iron weighing when new five to
six arrobas; the rest of the instrument gives a total weight of
234—288 lbs., and each head costs 26$000 to 27$000. After
three months or so they become much worn, and are transferred,
like the short breeches of the elder brother, to the Cadet at the
Praia. The Superintendent has imported steel heads from
England; each one valued at 106$300, and not one lasted out
the common "chapas de ferro" of Minas iron.

The "coffer" or rectangular trough in which the stamps work
is a wooden box lined with iron to receive a blow of 380 lbs.; it
is 26 to 30 inches long by 1 foot to 18 inches wide. All are protected
fore and aft by copper grates, with 6000 to 10,000 holes to the
square inch, and raised 20 to 23 inches above the coffer, to
prevent the fine powder passing away: from a short distance you
see the grey dust and water surging up around the stamp head.
A horizontal trough drops through a hole above the grating sufficient water to keep the charge wet in each battery; once a week
the grates, which are liable to clogging, must be removed, and
the gold sand washed out. The stamp labourers are divided into
two gangs, working day and night by alternate weeks.

This system of stamping loses free gold, which, when finely
laminated, is too light to sink, and floats off with the slimes.
Mr. Thos. Treloar, whose experience at Cocaes, Gongo Soco, and
other places, entitles his opinion to respect, has declared that 7
—8 per cent. of this thin plate gold disappears. Evidently the
sole remedy is to re-treat till deposition takes place.

Now commences the concentration process. The coffer-sup-
plying trough also gives water enough to wash the stamped and
pulverized matter down the strakes. These substitutes for the
earth trenches and "canôas," are wooden planes 26 feet long,
divided by ribs into shallow compartments, 3 feet long by 14
inches wide, with an angle of inclination of 1 inch per foot. Each
compartment is floored with an oblong of partially tanned bullock's
skin, or blanket when hide fails: it takes the place of the old
Brazilian grass sod. The tannery is near to and north of the
Ribeirão Bridge.

The principle is that the heavy but invisible gold in the slaty
sand adheres to the skin, whilst the lighter earthy particles are
washed away. The hair is against the course of the water, but the
little transverse lines of wrinkle, which time and use trace upon the

surface, are of more importance. Each ton of ore passing over the skins, leaves from one-third to one-half of a cubic foot of rich sand, and each cubic foot produces on an average 2 ounces of gold.

For the most part women attend the strakes and do the light work of watching the machinery, trimming the skins, and regulating the water; if this be neglected, the sand becomes clogged, and the gold floats over. The skins are divided into three upper or head skins, two middles, and two tails. The former, being the richest, are washed every two hours in one of the seven head sand boxes, whose keys are kept by the feitors. The large chest is divided into three compartments: the hides are first washed in the two side chambers; they are then drawn through the "swim-box" or middle space; and finally they are restored to the strakes. The middle and tail skins are washed every four hours, and the latter must be re-straked * before they are rich enough to be amalgamated with the head-skins.

Thus the finer sand is ready for amalgamation. But the coarser stuff that passes over the strake-skins still contains some 30 per cent. of gold. It is carried down by the launders to an ingenious self-acting apparatus, called a separator or classificator, adopted about four years ago, and much preferred to the old "concentrating ties." It is a wooden trough 12 feet long by 2½ wide, with four funnels perforated below: in these the stuff to be washed is gradually deposited; the heaviest particles settle in the first, where there is most watershed; the lightest in the last, where there is least, and the residue of impalpable slime runs through an open trapeze-shaped trough into the common drain, the Ribeirão.

The four tunnels discharge their contents into grinding circles of wood, stone paved, and about 8 feet in diameter. These are the "arrastres" or triturators,† protected by their sheds. A water-wheel works two horizontal arms, which drag by strong

---

* They are concentrated in "tailing-boxes," large troughs filled with water; these, when the bottoms are opened, wash the sands down the hides once more. The boxes are in pairs, one being closed for washing the hides whilst the other discharges the sand.

† Drag stones, from "arrastrar," to draw. In Mexico the rude contrivance was used for amalgamation, here it serves

only to triturate. There are three sets, the Routh, which receive the washings of the Addison and Herring stamps; this is a small building to the south-west of the main spalling floor. There are also the saw-mill arrastres in a lower detached building; they re-work the sand only when not employed in plank-cutting. The third are the amalgamation arrastres, attached to the amalgamation wheel.

chains four stones, each weighing a ton : the lode-stone is preferred for this purpose, as quartz does not grind well. After a thorough trituration the sand passes over the arrastres-strakes, is collected into tailing boxes, and is then prepared for the Amalgamation House.

But even after this second process it was found necessary further to reduce the refuse containing disseminated gold : this till 1855 was thrown into the stream : in 1856 the " Praia Works " were begun, and in 1858 they were ready for use. A dam was thrown across the Ribeirão to give a fall of water. The Arrastres sand was run along the right bank in a flume 500 feet long, 1 foot wide, and 9 inches deep. It was then taken up by a leat passing through a tunnel in the hill upon which stands Mr. Smyth's bungalow, and finally it is carried by launders to the lower works. Here it falls in a series of concentrating ties that separate the coarse from the fine stuff, and from 160 to 170 cubic feet of sand-water are delivered per minute. The sand is now re-stamped with a harder substance to assist the grinding. Formerly Cascalho-gravel — which contains quartz and iron — sand and alluvial deposits from the Ribeirão, were employed. Now they use quartz and killas in pieces about 2 inches long, and they find the unpyritic quartz the best.

At the main works the rich " head sand," which we have seen partially disentangled from the stone matrix, enters upon another phase. It is carefully kept moist, and defended from the atmosphere in wash tanks under water ; thus the flouring and powdering of the mercury are prevented. It is carried down from the boxes to the Amalgamation House in wooden bowls : the carriers are usually about twenty, with a reinforcement on Mondays. This is wholesome work in the open air ; but in the further process the youngest and stoutest hands are used, as " washing" doubtless affects the health. Inclined planes for conveying the sand and other economical processes have been proposed ; the Superintendent, however, sensibly cares most to show a good balance-sheet, and has little inducement to try expensive and precarious experiments.

The head sand is first deposited for measurement in boxes, each holding 16 cubic feet. Of these there are 16, and each connects by a funnel with its Freyberg or amalgamating barrel, whose contents are the same.* The sand is watered, and a small wheel causes the barrel to revolve for half an hour at the rate of 13—14 revolutions per minute. The " Freyberg " is then opened: if the paste be too wet the mercury will not mix well with the sand; the other extreme will divide the quicksilver too finely. When the mass is of proper consistency, 50—60 lbs. of mercury† are added to each barrel, which is expected to contain 32 ounces of gold.

Formerly the barrel process was continued 48 hours before the disengaged particles of concentrated sand were brought into complete contact with the mercury. Now the average is from 24 to 26 hours: the shorter time is in the hotter weather, and the richest gold requires the most work. After 24 hours a sample from the barrel is washed in the batêa to see if any free gold remains. In Brazilian mines the first " bateada " is always given for good luck to strangers.

When amalgamated, the muddy and partially liquid mixture is discharged from the barrel into the receiving trough placed immediately below, and here it sinks, freeing itself from the water. The object is now gradually to separate the mercury and amalgam from the mineral residue, the sand and the other impurities. The mass is washed down into a " lavadero " or " saxe," a machine composed of 10 troughs, each 16 inches long and 17 deep, reciprocating and working in wheels with a to-and-fro horizontal motion. Each compartment is charged with a bed of mercury, from 340 to 460 lbs., forming a stratum about 1 inch in depth. Two or three inches above the quicksilver is a passage through which the residuary sand and water are expelled by the movement. The free mercury rises and may be drawn off for use, whilst the amalgam sinks by its greater specific weight. Each compartment will separate in 8 hours its 16 cubic feet.‡

The fourth operation is " cleaning up," or separating the gold

* Some six different modes—iron pans, dolly-tubs, &c., have been tried, but the revolving barrel has finally been preferred; the others gave inferior results, with a greater loss of mercury.

† In 1846, the monthly loss of quicksilver was 35—70 lbs. In 1866, the consumption was 1091 lbs., or 39 ozs. per cubic foot of sand amalgamated. In May, 1867, 5200 lbs. have been used in amalgam, giving a loss of 95 lbs., or 0·41 lbs. per cubic foot. The price of quicksilver at Morro Velho is only 1$500 per lb., and it is cheaper to throw away the sick stuff than to treat it with sodium.

‡ The sand washed out of the last saxe compartment runs over strakes, and here the hides arrest stray portions of amalgam and "liss;" the latter is composed of various oxides and pearlish mercury, finely divided by the sulphate of the iron peroxide and the free sulphuric acid.

from the amalgam: this is done three times each month after " divisions," longer or shorter periods of 10 to 12 days. The upper part of the saxe is removed, boiling water is poured into each compartment, and thus the metal is more easily separated. Then the surface of the amalgam is covered with a stratum of coarse sand, from $\frac{1}{4}$ to $\frac{1}{2}$ an inch thick. After the hot water has been thrown out the sand is easily skimmed off, and the quicksilver becomes clean. The amalgam is then by strong twisting filtered through canvas cones of the stoutest Russian linen like coffee strainers, with stout iron rings round the mouths: the bags are subsequently treated to recover a little gold. The liquid quicksilver is thus forced out into a vessel ready prepared: the metal is considered pure, but minute inspection shows finely diffused gold. That which remains behind is still impure with mineral sand. Portions of the paste weighing 14—15 lbs. are rubbed in Wedgewood mortars with boiling water, which softens the mercurial alloy, and with native soap, which removes the impurities. Mercury is then added, the fluid amalgam is poured from pan to pan, both being of iron heated, and the surface dross or scum thus thrown up to the surface is removed. Boiling water and soap are reapplied till impurities disappear, and the metal looks bright with a silvery lustre.

Now balls of the pasty amalgam, weighing 15 ounces to 2 lbs., are kneaded into the shape of eggs, and are squeezed, wrung, and beaten in chamois leather till no free metal appears. The residue is a solid containing 42 per cent. of argentiferous gold * and 57—58 per cent. of mercury, with some impure matter, chiefly mineral sand. After this the balls, carefully weighed, are re-torted in the usual manner; the operation is completed after six or seven hours.

But the gold is still impure with iron and arsenic, nor has it the proper shape. It calls for the fifth form of treatment—the metallurgical.

The precious ore is now melted in crucibles of refractory clay made by M. Payen of Paris. Each is charged with $12\frac{1}{2}$ lbs. of alloy, and $\frac{1}{4}$ lb. of flux, borax, and bicarbonate of soda in equal proportions. It is then placed in an air furnace † heated by

---

* A few years ago the proportion of the precious metal was only 37 to 62—63.

† In 1862 a small laboratory and an assay office were built near the Amalgamation House. They contain two wind-furnaces (furnos altos) of good solidity, lined with cast-iron plates, two cupel furnaces of masonry, one dry bath, one gold melting room, and one weighing-room, separate.

charcoal, and a chimney or stack 26 feet high secures the degrees of temperature required. Complete fusion is effected in about 45 minutes. The crucible * is taken up with tongs, and the golden fluid is poured like a bar of soap into an oblong mould of cast iron previously warmed to expel moisture, and slightly greased.

Thus the babe is born and cradled.

It is born, however, with a caul. The skin is black with the slag of the fused salts, which have dissolved the impure matter of the golden charge. This surface is knocked off with the hammer, and the bar is found to have lost, from the crucible and other causes, from 6 to 8 oitavas, or ½ per cent. of its original weight. The ingots are cast three times per month, and 14 per diem is fair work. Each weighs 1600 oitavas, and assuming this at 7s. per oitava, the value will be 560l.†

And now the birth must be sent home. After each second month the bars are taken to the Company's office, and are there weighed by the Reduction officer in the presence of the Superintendent. They are then screwed down in small solid boxes of the fine hard yellow wood "vinhatico," each case containing three bars, and sealed with the Company's seal. The small packages are stowed away in as many mail-trunks, and are committed to the "Gold Troop." This is commanded by Mr. George Morgan, Jun., an experienced traveller, for whose kindness to my wife, on her return, I am most grateful. She would not have hesitated to travel accompanied only by unarmed blacks : there are few places

---

* After 3—4 meltings the crucibles are worn out, they are then crushed, and the gold in the little cracks of the material, and the fine globules on the surface of the porous clay, are recovered.

† The dry way is used in the carefully conducted assays necessary to discover the "loss in process," and the value of the ore treated during the divisions. The first step is to "sample," a delicate and important matter, unjustifiably neglected by the unscientific Cornish miner. Three times a day, with intervals of four hours, 20 cubic inches of stuff, taken from each coffer, are placed in the barrels till the mineral particles deposit themselves. The "separations," or specimens of the different lodes, are inspected at the assay office after every division. The sample is dried in a sand-bath, and a charge of two ozs. is weighed off. It then receives the flux (fundente), 500 grs. of red oxide of lead, two ozs. bicarbonate of soda, one oz. borax, one oz. common salt, and a little charcoal powder. Fusion is effected in an earthen crucible, with a small iron rod, that causes the lead to remain ductile, and the arsenic to separate from the sulphur, and collect at the top. The operation is always checked by a second sample. When its contents have been liquified in the fusion furnace, they are poured into an iron mould, where the scoriæ of the flux and the metalloids and minerals, arsenic, sulphur, iron, aluminium, silicium, and others, separate themselves. Finally, the cupel (cadinha) and muffle are used, and the button (culote) of argentiferous gold is the sample required.

where this can be done with perfect safety, even in civilized America.

Mr. Morgan is armed, and is escorted by two Tropeiro-guards, who have permission to carry pistols; the rest are drivers, with no weapons but their knives. Nothing could be easier than to scatter the little escort; a few shots from any hill-side would throw all the mules into confusion, and much treasure might be taken without bloodshed. That no such attempt has ever been made to plunder speaks very highly of Mineiro honesty, especially in a country where the police is merely nominal. It is related that, many years ago, a highwayman was captured after a short, successful career of bandittism; he was sent to Rio de Janeiro, ostensibly for judgment, but he was accidentally shot on the road. His death produced an excellent effect; had he reached Rio he would have escaped upon the same principle that causes Big Elk or Spotted Dog, after scalping a few dozen whites, to be fêted and flunkeyed at Washington.

Thus housed, the babe embarks for England. It had better far have remained in the Brazil, where such small population is much wanted.

CHAPTER XXVII.

THE WHITE MINER AND THE BROWN MINER.

"No flourishing and prosperous community of the different races of the European family has ever existed in a lower latitude than 36°."—*Mr. Crawfurd, Trans. Ethno. Soc.*, vol. i., part 2, p. 364.

IT may be said with truth that as a field for the white man no country equals the Brazil. In colonial days the pride of the people gave away their daughters to the Portuguese paupers, *pedibus qui venerat albis*, but who could prove gentility. In later times European clerks and mechanics have intermarried as a rule with the "first families." In this most democratic of empires, in this "monarchy fenced round with democratic institutions," this "republic disguised as an empire," all white men, not all free men, are equals, socially as well as politically. All are, to use the Spanish saying, "as noble gentlemen as the king, but not so rich." The aristocracy of the skin is so strong—despite the governmental apophthegm "all men are equal"—that nothing can make up for its absence.* Every "branco" is as good as his neighbour, upon the same principle that every scion of Basque-land has an equal title to "gentlemanship." This naturally, inevitably results from the presence of an inferior race and a servile caste. And thus it comes that society knows two divisions, and two only, free man and slave, or synonymously white man † and black man. Hence here, as in the United States, we observe the unnecessary insolence with which the prolétaire from Europe delights to assert his independence. I have been addressed by a runaway English seaman whom I had never seen, simply thus, "Burtin," &c., &c.

---

* The race in the Brazil being greatly mixed, allusions to colour in general society are considered to be bad taste. Strangers, however, will soon remark that families of pure white blood are proud of it beyond measure.

† "Meu branco"—my white—is the civil address used by Indians and Africans.

In the great Atlantic cities of the Brazil, and these only are, as a rule, known to foreigners, there are sections of the labour market where competition flourishes, and where, thanks to the Liberal party, there is a great and increasing jealousy of strangers. Not so in the interior and in the small towns. Nowhere can an honest hardworking man get on so well with such a minimum of money or ability. The services of a useful hand, whatever be his specialty or trick, will be bid for at once, and at the highest possible value, and will always remain in demand; and it is simply his own fault if employment does not lead on to fortune, and to what we may call rank. Convinced of this fact, whenever I hear a foreigner complain that he has failed in the Brazil, and rail against the people and their institutions, it is proof positive to me that the country has every right to complain of him—in fact that he is a "ne'er do weel," that he drinks, or he is an idler; he is incorrigibly dishonest; or finally, to be charitable, that he is an impossible man. This is unhappily far from being the usual belief;* but my personal experience of nearly three years, during which I have studied every phase of society between the palace and the cottage, entitles me to form an independent opinion.

Morro Velho alone will supply many instances of men who came out as simple miners and mechanics, and who by industry, sobriety, and good conduct, unaided by education or talent, have risen to positions which in an older country could not be achieved in a single generation. Some have gone forth from it to become superintendents of mining companies; others are local capitalists, and there are many instances of success on a smaller scale.

At the great mine, besides the officers, there are (June, 1867) eighty-six English miners, and fifty-five workmen and mechanics; the grand total of whites, including families, is 343.† Contracts are made in England, usually for six years, renewable by consent of both contracting parties. The wages of miners and mechanics vary from £8 to £10 per month of twenty-five working days; men of superior skill command more. The outward passage,

---

* Strangers are disposed, naturally enough, to exaggerate the jealousy of the people, and to complain of a combination against them. But let the complainers try any European country, and they will find, I am convinced, more obstacles in many, in few fewer, than in the Brazil. Trades unions, and other rank growths of over-population, are of course here unknown.

† In Appendix 1, Section C., the reader will find a "General Summary of Station List" for June, 1867.

costing £28 16s., is paid by the Company. During the first three years there is an increase of wages, depending upon good conduct, of £1 per mensem. The men are encouraged to take contracts, and "no progress no pay," secures double the amount of work done on "owner's account." They easily invest their savings at ten to fourteen per cent.; they remit money without cost to Rio de Janeiro, and in the banks there are some £3800 of small economies.

Each miner is bound in a penalty of £50, which bad behaviour forfeits, and £1 is deducted monthly for the "penalty fund." Eight shillings per mensem are taken for the contingency of the return passage, which costs £25; when, however, a man falls sick before the expiration of his engagement, the Company pays for his homeward journey, and his salary ceases from the day of his leaving the mine. This should be rendered compulsory upon all English associations in the Brazil, and thus we should avoid the degradation of seeing our fellow countrymen, after being dismissed by some petty official, wandering about houseless, friendless, barefooted, and in rags. In my day we were not allowed to take home a native servant from India without depositing the value of his return passage; either some similar law should be made by our Imperial Parliament, or the distressed British landsmen should be treated as "distressed seamen."*

When miners bring out their families to Morro Velho, there is no contract for the children, whose labour thus belongs to the parents. The newly arrived get credit at the store of Messrs. Alexander and Co., and, as has been shown, house rent amounts to a few shillings a year. The hand, as a rule, preserves his English tastes, which M. Francatelli and others ignore; he disdains cheap soups, he sneers at the cabbage stalk, he affects ducks and turkeys, port and sherry. In his own language he wants the best of everything, and plenty of it;

* I should propose that even men dismissed for ill conduct should be sent home at the expense of Companies that have employed them. This would lead to more circumspection in engaging servants with good certificates. As a rule the English operative "loses his head" during his few first months in the Brazil. He has escaped all class distinctions, he finds himself looked upon as an equal, and even received by those to whom in England he would touch his hat on the road-side. Accordingly he waxes "bumptious," he "cheeks" his superior, and before he has learned the language or the way to thrive, he is turned out, not to starve—there is no starving in the Brazil—but to eat the bread of beggary, to drink, and probably to rob.

he aspires to "spend with the best," and so does his wife.
In case of transgressing orders he is for the smaller offences
mulcted, for the greater dismissed.   The amount of fines is
settled at the daily "Officers' Conference," and the paper is
posted at the bridge.   I have seen a single mulct of £3 3s.;
this is true humanity, as it may save the culprit from the loss
of an excellent "berth."

Here the English labourer can do only from two-thirds to three-
fourths of his normal task in Europe; he has little manual labour,
and the fourteen to twenty miners who are at the same time below
ground, mostly act as supervisors, and mark or measure for the
blacks.   The day is eight hours, and only every third week is
night work.

The Englishman, generally speaking, here looks well, and
tolerably healthy, without, however, showing the colour and the
flesh which he has at home.   The Brazil is by far the most
salubrious of tropical climates, as far as these are known to
me; and the many pulmonary patients who, condemned to
death by the doctor in Europe, find strength and well being,
will doubtless agree with me.   But the robust man of the
Temperates requires acclimatization, and he lacks that preponderance of the nervous temperament which will be the portion
of his children.

One would suppose that Morro Velho is a paradise for those
who have led in England the hard lives of pitmen.   But though
the labourers are mostly, I believe, satisfied, it is not in human
nature, especially in British human nature, to avoid grumbling
at the transition from "bread, barley, and boiled turnips," to
beef and poultry.   There are cases of home sickness, an English-
woman pined away and died of nostalgia during our visit to the
mine, and it was proposed to send back to her natal fens
another who seemed likely to end in the same way.   Drunkenness
is comparatively rare, brandy and gin are hardly obtainable, and
the bouquet of the fatal cachaça deters many from the danger.
Being mostly from one county, the men preserve their peculiar
accent, and not a few of their superstitions.   "Dowsing," for
instance, has crossed the Atlantic, although the hazel used in the
Cornish form of rhabdomancy does not yet grow in the Brazil.

I have nowhere in the Brazil found the Englishman so thriving
as at Morro Velho; the wretched little colonies of Germans, and

dowsing with a rod or stick
dowse — search for underground
            water

others dispersed about the Empire, should take the hint and prefer one settlement of 3000 to ten of 300 souls. The apathy that haunts the Anglo-Scandinavian in tropical climates, is here exchanged for an amount of energy inferior only to that of his normal home-condition; his dipsomania is modified, if not cured, by occupation and society, excitement and discipline; and, finally, he is as a rule tolerably contented with his exile, because he is making money, and he may reasonably talk of revisiting the old country. At any rate he knows that he *can* go home. Of course, if he be a wise man,* his home for life will be in the Brazil, and if he be a good man, he will bring out as many of his friends as he can afford to bring. The man who fails in the Brazil suggests to me the grey-headed "full private"—the fault must be with some person, and it is probably to be found in him.

And now to the Brown Miner of "frontal race."

At first the free Brazilian showed a decided indisposition to work at Morro Velho; he had never known a regular employer or regular pay, without which no labour market can exist. He disliked the work of boring, being accustomed only to desultory agriculture, if indeed he had energy or inducement to attempt even that. In 1846 the proportion of this class was 20·23; in 1852 it had risen to 112·79. It was soon found out that a week's work meant a week's wage, that the labour and the remuneration were in constant relation; then houses were built for them upon the Company's grounds, and lodging was to be had for 0 $ 500 per mensem, where a labourer here averages 1 $ 500 per diem. The class increased rapidly to a total of 786, namely, 734 men and 52 women, who receive a little less pay; a few children, despite the provincial authorities who in their blindness resisted it, are employed in light work, such as collecting the tools for resharpening. The station list for June shows a grand total of 906 souls.† They are employed in the mechanical, the reduction and other departments, and the borers are now almost exclusively free Brazilians. Like their white brethren, they may work over-

---

* Especially a wise Cornishman, who knows the depressed state of his county, where extensive emigration to more hopeful lands has caused marriage to diminish, the birth-rate to decline, and mortality to increase.

† The ratio may be judged by the following figures:—

Officers . . .		22
European labourers . .		143
Native ,, . .		906
Negro ,, . .		1450
Total . .		2521

time, the day's task being eight hours, which reminds us of the four eights, the modern modification of the Sunday fowl in the " pot-au-feu."

Eight hours' work and eight hours' play,
Eight hours' sleep and eight shillings a day.

From one-half to two-thirds of them make one or two extra days' pay in the week. The task is two holes per diem, after which they are their own masters; the average depth is four palms, but this may be modified by the captain on duty according to the nature of the rock. They work in pairs, assisted by a boy; the latter holds the "boyer" or borer, an iron varying in length from one to four feet. They use the hammer dexterously, and accidents to the hand are rare.

The free labourers work with much more energy and intelligence than the slaves. The employers' chief complaint is their irregularity; on Sundays, fête days and Saints' days, or nearly a third of the year, they do nothing but ride about the country, gamble hard, and "hunt"* women. Among this class drinking has of late years greatly increased, and for more reasons than one, marriage should be encouraged.

It is not to be expected that the desultory habits of a life and the customs inherited from generations, can be totally changed in a few years. There is ample evidence of progress in the fact that neither mines nor railways in the Brazil can complain that labour is wanting.† Moreover, a race of skilled and practised hands is growing up, and it takes " comfortably" to the work as young men in the tin districts of Cornwall. And the " extraordinary dormant mineral wealth" of the country, once exploited by its possessors, will perpetuate and increase the class. Nothing now is wanted but a civilised School of Mines.

---

* "Caçar" is the slang Brazilian term.

† I am pleased to see that my energetic friend, Mr. J. J. Aubertin, Superintendent of the São Paulo country, has, after a residence of eight years, come to exactly the same conclusion. " Now on our own railway we cannot truly say that we have ever felt the want of labour ; yet when we first began there certainly was an indisposition, generally speaking, to work. But, by and by, when one and the other found out that a week's labour really meant a week's money, and that the work was there, and the constant master there too, to pay the money for the work, then the labourer began to comprehend his real position better. One told the other how the case was, how the remuneration for his toil really glittered in his hand on pay-day, and how he really earned his bread and independence ; and very soon disinclination gave place to willingness, and all wanted to come and learn to work, and get their money as their friends were doing" (p. 5. "Eleven Days' Journey in the Province of São Paulo. London, 1866). Similarly on the Bahia and S. Francisco Railway, where at times between 1858 and 1866 from 3000 to 4000 men were employed, free labour was rendered necessary by the terms of the concession.

And here we see distinctly before us the extinction of slavery in this magnificent Empire. The imported negro, the captive, the outcast, the criminal from Africa, has greatly improved his own lot by crossing the sea. But to the higher race which admitted him he has done incalculable injury, in many ways, moral as well as physical, chiefly by prepossessing it against all labour, and mostly against the best of all labour in a young country—agriculture. Where blacks work all work becomes servile, consequently the people has no "bold peasantry, its country's pride." Thus in all lands where the moribund "institution" still lingers, there is a class known in the Southern Union as "mean whites," and in the Brazil called "Vadios," or "Cappadocios"—idlers, vagabonds. I am aware that the North American "mean white" has often been represented meaner than he is, and that the importance of his class has been for party purposes greatly exaggerated, but nothing too strong can be said against the Vadio family. It lives sometimes upon the industrious, whose humanitarian and Catholic sentiments will not drive a vagrant from the door; more frequently the professional ne'er-do-weel can unfortunately command the labour of one, two, or a few slaves, male and female. He is thus a consumer, not a producer, and whilst he increases the population he introduces into it the myriad evils of mixed blood. Some of these mulatto households disgrace humanity.*

But the day is fast approaching when the Vadio will be compelled to work like other freemen. Already in the Brazil there are important branches of material industry in which the slave is used only as a hard necessity. As specimens I may quote the mining of diamonds and gold, the navigation of the great rivers of the interior, and the cattle breeding, which every year becomes more important, especially to the European emigrant. In the present phase, I venture to state, the negro is absolutely required for agriculture only, and even then he is merely provisional till immigration from Europe shall have set in with steady and copious flood. The great proprietors, some owning 3000 and 4000 head, look with horror at any sudden and premature measure that will desolate their immense plantations

---

* Those who deem this language too severe will consult St. Hil. (III. ii. 242—4). That excellent author speaks upon the tes- timony of a high Brazilian officer, and though he wrote in 1820, the picture is still true to life.

of coffee and cane, of tobacco and cotton.   They are not reassured by the accounts which reach them from the Southern United States, and their importance secures to them the consideration of the country.   Their attitude is legitimate, but this highly intelligent class will be the first to hail the arrival of the white hand.

The employment of free labour on a large scale will do much to remedy an evil which dates in the Brazil from three centuries. The great soldier and statesman, Martim Affonso de Souza, with wonderful political prescience, issued in 1532 an order that "not even to rescue* Indians should white men penetrate into the interior, without express permission from him or from his lieutenants; and that such permission should be given with great circumspection, and only to persons of good repute." This embargo was unwisely taken off on February 11, 1544, whilst he was serving in Hindostan, by his wife Donna Anna Pimental.   The consequence was an immediate dispersion of the colonists, who scattered themselves over the country between the Atlantic and the roots of the Andes, from the Plata to the Amazons, annihilated the aborigines instead of training them to labour, and brought in so many slaves that many a house in São Paulo could number 500 to 1000 head.   The good results were wonderful additions to geography, and immense discoveries of treasure.   On the other hand, the white settlers were decentralised to an extent that semi-barbarism was the consequence, and the backwoodsman who would not hear the sound of a neighbour's gun, left the wealth of the maritime regions wholly unexploited.   Even to this day the "Serra do Mar," within sight of the ocean, is mostly covered with virgin forests; it is known to contain extensive mineral deposits, but in rare cases has any part of them been worked.   In the present state of the Empire, centralisation round commanding points, and upon great lines of communication, both of river and rail, will be a national benefit.

* Resgatar, in plain English to buy as a slave.   I have quoted from p. 70 of the "Memorias para a Historia da Capitania de S. Vicente," by the celebrated Fr. Gaspar Madre de Deos.

CHAPTER XXVIII.

THE BLACK MINER.

GENERAL REFLECTIONS BEFORE LEAVING THE MINES.

" As the Indian is killed by the approach of civilisation, which he resists in vain,
so the black man perishes by that culture to which he serves as a humble
instrument."—*Count Oscar Reichenbach.*

I WILL not delay to consider whether race or climate,[*] religion,
or state of society, or the three combined, give rise to the
exceptionally humane treatment of the slave in the Brazil: but I
can pledge myself to the fact that nowhere, even in oriental
countries, has the "bitter draught" so little of gall in it. My
experience has never shown me a case of cruelty practised upon
slaves, and I have only heard of one severe flogging. On the
other hand I know many awful consequences of over-lenity. But
lately, at Aráraquára, in the Province of São Paulo, Benedicto, a
negro, was to be hanged for the barbarous murder of his master;
the hangman refused to act, and the criminal has been simply
shifted from the gallows and consigned to the galleys. I often
meet in the chain-gang, literally no penalty, a neighbour's slave,
who, working himself into a passion, causelessly stabbed to death
a black, to him unknown, and in presence of many witnesses,
drank, vampire like, his victim's blood: he is accompanied by a
brother assassin, who by way of freak killed the helpless old
Prior of the Carmo. It is therefore with some regret and much
astonishment that I read these lines, traced by so well informed

---

[*] One of Humboldt's good generalizations,
amongst many bad, is that "the facility of
being acclimated seems to be in the inverse
ratio of the difference that exists between
the mean temperature of the torrid zone,
and that of the native country of the traveller or colonist who changes his climate."
(Travels, i. chap. 3.) The distance may
be extended in a moral sense to races :

those who inhabit neighbouring latitudes
mix as a rule more intimately, and when
abroad are more' at home than peoples
whose foci are further removed. The English slaveholder mostly held himself aloof
from the African : the Brazilian, like his
forefather the Portuguese, admitted him
to far greater familiarity, and the result
was deplorable.

a pen: * "Virginia was a paradise compared with Cuba and Brazil. Some touch of softness in the lord, some gleam of pity in the mistress, had sufficed to keep the very worst planters of English blood free from the brutalities which were daily practised in the Spanish and Portuguese cities farther south." From obsolete consular reports, from the pages of old travellers, and from the writings of men who ran through the country, believed everything they heard, and, like M. Jacquemont, described "après une relâche de douze jours," in a region eight times larger than France, its capital, its navy, its coasting trade, its commerce, its finances, its government, its society, its servile condition, many cases might doubtless be collected.† But the relations between master and slave are modified by public opinion, and essentially by the progress of civilization. In the present day the Brazilian negro need not envy the starving liberty of the poor in most parts of the civilized world.

The slave in the Brazil has, by the unwritten law, many of the rights of a freeman. He may educate himself, and he is urged to do so. He is regularly catechized, and in all large plantations there is a daily religious service. If assailed in life or limb he may defend himself against his master, or any white man, and an over-harsh proprietor or overseer always runs considerable risk of not dying in bed. He is legally married, and the chastity of his wife is defended against his owner. He has little fear of being separated from his family : the humane instincts and the religious tenets of the people are strongly opposed to this act of barbarity. He has every chance of becoming a free man : manumission is held to be a Catholic duty, priestly communities are ashamed of holding slaves, and whenever there is a war the African is bought and sent to fight by the side of white recruits. Old usage allows

---

* "New America," vol. ii. chap. 31. Has the learned author studied the Black Code or the Provincial Laws of the English slave islands ? Even in 1815 Prince Max could say of the slaves in the Brazil, "on les traite généralement assez doucement."

† In this way one of the greatest offenders was the late Mr. Charles B. Mansfield ("esquire and M.A. of Clare Hall, Cambridge"); his liveliness, his trenchant style, his John Bullism, and the ample evidence of good intention in all the harm he did, caused the "noble worker," as his

editor called him, to be extensively read, believed, trusted ; and this increases the measure of his offence. The crudities and absurdities of an untravelled man, who, after a sedentary life, and a month in the New World, had the audacity to write a chapter (No. 4) headed "Brazil: Crime— Political Economy — Colonization — Slavery—Commerce," have been ably answered in an Ensaio Critico by Sr. A. D. de Pascual, Rio de Janeiro, Laemmert, 1861. But of the thousands who imbibe the poison how few will even see or hear of the antidote ?

him to purchase his liberty by his labour, and to invest his property in manumitting his wife and children.

I have scanty space for so important and far leading a subject as slavery in the Brazil.* But it may be briefly remarked that there is hardly an educated man in the country who would not right willingly see it abolished if he could find for it a substitute. All look forward to the great day of immigration and free labour. All, too, are aware of the fact that immigration and slavery can hardly co-exist. It is the same with Englishmen who, throughout the Empire, except in the great cities where they can hire servants, buy, and hold, and let, and hire slaves, despite the late venerable Lord Brougham's absurd Act of 1843.† And for the benefit of the wretches with oxidised skins, doomed by philanthropy to die in thousands at Ashanti, Dahome and Benin, not to mention a hundred other African Aceldamas and Golgothas, I venture to hope that the black continent may also be admitted to the boon of immigration. Under all circumstances the negro "coolie" temporarily engaged in the Brazil will benefit himself: confined to field work, not admitted to the house, and looked upon as a stranger in the land, he will benefit others.

Some years ago, when the "Negro's Complaint" still haunted

* The curious reader will find an excellent paper on "the Extinction of Slavery in Brazil," from a practical point of view, written by Sr. A. M. Perdigão Malheiro, translated by my friend Mr. Richard Austin, F.A.S.L., and published in the Anthropological Review, No. 20, Jan. 1868. The author, whose studies entitle his views to the greatest respect, estimates the slaves to number between the extremes 1,400,000 and 2,500,000, in 1864. In 1850 the number was 4,000,000. These figures ought effectually to lay the angry spirit of emancipation. If, however, the negroes must be killed off, why, then set them at once free. The measures at present to be adopted are to liberate all the slaves belonging to ecclesiastics, to tax heavily all city slaves and vagrants, to prevent large slaveholders being employed in high positions under government, and to satisfy Europe by fixing a definite time for the final solution of the problem. Lastly, we may observe that Messrs. Kidder and Fletcher calculate an emancipation of one million of slaves in the fifteen years between 1850 and 1866, whilst the productions of the country have increased at the rate of 30 per cent.

† It surprises me to read in Prince Max (i. 220) the cool way in which he recounts how M. Freyress buys and carries off an Indian boy. This was really a vile act to enslave one born free. "It is a startling and deplorable fact, and one that is calculated to lower our opinion of human nature, to witness the rapid adoption by those Europeans who leave their own country animated with the best and most generous principles respecting their fellow creatures, of the maxims and practices of hardened slaveholders." (Notes on the Slave Trade, by W. G. Ouseley, London, 1850.) It is more philosophical to seek and explain the cause than to be startled at or to deplore facts—simply signs that we do not read them aright. For my part, whenever I see a man leave England for the first time filled with the normal superlative and transcendental principles about holding persons to service, I expect a reaction to set in, and that his negroes will soon complain of his remarkable and unreasonable cruelty. For this cause, partly, the slaveholder in South Carolina did not like the "Yankee" overseer.

the public ear, when " black brother " was a mere catch-word and catch-pence in England, when the negro of sentiment and theory had worsted and ousted the negro of reason and practice, and when on this point, and perhaps on this point only, blatant Ignorance would not allow Knowledge to open her lips, sundry grossly impudent and infamous fabrications were circulated about all the English mining establishments in the Brazil.* The benevolent slanderer who wished to puff his own name, and the dismissed employé who would gratify his revenge, pandered to the popular prejudice, and dwelt unctuously upon the " adynamic condition " of the negro labourer, and his " cruel and murderous treatment " by the white. This was carried to such an extent that the Directors of the Great Mine were obliged to send out Dr. Walker, whose able report set the question at rest. But even to the present day, whenever an officer is "sacked" for insubordinacy or incapacity, the first threat he utters is something about " slaveholders."

I proceed now to give my account of the black miner as I found him at Morro Velho.

Without including 130 children of hired blacks, and who are not under contract, the establishment consists of 1450 head, thus distributed:

Company's blacks, 254 (109 men, 93 women, and 52 children); Cata Branca blacks, 245 (96 men, 87 women and 62 children); blacks hired under contract, 951.

In these numbers we may see a modification of Saint Hilaire's statement, " le service des mines ne convient pas aux femmes ; " † this might have been true under the old system, it is not so now. Generally in the Brazil men are preferred upon the sugar plantations, women on those that grow coffee, and as they are wanted for domestic purposes it is not so easy to hire them.

The " Company's Blacks " consider themselves the aristocracy, and look down upon all their brethren. Both they and the Cata Brancas are known by the numbers on their clothing; the hired

---

* See an "Introductory Letter to Sir Thomas Fowell Buxton, Bart., on the Frightful Horrors of Modern Slavery as practised by the Imperial Brazilian Association in their Mines at Gongo Soco." "I have sometimes thought," says Mr. Trollope, with great truth, "that there is no being so venomous, so bloodthirsty, as a professed philanthropist, and that when the philanthropist's ardour lies negro-wards, it then assumes the deepest dye of venom and bloodthirstiness." Witness the doubtless well-intentioned crowd which collected to call for the blood of Governor Eyre.

† Travels, III. i. 329. He has overdrawn the case. In hiring blacks the Superintendent warns owners that women must be accompanied by a greater number of men, and so we find that of the 951 hired, 602 are male and 349 are female.

negroes wear also M. V. marked on their shirts. The establishment expends per mens. £1400 upon contracts: I need hardly remark what a benefit this must be to the large proprietors of the neighbourhood. Thus the Commendador Francisco de Paula Santos lets under contract a total of 269 (including 173 children), his son-in-law Sr. Dumont 145 (97 adults and 48 children), and the Cocaes or National Brazilian Mining Association contributes 142 negroes and 13 children.

The figures given below will show the average of hire:* clothing, food, and medical treatment are at the Company's expense. Usually the agreement is for three to five years, during which period the slave cannot be manumitted. As a rule the Superintendent employs only robust men who have passed a medical examination, but he will take in doubtful lives under annual contract. The slave is insured by a deduction of 10$000 to 20$000 per annum for a fixed period; and if he die before the lease has expired the owner still receives his money—there are actually eighty-nine cases of this kind. Pay ceases only if the negro runs away: it is issued every third or sixth month, and the contractors can obtain one year's advance, at a discount of ten per cent.

As regards labour, all are classified according to their strength into first, second, and third-rate blacks. In 1847 permission to work overtime, that is to say, beyond nine hours forty-five minutes, was given to the first-rates. There is another division into surface and underground blacks. The former are smiths and mechanics, especially carpenters and masons, who work between 6 A.M. and 5 P.M., with one hour forty-five minutes of intermission for meals. The oldest and least robust are turned into gardeners, wood-fetchers, and grass-cutters. The regular working day at Morro Velho is as follows—

5 A.M. Reveillé sounded by the gong, and half an hour afterwards the Review.

6 A.M. Work.

8.15 A.M. Breakfast.

9 A.M. Work.

12.30 P.M. Dinner.

---

* Annual hire of first-class slaves	.	.	men	220 $ 000	women	100 $ 000
Not paying in case of death or flight	.	.	,,	230 $ 000	,,	110 $ 000
Annual hire of second-class slaves	.	.	,,	150 $ 000	,,	75 $ 000
Not paying in case of death or flight	.	.	,,	160 $ 000	,,	75 $ 000

1.15 P.M. Work.

2 P.M. Change guard. Blasting in the mine.

5.30 P.M. Mechanics' work ended.

8.30 P.M. Return to quarters. The slaves cook their own meals and eat supper at home. Saturday is a half-holiday: they leave off work at 2.30 P.M., and retire at 9 P.M.

The underground labourers are borers, stope cleaners, trammers who push the waggons, kibble-fillers, and timber-men: they are divided into three corps, who enter the mine at 6 A.M., 2 P.M., and 10 P.M. On Sunday the gangs shift places, so that only one week in three is night work. A rough estimate makes the number of the gang in the mine at the same time 620, including all hands. When work is over they proceed to the changing-house, and find a tepid bath at all hours. They put on their surface-clothes, and leave the mine suits either to be dried in the open air, or by flues during the rains. The precaution is absolutely necessary, though very difficult and troublesome to be enforced: the English miners shirk it, and the free Brazilians are the most restive, though they are well aware how fatal are wet garments.

The blacks lodge in the two villages situated half-way between the bottom of the river valley and the Morro Velho hill. Thus, while they escape malaria they are saved fatigue when going to, or coming from, work. They begin the day with coffee or Congonhas tea. Their weekly allowance, besides salt and vegetables, comprises 9 lb. of maize meal, 4½—5 lb. of beans, 13½ oz. of lard, and 2lb. of fresh beef. Meat of the best quality here averages 3 $ 000 per arroba, or twopence a pound, and the labourers purchase, at cost prices, the heads and hoofs, the livers and internals of the bullocks killed for the use of the establishment. The industrious have their gardens and clearings: they keep poultry and pigs, fattened with bran, which they receive gratis. Part they eat, the rest they sell to procure finery and small luxuries. " Carne Seca " and farinha are issued when the doctor orders. Nursing women have something added to the six-tenths of a plate of meal, one quarter of beans, and two ounces of lard, and children when weaned claim half rations. All the articles are of good quality, and if not a report is made to the Manager of Blacks.

Drink is not issued every day, nor may it be brought into the establishment. A well-conducted negro can obtain a dram once per diem with permission of the chief feitor or overseer. Each head of a department has a supply of "restilio," which he can distribute at discretion, and the mine captain can give a "tot" to any negro coming wet from duty. It is, however, difficult to correct the African's extreme fondness for distilled liquors, which in this light and exciting air readily affect his head, and soon prove fatal to him. He delights also in "Pángo," here called Ariri, the well-known Bhang (Cannabis sativa) of India, and of the east and west coast of Africa. He will readily pay as much as 1 $ 000 for a handful of this poison.

I never saw negroes so well dressed. The men have two suits per annum—shirt, and overalls of cotton for the hot, and of woollen for the cold season; the "undergrounds" receive, besides these, a stout woollen shirt, and a strong hat to protect the head. Each has a cotton blanket, renewed yearly, and if his dress be worn or torn, the manager supplies another. The women work in shifts of thin woollen stuff, and petticoats of stronger material; they usually wear kerchiefs round their neck, thus covering the bosom, and one shoulder, after the fashion of African "Minas," * is left bare. In winter capes of red broad-cloth are added to the Review costume.

The slave labourer is rewarded with gifts of money; he is allowed leave out of bounds, even to Sabará; he is promoted to offices of trust and of increased pay; he is made an overseer or a captain over his own people; at the Review he wears stripes and badges of distinction, and he looks forward to liberty.†

---

* I have explained this in Chap. 7.

† I was allowed to inspect the official list of black candidates for manumission (according to the Regulations issued by the Directors, January, 1845), and from it the following figures are borrowed :—

Mr. Keogh placed on the Manumission List—

In 1848 negroes and negresses			·	·	4	
,, 1849	,,	,,	·	· ·	4	
,, 1851	,,	,,	·	· ·	2	A total of 16.
,, 1852	,,	,,	·	· ·	2	
,, 1853	,,	,,	·	· ·	2	
,, 1854	,,	,,	·	· ·	2	

Dr. Walker.

In 1855 negroes and negresses			·	·	2	
,, 1856	,,	,,	·	· ·	2	Total 10.
,, 1857	,,	,,	·	· ·	2	
,, 1858	,,	,,	·	· ·	4	

The chief punishments are fines, which negroes, like Hindus, especially hate; the penalties, which now amount to 400$000, have been transferred to charitable purposes, and swell a small reserved trust-fund, intended to support the old and infirm. Other pains are, not being allowed to sell pigs, poultry, and vegetables; arrest within the establishment or confinement in a dry cell, with boards like a soldier's guard-room; fugitives are put in irons. Formerly the manager and the head captain, who required implicit obedience from the 500 hands of the underground department, could order a flogging. This was abolished, not, I believe, with good effect. Every head of a department can still prescribe the "Palmatorio," * but he must note and report the punishment to the Superintendent. Only the latter can administer a flogging with the Brazilian cat of split hide; and this is reserved for confirmed drunkenness, disobedience of orders, mutiny, or robbing fellow-workmen. The punishment list is sent in every fortnight, and as a rule is small. I especially noticed the civil and respectful demeanour of the Morro Velho blacks, who invariably touch their hats to a white stranger, and extend their hands for a blessing. They are neither impudent, nor cringing, nor surly, and, in my opinion, there is no better proof that they are well and humanely treated. I would here formally retract an opinion which I once thoughtlessly adopted upon the worst of grounds, "general acceptation." The negro cannot live in the presence of the civilized man: the Brazil proves that unless recruited from home the black population is not more viable than the "Red Indian." His rule and "manifest destiny" are those of all savages.†

Mr. Gordon.

In 1859 negroes and negresses	.	. 10		
,, 1860 ,,	,,	. . 16		
,, 1862 ,,	,,	. . 5		
,, 1863 ,,	,,	. . 5	Total 92.
,, 1864 ,,	,,	. . 2		
,, 1865 ,,	,,	. . 41		
,, 1866 ,,	,,	. 18		

Of these 6 lost the boon by intoxication, 2 were killed in the mine, and 14 died.

* The first "palmatorio" seen by me in the Brazil was at the house of an Englishman. It is a "paddle" of hard black wood, somewhat like that used at "knurr and spell," with a handle almost a foot long, and a flat circle about the size of a large oyster at the useful end, which is drilled with holes. Upon the gorilla-like hand of the negro it can hardly take the effect of that rattan which my old tutor, Mr. Gilchrist, was so fond of applying to his pupils' pink and white palms.

† By the excess of deaths over births, the negro population in the whole of the English Antilles undergoes every year a diminution of 4 in 1000 : in Tobago the annual decrease is 16 to 1000. Colonel Tulloch remarks, "Before a century the

Briefly to sum up the statistics of Morro Velho, in these its greatest golden days. The Company has outlived the thirty-seventh year, and during the last six it has paid upwards of £10,000 income-tax to the British Exchequer. The present outlay of the establishment is, in round numbers, £146,000 per annum, and the income £230,000. As a mine it has no parallel in the Brazil; the excavation has descended to zones unreached by other works, and, as has been seen, its breadth is without a parallel. It directly employs 2521 souls; indirectly double that number.

Besides the 343 English at Morro Velho there are at least 500 of our own countrymen scattered about the Province of Minas. All are destitute of protection; their marriages are to be contested in civil courts,* the nearest consulate for registration is that of Rio de Janeiro, and the cost of a journey to the coast and back would not be less than £50. There is the same difficulty touching wills and inheritances, especially in the case of the Company's officers, and the English medical men who live in the remoter parts of the Province. The French, Spanish, and Portuguese Governments have vice-consuls or consular agents at Barbacena and Ouro Preto, although none save the latter have many constituents. We shall probably see fit to follow their example.

And now adieu to Morro Velho, a place where I found, wonderful to relate, work carried on by night and by day in the heat of the Tropics, and in the heart of the Brazil.

---

negro race will be nearly extinct in the English colonies of the West Indies." (Anthropological Review, August, 1864, p. 169).

* A bill entitled "An Act to legalise certain marriages solemnized at Morro Velho in Brazil," and "to be cited for all purposes as 'the Morro Velho Marriage Act, 1867,'" remedies part of the inconvenience, but some kind of representation would remedy all.

CHAPTER XXIX.

TO "ROSSA GRANDE."*

Paiz de gentes e de prodigios cheio
Da America feliz porção mais rica.
Caramurú, 6, 49.

Mr. Gordon had obligingly offered to show me a seam of combustible matter of disputed substance. He organised everything for the trip: the animals were ten, allowing to each of us a change; our "Camarada," † or head man, was one Joaquim Borges; and "Miguel," now an old acquaintance, was assisted by a sturdy and very black black, João Paraopéba, named like Lord Clyde from the nearest river. The Superintendent was followed

---

* The following is an approximative itinerary from Morro Velho to Ouro Preto :—

Morro Velho to Raposos	.	. 1 hr.	45 min.	=	5 miles	14 miles.	Total 1st day's
,, Morro Vermelho	2	,,	40	,,	= 9 ,,		march 28 miles
,, Gongo Soco	. 3	,,	20	,,	= 10 ,,	14 miles.	in 8 h. 45 m.
,, Fabbrica	. 1	,,	0	,,	= 4 ,,		
Fabbrica to S. João do Morro	. 1	,,	0	,,	= 4 ,,	Total 2nd day, 17 miles in	
,, Brumado	. . 1	,,	0	,,	= 4 ,,	5 hours.	
,, Catas Altas	. 3	,,	0	,,	= 9 ,,		
Catas Altas to Agua Quente	. 0	,,	45	,,	= 2 ,,	Total 3rd day, 26 miles in	
,, Fonseca	. . 3	,,	0	,,	= 12 ,,	6 hours 45 minutes.	
,, Inficionado	: 3	,,	0	,,	= 12 ,,		
Inficionado to Bento Rodriguez	. 1	,,	0	,,	= 4 ,,		
,, Camargos	. 2	,,	0	,,	= 6 ,,	Total 4th day, 20 miles in	
,, Morro de Santa Anna	2	,,	15	,,	= 8 ,,	5 hours 45 minutes.	
,, Marianna	. . 0	,,	30	,,	= 2 ,,		
Marianna to Passagem	. 0	,,	30	,,	= 2 ,,	5th day.	
Passagem to Ouro Preto	. . 1	,,	0	,,	= 4 ,,	6th day.	
Ouro Preto to Casa Branca	. 3	,,	20	,,	= 12 ,,	Total 7th day, 23 miles in	
Casa Branca to Rio das Pedras	. 4	,,	0	,,	= 11 ,,	7 hours 20 minutes.	
Rio das Pedras to Sto. Antonio	. 3	,,	15	,,	= 9 ,,	Total 8th day, 13 miles in	
Sto. Antonio to Morro Velho	. 1	,,	30	,,	= 4 ,,	4 hours 45 minutes.	

Total . . 41 hr. 50 m.   133 miles.

† Properly a Camarado or Companion. In Portugal it is mostly given to an orderly (soldier) servant. In parts of the Brazil it is a familiar address to a friend, "my good fellow;" generally the name is assumed by every free man who condescends to "help," as New England says, not to serve you. Thus, if employed in lighting the town lamps, he will style himself "Camarada da luz"—help of the light. The Camarada, whose name reminds us of the "comradeship," or brotherhood of the old buccaneers, is a very important, and an exceedingly troublesome personage in Brazilian travel.

by his servant Antonio, gorgeous in the usual lively Minas livery, tall glazed hat and top-boots, turned up with gamboge-yellow; a large silver goblet, venerable article of luxury and ostentation, hung by a chain over his shoulder. Mr. L'pool accompanied us, and the journey was to last eleven days.

On July 10, 1867, we set out at 9 A.M., which may be called family-travelling hour at this season—and striking eastward passed the quarter known as the Praia de Bom Será. It consists of six lines of huts, with stays sunk in the ground, supporting a tiled roof upon a timber framework: thus the top is often finished, and the doors and window-frames are put up, before the side walls appear. The next process is to make the latter with wattle, and the clay is puddled in. This curious form of building is called "páo a pique," or parede de mão, "hand wall," from the dabbing required. Where the adobe or the pisé is known it takes the place of sticks and clay. Here live the free Brazilian borers, who, like a certain mining population further east, get screwed at times, and though they do not heave half a brickbat at, they wildly hoot with blue-red lips the passing stranger.

We then crossed by an unimportant bridge the Ribeirão, whose bed here widens, and everywhere shows signs of working: a peculiar white efflorescence, said to appear phosphorescent at night, frosts the dark refuse heaps. This was examined by Dr. Walker, who "found it to be nothing but sulphate of iron, which becomes white when deprived of its water of crystallization." Dr. Birt also reported that it was an "impure sulphuret of iron, or the white copperas of commerce, as gallic acid fully shows by converting it, when mixed, into ink." But Mr. Reay extracted a large proportion of arsenical pyrites from the ore generally, and especially from the Bahú. The "white stuff" is in fact a sublimate of arsenic, and, as will be seen, the boatmen pretend to trace it all along the Rio das Velhas. Further down the Praia are the works belonging to the Messrs. Vaz of Sabará: formerly they had many head of stamps, now reduced to a dozen, and a few Arrastres. They retreat the waste sand from the Great Mine, and the "Cascalho" hereabouts is said to be auriferous. Beyond them again are other Brazilian works, called "California."

We then ascended a steep rough hill, where there is a charming view of the settlement: the yellow soil is very mean, except in bottoms, and these are "cold" and flooded. On the left is the "Herring ride," which embalms the name of the first Superintendent; it is a pleasant wavy line circling round the hills, and coming out above the level of "Timbuctoo." Wheeling to the right we descended a stiff slope, rough and stony, sighting below us the basin of the Rio das Velhas; the stream was invisible, and the hollow looked like a vast cauldron whose seething lacked motion. The Rego dos Raposos * or Fox's Leap was then crossed, and near it lie the gold-crushing mill and the dwelling-house of the Capitão José Gomes de Araujo—a family which may be called the old lairds of Raposos. The formation is of pyritic matter, and partially decomposed quartz; there are veins and lodes, both auriferous, but none have yet been found to pay.

The slope ended in the usual abominable old Calçada; here, as in São Paulo, you know the approach to city, town, or village, by the extra vileness of the road. The reason is evident—the ways are more trodden and are not more mended. Over the heights around us were scattered a little coffee and two patches of leek-green sugar-cane. On the left bank of the Old Women's River we passed a decayed private chapel, an old gold-stamping mill, and a huge desolate manor-house belonging to the Araujos. More fortunate than Dr. Gardner, who had to make a long detour, we found a good timber bridge over the swift and swirling stream; it is 400 palms long, 14 broad, and 20 high—the last date of repair is 1864. The bulk of Raposos, or to give its title in full, "Nª Sª da Conceição de Raposos de Sabará," occupies a small bulge or basin in the riverine valley. It consists mostly of a villainous pavement and an Igreja Matriz. This church boasts the honour of being the first built in the Province of Minas; it was once very rich in silver plate, of which something still remains, and it owns its preservation to the care of its Vicar, "José de Araujo da Cunha Alvarenga," whose memory blossoms in the dust. It has two filial chapels, Santa Anna and Santo Antonio,

---

* The word is indifferently written Raposos or Rapozos. As a rule, in writing the same words, the Portuguese prefers the "s," and the Spaniard the "z." Thus the former would write "casa," the latter "caza." But the orthography in this as in many other points is by no means settled.

The Raposo fox is often confounded with the Cachorro do Mato, a yellowish-grey canine spread over the Southern American continent. Prince Max. (iii. 149) believes it to be the Agourachay of Azara, the grey fox of Surinam, and probably a climatal variety of the renard tricolor (Canis griseo-argenteus) of Pennsylvania.

near Sabará. The temple is built of the common hard clay slate, stuck together, not with lime but mud, which melts admirably during the rains: the two little towers are of red taipa or pisé, they are tiled like the church, but they are not white-washed—a symptom of exceeding penury in the Brazil. The parish was created in 1724, and contained two thousand souls whilst the gold-washing lasted; the number is now reduced to one-third.

We rode along the river-ledge into a wooded lane, and up an ugly hill, rough with loose blocks and round stones, and rich with dust of clay slate: barely passable now, what must it be in wet weather? Reaching the "Chapada," or plateau, we spurred fast over the one good league which we shall find to-day. We passed through a ruined farm with bare and broken walls. It was last inhabited by D. Reta, widow of one José Joaquim dos Frechos Lobo, and now it is church property, belonging to the "Irmandade do Santissimo" of Raposos. Beyond it is a rounded eminence, which caresses the eye of an old surveyor. To the north-west rises the massive, cross-crowned brow of Curral d'El-Rei; further west is the green-clad mount known as Morro do Pires: * to the south-south-west lies our acquaintance the Pico de Itabira, or the "Stone Girl," whilst fronting us, or southwards, runs the Serra de ¦ S. Bartholomeu, the eastern wall of the upper Rio das Velhas Valley. It here conceals the quaint top-knot of Itacolumi, and its regular ridge showed a sky-line blurred with thin rain, which now fell upon us for the first time in Minas Geraes. Perhaps these are the "showers of S. João," somewhat deferred, and interfering with the rights of St. Swithin. The vesicles of cloud were peculiarly well defined that day.

The tall hills and the quorn-shaped mountains are all bluff and running high to the west, which is also the strike of the stone out-crop. The cones and heights where the rain washes are streaked, jagged, and gullied, like those near S. João and S. José, with projecting stripes of laminated talcose-slate, dull, grey, hard, and rugged. This appears to be the skeleton of earth, and in places the formation is quaquaversal. On the summit I observed a trace of copper, which suggests that we

---

* Mr. Gordon found from the highest point of Morro do Pires that the Itacolumi bears exactly south-east.

are now upon the great field described by Dr. Couto.* The
more level places made my wife declare that she was once more
crossing the Wiltshire Downs. Gentle swells heave up the
surface, backed by bolder elevations, confused and billowy
ridges forming an irregular crescent on each side. They descend
steep to the little drains separating the mounds; and here we
look in vain for level water-meadows.

The vegetation of the broken Campo was the usual Cerrado,
dun and stunted, burnt and wind-wrung. Every hollow had
its dense coppice hanging from the sides, and forming thick
and thicketty jungle along the bottom. The stranger must not
attempt to penetrate these Capões. The mauve and yellow
bloom of the flowery forest was set off by the silver-lined
peltated leaves of the tall " Sloth-tree," one of the most
noticeable forms in the woodlands of the Brazil. I believe
that this " Cecropia" or Candelabra-tree belongs to the
second growth, but Dr. Gunning, whose experience is long
and respectable, declares that he has seen it in the " Mata
Virgem." Hereabouts the old woods have gone to make fuel
for Morro Velho. Yet the continual alternation of brake and
fell, of grass-land and shrubbery; the contrast of plateau and
dwarf plain with tall peak and bluff mountain, the diversity
of colour and the sunshine smiling through the tears of S.
João—here the people say the fox is being married—in England
the Devil is beating his wife—formed an effect the reverse of
monotonous.

The Sloth-tree (Arvore da Preguiça or Ayg) is so called because
that animal ascends it, especially by night, to eat the young
shoots and leaves till it looks like a skeleton. This Urticacea
is called by the Tupys Umbaúba or Umbahuba, also written
Anbaba, Ambauba, Imbaiba, and many other ways, but not
" Embeaporba," as Mr. Walsh does. Mr. Hinchcliff (" South
American Sketches" chap. xiii.) calls it Sumambaia, which means
a filix. The wild people make a difference between the Cecropia
palmata and the C. peltata (L.), specifying the latter as Ambai-

---

* He entered it about "Córregos," sixty
miles to the north, and found it consist of
ash-coloured rhomboids; paving the ground
over which his horse passed, without mixture of earthy matter, not in veins, but in
heaps, in rocks, in whole mountains, in entire
ranges. It is to Minas, he declares, what
silver is to Peru, and far more abundant
than iron, though in other parts of the
world bearing the proportion of one-tenth
to the ferruginous deposits.

tinga, or the "White," because the older leaves are lined with a
hoary down, are frequently upturned as if they were withered,
and patch the garment of the tree with white. The young foliage
is known by its burnished red tinge, which adds not a little to its
beauty.   The Brazilians also recognise two kinds, Roxa and
Branca.   The Cecropia is well known in Guiana and the Antilles,
where the people call it Coulequin and "bois de trompette." The
"Indians" employed this wood and the Gameleira for lighting
their fires with friction. The negroes easily remove the inner pith,
and use it not only for trumpets, but for tubes, spouts, and water-
pipes. The tree grows fast; in four months it is as thick as a man's
arm; it breaks easily, but it is a true wood, not a mere juicy stem;
and it is said to make good charcoal for gunpowder. The juice of
the buds is used as a refrigerant against diarrhœa, dysury, and
similar complaints; but I have never heard that " the flower is
highly prized as a remedy against snake-bites."

The C. palmata has a light grey, smooth, bare stem,
grass-green when very young, rarely perfectly straight and
tapering, generally somewhat bent, and often thirty feet high.
About the summit spring, at a right angle and slightly curving
upwards like the arms of a candelabrum, naked branches with
their large palmated leaves on long supports at the extremities,
like gigantic chesnut-leaves joined at the stalks.   The soil makes
a great difference in the shape of the tree: in certain rich lands
the bole appears shorter because the offsets commence sooner,
and in this case the primary boughs have a much greater number
of secondary branches. Great variety of appearance is given by
the bean-like bunches which hang to the stem of the white-lined
young leaves, and by the old foliage, which in decay waxes red
and finally black.   The C. peltata, which the people call red, has
more the appearance of a tree and less of a shrub : its stiff and
somewhat ungainly boughs spread more widely.   I have always
held the Cecropia to be the characteristic growth of the Capoeira :
it certainly is the king of the "bush."

The good league ended at a gateway, which leads from and to
nothing but a vile mile of broken dusty path.   It winds
unpleasantly close to deep gaps, shafts, and holes, which show
how much the country has been turned up, and which makes
you calculate the possibility of involuntary sepulture.   The
surface of the ground was clad with wild grass (Capim do

Campo), and bright with the pretty white flower of the Break-pot (Quebra panella), so called because it easily flares up and cracks the clay. A turn to the east showed us Morro Vermelho in the normal basin. The sphinx-shaped Red Mount, which gave the name, rises to the south-east of the Settlement : the lightning had lately destroyed its capping cross. The double-steepled church, with three black windows and abundant white-wash, spoke of prosperity; and as we wound downwards, up came the sound of the village bells, informing us that the energetic shepherd was calling his flock to spiritual pasture. The houses were scattered amongst masses of bananas tufted with palms. We came upon the Calçada —une fois sur la chaussée et le voyage est fini" may be said here as in Russia—and about noon we entered the Settlement.

Sr. Francisco Vieira Porto—popularly " Chico Vieira "—gave us breakfast and notices touching Morro Vermelho. The precise date of its foundation is unknown : it can hardly be older than the beginning of the eighteenth century. Gold was found there naturally alloyed with copper and iron : it was worked in about a score of places ;* and of these eight still do a little business. Industry gave it importance, and in all troubles and disorders the turbulent Mineiros took part with Caethé and Raposos against the Portuguese authorities, and the powers that were from home. The vivacity, compared with the size of these places, was sur-prising ; but in those days landed proprietors and mine-owners had not only negroes but multitudes of Red-skin slaves who liked nothing better than a row. In 1715 it armed itself and joined in open revolt the Villa Nova da Rainha (now Caethé) and Villa Real (Sabará). The mutineers refused to pay the quint of gold de-manded upon each pan, and required the remission of their usual tribute, which was only 960 lbs. of the precious metal. They had actually the insolence to appear before the Governor, the " Most Illustrious and Most Excellent Dom Boaz Balthasar da Silveira," and with abundant "barbaridade"—to use his own phrase—they shouted in his noble ear—" Viva O Povo !"—Long live the people.†

Morro Vermelho is now a mere Arraial, a long, straggling " encampment," like a fair or market, with one street, "the

---

* All duly named by the Almanack (1864-5).

† The Dom's letter addressed to the King, June 16, 1715, and describing the outrage, is printed in extenso by the Alma-nack of Minas, 1865, pp. 237—240.

general fault of villages in Minas,"* forming the highway up and
down which travellers must pass. It has a minimum of 100
houses and a maximum of 180: there are two upper-storeyed
dwellings, and I counted four Vendas or Groggeries. The people
suffer much from goître, and the place from want of communications; this greatly depresses their agriculture, their cattle-breeding, and their iron-smelting. Carts must make Morro Velho *viá* the
Rio das Pedras, or along two legs of a very acutangular triangle.

Mr. Gordon, the C.O., allowed us only an hour for breakfast:
the days were short, and night-travel amongst these hills is long.
We had no time to call at the pattern one-storeyed house near the
church, occupied by the vicar, Padre João de Santo Antonio; †
a reverend of excellent reputation, who in his town and his flock
makes them remember what comes next to godliness. We set
out at 1·30 P.M. up the rocky main thoroughfare, and crossed a
gruelly stream thick with gold-washing: like the Córrego da
Panella on the other side of the settlement, it is an influent of
the Rio das Velhas. Beyond it the rutty road spread far and wide
over the prism-shaped hill, and from its narrow crest we at once
dropped into a rich bottom-land.

In front rose the tall Serra of Roça Grande facing to the
setting sun; hence its cold temperature and its noble vegetation.
Here, contrary to the rule of the Maritime region, the north-west
is the rainy wind; the south-east brings dry weather. Thus
Gongo Soco on the northern side of the ridge averages 148
inches per annum to 68·28 that fall at Morro Velho on the
southern flank. On our left, and low down, was the large
fazenda of an Alferez Matheus Lopes de Magalhaes: the house,
the grounds, and the fine black cattle, show that the old Portuguese proprietor was a hard-working energetic man. Family
troubles, however, have compelled him to leave his home, and the
orchard, ‡ whose grapes and apples were famous, is now a waste.

---

* The reason is that the first houses
were always built on the banks of the auriferous streams where washing began.

† The brother of this ecclesiastic has
named himself "Demetrio Corrêa de Miranda." A chapter might be written upon
the subject of Brazilian names: as a rule
any man takes what he pleases, usually
the property of some great historic house,
and changes it when he likes. Sometimes
he goes so far as to publish the alteration
in the newspapers, but this is only when
he is in business. Often two and even
three brothers have different family names,
dropping a part, assuming the mother's
maiden name, or taking the name of an
uncle. The subject will, however, not
require the legislation which, in France,
was demanded by the important particle
"de."

‡ Pomar.

To the south-west is a deep excavation, the mine of "Juca Vieira;" the site is the flank of a rugged spine composed of quartz, reddish slate, ferruginous substance, and auriferous soil, forming pyrites. The Gongo Soco Company did not succeed with these diggings, which are now abandoned and choked with water.

Westward of this place, and adjoining the Rossa Grande property in the east, is the Repuxa* or Repucha Estate, five miles long by three broad. It belongs to jarring little owners who hold it by the "Datas"† or mineral concessions granted by the old Guarda-Móres, and it has been worked by a kind of Sociedade. In 1864 the Superintendent of the Sᵗᵃ Barbara Company at Pari recommended it through a London broker as a "splendid field for mining operations," and advised the sum of £40,000 to be laid out upon it. He reported the rock to consist of clay and talcose slate, with strata striking nearly east to west, and dipping 40°—50° south; the lode to be white and yellow quartz, with iron and arsenical pyrites; "Olhos" swells or bunches, which have given 50—60 oitavas per ton; and auriferous "Cáco," expected to graduate into pyritic produce below. As yet nothing has been done : perhaps, however, the project is not dead but sleeping.

Descending a steep, we found the land blooming with the Capim Melado, whose long glumes suggested heather. The hill was rough enough with rolling stones to puzzle an Arab. We then forded a streamlet and entered the Rossa Grande Estate. This until lately was part of the property belonging to the Marquess De Barbacena, a Brazilian gentleman well known in Europe. As we rode up, a miserable tail-race on our right, discharging some 300 gallons per minute, represented the only water supply; the path was evidently made with toe and heel, an "unsophisticated creation of nature," as is said of the highway in Siberia. Turning to the left, we passed a row of ground-floor out-houses more foully dirty than any I had seen that day. On the hill above, the inevitable Casa Grande had been commenced, but we

---

* The "x" in Portuguese sounding like "ch," or our "sh," allows the spelling to be confused, as in Cachaça or Caxaca, Cachoeira or Caxoeira, Chique Chique or Xique-xique.

† These "Datas" have been compared with the "Tin bounds" of Cornwall : the comparison is just as far as streaming goes, but not in mining.

went straight to head-quarters, which were temporary and humble. The Mining-Captain and Manager, Mr. Brokenshar, came and asked us to lunch : we declined with thanks, as we were short of time. "Then," said the host, "I've a bit of hot dinner in here—I shall wish you good-bye." He was evidently Cornish and cautious, nor did we like to put many questions. The place looked a failure : there were in sight fourteen very depressed white men, a few free Brazilians, and no slaves.

Thence we made for the stamps and inspected the stuff. The mine, which lies high up the hill-side, is a layer rather than a lode, dipping to the east, and cropping out of the north-north-western side of the Rossa Grande Ridge. The containing rock is a pinkish substance, coated with a thin layer* nearly all iron. Through it run veins of decomposed and easily powdered quartz of the sugary variety, expected to contain "Cáco." This cacophonous term is applied to quartz and oxide of, others say sulphate of, iron, and is held by miners to be a valuable stone. We also saw laminated iron-quartz containing a little iron pyrites, principally found in brown auriferous soil. The best gold-bearing substances in the formation are reddish oxide of iron and the "elephant tusk," a plate of dark micaceous impure iron, running parallel with the sugary quartz. Often there is a third layer of brown and decomposed iron oxide.

This mining property had long been in the market for £1600 without finding a purchaser. Presently a gentleman at Rio de Janeiro disposed of it for £22,000 (£11,000 in cash, and 2200 shares of £5 each fully paid up) to the Rossa Grande† Brazilian Gold-Mining Company Limited—the capital being £100,000. A Mining Captain who had known the place for twenty-eight years reported upon it in 1862, and declared that the estimates show 56 per cent. per annum upon a called-up capital of £40,000. According to the Prospectus the land extends on both sides of the Serra do Socorro, and thus it has, or is made to have, a rivulet at its disposal. The formation is quartz, brown oxide of iron, and arsenical pyrites, in a

---

* Called by the Brazilian miner "Capa."

† The original word is probably Roça, a clearing. But Rossa is the name in which the property was conveyed, and thus it is written by the "Almanak." Probably they were afraid that in Europe "Roça" would become "Roka."

containing rock of clay. Gold exists as tin and copper in England, where the talcose slate effects a mysterious conjunction with "granite."* The reporter also found a bit of quartz showing visible gold. There are said to be three distinct rock formations, all auriferous, besides one of Jacutinga, which is still unexplored. The first lode is white quartz and iron, the second is yellow quartz with auriferous arsenical pyrites and rich "Olhos," and the third is "Caco." The direction is east to west, and the dip 40° south.

Unfortunately assays from this lode do not give two oitavas per ton, which, in working on a large scale, means little or nothing.

---

* I saw no granite at these altitudes: the hard sandstone has probably been mistaken for it. So at Rio de Janeiro some one told me that the auriferous deposits of Minas were all granitic where gold had taken the place of mica.

CHAPTER XXX.

TO GONGO SOCO AND THE FABBRICA DA ILHA.

Overhead upgrew
Incomparable height of loftiest shade,
Cedar and pine and fir and branching palm.

Milton.

THE vast curtain of thin blue misty cloud, majestically drifting eastwards, did not raise its folds before 3 A.M.; luckily, for the sun that succeeded it made our clothes and riding gear smell distinctly of burning. We breasted a steep patch of "terra vermelha;" here "red land" is a ruddy argile, not, as in the Province of São Paulo, degraded volcanic matter. There was also "terra vermelha tatú," much affected by the armadillo,* and the rest was the common "maçape"† or "ball-foot" clay, more or less ferruginous. In places the ochre-tinted ground showed long streaks of "esmeril," not our emery, but a dust of magnetic iron which proves fertility of soil, which generally accompanies wash-gold, and which is, they say, associated with iridium or osmiure of iridium.‡ We are now in one of the dampest parts of Minas; it is the heart of the dry season, but pools still pit the greasy surface of the path.

Reaching a short level we run along the western slope of a ridge, and with many uncalled-for windings, such as travelling north when our course was south, we turned to the east. Beyond

---

* The common varieties given by Koster and others, are the "tatú bola" (Dasypus tricinctus), whose jointed armour enables it to ball itself like a hedgehog: the delicate meat is compared to that of the sucking pig; the "tatú verdadeiro," or true armadillo (D. novemcinctus), a larger species which cannot "ball;" the "tatú greba" (peba?) said to be anthropophagous (D. Gilvipes), and the "tatu Canastra" (D. gigas).

† The Brazilian farmer has, I have said, a distinct name for every variety of growth that clothes the vast expanse; and he as carefully distinguishes the several soils. I presume that "Maçapé" means "ball-foot:" it certainly balls the mules' hoofs, and renders riding in hot weather a succession of slides.

‡ This is positively asserted by José Bonifacio (p. 14, Viagem Mineralogica).

the summit of the Serra de Luis Soares we change water-shed, leaving the basin of the Rio das Velhas, or rather of the Rio de São Francisco, for that of the Rio Doce. The lands, once owned by the Gongo Soco Company, are now the property of the Commendador Francisco de Paula Santos. The road at once improves, it has been widened and partially drained; it is the Brazil *versus* England, and England is, I regret to say, "nowhere."

On the left was the junction of the Caethé* highway to Gongo Soco; we were shown the whereabouts of the town, at the base of the Serra da Piedade. I regretted that we had not time to visit it; the church is famous throughout the Province, and the place produces pottery of a superior quality, a blue clay which burns to a light greyish tint. But we had seen and were still to see, many a temple and a tuilerie.

The south-eastern side of this ridge is enriched by the over-falls from the western face; we now plunge into the true "Mato Dentro," or inner woodland formation. It is the fourth region, lying west of the Campos or Prairies, the Serra do Mar or Eastern Ghauts, and the Beiramar or Maremma; on this parallel it will extend west to the Cerro or true Diamantine formation, which reaches the luxuriant valley of the Rio de São Francisco. Originally the term "Mato Dentro," which is still applied to many settlements, was descriptive of the secular forests which lay "within" or inland of the grassy hills and prairie lands. These virgins of the soil have long been cleared away from many parts, and have been succeeded by tall second growth, stunted scrub, and the sterile fern.† Here and there, however, vast tracts of the primitive timber remain.

Mr. Walsh‡ proposes six regions or varieties of surface over

---

* Caa-été, or caa-reté, would literally signify "very bush," or "bush-much," true or good growth; hence a forest, applied either to the Mata Virgem or to the Mato Dentro. Many places in the Brazil have this name, which is also rendered in the vernacular "Capão bonito."

"Caété," derived from the same roots, is also a broad lettuce-like leaf from 3 to 5 palms long, and growing in rich damp grounds. The Indians made of this vegetation coverings for their provisions, such as war-farinha: the Brazilian trooper twists the leaf like the grocer's brown paper cone, and drinks from the rustic cup.

From "Caéthé" is derived the name of the South American wild hog, known as "Caetetu:" the last syllable is suu (also written suia and sôo), changed for euphony to tuu, and thus the word means literally "virgin-forest-game."

† "Toda essa terra se cobre, depois de meia duzia de plantacoës, de um feto (filix) a que chamão 'Sambambaia,' e que acontecido desemparão a terra," says Dr. Couto (p. 80).

‡ Vol. ii. pp. 299—312.

which his route lay. These are : 1. Beiramar ; 2. Serra Acima ; 3. Campos ; 4. Rocky metalliferous Serras, " a stony Arabia " ; 5. The Mato Dentro, which he describes as "low eminences covered with copse and brushwood, frequently interspersed with ferns and brambles"; and 6. " Bristly peaks and conical mountains of bare granite," for which read granular or quartzose " Itacolumite." * In the Cisandine valley of the Amazons River, Mr. R. Spruce finds five distinct series of vegetation, independent of the actual distribution of the running waters, and to a certain extent, of the geological and the climatic constitution of the country. He gives : 1. The Riparial Forests, which, with their scrub, live submerged for many months of every year ; 2. The Recent Forests ; 3. The Low or White Forests (caa-tingas ?), the remains of an ancient and highly interesting vegetation, which are now being encroached upon by a sturdier growth ; 4. The Virgin or Great Forests which clothe the fertile lands beyond the reach of inundations ; and, lastly, the Campos or Savannahs, regions of grassy and scrubby knolls, glades, and hollows.

We halted to admire the "floresta fechada "—closed forest— this pomp and portent of nature, this entire disorder of vegetation, through which the tropical sun shot rare shafts of golden light, and which kept the gloaming even at mid-day ; viewed from above the feathery leafage disclosed glimpses of yellow downs, grey rock-peaks, and blue ridges dotting the misty background, whilst the base was of impervious shade. The surface, wholly undrained and unreclaimed, is a forest mould, a layer of soft, spongy, chocolate-coloured humus, the earth of leaves, trunks, and root stools, in which the well-girt walker often sinks to the knee. After travelling through it, man learns to loathe the idea of a march amid a state of nature. Essentially uneven, the ground is a system of sombre sloping valleys and deep, abrupt ravines clothed in double shades, here soled with mud, there cut by a cool stream rolling its crystal down stone steps and over beds of pure sand, pebbles, and rock slabs. In some places it is diversified by cliffs and drops, in others knife-backs separate precipices on either side, and in others the stony bone pierces through the skin. The sections show a subsoil of rich

---

* The reader must be warned that these regions are not always distinctly marked : for instance, the metalliferous Serras (Cerro formation) alternate with the Mato Dentro.

red clay, embedding boulders of granite, gneiss, or greenstone,* or disposed in layers of argile, resting, as in the Maritime Range, upon the rock floor. Its climate is, during the day-time, a suffocating, damp heat, which causes a cold perspiration to follow the slightest exertion. The sun-beams rarely reach and never warm the mouldy ground, while the tree screens deprive earth of wholesome draughts. The nights and mornings are chill and raw; and during storms the electricity is excessive. Fevers abound, and the few human beings who live in the "greenwood" are a sickly race, sallow and emaciated, bent and etiolated, as if fresh from a House of Correction.

The altitude of the Mato Dentro is here that of the Maritime Range, the climate is similar, consequently there is a family likeness in the vegetation, which is fed fat upon abundant carbon, genial rain, and tropical sunshine. The dreams of the third and twelfth centuries, which, reviving the Hamadryads, restored to trees human spirits, here seem to be realised; everything growing wrestles and struggles for dear life, as if endowed with animal passions and bestial energy. In the clearings, where the bulwarks of verdure stand outlined, we are struck by many a peculiarity of the equatorial forest. The slim masts of the harder timber are planted in the ground like poles, the softer woods have giant flying buttresses raised from five to eight feet above the soil and forming the great roots below. The walls of the chamferings would enclose a company of soldiers; the wings here, as in Africa, are easily converted into planks, and the

---

* In the valleys, coombs or corries, these formations suggest "boulder-drift." Unfortunately the ravine floors and the "Tors" or rock-hummocks (roches moutonnées) are not "ice-dressed," or, at least, stone-scorings and striated, polished or grooved surfaces have not yet been observed. Professor Agassiz, the father of the glacial theory, remarks (Journey in Brazil, pp. 88 —89), "I have not yet seen a trace of glacial action, properly speaking, if polished surfaces and furrows are especially to be considered as such." He attributes the absence of striation and "slickenside" to the "abnormal decomposition of the surface-rock, which points to a new geological agency, thus far not discussed in our geological theories." He believes that the warm rains falling upon the heated soil must have a very powerful action in accelerating the decomposition of rocks; and he compares it with torrents of hot water striking for ages upon hot stones.

Few Brazilian travellers will accept this explanation of the absence of "grooving" and "burnishing." Almost all residents are agreed that in this country hard stone used for building, and other subaerial purposes, suffers notably less from atmospheric modification than it does in Europe. Nor is it easy to see how warm rain washing heated surfaces would affect the latter more powerfully than the tremendous force of alternate frosts and thaws of the so-called temperate regions.

It is, however, premature to discuss the subject of "ice-dressing" in the Brazil: the hammer must be freely used *in situ* before theorising can be of value.

Indians, an old missionary informs us, used them as gongs to recal stragglers by striking them with hatchets. The trunks are white-barked with etiolation, red-brown with various lichens and mosses, or spotted with a resplendent carmine-coloured growth.* They stand out like a palisade against the background of gloomy shade, and many of them are so tall that though the Indian arrow will top them, the shot-gun can do no harm. They shoot up boughless before spreading out, as high as possible, the better to fight the battle of life and to plunder their weaker neighbours of goodly sun and air, light and heat. The disposition of the few branches also is varied by the shape and tint of the leafage; some, the myrtles for instance, are marvellously symmetrical; others, the Malvaceæ and the Euphorbias, are picturesquely irregular; the result is a wonderful and a beautiful complication. Many species, I may venture to say, are unknown. The Myrtaceæ and Leguminosæ are the most numerous; the aristocracy is represented by Hymeneæ, Bauhinias, giant figs, towering Lauruses, and colossal Bignonias, which supply the hardest timber. The beauties are the Acacias, the Mimosas, the Lasiandras, and the slender-waisted palms, with bending forms and heads charged with tall silken plumes. The proletariat undergrowth is represented by Cassias charged with flower-tufts, Heliconias, ground-palms, tree-nettles (Jatrophas), Bigonias, Agaves, many kinds of Cactus, arundinaceous plants, and various Bamboos, often forty feet high, either unarmed or terrible with thorns. These form impenetrable *fourrés*, through which only an elephant's weight could break; the hunter must painfully cut for himself a path with the facão or bill, and he feels as if safely lodged in a vegetable jail.

The number, the variety, and the brightness of the flowers distinguish this Brazil forest from the more homely, though still beautiful growth, of the temperate regions, Canada and the Northern States of the Union. The general surface is a system of wonderful domes charged with brilliant points of light, glittering like vegetable jewels. It is now autumn, but the cold season here, as in Africa, takes upon itself the office of our spring, and thus spring and autumn mingle their charms. Some trees are still bare of leaf, others wear garments of ashen-grey or sere and

* John Mawe took with him to England some of this lichen, and tried, but in vain, to utilise the dye.

yellow; others are robed in rosy tints and burnished red. The normal colour is a dark heavy green; every shade of green, however, appears, from the lightest leek to the deepest emerald. While a few trees are in fruit many are still in flower, and here again is an endless diversity. The gold and purple blossoms first attract the eye; there is no want, however, of white and blue, pink and violet, crimson and scarlet. They load with perfume the moist heavy air, and once more there is every variety of odours, from the fragrance of the Vanilla and the Cipo Cravo, which suggests cloves, to the Páo de Alho, that spreads the smell of garlic over a hundred yards around it.

Most astonishing perhaps of all the forest features are the epiphytes, air-plants and parasites. The weak enwrap the strong from head to foot in rampant bristling masses, and hide them in cypress-like pillars of green. Even the dead are embraced by the living that swarm up, clasp, entwine, enwrap them, and stand upon their crests, the nearer to worship Sol and Æther. Every tall, gaunt, ghastly trunk, bleached with age and grimly mourning its departed glories, is ringed and feathered, tufted and crowned with an alien growth that sucks, vampire-like, its life-drops till it melts away in the hot moisture, and sinks to become vegetable mould. The least fracture or irregularity of stem or axil is at once seized upon by a stranger, that lives at the expense of the tree and assists at its death. Every naked branch is occupied by lines of brilliant flowers and tufty leaves of metallic lustre. Thus each venerable ancient of the virgin forests is converted into a conservatory, a botanical garden, "un petit monde," numbering a vast variety of genus and species, admirable in diversity of aspect, and clothed in a hundred colours—with truth, it is said, that a single trunk here gives more forms than a forest in Europe.

As a rule, orchids are not so abundant in the forests of the interior as in those nearer the sea, where they hang the wood with tufts of roses and immortelles. The upper branches of the tree are richest in pendent Cacti, and below them trails the bizarre, dull-grey Barba de páu* or Tillandsia. Further down flourish garlands and festoons of Arums and Dracontiums, Marantas and Caladiums, with succulent, dark-green, cordiform leaves.

---

* Also known as Barba de Velho : I have alluded to it in Chapter 3.

Most remarkable is the Bromelia, with coral-red calyx and the points of the folioles passing from flame-colour to purple-blue. There are bouquets of red, yellow, and orange flowers in spikes or umbels, now like the lily, then suggesting the hyacinth; they press close together, and sometimes one kind will take root upon another. The creepers are woody Bauhinias, Paullinias, and Banisterias, mixed with the withe-like convolvulus, the blue-flowered Ipomœa, much like our common convolvulus, the Vanilla, whose pods here feed the rats; the Grenadilla, studded with apples, and a variety of quaint and gaudy Passion-flowers. Many of them, Ampelidæ, Aristolochias, Malpighiaceæ, and others, are families either belonging to or best developed in this New World, and each has branched off into many a species. The ligneous vine-like llianas run up the masts with gigantic flat leaves, disposed at intervals like those of the dwarf English ivy. Not a few of them are thorny, and the people believe their wounds to be poisonous. Some throw down single fibres or filaments like a system of bell-wires fifty feet long; others, varying in thickness from a thread to a man's arm, trail across the path. These hang like the strained or torn rigging of a ship; those cling like monstrous boas to the bole till they reach a height where they can safely put forth their cappings of tufty leaves and flowers. The slightest sketch of their varieties would cover pages. The convolutions seem to follow no rule as regards the sun, although the southern side of a tree, like the northern in Europe, is here usually distinguished by a more luxuriant growth of moss and lichen. Our old friend, the Cipo Matador (Clusia insignis, "Mata páu"), that vegetable Thug, winds like a cable round the tree-neck which it is throttling. Many of the climbers pass down the trunks, take root anew, or run along a fallen forest-king, and swarm up the nearest support; from this they again descend, and thus they rope the forest with a cordage wonderful in its contrasts and complexities. Lowest upon the trees are the pendent fringes of delicate fernery, which are terrestrial as well as air-plants, mossing over every rock and giving life to the stone. In marshy places spring palm-like Equisetums, which easily over-top a man on horseback. The tree-ferns * are no unworthy

---

* It cannot be said in the Brazil that tree-ferns have a limited range: I find them everywhere in the humid climates between the sea shore and 3000 feet of altitude.

descendants of the Calamites, bundles of fibres, forty feet high; the eye dwells with pleasure upon the "antediluvian" type, comparing the smallness and the delicate cutting of the bending and waving folioles with the tallness and stiffness of the trunk; often, moreover, grimly armed with thorns.

These virgin forests have other dangers than fever and ague. It is necessary to encamp in them with care. Often some unwieldy elder, that has ended his tale of years, falls with a terrible crash, tearing away with him a little world. Where the ground is much "accidented" the dense huge vegetation of the lower levels fines off above into thin and scrubby caa-tinga and carrasco, where the winds bring no risk. During long-continued tropical rains tree shelter is of scant avail; at first only a fine spray descends, but this soon collects into huge drops and small spouts of water. Many of these growths are the despair of botanists; the infloration is found only on the top, and the wood is so hard that a day is easily wasted in felling. It is the same with the air-plants, which, carried from place to place by winds and birds, mostly grow far out of ladder reach.

Glorious in the sunshine, the Mato Dentro becomes weird and mysterious when the lurid red light bursts from the sunset clouds upon the mighty fret work of olive green. It is especially interesting when a storm gives deeper gloom to the depths of the alcoves, and presently startles all the sombre solitude. The forest is poor in large life, the grandest specimens are the poorest; as in Equatorial Africa, the inanimate will not allow the presence of the animate; we must, therefore, look for game in places where the forest outskirts meet cultivation. On the other hand, it is unpleasantly rich in the smaller life. And as we see vegetable forms ranging between the arctic cryptogams, mosses, and lichens that encrust the rocks, which are covered with the tropical Bromelias, and which shadow the palms, so we hear the scream of the hawk, the cry of the jay, and the tapping of many woodpeckers,* combined with the chatter of the parrot and the parroquet,† and the tolling of the bell-bird from the lofty treetop. "Ubi aves ibi angeli," said the older men, and we love the

---

* Especially Anabatis (Temminck) erythrophthalmus; A. atricapillus and A. leucophthalmus, a reddish-brown bird with a singular cry; it is described by Prince Max. iii. 32, and iii. 43.

† Parrots are rare in this region, and the macaw, that prime ornament of the virgin forest, has been killed out.

feathered biped, not only for itself, although loveable *per se*, but because its presence argues that of man. Nor must we forget, while noticing the "natural harmonies" in these leafy halls, the music of the "singing toad" in the swamp, and the frog concerts carried on in the water and the grass, on the earth and every fallen tree. At a distance it is a continuous recitativo with base and treble, interrupted at times by a staccato passage, which seems to be the cry of a child, the yelping of a cur, or the blow of a hammer upon an anvil. But even a list of small life, of the moths and butterflies, the beetles and the bees, the mosquitos and the abominable Marimbombo wasps, would delay us too long—we should not reach Gongo Soco to-night, or in this Chapter.

As we progressed slowly down the dark alley, admiring the " verdobscure" scene and the sunlight,

> . . . broken into scarlet shafts
> Amid the palms and ferns and precipices,

"O da Casa! any one at home!" cried a cheery voice behind us. We turned and recognised the Director of the Cuiabá Mine, Mr. James Pennycook Brown, F.R.G.S., whose acquaintance we had already made.

> Loose his beard and hoary hair
> Streamed, like a meteor, to the troubled air

as he rode up to join us. After a joyful greeting we dismounted to walk ; the path, skirting deep valleys and tangled ravines, showed much of the sublime and beautiful, but it was very muddy, steep, and slippery—in fact, it had little of the comfortable. At Cantagallo, highest mining station below the divide, we entered upon "Cánga," here an incrustation of brown hæmatite. It now paves the ground, there forms ledges projecting like roof-eaves; beneath it there may be claystone or Jacutinga, with or without gold.

Descending the hill we saw through the avenue of trees "Morro Agudo," a little peak blue with distance and bearing east with northing. Here, in the parish and district of São Miguel de Piracicaba, on an influent ten to twelve leagues from the true Rio Doce, is the iron foundry of M. Monlevade, a French settler of the old school. Though an octogenaire he turns out more work than any of his neighbours, and he supplies the Great Mine, despite the interval of eighty miles, with stamp heads and other rough appliances. His slaves are well fed, clothed, and lodged; by way of pay they employ the Sunday in washing gold from the stream, and they often make 1 $ 000 during the day; if compelled to work during the holiday they receive a small sum by way of indemnification.

Nearing the hill-foot, we turned abruptly down a steep to the left. On the right was a huge pit, red and yellow, whence the auriferous matter had been removed. Then appeared on the other side the upper ground of the once famous mine. The tall hill was rent and torn as if by an earth-slip, and showed a huge slide black as if charcoal had been shunted down it : at the bottom was a large rugged open cut such as Brazilian railways affect. The surface, as the sun withdrew, appeared the colour of lamp-soot. In this western portion was sunk Lyons's shaft, once the richest, and Gardner may still be justified in asserting that about half a mile to the eastward of the mine entrance the auriferous bed narrows to a point, but that "westward it appears inexhaustible."

We followed the bubbling waters of the Córrego de Gongo Soco till we came to the present workings. All is on a very small scale, confined to removing the pillars that were left, washing out the sides of the roadways, and taking up, where possible, portions of the old lines. Eighteen head of stamp, a feitor, and a few negroes are all the symptoms of present industry. The property, which runs one mile east to west, by about half that breadth north to south, now yields, they say, about 4 pounds Troy per annum, and the Commendador would, it is believed, sell it for a very moderate sum.

The shades of Captain Lyon and Colonel Skerrett must haunt this Auburn in "West Barbary," once so wealthy, now so decayed. It is melancholy to see ruins in a young land, grey hairs upon a juvenile head. The huge white store to the left of the path is shut up, the gardens have been wasted by the tame pig, the excellent stables are in tatters, whilst from the remnants of the negro Sensallas blind and crippled blacks came and received sixpences from Mr. Gordon as we passed. The Casa Grande of the "Lord High Commissioner," large as many a summer palace in Europe, looked abominably desolate, and though the place is still a "chapelry" the little steeple is shored up. The arched gateway of stone, the eastern limit of the mine proper, still stands, but the changing-house, where men shifted their garments, has melted away.

Contrasting with all this ruin was the prodigious vitality of nature. A fig-tree sprang fresh and green from the very middle of a slab * that might have made a table for Titans or a sarcophagus for Pharaohs. It was of regular shape, some 60 feet long, 15 broad, and about 4 in height; its material was iron and hard laminated clay. This " Baron's stone " should not be a " sine nomine Saxum." Another tree, a Canella (Laurus atra, one of the Laurineæ) has been allowed to remain near the entrance of the mine. The late Barão de Catas Altas used in his days of poverty to make it hold his horse, and, when the property became English, he requested that it might be spared.

We then passed down the beautiful vale of the Gongo Soco rill, some 4 miles long by half that breadth. On the left or north was the wooded range of Tijuco, highly ferruginous and auriferous, in fact, the mother of the gold. To the right was the stream valley, and my friends pointed out the place whence the deep adit for draining the mine should have been run up to the level of the Casa Grande. The bottom is garnished with timber and tree mottes; the undulating grassy sides show stones cropping out to the west; the upper heights are studded with thin Cerrados, and the picture is set in a semicircle of mountains.

Another turn to the left along the hill-side showed us the Gongo River of many names. It begins life as the Soccorro; it becomes the Barra de Caethé, the S. João de Morro Grande, and lastly the Santa Barbara, where it joins the great Piracicáva, and feeds the Rio Doce from the west. Up its valley we see the scatter of houses forming the Taboleiro Grande village, and higher up the gorge is the old settlement with the chapel of Soccorro, after which its grotto is called. The stream threads like a silver wire a black bed of degraded Jacutinga. Beyond it a white road winds up a block of hills to a mountain-tarn, known as the Lagôa das Antas. The lakelet is described as being without issue, shallow around the margin, and deep in the centre; its tapirs (antas) and caymans were soon destroyed by the miners who repaired there to

---

* Here called Lápa, which generally means a cave. It is our leh or lech, as it occurs in Crom-leh, the crumpled or crooked stone ; and in this part of Minas is generically applied to hard clay-slate.

wash their stolen gold, but it still contains leeches, somewhat smaller than those imported.

We were waxing tired after our long day of mist, drizzle, sunshine, and many emotions : the air became biting, and my wife declared that she held the halting place to be a myth. Still, long as the poplar avenue of the old French posting road, the path straggled over a soil of iron on the left bank of the Gongo River. At 6 P.M. we reached our destination, the Fabbrica da Ilha, which belongs to Sr. Antonio Marcos the Ranger. His son-in-law, Sr. João Pereira da Costa, received us with the normal Brazilian hospitality, and lost no time in supplying us with what our souls most lusted after, supper and sleeping gear.

I collected from Mr. Gordon and others the following items of information about the mysterious Jacutinga.*

The name is evidently derived from the well-known Penelope† called Jácu-tinga (P. Leucoptera) from the white spots upon its crested head and blue-black wings. This substance of iron-black, with metallic lustre, sparkles in the sun with silvery mica; the large pieces often appear of a dark reddish brown, but they crumble to a powder almost black. The constituents are micaceous iron schist ‡ and friable quartz mixed with specular iron, oxide of manganese, and fragments of talc. Pieces of the latter substance, large enough for small panes, occur in blue clay slate. The floor rock at Cocaes is fine micaceous peroxide of iron (specular iron), thin and tabular. This has never been reached at Gongo Soco, and the foot-wall is still unknown. It may be specular iron, for oligistic matter is found in small portions, and was stamped for free gold.

Much of the Jácutinga is foliated, and forms under pressure spheroidal oblong crystals never found perfect. It shows great differences of consistency ; some of it is hard and compact as hæmatite, and this must be stamped like quartz. In parts it feels soapy and greasy, not harder than fuller's earth ; it is easily wetted

---

* I have reason to believe that there are formations of Jacutinga in Habersham County, and about the north-east corner of Georgia.

† This handsome and fine-flavoured game bird is of many varieties, especially the Jacu-assu (big) the excellent J. pema, dark, which Prince Max writes Jacupemba, Penelope Marail, Linn., and J. Cáca, the smallest.

Ferreira says the Jacu-tinga (white) is " de côr preta," but with white spots upon the wings and head.

‡ Mr. Walsh applies the term "formação preta" to this gangue, but the Brazilians do not use the expression. He also calls Jacutinga "Corpo da formação," a term used rather in diamond washing than in gold washing.

and pulverised, but it is hard to dry. Its gold is readily separated by washing, and it is purified with nitric acid. The whole body of the lode is not worth removing; it is therefore best worked in underground galleries. The lines and veins are followed with pick and without blasting; their contents supply a soft and crumbling iron ore, which requires little stamping, and the "line gold" thus procured is of superior quality. Often by following the filaments which radiate to all directions from a common centre, the miner finds a nucleus or nugget of large size, but inferior in standard to the line gold, and losing more in the smelting-pot. The carat at Gongo Soco was 19—20. Some describe the gold as dark yellow with palladium, others say that it was deeply tinged with iron and coloured like lead. I have seen it of a bright brassy tint, and sometimes dingy red like worked unpolished copper.

Gongo Soco evidently "gave out" because men knew all about Jacutinga. But in this mine the gold was free and the plundering was enormous, some say to the extent of one-half the find. Tales are still told of miners going out on Sundays carrying guns filled with stolen ore, and the tin biscuit-cases that came empty into the mine sometimes took out from it thirteen pounds of the precious dust. There is yet much treasure hidden, and at times the lucky ones find little fortunes in pots and bottles. Gongo Soco is explained to mean "the gong, or bell, sounds not." Brazilians translate it " Escondrijo de ladroẽs "—den of thieves.

CHAPTER XXXI.

TO CATAS ALTAS DE MATO DENTRO.

E onde, estulto Velho, onde acharemos
O céo de Nitheroy ? As ferteis plagas
Do nosso Parahyba ? E as doces aguas
Do saudoso Carioca . . .?

Confederaçao dos Tamoyos, Canto IV.

WE slept comfortably at the little fazenda. It was the usual
country abode, a ground-floor used by negroes and animals,
a wooden staircase leading to the "sála" or guest room, and
behind it the gynæcium and kitchen, which are forbidden ground,
the sancta of the Dona. The front room is furnished with a
wooden table, always six inches too tall, a bench or two for the
humbler sort, and a dozen chairs with cane backs and bottoms ;
these are famous for wearing out overalls, and are instruments of
torture to those who remember the divan. The paperless walls
are adorned with hunting trophies, weapons, horse-gear, prints of
the Virgin, the saints, early Portuguese worthies, the siege of
Arronches, and Napoleon Buonaparte ; sometimes there is a
mirror and a Yankee clock, long and gaunt ; in the wild parts
there is a portable oratory, a diamond edition of a chapel, two
feet high, lodging proportional patron saints, prints, flowers, and
bouquets ; they defend the small sums and little valuables
entrusted to them by the owner. In the carpetless corner there
is often a large clay water-jar with a wooden cover, and a tin pot,
the drinking fountain. The family sleeps inside, the bedrooms
of the guests open upon the sála : these windowless alcoves—light
not being wanted at night and during the siesta,—are exactly
what old Rome bequeathed to her daughters, Portugal and Spain.
Each has one or two cots,* bottomed with rattan, hide, or board,
and mattresses stuffed with grass or maize leaves. The bed-

* Here called "Catre," evidently a corruption of the Hindostani khatli.

clothes are generally good, always clean, and the pillow-cases are
edged with broad pillow-lace. The dining-room is often in the
body of the house, where the feminine portion, congregating
behind the doors, can observe the stranger without being seen.
One of the peculiarities of the table is the absolute necessity of
a table-cloth; even if you are served with a mess of beans upon a
travelling box by a negro host, he will always spread a napkin.
The other is the presence of a tooth-pick holder of quaint shape,
which exercises much small German ingenuity. Our country
people often leave home with a mighty contempt for the cleanly
" palito," * which they amusingly term a dirty practice. In a
few months, however, they discover that it is indispensable in the
Tropics, but not having learned its use, they are by no means
pleasant to look upon whilst they use it. When the fazenda is on
the ground floor, the sála is a place of passage for vermin-bearing
sheep and goats, poultry and pigs; such was the Irish cabin of
the last generation, and the richest proprietors care little for this
nuisance, which the juniors and the seminude negrolings delight
to abate with sticks and stones.

Altogether the small fazenda lacks many things desirable to
the comfortable traveller. But in its roughness there is a ready
hospitality, and, if the master be a traveller or an educated man,
a hearty good will and a solicitude about the comfort of his guest
which I nowhere remember except in the Brazil.

Next morning we inspected the Fabbrica furnaces. On the
right bank of the Gongo River there is an outcrop of sandstone
slanting westward and roofing the Jacutinga, which can easily be
made either into pig (cast iron) or bar (wrought iron).† There is a
marvellous richness of this material, which reminded me of
Unyamwezi in Inner Africa; it extends for leagues over the
land, and Martius and St. Hilaire agree that this part of
Minas is, as Pliny said of little Elba, inexhaustible in its iron.
The mineral here contains from 50 to 84 per cent. of pure
metal, and that which we saw worked gives 60 per cent. What
would it pay in England, which must remain content with 20
to 35 per.cent. ?

* Palito, the little wood, the tooth-pick.
† " But it appears that the carbon here always escapes in the first instance (?), leaving, as Mr. Baird says, a very fine malleable iron behind, superior to any he had seen in the furnaces in England." Mr. Walsh (ii. 206).

The inner Brazil preserves the Catalan, or direct process of treating the ore by single fusion, now obsolete in older lands. Even the Munjólos* in Western, and the Maráve savages in Eastern, Africa, have improved upon it by adding a chimney for draught, a rude kind of wind-furnace.† Here the forge is a rough bench of masonry, ten feet long by two in height, and containing two or three funnel-shaped basins one foot in diameter, and open at the bottom before and behind. In the rear are the twiers or tuyères, the draught holes for the cold-water blast; a small stream falling through a rough tube forces the air into a wind-pipe and drains off below, whence it passes to work the forge-fire and the tilt-hammer. Unfortunately the blast cannot be controlled. The ore is broken into pieces about the size of a walnut, without previous roasting or sifting, and is mixed in the proportion of one-third to two-thirds of the charcoal, rudely measured by a basket; this mixture is placed in the furnace-basins, which are previously heated, and at times charcoal is added. As the iron melts it sinks, and the slag and other impurities are removed through the front holes opposite the twiers. The negro in charge attends to the fire, stirring up the mass from the top with a rod or poker, and he knows that the melting process is complete when the thick smoke and blue flame have changed to a clear white blaze.

The side opening at the bottom of the furnace-basin, which has been banked up with fine charcoal, is then cleaned, and the workman, with a pair of tongs, pulls out the "bloom" ‡ or "boss." It is chilled rather than quenched in a large water-bowl containing a layer of charcoal ashes, and now it has the appearance of an amygdaloid, the raisins of the pudding being the half-burnt fuel. The clinker is rejected, but there is no puddling to get rid of the abundant sulphur. This mineral will disappear under the hammer, showing how tenacious is the ore; an inferior quality would split. But also the wood charcoal, combining with the iron, has made a kind of steel; were sulphurous coal used with such a process, the produce would be almost worthless.

---

* See Chap. 24.

† A drawing of the Maráve forge is given in " O Muata Cazembe " (p. 38), the diary of the Portuguese Expedition of 1831-2 (Lisbon, Imprensa Nacional, 1854). We can hardly wonder, however, at the rudeness of the Brazilian process. In co-lonial days the people were forbidden to melt an ounce of iron : they walked upon it, but they were compelled to import their metal from Portugal.

‡ This lump of malleable iron is generally called a bala, locally a "lupa."

The last operation is now to place the "bloom" under the tilt-hammer, where it is dolleyed and stamped into the shape of a brick. No refining process is attempted beyond simple reheating to expel impurities and increase the hardness; it is then replaced under the hammer and drawn out to the required scantling. It goes to Morro Velho in bar, to be used as boyer iron. I have already remarked how it lasts out the stamps of English steel. But the rudest and simplest process suffices for such excellent ores—witness the Damascus steel forged by the rude Hindus in the hill-ranges of Bombay. Here an evident and easy improvement would be to build a stack or even a cylinder over the basins, and thus to heat the blast. It will be long before these men will be persuaded to employ the newly invented system of electro-magnets.

After an ample breakfast we struck down the River Valley, guided by Sr. da Costa; it was adorned with beautiful figs of the coolest and most refreshing green. On our left was a tall, turret-like outcrop of granular limestone mixed with "lápa," a hard clay slate. The mine was in a disordered condition and uncrystallised; in one place a horizontal vein cropped out from the main body.* Beyond this point the coarse ferruginous soil was a rabbit warren, burrowed in search of gold, now exhausted. Crossing the Gongo River, we rode up the one street of S. João do Morro Grande, whose newly finished Matriz, with the pepper-box and round-square belfries, we had sighted from afar. It is, comparatively speaking, an old place, and was raised from villagehood to parochial rank by a Royal Letter of January 28, 1752. The Serra de Cocaes, tall, stern, and cloud-capped, walls the left side of the valley, and on its slope is the little Gamelleiras Mine, working nine stamps, and belonging to the Capitão José de Aguiar and the Coronel Manuel Thomaz and brother.

It is curious to see how the soil near the stream has been tossed and tumbled about during the last 150 years; the present population could by no means have done it. "Hydraulicking" on an extensive scale was shown by long lines of leats, running

---

* Here Gardner (p. 494) was misled by M. von Helmreichen, who made the Serra north of the Gongo Soco Mine to run east to west, and to be " of a primitive character, the mass of its centre consisting of granite." Upon this he places schistose and clay slate, cropping out at about 45 deg.

along the hill-sides like the river beaches and the parallel roads of often-quoted Glen Roy. Above them mines and diggings, deepened by the rains of many a summer, have been cut into Vesuvian cliffs and craters of red clay.

We passed through the little village of "Capim Cheiroso," * whose "fley-craws," wind-worked figures on tall poles swinging their arms to frighten away birds, suggested the presence of Swiss. Beyond it is the São Francisco settlement, where three streamlets meet; near the junction are a little three-windowed chapel and a wooden bridge with a stone pier in mid-stream. The path ran up the pretty river plain, bright with sugar-cane, on the right bank of the Brumado stream. It had a look of home; the rivulet was, without overflowing, full—in these lands such streams are either o'erflowing or underflowing—and on the further bank wintry broom rose naked in the air. Reaching the much decayed village of Brumado, we saw on the left the road leading to Santa Barbara and the Párí Mine,† and we turn right-wards to the great house of Commendador João Alves de Sousa Coutinho. The retired courtier, a favourite of the first Emperor, gave us a hearty welcome and pressed us to stay.

Here we are close to the property of the Santa Barbara Gold Mining Company (Limited), of which a section of the public has assuredly heard. It was formed in 1861 to buy an estate and fazenda called the "Pari Gold Mine," or "Pari Lode," in the district of Piracicáva, parish of Sᵗᵃ Barbara,‡ from which it is distant about six miles. Its owner, Coronel João José Carneiro e Miranda, had long offered it for 5000*l*.; it was purchased for 12,000*l*., two-thirds in cash and the remainder in shares of 1*l*. each. Moreover 18,000*l*. were expended upon getting the mine into profitable working order, upon an adit for unwatering, and upon a new stamping mill of seventy-two heads. Thus the total outlay was just half the capital, 60,000*l*.

The proposer, who visited it in 1855,§ gave it a good name in

* "Sweet-smelling grass," a Cyperacca, Kyllinga odorata (Syst.).

† "Párí," pronounced much like the French Paris, is a fish trap.

‡ Sᵗᵃ Barbara, upon the western head waters of the Rio Doce, is said in the reports to be 14—15 miles due east of S. João do Morro Grande, 20 miles north by east from Gongo Soco, 24 miles from Cocaes, and

54 miles north-east of Morro Velho. According to St. Hil. (I. i. 214), who writes "Percicaba, or piracicaba," the Guarani words "Pira cy cabá" appear to signify "shining black fish."

§ In 1850, Dr. Walker reported that the lode resembled that of Morro Velho; that it was worked underground, but only by day, and that the ore was stamped,

his report.   The lode, hornblende, quartz, and arsenical pyrites, ran north to south, parallel with the clay slate containing rock.* At grass the width was 3—4 feet, but below it widened to 7—13. It has been worked to 100 fathoms, but the level was shallow, hardly 80 feet, and the only pump was a hand-pump.   The auriferous yield was to be upwards of four oitavas per ton.   By way of refresher, in April, 1863, a report by an ex-miner of Gongo Soco, who had thirty years' experience in Brazil, was sent home ; the worthy man assured all shareholders that the former proprietor, despite his " crude, imperfect, inefficient, and there- fore costly development," had realised a very handsome property. Corollary, what a fool he was to sell it !   Moreover, the principal agent, whose son was also one of the mining captains, reported that he was making five oitavas per ton ; other information was equally favourable, especially when volunteered by those who had local interests, such as a store, or a shop, to supply rose- coloured specs.

On the other hand, facts were unreasonable enough to prove that the hornblende which predominates over the pyritic forma- tion, though represented to be easy for boring, is an extremely refractory substance, making the quarrying very difficult, and neutralising the auriferous properties of the quartz.   After six years the agent withdrew.   The works are now in the hands of an ex-mechanic, two English miners, and a very few free Brazilians.   The slaves have been given up, and—sic transit gloria Sanctæ Barbaræ !   But she may become rediviva ; in such matters "impossible " must be erased from the dictionary ; and I have heard rumours that she is to be set on her feet once more.

After eating oranges and drinking orange-wine, we bade adieu to the Commendador, leaving with him that extremely *entêté* Mr. Brown.   A cross road to the west of the highway led up a short river valley with a charming "bit of view," crossed a "mud" or two, and placed us upon the open sunny Campo.   I always return to these pure and airy downs with pleasure, especially after a spell of the "shut forest."   Travellers complain that they are monotonous, but that depends upon the traveller.   As in the Arabian desert, objects are few, except to those who know

passed through arrastres, and straked in   * The underlay is stated to be 54°—55°
the usual way.   east.

where to find them and how to look for them, And there is nothing unsightly in the long rolling waves of ground, dotted over with the yellow apple of the Juá, the black woods in the lower levels, and the gradual sinking of the foreground into a smooth horizon of the purest blue.

Here for the first time rose high before us the Serra do Caráça,* more politely called da Maē dos Homens. We had turned its northern bluff without a clear prospect of its form, and we shall almost circle round it before we return to Morro Velho. Though it was so long in sight I was never weary of gazing upon it, despite the sage,

> Nil tam mirabile quidquam
> Quod non minuant mirarier omnes paulatim.

It is a grisly spectacle, that Big Face, a huge mass of iron slate towering several thousand feet † above the high downs. Its features are grotesquely seamed and dyked with broad and narrow bands of quartz ‡ standing out from the dark Itacolumite, and in places there were long vertical shaves of blue-black Jácutinga underlying the hard intercrust of mica slate. After yesterday's rain the ore had been washed out of the joints, making the slides and precipices look as if molten silver were flowing down a mountain of moulded iron, a grisly casting that disdains to show a sign of vegetation, and which seems to stand as if defying the elements for ever. The southern end, where the strata are almost perpendicular, assumes the appearance of a rhinoceros head ; nor are nasal horns wanting, the softer parts of the stone have scaled off, leaving a jagged line of tall pikes, like the " organs " of Rio Bay. Looking at it, as we do, from the west, it proclaims its inaccessibility; it is the wall of iron which Sikandar of Rum built against Yajuj and Majuj at Darband.

---

* Caráça is explained in Portuguese as Carranca (tetricus vultus) de Pedra (Voc. Port. & Latin of Padre Raphael Bluteau, 10 vols. folio). The word is feminine, but always takes the masculine affix, " O Caráça," the ugly face. This confirms the legend which derives its name from some pongo-faced negro, Quilombeiro, who first lived in its horrid heights. Mr. Henwood erroneously calls it " the Caraças." Mr. Walsh (ii. 312) is worse still : " Another was called ' Serra da Cara ' from its likeness to an enormous visage." St. Hil. (I. i. 218) observes that the word is at once Portuguese and Guarani. In the latter tongue, Cara and haça, or Caaraçaba, corrected to Caraça, mean a defile.

† Some say 3000 and even 4000 feet. St. Hil. (I. i. 285), who ascended the highest peak, lays down the height at nearly 6000 feet above sea-level.

‡ Mr. Halfeld informs us that the Caráça contains muriate of soda in the strata of Itacolumite.

This " Big Face Mountain" is the very pivot and centre of the mid-Minas gold mines, especially the pyritic formation : open the compass to a radius of $0°\ 30'$, sweep round, and the enclosed circle will all be more or less auriferous.   The Serra was examined botanically by Spix and Martius, followed by St. Hilaire : heavy rains kept Gardner away.   Mr. Gordon ascended by the southern face, and found a dangerous road, with round rolling stones, over ledges and along precipitous chasms : the pass by Allegria on the south-eastern side is also bad.   The best approach is from Brumado, which we have just seen, and up the easier northern slope.   On the summit is a plateau of some three square miles, soled by a swamp which dries up in winter ; around the margin of this water European vegetables grow to perfection.

As usual with remarkable mountains in Minas, the Caráça was long a hermitage where life must have been lively as that of a lighthouse-keeper thirty years ago.   A chapel in which mass was said for fifty miles round,* was begun in 1771, and dedicated to Nª Sª Maē dos Homens.   Near it was a monastery occupied by a brotherhood of eleven.   The works were all made by a certain Irmão Lourenço, who belonged to the regicide house of Tavora.   His portrait is still in the College, and he is remembered as a most worthy man who did not "make fire in the sea."   He lived there till past 1818, and at his death left to the king his hermitage, which became a seminary.   The congregation of the Mission of St. Vincent de Paul was presently established by Padre Leandro Rabello Peixoto e Castro, in virtue of the Royal Letter dated Jan. 21, 1820.   It languished till the present Bishop of Marianna, who had been one of the lecturers, returned to it as Principal, and found there very few pupils.   The diocesan collected funds for a little church and altar-stone to admit of the place being consecrated ; and the excellent prelate intends, it is said, to be buried in it.   The now well-known theological college occupies a secondary ridge on the north-west part of the plateau, and when residences were built the Propaganda sent priest-professors.   The Principal is M. Michel Sipolis, who has temporarily returned to France ; the Vice-Principal was his brother M. François Sipolis,

---

* So says Henderson, writing in 1821. In 1831, St. Hil. (I. i. 220) described the mountain plateau, which he visited in 1816 ; he also mentions "Frère Lourenço."

whom we shall frequently meet, and there were three other ecclesiastics, all well-educated men.

Our track lay up and down hills of yellow clay, thinly greened, and presently we fell into the Santa Barbara, or main road that leads from Ouro Preto to Diamantina. This, the most important line of communication in the Province, appears hereabouts a respectable highway; near the City of Diamonds it will become detestable. On the right was a ranch whose palms, coffee-shrubs and bamboos, larger than usual, argued a warmer climate.

Approaching a well-bridged stream, the " Ribeirão da Bitancourt," we saw from afar a phenomenon that puzzled us. At length, straining our eyes like so many D. Quixotes, we distinguished, not windmills, but a cavalcade of eleven Sisters of Charity in gull-wing caps, mounted on poor hack-mules, and travelling, like Canterbury Pilgrims, in single file under the escort of two priests. They had been sent from the Laranjeiras establishment at Rio de Janeiro to found a branch house at Diamantina. We halted and addressed mes sœurs : unfortunately, the only pretty Sister, who, moreover, sat her horse well, and who wore a neat riding-skirt, went forward, and would not join in the chat. M. François Sipolis, carrying his full-grown metal cross, was in command of the detachment, and recognised Mr. Gordon, and the Sisters my wife; loud and hot were the greetings. This priest, still young, had come to the Brazil in his salad days, and he has perhaps been too long here : I could hardly tell his nationality. The rear was brought up by a youth in soutane, with sallow greenish skin, and apparently a double supply of eyes, behind and before : he most diligently perused his breviary, while he took inward stock of everybody and everything. Thus, the King of Dahome's system of duplicate officials is not always despised by the civilised and the Jesuitic order touching the mission of their " apostles." *Misito illos vinos* is still carried out in the Brazil. I engaged myself to meet M. Sipolis at Diamantina : we then shook hands and parted *à l'aimable*.

After long sighting the grassy slopes below the settlement, we crossed a " lavapés "* in the shape of a bright little stream flowing

---

* " Wash feet." This name is given to the little stream nearest the settlement. It reminds one of olden Tuscany, where the peasant girl carried her shoes and stockings in hand till near the town, when she washed off the mud, and appeared in public like a " respectable person."

over its black Jácutínga bed; it rises in the Caráça, and forms one
of the head waters of the Rio Doce. Our hoofs clattered loud
over the rugged pavement of the silent "Catas Altas," called
"de Mato Dentro,"* although the forest has long ago been
cleared away. Mr. Gordon had sent his man forwards, and
we found all prepared at the "Hotel Fluminense e Bom Pasto
Feixado,"† kept by the Lieut.-Colonel João Emery. The son of
English parents, and thoroughly John Bull in burliness of look,
the host could speak only Portuguese. As he explained himself,
the face was British, but all the rest was Brazilian. It too often
happens in this Empire that the father and mother become accustomed to talk their mangled Lusitanian en famille, and thus
the children, with the harsh features and the freckled faces of the
far north, cannot answer the simplest question in the language
of their ancestors.

From the hotel we could easily see the diggings in the eastern
cheek of the Caráça. The upper stratum is a rich ochreous clay
some twenty feet deep, overlying fine micaceous slate, that rests
upon compact magnetic iron, and the latter has always been found
in far greater abundance than gold. In the lower beds run the
veins of ferruginous quartz which used to be split with fire and
stamped for precious metal. The eye chose out three huge excavations resembling craters and ranged in line, duly flanked by two
Casas Grandes. The easternmost is the "Pitangui," ‡ the Lavra do
Padre Vieira, which belongs to a Brazilian association and by
which flows the "lavapés." Next to it is Boã Vista, the Lavra do
Francisco Vieira, brother to the padre; it has lately done a little
business; and further on is an old houseless pit called "O
Machado." Besides these, the Brumadinho, the Bananal, and the
Durão, are spoken of by the people. They were mostly worked
out before 1801, and mining enterprise is now far beyond the
local purse. All supposed that we were going to buy, and whis-
pered, with the bated breath of a London police magistrate fresh
from Rome, the vast riches hidden in the mountain's lean bowels.

---

* Thus distinguished from Catas Altas
de Noroega.
† The Minas pronunciation of "fech-
ado." The first thing done by the sensible traveller on arriving is to ask and
look after the pasture. If he wishes to
make an early start, he must always place

his beasts in a "close pasture," where
ditch or palings prevent their straying.
‡ Some say that to the east of the Pitangui and the Morro de Agua Quente, is
"Cuiabá," a mine worked by the Gongo
Soco Company when their head-quarters
began to fail.

Whilst dinner was being served up, we easily visited the town, which dates from 1724 : since its mines failed it has become very poor, and the inhabitants support life by corn-growing and cattle-breeding. These simple and innocent occupations, Georgic and Bucolic, ought to make them happy; they look downcast as Melibœus or Corydon, and, as their dull lives are hardly worth keeping, they live long and die hard. The single street has, besides the Matriz Nª Sª da Conçeição, three chapels, a Rosario, a Sᵗª Quiteria, and a Bomfim. The porticoed mother church, which fronts a neat sloping square, is abundantly painted; even the balustrade round the tower is a deception not likely to deceive. The interior is quaintly and curiously ornamented with old twisted pillars, and, a novena being in prospect, cut and coloured paper extended from floor to roof. The rotulas* and balcony of the vicar, Padre Francisco Xavier Augusto da França, were crowded with ladies preparing for the festival. His reverence told me that he was entering his eightieth year. Why is it that after seventy a man must tell you his age inevitably, as if he had shot the albatross? He spoke of a parishioner who had lately died æt. 119, and he estimated his cure to extend over 3900 souls, of whom some 490 only were slaves.†

---

* The old wooden lattice work which formed a kind of hanging closet outside each window, and sometimes extending along the house face. Being handier than even an Affghan "Sangah" when a quiet shot was to be fired, they were suppressed in 1808, when the Court of Portugal changed quarters from Lisbon to Rio de Janeiro.

† The Almanack of 1865 believes the slave population not to exceed 488.

CHAPTER XXXII.

TO MARIANNA.

Torrão que de seu ouro se nomeava,
Por crear do mais fino ao pé das Serras ;
Mas que feito em fim baixo e mal prezado
O nome teve de " Ouro Inficionado."

Caramurú, 4, 21.

THE night was exceptionally cold, we slept soundly, and on the next day, a harmless Friday, we were on foot at an hour when the humid darkness seemed to be

Almost at odds with morning, which is which.

Instead of making "Inficionado" by the direct road to the south-south-east, we were to cover an equilateral triangle of twelve miles to "Fonseca," where the combustible matter is, and then to make our nighting place, as much further.

We resumed the Campo road, and after two miles with a few rough ascents and descents, we reached the little village Morro d'Agua Quente. While fording the streamlet, we were shown an island in which an English miner was buried. He had pledged himself to unwater the Agua Quente mine, and had set up some fine pumping gear, eighteen inches in diameter, made of wrought-iron plates from home. But even these failed ; he redeemed his word like the last of the Romans, by going to Kingdom Come. "There was," said the satirical Mr. B., "but one honest Cornishman in Minas, and he—went and hanged himself."

Mr. Gordon had some business to transact with a decent Brazilian body, the widow of an Irishman employed at Morro Velho—his other five relicts are not so easily managed. Meanwhile we put up at a little tavern kept by Sr. Leandro Francisco Arantez, an energetic young man who has a concession for working the seam which we had come to see. The Province is thoroughly alive to the necessity of supplanting seaborne coal by Brazilian, and has offered £2000 for the discovery of the grand desideratum. Sr. Arantez showed us with just pride the gold medal which had been conferred upon him in 1863, when he hit upon the doubtful substance : the reverse showed the head of H. I. Majesty, and Benè meritum premium was on the obverse. He told us his many troubles, how the people had discouraged him in every possible way, and had named his trouvaille "raiz de páu"—tree root. So in the Province of S. Paulo, when, at the end of the last generation, certain innovators proposed to abandon the valueless sugar growing, for coffee, they were derided as "planters of fruit."

Agua Quente—hot water—derives its name from a thermal spring, which was covered by an earthslip. In 1825, Caldcleugh spoke with an old man who remembered drinking "agua morna," lukewarm water, but he did not remember if it had any smell. Others declare that the heated element once appeared in the mine. As usual, the village has decayed, together with the cause of its origin : it has 68 houses within reasonable distance of one another. The Company's old store still exists at Bananal, near Agua Quente, but no work is done there. Above the mine is a peak, known as Morro d'Agua Quente, and from this our destination, "Fonseca," bears due south-east.

Accompanied by Sr. Arantez, we ascended a very steep hill that placed us upon the Chapada. Here the ground rang under the hoof as if iron plated ; in places it sounded hollow, suggesting that the thin crust might easily cave in, and such hereabouts is the formation generally. The appearance of the mineral reminded me of the laterite in Malabar and Western India, but here it is the richest hæmatite. Dr. Couto found the village of Agua Quente built upon immense deposits of copper ; sheets of the red variety, chequered and sprinkled with the ashy mineral, forming a chess-board of pleasing appearance. To the left was the Serra da Batêa, a southern butt-end of the great Serra do Frio.* On the right, and falling to the rear, looking exceptionally ribby, rose the peaked mountain, Caráça, down which the dangerous road is seen to wind.

Passing a small fazenda, "do Moreira"—not to be confounded

---

* This must not be confounded with the Cerro do Frio, further north, around the city of Cerro, or Serro, the old Villa do Principe.

with the Freguezia of Paulo Moreira, twelve leagues from Gongo
Soco, a little south of east—we found a basin separated by a
"knife-board" from one contiguous; both are gentle hollows
of considerable size. The easternmost showed at the side a
small winding stream, the young Piracicáva, and on its bank lay
Fonseca, a chapel and scattered huts, like a new mining locality.
Around, the land looked dry and sun-burnt: the dead brooms
and withered ferns covered in patches hundreds of acres, and
their dull sombre brown-grey will darken the brightest and
cheeriest landscape. This is a sign of a dry porous soil: the
tender root of the Samambaia* cannot penetrate the tough clay.
In the Brazil, where the fern is supposed to follow overfiring
and exhausting the ground, when once it has taken possession
the case is hopeless. In New Zealand the clover kills the fern
as the white man's rat destroys the native rat, and the European
fly drives away the Maori fly: perhaps it would do so here.
Now, the sole precaution is to cut the plants before they
branch, and to let beasts graze upon the roots, as we do in
England. In the Brazil, as in Tibet, peasants eat the young
shoots of a kind of fern ("Samambaia do Mato"): M. Huc
compared it—height of imagination!—with asparagus.

We descended to a "gulch," in which there is a little stream,
the Córrego de Ogó,† and the opening faced north-west by north.
This is the place where the coal was found, accompanying sand-
stone-grit and hæmatite. The dip of the rock is 70°; the strike
is west-south-west, and the cleavage planes are as nearly as
possible east to west. The water, as usual, here showed signs of
iron, and carbonate of lime appeared in the eastern wall, where
drops had trickled down. We found the same formation higher
up, and our guide told us that the coal was also in the Valley of
the Piracicáva, and in the western basin by which we had
ridden. We traced it a few yards down the Córrego, a ferruginous rill, which, after two miles, falls into the Piracicáva.
Here also was a quartzose and pyritic rock, which had given gold.
The precious metal was, however, "muito fi-i-i-no," as our com-

---

* Older writers prefer the less euphoric
Sambambaia, and Sambambaial, a (natural)
fernery. From one of these ferns (Mertensia
dichotoma), pipe stems are made, and fixed
to a little head of black clay.

† Ogó is described to be a base yellow
metal found in sand, and used to falsify
gold. Others tell us that it floats in water,
and is therefore probably mica, now called
popularly "Malacacheta." St. Hil. (I.
i. 341), speaks of a "sable brillant appelé
Ogó qui se trouve du côté de Sabará."

panion said, raising his voice almost an octave, to denote the superlative of fineness, that is to say, of minuteness.*

The combustible appears in small pieces and broken layers much mixed with clay and sandstone : we did not find a single block. It was mostly transition lignite, or brown coal, known in S. Paulo as "tipota :" distinctly modern, ligneous of appearance, and burning with the smell of wood. Other pieces from the same locality are smooth and black, like obsidian or sealing-wax, conchoidal in fracture, highly inflammable, and giving out thick smoke and gas in quantities. It is, in fact, our cannel coal, and it will be found useful when the old reverbere and the kerosine are clean forgotten. I recognised the formation, having already examined at the Fazenda of a certain Dr. Rafael, near Old Caçapava, in the Valley of the Parahyba River, Province of São Paulo, a very similar basin, whose lignite overlies cannel coal : here, however, at a greater depth, occurs anthracite, a veritable black diamond which does not soil the fingers, and which burns without smoke. Before working these places, the main consideration is whether the formation be sufficiently extensive to pay : the exploratory works should certainly not cost more than 200*l*. In Minas I nowhere observed the great deposits of sulphurous or bituminous shale which occupy the Valleys of the Southern Parahyba and the Upper Tiété, and which will some day supply the land with petroleum. These must be sought further east, and they will probably be found upon the lower courses of the Rio Doce, the Mucury, and the Jequitinhonha or Belmonte.

We then rode up the rough western wall of the eastern basin, and met with water everywhere, even near the top. This is a common feature both in Minas and S. Paulo ; the stranger is often surprised to see a crystal spring welling from the brow of a hill. The only trace of game was the "Frango do Campo," or Prairie Chicken, plumed like the water-rail, short-legged, and to be mistaken for a young hen that has escaped from the poultry-yard. The Siriéma, or Serpent-bird, ran before us in the path, and represented the turkey.

At the Fazenda do Moreira, Mr. Gordon bade us a temporary

---

* This custom, very general in the Brazil, probably descended from the aborigines, who expressed the superlative by intonation. St. Hil. (III. ii. 62), says that "Ouro fino" denotes "la belle qualité de cet or :" it may have this signification, or that given in the text.

adieu : he was to regain Morro Velho viâ Agua Quente, whilst we
intended to sleep at Inficionado. We descended a long hill,
passing near the bottom-water a small iron foundry, and by a
tedious ascent we made a Chapada, which, like that of the
morning, was a plain of iron, hollow-sounding as a pot. From afar
we saw the curling smoke of the settlement, and the black outlines
of " Cata Preta," * which was worked to little purpose by the Gongo
Soco Company, and which now belongs to the Commendador owner
of the mine. Then we dropped into a deep road, a hollow way, like
the lanes of fair Touraine, once so familiar to me, and presently
below us flowed the river, broad and clear, crossed by a tolerable
bridge. We lost no time in transferring ourselves to the hostelry
of Sr. Francisco Cesario de Macedo, at the southern end of the
village.

During the evening we walked out to see the " parishry of Nª
Sª de Nazareth do Inficionado "—of the Infected (gold). The
cognomen was given because the metal at first seemed excellent,
but presently showed the cloven foot. The "Infected" is now
the usual long, wretchedly-paved street or rather section of
high-road, whilst horse-shoeing and grain-selling at a dear rate
to bezonian travellers appear the principal industries. A dry
chafariz fronts the matriz, and there are two chapels, but never a
priest ; on the other side of the Piracicáva, a thin scaffolding still
surrounded the tall black cross, which was being duly armed.

The fashionable skin was a sallow brown, and people showed a
mixture of races, with much inter-marriage. Cripples and beggars
were unusually numerous. I saw two cases of hydrocephalus,
one with soft the other with hard head ; both creep upon the
ground, and have forgotten the use of their "immortal souls." At
Barbacena the mouth is worn open ; at S. João the tongue is
slightly protruded ; here the villagers "made at us a pair of
eyes" and laughed in our faces the laugh of semi-idiotcy, whilst
one of them audibly remarked that my "companion" † was "uma
senhora muita capaz"—highly trustworthy. The host, however,
was civil and obliging ; he did not even murmur when our

---

* The " Black Pit."

† The Brazilian gentleman speaks of his
wife as "Minha Mulher." The country
people call her "Companheira." The rest
say, "Minha Senhora"—my lady. So in
France, the bourgeois has a dame and a
demoiselle, but no femme or fille : in the
United States, not to speak of England, the
hotel books abound in "Mr. A. and lady"
—a useful prevarication if Mr. A. be *not*
travelling with his own spouse.

exceedingly careful fellow-traveller found a sixpence wrong in the mules' rations, and with loud " blatheration " performed the operation of docking.

Cata Preta boasts of one great birth. Fr. José de Santa Rita Durão was born there about 1737; this old worthy was the son of an energetic Portuguese colonist, and he died, as poets were wont to do, in the hospital of Lisbon, 1784. During these forty-seven years he wrote a number of poems, of which the best known is " O Caramurú,"* an epic in hendecasyllabics, numbering the normal ten cantos. Had the Lusiads never been created, this production would have become world-famous : as it is, the echo of the older and grander strain haunts the reader's ear. Even the sententious trick of the line terminating the stanza is preserved. For instance, the exordium—

> Of the stout spirit whom no toil could tame,
>   Nor daunt the rage of occidental waves ;
> Who the Reconcave,† ever dear to Fame,
>   Which still the haught Brazil's high city laves,
> Explored ; the " Thunder-Son," whose fearful name
>   Could rule and tame the savage Indian braves,
> I sing the valour proved by adverse fate—
> Who masters fortune, he alone is great.

The poem was hastily thrown off, and was printed in 1781. The Visconde de Almeida-Garrett, himself a most distinguished poet as well as prose writer and critic, says of it, " Where the poet has contented himself with simply expressing the truth, he has written most beautiful octaves, some of them even sublime." M. Ferdinand Denis, an early historiographer of Brazilian literature, declares it to be a "national epopee, which interests and excites the reader ; " and M. Eugène Garay de Monglave has translated it into French. It might, I think, appear in an English dress with much judicious curtailment, and with the prosaic portions reduced to plain prose.

On the next day—a thirteenth be it duly remembered—we left Inficionado at a late hour. Rain was brewing in front, the effect

---

* A certain Diogo Alvares of Viana was wrecked at Bahia, where the land swarmed with savages : by the use of his musket he rose, like Mr. Coffin of Abyssinia, to high rank amongst them. The Indian nickname is usually translated " Man of fire : " it properly signifies, " the electric eel." The " Son of Thunder " was the title given to Diogo Alvares, who married the " Princess " Paraguaçu.

† O Reconcavo is applied to the magnificent Bay of S. Salvador (da Bahia).

of the "Serra de Ouro Preto," which indulges in a perpetual night-cap of heavy wet. We began with the high-road, or, as it is here called, the "cart-road," to Marianna city, and we found some luxuries, such as the rivulets cleared of their large round stones. We were not, however, beyond the old wheel-tire with projecting iron knobs, which bite the slippery clay ground, and which over-work the trains upon the levels. Presently we turned into a bridle-path, exceptionally bad; our mules seemed to be climbing up and down stairs. The material is a glaring white quartzose sandstone, soft and laminated; it is easily trodden and weathered into holes and ledges. The formation is akin to the so-called Itacolumite which supplies Diamantina with its gems. There are mines around, rude diggings in clayey sand, mixed with coarse ferruginous gravel and debris from the schistose rocks of the Serra.

After an hour we descended to the hamlet "Bento Rodriguez," which lies between the forks of the river Gualaxo,* a vitreous stream in a ruddy pink bed, which contrasts charmingly with the lively verdure around. The eastern or further water, even at this season, was girth-deep: the ruins of a bridge were there, and a "pingela," which here represents the hanging bridge of Peru, showed that after rains the clear waters became unfordable. Another rise and fall led to a "Devil's Glen," a deep dark hollow, with strata highly tilted up, and a mountain burn plashing down the bottom, crossed by a single arch. About noon we reached Camargos, a small village with a stream in red sands below, and a very big church standing on a hill to pray, a veritable Pharisee. At this half-way house a little venda gave us shade; and a few words of civility and chatting about war-news produced oranges : our only expense for entertainment was 3d., the cost of a bottle of cachaça. The Brazil, like Russia and other young countries, is a place of exceeding cheapness for those who live, as the Anglo-Indian saying is, "country-fashion," on beans, charqui, and native rum. On the other hand, imported articles double their London prices, and anything out of the ordinary way is inordinately expensive. Those who think that they cannot

---

* Gualáxo do Norte, by Henderson written Guallacho. The water is so called from a neighbouring Fazenda, and it feeds the Rio Doce proper. We have now left the Valley of the Piracicava.

spend money here will marvel at the cost of beef-steaks and beer, fresh butter and English cheese.

Camargos—on this line towns and villages greatly resemble one another—sows and breeds like its neighbours : it has a small industry in the matter of gold, once so abundant, and it can also export iron. From this district came the tea which gained the gold medal in the Great Exhibition of 1862 :* we presently saw the plantations, rather shabby below, but rich in the higher lands, fronting the Bom Retiro Fazenda. I had not met with the shrub since leaving the Province of São Paulo, and it was the face of an old friend.

Ascending the Morro da Venda da Palha,† we enjoyed a noble view of enormous extent. To the north, under " a sky of wondrous height," rose the peak of " Itabira do Mato Dentro," a mere knob rising from the horizon plain, and distant, as the crow flies, forty-five miles. Eastward a tall blue screen, hardly distinguishable from the clouds, denoted the valley wall of the Rio Doce. In front surged the lumpy Serra de Ouro Preto, with a red road seaming, like a ribbon, its slopes of green.

From that point all was descent. The path became worse, and the half-devoured remnants of a cow lying across the line did not speak well for the new mines. Down the ruddy slope we fell into a country of Cánga and Jacutinga, like that of Gongo Soco. By degrees, the Morro de Santa Anna settlement, better known as the " D. Pedro Norte del Rey," a complicated absurdity, opened out before us. The site is a bleak and treeless hill-side, fronting east, " rugged as cliffs on the seashore," with its tall, naked face burrowed for gold ; an ugly contrast to the picturesque approach that characterises Morro Velho. On the upper level appears, *en profile*, the chapel, a white box, surrounded by the dull clay huts of the native workmen. Below it are the hospital, the houses of the officers, the white quarters of the English miners, the Casa Grande, large, neat, and well situated, and the " blacks' kitchen," a tall, white tenement, bald and bare. The latter surmounts a dwarf eminence rising from the valley sole, the " Córrego da

---

* The only complaint was that it wanted a certain aroma. This arose from its being too new. Moreover the specimens were so scanty that they could not be submitted to sufficient test. The principal tea grower of the Province is now the Senator Teixeira de Souza of Ouro Preto, the owner of Bom Retiro, or Fazenda do Tesoureiro.

† From Camargos to Marianna there is an older road, lying east of the line by which we travelled.

Canella," upon whose bottom land are the shops, smithy, carpentry, stamps, and other furniture. Here, too, were extensive washings made in the olden day.

Fortunately I had sent on Miguel with our introductory letter. The trooper met us before we reached the house, and now we learned for the first time that Mrs. Thomas Treloar, the Superintendent's wife, was not expected to live. She had passed thirty-three years in the Brazil, and had intended returning to an English home in June last. The "six months more" are sometimes as fatal in the Brazil as in Hindostan.

We retired from a sun " enough to roast a Guinea man," to the Venda, wretched as an inn in Styria, and considered the case. Dr. George Mockett, for whom also we had letters, was in attendance upon Mrs. Treloar; and her son-in-law, Mr. Francis S. Symons, Manager of the Passagem Mine, was momentarily expected. Nothing remained but to ride on two miles, and trust to the tender mercies of a Marianna hostelry.

We forded the Córrego da Canella twice, and passed over sundry hill-spurs. Here the houses thicken to a suburb, every second "ranch" shows stakes for tethering mules, and saddle-making is added to horse-shoeing. We remark that the whole road no longer presents the gloomy picture of ruins and deserted villages traced by Dr. Couto in 1801. But in those days, the mining population, mostly coloured, lingered about their exhausted diggings; now they have applied to other work. Everywhere we saw bullocks' hides stretched out in the usual Brazilian fashion upon a frame-work of sticks, the ground being too damp to permit pegging them down; thus they obtain the benefit of sun and wind, and they can easily be moved out of the rain. The skins, which in the dry season, after a few days' exposure, become hard and board-like, are used to cover mule loads by day, and to act couch at night: in the wilder parts they are the bed, sofa, and mattress, and in stools and settles they supplant the rattan.

Then we forded the "Ribeirão do Carmo,"* which divides the city proper from a large suburb, the "Bairro de Monsús:" higher up the stream there is a wooden bridge on stone piers,

---

* This is the River of Marianna, now popularly known as the "Rio Vermelho." We shall ascend its valley during the next two marches.

used during the rains. From this point is the prettiest view of the ecclesiastical capital, which reminded me of picturesque old Coimbra. The houses, here white, there red, pink and yellow, rise in steps from the right bank of the rivulet, which the poets have compared with the Mondego,* and appear based upon and mingled with rich green lines and clumps of the domed Jaboticabeira, palms, plantains, oranges, and bright-flowering shrubs.

Ascending a ramp, we left on the right the Ribeirão do Cattéte : gardens now bloom in its bed, but a long stone bridge proved that it has not always been dry. A vilely-paved street led us north-east to the Largo da Cadea, in whose centre still stands the pillory of colonial days, the first which I have seen in the Brazil. It shows the holes by which criminals were tied up, and it is surmounted by globe and crown, sword and scales, and the iron hooks to which limbs were suspended. The jail, also guild-hall, is a quaint, squat, old-fashioned building, with a complicated entrance curiously painted, and a few black soldiers were on guard. Fronting it is the Church of S. Francisco, tawdry in exterior : it is the temporary "Sé," the Cathedral being under repair. To its right is the Nª Sª do Carmo, with the usual round-square or pepper-caster towers.

Evidently we are in a city which is clerical and not commercial : the dulness is that of cathedral towns generally, from Itú in S. Paulo to Durham and Canterbury before the age of railways. "Formigões"—big black ants—as the black soutane'd students are called in waggishness, stroll through the thoroughfares, and loll listless about the shops. The store-keeper leans with elbows upon his counter, and stares vacantly at the street, or muses and smokes cigarettes in concert with a friend or friends, seated upon stools nearer the door. Negro urchins squat

---

* Claudio Manuel da Costa, of whom more hereafter, wrote a poem upon the Ribeirão do Carmo. When Apollo had stolen the nymph Eulina, this amorous drain cursed the god : the latter, in revenge, taught men to wound the bank for gold and precious stones, and to stain the crystal current with blood. At length, the Ribeirão, mad with despair, rushed down a rock and was dashed to pieces.

Dr. Henrique Cezar Muzzio, Chief Secre-

tary to the Presidency of Minas, and afterwards of São Paulo, has presented the original of this poem, "Villa Rica," to H. I. Majesty. Dr. Claudio died unmarried, but he left nieces : the latter attempted, when the Brazil became an Empire, to establish their rights, and applied to the usual officer, the "Procurador dos feitos da fazenda." Unhappily the papers had disappeared, and the cause was lost.

upon the steps, or try conclusions with vagrant pigs and dogs, which are apparently the main items of population : one of the creatures, who certainly had not heard of Joan Darc, bawled out " Godam," as we rode by.   Old black women hobbled about picking up rags and compost; and we remarked sundry white men going barefooted—a very unusual spectacle in the Brazil. Here and there a profusion of straight, glossy and well-greased hair, with a bright red blossom on the left side of the head,* and a face of very mixed blood, engaged in the " serious study of street scenery," inform the practised eye that, as might be expected where young men are "reading for the Church," Anonyma is as well known as to those who " live at Gondar."

Descending into the Largo da Praça, a grassy square, sloping eastward, we came upon the Hotel Mariannense, the best of the three inns.   The host, Sr. Antonio Ferreira, who complicates the Boniface with the Figaro—the reception room was in fact a barber's shop—began by charging us heavily for pasture and maize.   But we are now on the high road, where the leagues become better because shorter,† and the prices worse, because longer.   We ended with a bill which would have done honour to the Hôtel des Ambassadeurs, St. Petersburg.

The establishment was the typical estalagem or country inn of the old Brazil.   From the barber's room ran a long corridor to the back of the house, and it was so badly boarded that one risked falling through.   The bed chambers, with walls bare of everything but dirt, showed plank couches, a chair, and some-times a table.   The passage leads to the dining-room, distin-guished only by an armoire, whose glass front exposes spare china, cruets, condiments, a few bottles, and pots of provision. The normal " punch-bath " will not be ready for half an hour, the dinner for two hours : time is not worth a thought here, and regularity is next to impossible.   The negroes and negresses prefer staring, whispering, and giggling, to work, however light : there is never less than one screaming child to make night horrid ; and generally there are two fierce dogs that bark and bay responsively at the shadow of an opportunity.   The feeding

---

* The married wear the flower on the right side of the head.
† Here the league may be assumed at three geographical miles : as a rule, the further it is from the capital, the longer it waxes.

is that of the " venda;" there are " Irish potatoes," the " famine root," because we are in a city; and the lights are not lamps of Ricinus oil, but composition candles, for which we shall have to suffer in the purse.

And yet, to these three wretched inns there are nine churches!

CHAPTER XXXIII.

AT MARIANNA.

"La race Portugaise s'est emparée en Amerique de la contrée la plus admirable du monde, et que la Nature semble avoir pris plaisir à combler de tous ses bienfaits."— *Castelnau* (*Expédition*, iii. chap. 33).

In 1699, when João Lopes de Lima, a Paulista explorer, discovered gold in the "Rio Vermelho," which we have just forded, the miners built the "Arraial do Carmo." This became, in April 8, 1711, the "Villa de Albuquerque," under the Governor of that name, and in the same year it was changed to "Leal Villa de Nª Sª do Carmo." Public documents* granted precedence in all processions and public "Acts" to its Camara, as the senior Ædility in the Province. A royal letter from D. João V. (April 23, 1745) raised it to the rank of "Cidade Marianna," or "Marianopolis," so christened after the Austrian princess that sat upon the throne of Portugal. In 1750 the Quint alone exceeded 100 arrobas of gold per annum. This in 1799 fell to a little more than one-third.† But, as Dr. Couto remarks, the mitre then proved the best mine.

The finest view of the ecclesiastical city is from the southern rim of the basin, where the Church of São Pedro is being—or rather is not being—built. The plan shows some attempt at art, unlike the others which have grown out of being barns without acquiring the dignity of temples. It has two unequal bays, and attached to the southern, or greater, is a rectangular sanctuary. The clocherium, also composed of sandstone grit, resting upon solid foundations, awaits completion. The two bells are slung to the normal gallows outside, and there are graves which bother with their suggestive "Il faut mourir" those who are here for enjoyment. The façade bears the keys and episcopal hat and mitre.

* Dated July 17, 1723, and Feb. 21, 1729.

† More exactly 38 arrobas, 12 marcos, and 6 ounces.

The pilasters end barbarously in scrolls over the main entrance, and the side windows are not on the same plane. The body is partially covered with a zinc roof, which occasionally falls in, and the principal inhabitants are taperás—swifts or devilings.

Marianna lies below, couched on the pleasant western slopes, and extending to the sole of the valley, which is drained northwards by the serpentine Rio Vermelho. About the white mass of tenements lie diggings in red ground, and black Jácutinga heaps are the vestiges of its old youth. This basin, situated in a sub-range of the Serra do Itacolumi, which closes it on the south, is 2400 feet above sea-level. It suffers from the neblína, or morning fog, often deepening to a drizzle, but not so bad as that of Ouro Preto ; and it is succeeded by sun which glows in the cloudless sky till evening. It is reported that during the rains its bleak cold causes severe catarrhs. This, however, must be taken *cum grano*, as the equatorial clove-tree flourishes in the open air. Eight fountains supply the city with water slightly ferruginous, and where there is scarcity it arises from extensive disforesting.

We were reminded that Marianna is a bishopric* by a prodigious tumult and clatter of Angelas bells and chimes, a tutti of the steeples, on Saturday evening. On the Sunday there was a "Missa de Madrugada," or dawn-mass for the tattered many who did not like to show their rags at a later hour ; and shortly afterwards the Sisters of S. Vincent de Paul, a branch house of the Rue du Bac, set up the usual chaunt. At 8 A.M. there was mass, which began at 7·30 A.M., and thus the stranger was apt to miss it. At 9 A.M. there was high mass at the acting cathedral, and at 10 and 11 A.M. there was high mass in the other churches.

After breakfast we visited the city, which retains the character given to it by Gardner ; it appears almost deserted. The pavement was really bad—good only for the chiropodist. There were a few neat two-storeyed houses, but the greater part was ground-floor, made of scantling and whitewashed adobes, with half-windows, and not a few rotulas or lattices. Some of the fountains were old and quaint, fronted by carved and painted dolphins that contrast curiously with the neat modern castings and statues of the "Atlantic Cities" in the Brazil.

* Sede do Bispado de Minas.

We called upon the Bishop Monsignor Antonio Ferreira Viçoso at the Palace, a large old bungalow, with hat and arms over the door. The venerable ecclesiastic, now aged eighty, was still in feature and pronunciation a Portuguese : his eye was bright and intelligent, and his face calm and intellectual; he was dressed in the pink-red robe, according to the order which prescribes black to the priest, scarlet (typical of shedding his own blood*) to the cardinal, and white to the Pope. He received us most kindly, endured the ring-kissing with much patience, and led the way to a library, mostly theological, and adorned with fancy medallions and portraits of classical philosophers. Mgr. Gaume would have joyed to behold the caricature of poor epicures who committed the one unpardonable sin of declaring that the gods do not trouble themselves with mortal matters, and, therefore, that it is vain to hire for them priestly servants.

The "Reverendissimo" is highly spoken of, and has done much for ecclesiastical education in this and other Provinces. He lectured on philosophy at Evora, and on theology, mathematics, and languages at Angra dos Reis—where he had been a parish priest—at Rio de Janeiro, and at the Caraça. He then became successively Principal at the Seminaries of Angra, the Caraça, and Campo Bello.† He was promoted in January 22, 1844, by Gregory XVI., and was consecrated in the following May by the Bishop of Rio, Chrysopolis, and Pará. He took possession, by proxy, on April 28, 1844, and made his public entrance in early June. He has anointed, in the Cathedral of Marianna, two of his Caraça pupils to the bishoprics of Pará and Ceará, and he has lately visited Diamantina to perform the same office for its diocesan. More than once he has employed six to seven months, even during rainy weather, in inspecting his see, preaching, confessing, and administering chrism. We may safely join in the general prayer, "Deos conserve seus dias ! "

A short account of the Bishop's predecessors may not be uninteresting.‡ At the request of D. João V., Benedict XIV. dismembered the diocese of Marianna from that of Rio de Janeiro

---

* The Cardinalician purple has of late been solicited for the Archbishop of Bahia, the Primate of the Brazil. He will, if the honour be granted, be the first American that ever sat in the Holy College.

† A small place situated between Minas, S. Paulo and Goyaz.

‡ The Almanack for 1865 is answerable for any inaccuracies concerning the "Exms. Bispos de Marianna."

by the bull, "Candor lucis æternæ, Dec. 6, 1741.* The first diocesan was D. Frei Manoel da Cruz, D.C.L. of Coimbra, fourth bishop of Maranham, and friend and coadjutor of the famous—or infamous—P^e Gabriel Malagreda, the "devil's martyr"—"in Portug. pro fide occisus." When nominated, Sept. 15, 1745, D. F. Manoel travelled to Minas overland, in those days a dangerous journey, and rains and sickness occupied him, some say eleven months, others fourteen months and a few days. He finished the Matriz, now the Cathedral; he founded the Seminary, and he laid the first stone of S. Francisco in 1762. Directed to oppose, with "prudence, paternal love, and charity," the disorders of his herd, he was much complained of, but the King continued to repose in him the fullest confidence. He died Jan. 3, 1764, aged seventy-four, and he lies in the middle catacomb within the cathedral choir.

The second was D. Joaquim Borges de Figueirôa," a secular priest, who became Archbishop of Bahia before he reached Marianna. He was followed by D. Frei Bartholomew Manoel Mendes dos Reis, formerly resident bishop of Macáo; he also did not take personal possession, but he assisted in consecrating his successor. Then came three governors, one of whom, Ignacio Corrêa de Sá, the Doctoral Canon of the Cathedral, indited some singular threatening pastorals. "It is in your hands," he declared, "to show that your sins are not the cause of my departure, by hearing the word of God. If ye do so, then if the Lord be not pleased that we depart * * * He will send another to serve him with zeal and charity."

The fourth was D. Frei Domingos da Incarnação Pontével, a Friar-preacher, professor of philosophy and theology, and director of the Third Order of St. Dominic. He was confirmed by Pius VI., and he took charge Feb. 25, 1789. During his day happened the celebrated "Inconfidencia," in which the noblest son of Marianna, Claudio Manuel da Costa, of Paulista family (born 1729, died 1789), sacrificed his life for his native land. His portrait in the Episcopal Palace, Marianna, bears this distich—

> Quid præsul noster ? Nil est nisi pulvis in urnâ,
> Cordibus est nostris vivis et ipse manes.

---

* Pizarro says 1746. He also remarks that the second and the third bishop enjoyed at Lisbon the emoluments of this diocese. This suggests the modern practice of certain colonial episcopi, who have escaped blame when they deserve more of it than the "buccaneer bishops" so severely "banged" of late years.

He was succeeded by D. Frei Cypriano de S. José, a friar minor (Franciscan), of Arrabida, and a literary man. During his rule the Royal family landed in the Brazil. This Bishop died at Marianna, August 14, 1817, and on April 9, 1820, D. Frei José da SS. Trindade, of the Reformed Minors of S. Francisco of Bahia, was consecrated. The independence of the country having been declared, he assisted in the coronation ceremonies of the first Emperor, who, with the Empress D. Amelia, subsequently became his guests. He died in his diocese, September 28, 1835, and he lies in the Cathedral, near the first bishop. The seventh, D. Carlos Pereira Freire de Moura, did not live to take possession. The eighth we have just met.

An ecclesiastic accompanied us from the Palace after the episcopal blessing had been given, to the adjoining Seminary, where we were duly introduced to the Principal, Rev. João Baptista Carnaglioto, of Turin. The staff consists of a Vice-Principal and seven professors, with as many priests. About forty of the 180 pupils are now resident. The long vacation begins in July, and ends with October 1. The course of preparatory studies lasts five years, after which those destined for the church are sent to the Caráça, and the others to the various academies of the Empire, where doctors—in law, mathematics, and medicine—are manufactured by the gross. When first founded, the Seminary was placed under the Jesuit, Pe José Nogueira. It was reorganised by the present Bishop, the rectors being now diocesans of Ceará and Diamantina; and for a few months the director of the collegiate part was D. Pascual Paccini, Professor of Natural History in the Museum of Palermo, sent on a scientific mission to the Brazil. Dr. José Marcellino Roche Cabral, ex-editor of the once famous "Dispertador"—the Awakener—and a well-known writer, who had exchanged political for private life, was also a vice-director. The Most Reverend then divided the pupils into a major and a minor class, and entrusted both to the Fathers of the Mission. Charitable persons have bequeathed negroes and estates to the house, and its finances are managed by administrators under the Superior.

We walked through the establishment, which was remarkable for cleanliness and order; even the kitchen was neat. *Au reste*, there were the usual long double rows of small black iron bedsteads and red blankets, the travelling boxes ranged along the

walls, the long tables down long refectories, and the long scrip-
toria, with endless desks, and the huge, antiquated maps which
are seen in all such places. Upon the old doorway we were
shown the date, MDCCLX.—1760 is a hoar antiquity in this
the youngest of empires.

Lastly, we went to visit the Sisters of S. Vincent de Paul.
In 1749, the good Bishop, who is Superior of the Order in the
Brazil, collected alms, and established them in the city. They
now number fifteen. The house receives from the Government
six contos of reis per annum, and the law compels it to lodge,
board, and instruct forty orphans, duly nominated by the authorities. The reverend mother, elderly and compact, active and
bustling, received us cordially, and, with the rather startling
words, "Allons premièrement visiter le maître de la maison,"
led us to the convent chapel. We then inspected their school of
sixty-six boarders—girls of every age up to twenty, and even
upwards. The pupils pay 180$000 per annum, not including
washing and small extras. No signs of luxury, and few of comfort, appeared; on the other hand, the arrangements were excellent, and nothing could be cleaner. Next we saw the second
class, and the orphanry, numbering sixty-four. These in process
of time will be married to suitable persons, who are expected to
apply officially for wives. Lastly, passing through a good garden,
we visited the hospital patients,* forty-two in number, including
four men and six women—an unusual proportion—insane. They
were employed in making flowers and pillow-lace, of course for
sale; and all flocked up to kiss the Mother Superior's hand
with great show of respect and affection. After buying a few
mementoes, we went our ways.

Many Brazilians send their daughters to these places of instruction because they can get no better; but they do not like the
old monastic system, roughly adapted to modern days. They
fear to see their daughters buried alive "for the greater glory of
God, and of the Ladies of the Holy Heart." They openly exclaim against the system of espionage practised in these places,
and they have other objections which cannot with decency be
specified. As a rule, even in Europe, and in England especially,

---

* The usual number in hospital is thirty
to forty per annum. Many, however,
enter when past hope. In 1865-6 the
infirmary received forty sick, of whom
seventeen improved, thirteen died, and
the rest were cured.

the teaching of religious houses is fifty years behind the world. After a course of six to eight years' study, the girl " comes out " in a peculiar state of ignorance, and supplied with certain remarkable superstitions and ascetic ideas,* such as dislike to society, aspirations to the life of a religious, which in a young country like the Brazil cannot be too strongly deprecated, and an *engouement* for penance and mortification which everywhere should be obsolete. Of this house it is said that an orphan girl, one of the pupils, when called upon to sign her name could not write. The assertion found its way into an official paper, and opened the eyes of the public. For my part, I believe the place of these excellent women to be in the hospital, or by the sick bedside, where their heroism and devotion deserve the highest respect. Instruction is not their *forte*, and yet they vehemently desire it, because thus they can best mould the minds of the rising generation.

* I could name a house of education, a " convent-school," not far from London, where in the nineteenth century children learn that on Christmas Eve all animals kneel down and pray ; that thunder is the voice of the Deity—the merest fetishism ; and that opiates must not be given to a dying person, whose " agony " is the last temptation to voluptuousness, or the final chance of penitence—three specimens out of three hundred ! My experience is that in matters of pure faith or belief—that is to say, taking statements on trust—all nations are as nearly equal as their development of imagination, of the marvellous, permits them to be. Amongst the most civilised peoples in Europe it is right easy to point out tenets which, submitted to the eye of reason, appear identical with those held by the savages of the Bonny River.

CHAPTER XXXIV.

Quand ploon per San Médar
Ploon quarante ghiours pus tard.—(*Old Proverb.*)

St. Médard had been rainy, and so was St. Swithin. One
does not expect the weather-saints, be they SS. Bibbiana,
Mamert, Pancrase, or Servais, to serve alike for both hemi-
spheres. On the Saxon's fête we were visited by Mr. F. S.
Symons, who, despite his domestic troubles, hospitably insisted
upon our taking possession of his then empty house at Passagem.
We left Marianna that same morning, ascended the hill on which
St. Peter stands, and fell into the eastern slope upon a good
road, lately repaired by the Provincial Government. The
country has that monotonous beauty, primitive and savage, as
Atala or Iracema, of which our eyes are now wearying.
Our admiration of the inanimate is being fast exhausted; the
wildly beautiful, the magnificence of virgin forest, the uniform
grace of second growth, begins to pall upon us; we are tired of
grand mountain, picturesque hill, and even of softly undulated
prairie. The truth is, we want humanity; we want a little
ugliness, to speak plain English, by way of relief. Anthropos
and his works are to the land he holds, what life is to the body;
without them Nature lies a corpse or in a swoon. It is not
only the "inconstancy of man" that made Castelnau, in all
this splendid scenery, look forward to the icy tempests of the
Andes and to the shuddering caused by gulfs and arid deserts,
and by precipices fit only for the condor. I cannot but hold
that green is the most monotonous of colours, and that in a
warm, damp climate its effect is a peculiar depression. In the
desert of rock and clay there is a vitality and a vivacity of brain
which we never experience in India or in Zanzibar.

Presently we passed a neat building, the Mine Hospital.

After a couple of short miles, we turned to the left and entered the grounds of the Casa Grande. This bungalow formerly belonged to a proprietor and shareholder in the Passagem diggings. From afar it looks well, but a nearer inspection shows that it is roughly put together. A fine head of water pours from the bluff in front, and beyond it is shown a gap, a kind of brêche de Roland, where, in 1699, the two Paulista exploring parties, headed by Manoel Garcia, who discovered gold in a branch of the Ribeirão do Campo, and João Lopez de Lima, the founder of Marianna, unexpectedly met.

We spent three days at the head-quarters of the "Anglo-Brazilian Gold Mining Company (Limited)." Mr. Symons rode over from the Morro de Santa Anna as often as possible, and we had every reason to be grateful for the proverbial hospitality of the Cornu-Briton. Our first visit was to the "D. Pedro Norte Del Rey," by the road now familiar to us, and up the Valley of the Córrego da Canella, towards which the Morro de Santa Anna and the Morro de Maquiné both slope. The former is no longer worked; the free gold in quartz and the auriferous pyrites did not pay. The ground, however, is a burrow of shafts and levels, rendering it dangerous to stray from the path. The face of the mountain is covered with a layer of "cánga" some four feet thick; but the containing rock of the quartz is iron mica slate. We therefore proceeded to the latter, where the launders were flowing and the wheels were creaking merrily in the forest that gloomed high above us. The Buraco de Maquiné is the centre of three well-known old diggings; to its west is the Buraco do Tambor; eastward, the Matador,* and on the west the Mato das Cobras. Around it is a mass of mines—Bawden's, Cornelius' (new ground), Benicio's, Honorio's, Branco's, and the Minas de Sociedade, a very old digging.

The Maquiné hollow, which lies in a spur of the main hill to the north of the Morro de Santa Anna, is drained by a stream which falls into the Córrego da Canella. The gully shows in the same range six distinct deposits of Jacutinga, iron, mica,

---

* The Matador property has been worked by the ancients; now it belongs to the Company, and in due time will receive attention. A cross-cut was driven into the section called the Tambor; Jacutinga was found, but it proved to be unauriferous.

clay slate, decomposed quartz and gold ; the lode runs east to west, the dip is to the east,* and the underlay is northerly. Between the beds are layers of capa, or hard iron slate, dipping 5° to 6°. Number four gully is the highest part where exploration had begun ; number three, just below it, had been found "alive" with traces of gold, and number two (or the third from the top) varying in size from six inches to ten feet, is that which, after patient and persevering labour, has yielded such rich returns.

We rode up the hill accompanied by Mr. McRogers, the head mining captain, and saw the low ground to which the three deep adits will run. Mr. Thomas Treloar has taken due warning from his old place of employment, Gongo Soco. We were joined at the mouth of the mine by Mr. Hosken, another captain ; it is here the rule that one man must not enter. Jácutinga† gold is free, and, unlike the pyritic, requires every precaution against exposure ; in this matter it is as dangerous as the diamond, and, despite all carefulness, the negro will certainly find means of picking and stealing.

We entered No. 3 (from the top), or Hilcke's tram-level, the principal of the six which have been acquired by purchase or concession. The general direction was with the dip north 51° east, and four shoots or lines of gold have been found in it. The interior was literally walled with wood, cap pieces, and legs, with lathing of whole or split candeia trunks, and sometimes coarse planking to prevent the sides coming to. The sets of timbering were nowhere more than six feet apart. In the main levels, or arteries, first-class wood is used ; ordinary timber suffices for the stopes, and when the lode has been taken out the walls are allowed to come together. Under guidance of the captain we visited the cross-cuts driven northerly to communicate with the lode, side passages, and minor levels, which should be level, but which are distinctly the reverse. When lode is encountered, these are extended in its course, and are used for tramming out broken ore. Several levels have been driven and abandoned, as the workings penetrated below them. The prin-

---

* The easterly dip of the line of gold averages from 20° to 26°. One of the lines has been worked on 150 fathoms from outcrop.

† The Jacutinga is soft, and consists mainly of micaceous iron, friable quartz, sand, and clay, in a containing rock of slaty iron ore.

cipal are at present "Hilcke's" and "Alice's," intersecting the
lode, the former at 47, the latter at 128 fathoms. As a rule,
the walking was easy and even pleasant; the mine was exceptionally dry, and no hanging wall took away from the sense of
security. I noticed but a single blower—a crack in the side
which emitted gas; we tried to ignite it, but could not, and in
one place only the lights burned dim and blue. This speaks
well for the ventilation of the drivings. "Rises," or communications from one level to another, are made for shooting down
the ore broken in stope, and for convenience of breathing.
Air shafts are especially necessary in Jacutinga, the worst of
minerals for heat, which becomes intolerable. In some parts
the impure damp has extinguished the lamps and driven away
the miners; but this is rare.

After leaving the souterrain we saw some of the rich stuff
washed by women, labelled, locked up in safes, and sent down
to the lower stamps. Lately (1867) a nugget has been found
containing 512 oitavas of pure gold, and measuring eighteen by
eight inches. The common vein yields ten oitavas per ton, and
about 1800 tons are worked per month. Rich ore gives 800
oitavas (eight pounds, four ounces, Troy) per ton; twelve boxes,
or half a ton, have produced 1900 oitavas, and 700 pounds have
given eleven Brazilian pounds weight of gold. This is magnificent. But lines of gold in the fickle Jacutinga, reach fissures,
and frequently disappear. We carried off, by way of mementos,
small but very beautiful specimens of nuggets—*not* to the detri-
ment of the shareholders.

Remounting our mules, we passed a new building, the future
"changing barracks," where garments which may contain gold
will be deposited. After visiting the twelve head of upper stamps
where the rough Jacutinga is crushed and straked, we descended
to the lower stamp-house, where the rich ore is worked. When
pulverised, it is placed in a tacho, or long copper vessel, and
washed once more. Finally, it is taken up to the Casa Grande,
and packed up for travel.

An extraordinary meeting of the proprietors of this Company,
held July 23, 1862, sanctioned the purchase of the Morro de
Santa Anna, and sent out Mr. Thomas Treloar. The latter was
directed to place himself in communication with the agents,
Messrs. Moore & Co., of Rio de Janeiro, and the works began

in 1863.* Santa Anna proved a failure, the quartz being poor
and uncertain. The Superintendent had reported, "on the
Maquiné side we have more territorial than mining extent," but
the reverse was the case. An experienced miner had undertaken
to raise from the despised hollow 2000 oitavas per day, and was
offered a handsome sum in case of success, with the annexed
condition, "no gold, no remuneration." There were many
reports about the riches here buried. Tradition declares that
a Portuguese took out large quantities and went home, intending
to work the diggings on his return, which death prevented. It
is said that the "old men" found near the foot of the wooded
gap, sixty-four oitavas of gold after a burst of water, which
drained off into the Córrego. Thus guided, and directed, moreover, by his long experience, Mr. Treloar panned up the stream
and struck the lode. Maquiné was an afterthought; but the
energy and perseverance which conquered it deserve every credit.
It now employs 350 hands, white and black, and it is one of the
only two successes which can be claimed by English mining in
the Brazil.

According to Mr. Treloar's reports the Morro de Santa Anna
was so valuable that in 1762 the Government honoured it with
an especial law. By paying to the Treasury five per cent. of gold
extracted, any subject of Portugal could open a cross-cut to the
lode, and claim the surface ground for twenty-five palms, instead
of receiving it by the "data," which was about ninety fathoms.
Thus the mountain became the property of hundreds of people.
Santa Anna became as populous as Marianna; extensive diggings
were ignorantly driven; ventilation was neglected; hand labour
in a pilão, or mortar, was the only treatment known. The yield
fell off, and presently the major part became the property of a
few, from whom the Company bought it. The Buraco de
Maquiné also had a number of owners till it fell into the hands
of a certain Padre Píres.

We also visited the Passagem mining property, which lies on
the right of the high road to Ouro Preto. The site is a narrow
river valley, surrounded by low rolling hills and tall heights;
it is drained by the Marianna River, a mountain-torrent here,

---

* It began with 230 workmen, viz.,
12 Europeans, 65 free Brazilians, 123
negroes, and 30 negresses. In 1867 the
profits of the Company amounted to
£51,944 (at the average exchange).

flowing north-east, under high precipitous banks. This auriferous rock formation has been worked for nearly a century.
Caldcleugh described it in 1826. He found botryoidal manganese, with octahedral crystals of magnetic iron, in a ferro-
micaceous rock;* the metalliferous veins, which varied from six
inches to three feet in thickness, were of schorly quartz, arseni-
ate of cobalt, and pyrites, iron and arsenical, the latter called
by the miner "lead." The lower strata were dark mica-slate,
which higher up changes colour and blends with the simple
quartz rock. Under Baron von Eschwege the Company had a
capital of 20,000 crusados, and employed three overseers and
thirty-eight negroes; of course it hardly paid its expenses.
The rich stuff was carried in bowls to a mill of nine head of
stamps, and the coarser powder was subsequently levigated
between two horizontal iron plates worked by water—a more
scientific process, by-the-bye, than the present. Passages 100
feet long had been chiselled and blasted into the mica-slate; the
cog-pumps, however, could not unwater them. Capt. Penna,
the then Superintendent, proposed to drain the mine by a deep
adit, through which the stone could be hauled out; this was left
for the present Company to accomplish. In 1840 Gardner tells
us that the Arraial de Passagem had been built by gold
washings which the people had abandoned for growing provisions
to supply the capital. Since that time the property has belonged
to a score of men. A company, whose brain was the Commendador Paula Santos, worked the "Fundão" ground, and
sank, but to little purpose, the Vieira and the Rasgão adits.

The "Anglo-Brazilian Gold-Mining Company (Limited)"
began in January, 1865, with a capital of £100,000, half paid up,
and the shares are now at three-eighths premium, a favourable
sign. I have seen the Third Report of March 31, 1866, and
find it very satisfactory, promising a brilliant future. The works
are only beginning; everything is on a small scale, and the
speculation does not pay a dividend. But it is a "likely" affair,
which may still do great things, and I have no hesitation in
considering it even now a half success.

We put ourselves under the charge of Mr. Martin, head

---

* About Marianna the true Itacolumite
often passes into mica schist, and the
"phyllas satiné" contains garnet. There
is also a quantity of the curious flexible
stone erroneously called Itacolumite.

mining captain, who first showed us the plan. There is a large extent of mineral ground. All the diggings are on the right bank of the streamlet, which rises eighteen feet during the rains. The southernmost is the Fundão, whose surface is a swamp which swells to a lakelet in the lowest part of the riverine valley; it was once reported to be the richest, and is approached by "Foster's Shaft." Follow the Mineralogico and the Paredão grounds, each containing its mine, and to the north-east, or down stream, no limit has been assigned to the lode. The main lode can be traced, and has been wrought for miles in length.

Habited in correct "underground" costume, and each with lantern and stick, we entered the main or "Dawson's Shaft," or rather inclined plane, leading to the Mina Grande, which has three others for the extraction of stone—"Haymen's," Hanson's, and Foster's. Northward are in succession the Mina do Buraco Seco, the Mina do Barril, with the Barril adit, and the Mina do Congo. A transverse section through the deep adit shows a surface of humus and Jacutinga based on clay and iron-stone. The lode underlies the reddish and ferruginous mica-slate; the footwall is talcose slate, sandstone, and "killas," of blue and ruddy rock, whose quartz, here soft, there hard,* is at times interjected between the lodes. The dip of the vein is south-east 17° 30', and often shallower (15°), and the lodes run about north-east and south-west. The head-wall of the main lode (iron mica-slate) had been reached by old workings, some of which are still drowned out; a large accumulation of mud, crushed ground, and foreign matter, had to be cleared away. Thus the system of opening out the mines has been hitherto confined to sinking shafts on the footwall through the crushed workings of the former proprietors in order to encounter the lode. A large amount of the usual dead, unproductive matter has been got out. The lode and lodey stuff are said to be thirty-five feet thick,—namely, sixteen feet of main vein; a footwall of killas four feet "between the 'air and the 'oaf;'" and lastly, fifteen feet of canôa, short or rich body. The "pay dirt" gives per ton three to four oitavas of 23-carat gold, worth £3 12s. per ounce.

We found the eighty-three fathoms of tunnel steep and dark, but

---

* Locally called Congelada, that is to say, quartz, felspar, and other hard rock.

dry and comfortable; it was well timbered with beams and candeia trunks wherever the ceiling required propping. At length we reached a vaulted cavern, thirty-five fathoms of perpendicular depth. It was lit up with torches, and the miners—all slaves, directed by white overseers—streamed with perspiration, and merrily sang their wild song and chorus, keeping time with the strokes of hammer and drill. The heavy gloom, the fitful glare of the lights, the want of air, the peculiar sulphurous odour, and the savage chaunt, with the wall hanging like the stone of Sisyphus or the sword of Damocles, suggested a sort of material Swedenborgian hell, and accordingly the negret Chico faltered out when asked his opinion, " Parece O inferno!"

We then went down to the " deep adit," fourteen feet below the canôa, or rich lode, and driven to the right bank of the rivulet. The stone is trammed to the mouth, and hauled out; thence an inclined plane of wood, which runs up the nearly perpendicular ascent, and a whim conveys it to the stamp-houses. The matrix is evidently auriferous arsenical pyrites, much resembling that of Morro Velho; gold is rarely seen in the quartz, and sometimes "black Cáco" is found. The good picked stone is in the proportion of sixty per cent. Nineteen Europeans, including the Superintendent,* compose the white force; the others may be 380—400, men and women. The recruiting for the Paraguayan war, so near the capital, has greatly interfered with the supply of timber as well as hands. About fifty men work underground at once; each has a task of four palms or six palms, with extra pay for overtime, and the bore raises half a ton per diem, or a daily total of sixty to seventy tons. The stone raised varies from 1600 to 1800 tons per day, and the produce is from 3000 tons upwards.

When we were to grass we touched our pipes and examined the upper works. There were two hauling whims with mule-races, serving the four inclined planes which ran from the bottom of the mine to the spalling floors. There were forty-two head of stamps, of which thirty are new; they are divided into upper and lower, and the stuff is carried to them in platters on women's heads; after the third crushing the slime is allowed to run off. The arrastres and amalgamation have not yet been introduced. The

---

* Mr. Furst, an officer in the employment [of the Company, had lately died of typhus; the body became, it was said, "yellow as a guinea."

stamped sand, when fine enough, is washed in the batêa, and the gold is stored in locked-up troughs. The coarser stuff, before being replaced in the upper stamps, is levigated on sloping slabs in the "wash-house."

Very comfortable and pleasant was that Casa Grande, with its piano and plenty of books, not to speak of Bass and sherry. We had taken leave, and the mules stood saddled at the door, when Mr. Symons made up and asked me to read the burial service over his mother-in-law. At 3 P.M. we collected near the little ruined chapel that overlooks the narrow Valley of the Rio Vermelho. After not hearing for many years the " order " of the Church of England, I was struck by the coldness and deadness of the rite, the absence of consolation to the living, and the want of comfort to the dead, if "spiritists" speak the truth. And what is there appropriate in the "Lesson taken out of the fifteenth chapter of the former Epistle of St. Paul to the Corinthians," with its argu-mentative tone and its unintelligible allusion to being " baptized for the dead ? "* How far better is the short " office " used in the older western section of Christianity. The Cornishmen seemed resolved to add a little life to the ceremony. · When the reading was concluded they sang in a nasal tone a lengthy hymn, which gave them, I presume, some spiritual refreshment.

It was late in the afternoon when we set out for Ouro Preto, distant a short league. The whole length is more or less inhabited. So we read in 1801 that it was populous with little settlements and miners' huts built on heights near water. The line was then a fine calçada with an avenue of trees, which were, however, beginning to fail. Now it has changed for the worse ; it runs upon a kind of ledge. To the right is a confusion of red clay hills, covered with scrubby vegetation ; on the left, deep and in-visible in its rocky bed, flows the Rio Vermelho or Marianna

* Paul, 1 Corinthians, xv. 29. Amongst the Marcionites (A.D. 150), who were partly Manicheans, the rite was literally performed. When a man died, one of the sect sat in his coffin, and was asked by another whether he were willing to be baptised, and, consenting, he was baptised. The Cataphrygians, who followed the wild Montanus (A.D. 170) also baptised their dead ; and vainly the orthodox contended that the act was foolish and useless, since if it were valid a person might be baptised for a Jew or a Greek, and effect his con-version without the will of the recipient. Of modern days the practice has under-gone revival. See the " Book of Doc-trines and Covenants (of the Church of Jesus Christ of Latter-Day Saints ; selected from the Revelations of God. By Joseph Smith, President)" under the heads " Bap-tism for the Dead, acceptable only in the Temple ;" "Baptism for the Dead, the Nature of." I have also alluded to the rite in the " City of the Saints," chap. ix. p. 471.

River. The line is a gentle and regular ascent of red sand and
black earth, now muddy, then dusty. Scales of ferro-micaceous
slate glitter like powdered silver, and here they say occur scatters
of pale blue cyanite. The general direction is west, with a little
southing.*

We found Passagem, where several of the English miners lodge,
a little village with a certain air of neatness. A compatriot, who
from a labouring man had become a capitalist, here has a large
house. We had lived within a stone's throw of him during three
days. When we met, he invited us to become his guests, but he
had not energy enough to call. In three weeks, perhaps, he might
have succeeded. It is said that the first words learned by the
stranger in the Brazil are, " paciencia," " espere um pouco,"
and " amanhãa "—Patience, wait a wee, to-morrow. I may add
that some foreigners learn the lesson better than their teachers.
Men who live too long in the Tropics often fall into a nervous,
solitary habit of life ; in fact, the difficulty is not to do it.
Sr. Domingo Martens, of Whydah, left valuable silver plate lying
for years on the beach, because he would not or could not order
a guard of his army of slaves to bring up the boxes. I know a
traveller who spent three years in Inner Africa, always wishing
and intending to leave it, but lacking energy to give the word.
My excellent friend, Lieut.-Col. Hamerton, of Zanzibar, resolved
every night to pack up next morning, till, not being able to make
such exertion, he died.

About half-way we sighted a tall white fane, the Igreja do Alto
da Cruz, which in the gloaming looked like a Frankenstein, frightful
and gigantic, flat on its back, with its two legs *en l'air*. Another
mile showed on the right the Chafariz de Agua Ferrea, whose old
front and long inscription testified to the virtues of its chalybeate.
Near the entrance the road had been cut out of the solid rock ;
on the right, or northern side, was a quarry of white freestone
large enough to supply the Province, and tunnelled with long-
abandoned gold works, now used by the poor as pig-styes ; to the
left a parapet defended wayfarers from falling into the great dark
gully which, running west to east, drains the two parallel lines,
the southern Serra de Itacolumi and its opposite neighbour, the

---

* Burmeister's map makes Marianna
due east of Ouro Preto, which it is not.
In the last edition of Mr. A. Keith Johnston (Stanford, Charing Cross) Marianna is
placed south-south-east of Ouro Preto,
which is worse.

Serra de Ouro Preto. Both had been bored and excavated, riddled and honey-combed for veins and nests of auriferous quartz.

The situation of Ouro Preto, whose " ill-omened and ill-applied name " is pathetically noticed by Mr. Walsh, struck me at once as unlike any capital that I had yet seen.* We are accustomed to find race symbols and national character thoroughly developed in the political and administrative centre called a metropolis, and here we shall see that the old Villa Rica is not the less suggestive than Washington of the magnificent distances. It is nothing but a great village, a kind of " Aldeota," a single street built after the fashion of Minas along the highway, and near the water required for gold washing. Thus it resembles a provincial town, and there are many in Minas which equal it in population and exceed it in importance. Hence, also, life in these country settlements is a something

> * * * Duller than the fat weed
> That rots itself in ease on Lethe wharf.

The want of level ground causes the white houses that cluster on the rocks, whose salient angles face the torrent, to creep up and down the minor ridges which run perpendicularly from the main range, and to stand on steps cut out of the hill-sides. Here they lie scattered over the heights, there they disappear in the shades below us. The prospect wants all the grace and grandeur of a city. Yet it is singular, it is full of " surprises," and it is, to a certain extent, romantic and picturesque, thoroughly Mineiro.

We and our " following " found shelter at the house of the Commendador Paula Santos, Hospitaller or Receiver-general of the English at Ouro Preto, as was José Peixoto de Souza in the last generation. He was then at Rio de Janeiro, but his brother, Dr. José Marçal dos Santos, did the honours of the Golden City.

---

* Provincial capitals in the Brazil average 20,000 souls; some of them, Aracajú and Maceió for instance, much less; others, as Pernambuco and Bahia, much more.

CHAPTER XXXV.

VILLA RICA, NOW OURO PRETO (WEST END).

Difficiles terræ, collesque maligni.—Georgics.

THE following topographical description of the city was published in the "Annaes de Medicina" of 1848, by one of the illustrious "sons" of Ouro Preto, Dr. Eugenio Celso Nogueira. It is only fair to let him describe his home :—

"The capital of Minas is situated on the Serra de Ouro Preto, S. lat. 24° 24′ 6″, and W. long. (from the Sugarloaf of Rio de Janeiro) 0° 16′ 51″. Four hills, offsets from the same chain, form the base, and the irregularity of the site makes an exact description of the city a difficult task. Of the hills, some advance, others retire, leaving between them deep gorges. Those which are too steep for building purposes are covered with a poor vegetation, and are irregular with orifices due to time or to man's toil. The houses are built in unequal groups, rarely occupying the same plane ; hence the irregularity, which extends even to the street levels. Mostly they have an upper story, except in the suburbs, where the ground floor is the rule. In the city almost all can boast of glass windows and ceilings of bamboo-mat ; in the outskirts they are low and mean, some wanting even floors."

"Of the four hills, the most important is that of the Praça, raised 1620 toises* above sea level ; the Bairro of Ouro Preto, the lowest, numbers 1579, and the summit of Itacolumi 1960 toises. The city enjoys few clear and serene days ; throughout the year, especially during the rains, the sky is covered, and the

---

* The toise, I presume, is six French feet=76·755 inches, or 6·3946 feet English. Thus 1620 toises would be=10,362 feet. The Almanack gives 5245 (Lisbon) palms =3758 feet. Caldcleugh places the square (bar. 26·393, and therm. 69° 30′) 3969 feet above sea level. Gerber makes the Palace Court 1145 metres=3747 feet. My instruments (No. 1 and best, B.P. 206°, Temp. 65°, and No. 2, not so good, B.P. 206° 30′, Temp. 62°) range between 3180 and 3373 feet ; of these two I should prefer the latter, and give in round numbers the height of Ouro Preto 3400 feet.

clouds seem to have made their home upon the mountain tops."

This was written in 1843 ; since that time the climate has, they say, improved. But the altitude, the accidents of ground, and the peculiar position, make it subject to extremes of diurnal variation and to great uncertainty. Now it has the sun of Italy, then the fogs of England. The climate is distinctly sub-tropical, and northern races must be acclimatised before they can thrive in it. Yet it is cold; the equatorial fruits are poor; the pine-apple hardly ripens, whilst apples and quinces flourish. The temperature is hottest at 2 P.M., and coldest after midnight; the mean variations are from 58° to 84° F. in the shade ; the latter is rare, but the extremes would, I believe, tell a different tale. Evaporation is excessive, the result of feeble atmospheric pressure,* whilst the neighbourhood of the mountains exposes it to strong aërial currents from the Atlantic ; hence it is one of the dampest places in the Highlands of the Brazil. It is difficult to prevent broadcloth from being mildewed except in air-tight cases. As regards the healthiness of the climate opinions greatly differ. Of two Brazilian friends long resident here, one spoke highly in its favour, declaring that it had no endemic complaint : the other affirmed it to be dangerous, especially at the changes of season in April and November, and at all times fecund in goitres and consumption.

The plan attached to M. Gerber's book will, despite its defects,† enable us to find our way about the city, beginning at our temporary home.

The Commendador's house is buried amongst the hills at the lowest level of the one long street, and in a good central position. To the east is the well-built and parapetted stone bridge, the "Ponte dos Contos," crossing the Córrego of the same name. The rivulet winds from north to south till it joins the main drain, which we hear running below us as if over a dam. The Córrego bed is at this dry season a garden with tufty plots of strawberries and a noble Jaboticabeira myrtle, under which the "ranæ

---

* Dr. Franklin da Silva Massena, the engineer who studied engineering at Rome, calculates the atmospheric pressure on the human body to be 3·76 arrobas (12,032 lbs.) less than upon the seaboard of the Brazil. The annual mean temperature of Ouro Preto is generally laid down at 19°·9 (Cent.).

† The Planta Topographica do Ouro Preto is on too small a scale ; the streets are not named, nor are the hill-lines properly laid down.

palustres" make night vocal. The tenement is neat, with moulded windows and corniced roof, and the balcony is adorned with busts and a noble vine.

Our first walk will be up the Rua de São José, the thoroughfare leading with many a loop and bay, to the west and north-west. The place is classical. Close to our quarters is the small three-windowed house where lodged the unfortunate Alferes of Cavalry,[*] Joaquim José da Silva Xavier, nick-named (por alcunha) "Tira-dentes," or "Draw-teeth." This is not, as I supposed, an equivalent to our "Bell-the-Cat." The patriot was literally an arracheur de dents and a maker of artificial teeth. Several of his relatives are still at Alagôa Dourada, and they preserve his étui, the coarsest possible contrivance. He performed extraction "with subtle lightness," and he taught himself to make artificial teeth. The sight carries us back to the days of a popular movement, of which this great and heroic Province may reasonably be proud, as it led directly to the Independence of the Brazil.

The democratic nature of the outbreak, which the Government called the Conjuração (Conspiracy of Minas), or Levante de Minas (Rising of Minas), and which is now known popularly as the Incon-fidencia or Treason,[†] was evident, and as "sacred" as that of our Great Rebellion. The conspirators, when apprehended, made, it is true, protestations of loyalty, but their designs spoke for themselves. They resolved to proclaim their independence and liberty, and they proposed to abolish the highly obnoxious "Fifths" (Quintos), and other royal extortions; to cancel all Crown debts, to throw open the forbidden Diamantine lands, and to found a university at Villa Rica and a capital at São João d'El-Rei. They had devised a flag and arms, a triangle supposed to represent the Holy Trinity, whose mystery was the chief devotion of Tira-dentes; the motto was to be "Libertas quæ sera tamen,"[‡] and the symbol, an Indian breaking his fetters.

---

[*] Born 1757. Official documents call him ex-Ensign of the paid cavalry troops of the Minas Captaincy. The vulgar suppose that he was "Ensign," or Lieutenant of Artillery. He was captured on May 10, 1789, and placed by orders of the Viceroy in the Ilha das Cobras.

[†] An opprobrious term, adopted as a boast. St. Hil. (I. i. 202) calls it la pré-tendue conspiration, and declares "on ne découvrit aucune preuve." His account of the movement is poorer than Southey's.

[‡] Not a genius, as is popularly said. "Genio" and "Indio" in MS. would be easily confused. The Virgilian motto has fared very badly. Southey gives it "Liber-tas puæ sera tamen"—Senhor Norberto "Libertas quæ sero tamen." Sr. A. D. de Pascual (p. 60) writes "Libertas quæ sera tandem." The latter published in 1868 (Rio de Janeiro, Typ. do Imperial Instituto Artistico), a brochure entitled "Um Epysodio da Historia Patria. As Quattro derradeiras Noites dos Inconfidentes

Evidently the intention of the "Inconfidents" in their "embryonal attempt" was to establish a republic in Minas and the adjoining captaincies. This was in 1788, half a generation after the Boston Port Bill, the Starvation Plan, and the Tea-chests led to the King's war, and brewed a storm which upset and shattered the old colonial system of the world. The great Cromwell had taught the Anglo-Americans, and these in their turn, aided by the Encyclopedists and the "philosophers," had inoculated France with the sublimest ideas of liberty and independence. Hence the spirit of emancipation passed like an electric flash to the Brazil, where the "analogy of situation" was at once recognised. The Empire, I may here say, founded herself, and did not owe her existence, as the superficial remark is, to Napoleon the First. At that time the Governor and Captain-General of Minas Geraes was the Viscount of Barbacena,* and it must be owned that though he was an avaricious, corrupt, and unprincipled man, his vigour and address contrasted favourably with the feeble obstinacy and the failures of Burgoyne and Cornwallis. The circular touching the revenue which he addressed to the several Cámaras quite settled the grievance upon which the conspirators prepared to work. But his superior, the Viceroy of the "State of the Brazil," who succeeded at Rio de Janeiro D. Luiz de Vasconcellos e Souza, was the "stupid and taciturn" D. José de Castro, Count of Resende, the "pest of Portuguese nobility."

The Cabeças or leaders of the patriotic rebellion were thirty-two; such at least is the number sent for trial to Rio de Janeiro. There were not less than 1000 suspected, the flower of the land, clergy (of whom five were found guilty) as well as laity, all friends

---

de Minas Geraes (1792). The four last nights began with Tuesday, April 17, 1792. The author professes to quote from the MS. of a Franciscan Padre of the Santo Antonio Convent, who was sent with ten others on the night of the 18th and those following to console the eleven condemned to death. The Jesuits had introduced the custom of sending a minister of religion to be present whenever a capital sentence was read out, and on their expulsion the office passed to the Franciscans. Sr. Pascual informs the public by an Advertencia that he had purposed originally to write a drama; he has certainly in writing history preserved the dramatic form.

* D. Luiz Antonio de Mendonça Furtado. The name is thus given in MSS.; books usually prefer Furtado de Mendonça. The people believed that he had been sent out to recover arrears of the gold quint, amounting to 22,400 lbs. of gold. In July 11, 1788, he succeeded Luiz da Cunha de Menezes. The latter, who is satirised in the Cartas Chilenas, had some inkling of the republican tendencies then rife in Minas Geraes; but having many friends there, he contented himself, when returning to Portugal, with reporting the affair in a general way; hence dragoons and other troops were sent out to the disaffected colony.

if not relations.* We may imagine the horror-stricken state of the people when the movement failed. The notables were the proto-martyr "Tira-dentes," the arm of the conspiracy; Claudio Manoel da Costa, the brain; the poet, Thomaz Antonio Gonzaga, of whom more presently; and the seven condemned to death. These were, 1. Francisco de Paula Freire de Andrade, of the Bobadella family, Lieutenant-Colonel of the Cavalry Corps (Cavallaria Viva) of Ouro Preto, a man of high position and most interesting character. 2. His brother-in-law, José Alves Maciel, freemason, and first confidant of Tira-dentes, and who had travelled in the United States and in Europe;† his confessor describes him as a St. Paul persuading the others, and a St. Augustine directing to God his true confessions. 3. Ignacio José de Alvarenga Peixoto, ex-Ouvidor of Sabará and Colonel of the First Auxiliary Corps of the Campanha do Rio Verde. 4. The venerable Domingos de Abrêu Vieira,‡ Lieutenant-Colonel of the Auxiliaries of Minas Novas, who had seen his seventieth year. 5 and 6. José de Resende Costa, father and son. 7. Dr. Claudio Manoel da Costa, Crown Procurator and Commentator upon Adam Smith, Commissioner of Customs, and Father of Political Economy. 8. Lieutenant-Colonel (Auxiliary Cavalry) Francisco Antonio de Oliveira Lopes. 9. Luis Vás de Toledo (Piza). 10. Domingos Vidal de Barbosa, doctor or surgeon. 11. Salvador Carvalho Grugel do Amaral; and lastly (12), Tira-dentes. They

* The Almanack (1865, p. 51) gives twenty-four as the number of the Inconfidentes; of these twenty-one were found guilty. M. Ribeyrolles has published the trial in Portuguese and French. Dr. Mello Moraes (Brasil Historico, Rio de Janeiro, Dec. 18, 1864, and succeeding papers) has printed the whole Processo do Tiradentes. The original documents were, it is said, kept for many years sewn up in a leather bag amongst the archives of the Secretary of State for Home Affairs. But I believe this to be a mistake; the Visconde de Barbacena carried off to Europe all the documents which compromised him; many remained even in the Secretariat of Ouro Preto, and not a few have been published.

† There is, I am told, a despatch amongst those written from Paris by Thomas Jefferson to Washington, reporting that he had met at Passy two envoys from the Brazilian colony; of these, it is said, José Alves Maciel was one. According to General J. I. De Abreu e Lima (Compendio da Historia do Brasil, chap. 5, § 6) Maciel was probably the person mentioned by Jefferson when writing from Marseille on May 4, 1787, to "John Jay;" an extract of it is given in the Revista Trimensal do Instituto Historico (vol. iii. p. 209). Varnhagen (ii. 270) mentions the fact of Jefferson meeting at Nismes an ardent young Brazilian, José Joaquim da Maia, whose father was a mason at Rio de Janeiro. J. A. Maciel escaped better than his friends, because he was the son of a Capitão Mor, and was on good terms with the Captain-General.

‡ I am happy here to be able to record an instance of negro affection and gratitude. A slave, of name unknown, belonging to this officer, induced the authorities, by force of petitioning, to grant him permission of accompanying his master to jail and to exile in Africa. Sr. Pascual calls him a "black diamond" and a "faithful, noble, and saintly slave."

met, says their process, at Villa Rica, in the houses of Francisco
de Paula and of Dr. Claudio, and the sentence orders the place of
their "infamous conventicles" to be razed and salted.* They
had, it appears, determined to open the proceedings with the
watchword, "Hoje e o dia do baptizado;" others say "Tal dia
hé o baptizado" (To-day is the day of the baptized), (scil. republic).
Lieutenant-Colonel Andrade was to keep order with his troops,
Alvarenga, Oliveira, and Toledo, with their slaves and partizans,
were to excite the neighbouring towns; whilst Tira-dentes was to
sally forth with vivas for liberty, and to hasten for the Governor's
head to his country house near Cachoeira, where that dignitary
amused himself with farming.† Finally, Portugal was to be
officially informed that Minas Geraes had become an independent
republic.

According to Southey, who, not having heard the other part,
writes with an evident bias towards Portugal, the conspirators
"acted like madmen." Some of them seem to have done their
work in a half-hearted fashion, others to have been far too open
and confident, a few thought that saying was as good as doing,
and many looked upon the attempt as "hypothetic," not holding
the people ripe for liberty. It was, in fact, a "rude tyrocinio;"
on the other hand "it was a great enterprise, and everything
must have a beginning." The poet Gonzaga‡ spoke of Tira-
dentes as a poor devil, fit to become Jove or Neptune as to be the
chief of such a rebellion. One man upon his trial called it a
comedy; the Franciscan chronicler more aptly designated it a
tragedy. Revenge and treachery were rife as in the ranks of
Fenianism. The arch-delator was Colonel (of Auxiliaries) Joaquim
Silverio dos Reis Lairia Genses, one of the conspirators who
reported the plot verbally§ to the Governor. He owed 20,000

---

* The "razing" was not done, as it
was found more profitable to appropriate
the confiscated property. One door and the
little room occupied by Tira-dentes, were
pulled down and have since been destroyed.

† The conspirators declared that they
intended to arrest and deport, not to murder
him. This seems probable; but with such
a tête-montée as Tira-dentes, it is hard to
avoid excess or to foresee what may happen.
In such circumstances men mostly act upon
the instinct that the only way to get rid
of an enemy is to take his life. The Visconde de Barbacena was so unpopular that

when he visited Ouro Preto he was obliged
to take peculiar precautions. A room in
the present palace was divided by him into
eighteen different compartments, and no
one knew where he sat or slept.

‡ Lyras, ii. 38, 7—9. It is generally
believed, however, that Gonzaga applied
the words "pobre, sem respeito e louco"
only to save his friend. The confessor of
Santo Antonio describes him as "enthusiastic as a Quaker, and adventurous as a
Quixote."

§ Authorities are not agreed whether it
was done verbally or in writing.

cruzados to the Treasury, and he hoped by his treachery to obtain a remission of his debt. The documents signed for transmission to the Viceroy bear the names of the Mestre de Campo Ignacio Corrêa Pamplona and Lieutenant-Colonel Basilio de Britto Malheiro. This wretch demanded as the price of blood a pension and decorations. He was praised in the process as a loyal and Catholic vassal, and was left to starve at Pará, where he was driven by public indignation.

The accused were arrested on May 23, 1790, confined separately, and sent in a body to Rio de Janeiro. There they remained imprisoned, curious to relate, in the very same building where some years afterwards some of them took their seats as members of the National Assembly. Their confinement lasted till sentence was pronounced on April 18, 1792. Dr. Claudio Manoel da Costa, the "Amigo Glaucestre" of Gonzaga, was taxed by the Governor with treason, when he replied, alluding to the absorption of Portugal by Spain, "Traitor was your grandfather, who sold his country!" He was removed from the prison to a vaulted closet under the main staircase of the "Casa dos Contos." The permanent guard was changed, and he was murdered by the soldiers.* A report was spread that he hanged himself to a cupboard, after having opened a vein with the buckles of his breeches in order to write with his blood a distich on the wall, for he too was a poet.† The tale that his corpse was exposed on a taller gallows than usual in the Campo de São Domingos is fictitious; it was at once buried in unconsecrated ground, the Garden of the Quartel da Guarnição. But the vicar Vidal of the Menezes family, whose sister was grandmother to the present Senator Teixeira de Souza, of Ouro Preto, disbelieving the report of suicide, exhumed the body, and with the aid of two slaves, Agostinho and another, consigned it to the third catacomb in the High Chapel of the Matriz of Ouro Preto.†

---

* Tia Monica, a *sage femme*, happened to be passing professionally by the house just after the murder, and saw two of the soldiers dragging out the body of D. Claudio, a large-framed man, who was easily recognised. The Bobadella family tried in vain to save him.

† He was devotedly attached to Anacreon and Malherbe (et Rose elle a vecu, etc.) Among the confiscated articles belonging to Gonzaga were copies of these authors, bearing the name of Claudio Manuel. His poetry is well characterised in the Plutarco Brasileiro, i. 225—252. The Holy Office disliked the tone of his prose writings, and allowed few of them to be printed. The distich that showed the ruling passion strong in death never came to light.

‡ A soldier happened to die at the time, and according to some authorities the poet was interred in consecrated ground under the supposition that he was the defunct "praça."

Eleven of the conspirators, Gonzaga included, received sentence of death.   Seven of the ringleaders were condemned to be hanged at the Campo da Lampadosa, to be decapitated and quartered, with exposure of heads; their goods were confiscated, and, after the barbarous fashion of the time, their sons and grandsons were declared infamous.   Four others, Salvador Corneiro do Amaral Gurgel, José de Resende Costa,* father and son, and Dr. Domingos Vidal de Barbosa, were sentenced to hanging on a gallows taller than usual, like their friends, to beheading without exposure, but with loss of goods and attaint of issue.   The decree was read to them on the night of April 19, 1792.   Five were exiled for life to the Presidios or garrisons of Angola, and mulcted of half their property, with threats of death in case of their return.   The rest were temporarily banished, and two false accusers were flogged.   None could complain of their fate.   They knew the law; most of them were officials under government; they had staked their all upon the throw, and they had lost the game.

But it is said that the legal proofs were vile, and consequently that the sentence was iniquitous.   In those days the Viceroy was omnipotent, and the judges also, terrified by the example of France, carried on the proceedings with Draconic severity. Curious to observe, the Jeffries of the trial was the Desembargador Antonio Diniz da Cruz e Sylva, a poet still popular, whose Pindaric odes and heroico-comic piece, "O Hyssope," have become classical.†   But the Queen, D. Maria I., the first crowned head fated to visit the New World, was merciful: she commuted to perpetual banishment all the capital sentences of the Philippine Ordinances, except that of Tira-dentes; and thus of eleven heads only one fell.   Usually it is supposed that he was a mere tool of deeper men, punished in terrorem.   The tradition runs otherwise. He was the very type of Mineiro blood, of sympathetic presence, and sanguine-bilious temperament.   He had studied in the military schools of France,‡ and had there matured the project of a Pan-America by adding Minas to the list of Republics headed by

---

* Proprietor of the Sitio da Varginha, where one of the martyr's arms was put up, a property now belonging to the Dutra family.   His descendants in Africa claimed, on the ground of illegal sentence, its restitution, but did not succeed.

† Ferdinand Denis, ch. xxvi.   The Hyssope has been compared with the Lutrin,

and the poet has been called the Pindar of Portugal.   His assessors on this occasion were Antonio Gomes Ribeiro, the prosecutor, and the chancellor, Sebastião Xavier de Vasconcellos.

‡ The tradition is at fault; he never left the Brazil.

the United States. He died only forty-five years of age, energetic, and very "phrenetic." During the first year after his return home he had ridden five times, not on foot, as the tale is, in the interest of his darling project from Ouro Preto to Rio de Janeiro. At this place he was arrested. Upon his trial, although he left a wife and a little daughter, he had denied nothing; he accused no man; and finally he died, as political martyrs mostly do, like a hero.

The spot chosen for the execution of the Tooth-drawer, whom I can hardly call unfortunate, was then a wild space on the west of Rio de Janeiro, the Campo dos Ciganos, a place where gipsies and newly-imported negroes (negros novos) were buried. Six corps of infantry and two "companies" of cavalry, besides auxiliaries, a large armed force for a city of 50,000 souls, surrounded the scaffold, which stood exactly on the spot where the funeral coaches are now kept for hire. Crowds of people covered the plain, and massed themselves upon the skirts of the Santo Antonio hill. The son of the Count de Rezende (D. Luiz de Castro Benedicto), mounted on a horse shod with silver, commanded the troops. Whilst a Te Deum for the benefit of Her Majesty was chaunted at the Carmo, and loyal speeches were being made, the Brotherhood of the Santa Casa da Misericordia, as was then the custom, collected alms to be spent on masses for the repose of the victim's soul. The sum amounted to a "dobra," Sr. Pascual says five dobras, each 12$400 reis fortes, equal now to 100$000, showing the sympathies of the crowd. The heroic dentist, calm and grave, was led in the tunic of the condemned from the prison (now the Chamber of Deputies) by the Rua da Cadêa, the present Rua da Assembléa, and the Rua do Piolho, accompanied by two priests, and guarded by 100 bayonets.* He continued his adoration of the Trinity and the Incarnation till he reached the scaffold. There he presented his gold watch to the executioner. His last words, after repeating with his director the Athanasian Creed, were, "Cumpri a minha palavra, morro para a LIBERDADE" (I have kept my word—I die for liberty). The glorious confession was drowned by a ruffle of drums and clang of trumpets. At 11 A.M. he was hanged by the neck till dead, decapitated and quartered by a negro hangman and valets. His head and limbs were salted.

---

* According to Sr. Pascual, the Juiz de Fóra rode before him.

The former, of which poets have since sung as the "Cabeça do Martyr," was sent in a cask, and much decomposed, with an escort of dragoons to Ouro Preto, and placed upon a tall post (poste alto) which then stood at the north-eastern corner of the Rua Direita, fronting the main square. The windows were decked, and all the citizens were compelled to attend and shout "vivas" for the Queen. It is related that his brother, a priest,[*] shrank from the spectacle, and was compelled by force to stand and look and hurrah with the rest. His arms were sent to Parahyba and Barbacena, his legs were nailed to wooden posts (postes altos) on the Minas road, in the Sitio of the Varginha and the Freguezia de Cebollas,[†] "where the criminal had sowed the seed of revolution, and had committed his abominable practices." As he was a lodger, the value of the house was granted, but not paid, to its proprietor; it was ordered to be razed and thrown into the river, and the site to be ploughed and planted with salt, "that never again on that spot there might be building;" but interest preserved it. A Padrão,[‡] or Stone Column of Infamy, was set up, and this remained till 1821, when the citizens, excited by the new Constitution, assembled and abated the nuisance by pulling it down. In future days there will be a Mausoleum on this spot. At present Brazilians think little of these national glories; even the hill of Ypiranga has no monument to mark it amongst hills.

Thus tragically and with blood ended the "comedy," in the same year that witnessed the decapitation of the Bourbon "son of St. Louis;" and hardly had a single generation passed away when the Tree of Liberty and Independence, watered by the blood of the Republican Tira-dentes, shot up and overshadowed the land. Twenty-nine years after the savage scene above described the wild plain of the execution became the Rocio now known as the Praça da Constituição, and in sight of the spot where the gibbet was planted rises the statue of the first Constitutional Emperor of the Brazil, the Man of Ypiranga.

　　　　*　　　*　　　*　　　*　　　*　　　*

* Tira-dentes had two brothers who were priests.

† This place is on the road from Minas to Parahyba do Sul. It now belongs to the Deputy Sr. Martinho de Campos.

‡ The word is a corruption of Pedrão, a large stone. In the heroic days of Portuguese discovery these columns were planted by the adventurers, who thus took possession of the soil for the Crown, and Camoës tells us that Da Gama's armada was supplied with them.

According to Sr. Pascual, who is, I believe, in error, the head was placed in an iron cage (gaiola de ferro), and mounted upon a Padrão. He also relates that the brother of Tira-dentes, at 2 A.M., May 20, 1792, placed within the cage a stone with the symbolical inscription, "30   "Emvunah."

The Rua de S. José, beyond the widening where the proto-martyr lived, has a good modern macadam; it contrasts with the rest of the city, where the cruel pebbles are like our cobble stones—one seems to be "walking upon eye-balls." This main artery of the Western Quarter, the Bairro de Ouro Preto, shows the usual style of house, shop and store. The walls rise as if made of cards, straight from the ground, and in some of them a lower coloured band two or three feet deep resembles an external wainscot. Upon the roofs one line of tiles is placed convex, overlapping its concave neighbour, and the edges are closed with mortar;* joists from the wall support a horizontal planking upon which rest the eaves extended to defend the foundation; the underpart is finished with boarding and whitewashed, and if the house is of a Janota or dandy, the under edges of the tiles are painted vermilion. There are no tubes of derivation, and spouts large as an average hose pleasantly play upon your hat or your umbrella. Street literature hardly exists, signboards are rare and quaint, and the shops still preserve the homely little glass cases hung up to the jambs by day and taken down at night. The stores being ground-floor, tailors, shoe-makers, and artisans work at the doorway, or at the door-like windows which reach the ground, and employ half their time in chatting with the passing friend. English shops are common, and there is, as usual in these depôt towns, a small retail trade in everything that the mule trooper or the backwoodsman requires. I saw little of the decay which Mr. Walsh describes in 1829, and which made travellers declare that Villa Rica had become Villa Pobre. After the right-angled parallelograms, so offensive to the warped eye of the European traveller,† which characterise the new settlements of the Brazil, Ouro Preto has as much misshapen curvature and narrowness as can be desired. There will be every picturesque difficulty for water drainage and gas—somewhat a heavy price to pay for crookedness.

---

* A Chinese style. So the Kiaus of Borneo ("Life in the Forests of the Far East," by Spenser St. John. London, Smith and Elder. 1862. Vol. I. p. 263) split their bamboos in two, arrange the canes side by side with their concavities upward to catch the rain; then a row is placed convex to cover the edges of the others and prevent the water dripping through. It is an excellent hint to travellers where bamboos abound.

† I confess to admiring above all things a perfectly straight street, with a vertical swelling or depression, especially when there is a sag that allows the eye to fall upon it. Nor can it be presumed that a man is born with a taste for crooked streets and unparallelogramic squares.

Amongst the foreigners here established, we found an Englishman, Mr. Saul Spiers and his family. He dealt in jewellery and such matters generally, and here we saw specimens of the Minas topaz, of which the older authors, beginning with John Mawe, have left such careful descriptions. Here were three common varieties of this stone so rich in flaws, the wine-coloured, the brilliant straw-yellow, and the almost white; under the influence of "Fashion," and of extensive falsification, they soon became a drug in the markets of Europe, and are now no longer dug or indeed used except by watch makers. A few skins of ounces and wolves were procurable, but in the cities they are rare and very expensive. We also met Mr. David Morritzsohn, a German, once a shareholder in the land that now contains the Morro Velho Mine; he is now a delegate of the French Consulate at Rio de Janeiro. Further on is the best hotel, the Quatro Nacoẽs, kept by a Frenchman.

From the main street a long leg to the left or south leads to the hole in which is built Nᵃ Sᵃ do Pilar de Ouro Preto, the Matriz of this Quarter. The material of the old and primitive missionary pile is whitewashed stone and mud, with pilasters of grey-yellow sandstone and capitals painted chocolate. The main entrance fronting westward is somewhat bowed to the front,* and adorned with two columns of the Minas-Ionic, banded in the centre and resting upon an architectural nothing. Glass appears only in the façade, a calico-strip defends the rose-light, and the bell-towers are half-finished. The only praiseworthy parts are the old doors of solid wood, and these want washing and painting.

My wife, who entered the Matriz, describes it as being egg-shaped; round the upper part is a gallery opening into the body by four arches on each side, and one for the choir over the door. The ceiling of antique wood-work is carved and gilt, painted and frescoed; a curious box suggesting Punch and Judy, and hung near the choir between Heaven and Earth, contains the organ. There are two handsome pulpits, and four silver lamps dangle before the six side altars; the latter are of ancient taste, carved into angels and other grotesque figures.† A coat of arms well cut

---

* Here called "forma oitavada."

† On the right are,—

No. 1. Nᵃˢ Sᵃˢ dos Passos and das Dores; São João Baptista and Sᵗᵃ Rita.

No. 2. Sᵗᵃ Anna and Virgin; São José com Menino Deus and São Joaquim.

No. 3. A large Crucifix; São Miguel; São Francisco de Paula, and Santa Boaventura—Saint Good Luck, for whose mystery I have a respect verging upon adoration.

On the left are,—

in stone is placed near the ceiling over the Sanctuary rails. The Sanctuary, a mass of carved and gilt wood, has four tribunes; amongst its frescoes is a Last Supper on the ceiling, and tapers burn in large silver candlesticks in presence of the B^d Sacrament. The High Altar has a throne for the Santissima, surmounted on ordinary occasions by a statue of the Patroness, N^a S^a do Pilar, over whose head a crown is held by two angels; she is adequately supported by S. Pedro and S. Francisco de Borgia.

South of the Matriz, lined with tottering steep-roofed houses, is the Campo do Manéjo or parade ground, a kind of Praia or river-beach at the junction of the Córrego de Ouro Preto into the Funil stream from the south-west, and the latter has the honour of being named as the source of the great Rio Doce. The two form the Ribeirão do Carmo, Rio Vermelho or Marianna River. It rushes down a crack, a deep dark passage evidently draining an old lake or pond, which now appears to be a mere widening in the sandy bed. This place was once enormously rich; early in the present century, 12,000 slaves worked there, and the diggings supported the population of 30,000 souls. Even in Gardner's time, the half-naked "faiscador" could make a shilling a day by panning the sand and gravel, after removing the larger stones; now he may "dive" for ever like a duck, but he will find nothing.[*]

Beyond the Manéjo, a turn to the north leads to the N^a S^a do Rosario de Ouro Preto;[†] like the other churches, it is built upon a platform that levels the sloping ground. The body is divided into a pair of bays, the portico with stout piers is defended by a wooden railing painted red, and the space in front shows a fountain and a stone cross. Further to the east, a hill-top is

---

No. 1. N^a S^a da Conceição; the Guardian Angel (Anjo de Guarda), with Sta Isabel and the Menino Deus, all together; and São Sebastião.

No. 2. N^a S^a da Terra; Sta Ursula, Queen of the glorious Eleven Thousand; São Francisco de Assis, and São Domingos.

No. 3. Santo Antonio and Menino Deus; São Vicente de Ferreira, and São Gonçalo.

[*] Faisca de Ouro, primarily meaning a spark, is applied to a flattened particle or spangle of gold; it is opposed to Pisca de Ouro, a grain of gold smaller than the canjica, which again is less than the pepito, or nugget. The washer is called faiscador, and as his work is mostly under water he is said to mergulhar, or dive.

[†] In the other quarter there is another N^a S^a do Rosario, called do Alto. It was once very rich in plate, which has now disappeared. The tale is that the negro gold-diggers, who mostly affect this invocation, were allowed by their masters at the annual October fête of their patroness to load their wool with precious dust, and to wash it off in the holy-water stoup. When 12,000 to 14,000 men thus did, the "Golden Fleece" must have been no myth.

crowned with the Church of S. José; it has a single central tower, a clock stationary at 4·37, a heap of sand at the entrance, and one old man at work. Thence a long and steep paved ramp leads to the S. Francisco de Paula, upon which a man and a boy —they suggested Trafalgar Square—were putting a fresh front. There is no general panorama of Ouro Preto buried between its great parallel ranges, we must view it little by little, and here is a fine prospect of the Western Quarter limited by the two-towered chapel, Sr. Bom Jesus de Matosinhos, in the place called "As Cabeças."

Now going further north we cross a small stream by the "Pontilhão do Xaviers," a single arch; there is a good quarry of "freestone" up the ravine. Eastward lies a yellow ochre building, the barracks (Quartel) of the Police, once 600 strong, now volunteering in Paraguay. Their place is being taken by a new levy, which as yet numbers only 220. They are known by blue coats and red edgings (vivos), which for the National Guard are white, or fancy colour. Ouro Preto, being a capital, has its little troop of galley-slaves, who are seen in the streets working at the pavement under a master-mason. They do not beg like the Tuscan galeotto, but each man requires a guard, and beyond smoking and lounging, they do very little throughout the Brazil. This penalty, re-invented in the days of Charles VII., and made fashionable by Louis le Grand, wants extensive modification.

To complete the circle round the Bairro de Ouro Preto, we leave on the right a small single-towered temple, Nª Sª das Mercés (de Ouro Preto), whose façade bears a gilt figure and the inscription, "Ego Mater Pulchræ Dilectionis." To the south lies the cemetery of the brotherhood, abundant in weeds. The other tertiary orders of the capital are S. Francisco de Assis; S. Francisco de Paula, and Nª Sª do Carmo. We are now behind the Palace in the upper town, and we descend to the lower by a long stone ramp running to the west. The only remarkable building here is the "Quartel da Guarnicão fixa," a misnomer, as that garrison has gone to the war; the exterior is painted yellow, and inside is a hollow square, worse than the Scutari hospital in its worst days.

Physically Ouro Preto is unworthy of the vast Province which it commands; even in S. Paulo it would be only a second-rate town. The straggling and overgrown mining village numbers

6000 to 10,000 souls,* in 1500 houses. During its palmy days, between 1723 to 1753, the census gave 2400 tenements, and 30,000 inhabitants, of whom two-thirds were slaves; in 1800 it had already fallen to 19,000 to 20,000. In 1865 the whites were six to one black, now they are seven to one, and everything shows that the climate is not suited for the African.

Amongst its many disadvantages we may observe that carriages cannot be used, and that even riding is not safe in the city; there is no ground for extension, the streets are too narrow for rails, and the country is unfit for the iron horse. Hence we have the sights and sounds of a capital, the fair sex dressed in French toilettes,—

> " Gents corps, jolis, parés très richement."

Officers and men in uniform, civil and military, orderlies riding about, bells, guard-mounting, bugle sounds, and music ecclesiastic and military, whilst perhaps listening to the band stands some old negress habited in male cloak, with rusty chimney pot hat proudly perched upon a dingy kerchief. Literature can hardly be said to flourish when the Ouro-Pretanos cannot keep up a single bookseller's shop.† The late Abbé and energetic President, Councillor Joaquim Saldanha Marinho, has reformed the educational establishments and created five " Externatos." We have visited one at São João d'El Rei; the others are at Ouro Preto, Companha, Sabará, and Minas Novas. This has been an incalculable benefit. The illumination is poor, worse even than that of São Paulo; each lamp should be equal to six not to three stearine candles, and many of the posts are lying on the ground. The lands around it are unproductive, the gold-veined mountains cannot be worked except by companies, and the city is not wealthy. In Ouro Preto I did not see a single gold coin, and but for its minor industries it would resemble our miserable English colony on the Gold Coast. The city lives by the sweat of other brows, by its profession as a capital, and by

---

* I should prefer the number 8000. At the same time there is a considerable floating population, and on special occasions it may reach 10,000.

† In 1840 the Provincial Assembly established a preparatory college, with chairs for Latin, French, English, Philosophy, Mathematics, and Pharmacy. The Botanical Gardens, which, under the General Government, once spread 20,000 lbs. of tea about the country, have been let for 200 $000 per annum to a private proprietor. The people are fond of music, but that is everywhere the case in the Brazil.

the money which the Government expends upon its employés,
making the Province complain of " Empregocracia." Being on
the thoroughfare between the Imperial metropolis and the
Diamantine District, it has a certain amount of small commerce,
but this again is not likely to last. The sooner another site for
a capital is found the better, but it is not easy, I have already
said, to point out a central locality suitable for the purpose.

CHAPTER XXXVI.

OURO PRETO CONTINUED (EAST END).

Tu formosa Marilia, ja fizeste
Com teus olhos ditosas as campinas
Do turvo ribeirão em que nasceste.—(*Gonzaga, Lyra* xxix.)

On the other and far side of the bridge, where the city looks like a bit of old Abbeville, is the House of Millions * (Casa dos Contos), now the Thesouro, or the (Imperial) Treasury by excellence. It was built, as was the Commendador's house, by one João Rodriguez de Macedo, a very rich and important citizen, who kept open doors and lived in splendour. Like many others, he ruined himself by taking the contract of the "Disimos" or Tithes, which were confirmed by Pontifical Brief to the King of Portugal as Grand Master of the Order of Christ; and his debts threw his property into the tender hands of Government. He died almost mad and in penury. It is a fine large substantial pile, with bindings of grey stone, heavy balconies, and a Mirador or belvedere on the top. Below on the right is the Collectoria, where the provincial export dues are collected; on the left is the Branch Establishment of the Bank of Brazil,† whose President is Dr. Marçal, and behind it is the Post Office. *En passant* we were shown the place of Dr. Claudio Manoel's death. In the upper story is the General or Imperial Treasury, with all its complicated staff, inspector, chiefs of sections, writers first, second, and third, supernumerary writers (praticantes) and others; half a dozen to do the work of one—"loafing about" not included.

Thence we ascend the Rua dos Contos, a long straight ramp which sets out to the south-east, passing on the left a fountain,

* A name given by the people in the days when gold was lodged there.
† "Caixa Filial do Banco do Brazil." The capital was from the beginning and still is 100:000$000 (say £10,000), in notes of the Banco do Brazil. I would as willingly give other details; unhappily the Treasurer promised punctually to supply them to me, and as punctually neglected to do so.

one of the thirteen or fourteen in the city. It is curiously inscribed :—

> Is quæ potatum cole gens pleno ore Senatu
> Securi ut sitis a am (sic) facit ille sitis.

The water is better than the Latinity. On the right is a gay-looking building, the Mesa das Rendas, lately made a Provincial Treasury, showing a wilderness of clerks who, pen behind ears like the Secretary bird, work hard at the statistics of street communication.

The Rua Direita or High Street, which turns sharp east, is very steep and slippery, with narrow trottoirs. At the top is the Praça,* the square, there being no other. It is a long parallelogram sloping to the centre, which shows a monument to the Martyrs of Independence, lately built by subscription. It somewhat unpleasantly resembles the pillory of ancient days,† and we could not judge of base or capital, because both were en papillotes. It wants a figure of Liberty, Poetry or the Indian, "Brazil," or some other pretty heathen, for although a pillar supporting a statue is bad enough, a column that supports nothing is worse.‡ On the north is the Presidential Palace,§ finished by the Brigadier of Artillery, José Fernandes Pinto Alpoim, mentioned in the "Uruguay;" the scientific artillerist was also architect of the Viceregal, now the Imperial Palace at Rio de Janeiro. This Government House formerly accommodated the Gold Intendency in the lower part; the front looks like a "chateau-fort," a dwarf curtain connects two trifling bastions of the Vauban age, and its popguns used to overawe the exceedingly tumultuous town. The normal long stone ramp leads up to the entrance, which bears the Imperial arms and a gigantic "auri-verd banner." Here we called at the reception house between 11 A.M. and 1 P.M., upon the senior Vice-President and acting President, Dr. Elias Pinto Carvalho, a "liberal Historico," corresponding with our old Whig, born at Cruvello, and formerly Juge de Droit at Sabará. We were received in a fine large sála, with the inevitable sofa and double perpendicular

---

* Or Praça Publica. There are five Largos, or "Places," in the English, not the French, sense—mere widenings in the streets. Of the latter thirty-five are counted.

† The tradition is that the head of the heroic dentist was here placed—an error.

‡ Dr. Muzzio informs me that the Indian breaking his chains, who was to appear upon the flag, will take station here.

§ Palacio do Governo.

line of chairs ; there was little to remark but the inordinate size
of the "huge half-bushel-measure spittoons." His Excellency
promised to forward my journey, and really took the trouble to
write a long list of introductory letters, a kindness which I
hardly expected, and for which I beg to express my sincere
gratitude. At the Palace I also met the Secretary to Government, Dr. H. C. Muzzio, whose name has appeared in these
pages. He is deeply read in poetry, and especially in the history
of the "Inconfidencia;" to him my readers owe the first detailed
and correct account of this great historical episode which has
ever appeared in England.

We then visited the " Paço de Assembléa Legislativa Provincial"
on the north-east of the square. The hall was large and in good
repair, with seats for the President and the two Secretaries,
facing as usual the semi-circle of deputies' desks ; the public
accommodation was very limited, an advisable precaution where
discussion is apt to be exciting. South of the "Paço" is a plain
house, the Câmara Municipal. The southern side of the square
is occupied by a fine solid old building, the prison ; * the Mineiros
declare de Ouro Preto a Cadêa e agua—the best things at Ouro
Preto are the water and the jail—they boast of it as the finest in
the Empire ; perhaps it was, but now it cannot compare with the
newly established Houses of Correction. On the ground is a
fountain with a long inscription, and a double flight of stairs
runs up to the guarded entrance, flanked by barred windows.
The first and second stories have Ionic pillars, with huge and
ponderous volutes, and around the top is a massive stone balustrade, with a statue of Justice and other virtues at each corner;
nor has the lightning rod been neglected. The prisoners are 454
men and 12 women, a notable difference. We visited in the
upper story, the infirmary and the rooms for recruits disposed to
desert ; the drainage has lately been improved, but there was still
something to do in the way of cleanliness. The inmates showed
more industry than usual, and the head keeper, Sr. Joaquim
Pinto Rosa, wisely makes all his jail-birds learn some handicraft.
He ascended with us the winding staircase of the tall central
clock-tower, and from the leads we enjoyed a curious prospect.

The shape of the Golden City, or rather of what part we see,

---

* The old Bastille was in the middle of the square ; no vestiges of it now remain.

is that of a huge serpent, whose biggest girth is about the Praça, which also represents the Court or West-end. The extremities stretch two good miles, with raised convolutions, as snakes have in old books. The site is the lower slope of the Serra de São Sebastião, drained by the Funil in its break: this subrange is part of the " Ouro Preto " line, extending two leagues from east to west.* The " streeting " of both upper and lower town is very tangled, and the old thoroughfares, mere " wynds " and " chares," show how valuable once was building ground. Some fifteen churches,† mostly rise on detached and conspicuous points, and thus gain an appearance of elderly consequentialness. The houses hanging about the picturesque ravine, as near to the old mine-lake as possible, have necessarily one side taller than the other. Polychrome has the best effect: there are all varieties of colours, even the Imperial—gold and green—whilst one tenement is faced with imitation brickwork, white, red, and yellow.

All the view is hilly and " goldy," turned up and rummaged by the miner. Immediately south the Morro do Cruzeiro bears its cross, and here lies the highway to Rio de Janeiro. The gem of the prospect lies a few steps to the south, where we see upon the horizon, rising above its mountain wall, Itacolumi, the " Stone and Pappoose."‡ A tall black monolith projects its regular form against the sky, bending at an angle of 45°. By its side is a comparatively diminutive block, which the red men, picturesque in illiterate language, compared with a child standing near its mother. Perhaps the name alludes to some forgotten metamorphosis of Indian fable, and, perhaps again, this is the idea of some Mineiro poet who had not forgotten his bird. The slopes culminating in this apex are here bald, there grass-clad; tall Araucarias tell the severity of the cold, and if a cloud exist in the sky it is sure to find out " Itacolumi."

Deep in the hollow at the mountain foot, and backed by shady trees, is an uninteresting building, long, low, tiled and white-

---

* The substance is micaceous quartzose slate, resting on micaceous slate, with clay shale at intervals. Some travellers mention a base of gneiss, but I did not see this.

† There is at present an excessive economy of priests at Ouro Preto, only one-third being allowed to each church. About 1866 Padre França, the Chaplain of the Police, who also attended the prison,

was suppressed. They declare that his salary of 1:400$000 per annum was earned by celebrating one mass per fortnight. Caldcleugh mentions twelve churches.

‡ The name reminds us of the " Cow and Calf " at Ben Rhydding," which has no right to the " Ben." But how homely is the English compared with the Indian simile.

washed — very like a comfortable farm-house. Here lived and
died "Marilia," whose profane name was D. Maria Joaquina
Dorothéa de Seixas Brandão, the local Hero, Beatrice, Laura, or
Natercia, and who narrowly escaped being the Heloise of Minas.*
She was niece of Lieutenant-Colonel João Carlos Xavier da Silva
Ferrão, an aide-de-camp (adjudante d'ordens) to the Governor.
Books tell us that she was a "descendant from one of the
principal families in the land," † but this is denied by some at
Ouro Preto. Born in 1765, at sweet fifteen she was promised
by her uncle, a staunch Royalist, to the poet Gonzaga, then aged
forty-four, and there is a legend that her beauty hastened the
tragical denouement of the "Inconfidencia." A certain Colonel
Montenegro,‡ when "jawáb'd," as the Anglo Indian says,
taunted her with preferring to a "gentleman of fortune and
position," a poor "man who wrote books." She, girl-like, lost
her temper, and retorted that she preferred brains to money and
Montenegro. The latter denounced by letter the conspiracy to the
Viscount of Barbacena, who turned pale, placed the paper upon
the table, and left the room. His cousin, Fr. Lourenço, the
hermit of the Caráça, happened to be present; the missive was
blown to the floor, and the friar, picking it up, saw all at a
glance. He retired, sent for his friends in haste, told them
the treachery, and advised them to fly. They, however, hurried on
the movement, and rushing armed into the streets, attempted to
raise the cry of Liberty. The Governor, who being intimate with many of the accused, had, according to his party,
determined to retire from his post, was thus compelled to take
action.§ This tale is not told in any of the voluminous writings

---

* The first two parts of Gonzaga's Pastorals (Amores and Saudades) are entitled
"Dirçêu de Marilia," *i.e.*, to Dirçêu from
Marilia, and are thus "attributed" to the
lady. They are, however, the answers to,
and echoes of, the second three parts,
"Marilia de Dirçêu," *i.e.*, to Marilia from
Dirçêu, and it is generally believed that
they are the work of the editor, an unworthy
mystification. D. Maria probably never
wrote a line of verse, or perhaps prose, in
her life. "Marilia" is evidently Amaryllis,
and thus that well-known Brazilian Latinist,
Dr. Antonio de Castro Lopes, translates by

Rusticus haud, Amaryllis, ego, nec sole,
    geluque
Torridus, alterius qui servem armenta,
    bubulcus :

the first couplet of Lyra,—

Eu, Marilia, não sou algum vaqueiro,
Que viva de guardar alheio gado.

† The same is asserted by the Visconde
de Barbacena, May 23, 1789. Moreover,
the arms of the family are well known.

‡ The reader will bear in mind that all
this is merely local tradition. I record it
on account of its wide diffusion in popular
belief.

§ This certainly does not appear in the
Secret Correspondence of the Viscount of
Barbacena with the Viceroy D. Luiz de
Vasconcellos and with the Court of Lisbon.
The Franciscan chronicler before alluded to,
curiously defends Barbacena by declaring
that "he never was guilty of extortion,
and he governed Minas as Caligula ruled
Rome."

upon the "Inconfidencia," but I heard it everywhere in Minas, even upon the banks of the Saõ Francisco River.

Haplessly for the romance, Heloise was notably unfaithful to Abelard, as Abelard was faithless to Heloise.* The lovers whom "death could not part," and whose written protestations of constancy are legion, separated after the discovery of the rebellion: this is easily explained: amongst the Inconfidentes there had been some little talk of removing the stern aide-de-camp's head. They were, however, allowed to meet and bid farewell for ever—the scene is said to have been painful. And both did worse things. A certain Dr. Queiroga, Ouvidor of Ouro Preto, had the honour of supplanting, but not with a legal tender, the poet Gonzaga. By him D. Maria Dircêu, as she was called, had three children: Dr. (M.D.) Anacleto Teixeira de Queiroga; D. Maria Joaquina and D. Dorothéa, all blue-eyed and light-haired. At Ouro Preto she is now best known perhaps as the Mãi do Doutor Queiroga. In later years she lived retired, never left the house except for the church, and died (1853), aged eighty. Since that event the family has quitted Ouro Preto, and none could say where it had gone. She never would pronounce her lover's name, especially shunning the subject with strangers. On her death-bed she said to her confessor, "He (elle) was taken from me when I was seventeen." Those who knew her well described her as short of stature, and retaining in age finely formed features, and "a bocca risonha e breve"—the short smiling mouth—they agreed that her eyes were blue, and that her hair, which was white, had been meio-louro, blonde or light chestnut. Her lover, curious to say in four places, makes her locks the "hue of jetty night," and in four others, "crisp threads of gold," and the author of the favourite edition of the Lyras defends him as only friends can defend.†

* That is begging her right to the name of Heloise. The young and lamented author, A. P. Lopes de Mendonça (Memorias de Litteratura Contemporança, p. 375), is unjustly severe upon the hapless Marilia, not because she was unfaithful, but because she lived to the age of eighty-four (eighty). "This man, this poet, this tender soul, this passionate heart, this austere republican,"(?) this illustrious victim, this martyr to love and native land, lived through fifteen years of exile in Mozambique, far from her, far from the bride to whom he had devoted all

the sighs of his lyre, all the tears, all the torments of his misfortunes, whilst she continued to live careless and indifferent. She never thought of going to console him, of going to live with him, of going to die with him! O women! O women!" Moreover, he suspects that she used cold-cream.

† Marilia de Dircêu, Lyras de Thomaz Antonio Gonzaga, precedidos de uma noticia bibliographica, e do Juizo Critico dos Auctores Estrangeiros e Nacionaes, e das Lyras escriptas em resposta as suas, e accompan-

From the Praça we descended the Rua do Ouvidor to the south-east, and at a corner where four streets meet, fronting the Rua dos Paulistas, we remarked that the historic house of Claudio Manuel still wants the commemorative tablet. Perhaps the Ouro Pretanos think with the Greek that Ἀνδρῶν ἐπιφανῶν πᾶσα γῆ τάφος. Well does it deserve to bear a quotation from Plutarch, "Vitâ dignissimus est, quique morte suâ patriæ salutem quærit. It is a small five-windowed corner building, yellow, with green balconies. At the entrance is a dwarf hall; upstairs is a little square room with whitewashed walls, the studio of Vasconcellos,[*] and a second apartment, very similar, built round with old-fashioned brick seats, opens upon a roofed terrace or broad verandah. Here the Inconfidentes met to discuss their poetry, their projects, and their political aspirations; and from it there is an uninterrupted view to the home of D. Maria in the hollow.

The house began its life of fame by its connection with the "Revolution of the Three Poets," as the movement is still called by the people. They are Gonzaga, Claudio Manuel, and Colonel Ignacio José de Alvarenga Peixoto,[†] a man of the noblest character, a philosopher and a poet of "intemperate imagination," but perhaps the least high-seated in the Portuguese Parnassus of

hadas de Documentos Historicos. Por J. Norberto de Souza Silva. Two vols., 8vo. Garnier, Paris, e Rio de Janeiro, 1862. It is severely criticised by the scrupulous and painstaking Dr. Mello Moraes (Chorographia do Brazil, tom. iv. p. 612, of 1862), who charges the editor with the additions before alluded to, and many Musgravean corrections and conjectural emendations.

As regards the important question of the colour of Marilia's hair, Sr. Norberto remarks, certainly not in favour of his poet, that "lonro" (blonde) rhymes well with "ouro" and "thesouro," quoting the Spanish sarcasm,—

Fuerza del consonante, á lo que obligas
Que haces, que sean blancas las hormigas.

Anglicè.

Fault of the rhyme's compelling might,
That turns the ant from black to white.

The original MS. was not (as is generally said) burned by D. Maria; a copy in MS. was given by her family to Dr. José Vieira Couto de Magalhaes, actual President of Mato Grosso.

   * Mr. Walsh, ii. 214.

   † The pastoral Alcêu of Claudio Manuel, who called him cousin (primo). Born at Rio de Janeiro in 1748, he studied at Coimbra, and served the Crown as a magistrate at Cintra. Thence he returned home in 1776, and became Ouvidor in the Comarca of the Rio das Mortes. He preferred, however, retiring into the country and writing verses, which were highly esteemed by the amiable and liberal Viceroy, the Marquess de Lavradio. With a wife and four young children, he honourably sacrificed domestic happiness at the call of his country and his friends. On April 18, 1792, he was sentenced to death, which on May 2 was commuted to transportation for life, with confiscation of goods and attaint of issue to the second generation. He arrived at Ambáca, in Angola, a brokenhearted, white-haired man, white-haired when aged only forty-four, and there he died early in 1793. An ode inscribed to D. Maria I., another to Pombal, and a third in honour of his Alma Mater Coimbra, are admired as musical, facile in rhyme, and abounding in tranquil beauty. They will long be quoted in Cours de Littérature and Chrestomathics; the Parnasso Brasileiro (vol. i. 322—339) has given copious extracts from his other compositions.

the present day. There were two others more or less concerned in the affair, namely, Manuel Ignacio de Silva Alvarenga,* and Dr. Domingos Vidal de Barboso, who was banished for life to West Africa, and who died there also in 1793. This celebrated quintette may be called the heads of the Minas school.

In this house Gonzaga, the central figure of the poetic group, used to pass his time embroidering wedding-garments for D. Maria and himself.† Lately some of his letters have been found, ordering silk thread from various merchants. He was born at Oporto in August, 1744, and was there baptised on September 2. The Brazil claims him, as his father was a Brazilian official, and he himself calls the colony his home.

> Por deixar os patrios Lares
> Não me pesa o sentimento.‡

And he mentions his youth having been spent at S. Salvador da Bahia,

> Pintam que os mares sulco da Bahia
> Onde passei a flor da Minha idade,§

He studied law at Coimbra, he took magisterial office at Beja and other places in Portugal, and finally he became Ouvidor of Villa Rica—in those days a more important person than the President in these. His approaching marriage delayed him for two or three years, and he lingered even after he had been appointed Desembargador, or one of the Judges of the Supreme Court at Bahia, a delay which told strongly against him. The general belief is that the home government, whose consent to the union was then necessary, hesitated to give leave, because it did not wish the poet's influence to be settled in Minas. A legend still told within these walls, and I believe it is true, makes a muffled figure on the night of May 17, 1789, warn him of the approaching storm. He paid no regard to it: on the 22nd he dined at home in the Rua de Ouvidor ‖ with his friends, and on the next day all were under arrest.

---

* He has been noticed in Chapter ii.

† Aqui um lenço
   Eu te bordava.
"For thee a kerchief I did embroider." Part I., "Amores," Lyra 10. The words allude to the poet's occupation, but the author-editor places them in the mouth of Marilia.

‡ Vol. ii. Part 3, Lyra 3,—
"To leave my own paternal Lares,
   Little of regret I feel."

§ Vol. ii. Part 2, Lyra 7,—
"They (dreams) paint me ploughing through Bahian seas,—
Bahia, where my youth tide's flow'ret bloomed."

‖ On the left-hand side going down. It was the old residence of the Ouvidores, or Chief Justices, and is now a police office.

Gonzaga * was sent with the other accused to Rio de Janeiro. His friends were placed in the prison where the Chamber of Deputies now stands: he was confined in a dungeon (masmorra) in the Ilha das Cobras, and afterwards in the houses of the Third Order of Francisco da Penitencia. During his 1095 days of solitude he relieved his mind by scrawling upon his dungeon walls with desperate charcoal, candle or torch soot, and an orange-stick. He was subject to four several examinations,† and he complained bitterly of the virulent hatred of a private enemy, Basilio de Brito—now an unknown name—who had sworn to "follow him to the gates of death." The evidence against him was very conflicting, and almost wholly presumptive: at times hopes were held out to him, and he thought that his marriage might take place. He was reported to have undertaken a code of laws for the new Republic; on the other hand he was affirmed to have quarrelled with Tira-dentes, and the conspirators seem to have looked upon him as an outsider. His sentence, finally issued on April 18, 1792, dwells upon the fact that he was a "man of lights and talents," and he was evidently lost by his high reputation. For daring to be an eminent and intellectual mind he was banished for life to the Pedras de Angoche (Encogé), in West Africa: after the execution of Tira-dentes, the penalty was commuted to ten years' transportation to the deadly climate of Mozambique, with pain of capital punishment in case of return. The voice of the people, whose instincts are so true in these matters, has done him justice, and the favourite name of the movement is now the "Inconfidencia do Gonzaga."

On May 23, 1792, the third anniversary of his confinement, the unhappy poet left for ever, in the ship Nª Sª da Conceição Princeza de Portugal, the shores of his loved Brazil. At the pestiferous Mozambique his life was miserable, he tried vainly to practise law, and he lost the gift of poetry.‡ He forgot "Marilia bella," or perhaps on the principle "Saudades de mulher só mulher mata," six months after landing he married a rich mulatto girl who had nursed him through his fevers. "D. Juliana de Souza Mascarenhs" was aged nineteen, and signed her contract with a +, and she was addicted to beating her

* Spix and Martius have erroneously made him Ouvidor of "S. João del Rey."
† These Interrogatorios were dated Nov. 17, 1789 ; Feb. 3, 1790, and Aug. 1 and 4, 1791.
‡ Whatever he wrote there was stamped with nostalgia, and shared the decay of his intelligence.

husband. He became almost insane, and died in 1807,* aged
sixty-three : he was buried in the Cathedal of Mozambique, and
he wrote his own epitaph in the Lyras—

> Pôr-me-hão no sepulchro
> A honrosa inscripção :
> —" Se teve delicto,
> So foi a paixão,
> Que a todos faz réos." †

" The " Proscript of Africa " is described as a manner of
" Tommy Moore," a short stout figure, with blond hair, bright
and penetrating blue eyes, and a pleasing spirituel countenance :
his address, at once frank and courteous, won every heart. He
was a dandy, delighting in battiste shirts, laces, and embroidered
kerchiefs ; he left some forty coats, some peach-coloured, others
parrot-green—a wardrobe which suggests "Goldy's" bloom-
coloured preferences. The portrait prefixed to the favourite
edition was " eliminated from the depths of his self-conscious-
ness " by the artist, Sr. J. M. Mafra. It shows the poet very
precisely as he was not, tall, thin, twenty-four, not forty-eight,
with long dark flowing locks, melancholy regular features, and
irreproachable top-boots—in jail.

Gonzaga is still the popular Brazilian poet, and amongst the
Latins he will take rank with Metastasio. Some of his lyrics
are remarkably operatic—who does not remember the Italian of—

> São estes os sitiôs ?
> São estes, mas eu
> O mesmo não sou.¹

Almeida-Garrett laments his " fatal error " in not devoting himself to national subjects : yet his pastorals, like his politics, are
destined to a long life. His hand may evidently be traced in the
Cartas Chilénas : ‡ some judges declare that the master's touch

---

* Not in 1809, as MM. Wolf and A. P.
Lopes de Mendonça say.

† They shall 'grave on my tomb
　　These words of fair dealing,—
" If the crime was his doom
　　'Twas but error of feeling,
　　Which makes all to err."
　　" Lyras," Vol. ii. Part 2, 17.

‡ For instance, in the following lines
(" Epistola a Critillo," p. 25),—

" Nem sempre as aguias de outras aguias
　　nascem,

Nem sempre de leoẽs leoẽs se gerão :
Quantas vezes as pombas e os cordeiros
São partos dos leoẽs, das aguias partos."
　　　　　　Anglicè.
" Not always eagles are from eagles sprung,
Not always lions are by lions got ;
How often haps it that the doves and
　　lambs
Are born of lions, are of eagles born."

I have already alluded to this satire,
which will be read as long as there are
pompous governors and silly men in high

is not there, others opine that it is. He has left certain prose
juridical studies, especially on usury and education, which still
remain in MSS.

In poetry Gonzaga is always as he called himself, O bom
Dircêu. Remarkable for grace and naïveté his erotics contain
not a trace of coarseness : they are sentimental, dashed with a
tinge of melancholy, which of course deepens in the gloom of his
prison. As is the case with all the better Portuguese poets his
style is remarkably correct, and his language studiously simple,
withal sufficient. Recognizing the fatal facility of rhyme in his
mother tongue he binds himself, by stringent rules, in grave and
acute consonances, rejecting the former in his most laboured
pieces. The Lyras, like the productions of the Minas school
generally, are hardly to be translated adequately in foreign verse.*

The last great inhabitant of the house was the councillor and
senator Bernardo Pereira de Vasconcellos,† whose father, Dr. Diogo
Pereira Ribeiro de Vasconcellos, had bought it very cheaply when
the heirs-at-law lost their papers. The " Franklin " or "Adams "
of the Brazil was born at Ouro Preto, and died paralytic at Rio
de Janeiro, leaving a history, which is that of his young country's
liberty. Being unmarried, he bequeathed the tenement to his
sister, D. Dioga, of whom a terrible tale is told : she was afterwards married to a Frenchman, still living. Thence it passed into
the hands of the present owner, D. Jeronymo Maxiano Nogueira

---

places. It has all the mystery, and much
of the genius, of Junius. Claudio Manuel
and Ignacio José de Alvarenga Peixoto are
also suspected of having assisted in writing
the Cartas (Introduction to Cartas Chilénas, by Luiz Francisco da Veiza. Laemmert, Rio de Janeiro, 1863). Varnhagen
(Epicos Brasileiros, p. 401) suggests that
the author may have been Domingos Bar-
boza Caldas, who was banished to the Nova
Colonia. It is the custom to depreciate
these letters ; but no one can assert of the
author—

" The lessons he taught mankind were few,
And none that could make them good or
    true."

Dr. Muzzio, who I have said is a hard
student of poetry, believes that the Cartas
were written by the Minas school, and that
they show the hand of Gonzaga.

* MM. de Montglave and Chalas have
wisely preferred prose. M. Ruscalla, D.
Enrique Vedra, and Mr. Iffland, have given

them an Italian, Spanish, and German
dress (M. Ferdinand Denis, " Resumé de
l'Histoire Littéraire du Brésil," chap. 5,
p. 568, and Ferdinand Wolf, Le Brésil
Littéraire, chap. 7, p. 66). Of the three
principal Brazilian poets not one has yet
reached a country which reads thousands
of rhymes like these,—

" The Royal Poet has a few words to say
About working men and the railway ;
We have now got down the great Broad
    Gauge,—
I hope it will increase our trade."

† He must not be confounded with José
Teixeira da Fonseca Vasconcellos, First
President of Minas, and created Visconde
de Caethé ; the latter was one of those who,
on Jan. 9, 1822, elicited from D. Pedro I^{mo}
the exclamation famed in Brazilian history
as " O Fico "—"the ' I remain.' " B. P.
de Vasconcellos and his sister were popularly known as Jupiter and Juno.

Penedo. On the right is the Casa do Mercado, with mules tethered in front of the large verandah, and yellow walls. Opposite it stood the Pillory, which, some thirty years ago, was pulled down by some young men by way of spree. To the south of the little square is the Church of S. Francisco de Assis. The outside is handsome, but the projecting façade shows two Ionic pillars ungracefully converted into pilasters. Over the entrance are steatite carvings by the indefatigable "Aleijado," showing a vision of the Patron, and above is a sepulchran cross. The yellow doors are of solid wood, cut into the usual highly-relieved bosses. In the interior are the normal six side-altars, a profusion of pictures let into the whitewashed wall; a fanciful choir balcony; a large ceiling fresco of Santa Maria surrounded by angels, and the Trinity on life-size figures of painted wood. The pulpits at the entrance of the sacristy are of soapstone, well cut, and recalling to mind the far-famed " Prentice's bracket."

Further down to the south-east is the Nª Sª das Mercês dos Perdoẽs, so called to distinguish it from the other Church of Mercies : it is a single-towered building, still unfinished outside. To the north-east is Nª Sª da Conceição, the Matriz of the eastern parish, called " de Antonio Dias," from the famed old Taubatiense, who settled here in 1699, and of whom all but the name is forgotten. It was once the richest church in the place, now it is a long whitewashed building, gilt, but mean and tawdry. Here on Feb. 11, 1853, were deposited* the mortal remains of " Marilia formosa "—Rosa Mundi, non Rosa Munda, whose story I have been compelled to strip bare of all its romance. To the south-east is Nª Sª das Dôres, and far to the east rises the Alto da Cruz, before mentioned.

Returning to the Praça Publica we visit, on its west, the largest church in the "Imperial City of Ouro Preto," Nª Sª do Carmo. Based upon a high and solid platform, it is externally a huge barn, with a bay façade, decorated as to the entrance with cherubs and flowers in blue steatite, stuck on to the grey-yellow sandstone. The two belfries are of the round-square order, with pilasters where corners should be. It has glass windows, here a sign of opulence : the inside is remarkable only for gaudy

---

* I am told in the third catacomb on the Epistle side, a kind of family vault. Lately, when it was opened, a skull was shown as that of D. Maria; but it had evidently not been worn by an octogenarian.

hangings of crimson and gold; and the choir is supported by two
columns and a pair of pilasters shaped like gigantic balustrades,
a kind of "barrigudo" style, which deserves to be called the
Flunkey-calf Order. The little catacombs of the Brotherhood are
on the south, and detached. The Capital of the Gold and Diamond
Province has not yet a public cemetery, and her sons must still be
buried in their churches. This is somewhat too primitive for 1867.

In the street, to the north of the Carmo, is the theatre, known
by its yellow wash: it claims to be the oldest in the Empire.
The house belonged to a certain Coronel João de Sousa Lisbôa,
also a victim of the royal tithes: he was declared bankrupt, yet
it is said that the property, when sold, left no deficit. It has
lately been repaired at the expense of the Province, and it is
usually occupied by amateurs, who perform always respectably,
sometimes remarkably well. The very civil Impresario, a Portuguese, led us round the house, whilst his company were rehears-
ing. The interior is laid out in the democratic style of the
United States, here generally adopted; all the circles are open,
and a single central box, the President's, fronts the stage. I much
prefer this disposal to the European exclusiveness of pens and
pews; the prospect is more pleasing, and there is better ventilation, always a grand desideratum; moreover, civilisation here
does not demand the "dress-circle" to be kept "select," nor
does your coat determine whether you are god or swell.

To the far south of the theatre is the old Tyburn, the Morro da
Forca, or Gallows Hill.* It was levelled at an expense, they
say, of ten contos (£1000); for an intended Industrial Exhibition,
which proved the veriest failure. The projecting mound should
be visited for the sake of the view. Thence we fall into the Rua
de Sta Quiteria, execrating its slope and its abominable pavement,
and finally the Rua dos Contos lands us where we set out.

During our short stay at Ouro Preto, a glimpse at society left
many pleasant impressions, and we could hardly understand
those foreigners who complain that it is "not the style of thing
to which they are accustomed." We spent a musical evening of
many "modinhas," with the agreeable family of the ex-Secretary to
Government, José Rodrigues Duarte, whom I afterwards met on
the Rio dos Velhas; I also made the acquaintance of D. Antonio
de Assis Martins, of the Government Secretariat, and part editor

* The pillory was for whipping, exposing limbs, and minor punishments.

of the Almanak de Minas. Although a Conservative he has been
assisted by the Liberal authorities, and indeed such works deserve
not only local but general attention. They here represent the
issues of those historical societies, ever increasing in the States
of the North American Union, and they prove to the Old World
that the young, whilst looking to the Future, has not forgotten
the Past. In times to come the historian will derive from them
invaluable assistance.

Party feeling runs high at Ouro Preto, as it did amongst us
when unbreeched boys were asked—" Are you for Pitt or Fox?"
And here a word upon this most important subject in the Brazil.
Europeans and foreigners, who, hastening to make fortunes, hate
every excitement which can interfere with the money market, are
very severe upon the " arid and acrid politic" of the land.* They
never think that the excitement of partizanship is a phase through
which all juvenile societies and governments must pass, like the
hot youth of the individual.   " Un peuple nouveau, positif par
conséquence," has to provide for its physical wants, to establish
civil order, and to secure life and property: it will indulge in
wars, and other calamities must occur: the breathing time is
necessarily spent not in science and philosophy, the highest aims
of its later life, but in religious functions, and in adjusting its
political questions. And indeed these are the two noblest exercises of youthful human thought, thus embracing all interests
between heaven and earth—Um die Erde mit dem Himmel zu
verbinden. Nor should it be otherwise: the most wholesome
sign in a young people is a determination to enter into " the
affairs of the nation," affairs which older communities, finding
the machinery too complex for the general comprehension, are
fond of abandoning to professional thinkers. Of course this
laudable curiosity will often degenerate into violent and personal
party feeling, but none will condemn the useful because it is open
to abuse.

I find in the Brazil another symptom of strong and healthy
national vitality. Men wage irreconcilable war with the present;
they have no idea of the " Rest and be thankful" state. They

---

* The pleasant operation, parentally
called "telling you of your faults," is
nowhere endured with a better grace than
in the Brazil. There is nothing that a
stranger may not assail, provided he show
a friendly spirit, not a mere desire to
blame.

balance " Whatever is, is good " by the equation " Whatever is, is bad; " yet they are neither optimists nor pessimists. They have as little idea of " finality " as have New Yorkers. They will move and remove things quiet, and they will not leave well or ill alone. They are not yet, happily—

> Men of long enduring hopes,
> And careless what the hour may bring.

Were infanticide disgracefully prevalent amongst them—it is rare as in Ireland—they would find some means of checking it. They are determined to educate their children, unlike the lands where the political physicians allow the patient to perish whilst they wrangle over how to save him—what physic is to be or is not to be given. They will emancipate their women* and convert them into "persons." They provide against pauperism, and they study to bring the masses up to the high standard of Prussia and Belgium. They would assimilate their army to that of France, not preserve a "sham army," or an "army of deserters." They would model their navy upon that of the United States, not " Monitors,"—and so forth.

There is everything to hope from a race with prepossessions for progress towards such a high ideal. Of late years in England it has been the fashion of the many non-thinkers to be facetious about " ideas ; " † and yet I would ask what word best describes the suppression of the export slave-trade and its expression, the Sentimental or Coffin Squadron ? What but an idea is it to send thousands of missionaries bearing the " bread of life " to the heathen of Asia, Africa, America, and Australasia, whilst the children of the kingdom starve at home ? On the same principle some acute observer discovered that Napoleon Bonaparte always spoke of glory : Arthur Wesley invariably used the word duty. No truer measure of difference in mental stature between the Exile of St. Helena and the owner of

---

* At a time when common sense is demanding the political emancipation of women in England, it is curious to read an old book, the "Travels of Mirza Abu Taleb Khan" (1799-1803; Longmans, 1814), showing the superior liberty of the sex amongst Moslem races. He admirably accounts for the vulgar prevalent idea that the Asiatic wife is a slave, and proves that she has over her European sister immense advan-tages in the management of children, property, and servants, and in real freedom, despite apparent seclusion, which in modest women is always voluntary.

† Of course this does not apply to those who do think. "Rebellions are never really unconquerable until they have become rebellious for an idea," says Mr. J. S. Mill with profound truth.

Apsley House can well be imagined. Duty was at once enthroned, if not deified; it was real, solid, practical, English (which mostly means routineer); whilst glory was romantic, flimsy, flippant, French. The effect was to exaggerate the involuntary evils which Bacon* and Locke carried out to extremest doctrines, bequeathed with all their immense services to our national mind. Hence the bit of truth in the often quoted saying, "a nation of shopkeepers," which still stings too hard. The one-sided view of life made the eye say to the hand, "I have no need of thee." And worse still, it pitched unduly low the tone of thought by satisfying men with a moderate tangible desideratum, and by ordering the spirit to go so far and no farther. For what is Glory, rightly understood, but Duty nobly done, and honourably acknowledged by the world? Is it not the temple of Ideality, to be reached only by the steady plodding path of Reality?

---

* Thus a popular writer of the present day gravely informs us that Bacon's way is "the only way of procuring knowledge."

CHAPTER XXXVII.

Pelos ingremes trilhos tortuosos
Da Serra Altiva, que os Cabeços ergui
Calvos, arripiados.
        (*Joaquim Norberto de Souza Silva.*)

THE evening of the last day showed thick and heavy vapours surging up from the lowlands, and careering over the Peak. All judged it to be a sign of cold, perhaps of snow. I augured, and too rightly, that it was rain. Heavy showers fell at intervals during the night, and the morning was misty. We were to be guided by Sr. José da Costa Lana, an employé of the Commendador. He opined that the clay-paths or rock-streets would be slippery, and that the hangings of purple cloud upon the summit would conceal the view. We resolved, however, to take our chance, and about 8 A.M. we found ourselves upon the Marianna road.

Presently we turned off to the south, and making easting, reached the little church of Padre (João de) Faria (Fialho), another ancient colonist: a fine Cruzeiro or stone-cross stands in front of it. In the hollow lies the " mine of Padre Faria," now filled up with rubbish. It dates from the first Golden Age of Minas : the " old men " have run levels into the hard lode, and the position on a hill side will enable it to be unwatered without much pumping : therefore Mr. S. Ollivant, of Ouro Preto, proposes to exploit it by means of a Company. The main auriferous veins dip northwards, and the lateral branches form zigzags in all directions. The material is " Carvoeira " (place of coal) or rich Jacutinga, Pedra Muláta (Adularia), a felspar containing gold, sometimes in sight and sometimes not, and finely disseminated spots and lumpy lines of arsenical pyrites. The precious metal is found also in pot-holes (panellas), in cavities called "formigueiros" or ant-holes.   The assay gave a carat of 23 and 23·3, and the loss in treatment was 5 per cent.

Turning to the right, we crossed a spur of ground, and fell into the "Funil" Valley; over the torrent rushing down the deep black gap is thrown a very shaky bridge, with the "garde-fou" on the ground.   Here is a small cascade which perhaps merits its romantic name, "Cachoeira de Cintra." *   After a long elbow to the east, we turned westward, and began a serious ascent, which presently showed us a clump of white houses, in which we recognised Passagem.   Marianna and its pretty basin are hidden by a hill, but a quarter of a mile ride to the left shows them in bird's-eye plan.   From the episcopal city there is a line of ascent, but it is described as a kind of gulley, and many of the citizens had never heard of it.

On these heights we passed fellows with pistols slinking about the bush: they had probably been baulking the recruiting officer.   In the Brazil, where leagues are many and where men are few, people readily follow the precept of Montesquieu, "If you are accused of having stolen the towers of Nôtre-Dame, bolt at once."   Here "miserum est deprensi," not for that sin only, but for all offences.   There were two places, mere ledges of rock with loose stones, up which the mules had to spring like goats.   The vegetation dwindled as we rose higher, and the ground was clothed with the dwarf Sumará and other Bromelias.   These may be compared with the "arbres des voyageurs" in various regions. A full-grown plant gives a pint of water, collected between the stalk and the bases of the leaves.   When fresh it is pure, wholesome, and free from vegetable taste, but not "nectar."   After a time of drought the fluid becomes turbid, a fine black mould collects in it, and dead insects and live tadpoles, especially those of a small pale yellow frog (Hyla luteola), require it to be filtered.   The shrubby growth suggested the Carrapato-tick; but we are now above his level.

After an hour's ride we reached the last and highest spring, and here the two negroes, who carried the provision basket, declared they would await us, as we were now close to the "Stone." The proposition was at once overruled.   Itacolumi Peak rose straight before us, now a spectre looming tall through the grey

---

* A friend told Southey, the historian, that the lands around S. Paulo, the city, reminded him of Cintra. The comparison would have been juster if applied to the Itacolumi neighbourhood.

mist, then completely wrapped in cloud-swathe, then standing out with startling distinctness. It looked like a diamond edition of the " Serra do Caráça," and indeed the material is the same. It also reminded me of Pilot Knob, Mo., where 700 feet of specular iron are piled in " masses of all sizes, from a pigeon's egg to a middle-sized church." Both mother and child seem to change shape when viewed from each hundred yards. But a belt of impassable forest lay between us and our bourne, and these giants always look much nearer than they really are. Therefore we " sprang " the niggers.

Many places in the Brazil are called " Itacolumi." There are two others in Minas—one to the west of Itambé, called also from its seven summits " Sete Peccados Mortaes : " another is on the right bank of the Upper S. Francisco, south of Paranaguá, and there is a third and a fourth to the north-west of Maranhaõ. The word is properly rendered " Pedra e Menino," Stone and Pappoose (Red-skin child). Mr. Walsh mistranslates it " child of stone ; " and he is followed by Sr. Norberto de Souza Silva, who explains " Ita-conuni " by " Mancebo de Pedra." * It is also written " Itacolumy," and more exactly " Itacolumim." †

This Peak has given its name to a rock, or rather to three very different kinds of rock. The older writers apply " Itacolumite " to a white or yellow sandstone, flexible like a plate of gutta percha, termed a " great geological curiosity " by our press. It is found in Georgia and North Carolina, and it greatly resembles that of the Lower Himalaya, in which thin layers of the silicious granular matter are associated with small plates of talc. The " Pedra elastica " was described two centuries and a half ago by the Padre Anchieta. Dr. Charles Wetherill (American Journal of Science and Art) declares that the pre-

---

*   O alto cume
Do Itacolumi, gentil mancebo
Que o Indio converter-se *em pedra viva.*
        (*A Cabeça do Martyr*).
† Curious to say, Sr. B. J. da Silva Guimarães (p. 408, Poesias ; Rio de Janeiro, Garnier, 1865) declares that "Itacolumy" was a name substituted for "Itamonte" by the poet Claudio Manoel. Yves D'Evreux corrupts Curumim to " Kounoumy ; " perhaps, however, the sounds were hardly distinguishable. He gives as the ages of mankind,—1. Peïtan, babe ; 2. Kounoumy miry, child ; 3. Kounoumy, adolescent ; 4. Kounoumy Ouassou, man ; 5. Ava

(aba), middle-aged ; 6. Thouyuaë, old man. St. Hil. (III. ii. 261) gives " Curumim," garçon, in the dialect of the Aldêa do Rio das Pedras, and the Tupy Dictionary translates "Curumim" by Menino. The Indian *r* was changed to *l* by the colonists, who also docked the termination. I find a distinct labial nasalization like the Dewanagari ह, somewhat like a French *i* pronounced through the nose, and as in the Portuguese *Jardim.* The Iberian tongues take a pride in pronouncing all their letters, and it is regrettable to see a word written as it should *not* be spoken.

vailing opinion as to the elasticity of the stone resulting from
the presence of mica is erroneous, and that if a thin plate of this
sandstone be subjected to examination by the microscope, the
flexibility will be found to depend upon minute articulations
where the sand-grains interlock. In my specimens the stone
abounds in light yellow mica, and when the friable material
crumbles, the two main component parts at once separate. Near
São Thomé das Letras, before alluded to, there is a fine quarry
of this elastic variety. In the deeper parts the strata become
thin, and gradually pass into natural slabs of the finest quartzite,
stratified quartz, of course losing all elasticity.

This flexible stone is not the matrix of the diamond and the
topaz, although sometimes associated with it. Diamantine
"Itacolumite" is, as will presently appear, a hard talcose rock
of distinctly laminated quartz, white, red, or yellow, granular,
with finely disseminated points of mica: it is either stratified
or unstratified. In Minas the name is popularly given to
the refractory sandstone grits, and to a fine crystalline rock
evidently affected by intense heat. Curious to say, Itacolumi
Peak consists neither of this, nor of that, nor of the other, yet
its name has been given to all three.[*]

The last formations, laminated quartz and sandstone grits,
form with Itaberite, almost all the Highlands in this part of
the Brazil. Considerable confusion is often caused by the triple
use of the word. Thus M. Halfield[†] explains Itacolumite by
" quartzo-schistoso, schisto de quartzo, micachisto-quartzoso,
gelenk-quartz, and elasticher sandstein." In school-books each
author interprets it his own way. It would be well to limit it, as
Gardner does (Chap. 18) " to hard iron slate."

Leaving the water, we turned westward, passing the Capão dos
Inglezes or " Tree Motte" of English pic-nickers, which reminded
me of a certain estancia at Tenerife. I cannot find that any

---

[*] Allow me, as regards the term "Itacolumite," to quote what M. Boubée said
with great truth about the groups of the
Transitional formation known as Silurian
and Cambrian,—"I cannot understand the
necessity of going to seek in a corner of
England the type of divisions and a classi-
fication of so important a nature which is
found fully developed in Normandy and
Brittany, Cevennes, Ardennes, the Pyre-
nees generally, &c." Again, what can be
worse than to substitute "Devonian" for
"Old Red Sandstone," for a system which
extends not only over Northern Europe,
but also over Northern America. "Itacolumite" in its three several senses belongs to the globe, not to Minas Geraes, to
which but not by which it has been limited.

[†] Relatorio, on p. 78. He might have
termed it more correctly flexible Itacolumite, granular or quartzose Itacolumite,
and crystalline Itacolumite.

of the writing travellers have made the ascent, yet all the silent men have so done. About this Capão is a fine site for a small settlement: the hydropathist who "müss gebirge haben" will here find in the dry season the clearest air and the purest water.   Our next operation was to lose the way amongst paths ramifying to every rhumb, and we went too far west towards the Itatiaia village which gleamed white upon its hill.   At last, after a tough struggle over rocks and slides, we passed round to the south of the "Stone," and after three hours' riding stood a little above it.   The winding goat-track numbered some six to seven miles, and the direct distance cannot be more than three, for we heard the clocks of Ouro Preto striking the hour.

After a fight with the high winds I boiled the thermometer, which gave 5860 feet,* still showing that the culminating range in this section of the Brazil is, as in Eastern Africa, the Maritime Chain.†   We then proceeded to examine the singular formation, and the iron-stone so distracted my bearings, that they deserve little confidence.   The base is a short ridge, a latitudinal expansion, a vertebra in the "Serra Grande" or do Espinhaço, which here trends from south to north.   The material is "Jacutinga," soft micaceous and ferruginous schist, "Itacolumite" proper or hard iron slate, and quartzose micaceous slate, with a dip of 65°.   The "Ita" rises on the western side of a quoin-shaped mass, bluff to the west : it is one of the many pikes and organs which at lower elevations are seen bristling over this part of the chain, and it is surrounded by huge blocks and boulders of all shapes and sizes.   To judge by the eye, it lies 500 to 600 feet below the highest point of the parent-bluff, which, seen from the west, has a tabular form ; and thus the extreme height above sea level would be about 6400 feet.   The "Pedra" is a core of the hardest iron slate, black and polished like a metal casting, and the surface shows joints but no stratification, whilst the sides are striped by wind and weather into vertical and inclined striæ.   Formerly it

---

* The usual estimate is about 8000 palmas = 5733 English feet. Mr. Gerber has 1750 metres = 5727 feet, and Mr. Keith Johnston's last map 5750 feet.   My observations on a level with the summit of the Pedra gave 5860 feet above sea-level (B. P. 202°·50, Temp. 57°), or 2487 feet above Ouro Preto.   At the Hermit's Cave below the "Pappoose" I obtained 5095 (B. P.

203°·1, Temp. 59°) above sea-level, and 765 feet below the "Ita."

† Nearly half a century ago it was remarked that these Organ Mountains, where even small glaciers are found, would, like the Sant' Angelo Mountains of the Bay of Naples, supply the Fluminenses with ice, which they import at a high price.

could be ascended by a chain fastened to the summit; this aid has now disappeared, and nothing but a fly or a lizard could swarm up its smooth metal.

We then proceeded to view the " Columi." Seen from Ouro Preto it appears almost to touch the mother stone, a smooth slope intervening. It is found to be separated by a deep gap of loose humus, protruding rock, and decomposed vegetation, and the path is matted with a tangled growth of trees and shrubs, thorny bushes and llianas, which catch the legs like man-traps. Descending to the east, we stood opposite a dark mass of the same metallic formation and aspect as the upper feature; the shape was that of a gorilla's skull, not unlike, but about three times larger than the "Bosistow Logan Stone." Slipping down sundry rock-drops, we found below the eastern base a cross and a cave once inhabited by a hermit. A skull was lately picked up in this Troglodytic refuge, which the black guide called a "Sarão;"* and doubtless it has given shelter to many a Maroon.

Returning after a difficult climb to the breakfast-ground, we soon ascertained that the two negroes left to guard the provaunt had spent their time well—were drunk as drunk could be. They paid the penalty by not reaching home before midnight, and how they reached it at all without cat's eyes is still a puzzle to me. The last shred of mist had now been melted by the sun of noon, and the tall pillar glowed and glanced in the fervid rays like a bar of specular iron-stone. · A little to the east of north † lay the city of Ouro Preto, sitting stiffly upon the hard lap of São Sebastião, with feet dipping to the stream-bank on its south. Behind it lay the brown lines of the Morro de Santa Anna, craggy, with ruined chapel; a little to the west of north stretched the blue lines of the "Serra do Caráça," and north the Piedade range,‡ like a lumpy cloud, closed the horizon. On the southwest the jagged walls of S. José d'El-Rei struck the eye, and the rest was a tumbled surface of rounded hills subsiding into longer

---

* For Salão, a saloon. The skull was promised to me, or rather through me to the Anthropological Society of London. It was not sent, but this gentle hint may cause it to be forwarded. The direction of the Anthropological Society is No. 4, St. Martin's Place, London, W.C.

† M. Gerber's map places the Peak south-east of Ouro Preto. Mr. Johnston's puts it too far to the south-west. I took bearings, but when protracted they proved useless.

‡ Mr. Gordon took an observation from the eastern side of the Peak base, whence the western point of the Serra da Piedade bore due north.

and more level lines as they reached the rim of the basin in whose centre we stood.

The descent was far more pleasant than the ascent, not always the case in Brazilian mule-travelling. The beauties of an enchanting prospect lay full before us, and thus we could enjoy the "unfading and inexhaustible pleasure which the face of Nature always gives when presented under new and varying aspects." In the lower levels smokes by day and nightly blaze show that the grass is being fired; the proceeding, however, is punished at this season with "posturas" or fines, because the birds, especially the fine game Cadorna,* at which dogs point, are nesting. This sensible idea deserves to be carried out beyond the limits of city jurisdiction. The afternoon was magnificent, and we returned long before sunset, delighted with our excursion, and grateful to our guide, Sr. Lana, who had made the toil so great a pleasure.

---

* S. Hil. (III. ii. 203) suspects that the Cadorna is the Tynamus brevipes of Pohl, and that the Perdiz (Ynambú, or Inambu) is the T. rufiscens. Both words are taken from Portugal, and applied to birds of the New World, specifically, and often generically, different. The same was done with "pheasant," "partridge," and "quail" in Northern America and British India.

The other common kinds of Tinamus are the Juo (Tinamus noctivagus), described by Prince Max. A larger species is the Macúca (Tinamus Braziliensis).

CHAPTER XXXVIII.

THE MINEIRO.

Die klaren Regionen
Wo die Reinen Formen wohnen.
Schiller.

SECTION I.

THE MINEIRO HISTORICALLY VIEWED

BEFORE leaving the Imperial City, which is the modern type of old Minas, it appears advisable to give a sketch of its inhabitant, the Mineiro, who, like his ancestor the Paulista, is still the typical man in the Brazil.[*]

The first colonists from Portugal settled in S. Paulo in the earlier half of the sixteenth century. As happened to the refugees from England, the morgue of the old country represented them to be mere roturiers.[†] The accurate and painstaking Santista Fr. Gaspar Madre de Deus has, therefore, thought proper to investigate the origin of the settlers at Santos, now the port of S. Paulo, and he has proved that they belonged to honourable families in Portugal and Italy.

The blood was, in fact, too honourable; it brought with it an almost insane vanity, commonly called pride of birth, and the immediate result was a deterioration of race. White women were rarely imported to a country which was in a chronic state of savage

---

[*] My space will permit me to touch upon the subject very lightly; moreover, throughout these volumes a variety of anthropological notes have been recorded wherever the subject suggested them.

[†] Both Paulistas and Portuguese can now afford to smile at the witticisms of the old comedy-writer Garção.

Parece-me que estou entre Paulistas,
Que arrotando Congonha, me aturdiam
Co' a fabulosa illustre descendencia

De seus claros Avós, que de cá foram
Em jaleco e ceroulas.

" Methinks by Paulistas girt I stand,
Who full of windy 'Mate' stunn'd my ears
With fabulous illustrious descent
From ancestors renowned, who hence departed
In drawers and doublet."

Maté I have explained to mean Paraguay tea.

war, and the settlers, as a rule, disdained to intermarry with the
daughters of the Redskin. Yet, as in the United States, unions
with the free-born but barbarous blood * were never held to be
disgraceful, and in process of time some houses have come to
boast their descent from the "Indian Princess."

But when agriculture began in earnest the African was
imported, and the servile mixture, at all times and in all places a
dishonour amongst white races, who in this point obey an
unerring instinct, advanced at a rapid pace. I can quote the
case of a city in Minas where amongst three thousand, or including the vicinity, five thousand souls, there are only two families
of pure European blood. On the coast the colonists found
opportunities of marrying their daughters to men from the Old
World, and the lowest of "high-born beggars" was preferred to
the wealthiest and most powerful of mule-breeds. But in the
interior mulattism became a necessary evil. Hence, even to the
present day, there is a strange aversion to marriage, which, in so
young a country, forcibly strikes the observer. Men do not like
to "marry for ever," and the humane Latin law, which facilitates
the naturalisation of illegitimate children, deprives matrimony of
an especial inducement. Brazilian moralists have long since
taken the evil in hand, and have even proposed that public
employment should be refused to those living openly in a state of
concubinage. The day of sumptuary and domestic laws, however,
is now departed, and men no longer respect rulers who cannot
separate the private from the public lives of their subjects.

Presently to hunting red-skins was added another industry—
gold-digging. Before the end of the century which witnessed the
establishment of the first Portuguese colony, multitudes flocked
to the Far West, and thus much of the noblest Paulista blood
became Mineiro. The "turbulent riches of metals" did their
usual work; a vagrant horde, a "colluvies gentium," displayed all
the rowdyism and ruffianism which we of this day have witnessed
in California, San Francisco, and Carson City. As was said of
the Indians, the immigrants had neither "F., L., nor R"—Faith,
Law, nor Ruler—and the motto of the moving multitude seems to
have been—

> Quem dinheiro tiver,
> Fará o que quizer.†

---

* The Indians used to call negroes "Macácos da Terra"—monkeys of the land.

† Whoso money acquires,
May do all he desires.

As I am not writing a history of Minas, a mere sketch of events which distinguished her capital will show the spirit which animated the race.

Shortly after the "War of the Emboabas" the village of Antonio Dias was promoted, by the Act of June 8, 1711, to township, with the merited name of "Villa Rica." Between 1700 and 1713 the Royal Quint of gold had been raised upon the batêa or pan; in 1714, however, D. Braz Balthasar Silveira, in its stead, established capitation Fifths and toll-houses (Registros or Contagens). The latter aided in the collection by taking dues upon all imports. In 1718 they were dismembered from the Fifths and were farmed out. In 1719, when D. Pedro de Almeida, Conde de Assumar, Governor and Captain-General of Minas, proposed, instead of the poll-tax, to erect public mints and smelting-houses, serious troubles took place. At Ouro Podre, the richest place adjoining Ouro Preto, some two thousand men rose in arms, and about midnight of June 28, razed the foundations of the building that had been begun, and attempted to massacre the Ouvidor Geral of the Comarca, Martinho Vieira. This violent partisan fled, leaving his house to be plundered. On July 2 the mutineers compelled their Municipal Chamber to take the van, and, marching to the "Leal Villa de Nª Sª do Carmo." now Marianna, forced their fifteen conditions upon the Governor,* Some of the articles signed by the contending parties are quaint in the extreme. The authorities are accused of "working more miracles than Santa Lusia," in defrauding the people, whilst No. 11 runs thus: "They (the insurgents) require that the Companies of Dragoons shall feed at their own cost, and not at the expense of the public."

Thus the mutineers obtained their pardon, which was, of course, officially null. The ringleaders (os cabeças) returned to Villa Rica; and, in the pride of success, divided the spoils of war. The Mestre de Campo, Pascoal da Silva Guimarães, disposed of various appointments; his son, D. Manoel Mosqueira da Rosa, elected himself Ouvidor; and Sebastião da Veiga Cabral, becoming President of an independent organisation,

---

* The letter of the Count of Assumar, describing this "horroroso motim" is printed in the Almanack, 1865 (p. 101—104), and the conditions which he signed in Almanack, 1864 (p. 56). Southey (iii. 38, 158—161) has translated the Count's report almost literally, and has thus taken a one-sided view of the affair.

instanced, in a friendly way, the Governor to take refuge at São Paulo.

But the Count of Assumar was now prepared for energetic action. He sent a Company of Dragoons to Villa Rica, seized Cabral and despatched him to Rio de Janeiro. On July 15 he laid hands upon the rest of the "poderosos," "with many other accomplices, whose multitude caused him to forget their names;" amongst them, however, were Frei Vicente Botelho, Fr. Francisco de Monte Alverne, João Ferreira Diniz, and Felipe dos Santos. The latter had been sent to Cachoeira do Campo with the view of raising the people, described by their ruler, in his "grand way," as a "vil canalha." He was chosen as an example to terrify the captives, and was torn to pieces by four wild horses in the streets of the capital. Pascoal, the ringleader, was sent to Lisbon, where he brought an action against the Governor, and died before he could establish his innocence. The rest, "who had been blinded by the demon," were imprisoned, and their goods were burned without form of process on the hill of Ouro Podre, which thence took the name of Morro da Queimeda.*

Immediately after this affair, Minas Geraes was dismembered from the captaincy of S. Paulo, and Villa Rica was made her capital. On August 18, 1721, she received her first Governor and Captain-General, D. Lourenço de Almeida. He established the foundries and mints, which at once produced counterfeiting. In 1730 a society was established at Rio de Janeiro to defraud the Quint, and one Ignacio de Souza Ferreira, and Manuel Francisco, a man of rare mechanical ability, were sent out to find a proper location. They chose a "secular and fearful" forest at the foot of the Great Serra,† near the place now called S. Caetano da Moeda—of the Coin. The affair came to the ears of the Viceroy; he ordered the Governor of Minas to make inquiries, and presently two men turned "king's evidence." The house was surrounded by armed men, the chiefs were taken, and, in 1731, Manuel Francisco was sent to the scaffold. Justice was executed with such severity, and the accomplices were so

---

* The Hill of the Burning.

† Hence the range took the name of "Serra da Moeda"—of the Coin. There are still legends of treasure buried near the site where the stamping house stood. Other establishments for falsifying money were set up at Catas Altas de Mato Dentro, and elsewhere. The coined pieces were as pure as those issued by the Mint, but they had forgotten to pay the Royal Quint.

numerous, that Desembargadores were sent from Rio de Janeiro, and they brought actions against the authorities that had shown excess of zeal. In 1735 (Pizarro) the "Mint" of Villa Rica was abolished, and from that time forward only gold dust was in circulation.

This event, combined with the immense increase of contraband, rendered foundries and mints well-nigh useless. On March 20, 1734, a Junta of the people, assisted by delegates from the municipal bodies, met the second Governor, D. André de Mello de Castro, Conde das Galveas, accepted an annual composition of 100 arrobas, 3200 lbs. of gold. But the palmy days of "pick and pan" were ended. In the next year a capitation tax was levied, shops and stores were heavily burdened, and gold was rated at 1$500 per oitava. These measures caused the greatest dissatisfaction, and finally, by Royal Letter of Dec. 3, 1750, D. José re-established the Casas de Fundição, and accepted as Quint one hundred arrobas of gold.

But Portugal, the Paterfamilias, was very fond of borrowing, on every possible pretext, from the rich and unhappy bantling over the water. Imposts were devised to assist in rebuilding Lisbon after the earthquake of Nov. 1, 1755. These were continued by Royal Order of Jan. 4, 1796, when the Ajuda Palace was burnt down. The disimos or tithes were collected with such vigour that those who farmed them were, with rare exceptions, ruined. Tolls levied at ferries were sent to the Home Treasury, which was further swollen by fees paid on taking office, or rather by the sale of posts under government. The salt tax was made a burden. Stamped paper was not forgotten, and a forced "literary subsidy" was imposed by Royal Order to defray the charges of provincial education, which was never given. And, beginning with 1711, large subsidies, donations, and benevolences— voluntary, but under pain of the galleys—were required for the extraordinary expenses of the Court of Portugal. Such was the colonial system of those days, nor can any country in Europe charge its neighbour with conduct worse than its own. The inevitable end was to drive men to independence.*

* The Viscount of Barbacena had brought out the last orders for the voluntary subsidy in the matter of the Ajuda Palace; at a time when the arrears of Fifths amounted to 700 arrobas, 22,400 lbs. of gold, equal to all the actual circulation in the Province. On the trial of Gonzaga, it was proved that the poet had urged the Intendant to levy, not one year's Fifths, but the whole arrears. He pleaded that he had so acted in order

The memorable "Inconfidencia" was, it has been seen, the first blow struck. Liberty lay bleeding and exhausted for a time; but sixteen years after that tragedy D. Maria I. and D. João landed at Bahia, and the colony became at once the mother country. When the constitutional movement began, the Ouro Pretans arose with a will, and chose for their leader Lt.-Col. José Maria Pinto Peixoto. The last of the Governors and Captains-General, D. Manoel de Portugal e Castro, closed the gates of his Palace, the doors were burst open, and the cannon was taken out to command the streets. Next morning (Sept. 21, 1821) the people filled the square, shouting "vivas" for the Constitution. They required the Municipal Chamber to elect a Provisional Government, which at once entered upon its functions, headed, much against his will, by D. Manoel. A second Provisional Government was installed on May 20, 1822; political agitation continued, and the people would not recognize the future founder as provisional ruler of the Empire, or Prince Regent. D. Pedro, with his usual manliness and daring, alone and after an amusing scene at a place called the "Chiqueiro," preceding his escort, on April 9, 1822, entered the city; he was rewarded with an enthusiastic reception.* On Jan. 30, 1823, the Comarca do Ouro Preto was created, and Villa Rica retook her old name; which, however, had never been forgotten by the people. The first President of the Province of Minas Geraes, José Teixeira da Fonseca Vasconcellos, entered upon office Feb. 29, 1824.

Nine years after this event troubles broke out at Ouro Preto, but they were easily suppressed. In 1842 the disturbances were of a much more serious nature, and assumed a form bordering upon secession. Since that time the Mineiro has been tranquil. But the past should warn statesmen that a race so fiery † must have no reasonable subject of complaint, if it be expected to remain quiet and content. Its sole grievance at present is want of postal and telegrammic communication, of roads, railways—as has been seen, there is not yet a kilometre of rail—and river

---

to convince the Home Government that the measure was impossible, and thus to obtain a remission of the debt. But the judges were of opinion that his object had been to increase the irritation of the people, and more especially as the furious Tira-dentes had already mooted the question with an intention which he scorned to deny.

* The second visit was not so fortunate, and immediately after it the Emperor resigned.

† In this point they suggest the Basques, of whom the celebrated Gonzalo Fernandez de Córdova used to say that he would rather keep lions than govern them.

navigation ; with these improved it may confidently look to a great and glorious future.

Section II.

THE PHYSICAL MAN.

I will here offer a few remarks upon the descriptive anthropology of Minas Geraes.

Before the stranger has passed a month in the Brazil he begins to distinguish the native from the European. The Brazilian * bears the same physical relation to his ancestor the Portuguese as does the American of the Union to the Britisher. During the last three centuries and a-half the New-World European has developed a more nervous temperament ; he has become lighter in weight—the maximum mean in the masculine gender is usually assumed, in the Brazil, at four arrobas = 128 lbs., about nine stone —and rather wiry and agile than strong and sturdy. Hence the Brazilian calls himself "Pé de Cabra," † or goat-foot, opposed to the Portuguese, who is "Pé de Chumbo," foot of lead. The latter also is readily recognized by the thickness and coarseness of his nose,—"noscitur a naso," like the old Englander of sanguine and lymphatic diathesis in New England. Here the nervous temperament accuses itself in the thin, arched, and decided form of the organ, with the nostrils convoluted, and strongly marked alæ, and the high "bridge," which gives the Roman profile, full at once of energy and finesse.

The older comparative anthropologists, from the great monogenist Hippocrates to Buffon, Prichard, and Buckle,‡ made the great differentiator between nation and nation "climate ; " *i.e.*, the aggregate of all the external physical circumstances appertaining to each locality, in its relation to organic nature. And the first modern school being orthodox monogenists, boldly asserted that black and white skins—for the question was then but skin deep—were mere modifications of each other, produced by

---

* Brazileiro opposed to the Portuguez, or Filho do Reino, unpolitely called Portúga, Pé de Chumbo, Bicudo, Marinheiro, Gallego, and so forth.

† An opprobrious term invented by the enemies of Brazilian Independence, and accepted in a modified signification by the people.

‡ Who moreover (i. 567) speaks of the "fanciful peculiarity of race."

the complicated agencies which they evoked. This palpable absurdity was rejected by serious students almost as soon as it was propounded. Presently the anatomists and physiologists, pressing to the other extreme, everywhere detected fixity of type with race, and race only, in history. " Race is everything," said Dr. Knox.

I venture to opine that the truth lies between the two, and that both schools have generalised upon insufficient grounds. "Si l'anthropologie est encore si obscure, c'est peut-être qu'on a beaucoup trop raisonné sur cette science et trop peu observé." Thus says Auguste de St. Hilaire in 1819, and the dictum still deserves to be written in capital letters.

The notable approximation of the Ibero-Brazilian and the Anglo-American of the Union, two peoples sprung from two distinct and different ethnic centres, can hardly be explained except as the result of local causes, which have assimilated the advenæ to the autochthonic type, the so-called Red Man :[*] hence, for instance, the beauty, the smallness and the delicacy of the extremities, which is often excessive, degenerating into effeminacy: in the Portuguese and English the hands and feet are large, fleshy, and bony, evidently made by and for hard use. Hence, too, the so-called " hatchet-face," common to the citizens of the Empire and the Republic, the broad and prominent brow, the long thin cheeks, flat or concave, the features generally more sharply marked, and the protruded, massive, and often cloven chin, the quadrangular mentum, that striking peculiarity of " Indian" [†] blood. In both, too, the hair is evidently changed : it loses the Caucasian or Aryan "wave," and becomes straight, lank, glossy, and admirably thick. The whiskers are often "clear sown," and thus the facial pile is reduced to the "goatee," "which," says M. Maurice Sand, " donnerait l'air vulgaire à Jupiter lui-même." [‡]

---

[*] I am pleased to see that Eschwege denies the copper colour to the American races as a rule. They are born of a whitish yellow tinge, and they become a sunburnt brown.

[†] The word "Indian," as Mr. Charnock warns us, properly speaking, means one born in the Valley of the Indus. But what can the unfortunate anthropologist do in these young days, when such terms as Caucasian and Turanian, Semitic, Hamitic, and Japhetic, must still be used for want of better ?

[‡] I quote Mr. Sand without agreeing with him. The "goatee" is not only original ; it also suits the features.

All tribes of Indians are not confined to a thin pile about the mouth, and growing only three inches long. There was one clan whom the Portuguese called from their large beards, "Barbados." The same may be observed in Inner Africa.

This modification of form and approximation to the Indian type I hold to be a fact, and I cannot explain it except as the effect of climate, which, in Hindostan, develops the lymphatic, and, in Utah territory, the nervous temperament.* This belief in " Creolism " may be heretical, and, if so, the sooner it is stated and disproved the better.† But the instances popularly cited to prove the absolute permanence of race, as the Parsees in Western India, and the Jews in Aden—to quote a few of many—do not touch the question. These tribes have moved over a small area of ground : they have made little departure in latitude, less in longitude. My observations come from the New World, where, with the exception of those that have passed over the frozen Arctic Sea viâ Behring's Straits, all mammalia are specifically different from those of the so-called Old World. Under similar conditions a distinct Creolism has been remarked by travellers in Australia.

The Mineiro—meaning the man whose ancestors, or at least whose father is born in the country—is easily known even amongst

---

* The " temperament," also, is a purely empirical system, which will cease to be regarded when the chemistry of the blood, of which it is the effect, shall have been sufficiently studied. The subject is too extensive for a foot-note, but it may, I think, be shown that the Luso-Brazilian, as well as the Anglo-American, has been modified morally as well as physically by climate, and has assimilated in national character to the aborigines.

To the high development of the nervous diathesis we must attribute the remarkable facility with which mesmerism, or animal magnetism, acts both in the Empire and in the Republic. A practitioner at São Paulo found three out of nine students subject to the influence. Extraordinary cases are cited. At Maceió, in the Province of Alagôas, there is a girl, the niece of the Barão de J * * *, who, they say, can, by power of volition, give to a glass of water the smell, and, to a certain extent, the appearance of any liquor required—milk, wine, or liqueur : she has, moreover, produced in it distinct layers, each preserving its peculiarity. A committee of six medical men assisted at the trial, where, moreover, was a professional prestidigitateur, who confessed himself unable to understand, though he had often shown the trick in the way of trade, how the changes were

effected. Mr. Spenser St. John tells a similar story (ii. 262) of a woman in Borneo proper, who cooked one of his own eggs by simply breathing upon it.

It is now too late to ignore subjects so important as introvision, thought-reading, and medical clairvoyance. The majority of men, who have never witnessed the phenomena, will of course deride and dislike the subject. Not so he who seeks to understand the causes of things : he will hold it incumbent upon him to investigate the truth to the utmost, and he will modify his theories to facts, not facts to his theories.

† " The negroes who have been bred in the States, and whose fathers have been so bred before them, differ both in colour and form from their brothers who have been born and nurtured in Africa." (North America, by Mr. A. Trollope, Chapter 5.) Superficially we have all observed this. And the value of the observation is the greater because the author has no theory to support, and apparently is not an anthropologist. "Sous l'influence du contact de la race blanche (says M. Liais, L'Espace Céleste, p. 217), et surtout par l'effet du mélange qui tend à s'opérer, il se forme une race de noirs beaucoup plus intelligente que celle des nègres d'Afrique."

Brazilians, nor can his peculiarities be explained by "hot-air pipes and dollar-worship." He is a tall, lean, gaunt figure, which, when exaggerated, represents our popular long and lank D. Quixote. There is no want of the "intellectual baptism," innervation, vulgarly called "blood." The frame is sinewy and well formed for activity : it is straight as that of a Basque, not like the drill sergeant's, and even labouring men do little to bend them like our round-shouldered peasantry. The neck is long, and the larynx is prominent ; the thorax often wants depth. The hips and pelvis are mostly narrow ; the joints, wrists,* and ancles, are fine, and the legs are, as often happens amongst the Latin races, not proportioned in strength to the arms. Obesity is rare, as amongst the true Persians : it occasionally appears in men of advancing age, and it is considered nullo curabilis Banting. The short, square and stout-built Portuguese shape, osseous and muscular, is not, however, unfrequent. Amongst the offspring of English parents I saw seven of the gaunt nervous temperament and two of the John Bull.

Many of the women have plump and rounded forms, which run to extremes in later life, becoming pulpy or anatomical. Not a few possess that fragile, dainty, and delicate beauty which all strangers remark in the cities of the Union. The want of out-of-doors labour and exercise shows its effect in the Brazil as palpably as in the United States. The sturdy German fraus who land at Rio de Janeiro look like three American women rolled into one. Travellers are fond of recording how they see with a pang, girls and women employed in field work, and the sentiment is, I believe, popular. But they forget that in moderation there is no labour more wholesome, none better calculated to develop the form, or to produce stout and healthy progeny. They should transfer the feeling to those employed in the factory or the workshop.

The Mineiro's skin is of a warm dark brown, rarely lit up at the cheeks, and often yellow from disturbed secretion of bile, or from obstruction of the ducts, or from excess of choleic acid in the system, tinging the cutaneous blood vessels. It is, in fact, the tint of Portuguese Algarves, where the Moor so long had his home. Every variety of hue, however, is found, from

---

* According to Prince Max., i. 209—10, the women of the coast "Pourys" wore strings, or bark strips, round their wrists and ankles, "pour les rendre plus minces."

the buff colour of Southern Europe to the leathery tint of the mulatto. Here all men, especially free men who are not black, are white; and often a man is officially white, but naturally almost a negro. This is directly opposed to the system of the United States, where all men who are not unmixed white are black.

The skull is generally dolicocephalic, and it is rather coronal than basilar: rarely we find it massive at the base or in the region of the cerebellum: the sides are somewhat flat, and the constructive head is rare as a talent for architecture or mechanics. The cranium is rather the "cocoanut head" than the bull-head or the bullet-head. The colour of the hair is of all shades between chestnut and blue-black; red is rare; when blonde and wavy, or crisp and frizzly, it usually shows mixture of blood: it seldom falls off, nor does it turn grey till late in life—also a peculiarity of the aborigines.* With us the nervous temperament is mostly known by thin silky hair: here we have the former accompanied by a "mop." I have heard Englishmen in Brazil declare that their hair has grown thicker than it was at home :.† so Turks in Abyssinia have complained to me that their children, though born of European mothers, showed incipient signs of wool—they invariably attributed it to the dryness of the climate. Though hair in the Brazil is indeed an ornament to women, it seldom grows to a length proportionate with its thickness. The deep-set eyes are straight and well opened: when not horizontally placed there is a suspicion of Indian blood : the iris is a dark brown or black, and the cornea is a clear blue-white—not dirty-brown as in the negro. The eye-brows are seldom much arched, and sometimes they seem to be arched downwards : the upper orbital region projects well forward. The mouth is somewhat in the "circumflex-accent shape;" and the thin ascetic lips are drawn down at the corners, as in the New England and the

---

* The same is remarked of the negro both in the Brazil and at home.

† Some attribute the improvement to the use of Xoxó or Chochó, the oil extracted from the kernels of the Dendé palm-nut (Elæis guineensis, whose pericarp yields the palm oil of commerce). The kernels are pounded in a mortar and ground between stones till reduced to a fine pulp : the mass is then beaten up in a bowl with hot water, and the oily matter is skimmed off the surface. The Brazilians, before using it, place the Xoxó in another bowl with cold water, and expose it to the dew for eight or ten nights, changing the water daily. I am surprised that this article, so much used in Africa, and so much prized throughout the Tropics, has not found its way to England, where beargrease of mutton suet still holds its own.

asthmatic sufferers in England.   The teeth, of dead white, are unusually liable to decay : they require particular attention, and thus the dentist is an important person.*   Young men of twenty-five sometimes lose their upper incisors, a curious contrast of old mouth and young hair.

The expression of the Mineiro's countenance is more serious than that of the European.†   In his gait, the slouch of the boor is exchanged for the light springing step of the Tupy.   Hence he is an ardent sportsman, and the " country squire" delights in hunting parties, which extend from a week to two months.   The nomad instinct is still strong within him, and he is always ready to travel : curiously enough, foreigners blame this propensity, and quote the old proverb about the rolling stone.   All are riders from their childhood, and, like the northern backwoodsmen, they prefer the outstretched leg with only the toe-tip in the stirrup : this they say saves fatigue in a long journey ; moreover, as they sit only by balance, they can easily leave the animal when it falls. Our hunting seat and the hitched-up extremities of the Mongol would be to them equally unendurable.   It is to be observed that all the purely equestrian races ride either as if squatting or standing up ; and both equally abhor what we call the juste milieu. As rupture is almost unknown where the leg is stretched out to its length, I must attribute this accident, so common amongst our cavalry-men, to tight belting the waist and to carrying unnecessary weight.‡   Like the Bedouin and the Aborigines of the Brazil, the Mineiro is able to work hard upon a spare diet, but he will make up manfully for an enforced fast.   Self-reliant and confident, he plunges into the forest, and disdains to hive with others and to cling in lines to the river-bank.

The race is long-lived, as is proved by the many authenticated cases of centagenarianism.   Of the endemic diseases, the most remarkable are leprosy and goître.

---

* In a town of 15,000 souls, I have seen three dentists in one street.   As in Europe, so in the Brazil, the best are those from the United States ; it is painful to compare with their light and durable articles, the clumsy work of our country practitioners, and sometimes even of the Londoner.

† This is also an "Indian" peculiarity ; all travellers mention the gravity of the Red Man's look ; and some have commented upon the acquired "moodiness" of the expression in the United States.

‡ I borrowed from the people a "wrinkle" which might be adopted to advantage by our troopers.   When the animal is required to stand still, the rider, on dismounting, passes the bridle over its head, and allows it to lie upon the ground.   Horses and mules easily learn to take the hint.

Leprosy, here called morphéa, and the patient morphetico, is by no means so common in Minas as in S. Paulo, where it spares no age, sex, or station. Yet the races are of kindred blood : the climates are similar, and the diet is the same. Here it is comparatively rare amongst the higher classes, and as in India and Africa, I have never seen a European affected by it or by its modification, elephantiasis. Various causes are assigned to the origin of this plague, once common amongst us.* Some derive it from the Morbus Gallicum; others from diet, especially from excess of swine's flesh : so in Malabar it is supposed to attack those who mix fish and milk, which is held to be the extreme of bile-producing alimentation. All agree that it is hereditary. The attack commences with brown discolorations on the white skin, and ends with mortification of the members, necrosis of the bones, and death. Every drug has been applied to arrest its progress ; even the bite of a rattlesnake has been tried. In certain stages it is held to be highly contagious, and those suffering from it usually separate from their families. The leper-class in the Brazil is dangerous, actively and passively. We may remember that in France it was known as "ladre." It is evident that in this Province, as in São Paulo, lazar houses are greatly required.

If Minas has less leprosy, she is more afflicted with goître than her neighbour. The disease in Portugal is called "Bócio" and "Papeira," in the Brazil "Papos," † and the patient "Papudo." Pliny's assertion (ii. 37) " Guttur homini tantum et suibus intumescit, aquarum quæ petantur plerumque vitio," does not hold good here. Caldcleugh (ii., 258) saw goîtered goats at Villa Rica. Mr. Walsh (ii., 63) declares that it attacks not only men but also cattle, and that cows are often affected by it. I have owned a dog with an incipient goître, and have heard of its appearing in poultry. The people, as usual, attribute it to the water ; for instance, the rivers Jacaré and do Macúco are supposed to cause it by the "agglutination of vegetable matter." Castelnau observes that this morbid enlargement of the thyroid gland is

---

* In A.D. 1101, Matilda, wife of Henry I., founded the Lazar-house, now St. Giles. In the thirteenth century, France contained, according to Dr. Sprengel, deux mille leprosaries. Possibly this European leprosy would now be called by another name. Upon the subject of the dread malady in São Paulo, I shall have more to say when treating of that Province.

† Literally crops or maws.

common in "Itacolumite" countries; but that it does not, as in Europe, extend to great altitudes. It can hardly be explained by confined air, by deficiency of atmospheric pressure,[*] or by carrying loads on the head. It is believed to be hereditary. The Indians suffered much from it, and throughout the Mineiro highlands it is so prevalent, that no girl, they jocosely say, can be married if she has not her "papos." It begins early in both sexes; children in their teens have the rudiments of two or three protuberances which, in time, will become like dented air-cushions fastened round their necks. It is never arrested by surgical operations, and the only popular cure is salt, especially in the form of sea-baths, which they declare absorb the swelling. On the Rio das Velhas it is almost general; yet curious to say, on the Upper São Francisco, after the junction of the two streams, it becomes remarkably rare. Saline ground is wanting in the former, abundant in the latter valley, which seems to favour the vulgar idea. In the Brazil I have never found cretinism to accompany goître, so far verifying M. Koeberle, who looks upon the two complaints as distinct morbid conditions. Mr. Walsh, however, mentions one case.[†]

Fecundity in this Empire is the norma of animal as of vegetable nature. Were not colonisation a present necessity, the human race would soon populate, with a comparatively homogeneous people, the vast regions that await inhabitants. The Province of São Paulo is supposed to double her numbers in thirty years without the assistance of immigrants.[‡] Girls marry as did our

---

[*] I can hardly assert this positively: there are some arguments in favour of defective atmospheric pressure being one of the causes.

[†] Another disease which deserves mention is the virulent form of psora called Sarnas. When ill-treated, and when driven in, the consequences are always dangerous, and often fatal. It is ever difficult to cure, and it cannot be eradicated from the system without much more skill and perseverance than what is now the rule. In many parts of the Brazil it is as common as on the Congo River, where the Portuguese assert no stranger can long escape it.

[‡] Sr. Candido Mendez de Almeida gives the total population in the Brazil for 1868 as 11,030,000 souls, and Minas Geraes, 1,500,000. The Senador Pompeo, upon this subject the highest authority in the Brazil, gives the following estimate of her population in 1866 :—

	Free.	Slaves.	Savages.
The Court Municipality .	320,000	100,000	
Amazonas	69,000	1,000 }	
Pará	290,000	30,000 }	140,000
Maranhão	320,000	65,000 }	
Piauhy	210,000	22,000 }	5,000

grandmothers, at fourteen, and bear children till late in life. Unions between December of seventy and May of fifteen are common,* and the result is a wife coeval with her grandchildren by marriage. Connections of blood relations, such as uncle and niece, are not rare ; and, to the shame of the Catholic Church, it still grants dispensations to commit incest for a consideration. The results are not so terrible as in England, and especially in New England ; yet throughout the Brazil the finest population is always found in places which foreigners have most frequented.

The Mineira in her nursery song assigns a patriotic cause to her desire for issue—

> " Acalánta te ó menino,
> Dorme já para crescer,
> Que O Brazil precisa filhos—
> Independencia ou morrer.† "

Like her sister in New England and Ireland, she shows more philoprogenitiveness than amativeness ; and her diet is spare like that of the Scotch woman : ‡ these, on the rule that rich aristocracies decrease while poor communities multiply, may be part causes of her exceptional fertility. I have heard of apparently

	Free.	Slaves.	Savages.
Ceará	525,000	25,000	
Rio Grande de Norte .	210,000	20,000	
Parahyba . . .	250,000	30,000	
Pernambuco . .	1,000,000	250,000	
Alagôas	250,000	50,000	
Sergipe . . .	220,000	55,000	
Bahia	1,100,000	300,000	8,000
Espirito Santo . .	50,000	15,000	
Rio de Janeiro . .	750,000	300,000	
São Paulo . . .	750,000	85,000	
Paraná	80,000	10,000	8,000
Santa Catharina .	125,000	15,000	
S. Pedro . . .	340,000	80,000	
Minas	1,150,000	300,000	
Goyaz	135,000	15,000	15,000
Mato Grosso . .	40,000	6,000	24,000
Totals . .	8,134,000	1,784,000	200,000
Grand total . .	10,118,000		

* The husband will then address his wife as "Minha filha," something very terrible to Asiatic ears. The wife rarely calls her husband "husband :" she mostly prefers a paraphrase, as Compadre, or primo (cousin).

† Hush, my baby, lullaby,
Take thy sleep and quickly grow;
Needeth children the Brazil—
Independence or we die.

‡ In Scotland 100 children are born per annum of 348 women to 386 in England.

well-authenticated cases of superfetation.* The Mineira is an excellent mother, when superstition does not smother nature : but an "anjinho" or "innocente," a very young child, dies unregretted, because its future happiness is certain. The young are what we call "petted," or enfans terribles ; they are young gentlemen and ladies after the third year : en revanche through life, they preserve the greatest affection and respect for the mother, kissing her hand and asking her blessing every morning and night. In no country do progenitors sacrifice themselves so much to their progeny ; I knew a father who studied algebra in order to write an algebraic letter to his son. And nowhere are children more grateful : a lesson to that hateful being the "stern parent of Europe." Such a custom as "administering the innocents" is absolutely unknown. As in all new countries, the "infantry" grow up almost wild, and infinitely prefer the fazenda to the town ; so in the United States, the traveller first remarks the tameness of the horses and the wildness of the children.†

The dress of the Upper Ten is purely European. The Mineiro has cast aside the picturesque old Iberian costume, which was worn during the first quarter of the present century, the Spanish sombrero, plumed and broad-flapped, the short-mantled and gold-trimmed coat, the doublet or jacket of flowered cotton, and the large puffed breeches, with pink silk lining appearing through the slashes. The silvered horse-trappings are becoming obsolete, and though the spurs with crown-piece rowels are retained, they are mostly made in England. Morning-dress is unknown throughout the prim-mannered Empire : Brazilians will wear black clothes in the morning. A gentlemen never appears in the street, even at dawn, without chimney-pot tile (chapéo alto), black coat, waistcoat, and overalls black or white, cane or umbrella. Travellers must follow the semi-barbarous custom, and dress in broadcloth behind a bush before they enter a house. On the road the Mineiro will allow himself a Chile or Guayaquil (Panama)

---

* Not, however, that mentioned by Mr. Walsh, a hoax perpetrated upon him by my friend the Visconde de B——.

.† It was the same with the Tupys. Amongst the Sea Dyaks, "He is very wicked" is the greatest praise to a child. This also is the case amongst the so-called Kafir (Caffre) races : the more mis-chievous and boisterous the boy, the more proud is the father. Prof. Dabney (Life of Jackson, p. 15) alludes to the "relaxation of parental restraints which usually prevails in new countries ;"—he might add, amongst the uncivilised as opposed to semi-civilised races.

hat, and huge loose-topped boots, generally of half-tanned unblacked leather, which contain his slippers and other comforts. The linen, or rather cotton, is scrupulously clean,* with a propensity to starching and to dyeing sky-blue with indigo. The poor imitate the wealthy; but their garments are often home-woven and home-cut. The tailor "in partibus" charges about double what Stultz ever did.

The only relic of the national costume retained by the Mineira is seen only when she goes to mass. It is a mantilla of rich black silk, satin, or broadcloth, trimmed with stout home-made lace falling over the eyes; though lately patronised by H. H. the Pope, it is not held strictly correct in cities and towns. I have alluded to the frequency of bathing.† The sex delights in flowers and perfumes : in the wildest parts pots of basil, pinks, geranium, lavender, and sweet herbs are placed on troughs raised above the reach of pigs and poultry. They have an amiable predilection for diamonds and rich toilettes : a glance at a French milliner's bill in the Brazil shows the necessity of repressing the taste. At public balls the sumptuary law runs, "Ladies are politely requested to appear attired with the utmost simplicity," and sometimes even the use of gloves is deprecated.

SECTION III.

THE MORAL MAN.

Perhaps the best general view of this extensive subject will be given by the following official list of crimes which have come before juries of the Province during a period of ten years.‡

---

* In this point diametrically opposed to the Welsh, who are described as "scrupulously clean in everything but their persons."

† As a rule the Brazilian Indian in the wild state bathes every day at dawn, and afterwards whenever he wishes to cool himself.

‡ Many of these offences, it must be remembered, are committed by the servile population, which, under the excitement of the expected emancipation, is peculiarly prone to acts of violence. "The English are soon coming to set us free," I have heard said by negroes chattering at the fountain.

"On trouve chez les nègres beaucoup de dispositions et de persévérance pour s'instruire dans les arts et dans les sciences : ils ont même produit des personnages distingués." So says Prince Max. (i. 113—114), quoting Blumenbach, Beytrage zur Naturgeschichte (vol. i., p. 94). I must warn the reader against this vague assertion, which offers no manner of proof. In the days when those authors wrote, the mulatto was confounded with the negro ; moreover, the noble African races, namely, those mixed with Semitic blood, and leavened for a course of ages by connections with Southern Europe, were not distinguished from the pure African.

Table showing the Crimes committed in the Province of Minas Geraes, from 1855 to 1864.

PUBLIC CRIMES.

Years in which these crimes were committed	Against the free enjoyment and exercise of political rights.	Sedition.	Insurrection.	Resistance.	Flight and letting prisoners escape.	Disobedience.	Prevarication.	Bribery.	Excess or abuse of authority.	Omission or negligence in duty.	Irregularity of conduct.	Falseness.	Perjury.	Peculation.	False coining.	Destruction or injury to public goods.	Sum Total.
1855	...	...	...	3	12	1	...	...	...	1	3	...	1	2	1	1	...	25
1856	...	...	...	6	...	10	...	...	...	...	...	...	3	3	...	1	1	24
1857	...	...	...	6	4	...	...	1	...	...	2	...	1	4	1	...	1	20
1858	...	...	...	6	13	2	1	2	...	3	6	1	2	2	...	...	2	40
1859	...	...	...	6	14	1	1	...	...	...	1	...	3	3	...	...	1	30
1860	...	...	...	5	8	...	...	...	...	1	1	...	3	...	1	...	...	19
1861	3	...	...	2	4	...	...	...	...	...	...	...	3	1	1	...	...	14
1862	...	...	...	4	9	...	...	...	...	3	1	...	3	3	1	...	...	24
1863	2	1	...	8	11	...	1	...	...	4	1	1	3	3	2	...	...	37
1864	1	1	1	2	14	...	1	1	1	2	2	...	2	1	...	1	1	31
Sum Total	6	2	1	48	89	14	4	4	1	14	17	2	24	22	7	3	6	264

PRIVATE CRIMES.

Years in which these crimes were committed.	Against private liberty.	Homicide.	Attempt to murder.	Infanticide.	Wounds and physical offences.	Threats.	Breaking into private houses.	Rape.	Calumny and injury.	Polygamy.	Adultery.	Petty larceny.	Bankruptcy and other crimes against property.	Bodily injury.	Theft with violence.	Sum Total.
1855	...	80	15	...	139	16	1	1	1	1	...	...	14	5	9	14	296
1856	3	101	24	...	163	14	4	1	1	2	1	...	9	6	6	12	347
1857	6	108	36	...	163	26	1	2	1	5	1	...	8	3	14	9	383
1858	8	164	45	...	240	28	2	...	...	14	2	...	43	5	9	18	578
1859	5	163	44	1	266	37	3	5	2	16	...	...	24	14	15	35	630
1860	4	117	42	1	225	24	3	5	3	9	...	1	28	9	10	22	503
1861	1	80	36	...	85	8	...	2	2	2	...	2	7	4	5	22	256
1862	4	119	58	...	153	4	...	2	1	2	...	...	8	8	6	15	380
1863	2	135	40	1	150	10	1	6	...	1	1	...	12	1	4	12	376
1864	3	119	46	...	170	3	...	1	1	7	...	...	8	4	4	17	383
Sum Total	36	1186	386	3	1754	170	15	25	12	59	5	3	161	59	82	176	4132

POLITICAL CRIMES.

Years in which these crimes were committed.	Offences against religious morals and good manners.	Fabric and use of instruments to rob.	Illicit meetings.	Vagrancy.	Forbidden arms.	Abuse of the press.	Mutiny	Sum Total.
1855	...	...	2	...	43	...	...	45
1856	...	...	2	2	45	...	1	50
1857	...	...	4	3	35	...	4	46
1858	3	1	3	...	41	1	1	50
1859	...	...	2	...	52	...	...	54
1860	...	...	...	...	44	1	...	45
1861	...	...	...	...	2	...	...	2
1862	...	...	2	...	4	...	...	6
1863	...	...	1	...	7	...	...	8
1864	...	...	...	...	3	...	...	3
Total	3	1	16	5	276	2	6	309

General total.—1855, 366 ; 1856, 421 ; 1857, 449 ; 1858, 668 ; 1859, 714 ; 1860, 567 ; 1861, 272 ; 1862, 410 ; 1863, 421 ; 1864, 417 ; sum total, 4705.

Secretary of Police of Minas,
August 1, 1866.   ANTONIO XAVIER DA SILVA, Jun.,
Acting Secretary.

The document speaks for itself. I will only remark that the crimes against property are 204, against person 3299, out of 4705; and that to three cases of petty larceny there are 1186 murders. Yet Brazilian law protects, unlike ours, life and limb much more than goods and chattels. Here to raise a stick, even to use insulting language, is actionable, and the offence is severely punished. Foreigners say that it is better to kill a man in the Brazil than to wound him. It is criminal to shoot a burglar in the act of plundering your house. In England the law is grotesquely and scandalously in the other extreme, and the necessary tendency is to develop and foster the national vice, ruffianism and brutality.* The wife-beater and the street-malefactor, after the nearest possible approach to the homicide of an unoffending person, may rest assured that nowhere in the wide world they will be treated so kindly and considerately. But though they

---

* It is not long since the traveller was warned to beware of jealousy in Italy, ridicule in France, and the "lower orders" in England. France in 1866 had only one-sixth of the criminal trials by jury found necessary in England.

may flatten noses and break ribs for 5*l.* or a week of jail, they
must not touch watch or breast-pin, otherwise the Majesty of the
law will don its most terrible frown.

How is it, then, that in Minas—I may say in the Brazil generally—there is so little safety for life, which is so sedulously
protected ?

Amongst the rich, murders come from three causes, land,
political questions, and "affairs of the heart"—a member only
secondarily concerned in the matter—especially when the honour
of the family is concerned, and when only a shot or a stab
can set matters right.   The poor kill one another after quar-
rels about land, gambling losses, love, and liquor: the cachaçada or drunken fray often ends in bloodshed.   As a rule, all
males are armed : revolvers and bowie-knives when in cities are
worn concealed; in the interior no one walks or rides abroad
without a gun or long pistol (garrocha), and the knife never quits
his side.   Bloodshed is looked upon with little horror; practically there is not that regard and respect for human life, which
distinguish the older social state of Europe.   The affectionate
diminutive "facadinha" means a knife-thrust, and " uma morte-
zinha " (lit. " a little death ") is a murder, generally treacherous.
The moral impossibility of carrying out capital punishments—
of blotting out the criminal from the catalogue of living men—the
facility of breaking jail, and the scanty dread of hard labour with
the slave gang, are inducements to gratify revenge.   Lastly, most
of these criminals are uneducated; and if the prison is to be
closed, the school, and in this phase of civilisation, the parish
church, must be opened and kept open.   Let us ever remember
with M. Quetelet (Sur l'Homme, ii. 325) " c'est la société qui
prepare le crime, le coupable n'est que l'instrument qui l'execute."
" There goes my unfortunate self," exclaimed the good Fénelon,
when he saw a thief dragged to the gallows.

Some of the murders are scandalous.   We read, for instance,
in the city of Lavras that A. B. having a quarrel with C. D.,
wounded him five times, assassinated the municipal guard E. F.,
killed G. H., and severely injured I. K., who accompanied the
police magistrate to the spot.   In 1866 an M.D., married to the
grand-daughter of the Baron of R. V., an inoffensive man, well
spoken of, murdered him in the public square of the Freguezia
de S. Gonçalo da Campanha.   In the same year a Dr. A. B.,

riding with three friends in the vicinity of Philadelphia, was shot
dead from an ambuscade by C. B., who at once mounted his
horse and escaped. When I approached the Paulo Affonso Rapids
my men were discussing a murder which had taken place some
six weeks before. In this case there was the usual negro, and
more than one woman. The Senhora Isidora Maria da Conceição
preferred the Senhor 'Ferino (Zepherino) da Cruz to her lawful
spouse, the Senhor José Telles de Menezes, and the pair agreed
to put him out of the way. " 'Ferino" enlisted the sympathies
and assistance of his own wife, the Senhora Marianna Telles de
Barros, by telling her that the man to be killed had spoken
against her. "He must be slain!" exclaimed the duped lady.
The Brazilian Clytemnestra removed her husband's weapons, the
party knived their victim with many wounds, cut off his tongue
and ears, scalped him as Mohawks would have done, mutilated
him, and tying heavy stones to the arms, threw the body into the
Rio de São Francisco. It was found a fortnight afterwards apparently fresh, they said, evidently with a turn towards a minor
miracle. I asked the cause of the mutilation: the reply was
"para judearem," Jewishness. Here the Jewry still serves as a
synonym for all devilry.* The criminals are confined at Gere-
moába in the Province of Bahia, some twenty-five leagues from
the Porto das Piranhas; it is a country jail, peculiarly fitted for
effraction; moreover, any amount of perjury is at their disposal. A jury will be packed, and transit in rem judicatam will
probably settle the matter.

On the other hand the ratio of crime to population is trifling,
and, as has been shown, the law-loving, or rather the kindly
though fiery character of the Mineiro is shown by the state of
the police. With such and so small a repressive force, most
European countries would be uninhabitable. In 1866 England,
with a population of 20,000,000, yielded 19,188 criminal trials by
July, and 27,190 apprehensions for grave indictable offences.
Nowhere is travelling safer for foreigners who do not engage in
politics, amours, or law suits. Theft is unknown where strangers
have not settled: when I first descended the Ribeira de Iguape in

---

* So a man will often say " Judéo-nos,"
he has jewed us. Jew is still used here in
a sense which is utterly obsolete amongst
the educated classes in Europe. Had I a
choice of race, there is none to which I
would belong more willingly than the
Jewish—of course the white family.

1866 my boxes were left open. In 1867, after a little Anglo-American immigration, the people had become adepts in the art of picking and stealing, and every precaution had to be taken, even against free men. Amongst the Tupy tribes larceny was unknown, and in the interior of Minas it is still confined to slaves. Yves D'Evreux informs us that "Mondaron," or thief, was the greatest insult addressed to an Indian, and that the wild women preferred being called Patakere (meretrix) than Menondere.

The prevalence of intoxication surprised me. St. Hilaire testifies to the fact that in his time a drunken man was hardly ever seen. Gardner declared that, landing at Liverpool, he met in a few days more men in liquor than he had found amongst the Brazilians, black or white, during five years' travel. Prince Max. complains of the vice on several occasions,* but he was travelling amongst the wretched settlers of the Maremma, on the eastern coast.

My experience is as follows. In the Atlantic cities sobriety is the rule, especially amongst the educated,† and the climate hardly permits the abuse of stimulants to endure long. But in the interior the vegetable diet, the fatal facility of obtaining cheap and efficient liquor, the want of excitement, and the example of exiles, who find in the bottle their best friend, has made the lower orders, like those ruled by the Maine Liquor Law, a race of hard drinkers.

Old people have told me that in their youth the remark which capped the description of a reprobate, a "perdido," was, "and, it is said, he drinks." The dipsomania of Northern races afforded many a pleasantry now unfortunately obsolete. "Um Inglez bebado"—a drunken Englishman, "what a pleonasm! what tautology!" they exclaimed. "Tem sua baeta Inglez," he wears his English baize (or "frieze trusty"), was equivalent to "falla Inglez,"—he speaks English, in Portuguese Africa meaning

---

* Vol. ii. p. 364. "Le sejour de Villa-dos-Ilheos ne convenait pas aux Brésiliens que j'avais pris pour m'accompagner dans les forêts ; ils étaient tous grands buveurs d'eau de vie, et avaient occasionné plusieurs scènes désagréables." Vol. iii. 148. "La fainéantise et un penchant immodéré pour les boissons fortes sont les traits distinctifs du caractère de ces hommes" (the Vadio class). Also "Nous avons été souvent incommodés par des ivrognes, et nous avons eu quelquefois beaucoup de peine à nous débarrasser de ces hommes, qui nous gênaient singulièrement."

† It is only in this sense that I can understand Castelnau (i. 132), "L'ivrognerie est presque inconnu au Brésil."

"he's drunk." The Mineiro can no longer boast of that pleasant moral superiority. It is difficult to engage attendants, freemen as well as slaves, who do not habitually exceed, and if the "boss" show a bad example, the indulgence will pass all bounds. The "Tropeiro" and the boatman will begin the day with a dram, "para espantar O Diabo"—to fright the Fiend.* There is a second, "mata bicho"—kill-worm,† which, as the old pleasantry says, dieth not. After breaking fast at 7 or 8 A.M., a third, with sober men, follows dinner, from noon to 2 P.M., and often the night is spent by friends over a guitar (viola) and a garrafão (demijohn) of Cachaça. In a small village, after a fête-day, I have seen five or six men strewed on the road, and I have been repeatedly warned never to engage a crew for shooting rapids on the morning after a merry-making. Like Orientals, few men here drink temperately; those who drink drink hard, and those who avoid the vice are total abstainers—which tells its own tale. The consumption of ardent spirits exceeds, I believe, that of Scotland. Brazilians who are scandalised by the quantities that disappear, declare that the raw rum is used in baths. The Government would do well to publish the statistics of the subject, and these could easily be collected, as most of the distilleries are taxed, and Cachaça pays an octroi on entering the cities and towns. Anthropologists will remember the immense quantities of whiskey drunk in the United States, and it is curious to observe that the aborigines of the Brazil were extraordinarily addicted to intoxication. De Lery, the quaint old chaplain of Villegagnon, says (Voyage, 130—132): "Qu'il ne soit permis de dire arierre Alemans, Flamans, Lansquenets, Suisses et tous qui faites carhons et profession de boire, par de çà ; car tout ainsi que vous-mêmes, après avoir entendu comme nos

---

* H. S. M. is as much invoked as the "Diawl" in Wales.

† The expression "Matar O bicho," to kill the worm, is popular in every Portuguese colony. Its origin is thus explained. In the early part of the eighteenth century appeared a disease in Spain which made many victims. The physicians called it "mysterious," till a certain Dr. Gustavo Garcia, an old doctor who had retired from practice, proceeded to the autopsy of the dead, and found in the intestines a small worm still alive. He treated it with alcohol, which at once destroyed it; the

medicos took the hint, and every patient was at once dosed with a petit verre. From Madrid the habit and the expression passed to Portugal, and thence over the Portuguese world. Sr. Mendes de Faria, from whom these lines are borrowed, remarks, "Uns matam o bicho de manhã, outros ao jantar, muitos à noite, e a maior parte, em quanto lhes tinir um real na algibeira." "Some kill the worm in the morning, others at dinner time, many at night, and the majority as long as a coin rattles in their pockets."

Amériquains s'en acquittent, confesserez que vous n'y entendez rien au prix d'eux, aussi faut-il que vous leur cédiez en cet endroit."

The Mineiro, like the Paulista, is a religious man but a lax Catholic. Catholicism is here far removed from its legitimate centre, and has undergone some notable changes. At the same time he has, like the Paulista, a certain horror of any one non-Catholic. He is rather superstitious than fanatic, but all know how easily the former may pass into the latter phase. The persecuting element is not strong, although I have read the speech of a Provincial Deputy, who proposed to put to death a priest who became a convert or a pervert to "Protestantism." Hardly any one in these days builds a church—a wholesome sign of the times.* Many of the highly educated, if not the vulgar, advocate the marriage of the clergy, and the Regent Feijó wrote upon this subject a pamphlet, which was translated by an American missionary, Mr. Kidder. The parishioners have little objection to a Vigario who takes a wife and makes an honest man of himself. The climate is not favourable to chastity ; the race, especially where the blood is mixed, is of inflammable material, and the sayings and doings of slaves do not comport with early modesty. I need hardly say that the celibacy of the clergy is merely a matter of discipline, preserved in this day because it is, or is supposed to be, agreeable to the spirit of Christianity, and because it certainly is highly advantageous to the Church. On the other hand the superior dignity of virginity or sterility, either enforced or voluntary, is an idea revolting to reason and common sense, especially in a young country, where polygamy is morally justifiable, the evils being more than counterbalanced by the benefits.

In Minas and in the Brazil generally, where the " sabbath " is kept more strictly than in France and Southern Europe, we no

---

* I have already alluded more than once to this most important subject : let me here quote my lamented friend, Mr. H. T. Buckle (History of Civilisation, 2nd edit. ii. 174), with whose enlightened views I thoroughly agree.

" It is certain that in the middle ages there were, relatively to the population, more churches than there are now, the spiritual classes were far more numerous, the proselytizing spirit far more eager, and there was a much stronger determination to prevent purely scientific inferences from encroaching on ethical ones."

To this I would add, that there are countries where still lingers the gross mediæval superstition, namely, that after murdering a man, or beggaring a family, the most graceful thing to do is to expend part of the spoils in building a church and in feeing a priest. It is still one of the besetting " idols "—theological assumptions and metaphysical hypotheses.

longer find that abuse of fêtes, holy days, and saints' days, which in parts of the Old World still render useless half the month. Nor is the unmeaning practice of fasting carried to excess. The confessional is not abused except by the professional devote, and we seldom hear of a man who has recourse to his priest in all matters, trivial or important, secular or spiritual.* Briefly the people is ripe for religious reforms. Of these the principal would be an " irréligieux édit * : * qui autorise tous les cultes," all faiths should be permitted to build for their worship, temples, not houses. Civil marriages are allowed by law, a great advance beyond certain of the " nebulous " Hispano-Argentines, who, during the last few months, rose in riot against the innovation. But mixed marriages between Brazilians and foreigners must be relieved of certain drawbacks, such as compelling the issue to be brought up in the belief of Rome.† When the Church yields, the State cannot remain behind. Some day every immigrant citizen will be admitted to the highest posts under the government of which he volunteers to become a subject; now he can be a Senator but not a Deputy, that is to say, a colonel but not a captain. The Brazil will do well to consider the example of the United States, which have risen to their present state of prosperity by thorough and unlimited toleration : not because they are near Europe or enjoy a fine climate, or own a wealthy country, or can grant land by the square mile. All these advantages, to a greater extent, may, I believe, be found in the Empire.

* I shall reserve for another volume considerations on the present state of the secular clergy in the Brazil. As a rule they are grossly and unworthily abused by foreign, especially by English Catholics, who, as a rule, are Ultramontanes. My personal experience has taught me that they are far better than reading and hearsay entitled me to expect; they are sufficiently elevated in point of education above their flocks ; if not so "enlightened," they are far less bigoted than the stranger ecclesiastics now swarming to the Brazil ; and all, even their enemies, bear witness to their obligingness and hospitality. I am glad to find my opinion supported by the testimony of so good an observer as M. Liais (L'Espace Céleste, p. 220). "Il faut, au reste, reconnaître que dans ce pays le clergé Catholique a des opinions plus libérales et moins ultramontaines qu'en France. On l'a, en

général, calomnié. J'ai eu occasion, à Olinda surtout, de voir souvent des prêtres très recommandables sous tous les rapports."

† It will here occur to many that without an influential National Church an Empire can hardly be expected to last, and that complete toleration belongs to a limited Monarchy or a Republic. This is, I believe, true of the aristocratic form of Imperialism : in the democratic form, where the republic conceals itself under the mask of sovereignty, it appears a solecism, an anachronism. Before 1836, the Constitution of North Carolina declared that "no person who shall deny the being of God, or the *truth of the Protestant religion* (what may that be ?), shall be capable of holding any office or place of trust or profit." The Brazil, therefore, is still behind what North Carolina was a generation ago.

But they can never be thrown open to the world until complete equality in civil as in religious matters shall level all obstacles in the path of progress. There must, I believe, be some modification in the Brazilian Constitution before the nation can cease to be what the witty Frenchman termed it, " un peuple prospectus."

The Mineira lives in the semi-seclusion system which crossed the Atlantic from Iberia; it was there increased by the dominion of El Islam, which, on the other hand, borrowed some laxity from Christian example. " Femme file et ne commande pas." In none but the most civilised families do the mistress and daughters of the house sit down to the table with the stranger; amongst the less educated the déshabille is too pronounced to admit of reception without an almost total toilette. This state of things reminded me much of the Syrian Christians, who will not change their old system for the liberty, or, as they call it, the license of Europe. Men protect their women in two ways. Either, as Orientals, they keep them out of temptation; or, as we do, they expose them freely, but with the gaslight of publicity turned full upon them. Again in Europe there are minor differences of treatment. In France and Italy, in fact among the Latin races generally, the girl must not leave her mother's side; she may hardly walk out with her brother, who is held to be inefficient as a chaperon; but, once a wife, the surveillance is ended.* In England the maternal protection is unduly lax, and " flirtations " before marriage are not looked upon as offensive to society; thus those who enter the " holy state " are anything but virginal in mind. In Canada the freedom is carried to excess, quite as much perhaps as in the United States, but in the latter women are accompanied by the revolver and the bowie-knife.

As in tropical countries generally, the " awkward age " of long limbs and large extremities which immediately precedes the beauté du diable is unknown in Minas. The girls are never prettier than between thirteen and sixteen, when they are little women. Similarly there is no hobbledehoyhood and that hideous breaking of the voice which is apparently peculiar to the temperates.

I believe the state of the family to be in Minas, as in the Brazil

---

* I would not be understood here to repeat the absurd and disgraceful calumnies heaped upon French society in the beginning of the present century.

generally, exceptionally pure; and that, in this respect, many foreigners do the people a foul wrong. It would be amusing, if it did not provoke indignation, to hear a stranger, after a few months' residence, who can hardly speak a connected sentence of Portuguese, gravely supplement his want of experience by power of fancy, and quote the injurious saying which seems to have run from pole to pole, " Birds without song, flowers without perfume, men without honour, and women without honesty." Cities and large towns are mostly on a par as regards morality all the world over; a nation must be judged by its village and country life. Here a breach of virtue is almost impossible, opportunity is almost wholly wanting, and "chumbo na cabeça," or "faca no coração"* would certainly be the doom of the so-called " seducer." As in the United States and not in Iberia, the penalty in the Brazil falls upon the wrong person, the lover not the wife. This accords with the feeling in England, and, indeed, in most northern nations. Our Court of Divorce, if settling the case of Potiphar versus Potiphar and Joseph, would not permit the co-respondent to tell a tithe of the truth; he would, if unwise enough to attempt the defence of fact, be called an unmanly contemptible fellow by the judge, and he would go forth execrated of all England.

I may quote respecting the Mineira what the Countess Paula von Kollonitz† has said of the Mexican spouse. " The bulwark of relations by which a young wife is surrounded acts to a great extent as a protection to her: but, independently of that, I found them nearly always retiring and rigid, even to prudishness, when strangers were inclined to be presumptuous. Their marriages are really domestic and happy, married people are always seen together, and the husband lavishes gifts on his wife, which is considered a special mark of attachment." I may add that the exemplary conduct of the Brazilian women who have married English husbands speaks loudly in praise of the sex generally.

Dutch Bernard de Mandeville, whose plans for diminishing immorality—in the limited sense of the term—were so far before his age that they exposed him to a Middlesex Grand Jury in

---

* "Lead through the head : a knife in the heart." "I have resided at small towns in the interior, where the habits, and the general standard of morality of the inhabitants, were as pure as they are in similar places in England." The Naturalist on the Amazons (vol. i. p. 43).

† The Court of Mexico. Messrs. Saunders, Otley & Co.

1723, asserted, to the scandal of all "proper persons," that the
Hetæra class is numerous or few in exact ratio to the purity or
depravity of the family.   The loosest places in Europe are those
where the Agapemone is poorly kept up and frequented only by
strangers.*   The extreme prevalence of professional prostitution
in the country towns of the Brazil, as described by travellers
before 1820, and which gave the proverb "mulher e cachaça em
tudo lugar se acha," has now disappeared.   Yet in the
"chapelries," which are frequented on Sundays and festivals by
the "squirearchy," there will be three or four daughters of
Jerusalem, each making 150l. per annum, here equivalent to 500l.
in England; the money comes from the planters' sons, who in
Europe would apply to the wise woman or the cartomantiste—
which is worse.   And, as Cato knew, there is a great deal of
difference between public and private vice.

Poetical justice in the matter of the Hebrew is dealt out to the
Brazilian by Europe, which loves to call him the "Jew of South
America," and the same has been said of the New Englander.
Both races are essentially "smart," and "smartness," be it
observed, is rapidly finding its way eastward ; † both produce first-
rate men of business, and many have made colossal fortunes in
a few years.   The "pobre rico," or poor rich man, who lives like
a beggar and lends his hoards at 15—24 per cent. is not
unknown ; as a rule, however, money is freely spent, and there is
little of the grasping, tenacious covetousness vulgarly attributed
here to the Portuguese, amongst us to the Hebrew.   The highest
homage is paid to commerce ; half the titled men in the land have
been or are in trade, directly or indirectly ; a planter's house is
not finished without a shop on the ground-floor, and I have not
yet met a Fazendeiro who would not sell his estate, in whole or
in part, with slaves or without slaves.

St. Hilaire, who had become almost a Mineiro, found a want

---

* At Hyderabad, in Sindh, the break up
of rigid Moslem rule was followed by a
deluge of debauchery.   I well remember
that the dancing girls, in a pathetic memorial to Sir Charles Napier, declared that
the married women were "taking the
bread out of their mouths."   We at once
learn what New York is by reading in the
Census of 1865, that the unmarried are
423,121 ; the professional prostitutes known
to the police, 3,000 ; and the total number
of women who live by prostitution publicly
and privately, 25,000.   Here we have a
polyandry of at least 17 men to 1 woman.
One of the most depraved cities which I
have seen numbered 200,000 souls, and two
small "Agapemones."

† An excellent paper might be written
upon the effect which Anglo-America is
exercising upon the English mind for good
and for evil ; the former palpably predomi-
nating.

of cordiality when he left Minas.* My experience is the reverse of his. The Paulista, though reserved, is more at home with strangers than his cousin; the latter may be described as "acanhádo," which partially answers to our word "shy." There is a painful amount of ceremoniousness, which takes us back to the primitive punctiliousness of Minho e Douro. Both Provinces are equally hospitable, both dislike distance of manner, and both prefer the French manner of address to the English—as the difference was a third of a century ago. But on the road the Paulista pulls off his hat, gives you a hearty good-morning, and willingly answers every question. The Mineiro eyed us hard before touching his tile, often his hand hung suspended between saddle and head, childishly calculating whether the stranger would or would not acknowledge the salute. Sometimes he stared at me surlily and angrily, the women "made faces," and the men returned a sharp answer, which forbade all hope of intercourse. This, however, was my misfortune. The Paraguayan war made the people of the interior consider every foreigner as an agent of government, or travelling for some dark purpose. In one place I became the Chief of Police, a functionary who, as a rule, does not appear till some one is "wanted," and who makes even the innocent take to the bush. On the Rio de São Francisco I found myself President Lopez, and I was never less than a "recruiting officer," a character about as popular as the gauger in old Ayrshire when Robert Burns sang, or as the bailiff in Connemara when governed by Martin of Galway. Moreover with increased numbers of European visitors and settlers the Mineiro has not learned increased respect for foreigners, and no wonder. Familiarity with such men—I hasten to say that there are many notable exceptions—can breed only contempt.

Minas has produced the two parents of the Brazilian Epic, and her sons have distinguished themselves in arts and arms throughout the Empire. The intellectual range of the Mineiro has mostly been confined to the humanities. Modern science cannot be acquired in the Province, mechanics are unknown, but the belles-lettres are open to all. Like the Neo-Latins generally, they easily learn the cognate dialects, and their nimble but somewhat

---

* In II. i. chapter 2, and elsewhere.

desultory comprehension masters with ease the various introductory branches of mathematics. They have a very decided
sotaque or brogue, which at first is not easily understood. The
Paulista speaks with his mouth unduly open; his is the Doric, the
North-country dialect of the Brazil. The Mineiro closes his lips
and eats his words till they fail to catch the strangers' ear; it is
Lancashire versus Northumberland. This is doubtless derived
from old times, when there was great mixture of Indian blood
St. Hilaire (III. ii. 107, and ii. 263) makes it a characteristic of
the Red-skins. "Comme les diverses nations indiennes que
j'avais vues, jusqu'alors les Cayapós parlent du gosier et de la
bouche fermée." He is confirmed by all travellers, even from
the earliest ages. Prince Max. (iii. 166) says of the Camacans or
Menians, "Ils coupent brusquement la fin des mots, parlent bas
et la bouche à moitié ouverte."

I am unwilling to extend this Chapter by extracting from
official sources statistics of educational establishments and lists of
scholars. Throughout the Brazil these details look better upon
paper than in the flesh. But the subject is never neglected, and
the greatest "thinkers" do not consider it unworthy of their
highest attention. The school, "the mysterious laboratory where
the man and the child in collaboration prepare the future." Moreover it may be safely said that every poor man's son, except in
the remotest places, can obtain primary instruction, that the
three R's are generally studied, and that those unable to read
and write do not number as many as in England and France.*
Moreover, the total darkness still found among the lower orders
in Europe, the utter absence of all knowledge, is here confined to
idiots. Some Provinces, like Paraná, have shown their wisdom

---

* Throughout England, in 1840, only 58
per cent. could sign their names in the
marriage registers. In 1851 the population rose to 62 per cent., and in 1864 to
72 per cent. What can be expected when
the State devoted to education the miserable
sum of £636,806 per annum, about equal
to what is annually wasted upon the Sentimental or West African squadron? In
France, roughly speaking, one-third of the
population cannot read and write, and there
are 55 of the 89 Departments in which the
number of the illiterati ranges from 30 to
75 per cent. In 1855 the proportion
generally was 39·92 per cent. In 1864

the percentage of men who were analphabetic was 27·88 : that of women 41·45, the
general average being 34·66. Of the
criminal cases tried in Minas during 1865,
5 were well educated, 136 could read, and
187 were analphabetic : total, 328. In
1867, the respective numbers out of 290
were 1, 116, and 173.
  I am hardly astonished to see the late
Dr. Knox assert, "We have it from the
latest travellers, that the ignorance of the
so-called (?) Brazilian is something astound-
ing." (Ethnological Inquiries and Observations, Anthropological Review, Aug. 1863,
p. 252).

in compelling children to attend school; and this, I believe, will soon extend throughout the Empire. At present the fault is rather with the seniors than with the juniors, and parents have not had time to learn what education means.

Books and magazines being still rare and expensive, the newspaper is the staple of literary pabulum throughout Minas. In every shop from early dawn the master or his men may be seen wasting time—foreigners call it—over the periodicals. As the citizen of the United States, so the Brazilian finds amply sufficient enjoyment in a glass of water, here not iced, and a cigar, there a quid or chaw, accompanied by a newspaper. I may here venture to suggest a remarkable similarity between the highest forms of European society and that of the Empire and the Western Republic. What man of the world, especially what woman in Paris, ever reads anything but a newspaper or a magazine? Who in London life has time to turn over a page beyond the dailies, weeklies, and monthlies? In how many country-houses are the books upon the tables and on the shelves never touched by any one except the duster?

The reason is that the newspaper is progression, it is the literature of the Future. As Lamartine informed the French Chambers, it will, before the century ends, embrace all human thought, and become the word of man. When journalism shall be infinitely extended by machinery, and submit every day to the public eye every question treated in the fullest manner, the octavo must take the form of the broad sheet. As an old ex-editor I cannot agree with M. Emile de Girardin, "rather one day of office than ten years of journalism"—nor has he worked out his aspirations.

The especial glory of the nineteenth century is that it is rescuing education, learning, enlightenment, from the professionally savans and the Upper Ten Thousand; and sending it abroad as a gospel to mankind. And this will ever distinguish it as an era. Thus, in the beginning of man's religious life, the Lawgiver of the Hebrews took from the Egyptian priests, who had veiled it in the deepest obscurity of faith and practice, the idea of the One God, which has never been, and which can never be, lost to the human mind. ⎤ *interesting*

At the end of the last generation, Gardner found at Ouro Preto a couple of printing offices and four newspapers in small folio :

two of these were ministerial, and the "balance" was opposition;
both were wholly political. Now increased communication with
the metropolis has reduced the typographies to one, the "Typographia do Minas Geraes;"* the periodicals to two; this is also
an evidence of subsiding popular excitement. The "Constitucional" is Conservative; it appears once a week, generally on
Sunday, and the editors are Dr. Camillo da Cunha Figueiredo,
B.A., and Dr. Benjamin Rodrigues Pereira. The "Diario de
Minas," a daily (dating from January 1, 1868), as the name denotes,
is edited by a Liberal, D. João Francisco de Paulo Castro, whose
party has now long been in power. It is in the usual style of the
Brazilian country papers, a single sheet, four columned, twenty-
eight inches × fifteen. There is a leading article, which, like
that of the "Eatanswill Gazette," utterly smashes the opposition
and the rival. News and correspondence from Europe and from
the other Imperial provinces follow the arrival of the post; when
the Legislative Assembly is sitting, the Official Part contains the
speeches fairly reported, and there is generally something about
price current. Being in power, and probably well salaried, it can
afford to be calmer and to show more temper than the Conservative. Here, as elsewhere, the tone of the newspaper is the
expression of society. Allusions to kicking and horsewhipping,
scandalous personalities and violent language, are not unknown to
Brazilian journalism; but they are generally reprobated, and will
presently meet the fate of the "Satirist;" and even now the talk
is rarely taller than what we find in an Irish article upon some
subject of ephemeral interest. I have never seen anything to be
compared with the "Bombay Times," under Dr. Beust—the
"blatant beast" of the "Devil's Brother," or of a certain
London magazine which devoted itself during its short life to
Oriental subjects.

To a traveller, the most characteristic part of a newspaper is,
perhaps, its advertisements. He takes up the "Constitucional,"
there is a "mudança de nome," some man changing name simply

* In this is a "Corcunda" (High-Tory)
named Luiz Maria de Silva Pinto, who,
being aged 86 or 87, well remembers the
events of 1789. He always speaks with
great respect of the Royal clemency to the
authors of Brazilian independence. I have
remarked Southey's prepossessions in favour
of a country which converted the Brazil
into an agricultural and mining establishment. Curious to say, a Brazilian General,
J. I. de Abreu Lima (Compendio, Chapter
5, s. 6), speaks contemptuously of her
great movement, the Inconfidencia. "As-
sim se mallogrou o insensato projecto de
uma sociedade que mantinha no proprio
seio o germen de sua destruição."

to avoid confusion. A. B. C. D. de E. publicly returns general
thanks to those who received him hospitably during his last
journey—a graceful practice. The relations and friends of the
deceased Sr. Fulano de Tal are invited to meet at a solemn
requiem mass, celebrated for the repose of his soul, and they will
be there : this is headed with a profile sketch of a tomb, bearing
the inscription MORTE, overhung by a widow in a poke-bonnet, and
with the orphan sitting disconsolate upon the ground. "Fugido"
in the largest letters, 50 $ 000 in full-length figures, and an
anthropoid with a bundle over his shoulder and a switch in his
hand, show that a chattel has "made tracks" and is wanted. A
cardboard house and two unvegetable-like trees denote a "chácara," a "sitio," or a town-residence for sale. A piano, a few books,
some musical pieces, gloves, boots, lottery-tickets, and stationery
are recommended to the public. But the mass of the two pages
is filled with patent medicines. Under the titles of "the Lame
Walk," and the "Battle of Life," salsaparilla of Bristol modestly
disguises itself. The quina of Laroche and Blancard's pills, &c.,
disdain such pretences. And that Great Britain may be adequately represented, the wonder-working unguento and pildoras
(Spanish), or pilulas (Portuguese) — "bother the pills" — of
Holloway sprawl barefaced over at least two columns.

Finally, "a Pedido" denotes the communiqué. This correspondence is generally sent unsigned or footed by a fancy or a real
name, popularly known as the "testa de ferro :" he bears blame
for a consideration. It is the most rabid, if not the only rabid,
part of the issue.

CHAPTER XXXIX.

RETURN TO MORRO VELHO.

O mormaço
Causava agudas dôres de Cabeça,
Porque O clima não é do ameno Campo
Do aurifero paiz chamado *Minas.*
José Joaquim Corrêa de Almeida.

WE had given all possible time to the interesting capital, and
I was becoming anxious to reach the Rio de São Francisco before
the rains set in. Our return to Morro Velho would cover only
twelve short leagues, but as the country was new, two days were
devoted to it. The exit from Ouro Preto is *via* the Caminho da
Cachoeira, and after passing the church "Sr. Bom Jesus de
Matosinhos," we struck the open country. The day was heavy
with warm heat,* and a thick blue haze softened the rugged
profile of the Itacolumi chain. From that point the range began
to fade, and soon the romantic peak looked like a fragment of
slanting mist, based upon a long, light, azure cloud.

After two hours we reached the Ranch of José Henriques, a
little "povoado," where the road forks to Nª Sª da Nazareth
da Cachoeira do Campo, whose name has already occurred. We
took the right, or eastern path, and exchanged the Valley of the
Rio Doce for that of the Rio das Velhas. "Esbarrancados,"
huger than usual, pitted the slopes of the divide, and we crossed
a narrow natural isthmus between the yawning water-breaches,
whose sides were zoned with the usual rainbow tints, whilst a
thick shrubbery clothed the soles. Thence the path led down a
minor eastern head-water of the "Old Squaws." The water was
muddy, with up-stream washings, and ran in a bed of pink sand
and clay, dotted with white quartz—a kind of fancy rivulet.
From afar we had sighted the Arraial of Sᵗᵒ Antonio da

---

* Here called Mormaço.

Casa Branca and its white church, perched upon a hill; but it was two hours before we reached it, and were able to rest for half an hour on the steps of a kind of ranch. Dr. Couto says of this place, that it had flourished before 1801, but that a stone chapel was all that it had to show for its gold. The industries are now agriculture and cattle-breeding. Two instances of longevity were here quoted: one a "lavrador," or small proprietor, still robust, though 100 years old; and the other, ten years senior to him, was Genoveva Pereira Bastos, a sage femme, experienced in the profession—her grand-great-grand and great-great-grandchildren (teternetos) amounted to 120.

After passing the old chapel, we came upon a hilly country, of very mean soil, with a road neither good nor bad. Presently we crossed two contiguous bridges over the true head-waters of the Rio das Velhas. The muddy and deeply-bedded stream, forty feet broad, swirled grimly round a holm, upon which there was a house. It drains the narrow sack formed by the Serra do Capanéma,* by the Serra do Ouro Preto to the south, and to the east by the Serra de São Bartholomeu.

Thence we ascended a long hill, and found clouds drifting heavily from the north-west. The dull heat was now dispersed by raw wind, and rain came on, with a succession of storms which lasted uninterruptedly for thirty-six hours, making the clay greasy as tallow. To the right, and below us, lay the little village of São Vicente, with its two-towered church, some miners' quarters, and the "Casa Grande" of notable size, showing that an English Company has dropped its money there. From the green hills behind it a fine head of water, tumbling white, could be seen through the thick falling drops.

The "Morro de S. Vicente estate" belonged to D. Rosa, the widow of an English mechanic. About 1864, when the Sabará diggings, of which more presently, failed, it was bought by the "East Del Rey Company" at an expense of £36,000. Of this total two sums, £14,000 and £1700, reached the owner. Some of the shares have not been paid up, and the shareholders are not registered.

The dip of the lode is 28°, and the strike is east to west. The

---

* There is also a village of this name derived from an old Brazilian family. A certain Manoel da Costa Capanéma is found in the list of the "Inconfidentes:" he was a shoemaker and was pronounced innocent.

vein here and there runs between crystal and quartz, and the latter gives free gold, sometimes partially crystallized, and affording pretty cabinet specimens. The metal is found in " eyes," or rather in shoots running diagonally across the formation. It was first worked on the " open-cut " system, and afterwards by shafting. The stone is stamped and straked, and amalgamation is not used.

Failure is its actual state. Surface works have been heavy, whilst machinery and other underground appliances have been light; and the falling-in of the mine interrupted the pumping. A philanthropic banker of Falmouth, " a great anti-slavery man," determined to astonish and gratify the world by showing the grand results of free black labour. It reminds one of the merchant who, to cure sailors of their superstition, built and lost the ship " Friday." The issue, as might be expected, was pure perte, and the projector, disgusted with his project, soon disposed of his shares. They report that a new company is to be formed in England, and that São Vicente will again be put upon his trial. The little lode may pay if worked safely, that is to say, scientifically and economically.

We rode through rain striking upon our faces, and, as evening was gathering in, we entered by a long descent the " Arraialito," known as the Rio das Pedras. The single street showed to the east the Rosario Church, and westward the half-built Capella de Nª Sª de Conceição. There are also two smaller chapels; in fact, the churches are almost as numerous and far exceed in cubic contents the dwelling-houses—a pleasant aspect to the ecclesiastic, and an eye-sore to the economist.

We had sent on our Camaráda, Joaquim Borges, to order dinner and beds: luckily. At the door of the pigmy hostelry we caught sight of an elderly citizen in a hammer-claw, or swallow-tail black coat, and we found a party of Southerner immigrants wandering about in search of land. The leader was a Mississippi man, accompanied by two daughters and one son-in-law, two companions from the same State, and a Georgian who was hailing back for the Plate River, despite Indians, Gauchos, and other little difficulties. Mostly these strangers had been accustomed to the flats of Florida and the plains on the bank of the .Yazoo River. None of them came from the Midland States, where men raise cereals and cotton—at present, perhaps, the most important and certainly the safest industry in the Brazil.

I had already met several parties of these refugees, and they were not my last experience. The first impression made by our Transatlantic cousins—speaking only of the farmer and little educated class—is peculiar and unpleasant. In them the bristly individuality of the Briton appears to have grown rank. Their ideas of persons and things are rigid as if cast in iron; they are untaught, but ready to teach everything.* Each one thinks purely and solely of self, from the smallest acts and offices of life, such as entering a room or sitting. down at meals, to the important matter of buying land or of finding a home. All have eyes steadily fixed upon the main chance; every dodge to "get on" is allowable, provided that it succeeds; and there is no tie, except of blood, to prevent at any moment the party falling to pieces. Amongst themselves there is no geniality; of strangers they are suspicious in the extreme, and they defraud themselves rather than run the risk of being defrauded. Nothing appears to satisfy them; whatever is done for them might have been done a "heap deal better." As the phrase is, they expect roast pig to run before them, and even then they would grumble because the crittur was not properly fixed for them.

This is not an agreeable account of the pioneers now leading the great Anglo-American movement in the Brazil. Yet we presently find out that these are the men wanted by the Empire to teach practical mechanical knowledge, to create communications, and to leaven her population with rugged northern energy. Bred in a sub-tropical country, seasoned to fevers, and accustomed to employ negroes, they will find the Mediterranean Brazil an improved edition of their old homes. Nothing is to be said against the German in this country, except that he is too fond of farming, as he often did in the United States—an "imperium in imperio;" moreover, his political ideas are apt to be in extremes. The Frenchman, like the Portuguese, comes out empty, as the old saying is, and goes back full. The Englishman, except under Morro Velho discipline, languishes and drinks. As regards bodily labour, he is inferior to the negro. The Scotchman prefers great cities. The Irishman has been hitherto found unmanageable, but under the Anglo-American, who knows so

---

* One of them, and perhaps the best educated, had heard of Hannibal and the vinegar which split the Alps. I heard him recommend the plan to a Portuguese, and remember the face of the latter after the trial. In this part of the world vinegar is nearly as dear as wine.

well to drive and manage him, he will be a valuable hand, the muscle and the working power of the country.

It was impossible not to admire the pluck and spirit of these pilgrims. Everything was new and strange to them, they saw what they did not understand, they heard what they could not comprehend—it was quite indifferent to them. They mounted their wretched nags; they wandered about at night; they slept in the woods heedless of Maroons and "tigers," and they were brought in by the negroes to•the planters' houses, which they often mistook for hotels—in fact, they became a standing marvel to the land. An old man, with a foot and a half in the grave, unaccompanied by a servant, and riding not as the Rechabim rode, a garron, like the steeds of Agincourt, carrying a carpet-bag and a paper of bread, but without even a blanket, actually set out to descend the São Francisco River, cross to the head waters of the Tocantins, and float down to the Amazons. He had been wandering upwards of a year in the Brazil: he had not learned a sentence of Portuguese, and probably he never could. Like the British sailor, he instinctively determined that those who cannot understand good English will be better suited with it broken, "*Me* no sabby, *me* no carey, *me*—very peculiar *me*— no drink wine—vinho—*me* no drink coffee—caffé—*me* no drink spirits." This, aided by the presence of a mighty quid, was intended to enlighten the dullest understanding. His account of meeting in the backwoods with an English-speaking youth had its comic side. The latter pulled up his galloping nag, stared at the solitary figure dressed in a kind of winter greatcoat, collaring him to the head and skirting him to the heels; at the crumpled-up trousers; at the under-drawers, forming a "lucid interval;" and at the unblacked boots, with toes well turned out. Presently he found presence of mind enough to exclaim,—

" Who the h— are you ?"

" Guess," replied the senior, "that *that* don't concern *yeou.*"

" Where the d— are you going ?"

" Wal," was the rejoinder, "s'pose it don't much matter to *yeou.*"

" What are you doing, then ?"

" 'Calc'late, young man, that you had better move off that way, and I go this way," suiting the action to the word, and thus they parted.

He offered to accompany me, but I could not bring myself to

say yes. Hunger and thirst, fatigue and vigil, are all endurable, not so the bore.

> Garrulus hunc quando consumet cunque ; loquens
> Si sapiat, vitet—

This venerable egotist was candid enough to declare that he wanted my company as an interpreter. At every five minutes he would interrupt conversation with "Tell him so and so," or "Ask him this and that." He wanted me to sell his garron, to threaten that it should be turned loose upon the world if it could not fetch its price, to "swap" it for a canoe. *Malè salsus,* I translated him literally, and the expression of the Brazilian countenance, with a painful tendency to a guffaw—a "gargalhada"—which civility forbade, was a study. At the age of sixty-two he seemed to have outlived all sense of gratitude, and to say a good word of any one would, I believe, have killed him.

This Southerner emigration will be, to a certain extent, a natural selection from the United States, even as the population of the latter is a selection of species from Europe. What I mean is, that, whereas the old, the sick, and the feeble in mind and body remain at home; the young, the brave, and the adventurous, even the malcontent, the criminal, and the malefactor go forth in search of fortune, and find it.

The population of the Brazil, a land whose extent is equal to the United States, and whose natural advantages are far superior, is but little in excess of what the Republic could show in 1820—somewhat over ten millions, including negroes and "Red-skins." About that time began the great squatter movement to the south and west of the Mississippi Valley, which so wonderfully increased European immigration. The new comers found miserable little settlements of straggling "shanties," occupied by a few hundred mongrels, mulattos and mixed breeds, French and Spaniards, with the savage at their doors. Such, for instance, was St. Louis, Mo. In less than half a century it is a vast and wealthy city, with a magnificent future awaiting her. Many of the earliest immigrants returned from the Valley. They were disgusted with the wild life ; they wanted "comforts," and they did not like the vicinity of the tomahawk and the fever. But the strong men remained, and before 1860 they had attracted a population sufficient for an empire.

And thus it will be with the Brazil. Thus only can she expect to play a conspicuous part in the great drama of Human Progress.

On the next day we set out early through the wind and rain. In the afternoon we reached Morro Velho, where the heartiest welcome awaited us. We felt almost spoony enough to quote the spoony lines—

> Home ! there is magic in that little word,
> It is a mystic circle that surrounds
> Pleasures and comforts never known beyond
> Its hallowed limits.

CHAPTER XL.

TO SABARÁ.

Kennst du das Land wo die citronem blühn
Im dunkeln Laub die Gold-Orangen glühn ?

Goethe.

AFTER another comfortable fortnight at Morro Velho, I prepared to embark from Sabará. Mr. L'pool had now made his
book, and was—*Deo gratias—en route* to the coast. With a
peculiar cat-like feeling I bade adieu to the Casa Grande, where
we had found an English home in the Highlands of the Brazil.
My excellent compatriots, however, accompanied me to break
the shock of departure. The day was Tuesday, the weather
rainy—auspicious both—and I looked forward to being one of
the pioneers of a great national movement.

We crossed the Ribeirão, and ascended the northern, or " Old
Hill," by the " Mine Road," past features now familiar ; we
ducked heads to the pump-lift, and we glanced at the grist
or flouring-mill. M. Müller, who has charge, takes great pride
in its superiority to all others in the Province but one. On the
left were the villages of " Boa Vista " and " Timbuctoo," hollow
squares, in shape much resembling the " T'hembe " of Unyamwezi, and easily convertible into fortified posts, whose low, white
walls and heavy tiled roofs would give trouble. The interior
is divided into courts. The married have separate houses ;
the unmarried are divided into gangs of fifteen or twenty,
according to the size of the quarters, and the place set off for
the girls is called—from the utter absence of conventual discipline, I presume—the " Convent." These villages are under
the surveillance of four black captains, who are on duty by night
as well as by day ; they must exert themselves hard to ensure
anything of cleanliness, and some of the slaves are incorrigibly
swinish. All is perfect Inner African within the quarters : the

little fire burns on the hearth at midday, and each door has its
tall steps of rugged stone, upon which the inmates sit and smoke
and sun themselves.

Turning to the left we struck " Smyth's Road," which rounds
the hill in a civilised style. Westward, and distant about two
miles, is the Convalescent Station, " Campo Alegre," a rancho
for sick blacks, put up by themselves. It has not a vestige of
" prairie," but the hilly grounds supply in abundance coffee,
vegetables, and firewood. Beyond it we see the Paraopéba road
winding over the hills, and in front of us rises the goatee
" Morro do Curral d'El-Rei."

The " Curral " is the southernmost apex of a chain which
divides the Paraopéba and Upper São Francisco from the course
of the Rio das Velhas. Its general direction is north-north-
west, and it extends about 3°, or 180 miles; the various names,
beginning from the south of the range, are Serra do Salto, Serra
da Sella Ginete, and Serra do Espiritu Santo. Beyond the
confluence of the Rivers São Francisco and das Velhas it
prolongs itself by the Serra do Jenipápo and Serra do Itacolumi, after which it meets the Serra da Mata da Corda coming
from the south-west.

The Curral is curiously weathered into cliffs and jags* of the
usual volcanic shape, covered with green. It is a Proteus, here
looking like a regular pyramid, there like a quoin, and there
knob-shaped; it will remain visible for many a mile, and we
shall see it even from the river. It appears to me the northern
limit of the hilly metalliferous, especially the great pyritic, formations, and beyond it begin the flatter and more cultivable
soils, especially the great limestone fields; this, however, will
demand further investigation. A ride to the cross, hence two
miles northwards, and distant five to six by the road, gives a
view ennobled by physical size. The soil is poor, but the
immense quantity of rain caught by the cold Peak causes it to
be tolerably clothed. Towards the south we see nothing but
hills and hollows, suggesting the old simile of a raging sea
suddenly turned to earth; here there is nothing level but the
horizon. Below us are the Bananal tanks and leats, and a mule-
farm, where a patch of water is mistaken for a house. Nearer

---

* Serrote is the native name of this minor feature : it properly means a handsaw.

is the Taquaril, a deserted gold-mining estate now in process of
"rehabilitation." It lies very high up, and I should imagine
that the expense of water-supply would be enormous. Just
below the cross is "Mocámbo,"* a good bit of land. Northward
the rises and falls are those of a more tranquil ocean, and the
smooth green valley of Curral d'El-Rei shows a little white
village of cultivators and cattle-breeders, who number some 359
fires. It is one of the seven churches which can be seen on a
clear day; the others are S. Sebastião, Fidalgo, Contagem,
Capella Nova, Matosinhos, and Jaguára, to which some add an
eighth, Sta Luzia.

It is difficult to make cart roads over this up and down of
stiff clay. Even our mules do not find it easy to keep their
feet, and the pace is three miles an hour. We round a hill-side,
and sight for the first time Sabará, distant over eight miles.
This is one of those amene and charming prospects which so
often burst upon the Brazilian traveller's eye and form such a
relief after the general cachet of uniformity and monotony which
Solitude and Nature unrelieved by Art affix to its magnificence.
Like most of these places, it is fairest seen from afar, when
irregularity adds to its beauty. The large patch of milk-white
and red-roofed houses, with quintals, at once "compounds,"
gardens and orchards, rich with the deep, green verdure of the
orange and the myrtle, set off by the lighter banana, lies upon
a sloping bank in a kind of "Doab," or "Rincon," where two
streams form an angle. Its majestic background is the celebrated
Serra da Piedade,† a huge lump, generally capped by thick clouds.
To the east this stone-stripped wall bristles with organs or
needles, and we could not but observe its resemblance to the
metalliferous Serras of S. João and S. José. We were to enjoy
its imposing presence for some days; it began by weeping over
us a heavy shower, even as the Brazilian aborigines shed bitter
tears when they meet a friend.

The land of hard yellow clay is poorly clad; but, as usual,
the bottoms are well wooded and would grow cotton. There are

---

* This word means a stronghold of criminals and maroons. Constancio makes it
synonymous with Quilombo. Koster alludes to the Mocámbo, 2, xix.

† Curious to say, M. Gerber (Map, 1862)

has placed the Piedade south-west instead
of north-east of Morro Velho, and has left a
white space on the north of "Cuiabá." M.
Burmeister's map gives it correctly.

extensive *débris* of "Pisarra,"* a name given throughout the
Brazil to many different formations, laminated yellow argile, or
limonite, decomposed rock, and imperfect "killas." The clothing
of the uplands is the usual Cerrado of Barbatimão, wild guava
and "folha larga;" and the shorter growth is of tall Sapé
(Saccharum Sapé) and ferns. Congonha tea abounds, but near
the road it has been torn up by the muleteers. The clearings,
here called fazendas de fogoës † — stove-farms — show a little
sugar of poor quality. Cattle, it is said, suffer from the poisonous
plants, chiefly Rubiaceæ,‡ which appear in the second growth,
and which are known as "Herva de Rato." The tropeiras all
assert that when forage is scarce many of their animals are
killed by them, and they have several simples upon which they
rely. I believe, however, that very often the deaths result from
change of pasture; moreover, no man has yet been able to show
me the "ratsbane."

Turning into a bridle-way on the left of the road we came upon
the charcoal-burners who were working for Morro Velho. Here,
but not everywhere, they have abandoned the old pit in favour of
wood-heaps piled round with "Candeias" (Lychnophora, Mart.)
about four feet high, banked up with sods and clay. The system
is still very rude, and much carbon disappears with the oxygen
and hydrogen. We presently fell into the Valley of the Córrego
de Rapaunha which drains the southern face of the Curral.
The name, "Scrape-hoof," is one of many similar trivialities,
as "Farinha Podre," or rotten flour, "Rapa-queijo," scrape-
cheese, "Papa-farinha," grub-flour, "Gallinha choca," spent-hen,
and "Passa-tres," pass-three, because probably that number of
travellers first crossed it. They suggest the nomenclature of the
very Far West further north, and the Black Bob's Creek, Dead-
man's Flat, Monk's Trunky Creek, and Scabby Flat of romantic
Australia. Presently we turned to the right and entered private
grounds, the Fazenda de Andre Gomez: Seville oranges were
scattered over the earth, and the red-yellow flower of the Guandú
pea (Cajanus indicus) contrasted well with the coffee in spring

---

* Pisarrão when in larger masses or
flakes. St. Hil. (III. ii. 267) prefers "Pis-
sarão" to "Pisarão." Dr. Couto writes
Piçarra (p. 38) in the old style : he translates it talco negro, and defines it (p. 105)
to be hard or soft talcose stuff in leaves or
laminations.

† Or simply fogoës, as "tem bons
fogoës para plantar."

‡ St. Hil. III. i. 176, refers to the
Rubia noxia, and mentions these "Hervas
de Rato" in several places.

dress, long lines of stars and spangles, regular as if snow had fallen during the night, disposed along the twigs and set off by the foliage of metallic green. The property belongs to a distinguished Liberal, Monsenhor D. José Augusto Pereira da Silva, Vigario da Vara,* ranking in the clergy next to the Bishop, President of the Municipal Chamber of Sabará, and, in fine, the most influential person in this place.

The dignitary being out visiting, we struck the Praia, or beach of the Rio das Velhas. The swift yellow stream is foul with washing, and unhealthy with mineral water; its bed is deeply encased, and abounding in bad turns and shallows. A chain stretches across the water; and large shorings and scissars near an inclined plane and whim, show where Sr. Dumont's boat discharges the huge tree-trunks required by Morro Velho. Above this "Port Dumont," however, the river is unnavigable. As far up as Raposos, the valley shows spoil-banks and cascalho-heaps which had been rudely washed in the "Canôas" of the "old ones."

Half an hour's ride down the bed placed us at Santo Antonio do Arraial Velho. This was converted from a Capella Curada to a Parish, and annexed to Raposos by D. Frei Antonio de Guadaloupe, the well-remembered Bishop of Rio de Janeiro in 1736. It is therefore one of the oldest in the Province, but little remains of its former glories. The stone bridge (Ponte Velha) has clean disappeared, the little mud chapel is hardly whitewashed and half ruined, and though there are remnants of walls along the road, a few scattered huts suffice for the population. There was a "Venda" with the usual tall pole and Saint's picture, which made our friend Sr. Antonio Marcos remark that his patron had here become a Captain of Thieves, and a Teacher of the verb "Surripio." †

Presently, reaching a fine Fazenda, we had another surprise, the second on the same day. Sabará again appeared, and this time the scene was Switzerland. The foreground is a green flat, with a single noble tree; the river bends away to the right with graceful sweep, exposing the slope upon which sits the high-sited city, whose many steeples tell the pride and piety of the old

---

* An ecclesiastic with certain juridical powers : in matrimonial and other matters affecting the Church.

† A facetia derived from old Padre Vieyra, who made certain of his countrymen, conjugate "Rapio."

population. Behind it the huge Serra da Piedade curves to meet
the Curral ; and, in the nearer hills, black slides of Jácutinga
show that there is still iron-smelting in the land. High on the
right rises the feature so common in Minas, the tall black furnished cross, fronting the little white chapel to which pilgrimages
are made. This Morro da Cruz is 2800 feet, more exactly 858
metres (L.) above sea-level.

We entered the city by the normal bridge of the Brazilian
Provinces, too long, too low, and too old. It wants raising four
feet and shortening one-third, which is easily done. The breadth
of the whole bed is 108 metres, but the left bank is cumbered, at
the bend of the river, by a large and ever-increasing sand-bank,
where the furious Ribeirão de Sabará falls at an acute angle
into the Rio das Velhas.* Here, at about half the width of the
bridge up-stream, the water averages 44 instead of 108 metres,
and there is a quarter-built abutment which should be prolonged
to deepen the channel. The expense is estimated at £8000, but
at present there is a certain difficulty known as impecuniosity.
As usual, it is to be made of the fine Aroeira wood, which grows
to a great size down stream ; a scantling ten inches by ten, adding
immensely to the weight, and nothing to the strength of the
construction, seems to be an idea embedded in the Brazilian
mind. The Province of Minas has only one suspension-wire-
bridge with cables of 2·50 inches; it was thrown over the
Parahyba River, at Sapucaia, by a French engineer, M. Astier.
It may, for aught I know, be the sole specimen in the Empire.
Near Morro Velho good wire is always procurable, and on the
São Paulo Railway the cable is of 3 to 3·66 inches, and calculated
to bear a strain of twenty-two to thirty tons for a descent of 200
feet. Evidently the suspension bridge is a great economy hitherto
neglected.

The picturesque city is the usual long, narrow, mining settlement. It has grown out of wattle and dab to stone and
lime. Presently it will be marble. It covers about a mile from
east to west, with sundry windings and deviations. The whole is
paved, and the pavement is not worse than usual. It is divided
into the Old, or Eastern, Town, called " Igreja Grande," whilst

---

* Dr. Couto makes the Rio das Velhas
flow into the Valley of the Ribeirão de
Sabará, but the reverse is distinctly the
case. Both meet a little above the bridge
and dash at a hill through which they
seem to break.

the other is known as the "Barra." The two number six squares, twenty-two streets, and nine travessas, or cross streets. There is a tolerable theatre, where amateurs divert the public. Besides many private, there are four public fountains, which supply the purest water—a necessity here. The position of the city makes the climate exceptionally hot—in fact, Sabará and Morro Velho have the most tropical temperatures in Minas.[*] Many of the houses are painted—one is red, another pink, with pea-green shutters, and so forth. The Rua Direita has some good shops, where men in leather hats, like the "Matutos" of Pernambuco, gather to purchase goods, wet and dry, for the interior. There are, besides store-keeping, the local industries, lime-burning and making rude gold ornaments. The former comes from a quarry about a furlong below the bridge, the beginning of the calcareous formations, which extend to the São Francisco River. The late Colonel Vaz first called attention to it, and it belongs to the Rangel family.[†] As yet it has only been pulled at, and the expense of opening it will be some £200. It promises, however, well, and there is a good fall for the rubble. The lower strata are composed of a yellow-grey marble, not very sound, but which, probably, will improve when the workings shall be deeper. The gold employs many people, who turn out coarse rings, brooches, and so forth. The metal, however, is not nearly so pure as that of Diamantina.

We find tolerable lodgings in the Rua das Bananeiras, at the house of D. Maria dos Prazeres, and proceed to inspect the City. Our first visit is to the Largo da Cadeia, or do Rosario. In the centre of the square, upon four stone steps, stands the old pillory, surmounted by two weed-grown 'scutcheons. "Better have a Chafariz," remarks our guide, Major Candido José de Araujo Bruxado, despite his strong Conservative proclivities. To the north, on a commanding site, is the Rosario, a large unfinished shell of cut stone. On the west is the three-storied house of a local aristocrat, the Barão de Sabará, and it is supplied with a thunder-

---

[*] Sr. E. José de Moraes found the mean diurnal temperature of Sabará between March 13 and 23, 1862, to be 24°·78 (C.) and the altitude 700 metres. At Jaguára, 646 metres high, between April 18 and 29 the figure was 23°·33 (C.). At Trahiras (570 metres) the air was 22°·49, and the water was 20°·47 between May 12 and 31.

[†] The actual proprietor is Sr. José Severianno Coutinho Rangel. According to some authorities limestone is found higher up the Rio das Velhas.

rod, here much wanted. It rivals the Palacete of the Barão de Catas Altas, in the Rua Direita, which cost £2000, and now lets for 3$000 per month—at the then rate of exchange about £7 per annum. On the south is a quaint and ancient building, smooth stone below and adobe above, fronted by a deep balcony upon four wooden posts. The bell, and the Imperial Arms upon the floor, tell the Town House; the ugly faces at the roughly-barred windows below prove the prison. We have seen the best jails in the Province at Ouro Preto and S. João, and there is a third at Campanha; the rest are described by the fact that in 1863-4 there were no less than forty-two evasions. On the other hand, pauper prisoners are here, as everywhere in the Brazil, supported by the public; not left, as at Goa and Madeira, to the untender mercy of private charity.

Below the square we passed the neat house and grounds of the Desembargador, José Lopez da Silva Vianna, who died about two years ago. He was a D.C.L. of Coimbra, and his high reputation caused him to be chosen advocate for three "Gold Companies." On a rise beyond it is the Carmo Church, fronted by detached Catacombs;[*] the façade is ornamented with steatite, cut by the Aleijado. To the north is the Matriz of Nª Sª da Conceição. In former times it was leafed with gold, panned from the river, and the necessary tools were sent out from Portugal. Near it is the small and unpretending Igreja das Mercês. The other temples are the S. Francisco, black and unfinished; the little Sta Rita, in the Rua Direita; the Nª Sª do O; and the Hospicio and Convento of S. Francisco de Assiz, on an elevated site to the north. Till lately some Brothers of the Holy Land have been established here in their Hospicio da Terra Santa, and during the last ten years they have drained the Province of £20,000, for the benefit of a Jerusalem held by the Turks.[†]

From the Carmo there is an extensive view of the Ribeirão de Sabará, which higher up takes the name of Macahúbas.[‡] It is

---

[*] The catacomb system in the Brazil suggests the Camucis or Camucins, long earthen pots in which the chiefs of the savages were buried.

[†] Relatorio of 1865, p. 39. These missionaries were mostly Italians, and are said to have been independent of the Propaganda.

[‡] "Of the Macahúba," or Macaúba palm-tree, a (thorny?) variety of the Coqueiro (C. butyracea): negroes pronounce the word Bocauba, and in other Provinces Macahyba. Dr. Couto writes Mocauva, and the System by an error of accent Macaubá. According to St. Hil. the palm resembles, but is not identical with the Acrocomia sclerocarpa of Martius.

a violent torrent after rains, filling up its valley, and sweeping away the bridges, which are, therefore, reduced to "pingelas"— single planks or tree trunks. At present the shallow rill sings pleasant music as it courses briskly down the sandy bed, pitted and heaped with gravel once golden. The highlands on both sides are rough and scaly, producing little save ticks. Beyond the stream lies the inevitable "Casa Grande," large, white, and shut up. The "Emily Mine" is in a red ridge of irregular shape, pierced and tunnelled for gold, whilst the "Capão Mine" is hid by the base of a projecting hill. The houses in the street-road have large "compounds" stretching down to the stream below. Turning to the left is the rough path to the old "Intendencia," through which the gold passed, a large block of building, with the windows guarded by wooden rails, queer, bulging, and antique. Inside the ceilings show the "four quarters" of the globe, the fifth division being to it unknown. The place has lately been bought by Sr. Francisco de Paula Rocha, a Latin professor, who has made of it a boys' school.

Sabará, in old MSS. and books "Saberá," and fully written Saberá bussú—Saberá the Great—took its name from a cacique or chief found settled near the stream. Great wealth was extracted from the deep wells of both river-beds, which are said to be still unexhausted, and from the ferruginous gravel of the banks. The ore was first worked in 1699 to 1700, by the great Paulista explorer, Bartholomeu Bueno Silva, the "Old Devil." In 1707 Fr. Francisco de Menezes and a friend known as Conrado had contracted for the duties paid upon raw meat (carnes verdes), and their monopoly was opposed by the Paulista party, under "Julio Cesar" and D. Francisco de Rondon. The latter were persuaded to place their weapons in the public stores, and were attacked when defenceless. This led to the movement which made the famous and formidable "Caudilho,"[*] Manoel Vianna, a temporary dictator. The Governor Albuquerque, after settling the dispute, expelled the fighting friar from Minas, and the King signed on June 19, 1711, the celebrated letter forbidding all ecclesiastics, missionaries alone excepted, to enter the Province.

In 1711 the settlement obtained the honours of township as the "Villa Real" (de Sabará); and in 1714 it became the Cabeça,

---

[*] A guerilla chief, or captain.

or chef-lieu of a "Comarca." Of these immense subdivisions
of an immense captaincy, Minas Geraes had at first four, each
nearly equal in extent to England proper. Like the other head-
quarters of the Comarcas, Villa Rica, S. João d'El-Rei, and
Villa do Principe, it had its "Casa de fundição," or Gold-
Smelting Office, and this was not abolished till 1719-20. In
1788, according to Henderson, the city had 7656 souls, lodged
in 850 houses. That author relates from the Ouvidor's mouth a
priestly trick which reads badly. A holy woman, Harmonica by
name, began to live without food, and the good fathers raised
funds to build a house, and to establish a nunnery under the title
of Sᵗᵃ Harmonica. The judge, having reason to suspect that
her reverence would be killed, declared that the priests should
answer for her life, and the result was that she returned to her
regular meals like an ordinary Christian. The tale reminds us
of the blood of St. Januarius, which liquefied so kindly when
Murat overcame its reluctance by a platoon of infantry. In 1801
Dr. Couto gave the place a population of about 4000 souls; this
rose to 9347 * in 1819. By an Alvará, dated March 17, 1823, it
obtained the title of "Fidelissima," and in 1833, when there
were troubles in the capital, the citizens marched upon it. On
August 11, 1842, the Royalists failed to gain the eminence called
Cabeça de Boi, which was occupied by the battalions of Sᵗᵃ
Quiteria and Sᵗᵃ Luzia. Next day three columns of the insurgents attacked the city: Alvarenga's by the road from Raposos to
Arraial Velho ; Galvão's by the Rapa-queijo track ; and Lemos'
by that of Papa-farinha. Zeferino, the guerilla, assaulted the bridge
of Mãi-Domingos, over the Sabará rivulet, and, after twelve
hours of hard fighting, the Imperialists were driven away to
Caethé and Congonhas. This was the "Victory of Sabará,"
which was followed a few days afterwards by the crushing defeat
of Sᵗᵃ Luzia.

The municipality of Sabará is supposed now to contain 30,000
souls. The city lives chiefly upon the Morro Velho Mine, and,
as usual, it will neither make its own improvements, nor allow
others to make them for it. For instance, the "St. John Del
Rey Company" offered to repair the three leagues of precipitous
and dangerous road leading to Santa Luzia ; but the munici-

---

* It is as usual difficult to decide whether the numbers apply to the city or the
municipality.

pality, fearing the loss of certain dues, have left the line in all
its horrors and its shame. The barbarous feeling known as "des-
confiança"* thus, we see, still flourishes. There is a mortal
dulness about the place, despite its eight churches; it seems to
die every night, and to recover only half life in the morning. It
shows more "vadios," especially about its "Bridge of Coventry,"
—a favourite Brazilian lounge, where one prospects black and
brown washerwomen—than the visitor to London will see during
the first six items of the week; and if you ask them, "Why
stand you here all the day idle?" they will reply, if they reply at
all, "Because no man hath hired us"—i.e., we have nothing better
to do.

This great centre of gold-washing rose suddenly to wealth and
importance in the beginning of the last century. Its treasures
were nearly worked out in 1825, quite in 1846. Of late certain
English mines, concerning which more presently, gave it a partial
resuscitation. But its future is still to come. Between Sabará
and the capital of the Empire, as M. Liais has shown, there are
only 192 direct miles.† Moreover, the meridian is nearly the
same. The navigation of the Rio das Velhas, even now beginning, will place it in communication with the São Francisco River;
and it must become, with time, another St. Louis, Mo. I have
carefully described its decayed state, and travellers of the next
generation will read my description, long and somewhat tedious
as it is, with interest.

At Sabará my preparations were made for descending the Rio
das Velhas, and I found myself in the hands of a Portuguese
storekeeper, living in the Rua do Fogo, No. 28, named Manoel
Pereira de Mello Vianna, and popularly called "Piába,"‡ or the
Sprat. Unfortunately he had been in England; he spoke our
language, and thus he could exploit all the hapless Anglo-Ame-

---

* Suspicion : the uncivilized Brazilian
is remarkably "desconfiado," like the backwoodsman further north.

† More exactly 3° 12′ 39″. M. Liais
gives the true lat. of Sabará S. 19° 53′ 51″·7
(Niemeyer 19° 54′ 15″, and Gerber 19°
53′ 20″), and the long. west of Rio
1° 13′ 48″·6 (Gerber 0° 35′ 20″, and Wagner
0° 36′ 20″). The following table shows the
position of the three cities which demand
connection : they occupy nearly the same
arc of the great circle of the terrestrial

sphere :—

	S. Lat.	Longitude.
Rio de Janeiro	22° 53′ 51″	0° 0′ 0″
Barbacena	21° 13′ 9″	0° 49′ 45″
Sabará	19° 53′ 51″·7	1° 13′ 49″

‡ One of the Salmonidæ described by
Gardner : it is two to three inches long,
and a vivacious, bustling, peering sprat.
It is good bait for the "Maudim," and
other greedy fish, and it is eaten by
children.

ricans who fell into his hands. I translate his preposterous bill,* which ends with "My labour gratis." This reminded me of the "Nothin' charged for grief," in the Irish wake. Others may gain by my giving to it publicity. These people always suspect Government Expeditions, when the Brazilian Uncle Sam pays for all, as in the much-satirized surveys of the United States. They cannot believe that you travel at your own expense, instead of burdening the "Empire" or the "Province." How should they, who have never seen it done ? But I may justly complain when, in addition to his extortionate charges, the Piába sent me down a river like the Mississippi in a raft whose starboard canoe had a "racha," or leak, hardly stopped up with Sabará clay.

---

* The Most Illustrious   , debtor to Manoel Pereira de Mello Vianna.

Two new (very old) canoes	200 $ 000	(worth about half).
For having them poled up	33 $ 000	(they came from a few leagues below the town).
Two carpenters (6 days each)	26 $ 400	(the usual double).
Extra planks . . .	48 $ 993	
Awning cloth . . .	26 $ 400	
Sleeping cushion . .	9 $ 000	
Nails, saws, &c., &c. ' .	67 $ 586	

Total . . 411 $ 379

" Meu Trabalho gratis."   Sd. M. P. de M. Vianna.

CHAPTER XLI.

TO CUIABÁ.

Verás separar ao habil negro
Do pezado esmeril a grossa areia,
E ja brilharem os granetes de ouro
No fundo da batèa.
Lyras of Gonzaga.

I WILL conclude this volume with an excursion from Sabará to Cuiabá, made by Mr. Gordon and myself on July 4—5, 1867.

We set out eastward, and presently we crossed the red Sabará Rivulet by a long bridge, the Ponte Pequena or "de João Velho : its hand-rail is so low that a vicious mule would be tempted to try a spring. Thence we ascended the Lilliputian riverine valley, and presently we passed the "Folly," with a fine verandah on the hill-top to our right. This, the head-quarters of the "East Del Rey Mining Company, Limited," established in 1861, cost, they say, from £2000 to £2500. A sanguine account of the "immense size of the vein" went home, and the public was informed that "the lodes are in every respect similar in formation and character to those of the celebrated mine of Morro Velho ; the facilities for working them are, however, much greater, and the outlay required to bring them into a profitable state would be comparatively small." The property consisted of two estates, one the "Papa-farinha," afterwards called the "Emily," three miles long by one and a-half broad : here the out-crop was described as being 300 to 400 feet above the Sabará stream, which runs 100 fathoms north of it. The other was the "Capão," about half a mile south by west of the "Emily," and it was proposed to work both simultaneously.

Both grounds were ceded to the Company for a term of fifty years : the purchase of the whole mining plant, buildings, stamps, and wheels, was effected for £2500 ; and a royalty of three per cent. on the gold was made payable to the grantor. The latter, formerly of Minas Geraes, now of France, had bought the two, when Managing Director of the Cocaes Company, for £1200, and though he had employed upon them large gangs of blacks, the mines never produced anything that approached working costs. Furthermore, £10,000 were made payable to said grantor, when the shareholders should have received £10,000 in dividends; and a third and final £10,000 was to find its way in the same direction, when £20,000 should have been divided. Under these circumstances the Company was raised, with a capital of 30,000 shares, each £3.

But, when operations began, the lode, said to be twenty-four feet wide, was found irregular, and much better left untouched. Pyrites was rare, the general formation being a disturbed line of iron and manganese, quartz, and clay slate, in a containing rock of "killas." A shaft was run into the "Capão," and various trial levels to intersect the lode, were dug in the hill-side of the "Emily." A single small set of stamps—now removed—was set up, and even for these there was not employment. The published accounts show an expenditure of £36,000 at Sabará: and the good shareholders enjoy the satisfaction of having most comfortably lodged their employés in a Casa Grande. The "East Del Rey" has therefore walked off to "S. Vicente:" it now wants only a new name, new subscribers, and a new capital.

Here the little Macahúbas River drains the northern face of the Caethé hills and the southern front of the Serra da Piedade. This huge chine towers on our left with jags and saws, blocks and "cheese wrings," of tortuous, micaceous clay slate, resting upon a rough, hard, and reddish ironstone, mostly oxide, and in extreme abundance : here is, in fact, the northern buttress of that range whose southern apex we saw at Itabira do Campo. The vegetation forms a threadbare coat of thin grass, and low grey, scrubby shrub. The best ascent is from the east viâ Caethé ; the western side has a path, but it is abrupt and unsafe. On the summit, some two and a quarter leagues from Sabará, rises a small white church, which glistens like a pearl in the sparkling sun: conspicuous from afar it will be most useful to surveyors. The Piedade, like the Caraça and the Itacolumi, began civilized life with its hermit ; presently the cell expanded to a church, and lastly, D. João VI. presented to it an adjoining farm to be held allodially and in perpetuum. Many pilgrims still visit and offer candles in this "free, privileged, and manumised chapel." There is a dispute about the height of the Serra's crested head. Spix and Martius make it 5400 feet above sea-level—2400 below what Gardner assigned to the Organ Mountains or Maritime Range. MM. Liais and Halfeld differed about the comparative altitudes of the Piedade and the Itacolumi. Mr. Gordon took observations both on the Piedade and at Sabará, but his instrument appears to have been out of adjustment.[*]

This range is said strongly to reverberate sound, showing, according to some authors, that it is "fully charged with mineral." The ancients supposed consecrated rocks to emit significant and prophetic noises : we call to mind the "Kenidjack," or Hooting Cairn of Cornwall, and sundry others, where people are equally affected with folk-folly. The Brazilians quote many apparently authenticated cases of "Bramidos," or subterranean roarings, which they connect with the Mãe de Ouro or gold-pixy. Undoubtedly they often confuse the underground reports with the superficial sounds of an exaggerated storm, the roaring of the wind, and the muffled reply of the cold grey stones ; the shivering of the trees, and the falling of decomposed and scaled-off blocks, heard within doors, making the inmates exclaim, " How they snore—how they blow "—and causing them to shudder with panic-fear. We remember the " Schnarcher," or snorers, the two granite lumps on the Barenberg, where popular superstition placed the earth's centre. The subterranean thunders, unaccompanied by appreciable shocks, called the "Bramidos de Guanaxuato," have been mentioned by Humboldt. Those, however, are distinctly volcanic, but in many parts of the Brazil they seem to be heard in the limestone and the sandstone formation. Personally, I have not witnessed the phenomenon, but the mass of evidence is certainly for its existence.

Many a time we forded and re-forded the little mountain-burn with the golden sands and the fishy waters. At places there are currals or weirs of very poor construction, double and sometimes

---

* On the summit Pelissher's aneroid gave Bar. Reading 26·24. Temp. 77° = 3500 feet. At Sabará Bridge, on the level of the stream, Bar. reading 29·32. Temp. 78° = 568 feet. But M. Liais makes the latter 695 metres, or nearly 2300 feet, almost 500 below the Morro da Cruz, and these figures are evidently correct. M. Buril (L'Empire du Brésil) offers the following table of altitudes :—

Itambé	1816 metres above sea-level.
Piedade	1774	,,
Itacolumi	1754	,,
Itabira	1590	,,

treble. In other parts there were wretched dams, forming rude leats: they must be carried off by every flood. Here and there the stream was arrested by stakes driven into the gravelly bottom: upon these were piled brushwood and stones to slacken the current and induce it to deposit its gold. A single old "faiscador" or washer appeared: he looked like a gorilla caught in the open, and he glared at us as if we were so many Du Chaillus. His tools were the carumbeia or bowl for coarse gravel, the batêa or platter for the finer sand, and an almocafre, here pronounced almocorf.* This is the iron hoe which turns up the pebbles, and it appears in four shapes, the rounded-conical, the square, the lozenge, and the triangle. Where water abounds the gold is worked by the Monjólo,† a trapèze-shaped trough of sticks and stiff clay, the broad end raised at an angle of 35°, some three or four feet above the stream level. Into the upper part the auriferous gravel is thrown and water is ladled in, whilst a bit of skin placed at the lower and narrow end arrests the flattened scales and the minute grains, which are specifically about seven times heavier than the stone.‡

The River Valley closed in as we advanced, and became more picturesque: happily for us there were clouds; in these bottoms the heat is excessive, especially during the early warm season, August and September. We presently passed the Pompêo village, often mentioned by travellers: a wretched chapel and broken walls are all that remain of its old magnificence. Cald-cleugh found on the right bank of the streamlet a formation of chorite slate, with cleavage planes traversed, nearly at right angles, by broad, distinct, and well displayed veins of quartz, often auriferous. The upper soil showed a regular layer of quartz fragments: now much of it has been removed. Beyond Pompêo on the left still rises the old Cuiabá Company's Casa Grande, built by Mr. Edward Oxenford.

After fording the Ribeirão six times we sighted in an "impasse" before us the celebrated "horse-shoe." It is a savage rocky

---

* In dictionaries we find Almocafre and Almo Cafre, which Moraes explains "Sancho com bico ou ponta, usada na mineração." The word is probably the Arabic Mikhraf (مخرف) an instrument for gathering. The most common shape is the elliptic arch.

† St. Hil. (III. ii. 143) calls this rude contrivance cuyacá, probably a word peculiar to Goyaz: he omits the skin and thus he loses his gold.

‡ Many Monjólos are seen on the Rio das Velhas, where the people still believe in canjica, or nugget gold: since 1801, however, they have found very little of it.

hollow in the southern sub-chain of the Serra da Piedade, which
bristles high above it, and which is to the Cuiabá deposits what
the Serra is to those of S. José and the Curral to Morro Velho.
Towering some 220 feet in the air were certain "shoots," which
announced to us that we had reached our destination. A few
poor huts lay scattered about, and there was a little forge that
turns out knives and horse-shoes: the old mining proprietress
has outlived all luxury, and wears a man's coat over a tattered
chemise. At the end of the sixth mile * of tedious road, we passed
some twenty head of stamps and three "arrastres," with the
other usual appurtenances, and we dismounted at a ground-floor
tenement to be received with a true Scotch greeting by Mr.
Brown.

After what is locally called a " Bisnaga," we proceeded to visit
the Cuiabá works.† The ascent was severe up the eastern seg-
ment of the " Horse-shoe," which is said to contain six several
lodes running east and west. The lower part of the formation is
by far the richer, and it belongs to the Vaz family, who by
rude hand-work produced five oitavas of ore per ton. The
Company's portion, situated higher up, is known to be poor; and
northwards the lodes are much disturbed. As we rose we could
see the clay slate dipping from west to east, and the mountains
bluff to the west: it is not known how the strata underlie the
mineral formation.

We passed the " Serrote " or midway workings, a ridge running
nearly north to south, and what miners call " lurched " or heaved
off. Here, as is shown by the red ground, a large surface had
been washed. To the left and higher up was the little mining
village " Cuiabá." We entered the Terra Vermelha Gallery, the
highest digging, and about forty fathoms long: there being no
means of ventilation the smoke of the late blasting hung heavily.
I could not see any possibility of drainage, and I judged that the
water would soon stop further dead-works—sinking and driving.
The roof seemed to be solid, but prolonged excavation will soon

---

* Dr. Gardner says two leagues (I presume geographical) from Sabará. The
prospectus of the East Del Rey Company
made the latter place seven miles east of
"St. John Del Rey." I should read nine
—a total of fifteen to Cuiabá.

† A gourd in bottle shape is called

Cabaça, our Calabash : Cúia or Cúya is a
section of the same gourd used by the
indigens as a skillet or cup, and -abá,
means the place of. The capital of the
Matto Grosso Province is usually written
Cuyabá : the mine Cuiabá.

a ba → the
place of

necessitate timbering. The formation is that of Morro Velho, quartz and pyrites: but the latter is not equally disseminated, and the scraps are rich whilst the bulk is poor. The mundic is apparently copper pyrites, which may contain silver with arsenic. The Brazilians have different names for the rock, "Pedra de Campo," quartz boulders; "Olho de Porco," a blue quartz with iron pyrites and free gold;"* "Cáco," soft sugary quartz containing the precious ore in olhos or pockets; and "Lapa," the usual killas. As much as nine oitavas have been taken from three tons of stone. Much blasting is required, but the stuff being more brittle than that of Morro Velho, is easier to spall and stamp. Amalgamation works have not yet been used.

About midway is the "Shallow Adit," now fifteen years old, and some 109 fathoms long: it was driven to meet the "Serrote" and to unwater the mineral above that region. According to the Messrs. Vaz the ore is here rich. We found a primitive tramway, and the wooden rails where exposed to friction had guards of thin metal plates.† We then visited the lowest site, "Vivian's Level," alias "Mina do Cedro," thirty fathoms long. This will drain at a lower point the "Serrote" and the "Fonte Grande," which is close to it, on the left. Thus also stone can be got out at a moderate cost for the stamps. The line was in soft clay, and very wet: its western direction seemed to run under the "Fonte Grande" ravine and Córrego, which was on our left, and thence to pass straight into a worthless mass of killas. A dozen workmen or so were preparing to lay a tramway upon a newly cut road leading to the spalling-floors, which are seven fathoms below the shoots and these thirty above the stamps.

We had now done a fair day's work, and we were ready for our wage of rest. The house was not a Casa Grande, but none the less hospitable therefore, and Mrs. Gordon had not forgotten to supply us with a huge basket. The evening also at this elevation was delightfully cool and clear. Our good host, Mr. Brown, has been seven to eight years in the Brazil. He came out here as Receiver and Manager, under orders of the Court of Chancery, to the Cocaes Company, which, at the petition of its share-

---

* I have seen some splendid specimens of this rock brought from a site very near the city of S. Paulo.

† In the Brazil, where woods, hard as many metals, are abundant and cheap, it is strange that these rails have not generally been adopted for small works.

holders, was in process of " winding up." It was desirable to
"realize" and to settle affairs without any further call upon
actionnaires, who are not registered. He has preserved all his
energy, he boasts that his house contains the only private
printing-machine in the Province, and he proposes a Company
with a capital of £100,000 in 20,000 shares. The estate, a
peninsula between the Macahúbas and Gáia streams, is seven
miles long by two to three broad, and is well supplied with
wood and water. The six lodes have been little troubled,
although formerly a hundred head of stamps worked at once,
and the yield was 2—16 oitavas per ton—the stamp-sand being
simply panned. The ground belongs at present to many small
Brazilian owners, and a section of it, neither large nor valuable,
is part of the " Cocaes Estate." Meanwhile only one English
miner and forty to fifty free natives are employed; and mining,
—like farming, racing, or ballooning,—on a small scale, is not
apt to pay.

A few words concerning " Cocaes," alias the " National
Brazilian Mining Association "—even foreigners here have a
lust for high-sounding names. The little village Nª Sª do
Rosario de Cocaes* lies upon the Una River, in the same range
as Gongo Soco, which is about eight miles south by west: it is a
cold, humid, but healthy site, 3400 feet above sea level, distant
thirty-two miles from Sabará, and fifty from Ouro Preto.
Dr. Couto, who visited it in 1801, declares that the once rich
stream had then been worked out (todo lavado), and that the
miners had ascended the hills to find better washings : he
detected in the heights huge spoil-heaps of red, ash-coloured,
and purple copper. Here still resides the "intrusive President," José Felicianno Pinto Coelho da Cunha, who undertook
Minas in 1842, and who is now Barão de Cocaes,† commanding
the National Guard.

The lode is Jacutinga. It is here a micaceous iron schist,
or slate, dipping easterly at about 30°, striated, coloured pepper

---

* I did not visit Cocaes. Cocal, a word
found on the Rio de São Francisco, is a
plantation of Coca (Cocculus indicus, which
Moraes also calls Mata-piolho, and says is
used to narcotize fish). St. Hil. (I. i. 444)
suggests that it may be the plural of Cocão,
une sorte de bois du Brésil que l'on emploie
dans les charpentes." But the plural form

of Cocão is Cocões, not Cocaes.

† He is not wealthy, having divided
amongst his children almost all his property
except the house in which he lives. His
brother, Colonel Felicio José Pinto Coelho
da Cunha, was the first husband of the
celebrated beauty, the late Marqueza de
Santos.

and salt; now soft and friable, then hard and passing into ferruginous sandstone. The walls of the lode generally are blue clay-slate, and the foot-wall or under-wall is composed of fine specular micaceous iron, in large slabs bright as a mirror. The better shoots are tolerably rich. Of pyritic formations there are three, or some say two, longitudinal strikes through the mineral part of the estate: these dip west to east, and the underlay is about 40° south.

In 1830 the land had been surveyed by M. Ferdinand Halfeld, and belonged to several Brazilian proprietors, amongst whom the Barão de Cocaes was the chief man. Three years afterwards it was rented by the Company for a term of fifty years, and the lease has thus about sixteen to run. Mr. Macdonald, Chief Commissioner, and the Mining Captain, Mr. Thomas Treloar, began work in June, 1834. Under the rule of Mr. Roscoe, Mr. Goodair (a Portugal-born Englishman), the late Mr. Henry Oxenford, Senior (1847), and Dr. Gunning,—who went out as "Medical Missioner," to the Brazil!—the mine yielded some £100,000, but never paid its costs. When Gardner visited Cocaes the total expenses had been £200,000. The chief shaft was fifty fathoms deep, and the hands were thirty free Brazilians, thirty English miners, and 300 "Company's blacks." He admired the conspicuous church and the neat houses in rich gardens; declaring the village to be the prettiest that he had seen in Minas. In 1850 Dr. Walker found the water so deep that the mine was unmanageable. In 1851 there was a "run:" the walls came together, and the crushed timber carried away the pumping gear, choked up the engine shaft, and filled the level with fragments of rock. Mr. William Treloar wound up affairs. The unexpired lease of the Association may easily be taken up, but the 10 per cent. royalty must be reduced to 4, if profit is to be expected.

*   *   *   *   *   *   *

At Sabará we concluded our 500 miles of land journey through the richest and the most popular part of Minas Geraes. Here, however, ends the excursionist portion, much of which, I have said before, will soon form a section of the nineteenth-century Grand Tour. But what now comes is not yet exactly a pleasure trip down the Thames or up the Rhine: there are hot suns, drenching rains, and angry winds to be endured; there is before us a certain amount of hardship, privation, and fatigue, with just enough of risk to enliven the passage; and, finally, there are nearly 1300 miles to be covered by the craziest of crafts, caulked with Sabará clay.

END OF VOL. I.

WOMAN ✓
Floristella da Horta
widow — mine owner

Luzia

Voz
Aureliano
Joaquim
Pedro
Antonio
Luis
Leandro
Manoel
Felizardo
Pedro
Felipe

Freiria
Vieira
Azevedo
Ribeiro
Avanter
Cabral
dos Santos
Ferreira
daVara
da Silva

Rulof Antonio (38 in 1823?)

p190   16 days from RJ

NB also looking for Gov
3 15 /6

Villa Real
de Sabara
Villa
Real

Genovera

Made in the USA